Lecture Notes in Computer Science　14238

Advanced Research in Computing and Software Science
Subline of Lecture Notes in Computer Science

More information about this series at https://link.springer.com/bookseries/558

Argyrios Deligkas · Aris Filos-Ratsikas
Editors

Algorithmic Game Theory

16th International Symposium, SAGT 2023
Egham, UK, September 4–7, 2023
Proceedings

Springer

Editors
Argyrios Deligkas ⓘ
Royal Holloway University of London
Egham, UK

Aris Filos-Ratsikas ⓘ
University of Edinburgh
Edinburgh, UK

ISSN 0302-9743   ISSN 1611-3349   (electronic)
Lecture Notes in Computer Science
ISBN 978-3-031-43253-8   ISBN 978-3-031-43254-5   (eBook)
https://doi.org/10.1007/978-3-031-43254-5

This Springer imprint is published by the registered company Springer Nature Switzerland AG
The registered company address is: Gewerbestrasse 11, 6330 Cham, Switzerland

Paper in this product is recyclable.

Preface

This volume contains the papers and extended abstracts presented at the 16th International Symposium on Algorithmic Game Theory (SAGT 2023), held during September 4–7, 2023, at Royal Holloway University of London, UK. The purpose of SAGT is to bring together researchers from Computer Science, Economics, Mathematics, Operations Research, Psychology, Physics, and Biology to present and discuss original research at the intersection of Algorithms and Game Theory.

This year, we received 59 submissions, which were all rigorously peer-reviewed by the Program Committee (PC). Each paper was reviewed by at least 3 PC members, and evaluated on the basis of originality, significance, and exposition. The PC eventually decided to accept 26 papers to be presented at the conference.

The works accepted for publication in this volume cover most of the major aspects of Algorithmic Game Theory, including auction theory, mechanism design, markets and matchings, computational aspects of games, resource allocation problems, and computational social choice. To accommodate the publishing traditions of different fields, authors of accepted papers could ask that only a one-page abstract of the paper appeared in the proceedings. Among the 26 accepted papers, the authors of 3 papers selected this option.

Furthermore, due to the generous support by Springer, we were able to provide a Best Paper Award. The best paper award was decided by a three-member committee consisting of Edith Elkind (University of Oxford, UK), Vasilis Gkatzelis (Drexel University, USA), and Brendan Lucier (Microsoft Research, USA). The PC decided to give the award to the paper "Computational Complexity of Decision Problems about Nash Equilibria in Win-Lose Multi-Player Games" authored by Vittorio Biló, Kristoffer Arnsfelt Hasnen, and Marios Mavronicolas. The program also included three invited talks by distinguished researchers in Algorithmic Game Theory, namely George Christodoulou (Aristotle University of Thessaloniki and Archimedes/RC Athena, Greece), Michal Feldman (Tel-Aviv University, Israel), and Alex Teytelboym (University of Oxford, UK). In addition, SAGT 2023 featured a tutorial given by Philip Lazos (Input Output Global (IOG)) and Evangelos Markakis (Athens University of Economics and Business, Greece, and Input Output Global (IOG)).

We would like to thank all the authors for their interest in submitting their work to SAGT 2023, as well as the PC members and the external reviewers for their great work in evaluating the submissions. We also would like to thank Springer, Google, Input Output Global (IOG), and the Laboratory for Foundations of Computer Science (LFCS) of the School of Informatics at the University of Edinburgh for their generous financial support. We also thank the Dutch Research Council (NWO) for financially supporting the affiliated FaiRACAC 2023 workshop, held in conjunction with SAGT 2023, through the Veni project No. VI.Veni.192.153. We are grateful to the Computer Science Department of the Royal Holloway University of London for hosting the conference. Finally, we would also like to thank the staff of Springer for helping with the proceedings, and the OpenReview conference management system for facilitating the peer-review process.

July 2023

Argyrios Deligkas
Aris Filos-Ratsikas

Organization

Program Committee

Georgios Amanatidis	University of Essex, UK
Vittorio Bilò	University of Salento, Italy
Argyrios Deligkas (PC Co-chair)	Royal Holloway University of London, UK
Eduard Eiben	Royal Holloway University of London, UK
Tomer Ezra	Sapienza University of Rome, Italy
Angelo Fanelli	CNRS, France
Michail Fasoulakis	ICS-FORTH, Greece
John Fearnley	University of Liverpool, UK
Aris Filos-Ratsikas (PC Co-chair)	University of Edinburgh, UK
Federico Fusco	Sapienza University of Rome, Italy
Mingyu Guo	University of Adelaide, Australia
Sushmita Gupta	Institute of Mathematical Sciences, India
Daniel Halpern	Harvard University, USA
Thekla Hamm	TU Wien, Austria
Kristoffer Arnsfelt Hansen	Aarhus University, Denmark
Tobias Harks	University of Augsburg, Germany
Martin Hoefer	Goethe-Universität Frankfurt, Germany
Alexandros Hollender	EPFL, Switzerland
Ayumi Igarashi	University of Tokyo, Japan
Bart de Keijzer	King's College London, UK
Max Klimm	TU Berlin, Germany
Moran Koren	Ben-Gurion University of the Negev, Israel
Piotr Krysta	University of Liverpool, UK
Rucha Kulkarni	University of Illinois at Urbana-Champaign, USA
David Manlove	University of Glasgow, UK
Pascal Lezner	Hasso Plattner Institute, Germany
Minming Li	City University of Hong Kong, China
Maria Kyropoulou	University of Essex, UK
Bo Li	Hong Kong Polytechnic University, China
Themistoklis Melissourgos	University of Essex, UK
Evi Micha	University of Toronto, Canada
Gianpiero Monaco	University of Chieti-Pescara, Italy
Nikos Protopappas	University of Patras, Greece
Guido Schäfer	CWI, The Netherlands
Yixin Tao	London School of Economics, UK
Zoi Terzopoulou	Saint-Etienne School of Economics, France

Artem Tsikiridis	CWI, The Netherlands
Rohit Vaish	Indian Institute of Technology Delhi, India
Carmine Ventre	King's College London, UK
Adrian Vetta	McGill University, Canada
Cosimo Vinci	University of Salerno, Italy

Best Paper Award Committee

Edith Elkind	University of Oxford, UK
Vasilis Gkatzelis	Drexel University, USA
Brendan Lucier	Microsoft Research, USA

Organizing Committee

Argyrios Deligkas	Royal Holloway University of London, UK
Aris Filos-Ratsikas	University of Edinburgh, UK

Steering Committee

Elias Koutsoupias	University of Oxford, UK
Marios Mavronicolas	University of Cyprus, Cyprus
Dov Monderer	Technion, Israel
Burkhard Monien	University of Paderborn, Germany
Christos Papadimitriou	Columbia University, USA
Giuseppe Persiano	University of Salerno, Italy
Paul Spirakis (Chair)	University of Liverpool, UK

Additional Reviewers

Michelle Döring	Paraskevi Machaira
Kaito Fuji	Shivika Narang
Hans Gawendowicz	Oliviero Nardi
Merlin de la Haye	Vishwa Prakash
Halvard Hummel	Aditi Sethia
Nicolas Klodt	Nicholas Teh
Simon Krogmann	

Abstract of Invited Talks

A Proof of the Nisan-Ronen Conjecture

George Christodoulou

Aristotle University of Thessaloniki and Archimedes/RC Athena, Greece
gichristo@csd.auth.gr

Abstract. Noam Nisan and Amir Ronen conjectured that the best approximation ratio of deterministic truthful mechanisms for makespan-minimization for n unrelated machines is n. This work validates the conjecture.

Ambiguous Contracts

Michal Feldman

Tel Aviv University, Israel
mfeldman@tauex.tau.ac.il

Abstract. We introduce a model of *ambiguous contracts*, capturing many real-life scenarios where agents engage in contractual relations that leave some degree of uncertainty. Our starting point is the celebrated hidden-action model and the classic notion of a contract, where the principal commits to an outcome-contingent payment scheme for incentivizing an agent to take a costly action. An *ambiguous contract* generalizes this notion by allowing the principal to commit to a set of two or more contracts, without specifying which of these will be employed. A natural behavioral assumption in such cases is that the agent engages in a max-min strategy, maximizing her expected utility in the worst case over the set of possible contracts.

We show that the principal can in general gain utility by employing an ambiguous contract, at the expense of the agent's utility. We provide structural properties of the optimal ambiguous contract, showing that an optimal ambiguous contract is composed of simple contracts. We then use these properties to devise poly-time algorithms for computing the optimal ambiguous contract. We also provide a characterization of non-manipulable classes of contracts—those where a principal cannot gain by employing an ambiguous contract. We show that linear contracts—unlike other common contracts—are non-manipulable, which might help explain their popularity. Finally, we provide bounds on the *ambiguity gap*—the gap between the utility the principal can achieve by employing ambiguous contracts and the utility the principal can achieve with a single contract.

Joint work with Paul Duetting and Daniel Peretz.

Duality in Market Design

Alex Teytelboym

University of Oxford, UK
alexander.teytelboym@economics.ox.ac.uk

Abstract. Market participants often experience income effects because of financing costs or budget constraints. Yet income effects are often ignored in market design. I will describe how tools from consumer theory can be deployed to analyze income effects in matching markets and exchange economies with indivisibilities. These tools pave a way to designing markets for indivisibles that elicit and incorporate income effects.

Abstracts

Reputation-Based Persuasion Platforms

Itai Arieli, Omer Madmon, and Moshe Tennenholtz

Technion - Israel Institute of Technology, Israel
{iarieli,moshet}@technion.ac.il,
omermadmon@campus.technion.ac.il

Bayesian persuasion refers to a situation where a sender (e.g., a seller) attempts to influence the decision of a receiver (e.g., a buyer) by presenting them with information. One classic example is a seller trying to sell a product of uncertain quality to a buyer. The seller may have some aggregate knowledge about the preferences and likelihood of purchasing the product for a group of buyers, but may not be able to distinguish among individual buyers. In contrast, other parties, such as online selling platforms like Amazon and eBay, may have access to more specific information about each buyer and their likelihood of purchasing the product. These platforms can use this information to reveal relevant characteristics of individual buyers to the seller, improving the efficiency of the persuasion process. Our work aims to study this double information disclosure mechanism in a persuasion setting. We study this model in two different settings: a one-shot setting and a repeated setting, which is inspired by reputation considerations.

We consider the standard product adoption setting with a binary set of states of the world (high and low product quality) and a binary set of receiver actions (buying and not buying the product). Only the sender knows the product quality, and only the platform knows the user type. Our problem, then, is to find an information disclosure policy of the platform that maximizes the users' utility, under the assumption that the sender follows its own optimal recommendation policy. In the one-shot setting, we demonstrate how our model can be reduced to a seemingly unrelated model of market segmentation. This reduction provides an efficient solution for the one-shot persuasion platforms problem.

Next, we introduce the reputation-based persuasion platform problem, in which myopic users arrive sequentially. In this setting, the platform controls the sender's information about users and maintains a reputation for the sender, punishing it if it fails to act truthfully on a certain subset of signals. For the reputation-based setting, we provide a characterization of an optimal platform policy. This policy relies on the fact that in the high reputation state, it is optimal for the platform to adopt the segmentation which is similar to the one it provided in the one-shot case.

Acknowledgements. The work by Moshe Tennenholtz was supported by funding from the European Research Council (ERC) under the European Union's Horizon 2020 research and innovation programme (grant agreement 740435). Itai Arieli gratefully acknowledges support from the Israel Science Foundation (grant agreement 2029464).

Decentralized Attack Search and the Design of Bug Bounty Schemes

Hans Gersbach[1], Akaki Mamageishvili[2] and Fikri Pitsuwan[1]

[1] ETH Zürich and KOF, Leonhardstrasse 21, 8092, Zürich, Switzerland,
{hgersbach, fpitsuwan}@ethz.ch
[2] Offchain Labs, Zürich, Switzerland
amamageishvili@offchainlabs.com

Systems and blockchains often have security vulnerabilities and can be attacked by adversaries, with potentially significant negative consequences. Therefore, infrastructure providers increasingly rely on bug bounty programs, where external individuals probe the system and report any vulnerabilities (bugs) in exchange for rewards (bounty). We develop a simple contest model of bug bounty. A group of individuals of arbitrary size is invited to undertake a costly search for bugs. The individuals differ with regard to their abilities, which we capture by different costs to achieve a certain probability to find bugs if any exist. Costs are private information. We study equilibria of the contest and characterize the optimal design of bug bounty schemes. In particular, the designer can vary the size of the group of individuals invited to search, add a paid expert, insert an artificial bug with some probability, and pay multiple prizes.

We obtain the following results. First, we characterize the equilibria, establishing that any equilibrium strategy must be a threshold strategy, i.e. only agents with a cost of search below some (potentially individual) threshold participate in the bug bounty scheme. Second, we provide sufficient conditions for the equilibrium to be unique and symmetric. Third, we show that even inviting an unlimited crowd does not guarantee that the bug, if it exists, is found, unless there are agents which have zero costs, or equivalently have intrinsic gains from participating in the scheme. It may even happen that having more agents in the pool of potential participants lowers the probability of finding the bug. Fourth, adding a paid expert can increase or decrease the efficiency of the bug bounty scheme. Fifth, we illustrate how adding (known) bugs is another way to increase the likelihood that unknown bugs are found. When the additional costs of paying rewards are taken into account, it can be optimal to insert a known bug only with some probability. Sixth, we demonstrate that in a model with multiple prizes, having one prize (winner-takes-all) achieves the highest probability of finding the bug. Seventh, we identify circumstances when asymmetric equilibria occur. Lastly, we discuss how our baseline model can be extended to allow for multiple bugs, multiple experts, and heterogeneity of agents with respect to cost distributions, search times, and skills.

A full version of the paper is available at: https://arxiv.org/abs/2304.00077.

This research was partially supported by the Zurich Information Security and Privacy Center (ZISC) at ETH Zürich.

Weighted Fair Division with Matroid-Rank Valuations: Monotonicity and Strategyproofness

Warut Suksompong[1] and Nicholas Teh[2]

[1] National University of Singapore, Singapore
warut@comp.nus.edu.sg
[2] University of Oxford, UK
nicholas.teh@cs.ox.ac.uk

The problem of fairly allocating a set of scarce resources among interested parties is longstanding and fundamental in economics. Applications of fair division are wide-ranging, from allocating medical supplies to communities or schoolteachers to primary schools, to dividing assets in a divorce settlement and usage rights of a jointly invested facility.

Although the majority of the fair division literature assumes that all agents have the same entitlement to the resource, this assumption fails to hold in several practical scenarios. For instance, when allocating resources among communities of different sizes, larger communities naturally deserve a larger proportion of the shared resource pool. Following several recent papers, we study the allocation of indivisible goods to agents with weights corresponding to their entitlements.

Previous work has shown that, when agents have binary additive valuations, the maximum weighted Nash welfare (MWNW) rule is resource-, population-, and weight-monotone, satisfies group-strategyproofness, and can be implemented in polynomial time [2]. We generalize these results in two directions.

1. We show that the results continue to hold even for agents with *matroid-rank* (also known as *binary submodular*) valuations. Matroid-rank valuations generalize binary additive valuations and capture settings such as course allocation in universities or public housing allocation among ethnic groups.
2. We prove that the results hold generally for *weighted additive welfarist rules*, which select an allocation that maximizes a welfare notion given by the weighted sum of some increasing and concave function of the agents' utilities. MWNW is a weighted additive welfarist rule with the logarithm function.

Combined with results from prior work [1], our findings demonstrate that the maximum weighted harmonic welfare rule and its variations are arguably stronger candidate rules than MWNW for agents with arbitrary entitlements and matroid-rank (or binary additive) valuations.

The full version of this paper is available at http://arxiv.org/abs/2303.14454.

References

1. Montanari, L., Schmidt-Kraepelin, U., Suksompong, W., Teh, N.: Weighted envyfreeness for submodular valuations. **CoRR abs/2209.06437** (2022)
2. Suksompong, W., Teh, N.: On maximum weighted Nash welfare for binary valuations. Math. Soc. Sci. **117**, 101–108 (2022)

Contents

Computational Aspects and Efficiency
in Games

Computation of Nash Equilibria of Attack and Defense Games on Networks

Stanisław Kaźmierowski[(✉)] and Marcin Dziubiński[iD]

University of Warsaw, Faculty of Mathematics, Informatics and Mechanics,
Banacha 2, 02-097 Warsaw, Poland
s.kazmierowski@uw.edu.pl, m.dziubinski@mimuw.edu.pl

Abstract. We consider the computation of a Nash equilibrium in attack
and defense games on networks (Bloch et al. [1]). We prove that a Nash
Equilibrium of the game can be computed in polynomial time with
respect to the number of nodes in the network. We propose an algorithm that runs in $O(n^4)$ time with respect to the number of nodes of
the network, n.

Keywords: Games on networks · network interdiction · Nash
Equilibrium

1 Introduction

International drug trafficking [4,9], disrupting the movement of the enemy troops
[6,8], and terrorist attacks [10] involves strategic actors interacting over a network of bilateral connections. A class of scenarios of this type consists of a network of defenders (e.g. countries connected by common borders) and an attacker
attempting to move an undesirable object (e.g. a bomb or a package of drugs)
through a network to a targeted node (e.g. a targeted country). Each defender is
interested in his security but investment in protection spills over to subsequent
defenders on the potential routes of attack.

In a recent paper, Bloch, Chatterjee, and Dutta [1] introduce a game theoretic
model that captures such scenarios. In the model, an attacker (node 0) and n
defenders are all connected in a fixed network. The attacker chooses a target node
and an attack path in the network from her location (node 0) to the location of
a targeted node. In the event of a successful attack, the attacker gains the value
assigned to the target node. If successfully attacked, the targeted defender loses
his value while every other node on the path remains intact. To prevent potential
losses, every defender can invest in costly protection to increase the probability
of stopping a potential attack. An attack can be stopped by every defender on
the attack path. Bloch et al. [1] establish the existence of mixed strategy Nash
equilibria (NE) in the model and obtain a partial characterization of the NE as
well as a full characterization for the networks that form a line. They prove that
the set of nodes attacked with positive probability in NE is unique, and under
certain redefinition, the model has a unique NE. They provide a set of non-linear
equations describing the strategies in a NE when the set of nodes attacked with

A. Deligkas and A. Filos-Ratsikas (Eds.): SAGT 2023, LNCS 14238, pp. 3–21, 2023.
https://doi.org/10.1007/978-3-031-43254-5_1

positive probability is given. Whether this set can be computed efficiently and, consequently, whether a NE of the model can be computed efficiently, was left an open question.

Our Contribution. We provide an algorithm for calculating a Nash equilibrium (NE) of the model proposed in [1]. We prove that the algorithm runs in polynomial time with respect to the number of players. More in detail, we use the idea of reducing the network by removing the nodes that are not attacked under any NE, while maintaining all of the possible paths of attack. We identify a subset of defending nodes called *linkers* which are the subset of nodes that are never attacked in any NE. After removing the linkers from the network, every node can be reached by the attacker by a path of increasing values for the attacker. Using this observation, and building on the idea for computing NE for linear networks, where the nodes are connected in order of ascending values, presented in [1], we obtain a polynomial time algorithm that finds a NE of the model for any connected network.

Related Work. The problem of strategic transportation and interception of unwanted traffic through a network is known as the problem of network interdiction. In its classic formulation, the problem involves two players: an evader, who sends the traffic through the network, and the interceptor, whose objective is to stop the traffic. The problem of network interdiction has been studied extensively over the past years. In different models, the evader goal can be minimizing the length of the path from the source to the sink [7], avoiding detection by devices placed by the interdictor on the edges [12], or increasing the flow between the source and the sink [5,6,8]. The applications of network interdiction problem range from smuggling goods [4,9] and detecting the nuclear material [10] to disrupting the enemy troops movement [6,8]. See [3] and [11] for excellent surveys of this type of model.

The literature on NE computation is vast, and we restrict attention to the closest related works. [12] consider a zero-sum game model where the evader chooses any path on the graph and the interdictor chooses an edge in the graph. If this edge is on the path chosen by the evader, then the evader is detected with a fixed probability assigned to this edge. One of the contributions of [12] is reducing the linear programming problem which is a classic method for solving the zero-sum games to a polynomial number of constraints and variables when the considered size of strategy set of evader is of a possibly exponential size.

Closer to the model considered in this paper, is the model [2] in which each of the n defenders chooses whether to protect himself or not. The defenders are connected in the directed weighted graph with weights of the edges reflecting the probability of being contaminated by the incoming neighbours in case they are successfully attacked. There are two main settings considered, first where the direct attack is a result of a random event (e.g. a pandemic), and second, where the attacks are coordinated by an attacker with an incentive to maximize the number of infected nodes (e.g. hacker attacks). The authors propose a polynomial time algorithm for computing a NE for the models they consider.

2   The Model

We consider a game, introduced in [1], between an *attacker* (player 0) and n *defenders* (target nodes). We will use $[n] = \{1, 2, \ldots, n\}$ to denote the set of defenders. The attacker and the defenders are connected in a network modeled by an undirected graph, $G = \langle V, E \rangle$, where $V = [n] \cup \{0\}$ is the set of nodes and $E \subseteq \binom{V}{2}$ is the set of edges ($\binom{V}{2}$ denotes the set of all 2-element subsets of V). We assume that graph G is connected, meaning that every target is reachable from the attacker by some simple path p (i.e. a path where every node appears at most once).[1] Given a graph G, we will use $E(G)$ to denote the set of edges in G and $V(G)$ to denote the set of nodes in G.

The attacker attacks a selected defender in the network by reaching him through a path starting at 0 and ending at the defender. Each defender $j \in [n]$ has a value $b_j > 0$ describing his strategic importance to the attacker. If defender j is successfully attacked, the attacker receives a payoff of b_j.

If attacked successfully, the defender j obtains a negative payoff of $-d_j$. Each defender, anticipating a possible attack, can invest in protection (interception probability). Intercepting the attack means stopping the attacker, regardless of whether the defender is the target or simply lies on an attack path. The investment of defender j increases the probability $x_j \in [0, 1]$ of intercepting an attack and comes at a cost, $c_j(x_j)$. The cost of protection is an increasing, differentiable, and strictly convex function of the protection level and the cost of no protection is 0, i.e. $c_j(0) = 0$. We make the following assumption about the cost functions:

Assumption 1. *For every cost function $c_j(x_j)$ of defender $j \in [n]$, we assume that $c_j'(1) \geq d_j$ and $c_j'(0) = 0$.*

Assumption 1 implies that the only scenario in which the best response of the defender j might be the "perfect defense" (i.e. $x_j = 1$) is when he is the only attacked node.

In [1] it is assumed that the cost function $c_j(x_j) = x_j^2/2$ for the final presented results, but many important results are proven for a wider class of cost functions satisfying Assumption 1.

Defenders choose their interception probabilities independently and simultaneously with the attacker choosing a target $j \in [n]$ and an attack path p from 0 to j. Let $P(G)$ denote the set of all paths in graph G originating at the attacker node, 0, and $t(p)$ denote the terminal node of path p. Given any path $p \in P(G)$ and $j \in p$, the set of predecessors of j in p is $Pred(p, j) = \{k \in p : k \text{ lies on path } p \text{ between 0 and } j \}$. Fix a vector of interception investments $(x_1, \ldots, x_n)$. For any node j on path p, we let $\alpha_j(p, (x_i)_{i \in [n]})$ denote the probability that the attack along p reaches j

$$\alpha_j(p, (x_i)_{i \in [n]}) = \prod_{k \in Pred(p,j)} (1 - x_k).$$

---

[1] Throughout the paper when using the term path we will mean a simple path.

The probability that the attack on target j along path p is successful is given by

$$\beta_j(p, (x_i)_{i \in [n]}) = \alpha_j(p, (x_i)_{i \in [n]}) \cdot (1 - x_j).$$

The set of pure strategies of the attacker is defined by the set $P(G)$ of all paths originating at 0. The set of pure strategies of every defender $j \in [n]$, the level of protection, is the interval $[0, 1]$. Pair $(p, (x_i)_{i \in [n]})$ describes a pure strategy profile, with the payoff of the attacker given by

$$U(p, (x_i)_{i \in [n]}) = \beta_{t(p)}(p, (x_i)_{i \in [n]}) b_{t(p)},$$

and the payoff of defender j given by

$$V_j(p, (x_i)_{i \in [n]}) = \begin{cases} \beta_j(p, (x_i)_{i \in [n]})(-d_j) - c_j(x_j), & \text{if } j = t(p), \\ -c_j(x_j), & \text{otherwise.} \end{cases} \tag{1}$$

We allow the attacker to use mixed strategies, choosing a probability distribution π over all paths in $P(G)$. Let $\Delta(P(G))$ denote the set of all probability distributions over $P(G)$. The expected payoff of the attacker from a mixed strategy profile $(\pi, (x_i)_{i \in [n]}) \in \Delta(P(G)) \times [0, 1]^n$ is given by

$$U(\pi, (x_i)_{i \in [n]}) = \sum_{p \in P(G)} \pi(p) \beta_{t(p)}(p, (x_i)_{i \in [n]}) b_{t(p)}. \tag{2}$$

The expected payoff of defender j is given by

$$V_j(\pi, (x_i)_{i \in [n]}) = \sum_{\substack{p \in P(G) \\ t(p)=j}} \pi(p) \alpha_j(p, (x_i)_{i \in [n]})(1 - x_j)(-d_j) - c_j(x_j). \tag{3}$$

Following [1] we use the following assumption on defenders' importance.

Assumption 2. *For any two defenders i and j, $b_i \neq b_j$.*

This assumption means that no two defenders have the same strategic importance to the attacker. Moreover, without the loss of generality, we will assume that the defenders are numbered in increasing order with respect to their strategic importance to the attacker, i.e. $i < j \implies b_i < b_j$.

Definition 1 (Attack and defense game on a network). *Quadruple $(G, (b_i)_{i \in [n]}, (d_i)_{i \in [n]}, (c_i)_{i \in [n]})$ defines an attack and defense game on a network with network G, set of players $V(G)$, defenders' cost functions, c_j, attacker's evaluations, b_j, and defenders' evaluations d_j.*

We are interested in calculating (mixed strategy) Nash equilibria (NE) of attack and defense games on a network defined by Definition 1. A strategy profile $(\pi^*, (x_i^*)_{i \in [n]})$ is a NE if and only if for every mixed strategy $\pi \in \Delta(P(G))$ of the attacker, $U(\pi^*, (x_i^*)_{i \in [n]}) \geq U(\pi, (x_i^*)_{i \in [n]})$, and for every node $j \in [n]$ and every strategy $x_j \in [0, 1]$, $V_j(\pi^*, (x_j, (x_i^*)_{i \in [n] \setminus \{j\}})) \leq V_j(\pi^*, (x_i^*)_{i \in [n]})$.

3 Properties of the Nash Equilibria

In this section, we recall important properties of the NE of the attack and defense game on a network. The properties follow from [1] and are crucial for the computational results we obtain.

First, Bloch, Chatterjee, and Dutta [1] establish the existence of mixed strategy NE in the game.

Theorem 1 (Bloch et al. [1]). *The attack and defense game on a network always admits a Nash equilibrium in mixed strategies.*

Second, they establish sufficient and necessary conditions for the existence of pure strategy NE.

Lemma 1 (Bloch et al. [1]). *The described model yields NE in pure strategies if and only if the value b_n of node n satisfies*

$$b_n(1 - c_n'^{(-1)}(d_n)) \geq b_j \tag{4}$$

for all j such that there is a path p from 0 to j that does not contain n.

Note, that as c_n is a strictly convex, differentiable function, the inverse function $c_n'^{(-1)}$, of its differential, c_n', is well-defined.

Deciding whether the condition introduced in Lemma 1 is satisfied can be done in time $O(n)$ by the following straightforward algorithm. After removing the node n from the graph, all the nodes that remain connected to node 0 by a path form a set of nodes that can be reached by the attacker with a path that does not contain n. For this set of nodes, we check whether Inequality (4) is satisfied. If the condition is met then every profile where the attacker chooses a path p that terminates at node n, defender n chooses investment of $c_n'^{(-1)}(d_n)$ (value obtained from finding the derivative of payoff function of the n'th defender and comparing it to 0) and every other defender chooses investment of 0 is a pure strategy NE. From now on we will focus on the parameters of the model that do not yield NE in pure strategies.

3.1 Properties of Mixed Strategies Nash Equilibria

Given a game $\Gamma = (G, (b_i)_{i \in [n]}, (d_i)_{i \in [n]}, (c_i)_{i \in [n]})$, let

$$D_\Gamma(\pi, (x_i)_{i \in [n]}) \subseteq [n],$$

denote the set of all defenders attacked with positive probability under the strategy profile $(\pi, (x_i)_{i \in [n]})$. The following lemma about the independence of set $D_\Gamma(\pi, (x_i)_{i \in [n]})$ from a considered strategy profile $(\pi, (x_i)_{i \in [n]})$, that is a NE of Γ, follows from the proof of Theorem 2 [1].

Lemma 2 (Bloch et al. [1], Theorem 2). *Given the Assumption 2, for every attack and defense game on network* $\Gamma = (G, (b_i)_{i\in[n]}, (d_i)_{i\in[n]}, (c_i)_{i\in[n]})$, *and every two strategy profiles* $(\pi, (x_i)_{i\in[n]})$ *and* $(\pi', (x'_i)_{i\in[n]})$ *that are NE of* Γ,

$$D_\Gamma(\pi, (x_i)_{i\in[n]}) = D_\Gamma(\pi', (x'_i)_{i\in[n]}).$$

By Lemma 2, the set of nodes attacked with positive probability in equilibrium depends only on the game's parameters. Therefore, given a game $\Gamma = (G, (b_i)_{i\in[n]}, (d_i)_{i\in[n]}, (c_i)_{i\in[n]})$ we will denote this set by $D(\Gamma)$. We will call nodes in $D(\Gamma)$ *non-neutral nodes*. From proof of Theorem 2 [1], the set of non-neutral nodes is invariant under the vector of values $(d_i)_{i\in[n]}$ and the vector of cost functions $(c_i)_{i\in[n]}$ (as long as they satisfy Assumption 1). This is stated in the following lemma.

Lemma 3 (Bloch et al. [1]). *Let* $\Gamma = (G, (b_i)_{i\in[n]}, (d_i)_{i\in[n]}, (c_i)_{i\in[n]})$. *For any cost functions vector* $(c'_i)_{i\in[n]}$, *satisfying Assumption 1, and values vector* $(d'_i)_{i\in[n]}$ *it holds*

$$D(\Gamma) = D(\Gamma'),$$

where $\Gamma' = (G, (b_i)_{i\in[n]}, (d'_i)_{i\in[n]}, (c'_i)_{i\in[n]})$.

Following Lemma 3, for the remaining part of the paper, we will denote the set of nodes attacked in every NE of the game by $D(G, (b_i)_{i\in[n]})$. The set of nodes $[n] \setminus D(G, (b_i)_{i\in[n]})$ is never attacked under any NE. We call nodes in $[n] \setminus D(G, (b_i)_{i\in[n]})$ *neutral nodes*. We have the following observation.

Observation 1. *Every neutral node* j *maximizes his payoff in every NE by choosing a strategy* $x_j = 0$.

When the network, G, and the values of the nodes, $(b_i)_{i\in[n]}$ are clear from the context, we will use D instead of $D(G, (b_i)_{i\in[n]})$ to denote the set of non-neutral nodes and $[n] \setminus D$ to denote the set of neutral nodes.

For a non-neutral node, j, let P^j denote the set of all paths from 0 to j chosen by the attacker with positive probability in some NE of the game. Formally, path p from 0 to j in G belongs to P^j if and only if there exists a strategy profile $(\pi, (x_i)_{i\in[n]})$ that is a NE of the game, such that $\pi(p) > 0$. Bloch et al. [1] prove that any two paths in P^j can differ only on the set of neutral nodes. Moreover, non-neutral nodes on any two paths in P^j are aligned in the same sequence from the attacker to the target. This is stated by the following lemma.

Lemma 4 (Bloch et al. [1]). *For any two paths* p, p' *in* P^j,

$$Pred(p, j) \cap D(G, (b_i)_{i\in[n]}) = Pred(p', j) \cap D(G, (b_i)_{i\in[n]}).$$

Moreover, if $k, l \in Pred(p, j) \cap D(G, (b_i)_{i\in[n]})$ *then*

$$k \in Pred(p, l) \iff k \in Pred(p', l). \tag{5}$$

Following Lemma 4, for every non-neutral node j, we denote the unique sequence of his predecessors from D on any path in P^j by p^j. We call p^j *the equilibrium attack path of j*. The equilibrium attack paths are not always paths in the original graph, as they can lack some of the neutral nodes that are essential to their connectivity.

If a non-neutral node, $k \in D$, lies on an equilibrium attack path of another node non-neutral, $j \in D$, his equilibrium attack path, p^k, is a subsequence of p^j. This is stated by the following lemma.

Lemma 5 (Bloch et al. [1]). *Given two non-neutral nodes, k and j, if k is an element of p^j then p^k is a subsequence of p^j, i.e. that for some $m \in \{2, 3, \ldots, |p^j| - 1\}$, p^k is a sequence of first m elements of p^j.*

From Lemma 5, it follows that the set of nodes $\{0\} \cup D$ and the set of equilibrium attack paths $\{p_j\}_{j \in D}$ constitute a tree that is invariant under the vector of cost functions $(c_i)_{i \in [n]}$ (as long as they satisfy Assumption 1) and the vector of values $(d_i)_{i \in [n]}$. Therefore, for a given game $(G, (b_i)_{i \in [n]}, (d_i)_{i \in [n]}, (c_i)_{i \in [n]})$, we denote this tree by $T(G, (b_i)_{i \in [n]})$ and call it an *equilibrium attack tree*.

The concept of the equilibrium attack tree allows for the following redefinition of the game.

Definition 2 (Equilibrium attack tree game) . *An equilibrium attack tree game induced by the attack and defense game on network $(G, (b_i)_{i \in [n]}, (d_i)_{i \in [n]}, (c_i)_{i \in [n]})$ is the attack and defense game on network $(T(G, (b_i)_{i \in [n]}), (c_i)_{i \in D}, (b_i)_{i \in D}, (d_i)_{i \in D})$.*

In such a game, every defender is connected to the attacker by exactly one path – his equilibrium attack path. It means that every mixed strategy π of the attacker is described by vector $(q_i)_{i \in D}$, which determines the probabilities of attack on every node.

3.2   NE of the Equilibrium Attack Tree Game

Given an equilibrium attack tree game $(T(G, (b_i)_{i \in [n]}), (c_i)_{i \in D}, (b_i)_{i \in D}, (d_i)_{i \in D})$, let $D_0 \subseteq D$ denote the set of all the neighbours of 0 in tree $T(G, (b_i)_{i \in [n]})$. By [1], the first-order conditions that have to be fulfilled by any NE of the game are

$$x_j^* = 1 - \frac{U}{b_j}, \text{ if } j \in D_0, \tag{6}$$

$$x_j^* = 1 - \frac{b_{k(j)}}{b_j}, \text{ if } j \in D \setminus D_0, \tag{7}$$

$$q_j^* = \frac{c_j'\left(1 - \frac{U}{b_j}\right)}{d_j}, \text{ if } j \in D_0, \tag{8}$$

$$q_j^* = \frac{b_{k(j)} \cdot c_j' \left(1 - \frac{b_{k(j)}}{b_j}\right)}{U \cdot d_j}, \text{ if } j \in D \setminus D_0, \tag{9}$$

$$\sum_j q_j^* = 1. \tag{10}$$

where $k(j)$ is the direct predecessor of j in the equilibrium attack path p^j and U is the equilibrium utility of the attacker.

Equations (6) and (7) are obtained from the equations guaranteeing that the attacker is indifferent among the targets in the support.

$$b_j(1 - x_j^*) = U, \qquad\qquad \text{for } j \in D_0,$$
$$b_j(1 - x_j^*) = b_{k(j)}, \qquad\qquad \text{for } j \notin D_0.$$

Equations (8) and (9) are obtained from maximizing the payoff function of every defender defined in (11). First, we calculate the derivative

$$\frac{\partial V_j(q, x_1, \dots, x_n)}{\partial x_j} = \alpha_j x_j q_j^* d_j - c_j'(x_j). \tag{11}$$

The function $V_j(x_j)$ is concave, therefore it is only increasing in an interval where $\alpha_j x_j q_j^* d_j \geq c_j'(x_j)$. It follows from Assumption 1, that 0 is in this interval while 1 is not, therefore the derivative is equal to 0 in the maximum, hence

$$c_j'(x_j^*) = \alpha_j q_j^* d_j. \tag{12}$$

In any NE the attacker is indifferent over the strategies in the support, i.e.

$$U = b_j \alpha_j (1 - x_j^*).$$

After transforming this equation, we get

$$\alpha_j = \frac{U}{b_j(1 - x_j^*)}.$$

This means that the equation (12) states

$$c_j'(x_j^*) = \frac{U q_j^* d_j}{b_j(1 - x_j^*)},$$

hence

$$q_j^* = \frac{c_j'(x_j^*) b_j (1 - x_j^*)}{U \cdot d_j}.$$

Using equations (6) and (7) we get (8) and (9), respectively. Equation (10) states that the probabilities in any mixed strategy of the attacker sum up to 1. We conclude this subsection by stating the uniqueness of the solution to the introduced set of equations.

Theorem 2 (Bloch et al. [1]). *Given Assumption 2, the proposed set of first-order conditions (6)-(10) yields exactly one solution*

$$((q^*)_{i \in D}, (x_i)_{i \in D}, U) \in [0,1]^{|D|} \times [0,1]^{|D|} \times [0,1]$$

that is the unique NE of the equilibrium attack tree game.

3.3   Properties of the Equilibrium Attack Tree

In this subsection, we present the properties of the equilibrium attack tree that follows from Theorem 2. Consider a non-neutral node $j \in D \setminus D_0$. In the NE of the equilibrium attack tree game $(T(G, (b_i)_{i \in [n]}), (c_i)_{i \in D}, (b_i)_{i \in D}, (d_i)_{i \in D})$, node j is attacked through the equilibrium attack path $p^j = (0, p_1^j, p_2^j, \ldots, k(j), j)$, and the probability α_j of attacker successfully reaching the node j is

$$\alpha_j = \prod_{i \in \{p_1^j, p_2^j, \ldots, k(j)\}} (1 - x_i^*).$$

Using the (6) and (7), we get

$$\alpha_j = \left(1 - \left(1 - \frac{U}{b_{p_1^j}} \right) \right) \prod_{i \in \{p_2^j, \ldots, k(j)\}} \left(1 - \left(1 - \frac{b_{i-1}}{b_i} \right) \right)$$

$$= \frac{U}{b_{p_1^j}} \prod_{i \in \{p_2^j, \ldots, k(j)\}} \left(\frac{b_{i-1}}{b_i} \right) = \frac{U}{b_{k(j)}}. \tag{13}$$

The nodes in D, that can be a direct predecessor of a node j in his equilibrium attack path, are the non-neutral nodes that can be reached in graph G from j by any path that does not contain any other node from $\{0\} \cup D$. Let $N(j, D, G) \subset D$ denote the set of these nodes. Formally, non-neutral node i is in $N(j, D, G)$ if and only if there exists a path p from j to i in G that does not contain any nodes from $(D \cup \{0\}) \setminus \{i, j\}$.

Equilibrium attack paths are chosen by the attacker to maximize her payoff. Equation (13) states, that the smaller the value $b_{k(j)}$, of the direct predecessor of $k(j)$ of node $j \in D \setminus D_0$ on equilibrium attack path p^j, the greater the probability of reaching the node j by the attacker. We conclude this with the following observation, which states how the attacker chooses the equilibrium attack tree for a given graph G, set of nodes D_0 and their evaluations $(b_i)_{i \in D_0}$.

Observation 2 (Bloch et al. [1]).   *For any node $j \in D_0$, the attacker maximizes her payoff in the NE of the equilibrium attack tree game by attacking j directly. For any node $j' \in D \setminus D_0$ the attacker maximizes her payoff in the NE of the equilibrium attack tree game by attacking node j' along the equilibrium attack path where the direct predecessor of j' is node $i \in N(j, D, G)$ with the lowest value b_i.*

4   Computation of Mixed Strategy NE

The main challenge of computing a NE of a given attack and defense game, $(G, (b_i)_{i \in [n]}, (d_i)_{i \in [n]}, (c_i)_{i \in [n]})$ is computing the set of all non-neutral nodes, $D(G, (b_i)_{i \in [n]})$. To tackle this problem, we introduce the idea of network reduction by a subset of neutral nodes. We prove that reducing the network by any subset of neutral nodes retains a particular correspondence between the Nash equilibria of the original and the reduced model (in particular, both games yield the same equilibrium attack tree game). Using network reduction, we show that the equilibrium attack tree of the given game can be found in polynomial time when the set of non-neutral nodes is known. Next, we introduce an important subset of neutral nodes called *linkers*. After reducing the network by the set of linkers, the problem of finding the set of non-neutral nodes is easier. We propose an algorithm that allows for finding the set of non-neutral nodes of a given attack and defense game on a network. The algorithm generalizes the idea of finding the set of non-neutral nodes when the considered network is a linear graph with ascending values b_j, presented in [1], to finding this set when the considered network is an arbitrary graph. When the set of non-neutral nodes in the game $(G, (b_i)_{i \in [n]}, (d_i)_{i \in [n]}, (c_i)_{i \in [n]})$ is found, we calculate the NE of the corresponding equilibrium attack tree game. Finally, we show how to reconstruct a NE of a $(G, (b_i)_{i \in [n]}, (d_i)_{i \in [n]}, (c_i)_{i \in [n]})$ from the NE of the corresponding equilibrium attack tree game.

4.1   Network Reduction

For a given game $(G, (b_i)_{i \in [n]}, (d_i)_{i \in [n]}, (c_i)_{i \in [n]})$, its' set of non-neutral nodes D, and any neutral node $m \in [n] \setminus D$, let us construct a graph, called G *reduced by* m, obtained by removing node m and adding links between all pairs of neighbours of m that are not connected by an edge in G. We denote a graph G reduced by m by $G \setminus m$. Formally $V(G \setminus m) = V(G) \setminus \{m\}$ and $E(G \setminus m) = E(G) \setminus \{\{i, m\} : i \in V(G)\} \cup \{\{i, k\} : i \neq k \wedge \{i, m\} \in E(G) \wedge \{m, k\} \in E(G)\}$.

Let $h_m^G : P(G) \to P(G \setminus m)$ be a function such that, for a given path $p \in P(G)$,

$$h_m^G(p) = \begin{cases} p & \text{if } m \notin p, \\ p \setminus \{m\} & \text{otherwise.} \end{cases}$$

Function h_m^G maps paths emerging from 0 in graph G to paths emerging from 0 in graph $G \setminus m$.

Function h_m^G, defined for the set of the pure strategies of the attacker, naturally extends to a function $H_m^G : \Delta(P(G)) \to \Delta(P(G \setminus m))$ such that, for every probability distribution $\pi \in \Delta(P(G))$ over the set of paths in G,

$$H_m^G(\pi) = \sum_{p \in P(G)} \pi(p) \cdot h_m^G(p).$$

Lemma 6. *Let $\Gamma = (G, (b_i)_{i \in [n]}, (d_i)_{i \in [n]}, (c_i)_{i \in [n]})$. Node $m \in [n] \setminus D$ is a neutral node and strategy profile $(\pi^*, (x_i)_{i \in [n]}^*)$ is a NE of Γ if and only if the strategy profile $(H_m^G(\pi^*), (x_i)_{i \in [n] \setminus m}^*)$ is a NE of $\Gamma \setminus m = (G \setminus m, (c_i)_{i \in [n] \setminus \{m\}}, (b_i)_{i \in [n] \setminus \{m\}}, (d_i)_{i \in [n] \setminus \{m\}}).$*

Proof. Notice that the derivative of defender $j \in [n]$ payoff function, V_j, is given by

$$V_j'(x_j) = d_j \cdot \sum_{\substack{p \in P(G) \\ t(p)=j}} \pi(p) \, \alpha_j\left(p, (x)_{i \in [n]}\right) - c_j'(x_j).$$

Assumption 1 on costs functions guarantees that the maximum of V_j is inside the interval $(0, 1)$. As function V_j is concave, we can find this maximum by solving $V_j'(x_j) = 0$. We get

$$x_j = (c_j')^{-1}\left(d_j \cdot \sum_{\substack{p \in P(G) \\ t(p)=j}} \pi(p) \, \alpha_j\left(p, (x_i)_{i \in [n]}\right) \right). \tag{14}$$

In any NE, any defender j chooses the defense investment given by Equation (14) to maximize his payoff.

For the right to left implication, consider a NE $(\pi^*, (x_i^*)_{i \in [n] \setminus \{m\}})$ of a game $\Gamma \setminus m$. We will prove that when node m is neutral, every strategy profile $(\pi, (x_m = 0, (x_i^*)_{i \in [n] \setminus \{m\}}))$ that satisfies $H_m^G(\pi) = \pi^*$ is a NE of the game Γ. Notice that $x_m = 0$ implies that, for every path $p \in P(G)$,

$$\alpha_j(p, (x_i)_{i \in [n]}) = \alpha_j(h_m^G(p), (x_i)_{i \in [n] \setminus \{m\}}). \tag{15}$$

By (15) every defender $j \in [n] \setminus \{m\}$,

$$\sum_{\substack{p \in P(G \setminus \{m\}) \\ t(p)=j}} \pi(p) \alpha_j(p, (x_i)_{i \in [n] \setminus \{m\}}) = \sum_{\substack{p \in P(G \setminus \{m\}) \\ t(p)=j}} \sum_{\substack{p' \in P(G) \\ h_m^G(p')=p}} \pi(p') \alpha_j(p', (x_i)_{i \in [n]})$$

$$= \sum_{\substack{p \in P(G) \\ t(p)=j}} \pi(p) \alpha_j(p, (x_i)_{i \in [n]}).$$

As Equation (14) is satisfied for every defender $j \in [n] \setminus \{m\}$ by the strategy profile $(\pi^*, (x_i^*)_{i \in [n] \setminus \{m\}})$, notice that every defender $j \in [n]$ cannot increase his payoff by deviating from $(\pi, (x_m = 0, (x_i^*)_{i \in [n] \setminus \{m\}}))$ if the strategies of all the other players remain unchanged. Therefore, the only player that can benefit from changing her strategy in the strategy profile $(\pi, (x_m = 0, (x_i^*)_{i \in [n] \setminus \{m\}}))$ is the attacker.

Consider any path $p \in P(G)$ such that $\pi(p) = 0$. Notice, that

$$U(p, (x_m = 0, (x_i)_{i \in [n] \setminus \{m\}})) =$$
$$U(h_m^G(p), (x_i)_{i \in [n] \setminus \{m\}}) \leq U(\pi^*, (x_i)_{i \in [n] \setminus \{m\}}) = U(\pi, (x_m = 0, (x_i)_{i \in [n] \setminus \{m\}})), \tag{16}$$

hence the attacker also cannot increase her payoff by deviating from $(\pi, (x_m = 0, (x_i^*)_{i \in [n] \setminus \{m\}}))$. The inequality follows from the NE definition and both equalities follow from the Equation (15).

The strategy profile $(\pi, (x_m = 0, (x_i^*)_{i \in [n] \setminus \{m\}}))$ is a NE of the attack and defense game on network $\Gamma \setminus m$, because none of the players can increase their payoff by deviating from it.

The proof of reverse implication is analogous.   □

The reduction of the game extends to any set of neutral nodes by iterative reduction of neutral nodes one by one. First, note that for any game $(G, (b_i)_{i \in [n]}, (d_i)_{i \in [n]}, (c_i)_{i \in [n]})$, the corresponding set D of non-neutral nodes and any two neutral nodes $j, k \in D \setminus [n]$

$$H_k^{(G \setminus j)} \circ H_j^G = H_j^{(G \setminus k)} \circ H_k^G. \tag{17}$$

The reduction of the game extends to any set $S \subseteq ([n] \setminus D)$ of neutral nodes by iterative reduction of nodes from S one by one. Equation (17) guarantees that reduction by the set of nodes is invariant to the ordering in which we choose nodes from S.

Definition 3. *For a given game $(G, (b_i)_{i \in [n]}, (d_i)_{i \in [n]}, (c_i)_{i \in [n]})$, the corresponding set of non-neutral nodes D, any subset of neutral nodes $S \subseteq ([n] \setminus D)$, and any sequence $s = \{s_1, s_2, \ldots, s_{|S|}\}$ of all the nodes in S, the reduction of G by S with sequence s is defined as*

$$H_{S,s}^G = \begin{cases} H_{(S \setminus \{s_1\}),(s_2,\ldots,s_{|S|})}^{G \setminus s_1}, & \text{if } |S| > 2, \\ H_{s_2}^{G \setminus s_1}, & \text{if } |S| = 2. \end{cases}$$

As the reduction of the network is independent of the order of nodes from S, we denote it with H_S^G. Reducing the network by a given neutral node i can be done in $O(n^2)$ time and reducing the network by a given set of nodes, $S \subseteq [n]$, can be done in time $O(|S| \cdot n^2)$.

4.2   Linkers

We now introduce an important set of nodes called *linkers*. Let us call a node i a *linker* if he is not directly connected to the attacker and all of his neighbours' evaluations, b_j, are greater than b_i, i.e. $\{0, i\} \notin E(G)$ and $(\{i, j\} \in E(G) \implies b_j > b_i)$. All linkers are neutral nodes, which we state in the lemma below.

Lemma 7. *Every linker is a neutral node.*

Proof. Consider a linker $m \in [n]$ and any path $p \in P(G)$ such, that $t(p) = m$, i.e. m is a terminal node of p. Let $k(m)$ denote the direct predecessor of node m on path p. Notice that the probability $\beta_m(m, p)$ of the successful attack on node m through path p satisfies

$$\beta_m(p, (x_i)_{i \in [n]}) = (1 - x_i) \beta_{k(m)}(p \setminus \{m\}, (x_i)_{i \in [n]}) \le \beta_{k(m)}(p \setminus \{m\}, (x_i)_{i \in [n]}).$$

As $b_m < b_{k(m)}$ from the linker definition, for any strategy p, the strategy $p \setminus \{m\}$ yields a strictly greater payoff to the attacker. Therefore, the strategy p is not in the NE support of the attacker.

No path $p \in P(G)$ with terminal $t(p) = m$ is in the attacker support in any NE, hence considered node m is a neutral node.   □

Let $L(G) \subseteq [n]$ denote the set of all linkers in graph G. By Lemma 7, the set $L(G)$ is a subset of the set of all neutral nodes. Following the game reduction by the set of neutral nodes, we can reduce the graph G by $L(G)$ while retaining the correspondence between the NE of the original and the reduced model. We will call the graph $G \setminus L(G)$ a *proper* graph.

The following example illustrates reducing a graph by its linker.

Example 1. In the graph shown in Fig. 1, node 1 is a linker. We can reduce graph G by node 1, connecting all of 1's neighbours that are not directly connected. As a result, we get the proper graph shown in Fig. 2, where nodes 2 and 4 are now directly connected and every node is connected to the attacker with at least one ascending path of indices.

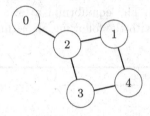

Fig. 1. Graph with a linker (node 1).   **Fig. 2.** Graph after removing the linker.

The following observation is a direct consequence of the properties of network reduction.

Observation 3. *Let* $\Gamma = (G, (b_i)_{i \in [n]}, (d_i)_{i \in [n]}, (c_i)_{i \in [n]})$, *graph* $G' = G \setminus L(G)$ *is the proper graph of* G, *and* $\Gamma' = (G', (c_i)_{i \in [n] \setminus L(G)}, (b_i)_{i \in [n] \setminus L(G)}, (d_i)_{i \in [n] \setminus L(G)})$. *Games* Γ *and* Γ' *yield the same equilibrium attack tree game.*

Determining whether a given node $i \in [n]$ is a linker can be done in time $O(n)$, hence finding the set $L(G)$ of all linkers can be done in time $O(n^2)$. As every node i in the proper graph has a neighbour j of a lower index, the following observation emerges.

Observation 4. *Every node in a proper graph is connected to the attacker with at least one path of ascending indices.*

As a consequence of Observation 4, we have the following lemma, characterizing the set of non-neutral nodes for proper graphs.

Lemma 8. *If graph G is proper, the set of non-neutral nodes D of the attack and defense game is $\{k, k + 1, \ldots, n\}$ for some $k \in [n]$.*

Proof. Let us assume that k is the lowest index of a node attacked with positive probability in NE. We will prove that every node with an index greater than k is also attacked with positive probability. Let us assume that node $k + 1$ is not attacked in NE. From Observation 4, we know there is at least one ascending path of nodes from 0 to $k + 1$. If there is such a path that does not contain k, then $k + 1$ has to be attacked. If he were not attacked, then he would not defend himself, and therefore attacking him would yield a greater payoff to the attacker than attacking node k. If every ascending path from 0 to $k + 1$ contains k, then again, $k + 1$ has to be attacked. If he was not attacked, he would not defend himself, and therefore the attacker could reach him with the same probability as the node k, but $k + 1$ would yield a greater payoff. The same reasoning for every other node with an index greater than k shows that if k is the lowest index of a non-neutral node, and graph G is proper, hence $D = \{k, k + 1, \ldots, n\}$.   □

4.3   Computation of the Equilibrium Attack Tree

Consider game $(G, (b_i)_{i \in [n]}, (d_i)_{i \in [n]}, (c_i)_{i \in [n]})$, with a proper graph G, and the corresponding set of non-neutral nodes, D. The equilibrium attack tree $T(G, (b_i)_{i \in [n]})$ can be found in polynomial time with the following algorithm.

Algorithm 1. Constructing equilibrium attack tree

    Input: proper graph G and a set $D \subseteq V(G)$
    Output: equilibrium attack tree T
1: $G' = G \setminus ([n] \setminus D)$
2: $T =$ empty graph
3: $V(T) = \{0\} \cup D$
4: **for** $j \in D$ **do**
5:     **if** $(0, j) \in E(G')$ **then**
6:        $E(T) = E(T) \cup \{(0, j)\}$
7:     **else**
8:        find $N(j, G')$ {the set of neighbours of j in graph G'}
9:        $i = \min(N(j, G'))$
10:      $E(T) = E(T) \cup \{\{i, j\}\}$
11:    **end if**
12: **end for**
13: **return** T

From Observation 4, we know that every node in a proper graph has at least one neighbour of a smaller index, hence in every iteration of the *for* loop, a new edge is added to the graph T. As the resulting graph T is a connected graph with $n + 1$ vertices and n edges, it is in fact a tree. From Observation 3 we know that graphs G and G' yield the same equilibrium attack tree. Observation 2 states that every neighbour of 0 in G' is directly connected to 0 in T, and every other node is connected in T to his neighbour in G' of the lowest index, which concludes the correctness of Algorithm 1 when the input set of nodes is the set of non-neutral nodes.

The dominant procedure when considering the time complexity of Algorithm 1 is finding the graph G', which can be done in $O((n - |D|) \cdot n^2)$.

4.4 Finding the Lowest Node Index in D

In this section, we consider game $(G, (b_i)_{i \in [n]}, (d_i)_{i \in [n]}, (c_i)_{i \in [n]})$, with a proper graph G, and show how to find the corresponding set of non-neutral nodes, D. Let k^* denote the lowest index of a node in D. We formulate the condition which is satisfied by k^* alone and test this condition for all the possible values of $k \in [n]$, finding k^*. Using Algorithm 1, for every $k \in [n]$ we can find the equilibrium attack tree T for graph G assuming that $D = \{k, k+1, \ldots, n\}$.

For every $k \in [n]$ we define a function $F_k : [0, b_n] \to \mathbb{R}_{\geq 0}$, such that, for a given payoff U of the attacker,

$$F_k(U) = \sum_i q_i^*(U, k),$$

where $q_i^*(U, k)$ is given by Equations (8) and (9), for $D = \{k, k+1, \ldots, n\}$. F_k has the following properties.

1. It is strictly decreasing in U, as every element of the sum is strictly decreasing in U.
2. $F_{k^*}(U^*) = 1$, where U^* denotes the attacker payoff at the equilibrium and k^* denotes the lowest index of a node attacked with positive probability in NE.

The condition on k^* is

$$F_{k^*}(b_{k^*}) \leq 1 < F_{k^*}(b_{k^*-1}), \tag{18}$$

as it implies

$$b_{k^*} \geq U^* > b_{k^*-1}. \tag{19}$$

The set of first-order conditions (6)-(9) guarantees that the payoff to the attacker is the same for every pure strategy in the support. The payoff from every pure strategy outside of the support is not greater than b_{k^*-1}, hence it is smaller than U^*. This means, that the attacker cannot increase her payoff by changing her strategy. Neither can the defenders, as each one of them already maximizes his payoff. Therefore, the strategy profile $((q^*)_{i \in D}, (x_i)_{i \in D})$ defined by Equations (6)-(10) describe the NE of equilibrium attack tree game $(T(G, (b_i)_{i \in [n]}), (c_i)_{i \in D}, (b_i)_{i \in D}, (d_i)_{i \in D})$ (which we know is unique from Theorem 2), with $D = \{k^*, k^* + 1, \ldots, n\}$.

4.5 Calculating the NE of an Equilibrium Attack Tree Game for a Proper Graph

Consider attack and defense game $(G, (b_i)_{i \in [n]}, (d_i)_{i \in [n]}, (c_i)_{i \in [n]})$, where graph G is proper. To calculate the strategy profile that is the NE of the corresponding equilibrium attack tree game, knowing that $D = \{k^*, k^* + 1, \ldots, n\}$, we need to find the payoff of the attacker U^*. This means solving the equation $F_{k^*}(U) = 1$

$$\sum_{i \in D_0} \frac{c_i'(1 - \frac{U}{b_i})}{d_i} + \sum_{i \in D \setminus D_0} \frac{b_{k(i)} \cdot c_i'(1 - \frac{b_{k(i)}}{b_i})}{U \cdot d_i} = 1. \tag{20}$$

In the case of the cost functions $c_i(x_i)$ being of the form $c_i(x_i) = x_i^2/2$, Equation (9) takes the form

$$\sum_{i \in D_0} \frac{1 - \frac{U}{b_i}}{d_i} + \sum_{i \in D \setminus D_0} \frac{b_{k(i)} \cdot 1 - \frac{b_{k(i)}}{b_i}}{U \cdot d_i} = 1.$$

This equation can be transformed into a quadratic equation after multiplying both sides by U, and it can be solved in linear time with respect to the number of nodes.

After establishing the payoff of the attacker, the last thing to do is to calculate the solutions of equations (6)-(9). Each equation can be solved in a constant time, as we only need to calculate the value of the function $x_i^2/2$ at a given point.

5 Calculating the Strategies in the NE for Any Graph

Consider $(G, (b_i)_{i \in [n]}, (d_i)_{i \in [n]}, (c_i)_{i \in [n]})$, where graph G is any connected graph. We showed how to find the set D and the NE $((q_i^*)_{i \in D}, (x_i^*)_{i \in D})$ of the attack equilibrium tree game $(T(G, (b_i)_{i \in [n]}), (c_i)_{i \in D}, (b_i)_{i \in D}, (d_i)_{i \in D})$ by first calculating the proper graph $G' = G \setminus L(G)$, then applying the method of finding the set of non-neutral nodes D and finally calculating the NE, $((q_i^*)_{i \in D}, (x_i^*)_{i \in D})\}$, of the corresponding equilibrium attack tree game. In this section, we show how to retrieve a strategy profile $(\pi, (x_i)_{i \in [n]})$ that is a NE of an attack and defense game on network, $(G, (b_i)_{i \in [n]}, (d_i)_{i \in [n]}, (c_i)_{i \in [n]})$, from the NE $((q_i^*)_{i \in D}, (x_i^*)_{i \in D})$ of the corresponding equilibrium attack tree game.

Let $R(i, j, G, D)$ denote the set of all paths p in G from $i \in D$ to $j \in D$, that do not contain any other node from D. To find the set $R(i, j, G, D)$ we remove nodes in $D \setminus \{i, j\}$ from G. If i and j are in two different components then $R(i, j, G, D) = \emptyset$. In general, set $R(i, j, G, D)$ can contain (exponentially) many different paths, and therefore can be difficult to find, however, we can obtain any of these paths in time $O(n^2)$. We will denote such a path by $r_{\{i,j\}}(G, D)$.

Considering an equilibrium attack path, $p^j \in P(T(G, (b_i)_{i \in [n]}))$, we create a path $p^{j,res} \in P(G)$ by replacing the edge between $m \in p^j$ and his predecessor $k(m) \in p^j$ with a path $r_{\{k(m),m\}}(G, D)$. From the reduction procedure, it follows

Nash Equilibria of Attack and Defense Games on Networks

that $r_{\{k(m),m\}}(G,D)$ exists for every such pair of nodes and it can be $\{m,k(m)\}$ if and only if $\{m,k(m)\} \in E(G)$. Let $\pi^* \in \Delta(P(G))$ be

$$\pi^*(p) = \begin{cases} q_j^*, & \text{if } p = p^{j,res}, \\ 0, & \text{otherwise.} \end{cases}$$

Observation 5. *Strategy profile* $(\pi^*, ((0)_{i \in [n] \setminus D}, (x_i^*)_{i \in D}))$ *describes a NE of* $(G, (b_i)_{i \in [n]}, (d_i)_{i \in [n]}, (c_i)_{i \in [n]})$.

This follows from the game reduction by the set of neutral nodes, as by reversing the reduction of G by set $D' = [n] \setminus D$, we can define the mapping $H_{D'}^G$ where $(H_{D'}^G)^{-1}(p^j) = p^{j,res}$ for every node $j \in D$, as for every j, and every mapping $H_{D'}^G$, $H_{D'}^G(p^{j,res}) = p^j$.

The procedure of reconstructing NE of the original game from the $((q_i^*)_{i \in D}, (x_i^*)_{i \in D})$ runs in time $O(|D| \cdot n^2)$, as it requires finding exactly $|D| \leq n$ paths $r_{i,j}(G,D)$.

6 Computational Complexity

A NE of the attack and defense game $(G, (b_i)_{i \in [n]}, (d_i)_{i \in [n]}, (c_i)_{i \in [n]})$ can be found by the following procedure.

Algorithm 2. Finding the NE of the general model

Input: attack and defense game $(G, (b_i)_{i \in [n]}, (d_i)_{i \in [n]}, (c_i)_{i \in [n]})$
Output: a NE of a given game

1: find the set $L(G)$ of all linkers in G
2: calculate the proper graph $G' = G \setminus L(G)$
3: **for** $k \in \{1, \dots, n\}$ **do**
4:     calculate $G_k' = G' \setminus \{1, \dots, k-1\}$
5:     construct equilibrium attack tree T_k for graph G_k' (Algorithm 1)
6:     construct function $F_k(U)$ using the equations (8) and (9)
7:     **if** inequality (18) holds **then**
8:         save $k^* = k$
9:         save $T_{k^*} = T_k$
10:        break
11:    **end if**
12: **end for**
13: calculate U^* solving (20)
14: calculate strategies of the attacker and the defenders solving the equations (6), (7), (8) and (9)
15: reconstruct the NE of the general game
16: **return** NE of the general game

The pessimistic time complexities of all the used procedures were established when the given procedure was introduced. The dominant operation of Algorithm 2 is the calculation of the reduced graph (line 4), which can require time

$O(n^3)$ in every iteration of the main loop. Therefore, the pessimistic run time of Algorithm 1 is $O(n^4)$.

Algorithm 2 can be easily generalized to compute Nash equilibria of the game for arbitrary cost functions (satisfying Assumptions 1) other than $c_i(x) = x^2/2$. In the case of such cost functions, the pessimistic time cost of Algorithm 2 is polynomial with respect to the number of players as long as Equation (20) can be solved in polynomial time.

7 Conclusions

In this paper, we proposed a method for finding a NE of attack and defense games on networks [1]. The proposed algorithm runs in polynomial time with respect to the number of nodes in the network.

The idea of reducing the network by the set of linker nodes that results in a proper graph, although simple, allows us to make an important observation that every node in a proper graph can be reached by the attacker by at least one ascending path. This idea can be used for the subclass of attack and interception games on networks, where the defenders make their decisions independently and only the target node is influenced by the attack. However, if the defenders could coordinate, it could happen that a linker node, although never attacked, is protected to defend more valuable nodes that can be reached only through this linker.

Acknowledgements. This work was supported by the Polish National Science Centre through grant 2018/29/B/ST6/00174.

References

1. Bloch, F., Chatterjee, K., Dutta, B.: Attack and interception in networks (forthcoming). Theoret. Econ. 1–51 (2023)
2. Chan, H., Ceyko, M., Ortiz, L.E.: Interdependent defense games: modeling interdependent security under deliberate attacks. In: Proceedings of the Twenty-Eighth Conference on Uncertainty in Artificial Intelligence, pp. 152–162. UAI 2012 (2012)
3. Collado, R.A., Papp, D.: Network interdiction - models, applications, unexplored directions. Technical report. RRR 4–2012, Rutgers University (2010)
4. Dell, M.: Trafficking networks and the Mexican drug war. Am. Econ. Rev. **105**(6), 1738–79 (2015)
5. Fulkerson, D.R., Harding, G.C.: Maximizing the minimum source-sink path subject to a budget constraint. Math. Program. **13**(1), 116–118 (1977)
6. Ghare, P.M., Montgomery, D.C., Turner, W.C.: Optimal interdiction policy for a flow network. Naval Res. Logist. Q. **18**(1), 37–45 (1971)
7. Golden, B.: A problem in network interdiction. Naval Res. Logist. Q. **25**(4), 711–713 (1978)
8. McMasters, A.W., Mustin, T.M.: Optimal interdiction of a supply network. Naval Res. Logist. Q. **17**(3), 261–268 (1970)

9. Mirzaei, M., Mirzapour Al-e-hashem, S.M.J., Akbarpour Shirazi, M.: A maximum-flow network interdiction problem in an uncertain environment under information asymmetry condition: application to smuggling goods. Comput. Indus. Eng. **162**, 107708 (2021)

10. Morton, D.P., Pan, F., Saeger, K.J.: Models for nuclear smuggling interdiction. IIE Trans. **39**(1), 3–14 (2007)

11. Smith, J.C., Song, Y.: A survey of network interdiction models and algorithms. Eur. J. Oper. Res. **283**(3), 797–811 (2020)

12. Washburn, A., Wood, K.: Two-person zero-sum games for network interdiction. Oper. Res. **43**(2), 243–251 (1995)

Stackelberg Vertex Cover on a Path

Katharina Eickhoff[ID], Lennart Kauther[(✉)][ID], and Britta Peis[ID]

Chair of Management Science, RWTH Aachen University, Aachen, Germany
{eickhoff,kauther,peis}@oms.rwth-aachen.de
https://www.oms.rwth-aachen.de

Abstract. A Stackelberg Vertex Cover game is played on an undirected graph $\mathcal{G}$ where some of the vertices are under the control of a *leader*. The remaining vertices are assigned a fixed weight. The game is played in two stages. First, the leader chooses prices for the vertices under her control. Afterward, the second player, called *follower*, selects a min weight vertex cover in the resulting weighted graph. That is, the follower selects a subset of vertices C^* such that every edge has at least one endpoint in C^* of minimum weight with respect to the fixed weights and the prices set by the leader. STACKELBERG VERTEX COVER (STACKVC) describes the leader's optimization problem to select prices in the first stage of the game so as to maximize her revenue, which is the cumulative price of all her (priceable) vertices that are contained in the follower's solution. Previous research showed that STACKVC is NP-hard on bipartite graphs, but solvable in polynomial time in the special case of bipartite graphs, where all priceable vertices belong to the same side of the bipartition. In this paper, we investigate STACKVC on paths and present a dynamic program with linear time and space complexity.

Keywords: Stackelberg Network Pricing · Vertex Cover · Dynamic Programming · Algorithmic Game Theory

1 Introduction

Stackelberg games – sometimes also called leader-follower games – are a tremendously powerful framework to capture situations in which a dominant party called the *leader* first makes a decision and afterward, the other players called *followers* react to the leader's move. An important detail thereby is that the leader has information about the followers' preferences and potential competitors. She thus tries to leverage this informational and temporal advantage to maximize her revenue. A typical example of such a scenario is a mono- or oligopolist dictating prices and the consumers adapting their consumption behavior accordingly. The concept of Stackelberg games traces back to the German economist Heinrich Freiherr von Stackelberg [23] who also coined the term.

This work is supported by the Deutsche Forschungsgemeinschaft (DFG, German Research Foundation) - 2236/2.

In many applications, the followers' preferences have a combinatorial structure and can be represented by a graph. For instance, the edges of the graph may represent all possible means of transport in a city, some of which, e. g., certain turnpikes, are under the control of the leader, and one follower wants to find a shortest or cheapest path between a designated source and destination. This would be an example of STACKELBERG SHORTEST-PATH (STACKSP) with a single follower. The leader then obtains revenue corresponding to the price of every edge under her control that is included in the shortest path selected by the follower. Labbè et al. [19] first introduced STACKSP to optimize turnpike returns. By doing so, they kicked off an entirely new branch of research on so-called *Stackelberg network pricing games*. In these, the leader controls a subset of the vertices or edges on which she can set prices in the first stage of the game. The other resources are assigned fixed prices. In the second stage of the game, one or several followers each select an optimal solution to the problem under consideration (e.g. SHORTEST-PATH, MINIMUM SPANNING TREE, MINIMUM WEIGHT VERTEX COVER, ...) based on the fixed prices, and the prices set by the leader. The goal of the leader is to select prices in the first stage of the game so as to maximize the resulting revenue, which is obtained from the prices of all resources she controls that are selected into the optimal solution(s) of the follower(s). As usual in the Stackelberg literature, we assume that the followers break ties in favor of the leader. Furthermore, we restrict our analysis to Stackelberg games in the single-follower setting.

Other common combinatorial graph structures that have been investigated under the Stackelberg framework include MINIMUM SPANNING TREE (MST) [4,10,11], MAX CLOSURE aka. project-selection [16], and MINIMUM WEIGHT VERTEX COVER (MWVC) [7,16]. Note that in the latter two problems, the leader controls part of the vertices, while in STACKSP and STACKMST the leader controls part of the edges. We provide further details on related work below. Stackelberg network pricing games are notoriously hard, and so a striking commonality of prior research on Stackelberg network pricing games is that they mostly obtained negative complexity results. For example, STACKSP and STACKMST are known to be APX-hard, even in the single-follower setting [10,15]. The few positive complexity results are often either FPT-algorithms where the number of priceable entities is parameterized, e. g., [4,22], or obtained under severe restrictions of the input. For instance, Briest et al. [7] showed that STACKELBERG VERTEX COVER (STACKVC) is solvable on bipartite graphs if all priceable vertices lie on the same side of the bipartition. Their result was later improved by Baïou and Barahona [2]. In contrast, Jungnitsch et al. [16] showed that STACKVC – the Stackelberg version of MWVC – is NP-hard on bipartite graphs when the priceable vertices are allowed to lie on both sides of the bipartition. This left the question whether STACKVC is solvable in polynomial time on special classes of bipartite graphs, like paths and trees.

In this paper, we show that STACKVC is solvable in linear time and storage on paths. It turns out that the algorithm and its analysis are quite involved; surprisingly so, given the extremely restrictive structure of a path. Our main contribution is the following theorem:

Theorem 1. STACKELBERG VERTEX COVER *can be solved on a path in strongly linear time and storage.*

Related Work. In this paragraph, we provide a brief overview of previous research on combinatorial problems in the Stackelberg framework.

Early research in the context of Stackelberg network pricing games was mostly concerned with edge-connectivity problems such as SHORTEST-PATH (SP) [1,5,15,19,22], MST [4,10,11], and SHORTEST-PATH-TREE [3,9]. Most of the results are concerned with hardness even w. r. t. approximability. For instance, to our best knowledge, the strongest hardness result for STACKSP is the impossibility to approximate STACKSP by a factor better than $(2-\epsilon)$ in polynomial time (assuming P $\neq$ NP) from Briest et al [5]. Similarly, Cardinal et al. [10] proved APX-hardness of STACKMST. There are also some results on the positive side but most of them require rather severe restrictions to the input. Possibly the most surprising general result is that a single-price strategy, i. e., a pricing scheme that assigns a uniform price to every priceable entity, suffices to obtain a logarithmic approximation factor [1,7]. This approximation guarantee remains – to our best knowledge – best-to-date.

A recent study by Cristi and Schroeder [12] analyzes the effect of allowing the leader to set negative prices in STACKSP. Since the influence of an edge goes beyond its direct neighbors, setting negative prices can actually increase the leader's overall revenue. Yet, it is easy to see that this is not true for STACKVC. Since including a vertex with weight less or equal than zero is always beneficial, a negative price cannot be better than selling the vertex for free.

Research on Stackelberg games is not limited to edge-selection problems, however. For instance, [6,20,21] examine KNAPSACK (KP) while [2,7,16] study MINIMUM WEIGHT VERTEX COVER (MWVC) in the Stackelberg setting. Since both these problems are already NP-hard in general [17], these publications either restrict to certain graph classes such as STACKVC on bipartite graphs, or in the case of STACKKP, assume that the follower uses an approximation algorithm to solve his problem.

Böhnlein et al. [8] extend the concept of Stackelberg games even further, allowing the follower to optimize an arbitrary convex program and thus capture non-binary preferences.

As we stated above, we restrict our analysis to the single-follower setting. In fact, among the references mentioned above, only a few consider the multi-follower setting. Some examples of this are [4,7,12,16,19,22]. Note that, in the multi-follower setting, one additionally needs to distinguish different variants of the model depending on whether or not the leader can sell copies of the same resource to multiple followers simultaneously and potentially obtain revenue for every copy. We refer to [16] for further details on this.

2   The Model

Let $\mathcal{G} = (V, E)$ be an undirected graph. Recall that $C \subseteq V$ is a *Vertex Cover (VC)* if every edge has at least one endpoint in C. Given weights $\omega \colon V \to \mathbb{R}_{\geq 0}$, a *minimum weight vertex cover (MWVC)* is a vertex cover C^* of minimal weight $\omega(C^*) := \sum_{v \in C^*} \omega(v)$.

In STACKELBERG VERTEX COVER (STACKVC) the vertex set is partitioned into $V = F \,\dot\cup\, P$, where F is the set of *fixed-price* vertices, and P is the set of *priceable* vertices. Initially, weights $\omega \colon F \to \mathbb{R}_{\geq 0}$ are only assigned to the fixed-price vertices. The vertices in P are under the control of the leader, who sets prices $\pi \colon P \to \mathbb{R}_{\geq 0}$ in the first stage of the game. Afterward, in the second stage of the game, the follower selects a MWVC with respect to the weights $\omega \colon V \to \mathbb{R}_{\geq 0}$, where the weight of every priceable vertex corresponds to the price set by the leader, i. e., $\omega(p) = \pi(p)$ for all $p \in P$.

In STACKVC the leader only obtains revenue for the priceable vertices contained in the follower's solution and aims to maximize her revenue. Both players are assumed to act fully rationally. Neighboring priceable vertices would force the follower to include at least one of them into a MWVC and thus, allow the leader to generate an arbitrarily high revenue. We therefore restrict our analysis to instances without adjacent priceable vertices. Similarly, vertices with a negative price will be included in any MWVC and can thus be removed by deleting all incident edges.

To circumvent infinitely small ϵ-values, we assume ties to be broken in favor of the leader, i. e., the follower chooses a MWVC that maximizes the leader's revenue. This assumption is common in Stackelberg literature. STACKVC then describes the optimization problem from the leader's perspective. That is, for a game on graph $\mathcal{G} = (V = F \,\dot\cup\, P, E, \omega)$, and initial weights $\omega \colon F \to \mathbb{R}$ on the fixed-price vertices, we want to solve:

$$\max_{\pi \in \mathbb{R}^P} \left\{ \sum_{p \in C^* \cap P} \pi(p) \,\middle|\, C^* \text{ is MWVC of } \mathcal{G} \text{ with } \omega(p) = \pi(p) \text{ for all } p \in P \right\}.$$

See Fig. 1 below for an exemplary instance of STACKVC on a path.

STACKVC on a Path. Unless stated otherwise, we always assume to be dealing with a path aka. line graph $\mathcal{P} = (V, E)$ with n vertices $v_1, \ldots, v_n$. W. l. o. g., we choose an arbitrary orientation of $\mathcal{P}$ and number the vertices from left to right, i. e., $\mathcal{P} = (v_1, \ldots, v_n)$. This provides us with a total order $\preceq$ of the vertices in V. That is, we have $v_i \preceq v_j$ whenever $i \leq j$. In this case, we call v_i a predecessor of v_j and similarly v_j a successor of v_i. In case we want to stress that $v_i \neq v_j$, i. e., $i < k$, we write $v_i \prec v_j$.

Let $p_1, \ldots, p_k$ denote the set of priceable vertices. We assume the priceable vertices to be numbered by their appearance on $\mathcal{P}$, i. e., $i < j$ if $p_i \prec p_j$. To improve readability, we may write π_i instead of $\pi(p_i)$ from hereon.

We denote the direct predecessor of v_i by $\mathrm{pred}(v_i)$, i.e., $\mathrm{pred}(v_i) := v_{i-1}$ for $i \geq 2$. Similarly, we define the direct successor of v_i by $\mathrm{succ}(v_i) := v_{i+1}$ for $i \leq n - 1$.

To simplify the notion of subpaths, we use $\mathcal{P}_{\prec v}$ to denote the subpath of $\mathcal{P}$ from v_1 to the direct predecessor $\mathrm{pred}(v)$ of $v = v_\ell$. That is, $\mathcal{P}_{\prec v} := (v_1, \dots, v_{\ell-1})$. For the subpath containing all vertices until v, but including v, we use $\mathcal{P}_{\preceq v} := (v_1, \dots, v_\ell)$. Analogously, for a set $S \subseteq V$, we define the sets $S_{\preceq v}$ and $S_{v \preceq}$ [$S_{\prec v}$ and $S_{v \prec}$] as the elements in S which are [proper] predecessors or successors of vertex v, respectively. Note that every path is a bipartite graph, where the parts correspond to the nodes with odd and even distance to v_1, respectively. We define $\mathrm{Part}(v)$ as the set of vertices that are on the same side of the bipartition as v. Remark that we do not apply any restrictions on the distribution of P w.r.t. bipartition of V.

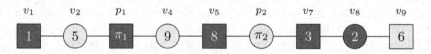

Fig. 1. A STACKVC instance with two priceable vertices. The MWVC C^* corresponding to the optimal pricing scheme $\mathbf{p}^* = (13, \infty)$ is highlighted in magenta.

Example 1. We illustrate the intrinsic complexity of STACKVC on paths using the example depicted in Fig. 1.

There are two priceable vertices p_1 and p_2 that lie on different sides of the partition, indicated by the round and square vertices. Depending on the choice of π_1 and π_2 either p_1, p_2, both, or none of them are included in the follower's solution. Remark that despite its very limited size, finding a pricing scheme that yields the maximum revenue of 13, in this case, is far from trivial.

For $\pi_1 \leq 5$, there is a MWVC including p_1 independent of the choice of π_2. This is because $\{v_1, p_1, v_5\}$ is a MWVC of $\mathcal{P}_{\preceq v_5}$ for this choice of π_1. Conversely, for $\pi_1 > 13$, $\{v_2, v_4\}$ is a MWVC of $\mathcal{P}_{\preceq v_4}$ and thus no MWVC of $\mathcal{P}$ contains p_1. For any price in between, either p_1 or p_2 is included in the follower's solution. Therefore, it makes sense to evaluate the same cases for p_2 for the choices $\pi_1 = 5$ and $\pi_1 = 13$. We refer to these prices as bounds and indeed they constitute the foundation of our algorithm for STACKVC on a path. Yet, one can clearly see that even with only two options per priceable vertex, simply evaluating every combination is not viable. By leveraging the problem's structure, we are, however, able to circumvent such an exponential blowup.

For this particular instance, $\pi_1 = 13$, $\pi_2 \geq 11$ (e.g. $\pi_2 = \infty$) yields the maximum possible revenue of 13. Note that under this pricing scheme, the leader does not obtain any revenue for p_2.

3   Sketch of the Algorithm

In this section, we sketch how Algorithm 1 (see pseudocode below) finds optimal prices for the leader given that the game is played on a path. In the subsequent sections, we describe the steps of the algorithm in further detail.

Before we start to describe our algorithm, let us shortly think how a MWVC of a path can be computed in the setting where *all* vertices are fixed-price vertices. Clearly, the problem is polytime solvable, since bipartite graphs allow for an efficient computation of a MWVC (Theorem of Kőnig-Egerváry [13,18]). In fact, one can even compute a MWVC of a path in linear time via the following dynamic programming approach: Traverse the path $\mathcal{P}$ from left to right and for every node v, check if there is a cheapest cover of the subpath $\mathcal{P}_{\preceq v}$ that includes v. If so, cut the path and repeat the procedure for the remaining path. The set C^* containing v and every second predecessor of it is a MWVC of $\mathcal{P}_{\preceq v}$. Note that, if the respective cheapest covers of $\mathcal{P}_{\preceq v}$ in- and excluding v have the same cost, we may either cut or continue.

In the Stackelberg setting, however, traversing the path in one direction and setting the prices does not yield optimal prices in general. Indeed, the leader obtains revenue for vertex p if there is a MWVC of the subpath up to p that includes p. Still, in most cases, p is included in a cover of the entire path for a price beyond that. This can be nicely observed in the instance depicted in Fig. 1. The maximum price for p_1 such that it is included in a MWVC of $\mathcal{P}_{\preceq p_1}$ is 4. Yet, it can be included for a price as high as 13 (when choosing π_2 accordingly). The primary challenge in STACKVC is, however, that the priceable vertices influence each other. If all priceable vertices are on one side of the bipartition, there is always an optimal solution including all priceable vertices. This vastly simplifies the problem. In fact, it turns the problem from NP-hard [16] to polytime solvable [7] on general bipartite graphs. The reason for this is that for instances with priceable vertices on both sides of the bipartition, the leader must first decide which priceable vertices she wants to be included in the follower's solution and then maximize her revenue given this selection. The instance discussed in Example 1 illustrates this nicely.

Overview. Due to the challenges described above, simple dynamic programming is not sufficient for solving STACKVC on a path. Nevertheless, we can employ it to compute lower and upper bounds for the priceable vertices (cf. Sect. 5). Note that the bounds of p_i depend on the prices $\pi_1, \ldots, \pi_{i-1}$ chosen for the previous priceable vertices. Consequently, a careful analysis is necessary, as we discuss later. We use these bounds for a benchmark case to tackle the combinatorial challenge of finding the optimal selection of priceable vertices that the leader wants the follower to include in his MWVC. We define the lower bound in a way such that matching the lower bound of a priceable vertex p_i guarantees that it is included in the follower's solution, i. e., the leader obtains the price of p_i as revenue. When setting the price to match the upper bound, p_i can still be included by reducing the revenue obtained for the next priceable vertex p_{i+1}. However, this is not always desirable. Therefore, we distinguish these options for each priceable vertex (cf. Sect. 6.1). To avoid an exponential blowup, we perform a sophisticated analysis to discard suboptimal options as soon as possible (cf. Sects. 6.2 and 6.3). By doing so, we can restrict ourselves to two potential pricing schemes at any time, giving us the desired linear complexity. In the end, we calculate the optimal prices for the leader by choosing the prices according to the optimal pricing scheme (given by the optimal option for each priceable vertex).

```
1 function StackVCP(P)
    Input: A path P = (v₁,...,vₙ) with k priceable vertices p₁,...,pₖ
           and vertex weights ω for the fixed-price vertices.
    Output: A revenue-maximizing pricing scheme π* ∈ ℝᵏ.
2   for i = 1 to k do
3   ⌊ α*[i], β*[i] = ComputeBounds(P, α*[1], ..., α*[i − 1])  // cf. Section 5
                    // compute optimal selection of priceable vertices
4   opt = CompareOptions(P, α*[1],...,α*[n]))                 // cf. Section 6.3
                        // compute optimal prices for given selection
5   π₁*,...,πₖ* = ResolvePrices(opt)                          // cf. Section 6.3
6   return π*
```

Algorithm 1: The outline of our algorithm for STACKVC on a path.

4 Structure of Minimum Weight Vertex Covers

In this section, we delve into the general structure of MWVCs of a path. We start with a simple lemma characterizing the cornerstones of such a cover.

Lemma 1. (cover condition). *Let v be the first vertex on $\mathcal{P}$ for which the following condition holds.*

$$\sum_{u \in \mathcal{P}_{\preceq v} \cap \mathrm{Part}(v)} \omega(u) \leq \sum_{u \in \mathcal{P}_{\preceq v} \backslash \mathrm{Part}(v)} \omega(u). \qquad \text{(cover condition)}$$

Then, $C^* := \mathrm{Part}(v) \cap \mathcal{P}_{\preceq v}$ is a MWVC of $\mathcal{P}_{\preceq v}$. Moreover, there is a MWVC of $\mathcal{P}$ containing C^*. If the inequality is strict, C^* is the unique MWVC of $\mathcal{P}_{\preceq v}$ and every MWVC of $\mathcal{P}$ includes C^*.

We call the inequality *(weak)* cover condition because it allows us to construct a cover for $\mathcal{P}_{\preceq v}$. We speak of the *strict* cover condition whenever the inequality is strict and thus, C^* is contained in any MWVC of the entire path $\mathcal{P}$. In the Stackelberg setting, fulfilling the weak cover condition often suffices to achieve the desired effect in terms of in- or excluding a specific vertex since we generally assume the follower to pick a MWVC in favor of the leader.

Proof. (*Proof of Lemma 1*). Observe that C^* and $\mathcal{P}_{\preceq v} \setminus C^*$ are the only vertex covers of $\mathcal{P}_{\preceq v}$ that do not contain any neighboring vertices. Since the cover condition holds at vertex v, we get

$$\omega(C^*) \leq \omega(\mathcal{P}_{\preceq v} \setminus C^*).$$

For the sake of contradiction, assume there was a MWVC C of $\mathcal{P}_{\preceq v}$ containing two neighboring vertices. W. l. o. g., let $x \prec y$ be the first neighboring vertices in C. Then, $C' := (\mathcal{P}_{\prec x} \cap \mathrm{Part}(y)) \cup C_{y \preceq}$ is a vertex cover of $\mathcal{P}_{\preceq v}$ which is strictly cheaper than C, since

$$\omega(\mathcal{P}_{\prec x} \cap \mathrm{Part}(y)) < \omega(\mathcal{P}_{\prec x} \cap \mathrm{Part}(x)) = \omega(C_{\preceq x}),$$

where the inequality holds since x does not satisfy the cover condition. Hence, C^* is a MWVC of $\mathcal{P}_{\preceq v}$ which contains v and the unique one if the strict cover condition is fulfilled.

Since a vertex cover of the entire path $\mathcal{P}$ must cover the edges in $\mathcal{P}_{\preceq v} \cup \{v, \mathrm{succ}(v)\} \cup \mathcal{P}_{v \prec}$, each MWVC $C^*_{v \prec}$ of $\mathcal{P}_{v \prec}$ completes C^* to a MWVC of $\mathcal{P}$ since C^* already covers $\mathcal{P}_{\preceq v} \cup \{v, \mathrm{succ}(v)\}$.

To see that C^* is contained in every MWVC $\widetilde{C}$ in case of strict inequality, note that $\widetilde{C}$ has to cover $\mathcal{P}_{\preceq v}$ as well. Moreover, if $\widetilde{C}_{v \preceq} \neq C^*$ replacing it with C^* would result in a cheaper vertex cover. □

Corollary 1. *We can split an instance at a vertex v satisfying the (weak) cover condition. That is, we can cut the path after v, find a MWVC for $\mathcal{P}_{\preceq v}$ including v, and independently compute a MWVC for $\mathcal{P}_{v \prec}$.*

Given that, the following statement follows immediately.

Corollary 2. *Let $v_1 \prec \cdots \prec v_\ell$ be all the vertices on $\mathcal{P}_{\preceq v_\ell}$ satisfying the cover condition such that only v_ℓ may satisfy the strict cover condition. Let $S_i := \{u \in \mathcal{P} \mid v_{i-1} \prec u \prec v_i\}$ denote the set of vertices between v_{i-1} and v_i. Furthermore, let C^* be a MWVC of $\mathcal{P}$. Then, $(S_i \cap \mathrm{Part}(v_i)) \subseteq C^*$ if and only if $v_i \in C^*$. Moreover, if v_ℓ satisfies the strict cover condition, v_ℓ is contained in every MWVC of $\mathcal{P}$.*

In the proof of Lemma 1, we use that v is the first vertex satisfying the (weak) cover condition. Yet, it suffices that no predecessor of v fulfills the strict cover condition to obtain a MWVC of $\mathcal{P}$ containing v. In that case, the cover may not be unique though.

Our algorithm cuts the instance whenever there is a vertex v satisfying the strict cover condition. It then treats the resulting instances $\mathcal{P}_{\preceq v}$ and $\mathcal{P}_{v \prec}$ separately.

To get a better understanding of the above statements, it may be helpful to consider the path depicted in Fig. 1. When plugging in $\pi^* = (13, \infty)$, no vertex v_i with $i < 7$ satisfies the cover condition. Hence, the respective other part of the bipartition constitutes a MWVC of $\mathcal{P}_{\preceq v_i}$. Vertex v_7 fulfills the cover condition and thus the set containing v_7 and every second of its predecessors constitutes a MWVC of $\mathcal{P}_{\preceq v_7}$. If this cover is chosen, it suffices to treat the remaining path separately.

5 Bounds for Priceable Vertices

As we motivated before, the leader generally wants to include a specific selection of priceable vertices in the follower's solution. In the following, we therefore derive bounds for each priceable vertex p_i telling us when a priceable vertex will be in- or excluded from a MWVC. First, we give the definition, then explain the derivation, and finally, show how the bounds can be computed efficiently.

Definition 1. (Lower and Upper Bounds). *Let p_i be a priceable vertex of $\mathcal{P}$. Given prices $\pi_1, \ldots, \pi_{i-1}$ for all preceding priceable vertices, we denote the lower and upper bound of p_i as*

(i) $\alpha^*[i](\pi_1, \ldots, \pi_{i-1})$ – the maximum price for p_i such that p_i is included in any MWVC of $\mathcal{P}$ independent of the prices $\pi_{i+1}, \ldots, \pi_k$ chosen for the remaining priceable vertices $p_{i+1}, \ldots, p_k$;

(ii) $\beta^*[i](\pi_1, \ldots, \pi_{i-1})$ – the maximum price π_i such that p_i can still be included in a MWVC of $\mathcal{P}$ by setting the prices of $p_{i+1}, \ldots, p_k$ accordingly.

Note that both bounds, $\alpha^*[i](\pi_1, \ldots, \pi_{i-1})$ and $\beta^*[i](\pi_1, \ldots, \pi_{i-1})$, are functions from $\mathbb{R}^{i-1} \to \mathbb{R}$. However, if the input $\pi_1, \ldots, \pi_{i-1}$ is fixed, we write $\alpha^*[i]$ and $\beta^*[i]$ for the sake of convenience.

The rationale for computing $\alpha^*[i]$ builds on Lemma 1. We search for the maximum price $\pi_i = \alpha^*[i]$ such that one node in $u \in \mathrm{Part}(p_i)$ between p_i and p_{i+1}, i.e., $p_i \preceq u \prec p_{i+1}$, satisfies the cover condition. We further ensure that when setting $\pi_i = \alpha^*[i]$, no vertex w from $\mathcal{P} \setminus \mathrm{Part}(p_i)$ between p_i and u satisfies the *strict* cover condition. Moreover, we cut the instance whenever the strict cover condition holds at some predecessor of p_i. This guarantees the existence of a MWVC including every $v \in \mathrm{Part}(p_i)$ with $p_i \preceq v \preceq u$.

To derive $\beta^*[i]$, we use a similar argument as above for $\alpha^*[i]$. However, this time, we want to find the maximum price such that no $w \in \mathcal{P} \setminus \mathrm{Part}(p_i)$ between p_i and p_{i+1} fulfills the strict cover condition. Note that the existence of such a node w would force p_i out of any MWVC.

On the same occasion, we make the following observation:

Observation 2. *Setting $\pi_i = \beta^*[i]$ suffices to obtain an optimal cover excluding p_i. It is thereby the minimum price guaranteeing the existence of a MWVC excluding p_i. We discuss later in Sect. 6.1 why this may be desirable.*
One important special case is the last priceable vertex p_k. For this vertex, the lower and upper bound always coincide, i. e., $\alpha^*[k] = \beta^*[k]$, by definition.

Algorithm 2 shows how the above principles can be implemented to compute the bounds efficiently. The main idea is to evaluate the cover condition for every vertex v and compute the difference or *gap* between the weights of the vertices from the two parts of the bipartition up to v:

Definition 2. *Let $p_i \in P$ be a priceable vertex and let $\pi_1, \ldots, \pi_{i-1}$ be the prices of the priceable predecessors of p_i. W. l. o. g., no vertex $u \prec p_i$ satisfies the strict cover condition (otherwise use $\mathcal{P} = \mathcal{P}_{u \prec}$ for the following definition). For a vertex v with $p_i \preceq v \prec p_{i+1}$ (or $p_i \preceq v$ if $i = k$), we define* gap(v) *as the absolute difference in weight of the two parts of the bipartition of $\mathcal{P}_{\preceq v}$. More concretely,*

$$\text{gap}(v) := \left| \omega(\mathcal{P}_{\preceq v} \setminus \text{Part}(v)) - \omega(\mathcal{P}_{\preceq v} \cap \text{Part}(v)) \right|, \tag{1}$$

where we use $\omega(p_j) = \pi_j$ for $j < i$ and $\omega(p_i) = 0$.

Note that, unless the cover condition is satisfied for some u between p_i and v, the difference is always non-negative for vertices in $\mathcal{P}_{p_i \preceq} \cap \text{Part}(p_i)$ and non-positive for vertices in $\mathcal{P}_{p_i \preceq} \setminus \text{Part}(p_i)$. Yet, we are only interested in its absolute value.

```
1  function ComputeBounds(P_{≺p_{i+1}}, π_1, ..., π_{i-1})
      Input: P_{≺p_{i+1}} = (v_1, ..., v_ℓ), prices π_1, ..., π_{i-1} for p_1, ..., p_{i-1}.
      Output: Lower bound α*[i] and upper bound β*[i] for p_i.
2     Cut instance at v ≺ p_i whenever the strict cover condition is
      fulfilled and repeat with P_{v≺}
3     Initialize ω(p_i) = 0, β[i, pred(p_i)] = ∞, α[i, pred(pred(p_i))] = 0
4     for v with p_i ≼ v ≺ p_{i+1} do        // if p_i = p_k, go through p_i ≼ v ≼ v_n
5        gap(v) = |ω(P_{≼v} \ Part(v)) - ω(P_{≼v} ∩ Part(v))|
6        if v ∈ Part(p_i) then
7           α[i, v] = max{gap(v), α[i, pred(pred(v))]}
8           β[i, v] = β[i, pred(v)]
9        else
10          α[i, v] = α[i, pred(v)]
11          β[i, v] = min{gap(v), α[i, pred(pred(v))]}
12       if α[i, v] > β[i, v] then
13          if v ∈ Part(p_i) then             // include p_i by cutting after v
14             α*[i] = β*[i] = β[i, v]
15          else           // include p_i by cutting after u with α[i, v] = gap(u)
16             α*[i] = β*[i] = α[i, v]
17          return α*[i], β*[i]
18    if i ≠ k then
19       α*[i] = α[i, v_ℓ], β*[i] = β[i, v_ℓ]
20    else                                // special treatment for p_k duo to end of path
21       if v_ℓ ∈ Part(p_i) then           // cut after u with α[i, u] = gap(u)
22          α*[i] = β*[i] = α[i, v_ℓ]
23       else                              // include p_i by excluding v_ℓ
24          α*[i] = β*[i] = β[i, v_ℓ]
25    return α*[i], β*[i]
```

Algorithm 2: Algorithm to compute $\alpha^*[i]$ and $\beta^*[i]$.

Intuitively speaking, the gap tells us how high we can set π_i until v triggers the (weak) cover condition. Consequently, we want to find a node $u \in \mathrm{Part}(p_i)$ with a very large gap such that no $w \in \mathcal{P} \setminus \mathrm{Part}(p_i)$ between p_i and u has a strictly smaller gap. Algorithm 2 essentially does exactly this.

Lemma 3. *Algorithm 2 computes the bounds $\alpha^*[i]$ and $\beta^*[i]$ as introduced in Definition 1.*

Proof. The proof follows from Lemma 1, Corollary 1, and Corollary 2 which apply because we cut the path whenever the strict cover condition is fulfilled at some node v. The remainder is a direct consequence of our argumentation above.

We provide an extensive proof covering the effects of intersecting bounds, i.e., $\alpha[i,v] \geq \beta[i,v]$ in the full version of this article [14]. □

For the instance in Fig. 1, we obtain the bounds $\alpha^*[1] = 5$ and $\beta^*[1] = 13$. The bounds for the second priceable vertex p_2 depend on the choice for π_1. For example, for $\pi_1 = \alpha^*[1]$, we obtain the bounds $\alpha^*[2] = 1$, and $\beta^*[2] = 3$, while for $\pi_1 = \beta^*[1]$ we obtain the bounds $\alpha^*[2] = 9$, and $\beta^*[2] = 11$.

6   Interactions Between Priceable Vertices

As we motivated earlier, the mutual influence of priceable vertices is the main challenge of solving STACKVC on a path. Nevertheless, in the previous section, we computed the bounds $\alpha^*[i]$ and $\beta^*[i]$ of each priceable vertex under the assumption that the prices of all preceding priceable vertices are fixed. In this section, we shed light on the interaction between priceable vertices and justify why the computation of bounds can be done in the way we explained before.

To do so, we first show that choosing prices outside the bounds cannot be beneficial (cf. Lemma 4). Moreover, we show that the price of p_i within the bounds does not affect the bounds for vertices $p_{i+2}, \ldots, p_k$ if π_{i+1} is set accordingly (cf. Lemma 5). Then, we investigate how the price π_i of one priceable vertex influences the bounds – and thus ultimately also the potential revenue – of the next priceable vertex p_{i+1}. We distinguish the membership of p_{i+1} in $\mathrm{Part}(p_i)$ (Sect. 6.1 and 6.2). Further, we observe that there is always an optimal scheme, in which the price π_i of each priceable vertex is either set its lower or upper bound w.r.t. $\pi_1, \ldots, \pi_{i-1}$ (cf. Sect. 6.1).

Lemma 4. *Let $\pi_1, \ldots, \pi_{i-1}$ be fixed, and $\alpha^*[i]$ and $\beta^*[i]$ be the optimal bounds computed by Algorithm 2 for p_i. The following statements hold:*

(i) *Choosing $\pi_i < \alpha^*[i]$ reduces the leader's maximum possible revenue on $\mathcal{P}$ compared to $\pi_i = \alpha^*[i]$.*

(ii) *Choosing $\pi_i > \beta^*[i]$ cannot improve the leader's maximum possible revenue on $\mathcal{P}$ compared to $\pi_i = \beta^*[i]$.*

The statement follows directly from the definition of the bounds (cf. Definition 1). A detailed proof can be found in the full version of this article [14].

Next, we show that choosing a price *strictly* between the bounds is not beneficial as well. Therefore, we show how π_i affects the bounds for the following priceable vertices. We use this later to narrow down the possible combinations of an optimal pricing scheme.

Lemma 5. *Let p_i, $i < k$, be a priceable vertex of $\mathcal{P}$ and the prices $\pi_1, \ldots, \pi_{i-1}$ of all preceding priceable vertices be fixed. We compare two prices π_i' and π_i'' for p_i in the interval $[\alpha^*[i], \beta^*[i]]$. Furthermore, let $x \in \mathbb{R}$ denote the difference between π_i'' and π_i', i.e., $\pi_i'' = \pi_i' + x$. The following statements hold:*

(i) *If $p_{i+1} \in \text{Part}(p_i)$, we get $\alpha^*[i](\pi_1, \ldots, \pi_{i-1}, \pi_i') = \alpha^*[i](\pi_1, \ldots, \pi_{i-1}, \pi_i'') - x$ and $\beta^*[i](\pi_1, \ldots, \pi_{i-1}, \pi_i') = \beta^*[i](\pi_1, \ldots, \pi_{i-1}, \pi_i'') - x$.*

(ii) *If $p_{i+1} \notin \text{Part}(p_i)$, we get $\alpha^*[i](\pi_1, \ldots, \pi_{i-1}, \pi_i') = \alpha^*[i](\pi_1, \ldots, \pi_{i-1}, \pi_i'') + x$ and $\beta^*[i](\pi_1, \ldots, \pi_{i-1}, \pi_i') = \beta^*[i](\pi_1, \ldots, \pi_{i-1}, \pi_i'') + x$.*

(iii) *Independent of whether $p_{i+1} \in \text{Part}(p_i)$, the bounds for $p_{i+2}, \ldots, p_k$ remain unchanged when π_{i+1} maintains the same distance to its bounds under both prices for π_i' and π_i'' for p_i. More concrete, if the price for p_{i+1} is set to $\pi_{i+1}' = \alpha^*[i](\pi_1, \ldots, \pi_{i-1}, \pi_i') + y$ or $\pi_{i+1}'' = \alpha^*[i](\pi_1, \ldots, \pi_{i-1}, \pi_i'') + y$ respectively, then $\alpha^*[j](\pi') = \alpha^*[j](\pi'')$ for all $j \geq i + 2$ where $\pi_\ell' = \pi_\ell''$ for all $\ell \in \{1, \ldots, i-1, i+1, \ldots, j-1\}$.*

To see that the statement holds, consider the definition of the bounds (Definition 1) and their connection to the gap (Definition 2). Again, the detailed proof is deferred to the full version [14].

To find leader-optimal prices, we must consider the effect of pricing a vertex within the described bounds. Therefore, we now analyze the implications of choosing different prices within the bounds. This allows us to boil down the choices of each p_i to three options. In Sect. 6.2, we describe the revenue corresponding to these options. Finally, in Sect. 6.3 we explain how to compare the revenues associated to these options efficiently.

6.1 Options

In the following, we narrow the reasonable pricing schemes, i.e., a combination of prices, for the leader. For this purpose, we distinguish whether p_{i+1} is in the same or in the opposing part of the bipartition as p_i.

Same Part. We begin with $p_{i+1} \in \text{Part}(p_i)$. Observe that p_i can be included directly by choosing $\pi_i = \alpha^*[i]$. According to Lemma 4, any price below this is disadvantageous. Any π_i in the interval $(\alpha^*[i], \beta^*[i])$ has the same effect, namely that p_i is included if and only if p_{i+1} is included as well. Looking at Lemma 5, we observe that increasing π_i decreases $\alpha^*[i+1]$ and $\beta^*[i+1]$ by the same amount that we increase π_i. Since we must include p_{i+1} to include p_i for any $\pi_i > \alpha^*[i]$, we can *shift* any excess revenue beyond $\alpha^*[i]$ from p_i to p_{i+1} by setting $\pi_i = \alpha^*[i]$.

Lemma 6. (Options for same part). *Let $i < k$ and $p_{i+1} \in \text{Part}(p_i)$. The following statements hold*

(i) Given that p_i should be contained in the follower's solution, $\pi_i = \alpha^*[i]$ is an optimal price for p_i.

(ii) Given that p_i should not be contained in the follower's solution, $\pi_i = \beta^*[i]$ is an optimal price for p_i.

Proof. To see assertion (i), remember that we cannot include p_i for a higher price without including p_{i+1}. If we include p_{i+1}, the revenue shifts from p_i to p_{i+1} (cf. Lemma 5(i)), there is no difference between setting π_i to $\alpha^*[i]$ or to any value between $\alpha^*[i]$ and $\beta^*[i]$.

To see assertion (ii), recall that by Definition 1, $\beta^*[i]$ suffices to exclude p_i. Furthermore, by Lemma 4 any price beyond it induces no change for the following vertices. □

In summary, we showed that whenever two consecutive priceable vertices p_i and p_{i+1} lie on the same side of the bipartition, $\alpha^*[i]$ is an optimal choice for π_i unless we want to exclude p_i. In that case, $\pi_i = \beta^*[i]$ is optimal. We now explore why excluding p_i might be desirable.

Opposing Part. We change the setting and now assume that $p_{i+1} \notin \mathrm{Part}(p_i)$. Furthermore, we consider $\pi_1, \ldots, \pi_{i-1}$ as fixed. Looking at the gap of π_i (cf. Definition 2) it is very apparent that increasing π_i also increases the gap at any successor of p_{i+1}. This directly translates to larger bounds and thus ultimately a higher price for p_{i+1}. This is rather intuitive since the vertices lie on different sides of the bipartition. Again, this effect is limited to $\pi_i \in [\alpha^*[i], \beta^*[i]]$.

Now, recall that for any $\alpha^*[i] < \pi_i \leq \beta^*[i]$, we must rely on p_{i+1} to include p_i. In particular, p_{i+1} must be excluded such that there can be a MWVC containing $\mathcal{P}_{\prec p_{i+1}} \cap \mathrm{Part}(p_i)$. Due to Lemma 5, choosing any price π_i in the interval $(\alpha^*[i], \beta^*[i]]$ is never better than setting $\pi_i = \beta^*[i]$. To see this, recall that if p_{i+1} is not part of the follower's solution, p_i is for any $\pi_i \leq \alpha^*[i]$ per definition.

Summarizing above observations, we obtain three reasonable choices for p_i if $p_{i+1} \notin \mathrm{Part}(p_i)$:

Lemma 7. (Options for opposing parts).

$O_1[i]$: *Renounce p_i to increase the revenue on p_{i+1} (by setting $\pi_i = \beta^*[i]$).*

$O_2[i]$: *Include p_i in a MWVC of $\mathcal{P}_{\prec v}$, $p_i \preceq v \prec p_{i+1}$ (by setting $\pi_i = \alpha^*[i]$).*

$O_3[i]$: *Include p_i by excluding p_{i+1} (by setting $\pi_i = \beta^*[i]$ and $\pi_{i+1} = \beta^*[i+1]$).*

Proof. The proof follows from Lemma 4, 5, and the above observations. □

Note that option $O_3[i]$ already fixes π_{i+1} and thus, there are no options for p_{i+1} in this case. Consequently, it may still be that p_{i+1} is excluded even if $p_{i+2} \in \mathrm{Part}(p_{i+1})$.

For simplicity, we refer to the options $O_1[i]$ and $O_3[i]$ regardless of whether $p_{i+1} \in \mathrm{Part}(p_i)$ or not. Yet, in case $p_{i+1} \in \mathrm{Part}(p_i)$, these options are irrelevant.

In the following, we explain how to appraise the revenue corresponding to the options $O_1[i] - O_3[i]$. Afterward, in Sect. 6.3, we elucidate how to evaluate them from an algorithmic perspective.

6.2   Appraising Revenue

Since the bounds and thus ultimately the potential revenue for priceable vertex p_i depends on the prices $\pi_1, \ldots, \pi_{i-1}$ of all priceable vertices preceding it, we define a *benchmark price* for all these vertices p_j with $j < i$ when evaluating π_i. Based on this benchmark, we anticipate the change in revenue for all following priceable vertices $p_{i+1}, \ldots, p_\ell$ when evaluating p_i. Independent from our choice of π_i, we continue evaluating the options for p_{i+1} as if π_i matched the benchmark.

Any benchmark between $\alpha^*[j]$ and $\beta^*[j]$ works. Yet, as we see later, assuming $\pi_j = \alpha^*[j]$ for any $j < i$ is the most convenient choice. We define as $\mathcal{R}_i$ the maximum revenue that the leader can obtain from vertices $p_i, \ldots, p_k$ when $\pi_j = \alpha^*[j]$ for all $j < i$. Similarly, we define $\mathcal{R}_i(O_\ell)$ as $\mathcal{R}_i$ when fixing one of the options $O_1[i] - O_3[i]$ for p_i.

Given that, we can compute the leader's revenue from p_i onward as follows.

Lemma 8. (Revenues for priceable vertices in same part). *Let p_i be a priceable vertex of $\mathcal{P}$ with $i \leq k - 1$ and $p_{i+1} \in \mathrm{Part}(p_i)$. Assuming $\pi_j = \alpha^*[j]$ for every $j < i$; the maximum revenue that the leader can obtain on $\mathcal{P}_{p_i \prec}$ always corresponds to choosing $O_2[i]$ introduced above:*

$$\mathcal{R}_i(O_2) = \alpha^*[i] + \mathcal{R}_{i+1}. \tag{R2'}$$

Note that we do not state how to the appraise the revenue of $O_1[i]$ and $O_3[i]$ since these options are generally inferior.

Proof. This follows directly using Lemma 5 and the considerations above.   □

Lemma 9. (Revenues for priceable vertices in opposing parts). *Let p_i be a priceable vertex of $\mathcal{P}$ with $i \leq (k - 1)$ and $p_{i+1} \notin \mathrm{Part}(p_i)$. Assuming $\pi_j = \alpha^*[j]$ for every $j < i$; the maximum revenue that the leader can obtain on $\mathcal{P}_{p_i \prec}$ given the options introduced above is:*

$$\mathcal{R}_i(O_1) = (\beta^*[i] - \alpha^*[i]) + \mathcal{R}_{i+1}, \tag{R1}$$

$$\mathcal{R}_i(O_2) = \alpha^*[i] + \mathcal{R}_{i+1}, \tag{R2}$$

$$\mathcal{R}_i(O_3) = \begin{cases} \beta^*[i] + (\beta^*[i+1] - \alpha^*[i+1]) + \mathcal{R}_{i+2} & \text{if } p_{i+2} \notin \mathrm{Part}(p_{i+1}), \\ \beta^*[i] - (\beta^*[i+1] - \alpha^*[i+1]) + \mathcal{R}_{i+2} & \text{if } p_{i+2} \in \mathrm{Part}(p_{i+1}), \\ \beta^*[i] & \text{if } i + 2 > k. \end{cases} \tag{R3}$$

We provide a detailed proof of this Lemma in the full version of this article [14]. Briefly speaking, the intuition is as follows: $\mathcal{R}_i(O_1)$ anticipates additional revenue for p_{i+1} that results from choosing $\pi_i = \beta^*[i]$; $\mathcal{R}_i(O_2)$ obtains $\pi_i = \alpha^*[i]$ as revenue for p_i; Finally, $\mathcal{R}_i(O_3)$ obtains $\pi_i = \beta^*[i]$ for p_i, no revenue for p_{i+1} but anticipates any revenue changes for p_{i+2} – if it exists – that are induced by choosing $\pi_{i+1} = \beta^*[i+1]$.

6.3   Compare Options and Resolve Prices

Putting everything together, we now discuss how the options introduced in Sect. 6.1 can be evaluated efficiently. Since the number of possible combinations is exponential in k, comparing all of them is computationally infeasible. Fortunately, Lemma 8 and Lemma 9 allow us to fix the optimal choice for p_i already when we consider p_{i+1}.

Recall that we assume $\pi_j = \alpha^*[j]$ as the benchmark price for all $p_j \in P$. Thus, we can also fix $\alpha^*[j]$, $\beta^*[j]$ for every priceable vertex. By anticipating any changes in revenue that arise from deviating from this benchmark, we can compare the revenue on the remaining path immediately.

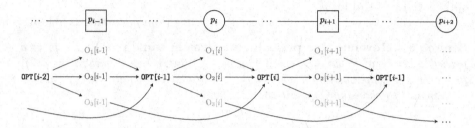

Fig. 2. A sequence of priceable vertices from alternating parts of the bipartition and their pricing options – as introduced in Sect. 6.1. Note that when applying the procedure described in Sect. 6.3 to compare the options, at most two branches remain open, at any time.

Comparing Options. The main idea is evaluating the revenue associated to $O_1[i]$ - $O_3[i]$ for every p_i. In case an option is contextually unavailable or generally inferior, we set the associated revenue to $-\infty$.

We can compare $O_1[i]$ and $O_2[i]$ right away. This allows us to asses whether excluding p_{i-1} is beneficial or not. This corresponds to comparing $O_1[i]$, $O_2[i]$, and $O_3[i-1]$. Consider Lemma 9 to see why this is viable. It remains to trace back which option for p_{i-1} led to this optimal revenue.

The important insight is that independent of which of the options is best, we find a clear optimal choice for π_{i-1}. Evaluating p_i might require opening a new branch but since there is only one option left for p_{i-1}, there are at most two open branches at any time. Figure 2 illustrates this. Additionally, we provide pseudocode describing this procedure in the full version of this article [14].

For the instance depicted in Fig. 1, we obtain the benchmark bounds $\alpha^*[1] = 5$, $\beta^*[1] = 13$ for the first and $\alpha^*[2] = \beta^*[2] = 1$ for the second (and last) priceable vertex. We then obtain $\mathcal{R}_1(O_1) = (13-5)+\mathcal{R}_{i+1} > 5+\mathcal{R}_{i+1} = \mathcal{R}_1(O_2)$ telling us that we can discard $O_2[i]$ immediately. Since p_2 is already the last priceable vertex, we obtain $\mathcal{R}_1(O_3) = 13$. To compare $\mathcal{R}_1(O_1)$ and $\mathcal{R}_1(O_3)$, we must evaluate $\mathcal{R}_2$. Since p_2 is the last priceable vertex, the lower and upper bound coincide and the only relevant option is $O_1[2]$. Hence, we obtain $\mathcal{R}_2 = \alpha^*[i] = \beta^*[i] = 1$. Now, we can tell that $O_3[1]$ is superior and hence the optimal choice for the leader is including p_1 for its upper bound by excluding p_2 (i.e., set π_2 to the upper bound). Note that the actual optimal price for p_2 is not the upper bound computed based on the benchmark prices but must rather be re-computed after plugging in the actual choice for π_1.

Resolving Prices. The optimal pricing scheme corresponds to optimal options for in- or excluding certain vertices from the follower's MWVC. We achieve this by setting the prices to lower or upper bounds. The bounds computed using the benchmark suffice to compare the different options, yet, they do not yield the actual prices. To compute these, we must consider the actual choice of π_j for every $j < i$ when computing the bounds of p_i. Again, we provide corresponding pseudocode in this paper's full version [14].

7   Proof of Theorem 1

In the following, we bring together all our insights from the previous section to prove our main contribution Theorem 1. The foundation of our algorithm are the bounds computed by the subroutine ComputeBounds (cf. Algorithm 2). Definition 1 states the impact of these bounds on a MWVC. The remaining statements in Sect. 5, in particular Lemma 3, justify their computation by Algorithm 2. The concept of these bounds rests upon our insights from Sect. 4 in which we dissected the structure of MWVCs of a path. The fundamental concept here is the cover condition introduced in Lemma 1. The cover condition allows us to determine when a vertex is part of a MWVC and thereby exhaust the potential revenue of a priceable vertex. Section 6 is devoted to solving the primary challenge of STACKVC on a path, namely the combinatorial problem of finding the optimal selection of priceable vertices to be included in the follower's solution. Lemma 4 and 5 justify our restriction of the leader's choices to the previously introduced bounds. We formalized this in Lemma 6 and 7. Lemma 5 also provides important insights on the interaction of priceable vertices which we use to appraise the revenue of the different options for each priceable vertex (cf. Lemma 8 and 9). An important step in this procedure was the definition of a benchmark price to make the options artificially comparable. Section 6.3, provides the details of how this comparison can be implemented efficiently. Once the optimal pricing decisions have been determined based on the benchmark prices, we must compute the actual corresponding prices.

Algorithm 1 aggregates all the above steps and together with the aforementioned statements attesting its correctness, it serves as proof of Theorem 1 with one small caveat that we discuss in the following.

Time Complexity. It is easy to see that Algorithm 1 in its present implementation has a time complexity in $\mathcal{O}(n^2)$. Responsible for the quadratic runtime, however, is only the computation of the bounds in the subroutine ComputeBounds (cf. Algorithm 2) which runs in $\mathcal{O}(n \cdot k)$. A savvier implementation of this subroutine gets along with less than two traversals of the path, thereby achieving (strongly) linear complexity. The enhancement bases on the following observation:

When setting the π_i to $\alpha^*[i](\pi_1, \ldots, \pi_{i-1})$ or to $\beta^*[i](\pi_1, \ldots, \pi_{i-1})$, we reach a vertex v at which $\mathrm{gap}(v) = 0$. We can cut the path after v, and compute the remaining bounds on $\mathcal{P}_{v \prec}$. The same holds if we set π_i to $\alpha^*[i]$ or $\beta^*[i]$, when executing ResolvePrices. In the worst case, v is always close to p_i and the bounds never intersect, so we always reach p_{i+1} before we know that we must cut at v and therefore traverse $v, \ldots, p_{i+1}$ two times.

With this optimization, we achieve the claimed strongly linear runtime since the branching scheme clearly runs in $\mathcal{O}(n)$ as well. Since we only store a constant number of variables for every priceable vertex, storage complexity is (strongly) linear as well.

8   Conclusion and Outlook

The main motivation of this paper is answering whether StackVC can be solved on some subclass of bipartite graphs, like paths or trees – a question that was also raised in [16]. Indeed, we can affirmatively answer this question for paths, as we state in Theorem 1. Thereby our algorithm is the first step to closing the complexity gap of StackVC on bipartite graphs. It was already known to be NP-hard on general bipartite graphs [16] and polytime solvable with the restriction that priceable vertices may only be on one side of the bipartition [7]. However, to the best of our knowledge, there have not been any positive results regarding the complexity of StackVC on bipartite graphs without any restrictions. The question whether StackVC can be solved efficiently also on trees remains open.

References

1. Balcan, M.F., Blum, A., Mansour, Y.: Item pricing for revenue maximization. In: Proceedings of the 9th ACM Conference on Electronic Commerce, pp. 50–59. EC 2008, Association for Computing Machinery, New York, NY, USA (2008)
2. Baïou, M., Barahona, F.: Stackelberg Bipartite Vertex Cover and the Preflow Algorithm. Algorithmica **74**, 1174–1183 (2015)
3. Bilò, D., Gualà, L., Proietti, G., Widmayer, P.: Computational aspects of a 2-Player Stackelberg shortest paths tree game. In: Papadimitriou, C., Zhang, S. (eds.) WINE 2008. LNCS, vol. 5385, pp. 251–262. Springer, Heidelberg (2008). https://doi.org/10.1007/978-3-540-92185-1_32
4. Bilò, D., Gualà, L., Leucci, S., Proietti, G.: Specializations and generalizations of the Stackelberg minimum spanning tree game. Theoret. Comput. Sci. **562**, 643–657 (2015)
5. Briest, P., Chalermsook, P., Khanna, S., Laekhanukit, B., Nanongkai, D.: Improved hardness of approximation for Stackelberg shortest-path pricing. In: Saberi, A. (ed.) Internet and Network Economics, pp. 444–454. Springer, Heidelberg (2010). https://doi.org/10.1007/978-3-642-17572-5_37

6. Briest, P., Gualà, L., Hoefer, M., Ventre, C.: On Stackelberg pricing with computationally bounded customers. Networks **60**(1), 31–44 (2012)
7. Briest, P., Hoefer, M., Krysta, P.: Stackelberg network pricing games. Algorithmica **62**, 733–753 (2012)
8. Böhnlein, T., Kratsch, S., Schaudt, O.: Revenue maximization in Stackelberg pricing games: beyond the combinatorial setting. Math. Program. **187**(1), 653–695 (2021)
9. Cabello, S.: Stackelberg Shortest Path Tree Game. Revisited. Institute of Mathematics, Physics and Mechanics (2012)
10. Cardinal, J., et al.: The Stackelberg minimum spanning tree game. In: Dehne, F., Sack, J.R., Zeh, N. (eds.) Algorithms and Data Structures, pp. 64–76. Springer, Heidelberg (2007). https://doi.org/10.1007/978-3-540-73951-7_7
11. Cardinal, J., Demaine, E.D., Fiorini, S., Joret, G., Newman, I., Weimann, O.: The Stackelberg minimum spanning tree game on planar and bounded-treewidth graphs. J. Comb. Optim. **25**(1), 19–46 (2011)
12. Cristi, A., Schröder, M.: Negative prices in network pricing games. Oper. Res. Lett. **50**(2), 99–106 (2022)
13. Egerváry, E.: Über kombinatorische Eigenschaften von Matrizen. Mat. Fiz. Lapok **38**, 16–28 (1931)
14. Eickhoff, K., Kauther, L., Peis, B.: Stackelberg vertex cover on a path (2023)
15. Joret, G.: Stackelberg network pricing is hard to approximate. Networks **57**(2), 117–120 (2011)
16. Jungnitsch, K., Peis, B., Schröder, M.: Stackelberg max closure with multiple followers. Math. Oper. Res. **47**, 3010–3124 (2021)
17. Karp, R.M.: Reducibility among combinatorial problems. In: Miller, R.E., Thatcher, J.W., Bohlinger, J.D. (eds.) Complexity of Computer Computations, pp. 85–103. Springer, Boston (1972). https://doi.org/10.1007/978-1-4684-2001-2_9
18. Kőnig, D.: Graphs and matrices. Mat. Lapok **38**, 116–119 (1931)
19. Labbé, M., Marcotte, P., Savard, G.: A Bilevel model of taxation and its application to optimal highway pricing. Manage. Sci. **44**(12–part–1), 1608–1622 (1998)
20. Pferschy, U., Nicosia, G., Pacifici, A.: A Stackelberg knapsack game with weight control. Theoret. Comput. Sci. **799**, 149–159 (2019)
21. Pferschy, U., Nicosia, G., Pacifici, A., Schauer, J.: On the Stackelberg knapsack game. Eur. J. Oper. Res. **291**(1), 18–31 (2021)
22. Roch, S., Savard, G., Marcotte, P.: An approximation algorithm for Stackelberg network pricing. Networks **46**(1), 57–67 (2005)
23. von Stackelberg, H.: Marktform und Gleichgewicht (Market and Equilibrium). Verlag von Julius Springer (1934). https://doi.org/10.1007/978-3-642-12586-7

Computational Complexity of Decision Problems About Nash Equilibria in Win-Lose Multi-player Games

Vittorio Bilò[1] , Kristoffer Arnsfelt Hansen[2] , and Marios Mavronicolas[3(✉)]

[1] University of Salento, Lecce, Italy
vittorio.bilo@unisalento.it
[2] Aarhus University, Aarhus, Denmark
arnsfelt@cs.au.dk
[3] University of Cyprus, Nicosia, Cyprus
mavronic@ucy.ac.cy

Abstract. We revisit the computational complexity of decision problems about existence of Nash equilibria in multi-player games satisfying certain natural properties. Such problems have generally been shown to be complete for the complexity class $\exists\mathbb{R}$, that captures the complexity of the decision problem for the Existential Theory of the Reals. For most of these problems, we show that their complexity remains unchanged even when restricted to *win-lose* games, where all utilities are either 0 or 1.

1 Introduction

The Nash equilibrium is the central solution concept for multi-player games; as a result, much research is being devoted to computational aspects of Nash equilibrium. Since, as already shown by Nash [23], every finite strategic form game has a Nash equilibrium, the most basic computational problem is that of computing *any* Nash equilibrium for a given game.

The computational complexity of this problem was settled in the seminal works by Daskalakis, Goldberg and Papadimitriou [14] and Chen, Deng and Teng [12] as being PPAD-complete for 2-player games, and by Etessami and Yannakakis [18] as being FIXP-complete for r-player games, when $r \geq 3$. Prior to these works, Abbott, Kane and Valiant [1] had established via a reduction that computing a Nash equilibrium in 2-player *win-lose* games, where all utilities are 0 or 1, is polynomially equivalent to the general case; so, it is also PPAD-complete. The computational complexity of computing a Nash equilibrium in r-player win-lose games has not been determined for $r \geq 3$.

In this work, we are interested in the decision problems of determining whether a given strategic form game has a Nash equilibrium satisfying certain

The second author is supported by the Independent Research Fund Denmark under grant no. 9040-00433B. The third author is supported by funds for the promotion of research at University of Cyprus.

natural properties; for example, does there exist a Nash equilibrium with all players' (expected) utilities are at least some given constant? Such problems have been studied extensively since they were first considered by Gilboa and Zemel [20]. We note that the equivalence between computing a Nash equilibrium for general 2-player games and 2-player win-lose games established in [1] does not, in general, preserve properties of Nash equilibria; thus, it has no complexity implications for such decision problems about 2-player win-lose games.

1.1 Previous Work

For 2-player games, the computational complexity of several such decision problems were shown NP-complete by Gilboa and Zemel [20]. Conitzer and Sandholm [13] revisited these problems and presented a unifying reduction to show them, together with additional problems, NP-complete, even for *symmetric* games. Bilò and Mavronicolas refined these results further, showing that these decision problems are NP-complete, even for symmetric, win-lose games [5]. To do so, Bilò and Mavronicolas designed suitable *gadget games* and used them to define a *game reduction* that allows for simple and uniform NP-hardness proofs.

For 3-player games, the computational complexity of such decision problems was only determined following the introduction of the complexity class $\exists \mathbb{R}$ in a seminal work by Schaefer and Štefankovič [24]. $\exists \mathbb{R}$ captures the computational complexity of the decision problem for the Existential Theory of the Reals, abbreviated as ETR. Schaefer and Štefankovič [24, Corollary 1] used a direct reduction from the decision problem for ETR to prove the first $\exists \mathbb{R}$-completeness result for a decision problem about Nash equilibria. Subsequently, a series of papers [4,6,19] proved $\exists \mathbb{R}$-completeness results for a range of decision problems about Nash equilibria:

- Garg *et al.* [19] proved a few additional $\exists \mathbb{R}$-completeness results by direct reductions from the result of Schaefer and Štefankovič [24]; further, they developed a *symmetrization* transformation [19, Section 5] to prove some additional $\exists \mathbb{R}$-completeness results for symmetric games.
- Subsequently, Bilò and Mavronicolas [6] extended the results of Garg *et al.* [19] to a catalogue of decision problems about both Nash equilibria and symmetric Nash equilibria. Similarly to 2-player games [5], their results were obtained via a general game reduction, again allowing for simple and uniform proofs of $\exists \mathbb{R}$-hardness by simply designing suitable gadget games.
- Lastly, Berthelsen and Hansen [4] developed a new series of $\exists \mathbb{R}$-hardness results by using an initial, much simpler reduction from ETR to a decision problem for 3-player games, thereby bypassing a rather involved transformation of Etessami and Yannakakis [18] that was used by Schaefer and Štefankovič. The 3-player game is such that the 2-player game resulting from it by fixing the strategy of either player 2 or player 3 is a *constant-sum* game. Taking advantage of the additional structure of the 3-player game, Berthelsen and Hansen used simple modifications of it to prove $\exists \mathbb{R}$-hardness results for 3-player zero-sum games, obtain new $\exists \mathbb{R}$-hardness results about general 3-player games and simplify previous proofs in [19] and [6].

1.2   Contribution and Methodology

We continue the study of the computational complexity of decision problems about Nash equilibria in win-lose multi-player games, as raised explicitly in previous work [5]. Our first result is that the initial reduction of Berthelsen and Hansen [4] can be adapted to the setting of win-lose games, simulating general outcomes by small win-lose gadget games and taking advantage of the additional structure of the 3-player game given by the reduction. It is, however, not clear how to do this in the win-lose setting. Instead we adapt the ideas of Bilò and Mavronicolas [6] to develop a win-lose version of their game reduction. We obtain results both for general games and for symmetric games.

   In both cases, we start with a *base game,* constructed by reduction from a particular ∃ℝ-complete problem. We then feed it, together with some *gadget game,* into a *game reduction* (resp., *symmetric game reduction* for symmetric games). Suitably choosing the gadget game for each decision problem we consider establishes their ∃ℝ-hardness in a simple and uniform way. These ∃ℝ-hardness results essentially settle an open problem from [5, Section 6].

1.3   Other Related Work

As an application of the proposed *approximate* Existential Theory of the Reals, Deligkas *et al.* considered decision problems about approximate Nash equilibria and proved quasi-polynomial upper bounds for them [15, Section 5.1]. The (in)approximability of NP-complete decision problems about (approximate) Nash equilibria has been studied in [3,16].

2   Preliminaries

2.1   Existential Theory of the Reals and the Class ∃ℝ

The *Existential Theory of the Reals* $\text{Th}_\exists(\mathbb{R})$, denoted by ETR, is the set of all true sentences over $\mathbb{R}$ of the form $\exists x_1, \ldots, x_n \in \mathbb{R} : \phi(x_1, \ldots, x_n)$, where ϕ is a quantifier-free Boolean formula with equalities and inequalities between polynomials with integer coefficients over the variables $x_1, \ldots, x_n$. The complexity class ∃ℝ was defined in the influential work by Schaefer and Štefankovič [24] as the closure of ETR under polynomial time, many-one reductions; so ETR is ∃ℝ-complete (by definition). Alternatively, and equivalently, ∃ℝ equals *(i)* the constant-free Boolean part of the class $\text{NP}_\mathbb{R}$ [9], which is the analogue of NP in the model of computation over the real numbers of Blum, Shub and Smale [8], and *(ii)* the analogue of NP in the model of computation by machines with access to unlimited *real-valued* memory [17]. It is straightforward to see that ETR is NP-hard (cf. [10, Proposition 8]). On the other hand, Canny [11] proved that ETR belongs to PSPACE. Hence, NP ⊆ ∃ℝ ⊆ PSPACE.

   QUAD denotes the decision problem asking whether a system of quadratic equations with integer coefficients has a solution over $\mathbb{R}$. Since any system of quadratic equations with rational coefficients is equivalent to a a single equation with a polynomial of degree at most 4 with rational coefficients, and the decision problem asking whether a polynomial of degree at most 4 with integer coefficients has a root over $\mathbb{R}$ is $\mathrm{NP}_{\mathbb{R}}$-complete [8, Main Theorem], QUAD is $\mathrm{NP}_{\mathbb{R}}$-complete. Since $\exists\mathbb{R}$ equals the constant-free, Boolean part of $\mathrm{NP}_{\mathbb{R}}$, it follows that QUAD is $\exists\mathbb{R}$-complete. Since a polynomial P with integer coefficients is computable by a straight-line program, whose length is polynomial in the input size of P, using the addition, subtraction, and multiplication operations with variables and the constant 1 as primitives, it follows:

Proposition 1. *The restriction of* QUAD *where* (1) *all quadratic equations have one the forms* $x_i = x_j + x_k$, $x_i = x_j x_k$, *or* $x_i = 1$, *and* (2) *the coefficients of quadratic equations are in the set* $\{-1, 0, 1\}$, *is* $\exists\mathbb{R}$-*complete.*

2.2 Strategic Form Games and Nash Equilibrium

An *r-player game* is a pair $\mathcal{G} = (\Sigma_i, \mathsf{U}_i)_{i \in [r]}$ such that for each $i \in [r]$, Σ_i is the *strategy set* and $\mathsf{U}_i : \Sigma_1 \times \ldots \times \Sigma_r \mapsto \mathbb{R}$ is the *utility function* of player i. A *strategy profile* $s = (s_1, \ldots, s_r)$ is a vector of strategies such that for each $i \in [r]$, $s_i \in \Sigma_i$ is the strategic choice of player i. We denote by $\mathsf{SP}(\mathcal{G}) := \Sigma_1 \times \ldots \times \Sigma_r$ the set of strategy profiles of game $\mathcal{G}$. For any player $i \in [r]$, $\mathsf{SP}_{-i}(\mathcal{G}) := \Sigma_1 \times \ldots \times \Sigma_{i-1} \times \Sigma_{i+1} \times \ldots \times \Sigma_r$ denotes the set of partial strategy profiles of $\mathcal{G}$ with respect to i; so $\mathsf{SP}_i(\mathcal{G})$ is deprived of i's strategy set. The game $\mathcal{G}$ is *win-lose* if for each $i \in [r]$, $\mathsf{U}_i : \mathsf{SP}(\mathcal{G}) \mapsto \{0, 1\}$. An r-player game $\mathcal{G} = (\Sigma_i, \mathsf{U}_i)_{i \in [r]}$ is *symmetric* if (1) all players share the same strategy set $\Sigma = \Sigma_1 = \cdots = \Sigma_r = \Sigma$, and (2) for each strategy profile s and every permutation π of $[r]$, $\mathsf{U}_i(s_1, \ldots, s_r) = \mathsf{U}_{\pi^{-1}(i)}(s_{\pi(1)}, \ldots, s_{\pi(r)})$; so, the utility of a player choosing some particular strategy is determined by the multiset of strategies chosen by the other players, with no discrimination among players.

A *mixed strategy* σ_i for player i is a probability distribution over Σ_i: a function σ_i such that for each $s \in \Sigma_i$, $\sigma_i(s) \geq 0$, and $\sum_{s \in \Sigma_i} \sigma_i(s) = 1$. The *support* of a mixed strategy σ_i for player i is the set $\mathsf{Supp}(\sigma_i) := \{s \in \Sigma_i : \sigma_i(s) > 0\}$ of strategies played with positive probability by player i in σ_i. A *mixed profile* $\sigma = (\sigma_1, \ldots, \sigma_r)$ is a vector of mixed strategies, one for each player, such that for each player $i \in [r]$, σ_i is her mixed strategy. Denote as $\mathsf{MP}(\mathcal{G})$ and $\mathsf{MP}_{-i}(\mathcal{G})$ the sets of mixed profiles of $\mathcal{G}$ and partial mixed profiles of $\mathcal{G}$ with respect to i, respectively. A mixed profile σ is *symmetric* if $\sigma_i = \sigma_j$ for each pair $i, j \in [r]$; denote this common mixed strategy as σ. For a mixed profile σ and a strategy profile s, we denote as $\mathbb{P}_\sigma(s) := \prod_{i \in [r]} \sigma_i(s_i)$ the probability that s is realized in σ. A strategy profile s is *enabled* in σ if $\mathbb{P}_\sigma(s) > 0$. The *expected utility* of player i for σ is $\mathsf{U}_i(\sigma) = \sum_{s \in \mathsf{SP}(\mathcal{G})} \mathsf{U}_i(s) \mathbb{P}_\sigma(s)$.[1] The *utility vector* of a mixed profile σ is the vector $(\mathsf{U}_1(s), \ldots, \mathsf{U}_r(s))$.

A mixed profile σ is a *Nash equilibrium* (NE) of $\mathcal{G}$ if, for each $i \in [r]$ and mixed strategy σ_i' for player i, it holds that $\mathsf{U}_i(\sigma) \geq \mathsf{U}_i(\sigma_{-i}, \sigma_i')$, that is, player i

---

[1] To keep notation simple, we use U_i to denote both the utility of player i when some certain strategy profile is realized and the expected utility of player i when some mixed profile is played.

cannot improve her expected utility by deviating to another mixed strategy. A *symmetric Nash equilibrium* of $\mathcal{G}$ is a Nash equilibrium of $\mathcal{G}$ which is also symmetric. By the properties of symmetric games (cf. [5, Lemma 2.1]), in any symmetric Nash equilibrium σ of a symmetric game, all players get the same expected utility; that is, $U_i(\sigma) = U_j(\sigma)$ for each $i \in [r]$. So, we sometimes drop the subscript i in the notation $U_i(\sigma)$ when referring to the expected utility of a player i in a symmetric Nash equilibrium of a symmetric game. The set of Nash equilibria of $\mathcal{G}$ is denoted as $\mathsf{NE}(\mathcal{G})$, while its set of symmetric Nash equilibria is denoted as $\mathsf{SNE}(\mathcal{G})$. By Nash's seminal results [23], any game with finitely many players and strategies has at least one Nash equilibrium and any symmetric game with finitely many players and strategies has at least one symmetric Nash equilibrium. Throughout this work, we shall make extensive use of the following well-known characterization of Nash equilibria (see, e.g., [22, Corollary 5.8]), stating that strategies in Nash equilibria are only supported on *best-replies*.

Lemma 2. *For an r-player game $\mathcal{G}$, the strategy profile σ is a Nash equilibrium if and only if for each player $i \in [r]$, $U_i(\sigma) = U_i(\sigma_{-i}, t)$ for each $t \in \mathsf{Supp}(\sigma_i)$ and $U_i(\sigma) \geq U_i(\sigma_{-i}, t)$ for each $t \notin \mathsf{Supp}(\sigma_i)$.*

A mixed profile σ is *Pareto optimal* if there exists no mixed profile σ' such that $U_i(\sigma) \leq U_i(\sigma')$ for all i, and $U_j(\sigma) < U_j(\sigma')$ for some j. In other words, σ is Pareto optimal if and only if it is not possible to increase the utility of some player without also decreasing the utility of some other player. If σ is both Parero optimal and a Nash equilibrium we say that σ is a*Pareto optimal Nash equilibrium*. A *strong Nash equilibrium* [2] (strong NE) is a strategy profile σ for which there is no non-empty coalition of players $B \subseteq [r]$ for which *all* players $i \in B$ can increase their utility by different strategies while assuming that players in $[r] \setminus B$ play according to σ. Clearly, a strong Nash equilibrium is also a Nash equilibrium. Central to our proofs is a definition refining [5, Definition 2.1].

Definition 3 (Positive utility property). *Fix an r-player game $\mathcal{G} = (\Sigma_i, U_i)_{i \in [r]}$. Player $i \in [r]$ has the positive utility property in $\mathcal{G}$ if, for each partial strategy profile $s_{-i} \in \mathsf{SP}_{-i}(\mathcal{G})$ with respect to i, there exists a strategy $t \in \Sigma_i$ such that $U_i(s_{-i}, t) > 0$. Game $\mathcal{G}$ has the positive utility property if every player $i \in [r]$ has the positive utility property in $\mathcal{G}$.*

For win-lose games, the positive utility property yields only Nash equilibria in which all players enjoying this property get a strictly positive expected utility.

Lemma 4 ([5, Lemma 2.2]). *Fix an r-player win-lose game $\mathcal{G} = (\Sigma_i, U_i)_{i \in [r]}$ and a player $i \in [r]$ with the positive utility property in $\mathcal{G}$. Then, for any $\sigma \in \mathsf{NE}(\mathcal{G})$, it holds that $U_i(\sigma) > 0$.*

2.3   Decision Problems

The decision problems about Nash equilibria in multi-player games considered in the literature [4, 6, 19, 24], are grouped together in four groups of problems of similar type, following [4]. Input to all is an r-player game $\mathcal{G}$ together with additional parameters, and the question is to decide existence of a Nash equilibrium σ satisfying a certain condition. We let u denote a rational number, k an integer, and $T_i \subseteq \Sigma_i$ a set of strategies of player i, for every i. Previous work proved membership in $\exists \mathbb{R}$ for all problems except for the two problems in the last group, for which we do not know whether they are even decidable (cf. [4, Section 3.4]). (The problem $\exists$IRRATIONALNE is expressible in the *Existential Theory of the Rationals*, denoted as $\mathrm{Th}_{\exists}(\mathbb{Q})$, which is not known to be decidable.)

Table 1. Decision Problems about Nash Equilibria

Problem	Condition
$\exists$NEWithLargePayoffs	$\mathsf{U}_i(\sigma) \geq u$ for all i.
$\exists$NEWithSmallPayoffs	$\mathsf{U}_i(\sigma) \leq u$ for all i.
$\exists$NEWithLargeTotalPayoff	$\sum_i \mathsf{U}_i(\sigma) \geq u$.
$\exists$NEWithSmallTotalPayoff	$\sum_i \mathsf{U}_i(\sigma) \leq u$.
$\exists$NEInABall	$\sigma_i(s_i) \leq u$ for all i and $s_i \in \Sigma_i$.
$\exists$SecondNE	σ is not the only NE.
$\exists$NEWithLargeSupports	$|\mathsf{Supp}(\sigma_i)| \geq k$ for all i.
$\exists$NEWithSmallSupports	$|\mathsf{Supp}(\sigma_i)| \leq k$ for all i.
$\exists$NEWithRestrictingSupports	$T_i \subseteq \mathsf{Supp}(\sigma_i)$ for all i.
$\exists$NEWithRestrictedSupports	$\mathsf{Supp}(\sigma_i) \subseteq \mathsf{T}_i$ for all i.
$\exists$NonParetoOptimalNE	σ is not Pareto optimal.
$\exists$NonStrongNE	σ is not a strong NE.
$\exists$ParetoOptimalNE	σ is Pareto optimal.
$\exists$StrongNE	σ is a strong NE.
$\exists$IrrationalNE	$\sigma_i(s_i) \notin \mathbb{Q}$ for some i and $s_i \in \Sigma_i$.
$\exists$RationalNE	$\sigma_i(s_i) \in \mathbb{Q}$ for all i and $s_i \in \Sigma_i$.

For symmetric games, we shall consider corresponding problems (replacing NE by SNE in their notation); they ask about the existence of a *symmetric* Nash equilibrium satisfying the conditions.

2.4 Gadget Games

The first gadget game simulates utilities outside $\{0, 1\}$ in 3-player win-lose games.

Definition 5 (Diagonal game). *Consider integers $m \geq 2$ and $0 \leq v \leq m$. The 3-player win-lose game $\mathcal{G}_{m,v}^{\mathrm{diag}}$ has a (common) set of strategies $\Sigma_1 = \Sigma_2 = \Sigma_3 = \mathbb{Z}_m = \{0, 1, \ldots, m-1\}$, and (i) $\mathsf{U}_1(\boldsymbol{s}) = 1$ if and only if $(s_1 + s_2 + s_3 \bmod m) < v$, and and (ii) $\mathsf{U}_2(\boldsymbol{s}) = \mathsf{U}_3(\boldsymbol{s}) = 1 - \mathsf{U}_1(\boldsymbol{s})$.*

Note that when fixing the strategy of player 2, the resulting game between player 1 and player 3 is *constant-sum*; likewise, when fixing the strategy of player 3, the resulting game between player 1 and player 2 is constant-sum.

Lemma 6. *Consider a mixed profile* σ *of* $\mathcal{G}_{m,v}^{\mathrm{diag}}$*, where at least one player is playing each strategy uniformly. Then,* $\mathsf{U}_1(\sigma) = v/m$*. If* σ *is a Nash equilibrium, then* $\mathsf{U}_1(\sigma) = v/m$*.*

The next gadget game, defined in [6, Section A.1], has a unique Nash equilibrium with large support.

Definition 7 (Lineup game). *For* $m \geq 2$ *and* $r \geq 2$*, the* r*-player win-lose game* $\mathcal{G}_{r,m}^{\mathrm{lineup}}$ *has a (common) set of strategies* $\Sigma_1 = \cdots = \Sigma_r = \mathbb{Z}_m$*, and (i)* $\mathsf{U}_r(s) = 1$ *if and only if* $s_r = s_1$*, and (ii) for* $i < r$*,* $\mathsf{U}_i(s) = 1$ *if and only if* $s_i \equiv s_{i+1} - 1 \pmod{m}$*.*

Lemma 8 ([6, Lemma 7.1]). *Let* $m \geq r \geq 3$ *such that* $m \not\equiv 0 \pmod{r-1}$*. Then,* $\mathcal{G}_{r,m}^{\mathrm{lineup}}$ *has the positive utility property and a unique Nash equilibrium* σ *satisfying, for every* $i \in [r]$*,* $\sigma_i(j) = \frac{1}{m}$ *for each* $j \in \Sigma$ *and* $\mathsf{U}_i(\sigma) = \frac{1}{m}$*.*

The next gadget game is similar to the Lineup game and has a unique *symmetric* Nash equilibrium with large support, although it may have other non-symmetric Nash equilibria.

Definition 9 (Predecessor game). *Fix integers* $m \geq 2$ *and* $r \geq 2$*. The* r*-player symmetric win-lose game* $\mathcal{G}_{r,m}^{\mathrm{pred}}$ *has a common set of strategies* $\Sigma = \mathbb{Z}_m$ *and for every* $i \in [r]$*,* $\mathsf{U}_i(s) = 1$ *if and only if there is a player* $j \neq i$ *with* $s_i \equiv s_j - 1 \pmod{m}$*.*

Lemma 10 *For* $m \geq 2$ *and* $r \geq 2$*,* $\mathcal{G}_{r,m}^{\mathrm{pred}}$ *has the positive utility property and a unique symmetric Nash equilibrium* σ *with* $\sigma(j) = 1/m$ *for each* $j \in \Sigma$ *and* $\mathsf{U}(\sigma) = 1 - (1 - \frac{1}{m})^{r-1}$*.*

The next gadget game [5, Section 4.2] has no rational Nash equilibria:

Definition 11 (Irrational game). *The 3-player win-lose game* $\mathcal{G}^{\mathrm{Irr}}$ *has strategy sets* $\Sigma_1 = \Sigma_2 = \{0,1\}$ *and* $\Sigma_3 = \{0,1,2\}$ *and utilities depicted in Table 2.*

Table 2. The win-lose game $\mathcal{G}^{\mathrm{Irr}}$ with a single, irrational Nash equilibrium.

Profile	Utilities	Profile	Utilities	Profile	Utilities
(0,0,0)	(1,0,1)	(0,0,1)	(1,1,0)	(0,0,2)	(0,1,0)
(0,1,0)	(0,1,0)	(0,1,1)	(1,0,0)	(0,1,2)	(0,0,1)
(1,0,0)	(0,0,1)	(1,0,1)	(0,1,1)	(1,0,2)	(1,0,0)
(1,1,0)	(1,1,0)	(1,1,1)	(0,0,1)	(1,1,2)	(1,1,0)

Proposition 12 ([5, Proposition 4.2]). *The game* $\mathcal{G}^{\mathrm{Irr}}$ *has the positive utility property and a unique Nash equilibrium* σ*, which is irrational.*

We next prove that it is possible to add an arbitrary number of dummy strategies to the strategy set of all players in a win-lose game with the positive utility property so as to obtain another win-lose game with the positive utility property having the same set of Nash equilibria; so, clearly, all added dummy alternatives are played with probability 0 in any Nash equilibrium. This symmetry-preserving transformation will be used to transform gadget games into similar gadget games with arbitrarily large strategy sets.

Definition 13 (Strategy padding). *For an r-player win-lose game $\mathcal{G} = (\Sigma_i, \mathsf{U}_i)_{i \in [r]}$ and sets of strategies $(\Sigma_i'')_{i \in [r]}$ with $\Sigma_i \cap \Sigma_i'' = \emptyset$ for each $i \in [r]$, the r-player win-lose game $\mathcal{G}' = (\Sigma_i', \mathsf{U}_i')_{i \in [r]}$ has, for each $i \in [r]$, $\Sigma_i' = \Sigma_i \cup \Sigma_i''$ and for each $s \in \mathsf{SP}(\mathcal{G}')$,*

$$\mathsf{U}_i'(s) = \begin{cases} \mathsf{U}_i(s) & \text{if } s \in \mathsf{SP}(\mathcal{G}), \\ 0 & \text{if } s \notin \mathsf{SP}(\mathcal{G}) \text{ and } s_i \notin \Sigma_i, \\ 1 & \text{if } s \notin \mathsf{SP}(\mathcal{G}) \text{ and } s_i \in \Sigma_i. \end{cases}$$

Lemma 14. *Assume that $\mathcal{G}$ has the positive utility property. Then, the win-lose game $\mathcal{G}'$ constructed as in Definition 13 has the positive utility property and satisfies $\mathsf{NE}(\mathcal{G}') = \mathsf{NE}(\mathcal{G})$. When $\Sigma_i'' = \Sigma_j''$ for each $i, j \in [r]$ and $\mathcal{G}$ is symmetric, then $\mathcal{G}'$ is symmetric as well.*

3 General Win-Lose Games

3.1 The Base Game

The construction of the base game is by reduction from an instance I of QUAD, which is an adaptation of a construction by Hansen [21] and Berthelsen and Hansen [4] to the win-lose setting. We denote by Δ_c^n the *standard corner n-simplex* $\{x \in \mathbb{R}^n \mid x \geq 0 \wedge \sum_{i=1}^n x_i \leq 1\}$ and by Δ^n the *standard n-simplex* $\{x \in \mathbb{R}^{n+1} \mid x \geq 0 \wedge \sum_{i=1}^{n+1} x_i = 1\}$. We shall also identify $x \in \Delta_n$ with the probability distribution σ over the set $\{1, 2, \ldots, n+1\}$ given by $\sigma(i) = x_i$.

Hansen [21, Propositions 2 & 3] gave a reduction from QUAD to deciding if a system of homogeneous bilinear equations has a solution, where each pair of variables belong to the standard simplex. By Proposition 1, we assume that the system given by an instance I of QUAD consists of quadratic polynomials with coefficients from the set $\{-1, 0, 1\}$. Inspecting the reduction in [21, Propositions 2 and 3] reveals that the resulting bilinear system consists of polynomials with coefficients from the set $\{-1, -\frac{1}{2}, 0, \frac{1}{2}, 1\}$. We then scale all polynomials by 2 to obtain an equivalent system with integer coefficients at most 2. Thus, we have:

Proposition 15 ([21, Proposition 2 and Proposition 3]). *It is $\exists\mathbb{R}$-complete to decide if a system of homogeneous bilinear equations $q_k(x, y) = 0$, $k = 1, \ldots, \ell$ with integer coefficients of magnitude at most 2 has a solution $x, y \in \Delta^n$. It remains $\exists\mathbb{R}$-hard under the promise that either the system has no such solution* *or a solution (x, x) exists, where x belongs to the relative interior[2] of Δ^n and further satisfies $x_i \le \frac{1}{2}$ for all i.*

From a given bilinear system $\mathcal{S}$, we construct a 3-player game $\mathcal{G}(\mathcal{S})$ (denoted as $\mathcal{G}'_0(\mathcal{S})$ in [4, Definition 1], but also defined implicitly in [21, Theorem 1]).

Definition 16 (The 3-player game $\mathcal{G}(\mathcal{S})$). *Let $\mathcal{S}$ be a system of homogeneous bilinear polynomials $q_k(x, y) = \sum_{i=1}^{n+1} \sum_{j=1}^{n+1} a_{ij}^{(k)} x_i y_j$, $k = 1, \ldots, \ell$, with integer coefficients, in the variables $x = (x_1, \ldots, x_{n+1})$ and $y = (y_1, \ldots, y_{n+1})$. The 3-player game $\mathcal{G}(\mathcal{S})$ has $\Sigma_1 = \{1, -1\} \times \{1, 2, \ldots, \ell\}$ and $\Sigma_2 = \Sigma_3 = \{1, 2, \ldots, n+1\}$. The utility functions are $U_1((s, k), i, j) = -U_2((s, k), i, j) = -U_3((s, k), i, j) = sa_{ij}^{(k)}$, $s \in \{1, -1\}$.*

The strategy (s, k) of player 1 corresponds to the polynomial q_k together with a sign s, the strategy i of player 2 to the variable x_i, and the strategy j of player 3 to the variable y_j. Thus, mixed strategies of player 2 and player 3 are identified with assignments to $x, y \in \Delta^n \subseteq \mathbb{R}^{n+1}$. We observe:

Lemma 17 ([4, Lemma 1]). *For every $(s, k) \in \Sigma_1$, any strategy profile (x, y) of player 2 and player 3 satisfies the equation*

$$U_1((s, k), x, y) = -U_2((s, k), x, y) = -U_3((s, k), x, y) = sq_k(x, y) . \tag{1}$$

Hence, $U_1(z, x, y) = U_2(z, x, y) = U_3(z, x, y) = 0$ when z is the uniform distribution on S_1, so that the utility profile in any Nash equilibrium is of the form $(u, -u, -u)$, where $u \ge 0$.

Note that if (x, y) is a strategy profile for player 2 and player 3 such that (x, y) is *not* a solution to the system $\mathcal{S}$, then player 1 may choose (k, s) such that $u_1((s, k), x, y) = sq_k(x, y)$. Solutions to $\mathcal{S}$ are related to Nash equilibria in $\mathcal{G}$:

Proposition 18 ([4, Proposition 3]). *Let $\mathcal{S}$ be a system of homogeneous bilinear polynomials $q_k(x, y)$, $k = 1, \ldots, \ell$. If $\mathcal{S}$ has a solution $(x, y) \in \Delta^n \times \Delta^n$, then letting z be the uniform distribution on Σ_1, the strategy profile $\sigma = (z, x, y)$ is a Nash equilibrium of $\mathcal{G}(\mathcal{S})$ in which every player receives utility 0. If, in addition, (x, y) satisfies the promise in Proposition 15, then σ is fully mixed, player 2 and player 3 use identical mixed strategies, and no strategy is chosen with probability more than $\frac{1}{2}$ by any player. Conversely, if (z, x, y) is a Nash equilibrium of $\mathcal{G}(\mathcal{S})$ in which every player receives utility 0, then (x, y) is a solution to $\mathcal{S}$.*

When $\mathcal{S}$ is given as in Proposition 15, the utilities in $\mathcal{G} = \mathcal{G}(\mathcal{S})$ are integers of magnitude at most 2. We shall next transform $\mathcal{G}(\mathcal{S})$ to a win-lose game $\widehat{\mathcal{G}} = \widehat{\mathcal{G}}(\mathcal{S})$, by replacing each outcome by a diagonal game $\mathcal{G}_{4,v}^{\text{diag}}$ (Definition 5). To explain the idea, consider the game $\mathcal{G}'$ obtained from $\mathcal{G}$ by first increasing all individual

---

[2] The *relative interior* of Δ^n is the set $\text{relint}(\Delta^n) = \{x \in \Delta^n \mid N_\epsilon(x) \cap \text{aff}(\Delta^n) \subseteq \Delta^n$ for some $\epsilon > 0\}$, where $\text{aff}(\Delta^n)$ is the *affine hull* of Δ^n and $N_\epsilon(x)$ is a ball of radius ϵ centered at x.

utilities by 2 and hereafter scaling by $\frac{1}{4}$. Thus, all utility vectors of $\mathcal{G}'$ are of the form $(v/4, 1 - v/4, 1 - v/4)$ for some $v \in \{0, 1, \ldots, 4\}$, which, by Lemma 6, correspond to the utilities of the game $\mathcal{G}_{4,v}^{\text{diag}}$ in a Nash equilibrium. The next game represents $\mathcal{G}'$ as a win-lose game.

Definition 19 (The win-lose game $\widehat{\mathcal{G}}(\mathcal{S})$). *Let $\mathcal{S}$ be a system of homogeneous bilinear equations with integer coefficients of magnitude at most 2. Let $\mathcal{G} = \mathcal{G}(\mathcal{S}) = (\Sigma_i, \mathsf{U}_i)_{i \in [3]}$ be the 3-player game given by Definition 16. Denote, for an integer $0 \leq v \leq 4$, by $\mathsf{U}_i^{\text{diag}}[v]$ the utility function of player i in the game $\mathcal{G}_{4,v}^{\text{diag}}$ given in Definition 5. The 3-player win-lose game $\widehat{\mathcal{G}} = \widehat{\mathcal{G}}(\mathcal{S}) = (\widehat{\Sigma}_i, \widehat{\mathsf{U}}_i)_{i \in [3]}$ has $\widehat{\Sigma}_i = \Sigma_i \times \mathbb{Z}_4$ and and $\widehat{\mathsf{U}}_i((s_1, t_1), (s_2, t_2), (s_3, t_3)) = \mathsf{U}_i^{\text{diag}}[2 + \mathsf{U}_1(s_1, s_2, s_3)](t_1, t_2, t_3)$, for each player $i \in [r]$.*

We first observe that player 1 has the positive utility property in $\widehat{\mathcal{G}}(\mathcal{S})$.

Lemma 20. *For a mixed profile $\boldsymbol{\sigma}$ in $\widehat{\mathcal{G}}(\mathcal{S})$ such that σ_1 is the uniform strategy, $\widehat{\mathsf{U}}_1(\boldsymbol{\sigma}) = \frac{1}{2}$.*

We now analyze the Nash equilibria in $\widehat{\mathcal{G}}(\mathcal{S})$ where each player receives utility $\frac{1}{2}$.

Proposition 21. *Let $\mathcal{S}$ be a system of homogeneous bilinear polynomials $q_k(x, y)$ with integer coefficients of magnitude at most 2. If $\mathcal{S}$ has a solution $(x, y) \in \Delta^n \times \Delta^n$, then, letting $\boldsymbol{\sigma} = (\sigma_1, \sigma_2, \sigma_3)$ be the mixed profile where σ_1 is the uniform distribution on $\widehat{\Sigma}_1$, σ_2 plays (i, t_2) with probability $x_i/4$, and σ_3 plays (j, t_3) with probability $y_j/4$, $\boldsymbol{\sigma}$ is a Nash equilibrium of $\widehat{\mathcal{G}}(\mathcal{S})$ in which every player receives utility $\frac{1}{2}$. If, in addition, (x, y) satisfies the promise of Proposition 15, then $\boldsymbol{\sigma}$ is fully mixed, player 2 and player 3 use identical strategies, and no strategyaction is chosen with probability more than $\frac{1}{8}$ by any player. Conversely, if $\boldsymbol{\sigma} = (\sigma_1, \sigma_2, \sigma_3)$ is a Nash equilibrium of $\widehat{\mathcal{G}}(\mathcal{S})$ in which every player receives utility $\frac{1}{2}$, then (x, y) is a solution to $\mathcal{S}$, where $x_i = \text{Pr}_{\sigma_2}[\{(i, t_2) : t_2 \in \mathbb{Z}_4\}]$ and $y_j = \text{Pr}_{\sigma_3}[\{(j, t_3) : t_3 \in \mathbb{Z}_4\}]$.*

The $\exists\mathbb{R}$-hardness of $\exists$NEWITHLARGEPAYOFFS follows from the construction in Proposition 21. We also directly obtain two additional $\exists\mathbb{R}$-hardness results, which will be also restated later, as consequences of the game reduction.

Corollary 22. $\exists$NEWITHLARGEPAYOFFS $\exists$NEWITHSMALLPAYOFFS *and* $\exists$NEWITHLARGETOTALPAYOFF *are $\exists\mathbb{R}$-complete for 3-player win-lose games.*

3.2   The Game Reduction

Let $\widehat{\mathcal{G}} = (\widehat{\Sigma}_i, \widehat{\mathsf{U}}_i)_{i \in [3]}$ be the 3-player win-lose game defined in Proposition 21. By Lemma 20, player 1 has the positive utility property in $\widehat{\mathcal{G}}$. As $|\widehat{\Sigma}_1|$ is even, we consider a bipartition $(\widehat{\Sigma}_1^1, \widehat{\Sigma}_1^2) = (\{1\} \times \{1, \ldots, \ell\}, \{-1\} \times \{1, \ldots, \ell\})$ of $\widehat{\Sigma}_1$ into two subsets of the same cardinality. The game reduction is parametric: given game $\widehat{\mathcal{G}}$ and a 3-player win-lose game $\widetilde{\mathcal{G}} = (\widetilde{\Sigma}_i, \widetilde{\mathsf{U}}_i)_{i \in [3]}$ with the positive utility property and such that $|\widetilde{\Sigma}_i| \geq |\widehat{\Sigma}_i|$ for each $i \in [3]$, we construct a 3-player game $\mathcal{G} := \mathcal{G}(\widehat{\mathcal{G}}, \widetilde{\mathcal{G}}) = (\Sigma_i, \mathsf{U}_i)_{i \in [3]}$ as follows:

1. For each $i \in [3]$, the strategy set of player i is $\Sigma_i = \widehat{\Sigma}_i \cup \widetilde{\Sigma}_i \cup \{\tau\}$, where we assume $\widehat{\Sigma}_i := \{\widehat{a}_i(j) : j \in [\widehat{m}_i]\}$ and $\widetilde{\Sigma}_i := \{\widetilde{a}_i(j) : j \in [\widetilde{m}_i]\}$, with $\widetilde{m}_i := |\widetilde{\Sigma}_i| \geq \widehat{m}_i := |\widehat{\Sigma}_i|$. For a player $i \in [3]$ and a strategy $s \in \Sigma_i$, $\mathbb{I}_{\widetilde{\Sigma}_i}(s)$ denotes the indicator function which equals 1 if $s \in \widetilde{\Sigma}_i$ and 0 otherwise.
2. For each strategy profile $s \in \mathsf{SP}(\mathcal{G})$, the players' utilities are defined below, where $\widehat{P}(s) = \{i \in [3] : s_i \in \widehat{\Sigma}_i\}$ (resp. $\widetilde{P}(s) = \{i \in [3] : s_i \in \widetilde{\Sigma}_i\}$) denotes the set of players choosing a strategy inherited from $\widehat{\mathcal{G}}$ (resp., $\widetilde{\mathcal{G}}$) in s:

Case	Property of s	Utility Vector $\mathsf{U}(s)$
(1)	$s \in \mathsf{SP}(\widehat{\mathcal{G}})$	$\mathsf{U}(s) = \widehat{\mathsf{U}}(s)$
(2)	$s \in \mathsf{SP}(\widetilde{\mathcal{G}})$	$\mathsf{U}(s) = \widetilde{\mathsf{U}}(s)$
(3)	$s_1 \in \widehat{\Sigma}_1^2$, $s_2 = \tau$, $s_3 \in \widehat{\Sigma}_3$	$(0,1,0)$
(4)	$s_1 \in \widehat{\Sigma}_1^1$, $s_2 \in \widehat{\Sigma}_2$, $s_3 = \tau$	$(0,0,1)$
(5)	$s_i = \widetilde{a}_i(j)$, $j \in [\widehat{m}_i]$, $s_{-i} \in \mathsf{SP}_{-i}(\widehat{\mathcal{G}})$	$\mathsf{U}_i(s) = \widehat{\mathsf{U}}_i(s_{-i}, \widehat{a}_i(j))$, or 0 if $j \neq i$
(6)	$|\widetilde{P}(s)| \in \{1,2\}$, $|\widehat{P}(s)| < 2$	$\mathsf{U}_i(s) = \mathbb{I}_{\widetilde{\Sigma}_i}(s_i)$
(7)	None of the above.	$(0,0,0)$

(Note that, by Lemma 14, the requirement on the cardinalities of the players' strategy sets in $\widetilde{\mathcal{G}}$ is not a limitation of the reduction.)

By Case (1) (resp., Case (2)), when all players choose a strategy from $\widehat{\mathcal{G}}$ (resp., $\widetilde{\mathcal{G}}$), thus realizing a strategy profile $s \in \mathsf{SP}(\widehat{\mathcal{G}})$ (resp., $s \in \mathsf{SP}(\widetilde{\mathcal{G}})$), they get the same utility they have for s in $\widehat{\mathcal{G}}$ (resp., $\widetilde{\mathcal{G}}$). So both $\widehat{\mathcal{G}}$ and $\widetilde{\mathcal{G}}$ are subgames of $\mathcal{G}$. Case (3) defines the set of profiles in which player 2 receives utility 1 by playing strategy τ: they are all and only the profiles in which player 1 plays in $\widehat{\Sigma}_1^2$ and player 3 plays in $\widehat{\Sigma}_3$. Similarly, Case (4) defines the set of profiles in which player 3 receives utility 1 by playing strategy τ: they are all and only the profiles in which player 1 plays in $\widehat{\Sigma}_1^1$ and player 2 plays in $\widehat{\Sigma}_2$. Cases (3) and (4) together provide one of the two players 2 and 3 with a deviation guaranteeing an expected utility larger than $1/2$ in any mixed profile for $\widehat{\mathcal{G}}$ in which player 1 splits unevenly her probability mass between sets $\widehat{\Sigma}_1^1$ and $\widehat{\Sigma}_1^2$. By Case (5), for any player i and partial profile $s_{-i} \in \mathsf{SP}_{-i}(\widehat{\mathcal{G}})$ inherited from $\widehat{\mathcal{G}}$, the jth strategy of player i in $\widehat{\Sigma}_i$ is mimicked by her jth strategy in $\widetilde{\Sigma}_i$. (This is the reason we need the assumption that $\widetilde{m}_i \geq \widehat{m}_i$ for each $i \in [3]$.) Case (6) assigns utility 1 to all players choosing a strategy from $\widetilde{\mathcal{G}}$ in every strategy profile that cannot be obtained from a strategy profile in $\mathsf{SP}(\widehat{\mathcal{G}}) \cup \mathsf{SP}(\widetilde{\mathcal{G}})$ through the deviation of a single player. Cases (5) and (6) together incentivize the players towards choosing a strategy from subgame $\widetilde{\mathcal{G}}$ whenever some strategy profile outside subgame $\widehat{\mathcal{G}}$ is realized in a given mixed profile for $\mathcal{G}$.

Since all utilities are either inherited from games $\widehat{\mathcal{G}}$ and $\widetilde{\mathcal{G}}$ or come from the set $\{0,1\}$, $\mathcal{G}$ is win-lose. Note that strategy τ is a weakly dominated strategy for player 1, as there is no strategy profile s with $s_i = \tau$, such that $\mathsf{U}_1(s) = 1$.

However, we keep strategy τ in Σ_1, as this allows to refer to all players in a unified way in the following lemmas.

Lemma 23. *Player 1 has the positive utility property in $\mathcal{G}$.*

Lemmas 4 and 23 together imply:

Corollary 24. *For any $\sigma \in \mathsf{NE}(\mathcal{G})$, $\mathsf{U}_1(\sigma) > 0$.*

We now characterize the set of Nash equilibria of $\mathcal{G}$; it turns out to be a subset of $\mathsf{NE}(\widehat{\mathcal{G}}) \cup \mathsf{NE}(\widetilde{\mathcal{G}})$. We prove that all Nash equilibria for $\widetilde{\mathcal{G}}$ are preserved in $\mathcal{G}$:

Lemma 25. *Any Nash equilibrium for $\widetilde{\mathcal{G}}$ is also a Nash equilibrium for $\mathcal{G}$.*

We next prove that all and only the Nash equilibria for $\widehat{\mathcal{G}}$ in which player 1 evenly splits her probability mass between $\widehat{\Sigma}_1^1$ and $\widehat{\Sigma}_1^2$ and both players 2 and 3 receive utility 1/2 are preserved in $\mathcal{G}$.

Lemma 26. *A Nash equilibrium σ for $\widehat{\mathcal{G}}$ is a Nash equilibrium for $\mathcal{G}$ if and only if $\sum_{s \in \widehat{\Sigma}_1^1} \sigma_1(s) = 1/2$ and $\mathsf{U}_i(\sigma) = 1/2$ for each $i \in \{2,3\}$.*

We conclude the characterization of the set of Nash equilibria for $\mathcal{G}$ by proving, through a sequence of lemmas, that no equilibria other than the ones inherited from $\widehat{\mathcal{G}}$ and $\widetilde{\mathcal{G}}$ exist. We start with a characterization of the Nash equilibria for $\mathcal{G}$ in which one player chooses only strategies from $\widetilde{\mathcal{G}}$.

Lemma 27. *Fix $\sigma \in \mathsf{NE}(\mathcal{G})$ such that $\mathsf{Supp}(\sigma_i) \subseteq \widetilde{\Sigma}_i$ for some $i \in [3]$. Then, $\sigma \in \mathsf{MP}(\widetilde{\mathcal{G}})$.*

We next prove that there is no Nash equilibrium for $\mathcal{G}$ in which some player chooses strategy τ.

Lemma 28. *For any $\sigma \in \mathsf{NE}(\mathcal{G})$ and $i \in [3]$, $\tau \notin \mathsf{Supp}(\sigma_i)$.*

We now prove that there is no Nash equilibrium for $\mathcal{G}$ in which some player chooses strategies from both $\widehat{\mathcal{G}}$ and $\widetilde{\mathcal{G}}$.

Lemma 29. *For any $\sigma \in \mathsf{NE}(\mathcal{G})$ and $i \in [3]$, either $\mathsf{Supp}(\sigma_i) \subseteq \widehat{\Sigma}_i$ or $\mathsf{Supp}(\sigma_i) \subseteq \widetilde{\Sigma}_i$.*

We now prove that $\mathcal{G}$ has no equilibria other than those inherited from $\widehat{\mathcal{G}}$ and $\widetilde{\mathcal{G}}$.

Lemma 30. *It holds that $\mathsf{NE}(\mathcal{G}) \subseteq \mathsf{NE}(\widehat{\mathcal{G}}) \cup \mathsf{NE}(\widetilde{\mathcal{G}})$.*

Putting everything together, we obtain:

Theorem 31. *A mixed profile $\sigma \in \mathsf{MP}(\mathcal{G})$ is a Nash equilibrium for $\mathcal{G}$ if and only if it is either a Nash equilibrium for $\widetilde{\mathcal{G}}$ or a Nash equilibrium for $\widehat{\mathcal{G}}$ such that $\sum_{s \in \widehat{\Sigma}_1^1} \sigma_1(s) = 1/2$ and $\mathsf{U}_i(\sigma) = 1/2$ for each $i \in \{2,3\}$.*

3.3   ∃ℝ-Hardness Results

Let $\mathcal{G}'$ be the trivial 3-player win-lose game in which all players have a unique strategy and receive utility 1. Clearly, $\mathcal{G}'$ has the positive utility property and a unique Nash equilibrium σ, which is Strong and Pareto optimal and such that, for each player $i \in [r]$, $\mathsf{U}_i(\sigma) = 1$ and $|\mathsf{Supp}(\sigma_i)| = 1$. Let $\widetilde{\mathcal{G}}$ be the 3-player win-lose game with the positive utility property obtained from $\mathcal{G}'$ by exploiting Lemma 14. By using $\widetilde{\mathcal{G}}$ within the reduction in Sect. 3.2, Theorem 31 implies:

Corollary 32. *The following problems are ∃ℝ-complete for 3-player win-lose games:*

- ∃NEWITHSMALLPAYOFFS
- ∃NEWITHSMALLTOTALPAYOFF
- ∃NEINABALL
- ∃SECONDNE
- ∃NEWITHLARGESUPPORTS

- ∃NEWITHRESTRICTINGSUPPORTS
- ∃NEWITHRESTRICTEDSUPPORTS
- ∃NONPARETOOPTIMALNE
- ∃NONSTRONGNE

Next we consider the Lineup gadget game $\mathcal{G}_{3,m}^{\text{lineup}}$ (Definition 7). By Lemma 8, when $m \geq 3$ is odd, $\mathcal{G}_{3,m}^{\text{lineup}}$ has the positive utility property and a unique Nash equilibrium σ such that for each player i, $\mathsf{U}_i(\sigma) = 1/m$ and $|\mathsf{Supp}(\sigma_i)| = m$. Using $\widetilde{\mathcal{G}}$ with a suitably large choice of m within the reduction in Sect. 3.2, Theorem 31 implies:

Corollary 33. *The following problems are ∃ℝ-complete for 3-player win-lose games:*

- ∃NEWITHLARGEPAYOFFS
- ∃NEWITHLARGETOTALPAYOFF

- ∃NEWITHSMALLSUPPORTS

We now prove that ∃IRRATIONALNE is ∃ℝ-hard. We use the trivial gadget game $\mathcal{G}'$ as in Corollary 32, where we instead ensure, following [4, Theorem 6], that no Nash equilibrium σ in $\widehat{\mathcal{G}}$ (as stated in Theorem 31) is rational.

Corollary 34. ∃IRRATIONALNE *is ∃ℝ-hard for 3-player win-lose games.*

We now prove that the problem ∃RATIONALNE is ∃ℚ-hard, analogously to [4, Theorem 7] for win-lose games. The basic complete problem for ∃ℚ is, analogously to ∃ℝ, to decide if a system of quadratic equations with integer coefficients has a solution over ℚ, denoted as QUAD$_\mathbb{Q}$. A technical obstacle to obtain such a result by reusing the reduction from QUAD is that we do not know a bound on the magnitude of coordinates of rational solutions to quadratic equations, which is a critical part for the proof of Proposition 15. Instead we start from a promise version of QUAD$_\mathbb{Q}$ and construct a reduction to ∃RATIONALNE using the game reduction together with $\mathcal{G}^{\text{Irr}}$ (Definition 11).

Definition 35. QUAD$_\mathbb{Q}(\mathrm{B}(\mathbf{0}, 1))$ *is the promise problem given by* QUAD$_\mathbb{Q}$ *together with the promise that if the given quadratic system has a solution over* ℚ*, then a solution over* ℚ *exists in the unit ball* $\mathrm{B}(\mathbf{0}, 1)$.

As in Proposition 1, we rewrite the system using additional variables into a system of quadratic equations with coefficients only from the set $\{-1, 0, 1\}$. While this makes the promise in Definition 35 to no longer hold, we preserve a bound on the magnitude of coordinates in a rational solution to the system of quadratic equations. We then proceed analogously to the proof of [4, Theorem 7], incorporating simple scaling and translation, to obtain a reduction from the promise problem of Definition 35 to the analogue over $\mathbb{Q}$ of the promise problem of Proposition 15. Now using the game reduction together with the gadget game $\mathcal{G}^{\mathrm{Irr}}$, we have, in analogy to [4, Theorem 4], the following $\exists\mathbb{Q}$-hardness result:

Corollary 36. *There is a polynomial time reduction from the promise problem* $\mathrm{QUAD}_{\mathbb{Q}}(\mathrm{B}(\mathbf{0}, 1))$ *to* $\exists\mathrm{RATIONALNE}$ *and the output is a 3-player win-lose game. Hence,* $\exists\mathrm{RATIONALNE}$ *is* $\exists\mathbb{Q}$-*hard for 3-player win-lose games.*

4 Symmetric Win-Lose Games

4.1 The Base Game

We shall observe that the symmetrization transformation of [4] applies also to the setting of win-lose games. We construct a symmetrization $\widehat{\mathcal{D}}$ of $\widehat{\mathcal{G}}$: The common strategy set of each player is the disjoint union $\widehat{\Sigma} = \widehat{\Sigma}_1 \dot\cup \widehat{\Sigma}_2 \dot\cup \widehat{\Sigma}_3$. When the players play strategies a_1, a_2 and a_3 and there exists a permutation π of $\{1, 2, 3\}$ satisfying $a_i \in \widehat{S}_{\pi(i)}$ for all i, then player i receives utility $\widehat{u}_{\pi(i)}(a_{\pi^{-1}(1)}, a_{\pi^{-1}(2)}, a_{\pi^{-1}(3)})$. Otherwise, player i receives utility 0. So $\widehat{\mathcal{D}}$ is symmetric win-lose. Thus, we have:

Proposition 37. *If* $\boldsymbol{\sigma} = (\sigma_1, \sigma_2, \sigma_3)$ *is a Nash equilibrium in* $\widehat{\mathcal{G}}$ *in which every player receives utility* $\frac{1}{2}$, *then the symmetric strategy profile* $\boldsymbol{\sigma}'$ *in which a player chooses* $i \in \{1, 2, 3\}$, *each with probability* $\frac{1}{3}$, *and plays a strategu according to* σ_i, *is a symmetric Nash equilibrium in* $\widehat{\mathcal{D}}$ *in which all players receive utility* $\frac{1}{9}$.

Conversely, if $\boldsymbol{\sigma}'$ *is a symmetric Nash equilibrium in* $\widehat{\mathcal{D}}$ *in which every player receives utility* $\frac{1}{9}$, *then* $\boldsymbol{\sigma} = (\sigma_1, \sigma_2, \sigma_3)$, *where* σ_i *is the conditional distribution on* $\widehat{\Sigma}_i$ *obtained from* $\boldsymbol{\sigma}'$ *given that a strategy from* $\widehat{\Sigma}_i$ *is played, is a Nash equilibrium in* $\widehat{\mathcal{G}}$ *in which every player receives utility* $\frac{1}{2}$.

This immediately implies the $\exists\mathbb{R}$-hardness of $\exists\mathrm{SNEWITHLARGEPAYOFFS}$ and $\exists\mathrm{SNEWITHLARGETOTALPAYOFF}$ (We shall, however, restate it later.)

Corollary 38. $\exists\mathrm{SNEWITHLARGEPAYOFFS}$ *and* $\exists\mathrm{SNEWITHLARGETOTALPAYOFF}$ *are* $\exists\mathbb{R}$-*complete for 3-player symmetric win-lose games.*

4.2 The Symmetric Game Reduction

Let $\widehat{\mathcal{G}} = (\widehat{\Sigma}_i, \widehat{U}_i)_{i \in [3]}$ be the 3-player win-lose symmetric game defined in Proposition 37 (renaming $\widehat{\mathcal{D}}$ to $\widehat{\mathcal{G}}$). Consider a partition $(\widehat{\Sigma}^1, \widehat{\Sigma}^2, \widehat{\Sigma}^3)$ of $\widehat{\Sigma}$ into three non-empty subsets. The symmetric game reduction is parametric: Given game $\widehat{\mathcal{G}}$ and a 3-player symmetric win-lose game $\widetilde{\mathcal{G}} = (\widetilde{\Sigma}, \widetilde{U})$ such that $|\widetilde{\Sigma}| \geq |\widehat{\Sigma}|$, it constructs a 3-player symmetric win-lose game $\mathcal{G} := \mathcal{G}(\widehat{\mathcal{G}}, \widetilde{\mathcal{G}}) = (\Sigma, U)$ as follows:

1. The common strategy set is $\Sigma = \widehat{\Sigma} \cup \widetilde{\Sigma} \cup \{\tau^1, \tau^2, \tau^3\}$, where we assume $\widehat{\Sigma} := \{\widehat{a}(j) : j \in [\widehat{m}]\}$ and $\widetilde{\Sigma} := \{\widetilde{a}(j) : j \in [\widetilde{m}]\}$, with $\widetilde{m} := |\widetilde{\Sigma}| \geq \widehat{m} := |\widehat{\Sigma}|$. Given a player $i \in [3]$ and a strategy $s \in \Sigma$, $\mathbb{I}_{\widetilde{\Sigma}}(s)$ denotes the indicator function which equals 1 if $s \in \widetilde{\Sigma}$ and 0 otherwise;
2. For each strategy profile $s \in SP(\mathcal{G})$, the utility of each player is defined below, where $\widehat{P}(s) = \{i \in [3] : s_i \in \widehat{\Sigma}\}$ (resp. $\widetilde{P}(s) = \{i \in [3] : s_i \in \widetilde{\Sigma}\}$) denotes the set of players choosing a strategy inherited from $\widehat{\mathcal{G}}$ (resp. $\widetilde{\mathcal{G}}$) in s:

Case	Property of s	Utility Vector $U(s)$
(1)	$s \in SP(\widehat{\mathcal{G}})$	$U(s) = \widehat{U}(s)$
(2)	$s \in SP(\widetilde{\mathcal{G}})$	$U(s) = \widetilde{U}(s)$
(3)	$s_i = \tau^j$, $s_{i'} \in \widehat{\Sigma}^j$, $\forall i' \neq i$	$U_i(s) = 1$, $U_{i'}(s) = 0\ \forall i' \neq i$
(4)	$s_i = \widetilde{a}(j)$, $j \in [\widehat{m}]$, $s_{-i} \in SP_{-i}(\widehat{\mathcal{G}})$	$U_i(s) = U_i(s_{-i}, \widehat{a}(j))$, $U_j(s) = 0\ \forall j \neq i$
(5)	$|\widehat{P}(s)| \in \{1, 2\}$, $|\widehat{P}(s)| < 2$	$U_i(s) = \mathbb{I}_{\widetilde{\Sigma}}(s_i)$
(6)	none of the above cases	$(0, 0, 0)$

By Case (1) (resp., Case (2)), when all players choose a strategy from $\widehat{\mathcal{G}}$ (resp., $\widetilde{\mathcal{G}}$), thus realizing a strategy profile $s \in SP(\widehat{\mathcal{G}})$ (resp., $s \in SP(\widetilde{\mathcal{G}})$), they get the same utility they have on s in $\widehat{\mathcal{G}}$ (resp., $\widetilde{\mathcal{G}}$). So $\widehat{\mathcal{G}}$ and $\widetilde{\mathcal{G}}$ are subgames of $\mathcal{G}$. Case (3) defines the only case in which a player receives non-zero utility by playing a strategy in $\{\tau^1, \tau^2, \tau^3\}$. Specifically, a player playing τ^j receives utility 1 if and only if the other two players are both playing a strategy from $\widehat{\Sigma}^j$; in such a case, these two players get utility 0. By Case (4), for any player i and partial profile $s_{-i} \in SP_{-i}(\widehat{\mathcal{G}})$ inherited from $\widehat{\mathcal{G}}$, the jth strategy in $\widehat{\Sigma}$ is mimicked by the jth strategy in $\widetilde{\Sigma}$. (This is the reason we need the assumption that $\widetilde{m} \geq \widehat{m}$.) Case (5) assigns utility 1 to all players choosing a strategy from $\widetilde{\mathcal{G}}$ in every strategy profile that cannot be obtained from a strategy profile in $SP(\widehat{\mathcal{G}}) \cup SP(\widetilde{\mathcal{G}})$ through the deviation of a single player. Cases (4) and (5) together incentivize the players towards choosing a strategy from subgame $\widetilde{\mathcal{G}}$ whenever some strategy profile outside subgame $\widehat{\mathcal{G}}$ is realized in a mixed profile for $\mathcal{G}$.

Since all utilities are either inherited from games $\widehat{\mathcal{G}}$ and $\widetilde{\mathcal{G}}$ or come from the set $\{0, 1\}$, $\mathcal{G}$ is win-lose. As Cases from (3) to (6) do not discriminate among players, $\mathcal{G}$ is symmetric when $\widehat{\mathcal{G}}$ and $\widetilde{\mathcal{G}}$ are. We now characterize the set of symmetric Nash equilibria of $\mathcal{G}$; it turns out to be a subset of $SNE(\widehat{\mathcal{G}}) \cup SNE(\widetilde{\mathcal{G}})$.

Lemma 39. *Any Nash equilibrium for $\widetilde{\mathcal{G}}$ is a Nash equilibrium for $\mathcal{G}$.*

We next prove that all and only the symmetric Nash equilibria for $\widehat{\mathcal{G}}$ in which the probability mass is evenly split among $\widehat{\Sigma}^1$, $\widehat{\Sigma}^2$ and $\widehat{\Sigma}^3$ and, additionally, all players get utility $1/9$, are preserved in $\mathcal{G}$.

Lemma 40. *A symmetric Nash equilibrium $\boldsymbol{\sigma}$ for $\widehat{\mathcal{G}}$ is a Nash equilibrium for $\mathcal{G}$ if and only if $\sum_{s \in \widehat{\Sigma}^1} \sigma(s) = \sum_{s \in \widehat{\Sigma}^2} \sigma(s) = \sum_{s \in \widehat{\Sigma}^3} \sigma(s) = 1/3$ and $\mathsf{U}(\boldsymbol{\sigma}) = 1/9$.*

We conclude the characterization of the set of symmetric Nash equilibria for $\mathcal{G}$ by proving that no symmetric Nash equilibria exist other than those inherited from $\widehat{\mathcal{G}}$ and $\widetilde{\mathcal{G}}$.

Lemma 41. *It holds that $\mathsf{SNE}(\mathcal{G}) \subseteq \mathsf{SNE}(\widehat{\mathcal{G}}) \cup \mathsf{SNE}(\widetilde{\mathcal{G}})$.*

Putting everything together, we obtain:

Theorem 42. *A mixed profile $\boldsymbol{\sigma} \in \mathsf{MP}(\mathcal{G})$ is a symmetric Nash equilibrium for $\mathcal{G}$ iff it is either a symmetric Nash equilibrium for $\widetilde{\mathcal{G}}$ or a symmetric Nash equilibrium for $\widehat{\mathcal{G}}$ such that $\sum_{s \in \widehat{\Sigma}^j} \sigma(s) = 1/3$ for each $j \in [3]$ and $\mathsf{U}(\boldsymbol{\sigma}) = 1/9$.*

4.3 ∃ℝ-Hardness Results

Let $\mathcal{G}'$ be the trivial 3-player symmetric win-lose game, where all players have a unique strategy and receive utility 1. $\mathcal{G}'$ has a unique symmetric Nash equilibrium $\boldsymbol{\sigma}$, which is Strong and Pareto-optimal, and has $\mathsf{U}(\boldsymbol{\sigma}) = 1$ and $|\mathsf{Supp}(\boldsymbol{\sigma})| = 1$. Let $\widetilde{\mathcal{G}}$ be the 3-player symmetric win-lose game obtained from $\mathcal{G}'$. Using Lemma 14 and embedding $\widetilde{\mathcal{G}}$ in the symmetric game reduction, Theorem 42 implies:

Corollary 43. *The following problems are ∃ℝ-complete for 3-player symmetric win-lose games:*

- ∃SNEWithSmallPayoffs
- ∃SNEWithSmallTotalPayoff
- ∃SNEInABall
- ∃SecondSNE
- ∃SNEWithLargeSupports

- ∃SNEWithRestrictingSupports
- ∃SNEWithRestrictedSupports
- ∃NonParetoOptimalSNE
- ∃NonStrongSNE

For symmetric games, by Lemma 10, the predecessor game $\mathcal{G}^{\mathrm{pred}}$ (Definition 9) may replace the role the lineup game had in the proof of Corollary 33 to yield:

Corollary 44. *The following problems are ∃ℝ-complete for 3-player symmetric win-lose games:*

- ∃SNEWithLargePayoffs
- ∃SNEWithLargeTotalPayoff

- ∃SNEWithSmallSupports

For ∃IrrationalSNE similarly to the proof of Corollary 34, we obtain:

Corollary 45. ∃IRRATIONALSNE *is ∃ℝ-hard for 3-player symmetric win-lose games.*

For ∃RATIONALSNE similarly to the proof of Corollary 34, we use as gadget game, the symmetric game obtained by applying the symmetrization transformation of Garg *et al.* [19, Section 5] to the game $\mathcal{G}^{\mathrm{Irr}}$; the result is a 3-player win-lose game without rational symmetric Nash equilibria.

Corollary 46. *There is a polynomial time reduction from* QUAD$_\mathbb{Q}$(B$(\mathbf{0}, 1)$) *to* ∃RATIONALSNE *with output a 3-player symmetric win-lose game. Hence,* ∃RATIONALSNE *is ∃ℚ-hard for 3-player symmetric win-lose games.*

5   Conclusion and Open Problems

Combining and extending the ideas from previous works [4,6], we have refined most of the known hardness results for decision problems about the existence of Nash equilibria in multi-player games satisfying natural properties to the win-lose setting. An important direction for future research is to identify ∃ℝ-hard decision problems about Nash equilibria that remain ∃ℝ-hard in the win-lose setting. We list a few interesting ones here:

1. ∃PARETOOPTIMALNE, ∃STRONGNE and their symmetric variants, which our work leaves open.
2. ∃NONSYMMETRICNE is the decision problem asking, given a symmetric game, whether it has a *non-symmetric* Nash equilibrium; it is ∃ℝ-hard for 3-player games [4, Theorem 11].
3. The ∃ℝ-hardness results, as well as the hardness results for classes related to ∃ℝ (such as ∀ℝ), shown in [7], for deciding existence of an *evolutionarily stable strategy*.
4. Similarly, the FIXP$_a$-hardness results of computing a Nash equilibrium in symmetric 3-player games shown in [19, Sections 6 & 7].

References

1. Abbott, T.G., Kane, D.M., Valiant, P.: On the complexity of two-player win-lose games. In: FOCS, pp. 113–122 (2005). https://doi.org/10.1109/SFCS.2005.59
2. Aumann, R.J.: Acceptable points in games of perfect information. Pacific J. Math. **10**(2), 381–417 (1960). https://doi.org/10.2140/pjm.1960.10.381
3. Austrin, P., Braverman, M., Chlamtac, E.: Inapproximability of NP-complete variants of Nash equilibrium. Theory Comput. **9**, 117–142 (2013). https://doi.org/10.4086/toc.2013.v009a003
4. Berthelsen, M.L.T., Hansen, K.A.: On the computational complexity of decision problems about multi-player Nash equilibria. Theory Comput. Syst. **66**(3), 519–545 (2022). https://doi.org/10.1007/s00224-022-10080-1
5. Bilò, V., Mavronicolas, M.: The complexity of computational problems about Nash equilibria in symmetric win-lose games. Algorithmica **83**(2), 447–530 (2021)

6. Bilò, V., Mavronicolas, M.: ∃ℝ-complete decision problems about (symmetric) Nash equilibria in (symmetric) multi-player games. ACM Trans. Econ. Comput. **9**(3), 14:1-14:25 (2021). https://doi.org/10.1145/3456758

7. Blanc, M., Hansen, K.A.: Computational complexity of multi-player evolutionarily stable strategies. In: Santhanam, R., Musatov, D. (eds.) CSR 2021. LNCS, vol. 12730, pp. 1–17. Springer, Cham (2021). https://doi.org/10.1007/978-3-030-79416-3_1

8. Blum, L., Shub, M., Smale, S.: On a theory of computation and complexity over the real numbers: NP-completeness, recursive functions and universal machines. Bull. Am. Math. Soc. **21**(1), 1–46 (1989)

9. Bürgisser, P., Cucker, F.: Exotic quantifiers, complexity classes, and complete problems. Found. Comput. Math. **9**(2), 135–170 (2009)

10. Buss, J.F., Frandsen, G.S., Shallit, J.O.: The computational complexity of some problems of linear algebra. J. Comput. Syst. Sci. **58**(3), 572–596 (1999). https://doi.org/10.1006/jcss.1998.1608

11. Canny, J.F.: Some algebraic and geometric computations in PSPACE. In: STOC, pp. 460–467. ACM (1988). https://doi.org/10.1145/62212.62257

12. Chen, X., Deng, X., Teng, S.H.: Settling the complexity of two-player Nash equilibrium. J. ACM **56**(3), 14:-14:57 (2009)

13. Conitzer, V., Sandholm, T.: New complexity results about Nash equilibria. Games Econom. Behav. **63**(2), 621–641 (2008). https://doi.org/10.1016/j.geb.2008.02.015

14. Daskalakis, C., Goldberg, P.W., Papadimitriou, C.H.: The complexity of computing a Nash equilibrium. SIAM J. Comput. **39**(1), 195–259 (2009). https://doi.org/10.1137/070699652

15. Deligkas, A., Fearnley, J., Melissourgos, T., Spirakis, P.: Approximating the existential theory of the reals. J. Comput. Syst. Sci. **125**, 106–128 (2022). https://doi.org/10.10616/j.jcss.2021.11002

16. Deligkas, A., Fearnley, J., Savani, R.: Inapproximability results for constrained approximate Nash equilibria. Inf. Comput. **262**, 40–56 (2018). https://doi.org/10.1016/j.ic2018.06.001

17. Erickson, J., van der Hoog, I., Miltzow, T.: Smoothing the gap between NP and ∃ℝ. In: FOCS, pp. 1022–1033 (2020). https://doi.org/10.1109/FOCS46700.2020.00099

18. Etessami, K., Yannakakis, M.: On the complexity of Nash equilibria and other fixed points. SIAM J. Comput. **39**(6), 2531–2597 (2010)

19. Garg, J., Mehta, R., Vazirani, V.V., Yazdanbod, S.: ∃ℝ-completeness for decision versions of multi-player (symmetric) Nash equilibria. ACM Trans. Econ. Comput. **6**(1), 1:1–1:23 (2018). https://doi.org/10.1145/3175494

20. Gilboa, I., Zemel, E.: Nash and correlated equilibria: some complexity considerations. Games Econom. Behav. **1**(1), 80–93 (1989). https://doi.org/10.1016/0899-8256(89)90006-7

21. Hansen, K.A.: The real computational complexity of minmax value and equilibrium refinements in multi-player games. Theory Comput. Syst. **63**(7), 1554–1571 (2019). https://doi.org/10.1007/s00224-018-9887-9

22. Maschler, M., Solan, E., Zamir, S.: Game Theory. Cambridge University Press, Cambridge (2013)

23. Nash, J.: Non-cooperative games. Ann. Math. **2**(54), 286–295 (1951). https://doi.org/10.2307/1969529

24. Schaefer, M., Štefankovič, D.: Fixed points, Nash equilibria, and the existential theory of the reals. Theory Comput. Syst. **60**, 172–193 (2017)

Arbitrary Profit Sharing in Federated Learning Utility Games

Eirini Georgoulaki[1] and Kostas Kollias[2(✉)]

[1] Technische Universität Berlin, Berlin, Germany
eirini@math.tu-berlin.edu
[2] Google Research, Mountain View, CA, USA
kostaskollias@google.com

Abstract. *Arbitrary cost-sharing* is a model in which the players of a resource selection game get to declare the payments that they will make, rather than have the payments be determined by a cost-sharing protocol. Arbitrary cost-sharing has been studied in various contexts, such as congestion games, network design games, and scheduling games. The natural counterpart of arbitrary cost-sharing in the context of a utility game is *arbitrary utility-sharing*, meaning that each player will request a certain utility as a reward for her efforts in generating welfare for the system. This concept has received much less attention in the literature. In this paper, we initiate the study of arbitrary sharing in utility games, placing emphasis on the special case of *federated learning utility games*, in which players form groups that jointly execute a learning task and each player contributes certain types of data to each group. We present results on the price of anarchy and price of stability, showing that the price of anarchy is 2 and that arbitrary utility sharing is the only known method to achieve price of stability 1 with budget-balanced payments.

Keywords: Arbitrary sharing · utility games · price of anarchy · price of stability

1 Introduction

In utility games [23,25] sets of agents produce welfare and receive a reward in return. It is naturally expected that these agents (also henceforth called players) will act in a way that maximizes this individual reward. The assumption is that eventually they will play a Nash equilibrium outcome, i.e., a solution such that no player is better off by unilaterally deviating to a different action. Vetta [25] proved that in such games and under mild conditions, the worst case inefficiency of a Nash equilibrium when compared against the optimal solution, termed the *price of anarchy*, is bounded by 2, i.e., the optimal solution of the optimization version of the problem will have welfare at most 2 times that of any Nash equilibrium. The described model is of course very general and it is interesting to study more structured versions. One such version is the *federated learning (FL) utility-sharing game* studied in [16]. In this game, agents form groups to complete a learning task. The task comprises of smaller subtasks which are considered elements that need covering by the players. In the learning context, one can think of these as certain types of training examples that the agent may or many not possess in their data.

The work in [16] studied various utility-sharing methods for the FL utility-sharing game. This included the *egalitarian* method, where all players covering an element share its value equally, the *marginal gain* method, where players arrive in order and each agent is rewarded for the new elements that she covers upon arrival, and the *marginal loss* method where each agent is rewarded with the value lost if she were to leave the group. Note that the marginal loss method has a fundamental difference when compared to the other two: it is not *budget-balanced*, meaning that the value of an element may not be fully distributed to the players covering it. In fact, if we assume that all elements in a group are covered by more than one players, then no utility is given back to the players as reward. The other two methods are naturally budget-balanced.

In this work we will study a slightly different model for distributing utility back to the players in such games: *arbitrary utility-sharing*. Under this regime, the way that the players share the utility of a group is not dictated by a centralized method, instead it is the players themselves who declare the reward that each one requests for each element to which they contribute. If the requested rewards do not surpass the element's value, then the allocation goes through whereas if they are above it, there is disagreement and no utilities are granted back to the players. In this sense, the action of a player is a pair that consists of the group that the player selects and the reward that the player requests for each element that she covers.

1.1 Our Results

We begin our study with the *price of stability*, the well-known optimistic counterpart of the price of anarchy, where the optimal solution is compared against the best (rather than the worst) Nash equilibrium of each instance. We show that arbitrary utility sharing achieves the best possible price of stability, namely 1, in a budget balanced manner. In fact we show something stronger: Under arbitrary utility-sharing, *any* budget-balanced rewards in a socially optimal solution induce a Nash equilibrium. Hence, in the process, we also show that the method guarantees the existence of Nash equilibria. We also remark that our proof can be easily generalized to handle group welfare functions that are submodular in the player set.

Next we show that the price of stability of egalitarian sharing is at least 1.123, which proves that all previously studied methods fail to achieve price of stability 1 in a budget-balanced manner (marginal loss was shown to have a price of stability at least 1.581 in [16] and marginal gain is not budget balanced), making arbitrary sharing the only known method to do so.

We then turn to the price of anarchy and present a lower bound that converges to 2 as the size of the instance increases, matching the upper bound of [25] which, as we show, applies to arbitrary sharing as well.

1.2 Related Work

The FL utility game was introduced by Gollapudi et al [16]. The utility-sharing methods against which we contrast arbitrary-sharing were also defined in the same work. Other game-theoretic models in the federated learning context include [8,9].

Utility games were introduced by Vetta [25] to model strategic agents who produce submodular social welfare in a team, and seek to maximize their individual utility or payoff in return. For this general setting, Vetta showed an upper bound of 2 on the price of anarchy, subject to some mild conditions on the agent payoff functions. Marden and Wierman [23] studied utility sharing methods in a general distributed utility maximization model, and Harks and Miller [17] studied cost sharing methods in networking applications. Bachrach *et al.* [5] considered the effect of *positive* externalities among players working on multiple projects simultaneously, but restricted by an effort budget. In [22], the authors study a special case of utility games where the welfare produced by a resource is a function of the number of players on it, and prove that under certain conditions (e.g., symmetric players), the price of anarchy drops below 2.

We now mention related work in terms of the corresponding optimization problem – make an assignment of players to teams to maximize overall social utility, where the utility on every team is given by a weighted coverage function. This problem is called *submodular welfare maximization with coverage functions.* The best approximation ratio in the general case is $\frac{e}{e-1} \simeq 1.58$ [6,11,12].

Arbitrary-sharing has been studied in the context of cost-minimization games, such as scheduling, congestion games, and network design games [1–4,7,10,19,21]. Even though in network design games arbitrary cost-sharing will usually perform worse than egalitarian cost-sharing, an interesting special case of network design games where the price of anarchy improves has been identified in the face of real-time scheduling games [14,24]. The works in [18,20] study classes of games with non-decreasing per player costs.

2 Model

In the FL utility game there is a set of groups T for the players N to join. The utility produced in each group is given by a coverage function, i.e., there is set of elements S that need to be covered in each group, and each $s \in S$ offers unit utility. These can be interpreted as learning tasks or as learning instances that the players can contribute to the group. Each player i can contribute to a subset of these elements $S_i \subseteq S$. Then the elements covered in group $t \in T$ are given by $S_t = \cup_{i \in t} S_i$, and the utility produced is $U_t = |S_t|$. This is precisely a coverage function over the federated players in the group; we say that group t *covers* element s if $s \in S_t$.

From a social perspective, the goal is to maximize the total utility produced by all groups,

$$U = \sum_{t \in T} U_t = \sum_{t \in T} |S_t|.$$

We will call U the *social welfare* or *objective value*.

Each player i is interested in maximizing her own payoff, denoted u_i, which depends on the utility sharing mechanism. An assignment of players to groups is a *Nash equilibrium* when no player can improve her payoff by unilaterally deviating to a different group. The metrics that we study in this paper are the *price of stability* and the *price of anarchy*, which are the worst case ratios (over all instances of the FL utility sharing game) of the social welfare in the optimal assignment over the social welfare in the best and worst Nash equilibrium respectively.

In this work we mainly propose and study the *arbitrary utility sharing* method for this game, however we also present a result on the standard *egalitarian sharing* method [16]. In egalitarian utility sharing the value of a covered element is equally distributed among those covering it. In arbitrary utility sharing, each player gets to request payments for the elements that she covers. In this regard, the strategy of a player is not only the group that she joins (as is the case in egalitarian and marginal gain utility sharing) but also the utility that she requests in return for each element that she covers.

2.1 Handling Degenerate Solutions in the Arbitrary Sharing Model

Similarly to the cost minimization setting (e.g., [13,15]), arbitrary sharing can suffer from degenerate solutions where the player are stuck in disagreement about how to split an element's utility. For example, even in a game with a single group, a single element, and 3 players covering the element, it is possible for all 3 to request a payment greater than $1/2$. With any unilateral deviation to another payment request, the total payments requested remain greater than 1 and disagreement persists, hence we get an infinitely bad Nash equilibrium. We address this deficiency in the model similarly to [15]. The first modification is to define the utility of the players in a group that includes disagreements to be -1, instead of 0. The second is to introduce the strategy of not participating in the game, which offers a utility of 0. This is a natural amendment to the model given that it can be enforced using penalties. In fact, even without any designer-enforced penalties, it can be considered natural behavior for players to prefer to not participate in the game rather than stay in a group that does not produce any utility due to disagreements. Under these modifications, we get the following proposition.

Proposition 1. *Any Nash equilibrium in arbitrary sharing FL utility games has budget balanced payments for all elements.*

Proof. First it is easy to see that an equilibrium will not include any disagreement (i.e., an element where the total requested payments are greater than 1) since a player in such a group would prefer to take the non-participation option and increase her utility from -1 to 0. It is also trivial to see that there cannot be elements for which the total payments requested are less than 1 since any player would have an incentive to request a greater payment. □

3   Price of Stability in FL Utility Games

We first prove that the price of stability of arbitrary utility sharing in FL games is 1. In fact we prove the stronger statement given by the following theorem.

Theorem 1. *A social welfare maximizing assignment of players to groups and any budget balanced payment requests over it yield a Nash equilibrium for arbitrary sharing in FL utility games.*

Proof. Here we will merely prove that any beneficial deviation from such a solution will also increase the social welfare, yielding a contradiction. Consider a player i deviating from group t to group t', increasing her utility from $u_{i,t}$ to $u_{i,t'} > u_{i,t}$ in the process. Let $S_{i,t}$ be the set of elements that i covers by herself in t. By Proposition 1, i receives the whole value of the elements in $S_{i,t}$, i.e., $u_{i,t} \geq |S_{i,t}|$. Similarly, let $S_{i,t'}$ be the elements that i covers alone in t' after deviating there. By Proposition 1 we know that i will receive the whole value for these elements. We also know that i cannot ask for any positive reward for any other element in t' as, given that their values have been fully distributed to the players already covering them, there would be disagreement in the newly generated assignment. This means $u_{i,t'} = |S_{i,t'}|$. From the above, we get:

$$|S_{i,t}| \leq u_{i,t} < u_{i,t'} = |S_{i,t'}|.$$

When i deviates, the elements in $S_{i,t}$ will be removed from the social welfare, whereas the elements in $S_{i,t'}$ will be added to it. Hence, the above inequality shows that social welfare will increase, yielding the contradiction.   □

Remark 1. We note that the proof of Theorem 1 can be easily generalized to handle arbitrary submodular functions for group utilities. The only necessary condition is that each player receives a payment equal to the marginal increase that her presence causes to the group welfare (in the FL context this is equivalent to each player receiving the full payment for the elements that she covers by herself). Then it similarly follows that any beneficial deviation would also improve social welfare.

Theorem 2. *The price of stability of egalitarian sharing in FL utility games is at least 1.123.*

Proof. Consider a game with players $N = \{1, 2, \ldots, n + 1\}$ and elements $S = \{1, 2, \ldots, 2n\}$. Each player $i = 1, 2, \ldots, n$ covers elements $\{1, 2, \ldots, n, n+i\}$, i.e., the first half of the elements and element $n + i$. Player $n + 1$ covers all elements. The game has two groups. An assignment such that player $n + 1$ is alone in one group and all other players are together in the other group maximizes social welfare as it covers all elements in both groups with total utility $4n$.

Now let us consider a Nash equilibrium outcome (note that one is guaranteed to exist for egalitarian sharing as shown in [16]). Let $\alpha \in [0, 1]$ be a parameter such that the number of other players who share the group of player $n + 1$ is

αn. Consider any player i in the group that does not include player $n + 1$. Her utility is equal to:

$$\frac{n}{(1 - \alpha)n} + 1,$$

since she shares n elements (namely, elements $1, 2, \ldots, n$) with another $(1-\alpha)n - 1$ players and she covers one element by herself (namely, element $n+i$). If player i were to deviate to the other group, which includes player $n + 1$ and another αn players, she would have utility equal to:

$$\frac{n}{\alpha n + 2} + \frac{1}{2},$$

since she would share the first n elements with another $\alpha n + 1$ players and element $n + i$ only with player $n + 1$. By the equilibrium condition we get

$$\frac{n}{(1 - \alpha)n} + 1 \geq \frac{n}{\alpha n + 2} + \frac{1}{2} \Rightarrow \frac{1}{1 - \alpha} \geq \frac{1}{\alpha + \frac{2}{n}} - \frac{1}{2}.$$

As $n \to \infty$, the condition is satisfied when:

$$\alpha \geq \frac{5 - \sqrt{17}}{2} + \epsilon,$$

for arbitrarily small $\epsilon > 0$. Let $\hat{\alpha}$ be precisely the value on the right hand side. Then, in every equilibrium, there are at least $\hat{\alpha}n$ players who are joining player $n + 1$ in her group, leaving at least $\hat{\alpha}n$ elements uncovered in the other group. This means that the social welfare in any equilibrium assignment is at most

$$4n - \hat{\alpha}n = \left(4 - \frac{5 - \sqrt{17}}{2} + \epsilon \right) n.$$

This in turn gives a price of stability that is at least:

$$\frac{4n}{4n - \hat{\alpha}n} = \frac{4}{4 - \frac{5 - \sqrt{17}}{2} + \epsilon} \approx 1.123.$$

$\square$

These results imply that arbitrary sharing is the only known budget balanced method that achieves price of stability 1 in such games. The other two methods that have been studied beyond arbitrary and egalitarian sharing are marginal gain and marginal loss. The former was shown in [16] to have price of stability at least $e/(e - 1)$ and the latter is not budget balanced.

4   Price of Anarchy of Arbitrary Sharing in FL Utility Games

The standard upper bound of 2 on the price of anarchy in utility games [25] applies to FL utility games with arbitrary sharing as well, since they satisfy the property that a player is rewarded with at least her marginal contribution to the social welfare (by applying Proposition 1 on the elements that a player covers by herself). We now prove the lower bound in the theorem that follows. Our lower bound construction resembles the technique used in [16] for egalitarian sharing but some of the technical details differ.

Theorem 3. *The price of anarchy of arbitrary sharing in FL utility games is* 2.

Proof. We construct an instance and an assignment of players to groups that is an equilibrium and whose social welfare is a $\frac{1}{2}$ fraction of the optimal solution. We begin with an overview of this construction, and then give details of each step. First, we create a simple instance parameterized by an integer x (the meaning of which we explain later), and an assignment of players to groups with utility $\frac{x+1}{2x+1}$ times the optimal. Our assignment in this preliminary game will *not* be an equilibrium. We then modify the instance in two stages, where we preserve the ratio $\frac{x+1}{2x+1}$ w.r.t. the optimal solution, while creating sufficient structure to argue that the final assignment is an equilibrium for any x. Then letting $x \to \infty$ will yield the price of anarchy lower bound of 2.

Throughout the construction, we will have the players request their egalitarian shares, i.e., all players request an equal share of the unit utility given by an element that they cover. Note that this does not make the construction an instance of egalitarian sharing since the utilities players get by deviating are not the same as in the egalitarian sharing case.

Checking whether the final assignment is an equilibrium can be a complicated task in general, since there will eventually be a large number of players and possible deviations in the game. Our two-stage transformation will ensure, however, that this task reduces to verifying a single inequality. This will be achieved by imposing symmetry across players (first transformation) and symmetry across possible deviations of a player (second transformation). We now present the four stages of our proof (initialization, imposing player symmetry, imposing deviation symmetry, and picking the value of x) in detail.

Stage 1: Initialization. Our preliminary game uses the parameter $k = 2x + 1$. There are k elements $s_1, s_2, \ldots, s_k$, and k *types* of players where a player of type i can *only* cover element s_i. There are k players for each type, i.e., a total of k^2 players. The number of groups is also k. The utility produced by covering any single element in a group is 1.

We will crucially maintain two properties of the assignment. The first property imposes symmetry over how players are divided among groups.

Property 1. Note that there are $k = 2x + 1$ players who can cover an element. Our assignment will ensure that every element is covered by 2 players in x groups, by 1 player in 1 group, and remains uncovered in x groups. We will also ensure that every group has $k = 2x + 1$ players. These k players in any group will cover elements as follows: x elements will be covered by 2 players, 1 element will be covered by 1 player, and x elements will remain uncovered.

Note that the above property ensures that every group only covers $x+1$ elements out of the total of $k = 2x + 1$ elements. Similarly, every element is covered in only $x + 1$ groups out of the total of $k = 2x + 1$ groups.

The second property relates our assignment to an optimal assignment (call it OPT). To encode OPT, let us use k colors $c_1, c_2, \ldots, c_k$, where all players assigned to group i by OPT are said to have color c_i.

Property 2. OPT will satisfy the property that there is exactly one player with color c_i who can cover a specific element s_j, for any i and j. In other words, the $k = 2x + 1$ players who can cover any specific element will be divided among the $k = 2x + 1$ groups, thereby ensuring that all elements in all groups are covered. Contrast this to our assignment that only covers $x + 1$ elements in every group, and $x + 1$ groups cover every element, according to Property 1. Finally, in our assignment, there will be exactly one player of each color c_i in every group t. In other words, the overlap between any group in our assignment and any group in OPT will be exactly one player.

As noted above, Property 1 implies that the coverage of our assignment is $\frac{x+1}{2x+1}$ times the total number of elements, while Property 2 ensures that the optimal solution covers every element. However, it is not apriori clear that these properties can be satisfied by an assignment: the next lemma asserts this.

Lemma 1. *Given k groups, k elements, and, for each element, k players who can cover only that element, there is an assignment of the players to the groups and a coloring that satisfies Properties 1 and 2.*

Proof. (See Fig. 1 for an illustration of the $x = 1$ case.) The first group's structure is as follows: elements $s_1, s_2, \ldots, s_x$ are covered by two players, element s_{x+1} is covered by one player, and elements $s_{x+2}, s_{x+3}, \ldots, s_k$ are left uncovered. For this first group, we use any coloring that has a different color for each of the k players. The structure and coloring of the second group is obtained by performing a left circular shift to the first group's structure, i.e., $s_k, s_1, s_2, \ldots,$ s_{x-1}, are covered by 2 players, s_x is covered by 1 player, and $s_{x+1}, s_{x+2}, \ldots,$ s_{k-1}, are left uncovered. Colors are also shifted, i.e., the color(s) of the player(s) covering s_i in the first group is applied to the player(s) covering s_{i-1} (s_k, if $i = 1$) in the second group. We continue with similar left circular shifts to define the remaining groups. This assignment and coloring satisfies Properties 1 and 2. $\square$

We have now completed the first stage; we will call this the *preliminary assignment*. By Property 2, the optimal assignment covers all elements; hence, the ratio of the coverage of this preliminary assignment to the optimum is $\frac{x+1}{2x+1}$. However, this assignment is not an equilibrium, since players sharing an element have unilateral incentive to deviate to a group where the corresponding element is not covered. We now proceed to the next stages, which will modify this assignment to an equilibrium.

Stage 2: Imposing Player Symmetry. During this stage, we will augment the game by adding new elements. In our preliminary assignment, not all players

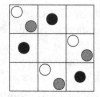

Fig. 1. The preliminary assignment for $x = 1$. Groups are rows, elements are columns. Cell (i, j) corresponds to group i, element s_j. OPT has all white players in group 1, all gray players in group 2, and all black players in group 3. The occupancy is symmetric across rows and columns and each color appears once per row and column.

have the same payoff since some of them share an element with a group-mate while others do not. In this stage, we impose symmetry across players: every player will share exactly $2x$ elements with another player and will cover exactly 1 element by herself. To do this, we create k copies of our preliminary assignment, and exchange roles between players in the different copies in a way that they all end up being symmetric. We will call this the *intermediate assignment*.

The first copy is identical to the preliminary assignment. In the second copy, we take the preliminary assignment and perform a circular shift on the colors, i.e., we change color c_i to color c_{i+1} (color c_k changes to c_1). Next, we rename the elements so that they are distinct from those in the first copy. We continue this process of doing a circular shift on the colors and renaming the elements in each subsequent copy until we have k copies in total. (See Fig. 2 for all the copies of the $x = 1$ case.) The intermediate assignment is constructed by appending all k copies (recall that the elements are distinct in the copies), and merging all players in the same group with the same color into a single player.

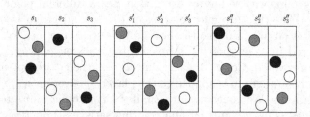

Fig. 2. The intermediate assignment for $x = 1$. The first copy is the original preliminary assignment. In the second one, white becomes gray, gray becomes black, black becomes white. In the third we shift the colors again. All three together form the intermediate assignment.

Note that Properties 1 and 2 continue to hold; in particular, this implies that the intermediate assignment covers a $\frac{x+1}{2x+1}$ fraction of elements in each group, while OPT covers every element in every group. Moreover, since every color assumes the role of every other color in the preliminary assignment in one of the copies, it follows that every player covers $2x$ elements with another player and 1 element by herself in the intermediate assignment. This implies that the players are symmetric in their coverage and payoff in their current group. However, the possible deviations of a player to another group are not symmetric, i.e., the payoff of a player depends on the group that the player moves to. In the next stage, we impose symmetry on the deviations of players, thereby reducing the equilibrium condition to a single inequality.

Stage 3: Imposing Deviation Symmetry. In this stage, we repeatedly perform an operation that we call *group structure switch*. Switching the structure of group t to that of t' involves taking each player in t, stripping her of her existing elements, and granting her the elements of the player in t' with the same color. By Property 2, this player in t' is uniquely defined given a specific player in t. A *group structure permutation* is said to be performed when we switch the structure of every group t to the structure of group $\pi(t)$, where π is a permutation on the groups T.

For every possible permutation π, we generate a copy of the intermediate assignment and perform a group structure permutation based on π. As we did in the previous stage, we rename elements so that they are different for each permuted copy and incorporate all $k!$ copies into our game by merging players in the same group with the same color into a single player with $k \cdot k!$ elements. This generates our *final assignment*. (See Fig. 3 for the copies corresponding to the six permutations for the $x = 1$ case.)

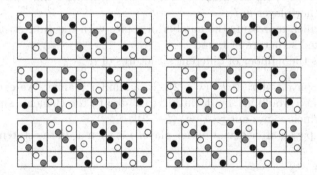

Fig. 3. All 6 versions of the intermediate assignment for $x = 1$. The first one is the original intermediate assignment. The rest are all possible permutations of the group structures (i.e., rows). All 6 together form the final assignment with 9 players: one white, one gray, and one black player in each group.

Again, note that Properties 1 and 2 continue to hold; as a consequence, each group only covers a $\frac{x+1}{2x+1}$ fraction of the elements in the final assignment whereas OPT covers every element in every group. Additionally, every deviation of a player to another group now result in exactly the same utility; therefore, not only are the players symmetric in their current group, but their deviation to any other group is also symmetric.

Lemma 2. *In the final assignment, the utility of any player i who deviates to a group t' that is not her assigned group t is $(2x^2 + x)k(k-2)!$.*

Proof. Consider a player i, and call her assigned group t. Fix some structure for t in an intermediate assignment, and focus on all versions of the intermediate assignment in which group t has that structure. There will be $(k-1)!$ such versions. Consider any element s that is covered by i and another player in this structure. Our first goal is to determine the coverage of element s in any other group t' in each of the $(k-1)!$ versions of the intermediate assignment that we are considering.

The copies of t' in the $(k-1)!$ versions we are considering can assume one of $k-1$ possible structures, excluding the structure that we have fixed for t. Each one of these $k-1$ possible structures for t' appears an equal number of times, i.e., $(k-2)!$ times. By Property 1, $x-1$ of these $k-1$ structures have 2 players covering element s. (Note that t itself has 2 players covering s, hence the number is $x-1$ and not x.) Similarly, in 1 of these structures, s is covered by a single player, and it is not covered at all in x structures. This implies that the payoff of i due to s, if she deviates to t', will be x when we sum across one copy of each structure of t', since she will only be able to claim a unit of reward for the elements that have not already been covered. For the overall payoff of i after deviation to t' due to elements shared with another player in t, we need to multiply this expression by:

- $2x$, which represents the number of different elements s that are covered by i and another player in t,
- $(k-2)!$, which represents the number of copies with the same structure of t', given a fixed structure of t, and
- k, which is the number of different structures of t.

This yields a payoff of $x \cdot 2xk \cdot (k-2)!$. In a similar manner, we can calculate the payoff that i would get by deviating to t' due to the elements she uniquely covers in t, which comes out to $x \cdot k \cdot (k-2)!$.

The total payoff after deviation for player i is then as in the statement of the lemma. □

Stage 4: Choice of parameter x. Note that the payoff of a player in the final assignment is $(x+1)k!$, since the payoff in every copy of the intermediate assignment is $x+1$ and there are $k!$ copies (recall that we have designated that players request equal shares in the equilibrium). Therefore, by Lemma 2, the equilibrium condition is:

$$(2x^2 + x)k \cdot (k-2)! \leq (x+1)k!.$$

Since $k = 2x + 1$, this simplifies to $(x+1)2x \geq 2x^2 + x$, which trivially holds for any x. We then get a $\frac{2x+1}{x+1}$ lower bound on the price of anarchy, which is arbitrarily close to 2 as $x \to \infty$. This completes the proof. □

References

1. Anshelevich, E., Caskurlu, B.: Exact and approximate equilibria for optimal group network formation. Theor. Comput. Sci. **412**(39), 5298–5314 (2011)
2. Anshelevich, E., Caskurlu, B.: Price of stability in survivable network design. Theory Comput. Syst. **49**(1), 98–138 (2011)
3. Anshelevich, E., Dasgupta, A., Tardos, É., Wexler, T.: Near-optimal network design with selfish agents. Theory Comput. **4**(1), 77–109 (2008)
4. Anshelevich, E., Karagiozova, A.: Terminal backup, 3d matching, and covering cubic graphs. SIAM J. Comput. **40**(3), 678–708 (2011)
5. Bachrach, Y., Syrgkanis, V., Vojnovic, M.: Incentives and efficiency in uncertain collaborative environments. In: WINE, pp. 26–39 (2013)
6. Calinescu, G., Chekuri, C., Pal, M., Vondrak, J.: Maximizing a submodular set function subject to a matroid constraint (extended abstract). In: IPCO, pp. 182–196 (2007)
7. Cardinal, J., Hoefer, M.: Non-cooperative facility location and covering games. Theor. Comput. Sci. **411**(16–18), 1855–1876 (2010)
8. Donahue, K., Kleinberg, J.M.: Model-sharing games: analyzing federated learning under voluntary participation. In: Thirty-Fifth AAAI Conference on Artificial Intelligence, AAAI 2021, pp. 5303–5311. AAAI Press (2021)
9. Donahue, K., Kleinberg, J.M.: Optimality and stability in federated learning: a game-theoretic approach. In: Annual Conference on Neural Information Processing Systems 2021, NeurIPS 2021, 6–14 December 2021, virtual, pp. 1287–1298 (2021)
10. Epstein, A., Feldman, M., Mansour, Y.: Strong equilibrium in cost sharing connection games. Games Econ. Behav. **67**(1), 51–68 (2009)
11. Filmus, Y., Ward, J.: The power of local search: maximum coverage over a matroid. In: STACS, pp. 601–612 (2012)
12. Filmus, Y., Ward, J.: Monotone submodular maximization over a matroid via non-oblivious local search. SIAM J. Comput. **43**(2), 514–542 (2014)
13. Georgoulaki, E., Kollias, K., Tamir, T.: Equilibrium inefficiency in resource buying games with load-dependent costs. In: Algorithmic Game Theory - 13th International Symposium, SAGT 2020, Augsburg, Germany, 16–18 2020 September, Proceedings (2020)
14. Georgoulaki, E., Kollias, K.: On the price of anarchy of cost-sharing in real-time scheduling systems. In: Web and Internet Economics - 15th International Conference, WINE 2019, New York, NY, USA, 10–12 December 2019, Proceedings (2019)
15. Georgoulaki, E., Kollias, K., Tamir, T.: Equilibrium inefficiency and computation in cost-sharing games in real-time scheduling systems. Algorithms **14**(4), 103 (2021)
16. Gollapudi, S., Kollias, K., Panigrahi, D., Pliatsika, V.: Profit sharing and efficiency in utility games. In: ESA (2017)
17. Harks, T., Miller, K.: The worst-case efficiency of cost sharing methods in resource allocation games. Oper. Res. **59**(6), 1491–1503 (2011)
18. Harks, T., Peis, B.: Resource buying games. Algorithmica **70**(3), 493–512 (2014)
19. Hoefer, M.: Non-cooperative tree creation. Algorithmica **53**(1), 104–131 (2009)
20. Hoefer, M.: Competitive cost sharing with economies of scale. Algorithmica **60**(4), 743–765 (2011)
21. Hoefer, M.: Strategic cooperation in cost sharing games. Int. J. Game Theory **42**(1), 29–53 (2013)

22. Marden, J.R., Roughgarden, T.: Generalized efficiency bounds in distributed resource allocation. In: CDC, pp. 2233–2238. IEEE (2010)
23. Marden, J.R., Wierman, A.: Distributed welfare games. Oper. Res. **61**(1), 155–168 (2013)
24. Tamir, T.: Cost-sharing games in real-time scheduling systems. In: Web and Internet Economics - 14th International Conference, WINE 2018, Oxford, UK, 15–17 December 2018, Proceedings, pp. 423–437 (2018)
25. Vetta, A.: Nash equilibria in competitive societies, with applications to facility location, traffic routing and auctions. In: FOCS (2002)

The Contest Game for Crowdsourcing Reviews

Marios Mavronicolas[1]([⊠])[iD] and Paul G. Spirakis[2][iD]

[1] Department of Computer Science, University of Cyprus, Nicosia, Cyprus
`mavronic@ucy.ac.cy`
[2] Department of Computer Science, University of Liverpool, Liverpool, UK
`P.Spirakis@liverpool.ac.uk`

Abstract. We consider a *contest game* modelling a contest where reviews for a *proposal* are crowdsourced from n *players*. Player i has a *skill* s_i, strategically chooses a *quality* $q \in \{1, 2, \ldots, Q\}$ for her review and pays an *effort* $f_q \geq 0$, strictly increasing with q. Under *voluntary participation,* a player may opt to not write a review, paying zero effort; *mandatory participation* does not provide this option. For her effort, she is awarded a *payment* per her *payment function,* which is either *player-invariant,* like, e.g., the popular *proportional allocation,* or *player-specific;* it is *oblivious* when it does not depend on the numbers of players choosing a different quality. The *utility* to player i is the difference between her payment and her *cost,* calculated by a *skill-effort* function $\Lambda(s_i, f_q)$. Skills may vary for *arbitrary players; anonymous players* means $s_i = 1$ for all players i. In a *pure Nash equilibrium,* no player could unilaterally increase her utility by switching to a different quality. We show the following results about the existence and the computation of a pure Nash equilibrium:

- We present an exact potential to show the existence of a pure Nash equilibrium for the contest game with arbitrary players and player-invariant and oblivious payments. A particular case of this result provides an answer to an open question from [6]. In contrast, a pure Nash equilibrium might not exist *(i)* for player-invariant payments, even if players are anonymous, *(ii)* for proportional allocation payments and arbitrary players, and *(iii)* for player-specific payments, even if players are anonymous; in the last case, it is $\mathcal{NP}$-hard to tell. These counterexamples prove the tightness of our existence result.
- We show that the contest game with proportional allocation, voluntary participation and anonymous players has the *Finite Improvement Property,* or *FIP;* this yields two pure Nash equilibria. The *FIP* carries over to mandatory participation, except that there is now a single pure Nash equilibrium. For arbitrary players, we determine a simple sufficient condition for the *FIP* in the special case where the skill-effort function has the product form $\Lambda(s_i, f_q) = s_i \, f_q$.
- We introduce a novel, discrete concavity property of player-specific payments, namely *three-discrete-concavity,* which we exploit to

The first author is supported by research funds at University of Cyprus. The second author is supported by ESPRC grant EP/P02002X/1.

devise, for constant Q, a polynomial-time $\Theta(n^Q)$ algorithm to compute a pure Nash equilibrium in the contest game with arbitrary players; it is a special case of a $\Theta\left(n\,Q^2\,\binom{n+Q-1}{Q-1}\right)$ algorithm for arbitrary Q that we present. Thus, the problem is $\mathcal{XP}$-tractable with respect to the parameter Q. The computed equilibrium is *contiguous*: players with higher skills are contiguously assigned to lower qualities. Both three-discrete-concavity and the algorithm extend naturally to player-invariant payments.

1   Introduction

Contests [39] are modelled as games where strategic contestants, or *players*, invest efforts in competitions to win valuable prizes, such as monetary awards, scientific credit or social reputation. Such competitions are ubiquitous in contexts such as promotion tournaments in organizations, allocation of campaign resources, content curation and selection in online platforms, financial support of scientific research by governmental institutions and question-and-answer forums. This work joins an active research thread on the existence, computation and efficiency of (pure) Nash equilibria in games for crowdsourcing, content curation, information aggregation and other tasks [1,2,4–6,12,14–18,21,25,40].

In a *crowdsourcing contest* (see, e.g., [8,13,33]), solutions to a certain task are solicited. When the task is the evaluation of proposals requesting funding, a set of expert advisors, or *reviewers,* file peer-reviews of the proposals. We shall consider a contest game for crowdsourcing reviews, embracing and wide-extending a corresponding game from [6, Section 2] that was motivated by issues in the design of blockchains and cryptocurrencies. In the contest game, funding agencies wish to collect peer-reviews of esteem *quality*. *Costs* are incurred to reviewers; they reflect various overheads, such as time, participation cost or reputational loss, and are supposed to increase with the reviewers' *skills* and *efforts*. Both skills and efforts are modelled as discrete; such modelling is natural since, for example, monetary expenditure, the time to spend on projects, and man-power are usually measured in discrete units. Naturally, efforts increase with the achieved qualities of the reviews. Efforts map collectively into *payments* rewarded to the reviewers to counterbalance their costs. We proceed to formalize these considerations.

1.1   The Contest Game for Crowdsourcing Reviews

We assume familiarity with the basics of finite games, as articulated, e.g., in [24]; we shall restrict attention to finite games. In the *contest game for crowdsourcing reviews,* henceforth abbreviated as the *contest game,* there are n *players* $1, 2, \ldots, n$, with $n \geq 2$, simultaneously writing reviews for a *proposal.* Each player $i \in [n]$ has a *skill* $s_i > 0$. Players are *anonymous* if their skills are the same; then, take $s_i = 1$ for all $i \in [n]$. Else they are *arbitrary*.

The *strategy* q_i of a player $i \in [n]$ is the *quality* of the review she writes; she chooses it from a finite set $\{1, 2, \ldots, Q\}$, with $Q \geq 2$. For a given *quality vector* $\mathbf{q} = \langle q_1, \ldots, q_n \rangle$, the *load* on quality q, denoted as $N_{\mathbf{q}}(q)$, is the number of players choosing quality q; so $\sum_{q \in [Q]} N_{\mathbf{q}}(q) = n$. A partial quality vector $\mathbf{q}_{-i}$ results by excluding q_i from $\mathbf{q}$, for some player $i \in [n]$. Players$_{\mathbf{q}}(q)$ is the set of players choosing quality q in $\mathbf{q}$. f_q is the *effort* paid by a player writing a review of quality q; it is an increasing function of q with $f_1 < f_2 < \ldots < f_Q$. *Mandatory participation* is modeled by setting $f_1 > 0$; under *voluntary participation,* modeled by setting $f_1 = 0$, a player may choose not to write a review and save effort.

Given a quality vector $\mathbf{q}$ and a player $i \in [n]$, the *payment* awarded to player $i \in [n]$ for her review is the value $P_i(\mathbf{q})$ determined by her *payment function* P_i, obeying the *normalization condition* $\sum_{k \in [n]} P_k(\mathbf{q}) \leq 1$. Payments are *oblivious* if for any player $i \in [n]$ and quality vector $\mathbf{q}$, $P_i(\mathbf{q}) = P_i(N_{\mathbf{q}}(q_i), f_{q_i})$; that is, $P_i(\mathbf{q})$ depends only on the quality q_i chosen by player i and the load on it. Note that oblivious payments are not necessarily player-invariant as for different players $i, k \in [n]$, it is not necessary that $P_i = P_k$. Payments are *player-invariant* if for every quality vector $\mathbf{q}$, for any players $i, k \in [n]$ with $q_i = q_k$, $P_i(\mathbf{q}) = P_k(\mathbf{q})$; thus, players choosing the same quality are awarded the same payment. A player-invariant payment function $P_i(\mathbf{q})$ can be represented by a two-argument payment function $P_i(q, \mathbf{q}_{-i})$, for a quality $q \in [Q]$ and a partial quality vector $\mathbf{q}_{-i}$, for a player $i \in [n]$. We consider the following player-invariant payments:

- The *proportional allocation* $\mathsf{PA}_i(\mathbf{q}) = \dfrac{f_{q_i}}{\sum_{k \in [n]} f_{q_k}}$; thus, $\sum_{i \in [n]} \mathsf{PA}_i(\mathbf{q}) = \dfrac{\sum_{i \in [n]} f_{q_i}}{\sum_{i \in [n]} f_{q_i}} = 1$. Proportional allocation is widely studied in the context of contests with smooth allocation of prizes (cf. [39, Section 4.4]). For proportional allocation with voluntary participation (by which $f_1 = 0$), in the scenario where all players choose quality 1, the payment to any player becomes $\frac{0}{0}$, so it is indeterminate. To remove indeterminacy and make payments well-defined, we define the payment to any player choosing quality 1 in the case where all players choose 1 to be 0. Note that proportional allocation is not oblivious.

- The *equal sharing per quality* $\mathsf{ES}_i(\mathbf{q}) = C_{\mathsf{ES}} \cdot \dfrac{f_{q_i}}{N_{\mathbf{q}}(q_i)}$; so f_{q_i} is shared evenly by players choosing q_i. Since $\sum_{i \in [n]} \mathsf{ES}_i(\mathbf{q}) = C_{\mathsf{ES}} \cdot \sum_{i \in [n]} \dfrac{f_{q_i}}{N_{\mathbf{q}}(q_i)}$, we take $C_{\mathsf{ES}} = \left(\max_{\mathbf{q}} \sum_{i \in [n]} \dfrac{f_{q_i}}{N_{\mathbf{q}}(q_i)} \right)^{-1}$. Note that the equal sharing per quality is different from the standard equal sharing, by which *all* players choosing quality at least some $q \in [Q]$ share f_q equally. Thus, standard equal sharing is not oblivious, while the equal sharing per quality is.

- The $K\mathsf{Top}$ *allocation* $K\mathsf{Top}_i(\mathbf{q}) = C_{K\mathsf{Top}} \cdot \begin{cases} 0, & \text{if } q_i \leq Q - K \\ \dfrac{f_{q_i}}{N_{\mathbf{q}}(q_i)}, & \text{if } q_i > Q - K \end{cases}$; so players choosing a quality q higher than a certain quality $Q - K$ share f_q evenly. Since $\sum_{i \in [n]} K\mathsf{Top}_i(\mathbf{q}^\ell) = C_{K\mathsf{Top}} \sum_{q_i > Q-K} \dfrac{f_{q_i}}{N_{\mathbf{q}}(q_i)}$, we take

$C_{K\text{Top}} = \left(\max_{\mathbf{q}^\ell} \sum_{q_i > Q-K} \dfrac{f_{q_i}}{N_{\mathbf{q}}(q_i)} \right)^{-1}$. Note that the KTop allocation is different from the standard KTop allocation, considered in, e.g., [14,22,40], by which *all* players choosing quality higher than $Q - K$ share f_q equally; so the utility of a player i choosing a quality $q_i > Q - K$ in $\mathbf{q}$ is $\dfrac{f_{q_i}}{\sum_{q>Q-K} N_{\mathbf{q}}(q)}$. Thus, the standard KTop allocation is not oblivious, while the KTop allocation is.

A generalization of a player-invariant payment function results by allowing the payment to player $i \in [n]$ to be a function $P_i(i, \mathbf{q})$ of both i and $\mathbf{q}$; it is called a *player-specific* payment function. The *cost* or *skill-effort function* Λ : $\mathbb{R}_{\geq 1} \times \mathbb{R}_{\geq 0} \to \mathbb{R}_{\geq 0}$, with $\Lambda(\cdot, 0) = 0$, is a monotonically increasing, polynomial-time computable function in both skill and effort.

For a quality vector $\mathbf{q}$, the *utility function* is assumed to be of quasi-linear form with respect to payment and cost and is defined as $U_i(\mathbf{q}) = P_i(\mathbf{q}) - \Lambda(s_i, f_{q_i})$, for each player $i \in [n]$. In a *pure Nash equilibrium* $\mathbf{q}$, for every player $i \in [n]$ and deviation of her to strategy $q \in [Q]$, $q \neq q_i$, $U_i(\mathbf{q}) \geq U_i(q, \mathbf{q}_{-i})$; so no player could increase her utility by unilaterally switching to a different quality. We consider the following problems for deciding the existence of a pure Nash equilibrium and computing one if there is one:

- ∃PNE WITH PLAYER-INVARIANT AND OBLIVIOUS PAYMENTS
- ∃PNE WITH PLAYER-INVARIANT PAYMENTS
- ∃PNE WITH PROPORTIONAL ALLOCATION AND ARBITRARY PLAYERS
- ∃PNE WITH PROPORTIONAL ALLOCATION AND ANONYMOUS PLAYERS
- ∃PNE WITH PLAYER-SPECIFIC PAYMENTS

The most significant difference between the contest game and the contest games traditionally considered in Contest Theory [39] is that the it adopts players with a *discrete* action space, choosing over a finite number of qualities, while the latter focus on players with a *continuous* one. (See [11] for an exception.) Alas, the contest game is comparable to classes of contests studied in Contest Theory [39] with respect to several characteristics:

- Casting qualities as individual contests, the contest game resembles *simultaneous contests* (cf. [39, Section 5]), in which players simultaneously invest efforts across the set of contests.
- While in an *all-pay contest* (cf. [39, Chapter 2]) all players competing for a non-splittable prize must pay for their bid and the winner takes all of it, all players are awarded payments, summing up to at most 1, in the contest game.
- The utility $U_i(\mathbf{q}) = P_i(\mathbf{q}) - \Lambda(s_i, f_{q_i})$ in the contest game can be cast as *smooth* (cf. [39, Chapter 4]): *(i)* each player receives a portion $P_i(\mathbf{q})$ of the prize according to an allocation mechanism that is a smooth function of the invested efforts $\{f_q\}_{q \in [Q]}$ (except when all players invest zero effort (cf. [39, start of Sect. 4], which may happen under proportional allocation with voluntary participation) and *(ii)* utilities are quasilinear in payment and cost; in this respect, U_i corresponds to a *contest success function* [37].

We shall need some definitions from Game Theory, applying to finite games with players i maximizing utility U_i. All types of potentials map profiles to numbers. A game is an *(exact) potential game* [27] if it admits a *exact potential* Φ: for each player $i \in [n]$, for any pair q_i and q_i' of her strategies and for any partial profile $\mathbf{q}_{-i}$, $U_i(q_i', \mathbf{q}_{-i}) - U_i(q_i, \mathbf{q}_{-i}) = \Phi(q_i', \mathbf{q}_{-i}) - \Phi(q_i, \mathbf{q}_{-i})$. A game is an *ordinal potential game* [27] if it admits a *ordinal potential* Φ: for each player $i \in [n]$, for any pair q_i and q_i' of her strategies and for any partial profile $\mathbf{q}_{-i}$, $U_i(q_i', \mathbf{q}_{-i}) > U_i(q_i, \mathbf{q}_{-i})$ if and only if $\Phi(q_i', \mathbf{q}_{-i}) > \Phi(q_i, \mathbf{q}_{-i})$. A game is a *generalized ordinal potential game* [27] if it admits a *generalized ordinal potential* Φ: for each player $i \in [n]$, for any pair q_i and q_i' of her strategies, and for any partial profile $\mathbf{q}_{-i}$, $U_i(q_i, \mathbf{q}_{-i}) > U_i(q_i', \mathbf{q}_{-i})$ implies $\Phi(q_i, \mathbf{q}_{-i}) > \Phi(q_i', \mathbf{q}_{-i})$. So a potential game is a strengthening of an ordinal potential game, which is a strengthening of a generalized ordinal potential game. Every generalized ordinal potential game has at least one pure Nash equilibrium [27, Corollary 2.2].

We recast some definitions from Game Theory in the context of the contest game. An *improvement step* out of the quality vector $\mathbf{q}$ and into the $\mathbf{q}'$ occurs when there is a unique player $i \in [n]$ with $q_i \neq q_i'$ such that $U_i(\mathbf{q}) < U_i(\mathbf{q}')$; so it is profitable for player i to switch from q_i to q_i'. An *improvement path* is a sequence $\mathbf{q}^{(1)}, \mathbf{q}^{(2)}, \ldots$, such that for each quality vector $\mathbf{q}^{(\rho)}$ in the sequence, where $\rho \geq 1$, there occurs an improvement step out of $\mathbf{q}^{\rho}$ and into $\mathbf{q}^{(\rho+1)}$. A *finite* improvement path has finite length. The *Finite Improvement Property*, abbreviated as *FIP*, requires that all improvement paths are finite; that is, there are no cycles in the directed *quality improvement graph*, whose vertices are the quality vectors and there is an edge from quality vector $\mathbf{q}^{(1)}$ to $\mathbf{q}^{(2)}$ if and only if an improvement step occurs from $\mathbf{q}^{(1)}$ to $\mathbf{q}^{(2)}$. Every game with the *FIP* has a pure Nash equilibrium: a *sink* in the quality improvement graph; there are games without the *FIP* that also have [27]. By [27, Lemma 2.5], a game has a generalized ordinal potential if and only if it has the *FIP*.

1.2 Results

We study the existence and the computation of pure Nash equilibria for the contest game. *When do pure Nash equilibria exist for arbitrary players, player-invariant or player-specific payments and for arbitrary n and Q?* For the special case of the contest game with proportional allocation payments and a skill-effort function $\Lambda(s_i, f_q) = s_i f_q$, this has been advocated as a significant open problem in [6, Section 6]. *What is the time complexity of deciding the existence of a pure Nash equilibrium and computing one in case there exists one? Is this complexity affected by properties of the payment or the skill-effort function, or by numerical properties of skills and efforts, and how?* We shall present three major results:

- Every contest game with arbitrary players and player-invariant and oblivious payments has a pure Nash equilibrium, for any values of n and Q and any skill-effort function Λ (Theorem 1). We devise an *exact potential* [27] for the contest game and resort to the fact that every *potential game* has a pure Nash equilibrium [27, Corollary 2.2]. By Theorem 1, the contest game with equal sharing per quality and KTop allocation has a pure Nash equilibrium. However, existence does not extend beyond player-invariant *and* oblivious payments: We prove the tightness of our existence result (Theorem 1) by exhibiting simple contest games with no pure Nash equilibrium when:

- Payments are player-invariant but not oblivious, even if players are anonymous (Proposition 3).
- Payments are proportionally allocated and players are arbitrary (Proposition 4).
- Payments are player-specific, even if players are anonymous (Proposition 6). The $\mathcal{NP}$-completeness of deciding the existence of a pure Nash equilibrium follows by a simple reduction from the problem of deciding the existence of a pure Nash equilibrium in a succinctly represented strategic game [32, Theorem 2.4.1] (Theorem 7).

- We show that the contest game with proportional allocation, voluntary participation and anonymous players has the *FIP* (Theorem 8). The contest game is found to have two pure Nash equilibria in this case. A simplification of the proof for voluntary participation establishes the *FIP* for mandatory participation (Theorem 10); the number of pure Nash equilibria drops to one. As the key to establish these results, we show the *No Switch from Lower Quality to Higher Quality* Lemma: in an improvement step, a player necessarily switches from a higher quality to a lower quality (Lemma 9).

These results are complemented with a very simple, $\Theta(1)$ algorithm that works under proportional allocation, for arbitrary players, with $\Lambda(s_i, f_q) = s_i\, f_q$ and making stronger assumptions on skills and efforts to compute a pure Nash equilibrium (Theorem 12). The algorithm simply assigns all players to quality 1; so it runs in optimal time $\Theta(1)$.

- Finally, we consider a player-specific payment function that is also *three-discrete-concave*: for any triple of qualities q_i, q_k and q, the difference between the payments when incrementing the load on q and decrementing the load on q_i is at most the difference between the payments when incrementing the load on q_k and decrementing the load on q. Three-discrete-concave functions make a new class of discrete-concave functions that we introduce; similar classes of discrete-concave functions, such as *L-concave*, are extensively discussed in the excellent monograph by Murota [28]. We present a $\Theta\left(n \cdot Q^2 \binom{n + Q - 1}{Q - 1}\right)$ algorithm to decide the existence of and compute a pure Nash equilibrium for three-discrete-concave player-specific payments and arbitrary players (Theorem 14).

Exhaustive enumeration of *all* quality vectors incurs an *exponential* $\Theta(Q^n)$ time complexity. To bypass the intractability, we focus on *contiguous* profiles, where any players i and k, with $s_i \geq s_k$, are assigned to qualities q and q', respectively, with $q \leq q'$; they offer a significant advantage: the cost for their exhaustive enumeration drops to $\Theta\left(\binom{n + Q - 1}{Q - 1}\right)$. We prove the *Contigufication Lemma*: any pure Nash equilibrium for the contest game can be transformed into a contiguous one (Proposition 15). So, it suffices to search for a contiguous, pure Nash equilibrium. The algorithm is polynomial-time $\Theta(n^Q)$

for *constant* Q; so the problem of computing a pure Nash equilibrium for the contest game with player-specific payments is $\mathcal{XP}$-tractable with respect to the parameter Q.

We extend the algorithm for three-discrete-concave player-specific payments to obtain a $\Theta\left(\max\{n, Q^2\} \cdot \binom{n + Q - 1}{Q - 1}\right)$ algorithm for three-discrete-concave player-invariant payments (Theorem 20). The improved time complexity for arbitrary Q in comparison to the case of three-discrete-concave player-specific payments is due to the fact that the player-invariant property allows dealing with the payment of only one, instead of all, of the players choosing the same quality.

1.3 Related Work and Comparison

The contest game is inspired by an interesting contest game introduced in [6]. While [6] focuses on proportional allocation and uses as cost function the product of skill and effort, the contest game studied here allows the cost function to be an arbitrary function of skill and effort, and the payment function to be any player-invariant, player-specific or oblivious payment function. Although we have considered a single proposal in our contest game, multiple proposals can also be accommodated, as in [6].

Casting qualities as *resources*, the contest game resembles *unweighted congestion games* [31]; adopting their original definition in [31], there are, though, two significant differences: *(i)* players choose sets of resources in a (weighted or unweighted) congestion game while they choose a single quality in a contest game, and *(ii)* the utilities (specifically, their payment part) depend on the loads on *all* qualities in a contest game, while costs on a resource depend only on the load on the resource in an congestion game. However, their dissimilarity is trimmed down when restricting the comparison to contest games with an oblivious payment function, where a payment depends only on the load on the particular quality, and to *singleton* (unweighted) congestion games, first introduced in [30], where each player chooses a single resource. Note that the payments in a contest game with an oblivious payment function may be player-specific, while, in general, costs in a singleton congestion game are not.

Congestion games with player-specific payoffs were introduced by Milchtaich [26] as singleton congestion games where the payoff to a player choosing a resource is given by a player-specific payoff function. (In fact, player-specific payments in this paper have been inspired by player-specific payoffs in [26].) In [26, Theorem 2], it is shown that, under a standard monotonicity assumption on the payoff function, these games always have a pure Nash equilibrium. An example is provided in [26, Section 5] of a congestion game with player-specific payoffs that lacks the *Finite Improvement Property (FIP)*. In contrast, Theorem 1 shows that the contest game with a player-invariant and oblivious payment function, a special case of a congestion game with player-specific payoffs, has a potential function; thus, it identifies a subclass of congestion games with player-specific payoffs that does have the stronger *FIP*.

Gairing *et al.* [20] consider cost-minimizing players and *non-singleton* congestion games with player-specific costs; [20, Theorem 3.1], shows that there is a potential for the strict subclass of congestion games with *linear* player-specific costs of the form $f_{ie}(\delta) = \alpha_{ie} \cdot \delta$, where $\alpha_{ie} \geq 0$, for a player i and a resource e; δ is the number of players choosing resource e. For the potential function result (Theorem 1) for the contest game with a player-invariant and oblivious payment function, we consider player-specific utilities of the form $U_i(q) = P_i(i, N(q)) - \Lambda(s_i, f_q)$, where $P_i(i, N(q)) \geq 0$ is not necessarily linear and Λ is a non-negative function, which is independent of $N(q)$ and could be non-monotone. While [20, Theorem 3.1] assumed *linear* player-specific costs, Theorem 1 extends it, due to the subtracted term $\Lambda(s_i, f_q)$. However, it also restricts [20, Theorem 3.1], since the contest game is singleton and P_i is assumed player-invariant.

The contest games considered in the proofs of the existence of pure Nash equilibria for [6, Theorems 1 and 3] assume $Q = 3$ and $Q = 2$, respectively, and consider proportional allocation, voluntary participation and a skill-effort function $\Lambda(s_i, f_q) = s_i f_q$, for any player $i \in [n]$ and quality $q \in [Q]$. Pure Nash equilibria are ill-defined in their considered cases as their definition ignores the indeterminacy arising when all players choose quality 1. Besides this correctness issue, Theorem 1 extends the context of the claimed [6, Theorem 3] from the case $Q = 2$ to arbitrary Q and to an arbitrary skill-effort function, and considers any player-invariant and oblivious payment function in place of proportional allocation. In the context we consider, Theorems 8 and 10 generalize the claimed [6, Theorem 1] from $Q = 3$ to arbitrary Q, while they significantly strengthen the claims about their (ill-defined) Nash equilibria, since *(i)* they establish the *FIP*, which is a property stronger than the existence of a pure Nash equilibrium, *(ii)* they simultaneously cover both voluntary and mandatory participation, and *(iii)* they explicitly determine the pure Nash equilibria and their number, while the outlined convergence arguments for claiming [6, Theorem 1] do not.

The contest game is related to *project games* [5], where each *weighted* player i selects a single *project* $\sigma_i \in S_i$ among those available to him, where several players may select the same project. Weights w_{i,σ_i} are *project-specific*; they are called *universal* when they are fixed for the same project and *identical* when the fixed weights are the same over all projects. The utility of player i is a fraction r_{σ_i} of the proportional allocation of weights on the project σ_i. Projects can be considered to correspond to qualities in the contest game, which, in contrast, has, in general, neither weights nor fractions but has the extra term $\Lambda(s_i, f_q)$ for the cost.

For the contest game in [16], there are m *activities* and player $i \in [n]$ chooses an *output vector* $\mathbf{b}_i = \langle b_{i1}, \ldots, b_{im} \rangle$, with $b_{i\ell} \in \mathbb{R}_{\geq 0}$, $\ell \in [m]$; the case $b_{i\ell} = 0$ corresponds to voluntary participation. In contrast, there are no activities in the contest game; but one may view the single proposal and quality vectors in it (as well as in the contest game in [6]) as an activity and output vectors, respectively. There are $C \geq 1$ *contests* awarding prizes to the players based on their output vectors; allocation is equal sharing in [16], by which players receiving a prize share are "filtered" using a function f_c associated with contest c. The special case of the contest game in [16] with $C = 1$ can be seen to correspond to a contest game in our context; nevertheless, to the best of our understanding, no results transfer between the contest games in [16] and in this paper, as their definitions are different; for example, we do not see how to embed output vectors in our contest game, or skill-effort costs in the contest game in [16].

Listed in [39, Section 6.1.3] are more examples of player-invariant payments, including *proportional-to-marginal contribution* (motivated by the marginal contribution condition in *valid utility games* [38]) and *Shapley-Shubick* [34, 35]. Games employing proportional allocation, equal sharing and K-Top allocation have been studied, for example, in [5, 10, 18, 29, 41], in [16, 25] and in [14, 22, 40], respectively. Accounts on proportional allocation and equal sharing in simultaneous contests appear in [39, Section 5.4 & Sect. 5.5], respectively. Player-invariant payments enhance *Anonymous Independent Reward Schemes (AIRS)* [9], where payments, termed as *rewards,* are only allowed to depend on the quality of the individual review, or *content* in the context of user-generated content platforms.

A plethora of results in Contest Theory establish the inexistence of pure Nash equilibria in contests with continuous strategy spaces; see, e.g., [3] or [33, Example 1.1]. Still for continuous strategy spaces and for proportional allocation, existence, uniqueness and characterization of pure Nash equilibria is established in [39, Theorem 4.9] for two-player contests and in [23] for contests with an arbitrary number of players, assuming additional conditions on the utility functions. All-pay contests with discrete action spaces were considered in [11]. In our view, the analysis of contest games with discrete action spaces is more challenging; it requires crisp combinatorial arguments, instead of concavity and continuity arguments, typically employed for contests with continuous action spaces.

2 (In)Existence of a Pure Nash Equilibrium

We show:

Theorem 1. *The contest game with arbitrary players and player-invariant and oblivious payments has an exact potential and a pure Nash equilibrium.*

Proof. Define the function $\Phi : \{\mathbf{q}\} \to \mathbb{R}$ as

$$\Phi(\mathbf{q}) = \sum_{q \in [Q]} \Gamma(\mathsf{N}_{\mathbf{q}}(q)) - \sum_{k \in [n]} \Lambda(s_k, \mathsf{f}_{q_k}),$$

where the function $\Gamma : \mathbb{N} \cup \{0\} \to \mathbb{R}$ will be defined later. We prove that Φ is an exact potential. Consider a player $i \in [n]$ switching from strategy q_i, to strategy $\widehat{q}_i$, while other players do not change strategies. So the quality vector $\mathbf{q} = \langle q_1, \ldots, q_{(i-1)}, q_i, q_{i+1}, \ldots, q_n \rangle$ transforms into $\widehat{\mathbf{q}} := \langle q_1, \ldots, q_{i-1}, \widehat{q}_i, q_{i+1}, \ldots, q_n \rangle$; thus, $\mathsf{N}_{\widehat{\mathbf{q}}}(q_i) = \mathsf{N}_{\mathbf{q}}(q_i) - 1$, $\mathsf{N}_{\widehat{\mathbf{q}}}(\widehat{q}_i) = \mathsf{N}_{\mathbf{q}}(\widehat{q}_i) + 1$ and $\mathsf{N}_{\widehat{\mathbf{q}}}(\widetilde{q}) = \mathsf{N}_{\mathbf{q}}(\widetilde{q})$ for each quality $\widetilde{q} \neq q_i, \widehat{q}_i$. To simplify notation, denote q_i and $\widehat{q}_i$ as q and $\widehat{q}$, respectively. So,

$$\mathsf{U}_i(\mathbf{q}) - \mathsf{U}_i(\widehat{\mathbf{q}}) = [\mathsf{P}_i(\mathbf{q})]_{[\mathsf{N}_{\mathbf{q}}(q), \mathsf{N}_{\mathbf{q}}(\widetilde{q})]} - [\mathsf{P}_i(\widehat{\mathbf{q}})]_{[\mathsf{N}_{\mathbf{q}}(q)-1, \mathsf{N}_{\mathbf{q}}(\widetilde{q})+1]} + \Lambda(s_i, \mathsf{f}_{\widehat{q}}) - \Lambda(s_i, \mathsf{f}_q),$$

where $[P_i(\mathbf{q})]_{[N_\mathbf{q}(q),N_\mathbf{q}(\widehat{q})]}$ and $[P_i(\mathbf{q})]_{[N_\mathbf{q}(q)-1,N_\mathbf{q}(\widehat{q})+1]}$ are the payments awarded to i when the loads on q and $\widehat{q}$ are $(N_\mathbf{q}(q),N_\mathbf{q}(\widehat{q}))$ and $(N_\mathbf{q}(q)-1,N_\mathbf{q}(\widehat{q})+1)$, respectively, while loads on other qualities remain unchanged. So $[P_i(\mathbf{q})]_{[N_\mathbf{q}(q),N_\mathbf{q}(\widehat{q})]} = P_i(\mathbf{q})$ and $[P_i(\mathbf{q})]_{[N_\mathbf{q}(q)-1,N_\mathbf{q}(\widehat{q})+1]} = P_i(\widehat{\mathbf{q}})$. Clearly,

$$\Phi(\mathbf{q}) - \Phi(\widehat{\mathbf{q}})$$
$$= \Gamma(N_\mathbf{q}(q)) - \Gamma(N_\mathbf{q}(q) - 1) - (\Gamma(N_\mathbf{q}(\widehat{q}) + 1) - \Gamma(N_\mathbf{q}(\widehat{q}))) + \Lambda(s_i, f_{\widehat{q}}) - \Lambda(s_i, f_q).$$

Now define the function Γ such that for a quality vector $\mathbf{q}$, for each quality $q \in [Q]$, $\Gamma(N_\mathbf{q}(q)) - \Gamma(N_\mathbf{q}(q)-1) = [P_i(\mathbf{q})]_{[N_\mathbf{q}(q),N_\mathbf{q}(\widehat{q})]}$. We set $\widehat{q}$ for q and $N_\mathbf{q}(\widehat{q})+1$ for $N_\mathbf{q}(q)$ to obtain

$$\Gamma(N_{\widehat{\mathbf{q}}}(\widehat{q}) + 1) - \Gamma(N_{\widehat{\mathbf{q}}}(\widehat{q})) = [P_i(\widehat{\mathbf{q}})]_{[N_\mathbf{q}(q)-1,N_\mathbf{q}(\widehat{q})+1]},$$

if $N_\mathbf{q}(q) \geq 1$, and $\Gamma(0) = 0$. Note that Γ is well-defined: the left-hand side is a function of $N_\mathbf{q}$ only, as also is the right-hand side since $P_i(\mathbf{q})$ is independent of *(i)* i, since P is player-invariant, and *(ii)* the loads on qualities other than q, since P is oblivious. An explicit formula for $\Gamma(N_\mathbf{q}(q))$ follows from its definition:

$$\Gamma(N_\mathbf{q}(q)) = \left(\Gamma(N_\mathbf{q}(q) - 2) + [P_i(\mathbf{q})]_{[N_\mathbf{q}(q)-1,N_\mathbf{q}(\widehat{q})+1]}\right) + [P_i(\mathbf{q})]_{[N_\mathbf{q}(q),N_\mathbf{q}(\widehat{q})]} = \cdots$$
$$= [P_i(\mathbf{q})]_{[1,N_\mathbf{q}(q)+N_\mathbf{q}(\widehat{q})-1]} + [P_i(\mathbf{q})]_{[2,N_\mathbf{q}(q)+N_\mathbf{q}(\widehat{q})-2]} + \cdots + [P_i(\mathbf{q})]_{[N_\mathbf{q}(q),N_\mathbf{q}(\widehat{q})]}$$

Hence, by definition of Γ,

$$\Phi(\mathbf{q}) - \Phi(\widehat{\mathbf{q}}) = [P_i(\mathbf{q})]_{[N_\mathbf{q}(q),N_\mathbf{q}(\widehat{q})]} - [P_i(\widehat{\mathbf{q}})]_{[N_\mathbf{q}(q)-1,N_\mathbf{q}(\widehat{q})+1]} + \Lambda(s_i, f_{\widehat{q}}) - \Lambda(s_i, f_q).$$

Hence, $\Phi(\mathbf{q}) - \Phi(\widehat{\mathbf{q}}) = U_i(\mathbf{q}) - U_i(\widehat{\mathbf{q}})$, Φ is an exact potential and a pure Nash equilibrium exists.

Since Γ, P and Λ are poly-time computable, so is also the exact potential Φ used for the proof of Theorem 1 since it involves summations of values of Γ, P and Λ. Hence, $\exists$PNE WITH PLAYER-INVARIANT AND OBLIVIOUS PAYMENTS $\in \mathcal{PLS}$.

Open Problem 2 *Determine the precise complexity of* $\exists$PNE WITH PLAYER-INVARIANT AND OBLIVIOUS PAYMENTS. *We remark that no $\mathcal{PLS}$-hardness results for computing pure Nash equilibria are known for either singleton congestion games [26] or for project games [5], which, in some sense, are also singleton as the contest game is; moreover, all known $\mathcal{PLS}$-hardness results for computing pure Nash equilibria in congestion games apply to congestion games that are not singleton. These remarks appear to speak against $\mathcal{PLS}$-hardness.*

We next show that existence of pure Nash equilibria is not guaranteed if P is not player-invariant and oblivious simultaneously. We start by showing:

Proposition 3. *There is a contest game with mandatory participation, player-invariant payments and anonymous players that has neither the FIP nor a pure Nash equilibrium.*

We continue to prove:

Proposition 4. *There is a contest game with mandatory participation, proportional allocation and arbitrary players that has neither the FIP nor a pure Nash equilibrium.*

> **Open Problem 5** *Determine the precise complexity of* ∃PNE WITH PLAYER-INVARIANT PAYMENTS *and* ∃PNE WITH PROPORTIONAL ALLOCATION AND ARBITRARY PLAYERS. *We are tempted to conjecture that both are* $\mathcal{NP}$-complete.

We now turn to player-specific payments. We show:

Proposition 6. *There is a contest game with player-specific payments and anonymous players that has neither the FIP nor a pure Nash equilibrium.*

We continue to show, using a reduction from the $\mathcal{NP}$-complete problem of deciding the existence of a pure Nash equilibrium in a (finite) succinctly represented strategic game [32, Theorem 2.4.1].

Theorem 7. ∃PNE WITH PLAYER-SPECIFIC PAYMENTS *is* $\mathcal{NP}$-complete, *even if players are anonymous.*

3   Proportional Allocation

3.1   Anonymous Players

We show:

Theorem 8. *The contest game with proportional allocation, voluntary participation and anonymous players has the FIP and two pure Nash equilibria.*

Proof. It suffices to prove that there is no cycle in the quality improvement graph. Recall that voluntary participation means $f_1 = 0$. We prove that improvement is possible only if, subject to an exception, the deviating player is switching from a higher quality to a lower quality:

Lemma 9 (No Switch from Lower Quality to Higher Quality). *Fix a quality vector* $\mathbf{q}$ *and two distinct qualities* $\widetilde{q}, \widehat{q} \in [Q]$ *with* $\widetilde{q} < \widehat{q}$. *In an improvement step of a player out of* $\mathbf{q}$, $N_{\mathbf{q}}(\widetilde{q})$ *increases and and* $N_{\mathbf{q}}(\widehat{q})$ *decreases.*

Under mandatory participation, it no longer holds that $f_1 = 0$, and Case **2.** in the proof of Lemma 9 does not arise; as a result, the node $(n − 1, 1)$, corresponding to $N_q(1) = n − 1$, $N_q(2) = 1$ and $N_q(q) = 0$ for each quality $q \in [Q]$ with $q > 2$, is not a sink anymore since the unilateral deviation of a player from quality 2 to quality 1 is now an improvement since $f_1 > 0$. So we have now a unique pure Nash equilibrium, where all players choose quality 1. The rest of the proof of Theorem 8 transfers over. Hence, we have:

Theorem 10. *The contest game with proportional allocation, mandatory participation and anonymous players has the FIP and a unique pure Nash equilibrium.*

Given the counter-example contest game in Proposition 4, Theorem 10 establishes a *separation* with respect to the *FIP* property and the existence of a pure Nash equilibrium between arbitrary players and anonymous players, under mandatory participation and proportional allocation. Theorems 8 and 10 imply:

Corollary 11. *The contest game with proportional allocation and anonymous players has a generalized ordinal potential.*

3.2   Mandatory Participation

We show:

Theorem 12. *There is a $\Theta(1)$ algorithm that solves* ∃PNE WITH PROPOR-TIONAL ALLOCATION AND ARBITRARY PLAYERS *with lower-bounded skills* $\min_{i \in [n]} s_i \geq \frac{f_2}{f_2 − f_1}$ *and skill-effort functions* $\Lambda(s_i, f_q) = s_i f_q$, *for all players* $i \in [n]$ *and qualities* $q \in [Q]$.

Since $\frac{f_2}{f_2 − f_1} > 1$, the assumption made for Theorem 12 that all skills are lower-bounded by $\frac{f_2}{f_2 − f_1}$ in Theorem 12 cannot hold for anonymous players where $s_i = 1$ for all players $i \in [n]$. This assumption is reasonable for real contests for crowdsourcing reviews where a minimum skill is required for reviewers in order to eliminate the risk of receiving inferior solutions of low quality. Indeed, crowdsourcing firms can target crowd contributors based on exhibiting skills, like performance in prior contests. Finally, note that the assumption made for Theorem 12, enabling the existence of a pure Nash equilibrium, could *not* hold for the counter-example contest game in Proposition 4.

4   Three-Discrete-Concave Payments and Contiguity

Say that the load vector N_q is *contiguous* if players 1 to $N_q(1)$ choose quality 1, players $N_q(1) + 1$ to $N_q(1) + N_q(2)$ choose quality 2, and so on till players $\sum_{q \in [Q−1]} N_q(q) + 1$ to n choose quality $q_{last} \leq Q$ such that for each quality $\widehat{q} > q_{last}$, $N_q(\widehat{q}) = 0$; so for any players i and k, with $i < k$, choosing distinct qualities q and q', respectively, we have $q < q'$. Clearly, a contiguous load vector determines by itself which $N_{\mathbf{q}}(q)$ players choose each quality $q \in [Q]$.

Say that an *inversion* occurs in a load vector $N_{\mathbf{q}}$ if there are players i and k with $i < k$ choosing qualities q_i and q_k, respectively, with $q_i > q_k$; thus, $s_i \geq s_k$ while $f_{q_i} > f_{q_k}$. Call i an *inversion witness*; call i and k an *inversion pair*. Clearly, no inversion occurs in a load vector $N_{\mathbf{q}}$ if and only if $N_{\mathbf{q}}$ is contiguous.

Given a contiguous load vector $N_{\mathbf{q}}$, denote, for each quality $q \in [Q]$ such that $\mathsf{Players}_{\mathbf{q}}(q) \neq \emptyset$, the minimum and the maximum, respectively, player index $i \in \mathsf{Players}_{\mathbf{q}}(q)$ as $\mathsf{first}_{\mathbf{q}}(q)$ and $\mathsf{last}_{\mathbf{q}}(q)$, respectively. Clearly, $\mathsf{first}_{\mathbf{q}}(q) = \sum_{\hat{q}<q} N_{\mathbf{q}}(\hat{q}) + 1$ and $\mathsf{last}_{\mathbf{q}}(q) = \sum_{\hat{q}\leq q} N_{\mathbf{x}}(\hat{q})$; so $\mathsf{first}_{\mathbf{q}}(1) = 1$ for $N_{\mathbf{q}}(1) > 0$ and $\mathsf{last}_{\mathbf{q}}(Q) = n$ for $N_{\mathbf{q}}(Q) > 0$.

Order the players so that $s_1 \geq s_2 \geq \ldots \geq s_n$. Recall that $f_1 < f_2 < \ldots < f_Q$. Represent a quality vector $\mathbf{q}$ as follows:

- Use a *load vector* $N_{\mathbf{q}} = \langle N_{\mathbf{q}}(1), N_{\mathbf{q}}(2), \ldots, N_{\mathbf{q}}(Q) \rangle$.
- Specify which $N_{\mathbf{q}}(q)$ players choose each quality $q \in [Q]$.

To simplify notation, we shall often omit to specify the players choosing each quality $q \in [Q]$. Thus, we shall represent a quality vector $\mathbf{q}$ by the load vector $N_{\mathbf{q}}$.

4.1 Player-Specific Payments

Recall that a player-specific payment function $P_i(\mathbf{q})$ can be represented by a two-argument payment function $P_i(i, \mathbf{q})$, where $i \in [n]$ and $\mathbf{q}$ is a quality vector. We start by defining:

Definition 13. *A player-specific payment function* P *is three-discrete-concave if for every player $i \in [n]$, for every load vector $N_{\mathbf{q}}$ and for every triple of qualities $q_i, q_k, q \in [Q]$,*

$$P_i(i, (N_{\mathbf{q}}(1), \ldots, N_{\mathbf{q}}(q_i), \ldots, N_{\mathbf{q}}(q_k) - 1, \ldots, N'_{\mathbf{q}}(q) + 1, \ldots, N'_{\mathbf{q}}(Q)))$$
$$+ P_i(i, (N_{\mathbf{q}}(1), \ldots, N_{\mathbf{q}}(q_i) - 1, \ldots, N_{\mathbf{q}}(q_k), \ldots, N_{\mathbf{q}}(q) + 1, \ldots, N_{\mathbf{x}}(Q)))$$
$$\leq 2 P_i(i, (N_{\mathbf{q}}(1), \ldots, N_{\mathbf{q}}(q_i), \ldots, N_{\mathbf{q}}(q_k), \ldots, N_{\mathbf{q}}(q), \ldots, N_{\mathbf{q}}(Q))) .$$

We show:

Theorem 14. *There is a $\Theta\left(n \cdot Q^2 \binom{n+Q-1}{Q-1}\right)$ algorithm that solves $\exists$PNE* WITH PLAYER-SPECIFIC PAYMENTS *for arbitrary players and three-discrete-concave player-specific payments; for constant Q, it is a $\Theta(n^Q)$ polynomial algorithm.*

Proof. We start by proving:

Proposition 15 (Contigufication Lemma for Player-Specific Payments). *For three-discrete-concave player-specific payments, any pair of (i) a pure Nash equilibrium $N_{\mathbf{q}} = \langle N_{\mathbf{q}}(1), \ldots, N_{\mathbf{q}}(Q) \rangle$ and (ii) player sets $\mathsf{Players}_{\mathbf{q}}(q)$ for each quality $q \in [Q]$, can be transformed into a contiguous pure Nash equilibrium.*

Proof. If no inversion occurs in $N_\mathbf{q}$, then $N_\mathbf{q}$ is contiguous and we are done. Else take the earliest inversion witness i, together with the earliest player k such that i and k make an inversion. We shall also consider a player $\iota \in [n] \setminus \{i, k\}$. Since payments are player-specific, $U_i(N_\mathbf{q}) = P_i(i, N_\mathbf{q}) - \Lambda(s_i, f_{q_i})$ and $U_k(N_\mathbf{q}) = P_k(k, N_\mathbf{q}) - \Lambda(s_k, f_{q_k})$. Clearly,

1. Player i does not want to switch to quality $q \neq q_i$ if and only if

$$\Lambda(s_i, f_{q_i}) - \Lambda(s_i, f_q) \leq P_i(i, (N_\mathbf{q}(1), \ldots N_\mathbf{q}(q), \ldots, N_\mathbf{q}(q_i), \ldots, N_\mathbf{q}(Q)))$$
$$-P_i(i, (N_\mathbf{q}(1), \ldots, N_\mathbf{q}(q) + 1, \ldots, N_\mathbf{q}(q_i) - 1, \ldots, N_\mathbf{q}(Q))).$$

2. Player k does not want to switch to quality $q \neq q_k$ if and only if

$$\Lambda(s_k, f_{q_k}) - \Lambda(s_k, f_q) \leq P_k(k, (N_\mathbf{q}(1), \ldots N_\mathbf{q}(q_k), \ldots, N_\mathbf{q}(q), \ldots, N_\mathbf{q}(Q)))$$
$$-P_k(k, (N_\mathbf{q}(1), \ldots, N_\mathbf{q}(q_k) - 1, \ldots, N_\mathbf{q}(q) + 1, \ldots, N_\mathbf{x}(Q))).$$

3. Player ι does not want to switch to quality $q \neq q_\iota$ if and only if

$$\Lambda(s_\iota, f_{q_\iota}) - \Lambda(s_\iota, f_q) \leq P_\iota(\iota, (N_\mathbf{q}(1), \ldots N_\mathbf{q}(q), \ldots, N_\mathbf{q}(q_\iota), \ldots, N_\mathbf{q}(Q)))$$
$$-P_\iota(\iota, (N_\mathbf{q}(1), \ldots, N_\mathbf{q}(q) + 1, \ldots, N_\mathbf{q}(q_\iota) - 1, \ldots, N_\mathbf{q}(Q))).$$

Swap the qualities chosen by players i and k; so they now choose q_k and q_i, respectively. Choices of other players are preserved.

Denote as $N_{\mathbf{q}'}$ the resulting load vector; clearly, for each $\widehat{q} \in [Q]$, $N_{\mathbf{q}'}(\widehat{q}) = N_\mathbf{q}(\widehat{q})$. We use **1**, **2** and **3** to prove:

Lemma 16. *The earliest inversion witness in* $\mathbf{q}'$ *is either i or some player* $\widehat{i} > i$.

We continue to prove:

Lemma 17. $N_{\mathbf{q}'}$ *is a pure Nash equilibrium if and only if* $N_\mathbf{q}$ *is.*

Now the earliest inversion witness, if any, in $\mathbf{q}'$ is either i, the earliest witness of inversion in $\mathbf{q}$, making an inversion pair with a player $\widehat{k} > k$, or greater than i. It follows inductively that a pure Nash equilibrium exists if and only if a contiguous pure Nash equilibrium exists.

By Proposition 15, it suffices to search over contiguous load vectors. Fix a load vector $N_\mathbf{q}$ and a quality $q \in [Q]$ such that $\mathsf{Players}_\mathbf{q}(q) \neq \emptyset$. No player choosing quality q wants to switch to the quality $q' \neq q$ if and only if for all players $i \in \mathsf{Players_q}(q)$,

$$\Lambda(s_i, f_q) - \Lambda(s_i, f_{q'})$$
$$\leq \mathsf{P}_i(i, \mathsf{N_q}) - \mathsf{P}_i(i, (\mathsf{N_q}(1), \ldots, \mathsf{N_q}(q) - 1, \ldots, \mathsf{N_q}(q') + 1, \ldots, \mathsf{N_q}(Q))) \,. \text{(C.1)}$$

Since P is player-specific, $\mathsf{P}_i(i, \mathsf{N_q})$ and $\mathsf{P}_i(i, (\mathsf{N_q}(1), \ldots, \mathsf{N_q}(q) - 1, \ldots, \mathsf{N_q}(q') + 1, \ldots, \mathsf{N_q}(Q)))$ are not constant over all players choosing quality q in $\mathsf{N_q}$ and switching to quality q' in $(\mathsf{N_q}(1), \ldots, \mathsf{N_q}(q) - 1, \ldots, \mathsf{N_q}(q') + 1, \ldots, \mathsf{N_q}(Q))$, respectively. Hence, no player choosing quality $q \in [Q]$ wants to switch to a quality $q' \neq q$ if and only if (C.1) holds for all players $i \in \mathsf{Players_q}(q)$.

To compute a pure Nash equilibrium, we enumerate all contiguous load vectors $\mathsf{N_q} = \langle \mathsf{N_q}(1), \mathsf{N_q}(2), \ldots, \mathsf{N_q}(Q) \rangle$, searching for one that satisfies (C.1), for each quality $q \in [Q]$ and for all players $i \in \mathsf{Players_q}(q)$; clearly, there are $\binom{n + Q - 1}{Q - 1}$ contiguous load vectors (cf. [7, Section 2.6]). For a player-specific payment function, checking (C.1) for a quality $q \in [Q]$ entails no minimum computation but must be repeated n times for all players $i \in [n]$; checking that the inequality holds for a particular $q' \neq q$ takes time $\Theta(1)$, so checking that it holds for all qualities $q' \neq q$ takes time $\Theta(Q)$, and checking that it holds for all $q \in [Q]$ takes time $\Theta(Q^2)$. Thus, the total time is $\Theta\left(n \cdot Q^2 \cdot \binom{n + Q - 1}{Q - 1}\right)$. For constant Q, this is a polynomial $\Theta(n^Q)$ algorithm.

By Proposition 15, a contiguous load vector satisfying (C.1) for each quality $q \in [Q]$ exists if and only if it will be found by the algorithm enumerating all contiguous load vectors. Hence, the algorithm solves ∃PNE WITH PLAYER-SPECIFIC PAYMENTS.

4.2   Player-Invariant Payments

Recall that a player-invariant payment function $\mathsf{P}_i(\mathbf{q})$ can be represented by a two-argument payment function $\mathsf{P}_i(q, \mathbf{q}_{-i})$, where $q \in [Q]$ and $\mathbf{q}_{-i}$ is a partial quality vector, for some player $i \in [n]$. In correspondence to three-discrete-concave player-specific payments, we define:

Definition 18. *A player-invariant payment function* P *is three-discrete-concave if for every player* $i \in [n]$, *for every load vector* $\mathsf{N_q}$ *and for every triple of qualities* q_i, q_k, $q \in [Q]$,

$$\mathsf{P}_i(q, (\mathsf{N_q}(1), \ldots, \mathsf{N_q}(q_i), \ldots, \mathsf{N_q}(q_k) - 1, \ldots, \mathsf{N_q}(q) + 1, \ldots, \mathsf{N_q}(Q)))$$
$$+ \mathsf{P}_i(q, (\mathsf{N_q}(1), \ldots, \mathsf{N_q}(q_i) - 1, \ldots, \mathsf{N_q}(q_k), \ldots, \mathsf{N_q}(q) + 1, \ldots, \mathsf{N_q}(Q)))$$
$$\leq 2\,\mathsf{P}_i(q_i, (\mathsf{N_q}(1), \ldots, \mathsf{N_q}(q_i), \ldots, \mathsf{N_q}(q_k), \ldots, \mathsf{N_q}(q), \ldots, \mathsf{N_q}(Q)))\,.$$

In correspondence to Proposition 15, we prove a Contigufication Lemma for three-discrete-concave player-invariant payment functions:

Proposition 19 (Contigufication Lemma for Player-Invariant Payments). *For three-discrete-concave player-invariant payments, any pair of (i) a pure Nash equilibrium $\mathsf{N_q} = \langle \mathsf{N_q}(1), \ldots, \mathsf{N_q}(Q) \rangle$ and (ii) player sets $\mathsf{Players_q}(q)$ for each quality $q \in [Q]$, can be transformed into a contiguous pure Nash equilibrium.*

By Proposition 19, it suffices to search over contiguous load vectors. Fix a load vector $\mathsf{N_q}$ and a quality $q \in [Q]$ such that $\mathsf{Players_q}(q) \neq \emptyset$. No player choosing quality q wants to switch to the quality $q' \neq q$ if and only if for all players $i \in \mathsf{Players_q}(q)$,

$$
\begin{aligned}
&\Lambda(s_i, f_q) - \Lambda(s_i, f_{q'}) \\
&\leq P_i(q, \mathsf{N_q}) - P_i(q', (\mathsf{N_q}(1), \ldots, \mathsf{N_q}(q) - 1, \ldots, \mathsf{N_q}(q') + 1, \ldots, \mathsf{N_q}(Q))) \,. \quad \text{(C.2)}
\end{aligned}
$$

Since P is player-invariant, $P_i(q, \mathsf{N_q})$ and $P_i(q', (\mathsf{N_q}(1), \ldots, \mathsf{N_q}(q) - 1, \ldots, \mathsf{N_q}(q') + 1, \ldots, \mathsf{N_q}(Q)))$ are constant over all players choosing quality q in $\mathsf{N_q}$ and switching to quality q' in $(\mathsf{N_q}(1), \ldots, \mathsf{N_q}(q) - 1, \ldots, \mathsf{N_q}(q') + 1, \ldots, \mathsf{N_q}(Q))$, respectively. Hence, no player $\widehat{i}$ choosing quality $q \in [Q]$ wants to switch to a quality $q' \neq q$ if and only if (C.2) holds for each quality $q' \neq q$, where $\widehat{i} \in \mathsf{Players_q}(q)$ is arbitrarily chosen.

To compute a pure Nash equilibrium, we enumerate all contiguous load vectors $\mathsf{N_q} = \langle \mathsf{N_q}(1), \mathsf{N_q}(2), \ldots, \mathsf{N_q}(Q) \rangle$, searching for one that satisfies (C.2), for each quality $q \in [Q]$ and for a player $\widehat{i} \in \mathsf{Players_q}(q)$; clearly, there are $\binom{n+Q-1}{Q-1}$ contiguous load vectors (cf. [7, Section 2.6]. For player-invariant payments, checking (C.2) for a quality $q \in [Q]$ entails the computation of the minimum of a function on a set of size $\mathsf{N_q}(q)$; computation of the minima for all qualities $q \in [Q]$ takes time $\sum_{q \in [Q]} \Theta(\mathsf{N_q}(q)) = \Theta\left(\sum_{q \in [Q]} \mathsf{N_q}(q)\right) = \Theta(n)$. Thus, the total time is $\binom{n+Q-1}{Q-1} \cdot (\Theta(n) + \Theta(Q^2)) = \Theta\left(\max\{n, Q^2\} \cdot \binom{n+Q-1}{Q-1}\right)$.

By Proposition 15, a contiguous load vector satisfying (C.2) for each quality $q \in [Q]$ exists if and only if it will be found by the algorithm enumerating all contiguous load vectors. Hence, it follows:

Theorem 20. *There is a $\Theta\left(\max\{n, Q^2\} \cdot \binom{n+Q-1}{Q-1}\right)$ algorithm that solves $\exists$PNE WITH PLAYER-INVARIANT PAYMENTS for arbitrary players and three-discrete-concave player-invariant payments; for constant Q, it is a $\Theta(n^Q)$ polynomial algorithm.*

5   Open Problems and Directions for Further Research

This work poses far more challenging problems and research directions about the contest game than it answers. To close we list a few open research directions.

1. Study the computation of *mixed* Nash equilibria. Work in progress confirms the existence of contest games with $Q = 3$ and $n = 3$ that have only one mixed Nash equilibrium, which is irrational. We conjecture that the problem is $\mathcal{PPAD}$-complete for $n = 2$.
2. Determine the complexity of computing *best-responses* for the contest game. We conjecture $\mathcal{NP}$-hardness; techniques similar to those used in [16, Section 3] could be useful.
3. Formulate incomplete information contest games with discrete strategy spaces and study their Bayes-Nash equilibria. Very likely ideas from Bayesian congestion games [19] will be helpful. Study existence and complexity properties of pure Bayes-Nash equilibria.
4. In analogy to weighted congestion games [26,31], formulate the *weighted* contest game with discrete strategy spaces, where reviewers have *weights,* and study its pure Nash equilibria.

Acknowledgements. We would like to thank all anonymous referees to this and previous versions of the paper for some very insightful comments they offered.

References

1. Abbassi, Z., Hedge, N., Massoulié, L.: Distributed content curation on the web. ACM Trans. Internet Technol. **14**(2–3) (2014). Article 9
2. Armosti, N., Weinberg, S.M.: Bitcoin: a natural oligopoly. Manage. Sci. **68**(7), 4755–4771 (2022)
3. Baye, M.R., Kovenock, D., De Vries, C.G.: The all-pay auction with complete information. Econ. Theor. **8**(2), 291–305 (1996)
4. Benadè, G., Nath, S., Procaccia, A., Shah, N.: Preference elicitation for participatory budgeting. Manage. Sci. **67**(5), 2813–2827 (2021)
5. Bilò, V., Gourvés, L., Monnot, J.: Project games. Theoret. Comput. Sci. **940**, 97–111 (2023)
6. Birmpas, G., Kovalchuk, L., Lazos, P., Oliynykov, R.: Parallel contests for crowdsourcing reviews: existence and quality of equilibria. In: Proceedings of the 4th ACM Conference on Financial Technologies, pp. 268–280 (2022)
7. Charalambides, Ch.A.: Enumerative Combinatorics. Chapman & Hall/CRC, Boca Raton (2002)
8. Chawla, S., Hartline, J.D., Sivan, B.: Optimal crowdsourcing contests. Games Econ. Behav. **113**, 80–96 (2019)
9. Chen, M., Tang, P., Wang, Z., Xiao, S., Yang, X.: Optimal anonymous independent reward scheme design. In: Proceedings of the 31st International Joint Conference on Artificial Intelligence, pp. 165–171 (2022)
10. Cheng, Y., Deng, X., Qi, Q., Yan, X.: Truthfulness of a proportional sharing mechanism in resource exchange. In: Proceedings of the 25th International Joint Conference on Artificial Intelligence, pp. 187–193 (2016)
11. Cohen, C., Sela, A.: Contests with ties. B. E. J. Theoret. Econ. **7** (2007). Article 43
12. Deng, X., Li, N., Li, W., Qi, Q.: Competition among parallel contests. ArXiv:2210.06866, October 2022

13. Di Palantino, D., Vojnović, M.: Crowdsourcing and all-pay auctions. In: Proceedings of the 10th ACM Conference on Electronic Commerce, pp. 119–128 (2009)
14. Easley, D., Ghosh, A.: Incentives, gamification, and game theory: an economic approach to badge design. ACM Trans. Econ. Comput. 4(3), 16.1–16.26 (2016)
15. Elkind, E., Ghosh, A., Goldberg, P.W.: Contest design with threshold objectives. In: Proceedings of the 17th Conference on Web and Internet Economics, p. 554, December 2021. Also: arXiv:2109.03179v2
16. Elkind, E., Ghosh, A., Goldberg, P.W.: Simultaneous contests with equal sharing allocation of prizes: computational complexity and price of anarchy. In: Proceedings of the 15th International Symposium on Algorithmic Game Theory, pp. 133–150, September 2022
17. Elkind, E., Ghosh, A., Goldberg, P.: Contests to incentivize a target group. In: Proceedings of the 31st International Joint Conference on Artificial Intelligence, pp. 279–285, July 2022
18. Feldmann, M., Lai, K., Zhang, L.: The proportional share allocation market for computational resources. IEEE Trans. Parallel Distrib. Syst. 20(8), 1075–1088 (2009)
19. Gairing, M., Monien, B., Tiemann, K.: Selfish routing with incomplete information. Theory Comput. Syst. 42(1), 91–130 (2008)
20. Gairing, M., Monien, B., Tiemann, K.: Routing (Un-)splittable flow in games with player-specific affine latency functions. ACM Trans. Algorithms 7(3) (2011). Article 31
21. Ghosh, A., McAfee, P.: Incentivizing high-quality user-generated content. In: Proceedings of the 20th International Conference on World Wide Web, pp. 137–146 (2011)
22. Jain, S., Chen, Y., Parkes, D.C.: Designing incentives for question-and-answer forums. Games Econom. Behav. 86, 458–474 (2014)
23. Johari, R., Tsitsiklis, J.N.: Efficiency loss in a network resource allocation game. Math. Oper. Res. 29(3), 402–435 (2004)
24. Karlin, A., Peres, Y.: Game Theory. American Mathematical Society, Alive (2017)
25. May, A., Chaintreau, A., Korula, N., Lattanzi, S.: Filter & follow: how social media foster content curation. ACM SIGMETRICS Perform. Eval. Rev. 42(1), 43–55 (2014)
26. Milchtaich, I.: Congestion games with player-specific payoff functions. Games Econom. Behav. 13(1), 111–124 (1996)
27. Monderer, D., Shapley, L.S.: Potential games. Games Econom. Behav. 14(1), 124–143 (1996)
28. Murota, K.: Discrete Convex Analysis, SIAM Monographs on Discrete Mathematics and Applications, vol. 10 (2003)
29. Pálvölgyi, D., Peters, H., Vermeulen, D.: A strategic approach to multiple estate division problems. Games Econom. Behav. 88, 135–152 (2014)
30. Quint, Th., Shubik, M.: A Model of Migration, Cowles Foundation Discussion Paper 1088, Yale University (1994)
31. Rosenthal, R.W.: A class of games possessing pure-strategy nash equilibria. Internat. J. Game Theory 2(1), 65–67 (1973)
32. Sahni, S.: Computationally related problems. SIAM J. Comput. 3(4), 262–279 (1974)
33. Segev, E.: Crowdsourcing contests. Eur. J. Oper. Res. 281, 241–255 (2020)
34. Shapley, L.: A value for n-player games. In: Kuhn, H., Tucker, A. (eds.) Contributions to the Theory of Games. Princeton University Press (1962)

35. Shubick, M.: Incentives, decentralized control, the assignment of joint costs and internal pricing. Manage. Sci. **8**(3), 325–343 (1962)
36. Siegel, R.: All-pay auctions. Econometrica **77**(1), 71–92 (2009)
37. Skaperdas, S.: Contest success functions. Econ. Theor. **7**(2), 283–290 (1996)
38. Vetta, A.: Nash equilibria in competitive societies, with applications to facility location, traffic routing and auctions. In: Proceedings of the 43rd IEEE Symposium on Foundations of Computer Science, pp. 416–425 (2002)
39. Vojnovič, M.: Contest Theory - Incentive Mechanisms and Ranking Methods, Cambridge University Press, Cambridge (2015)
40. Xia, Y., Qin, T., Yu, N., Liu, T.Y.: Incentivizing high-quality content from heterogeneous users: on the existence of nash equilibrium. In: Proceedings of the 28th AAAI Conference on Artificial Intelligence, pp. 819–825 (2014). Also: arXiv:1404.5155v1
41. Zhang, L.: The efficiency and fairness of a fixed budget resource allocation game. In: Proceedings of the 32nd International Colloquium on Automata, Languages and Programming, pp. 485–496 (2005)

Entrepreneurship Facility-Activation Games

Shaul Rosner$^{(\boxtimes)}$ and Tami Tamir

School of Computer Science, Reichman University, Herzliya, Israel
shaul.rosner@post.runi.ac.il, tami@runi.ac.il

Abstract. Entrepreneurship has long been a driving force for innovation and economic growth. While it has been extensively studied by economists, it has not received much attention in the AGT community.

We define and study an *entrepreneurship facility-activation game*, played by a single entrepreneur and n users. The entrepreneur may activate and close facilities, and each user should select one active facility. This setting combines a weighted singleton congestion game played by the users, with a revenue maximization game played by the entrepreneur, who dynamically determines the set of active facilities in response to the users' assignment.

We analyze the resulting game from multiple perspectives. From the entrepreneur's perspective, maximizing her profit, we provide an asymptotically tight $\Theta(\sqrt{n})$-approximation algorithm with and without stability restrictions.

For the total welfare problem of minimizing the total users cost and facilities activation cost, we provide tight linear bounds for the PoA and PoS. Additionally, we analyze the computational complexity of both the social optimum and the cheapest stable solution. We distinguish between games with weighted and unweighted users, with and without symmetric strategies, and between arbitrary and uniform facility activation costs.

Our results highlight the challenges of revenue maximization for entrepreneurs and the high impact of entrepreneurship on the total welfare and the equilibrium efficiency.

Keywords: Congestion Games · Revenue Maximization · Entrepreneurship · Equilibrium Inefficiency

1 Introduction

Entrepreneurship has long been a driving force for innovation and economic growth. As a result, understanding the dynamics of entrepreneurship is of great importance. In this paper we define and study an *Entrepreneurship Facility-Activation game* (Entrepreneurship game) which corresponds to an environment in which both an entrepreneur and the users of the facilities she activates behave strategically.

© The Author(s), under exclusive license to Springer Nature Switzerland AG 2023
A. Deligkas and A. Filos-Ratsikas (Eds.): SAGT 2023, LNCS 14238, pp. 90–108, 2023.
https://doi.org/10.1007/978-3-031-43254-5_6

Consider, for example, regulated mobile telecommunications infrastructure and services. Government-owned mobile networks provide services to all citizens. In contrast, a private company can also operate mobile telecommunications networks. This private mobile network operator may invest in building and maintaining mobile infrastructure, such as cell towers, and offer mobile services to customers. The citizens have the option to choose between using the network owned by the government or selecting one of the networks operated by the private operator. In our Entrepreneurship game, the entrepreneur controls a set of facilities that can be activated or closed during the game, while users must decide which facilities to use based on their individual preferences and the current state of the game. The entrepreneur's goal is to maximize her profit, which depends on the revenue generated from active facilities and the costs associated with activating and maintaining them. The users instead aim to minimize their costs independent of the cost invested by the entrepreneur.

This setting creates an interplay between the entrepreneur and the users, as the entrepreneur must constantly evaluate the expected profit from each facility based on its activation cost and potential demand from users. Meanwhile, users do not necessarily make the choice the entrepreneur expects. This dynamic reaction closely resembles real-world scenarios where an entrepreneur, or provider of a service, must decide which products or services to invest in and maintain, while consumers must choose which products or services to use.

Our model is based on key principles of entrepreneurial decision-making and consumer behavior. A critical aspect of this is the trade-off an entrepreneur faces between expanding her offerings and maintaining the profitability of existing products or services.

For instance, when investing in public transportation, an entrepreneur may establish routes between various locations. Introducing a new route may attract users who were previously not customers of the entrepreneur's services. However, operating a new route has a cost, and even if the new route is profitable some customers who previously used other routes operated by the entrepreneur may switch to the new route, reducing the profitability of the older routes. Therefore, the entrepreneur must strategically decide which services to activate, maintain, or shut down based on the expected demand from users and the associated costs, and react to the changes in the market.

In this paper we attempt to model the behavior of entrepreneurs and users. We investigate the existence of stable outcomes, as well as their inefficiency. We do this both from the point of view of the entrepreneur attempting to maximize her profit, without taking the users utilization into account, as well as from the point of view of the whole system – taking into account both the users' quality of service and the total activation cost.

As we show, even though every entrepreneurship game has a stable profile, the equilibrium inefficiency in both entrepreneur profits and user costs is very high, causing potentially high costs for the users, as well as low profits for the entrepreneur. We show tight bounds for these values, in a general setting, as well as in restricted classes of instances. Our results highlight the difficulty of making good investments as an entrepreneur, even in a relatively simplistic environment.

2   Model and Preliminaries

An *Entrepreneurship Game* is given by $G = \langle N, M, \{M_j\}_{j \in N}, \{w_j\}_{j \in N}, \{c_i\}_{i \in M} \rangle$, where N is a set of n *users*, and M is a set of $m + 1$ *facilities*, $\{a_0, a_1, \ldots, a_m\}$. Throughout the paper, we use j when indexing users, and i when indexing facilities.

The facilities $M \setminus \{a_0\}$ are controlled by an entrepreneur who may activate or close each of them during the game. Every facility $i \in M$ has an activation cost $c_i \geq 0$. For every $j \in N$, $M_j \subseteq M$ is the set of feasible facilities of user j, and w_j is the weight of user j. Let $W = \sum_{j \in N} w_j$ be the total users' weight. For every facility $i \in M$, denote by $all(i)$ the total weight of users for which facility i is feasible, that is, $all(i) = \sum_{j | i \in M_j} w_j$. We assume that for every i, $c_i \leq all(i)$. A facility that does not fulfill this condition is removed from the game.

The facility a_0 is the *civil facility*. The civil facility is not controlled by the entrepreneur, and can be viewed as a competitor of the entrepreneur. The civil facility has activation cost $c_0 = 0$, and it is feasible to all users, that is $a_0 \in M_j$ for every $j \in N$, and equivalently $all(0) = W$.

A profile of an entrepreneurship game describes the current assignment of the users, and a status indicator for every facility $i \in M$. Formally, a profile is a tuple (p, s) where $p = \langle p_1, p_2, \ldots, p_n \rangle$ and $s = \langle s_0, s_1, \ldots, s_m \rangle$. For all $j \in N$, $p_j \in M_j$, and for all $i \in M$, $s_i \in \{0, 1, -1\}$. A facility i is *active* if $s_i = 1$, and is inactive otherwise. $s_i = 0$ if facility i was never activated, and $s_i = -1$ if facility i was previously active, but then was deactivated. The civil facility is always active, that is, $s_0 = 1$ throughout the whole game. Let $M_{active}(p, s) = \{i | s_i = 1\}$ be the set of active facilities in profile (p, s). When either p or s are clear from the context, we omit them.

For a user j, p_j denotes the facility that serves j. Every facility that is serving a user must be active. Note that for every $j \in N$, $a_0 \in M_{active} \cap M_j$, so it cannot be that $M_{active} \cap M_j = \emptyset$. If $p_j = a_0$, we say user j is served by the civil facility. Let $J_0(p, s)$ denote the set of users served by the civil facility in profile (p, s).

For a facility $i \in M$, the *load* on i in p, denoted $L_i(p)$, is the total weight of the users assigned to facility i in p, that is, $L_i(p) = \sum_{\{j | p_j = i\}} w_j$. As is common in the study of congestion games, we assume that the service provided to the users assigned to a facility reduces with the congestion on it. Formally, the cost of user j in profile (p, s) is $C_j(p) = L_{p_j}(p)$. Note that this cost is independent of the facility's activation cost and only depends on the congestion.

The *profit* of the entrepreneur, which she aims to maximize, depends on two factors: the revenue from her active facilities, given by the total weight of their assigned users, and her expenses, given by the activation costs of the active facilities. Specifically, the profit of the entrepreneur is $\sum_{j \notin J_0} w_j - \sum_{i \in M_{active}} c_i = \sum_{i \in M_{active} \setminus \{a_0\}} (L_i - c_i)$. Note that the entrepreneur can have a profit of 0 by not activating any facility. A facility i in M_{active} is a *sound investment* if its activation cost is not more than the total weight of users assigned to it.

For the entrepreneur, it is never profit-increasing to activate a facility, as no user can be assigned to it at the time of activation. For an inactive facility i with $s_i = 0$, the entrepreneur can calculate her expected profit from i by using her knowledge of the current profile and the users' strategies. Formally, the expected profit of the entrepreneur from facility i with $s_i = 0$ is $f_i - c_i$ where $f_i = min(\frac{L_0}{2}, \sum_{j \in J_0 | i \in M_j} w_j)$. Intuitively, the entrepreneur expects users assigned to the civil facility that can choose i, to prefer it as long as its load is less than the load on the civil facility.

Activating a facility with a positive expected profit is considered beneficial for the entrepreneur. The entrepreneur can also close an active facility. Formally, if $L_i(p) < c_i$, then closing facility i is beneficial for the entrepreneur. When an active facility is closed by the entrepreneur, we set $s_i = -1$, indicating the investment is unsound. In our model, the entrepreneur will never attempt to activate a facility that has previously shown to be an unsound investment. When facility i is closed, all the users assigned to it are moved to the civil facility a_0.

A strategy is a *best response* (BR) for user j if it minimizes j's cost, as defined above, given the strategies of all other players. A strategy is a BR for the entrepreneur if it maximizes her expected profit, as defined above. In our model, the entrepreneur cannot change the activation of multiple facilities in one deviation. Best-Response Dynamics (BRD) is a local-search method where in each step some player is chosen and plays its best improving deviation (if one exists), given the strategies of the other players. In our model, users have higher priority in performing a deviation, thus, the entrepreneur may deviate from her current strategy only if no user has a beneficial deviation. This ensures that the entrepreneur does not change the set of active facilities before the profit they contribute is known and stable.

The focus in game theory is on the *stable* outcomes of a given setting. The most prominent stability concept is that of a Nash equilibrium (NE): a profile such that no player can improve its objective by unilaterally deviating from its current strategy, assuming that the strategies of the other players do not change. Formally, a profile p is a NE if, for every $j \in N$, p_j is a BR for user j, and the entrepreneur does not have a beneficial deviation.

For the analysis of social cost - as is common in facility location problems [23], we sum the user costs, and the activation costs of active facilities. Formally, the social cost of a profile is $cost(p, s) = \sum_{j \in N} C_j + \sum_{i \in M_{active}} c_i$. A *social optimum* of a game G is a profile that attains the lowest possible social cost. We denote by $SO(G)$ the cost of a social optimum profile; i.e., $SO(G) = \min_{(p,s)} cost(p, s)$.

It is well known that decentralized decision-making may lead to sub-optimal solutions from the point of view of society as a whole. We quantify the inefficiency incurred due to self-interested behavior according to the *price of anarchy* (PoA) [16] and *price of stability* (PoS) [2] measures. The PoA is the worst-case inefficiency of a pure Nash equilibrium, while the PoS measures the best-case inefficiency of a pure Nash equilibrium. Formally,

Definition 1. *Let $\mathcal{G}$ be a family of games, and let G be a game in $\mathcal{G}$. Let $\Upsilon(G)$ be the set of pure Nash equilibria of the game G. Assume that $\Upsilon(G) \neq \emptyset$.*

- *The* price of anarchy *of G is the ratio between the maximal cost of a PNE and the social optimum of G. That is, $PoA(G) = \max_{(p,s) \in \Upsilon(G)} cost(p, s)/SO(G)$. The* price of anarchy *of the family of games $\mathcal{G}$ is $PoA(\mathcal{G}) = sup_{G \in \mathcal{G}} PoA(G)$.*

- *The* price of stability *of G is the ratio between the* minimal *cost of a PNE and the social optimum of G. That is,* $PoS(G) = \min_{(p,s) \in \Upsilon(G)} cost(p,s)/SO(G)$. *The* price of stability *of the family of games $\mathcal{G}$ is* $PoS(\mathcal{G}) = sup_{G \in \mathcal{G}} PoS(G)$.

In our analysis, the set $\Upsilon(G)$ of NE profiles, does not include 'artificial' profiles in which facilities are arbitrarily unavailable. Formally, let (p^0, s^0) denote the *baseline profile* in which all the users are assigned to the civil facility. That is, for every user j, $p_j^0 = a_0$, and for every facility $i > 0$, $s_i^0 = 0$. Since we aim to analyze a setting in which an entrepreneur suggests her services in the presence of a civil facility, we only consider a profile (p, s) with $s_i = -1$ for some facility i, if (p, s) can be reached by a series of beneficial deviations from the baseline profile. Without this restriction, it is possible to easily construct games with high equilibrium inefficiently, simply because the social optimum uses facilities that are not available in the game. By considering only profiles in which facilities cannot be closed arbitrarily we isolate the inefficiency due to selfish behaviour (of both the entrepreneur and the users), and not due to an arbitrary non-feasible status of the facilities. In Sect. 6, we discuss further the rational behind studying this model, and mention several alternatives.

2.1   Our Results

We study entrepreneurship games from two perspectives. First, from the viewpoint of an entrepreneur who wishes to maximize her profit, and faces a variant of a facility location game, and second, from the viewpoint of the society, that wishes to combine low cost for the users with low cost for the entrepreneur. Some of our results refer to restricted classes of games. In a game with unweighted users, $\forall j \in N, w_j = 1$. In a game with symmetric users, all users have the same strategy space, that is, for all $j \in N, M_j = M$. In a game with uniform activation costs, there exists a value $c > 0$ such that $\forall i \in M \setminus \{a_0\}, c_i = c$.

In Sect. 3, we provide basic but important observations. Specifically, we prove the existence of NE profiles, and convergence of BRD. We then provide a bound of W for the activation cost and a bound of nW for the total cost of every NE profile, as well as a lower bound of W for the social cost of a SO profile.

In Sect. 4, we analyze the game from the entrepreneur's perspective. First, in Sect. 4.1 we consider the problem of finding a profile with maximal entrepreneur profit. We discuss the relation between this problem and the uncapacitated facility location (FL) problem, and explain why common techniques used for FL-approximation are not useful in our setting. We show a $\sqrt{n}$-approximation algorithm for this problem and prove it is asymptotically tight for both weighted and unweighted users. Next, in Sect. 4.2 we limit our search to NE profiles and give an asymptotically tight $3\sqrt{n}$-approximation algorithm for maximum profit NE in an entrepreneurship game with unweighted users. In Sect. 4.3 we present optimal algorithms for a game with symmetric users and show that our lower bounds apply for games with uniform activation cost as well.

In Sect. 5 we analyze the total welfare problem. Rather than looking strictly at maximizing the entrepreneurs profit, we aim to minimize the total cost paid by both the users and the entrepreneur. This analysis is divided between unweighted and weighted users. We show that it is NP-hard to even approximate a NE profile within a sub-linear factor, even for unweighted users. We then show bounds for the PoA and PoS, which are all $\Theta(n)$.

In light of the negative results for general instances, we analyze entrepreneurship games with symmetric users. While the problem remains hard with linear equilibrium inefficiency for weighted users, we provide a polynomial algorithm for finding the lowest cost NE for unweighted users and give $\Theta(\sqrt{n})$ bounds for the equilibrium inefficiency. We also analyzed the class of games with uniform activation costs, and show that our negative results remain valid, with slightly lower values for the PoA and the PoS.

Our results for the total welfare problem are summarized in Table 1. We remark that some of the bounds hold only for a sufficiently large number of users n. We conclude in Sect. 6 with a discussion of the significance of our analysis. Furthermore, we propose potential directions for future work to expand our understanding of other aspects of entrepreneurship. Due to space constraints, many of the proofs are omitted.

Table 1. Our results for the total welfare problem (Sect. 5). All the bounds on the equilibrium inefficiency are tight. The exact values of the PoA and PoS in unweighted games are bit lower than $\frac{n}{2}$ and slightly different for the PoA, the PoS, and for general or uniform activation cost instances. (†) The computational complexity of calculating a lowest cost NE profile, or the approximation factor for which it is hard.

Game Class	Unweighted			Weighted		
	PoA	PoS	Complexity[(†)]	PoA	PoS	Complexity[(†)]
General	$\approx \frac{n}{2}$	$\approx \frac{n}{2}$	$\Theta(n^{1-\epsilon})$	n	$n-2$	$\Theta(n^{1-\epsilon})$
Symmetric	$\Theta(\sqrt{n})$	$\Theta(\sqrt{n})$	Polynomial	n	$\frac{n}{2}$	Strongly-NPC

2.2 Related Work

To the best of our knowledge, no similar model to the one analyzed in our entrepreneurship game has been studied before. Nevertheless, there is a wide literature on the impact of entrepreneurs in economic models (e.g., [6,9]). These studies consistently highlight the positive effect of entrepreneurship on productivity and economic growth.

A problem similar to the profit maximization problem faced by our entrepreneur (Sect. 4) was considered in [1,24], which deal with profit maximization in the hub-location problem. However, the users in their analysis, which are units of demand, are not affected by the congestion on their selected facility, making the analysis of their choice different. A game-theoretic analysis of the hub location problem is given in [21,22], where the hub location problem is analyzed similarly to a Stackelberg game. Specifically, a big firm first locates a new hub on a plane as a leader, and the other firms locate their hubs afterwards.

Our model of entrepreneurship games is inspired by the (uncapacitated) facility location (FL) problem, which is one of the most well-studied problems in the operations research literature, dating back to [3,18] among others. In its simplest form, the problem is as follows: we wish to find optimal locations among a set of m locations at which to build facilities to serve a given set of n users, where building a facility at location i incurs a cost of f_i, and user j assigned to facility i incurs a cost of $d_{i,j}$, the distance between i and j. The general problem is as hard as weighted set-cover. A simple greedy algorithm guarantees $O(\log n)$-approximation [7]. Better approximation results exists with metric service costs [15,19,23].

In Sect. 4.1 we highlight the differences between the FL problem and our setting. One significant distinction from the traditional FL problem is that in our model, the cost incurred by users depends on the congestion on the facility. An FL problem where congestion arises at facilities and affects the users delay is considered in [8]. An alternative way to incorporate negative congestion, by making the activation cost of a facility a function of the number of clients assigned to it, is discussed in [12]. In both papers, the analysis is of a cost minimization problem, and not as a game.

Other related work deals with FL games. In the cooperative cost-sharing FL game, users share the cost of building facilities in certain locations [14]. In the competitive FL game service-providers select locations to place their facilities in order to maximize their profits, and set prices for each user. The clients select a facility and have private value for accepting the providers' prices [25]. Both variants are not directly related to our model. In [17] a two-stage facility location game is analyzed, that is similar to our model in that users attempt to minimize congestion on facilities, while facilities aim to maximize the total user weight assigned to them.

When isolating the users perspective in our game, we get that the users face a *congestion game* with singleton strategies played on the currently active facilities. In a congestion game [20], a set of resources is used by a set of players who need to use these resources. Players' strategies are subsets of resources. Each resource has a latency function which, given the load generated by the players on the resource, returns the cost of the resource. In *singleton* congestion games players' strategies are single resources. In *weighted* congestion games, each player j has a *weight* w_j, and its contribution to the load on the resources it uses as well as its cost are multiplied by w_j [5]. A lot of research has been conducted on the analysis of congestion games, and in particular, weighted singleton congestion games, that are often described as a job scheduling game [26]. The questions that are commonly analyzed are Nash equilibrium existence, the convergence of BRD to a NE, and the loss incurred due to selfish behavior [4,10,11,13].

3 General Properties

In this section, we present some useful properties of entrepreneurship games. The results are for games with weighted users, and are clearly valid also for unweighted games.

We first show that every entrepreneurship game is guaranteed to have a NE. More specifically, we prove that any application of BRD converges to a NE.

Theorem 1. *For every entrepreneurship game G, for every initial profile (p, s), BRD converges to a NE.*

Next, we bound the total activation cost and the social cost of any NE profile. Recall that $W = \sum_j w_j$ is the total users' weight. Denote by W_0^p the total weight of the users served by the civil facility in profile p, that is, $W_0^p = \sum_{j \in J_0} w_j$.

Claim 2. *In any NE profile (p, s), the total activation cost of the facilities in $M_{active}(p, s)$ is at most $W - W_0^p$.*

Claim 3. *For any entrepreneurship game G with $n \geq 2$, for every NE profile (p, s), $cost(p, s) \leq nW$.*

Finally, we provide a lower bound on the cost of any SO profile.

Claim 4. *For any entrepreneurship game G, $cost(SO) \geq W$.*

4 The Entrepreneurship Perspective

In this section we consider entrepreneurship games from the entrepreneur's perspective. The goal of the entrepreneur is to maximize her profit. The entrepreneur's profit in profile (p, s) is denoted by $profit(p, s)$ and is given by $\sum_{j \notin J_0(p)} w_j - \sum_{i \in M_{active}(p,s)} c_i$. When analyzing the maximum profit problem we assume that the entrepreneur determines both the set of active facilities and the users' assignment. However, when analyzing the most profitable NE profile, the entrepreneur does not control the users, and they selfishly select their assignment.

Throughout this section, a profile is given by an assignment p, where the facilities' status s simply corresponds to the set of active facilities. Let OPT denote a profile achieving maximal profit. We abuse notation and denote by OPT both the profile and its associated profit. Similarly, let OPT_{NE} denote a NE profile achieving maximal profit (and its profit).

4.1 The Entrepreneur's Max-Profit Problem

The problem of maximizing the profit in an entrepreneurship game may seem similar to well-known NP-complete optimization problems like the weighted set cover problem and the uncapacitated facility location (FL) problem, which have simple logarithmic approximations using a greedy algorithm. Recall that an uncapacitated FL problem is given by a set N of users, a set F of potential facility locations, each associated with a non-negative activation cost c_i, and a distance function $d : N \times F \rightarrow \mathbb{R}^+$. The objective is to find a subset $S \subseteq F$ of active facilities such that $\sum_{i \in S} c_i + \sum_{j \in N} \min_{i \in S} d(j, i)$ is minimal. That is, minimizing the total activation cost and the total distance between each user and their closest facility.

Our profit maximization problem can be described as an uncapacitated FL problem by setting the following distance function: For every user j and every

$i > 0$ (non-civil facility), let $d(j,i) = -w_j$ if $a_i \in M_j$ and $d(j,i) = 1$ otherwise. For a_0, let $d(j,0) = 0$. Note that in every optimal solution, the minimal distance of a user j from an open facility is $-w_j$ if at least one facility in M_j is open, and 0 otherwise. Therefore, an optimal solution corresponds to minimizing $\sum_{i \in M_{active}(p)} c_i - \sum_{j \notin J_0(p)} w_j$. This is equivalent to minimizing $\sum_{i \in M_{active}(p)} c_i + W - W_0^p$. Since W is fixed, this is equivalent to maximizing $\sum_{j \notin J_0(p)} w_j - \sum_{i \in M_{active}(p)} c_i$, that is, maximizing the entrepreneur's profit.

Unfortunately, although the optimal solutions for our problem and the uncapacitated FL problem are identical, we cannot apply the standard techniques used for FL-approximation to our setting. This is due to the analysis not holding for negative values, and the possibility of not covering an unprofitable element in our setting. Similar issues arise when trying to cast the problem as a weighted set cover problem.

The following example shows that in an entrepreneurship game, a greedy algorithm, that opens facilities one after the other, may only result in a $\sqrt{n}$-approximation of the maximum profit. This example fits both a greedy rule that chooses a facility for which the added *marginal profit* is maximal, and a greedy rule that chooses a facility for which the *profit-per-user* is maximal. For uncapacitated FL and for weighted set-cover, a greedy algorithm based on maximal profit-per-user provides an $O(\log n)$-approximation [7].

Example 1. Given $b \in \mathbb{N}$, consider an entrepreneurship game with $n = b^2$ unweighted users. There are $b + 1$ non-civil facilities, where for every $1 \le i \le b$, $c_i = b - 1$, and $c_{b+1} = b - 1 - \epsilon$, for some small $\epsilon > 0$. For every $1 \le j \le b$, $M_j = \{a_0, a_j, a_{b+1}\}$. The remaining $b(b-1)$ users are divided into b sets, where for each set $1 \le i \le b$ of $b - 1$ users, each user j has $M_j = \{a_0, a_i\}$.

Denote by v_i the number of unassigned users that can be assigned to facility i. Initially, for each facility $1 \le i \le b$, $\frac{v_i}{c_i} = \frac{b}{b-1}$, and for a_{b+1} we have $\frac{v_{b+1}}{c_{b+1}} = \frac{b}{b-1-\epsilon}$. Additionally, for every $1 \le i \le b$, $v_i - c_i = 1$, while $v_{b+1} - c_{b+1} = 1 + \epsilon$. Therefore, both a greedy algorithm choosing the facility with maximum profit, and a greedy algorithm choosing the facility with maximum profit-per-user, will assign users to facility a_{b+1}. Once b users are assigned to a_{b+1}, the number of unassigned users that may be assigned to a_i, for $1 \le i \le b$, is $b - 1$. Thus, no additional facility can have a positive profit. Therefore, both greedy rules lead to a profile with a profit of $1 + \epsilon$. Conversely, the profile where for every facility $1 \le i \le b$, all b users in $all(i)$ are assigned to a_i, has a total profit of b. Thus, greedy achieves profit $\frac{(1+\epsilon)OPT}{b} \approx \frac{OPT}{\sqrt{n}}$.

Moreover, it is possible to construct an instance where both greedy approaches fail to achieve even a $\sqrt{n}$-approximation. We present a $\sqrt{n}$-approximation algorithm, and prove it is asymptotically tight up to any polynomial factors. Algorithm 1 below calculates a profile p, such that $profit(p) \ge \frac{1}{\sqrt{n}} OPT$.

In the initial baseline profile, all users are assigned to facility a_0. In every iteration $k \ge 1$, the algorithm computes two profiles. The first profile, denoted p^k, is obtained by adding to the previous profile p^{k-1} a new facility i for which the profit-per-user is maximal, if all unassigned users for which i is feasible would select facility i as their strategy. The second profile, denoted p'^k, is obtained by adding to p^{k-1} a new facility i such that the added marginal profit is maximal, if all unassigned users for which i is feasible would select facility i as their strategy. This second profile, p'^k, is kept as a candidate for the maximum profit profile and is not extended in further iterations. The first profile, p^k, is extended in further iterations, and is not considered as a candidate output.

The algorithm continues iterating until no additional facility can add profit. At this point, the candidate profile with the highest profit is returned as output.

Algorithm 1. Approximating a maximal profit profile in an entrepreneurship game

---

1: Let $p^0 = p'^0$ be the baseline profile.
2: Let $k = 0$.
3: For every facility a_i, let $v_{i_{k+1}} = v_{i_1} = \sum_{j \in J_0(p^0) \mid i \in M_j} w_j$.
4: Let $a_{i^*_{k+1}} = a_{i^*_1} \in M \setminus M_{active}$ be the facility a_i for which $\frac{v_{i_1}}{c_i}$ is maximal.
5: Let $a_{i^{*\prime}_{k+1}} = a_{i^{*\prime}_1} \in M \setminus M_{active}$ be the facility a_i for which $v_{i_1} - c_i$ is maximal.
6: **while** $v_{i^*_{k+1}} > c_{i^*_{k+1}}$ **do**
7:     Let $k = k + 1$.
8:     Let p^k be the profile obtained from p^{k-1} by activating $a_{i^*_k}$, and moving every
       user $j \in J_0$ for which $a_{i^*_k} \in M_j$ from a_0 to $a_{i^*_k}$.
9:     Let p'^k be the profile obtained from p^{k-1} by activating $a_{i^{*\prime}_k}$, and moving every
       user $j \in J_0$ for which $a_{i^{*\prime}_k} \in M_j$ from a_0 to $a_{i^{*\prime}_k}$.
10:    Consider p^k. For every facility a_i, let $v_{i_{k+1}} = \sum_{j \in J_0(p^k) \mid i \in M_j} w_j$.
11:    Calculate $a_{i^*_{k+1}}, a_{i^{*\prime}_{k+1}}$ with respect to p^k.
12: **end while**
13: Return the most profitable profile in $\{p'^\ell\}_{0 \le \ell \le k}$.

Theorem 5. *Algorithm 1 returns a profile p such that $profit(p) \ge \frac{1}{\sqrt{n}} OPT$.*

Proof. Let k be the number of facilities activated by the entrepreneur during the algorithm. If $profit(p'^k) \ge \frac{1}{\sqrt{n}} OPT$, we are done. The analysis below refers to the case that $profit(p'^k) < \frac{1}{\sqrt{n}} OPT$. We prove that in this case some profile in $\{p'^\ell\}_{0 \le \ell < k}$ has profit at least $\frac{1}{\sqrt{n}} OPT$.

For every $\ell \le k$, let A_ℓ denote the set of users assigned to $a_{i^*_\ell}$ in profile p^ℓ. Let F^*_ℓ be the set of facilities to which the users of A_ℓ are assigned in OPT. Let $\mathcal{F}^*_\ell = F^*_\ell \setminus \bigcup_{\ell' < \ell} F^*_{\ell'}$. In other words, $\mathcal{F}^*_\ell$ is the set of facilities that serve in OPT users of A_ℓ but no users of $A_1, \ldots, A_{\ell-1}$.

For every $\ell \le k$ denote the profit from facility $a_{i^*_\ell}$ in profile p^ℓ by $\mathcal{P}_\ell = L_{i^*_\ell}(p^\ell) - c_{i^*_\ell}$.

Observation 6. *If* $profit(p'^k) < \frac{1}{\sqrt{n}}OPT$, *then there exists* $q \le k$ *such that the total profit contributed to* OPT *by facilities of* $\mathcal{F}_q^*$ *is more than* $\sqrt{n}\mathcal{P}_q$.

Proof. In OPT, for every open facility, $c_a < L_a$, as otherwise closing this facility increases the entrepreneur profit. The halting condition of the algorithm, which results in profile p'^k, is that there is no facility for which $v_{i_{k+1}^*} > c_{i_{k+1}^*}$. In other words, it is not beneficial to open an additional facility, even if all the users for which it is feasible will migrate from a_0 into it. Therefore, for every facility $a \ne a_0$ active in OPT, at least one user assigned to a in OPT is assigned to a facility other than a_0 in p'^k, and contributes to the entrepreneur's profit in p'^k. Thus, the facilities in $\bigcup_{0 \le \ell \le k} F_\ell^* = \bigcup_{0 \le \ell \le k} \mathcal{F}_\ell^*$ contribute the total profit of OPT. If for every $q \le k$, the total profit contributed to OPT by facilities of $\mathcal{F}_q^*$ is at most $\sqrt{n}\mathcal{P}_q$, then the total profit of OPT is bounded by $\sqrt{n}\sum_{\ell=1}^{k}\mathcal{P}_\ell = \sqrt{n} \cdot profit(p'^k)$. Since $profit(p'^k) < \frac{1}{\sqrt{n}}OPT$, we get a contradiction. $\square$

Assume that $profit(p'^k) < \frac{1}{\sqrt{n}}OPT$, and let q be the minimal index of a facility for which $\mathcal{P}_q$ is at least the profit contributed by facilities in $\mathcal{F}_q^*$ in OPT. By Observation 6, such a facility exists.

By definition of $\mathcal{F}^*$, all users assigned to $\mathcal{F}_q^*$ in OPT are unassigned in profile p^{q-1}. Therefore, in profile p^{q-1} there is at least one facility a_i for which $v_{i_q} - c_i \ge \sqrt{n} \cdot \frac{\mathcal{P}_q}{L_{i_q^*}(p^q)}$. Therefore, $profit(p'^q) \ge \sum_{i=1}^{q-1}\mathcal{P}_i + \frac{\sqrt{n}\mathcal{P}_q}{L_{i_q^*}(p^q)}$.

Additionally, since the facilities $a_{i_{k+1}^*}$ are chosen to maximize the profit-per-user, the total profit contributed by unassigned users in iteration q that are not assigned to facilities in $\mathcal{F}_q^*$ in OPT is at most $L_0(p^{q-1}) \cdot \frac{\mathcal{P}_q}{L_{i_q^*}(p^q)} \le n \cdot \frac{\mathcal{P}_q}{L_{i_q^*}(p^q)}$. Therefore, since users assigned to a_{i_q} in profile p^q that are assigned to facilities not in $\mathcal{F}_q^*$ in OPT already have their profit covered by previous iterations of the algorithm, $OPT \le \sum_{i=1}^{q-1}\sqrt{n}\mathcal{P}_i + \frac{n\mathcal{P}_q}{L_{i_q^*}(p^q)}$. This proves the profit of profile p'^q is a $\sqrt{n}$-approximation of OPT. $\square$

Example 1 shows that the above analysis of the algorithm is tight. That is, there are games for which Algorithm 1 provides a $\sqrt{n}$-approximation. Moreover, we show that this approximation is asymptotically tight, even for games with unweighted users.

Theorem 7. *For every* $\epsilon > 0$, *it is NP-hard to approximate the maximal profit within a factor better than* $\approx (\sqrt{2n})^{1-\epsilon}$.

Proof. Recall the maximum independent set problem (MIS). The input is an undirected graph (V, E), and the goal is to find a maximum cardinality subset of vertices $S \subseteq V$ such that for every edge $(u, v) \in E$, at most one of u and v is in S. It is well known that unless $P = NP$, for every $\epsilon > 0$, it is NP-hard to approximate MIS within factor $|V|^{1-\epsilon}$ [27].

Given a graph $G' = (V, E)$, we construct an entrepreneurship game G_{hard}, with $|V|$ non-civil facilities and $|E|$ users. The set of facilities is $\{a_0, a_1, \dots, a_{|V|}\}$. For $1 \le i \le |V|$, facility i corresponds to $v_i \in V$, and its cost is $c_i = deg(v_i) - 1 + \epsilon$. The users correspond to the edges, where for user j corresponding to $(v_{i_1}, v_{i_2}) \in$

E, let $M_j = \{a_0, a_{i_1}, a_{i_2}\}$. Note that a facility is profitable only if it is assigned all users that can be assigned to it. In this case, the profit from the facility is $1 - \epsilon$. Consider two facilities v_{i_1} and v_{i_2} such that $(v_{i_1}, v_{i_2}) \in E$. Since there is a user that can be assigned to at most one of these facilities, at most one of v_{i_1} and v_{i_2} can be profitable in any profile. Therefore, the entrepreneur will only activate a set of facilities that corresponds to an independent set in G', and the profit from activating an independent set $U \subseteq V$ is exactly $|U|(1 - \epsilon)$. Note that G_{hard} has $|E|$ users, and since $|E| \le \frac{1}{2}|V|(|V| - 1)$, G_{hard} has at most $\frac{1}{2}|V|(|V| + 1)$ users, that is, $|V| \approx \sqrt{2n}$. Unless $P = NP$, there can be no approximation better than $|V|^{1-\epsilon}$ for the maximum independent set problem [27]. Therefore, as a profile with a profit of $k(1 - \varepsilon)$ corresponds to an independent set of size k, it is NP-hard to approximate the maximum profit in an entrepreneurship game with unweighted users within a factor better than $(\sqrt{2n})^{1-\epsilon}$.   □

4.2   The Entrepreneur's Most Profitable NE Problem

We turn to discuss the problem of calculating a most profitable NE. The hardness proof in Theorem 7 can be extended to show the following.

Theorem 8. *For every $\epsilon > 0$, it is NP-hard to approximate the highest profit of a NE within a factor better than $\approx (\sqrt{2n})^{1-\epsilon}$.*

We provide a $3\sqrt{n}$-approximation algorithm for the maximal profit NE in games with unweighted users. The algorithm consists of two phases: First, some not necessarily stable profile is computed, and second, this profile is turned into a stable one. The following claim is required for the second phase.

Claim 9. *Given a profile $\hat{p}$ of an entrepreneurship game, in which every non-civil facility is assigned at most $\lceil \frac{n}{2} \rceil$ users, a NE profile $\hat{p}^{NE}$ with $profit(\hat{p}^{NE}) \ge \frac{1}{3}profit(\hat{p})$ exists and can be computed efficiently.*

Recall Algorithm 1 that computes a $\sqrt{n}$-approximation to OPT. The returned profile may assign more than $\lceil \frac{n}{2} \rceil$ users on some facility. We tune Algorithm 1 as described in Step 1 of Algorithm 2 below, such that it produces a $\sqrt{n}$-approximation to OPT_{NE}. The resulting profile fulfills the bounded load constraint required in Claim 9, and is converted to a NE in Step 2.

Algorithm 2. Approximating a maximal profit NE profile in an unweighted entrepreneurship game

---

1: Run Algorithm 1 with the following modifications:
    (i) in Steps 3 and 10, for all k, $v_{i_k} = \max\{\lceil \frac{n}{2} \rceil, |\{j \in J_0(p^k | i \in M_j\}|\}$,
    (ii) in Steps 8 and 9 at most $\lceil \frac{n}{2} \rceil$ users (chosen arbitrarily) are moved from a_0 to $a_{i_k^*}$ and $a_{i_k^{*'}}$, respectively.
2: Convert the output profile, $\hat{p}$, to the NE guaranteed by Claim 9.

Theorem 10. *Algorithm 2 returns a NE profile with profit at least $\frac{1}{3\sqrt{n}}OPT_{NE}$.*

Remark: It is possible to extend the algorithm to handle also games with weighted users. The underlying partition problem adds an additional constant factor to the approximation ratio.

4.3 · Games with Symmetric Users or Uniform Activation Cost

In a game with symmetric users, the entrepreneur clearly maximizes her profit when all the users are assigned to a single facility $a \neq a_0$ with $c_a = min_{i>0}c_i$. Calculating OPT_{NE}, the most profitable NE, is slightly more complicated, and we present an efficient optimal algorithm for this task.

Theorem 11. *In any entrepreneurship game G with unweighted symmetric users, calculating $OPT_{NE}(G)$ can be done in $O(m \log m)$.*

Proof. Let G be a entrepreneurship game with unweighted symmetric users. Sort the facilities such that $c_1 \leq \cdots \leq c_m$. Note that if k facilities are active, then the revenue of the entrepreneur is maximized if these facilities are $\{a_0, \ldots, a_{k-1}\}$. Moreover, given k, the profile in which there are $\lfloor \frac{n}{k} \rfloor$ users assigned to a_0, and $\lceil \frac{n}{k} \rceil$ or $\lfloor \frac{n}{k} \rfloor$ users assigned to each facility $a_1, \ldots, a_k$, is a NE and is the most profitable NE with k active facilities. The entrepreneur's profit in such a profile is $\gamma(k) = n - \lfloor \frac{n}{k} \rfloor - \sum_{i=0}^{k-1} c_i$. Clearly, $\gamma(0) = 0$, and for every $1 \leq k \leq m$, it is possible to calculate $\gamma(k)$ given $\gamma(k-1)$ in constant time, and to identify the index k^* for which $\gamma(k^*)$ is maximal. □

For the class of games with uniform activation cost, the hardness proofs given in Theorem 7 and Theorem 8, can be modified to show that it is unlikely to have a $(\sqrt{n})^{1-\epsilon}$-approximation algorithm for calculating either OPT or OPT_{NE}. Specifically, given input (V, E) for the MIS problem, let $\Delta = \max_i deg(v_i)$. In the reduction, set the activation costs of all facilities to be $\Delta - 1 + \epsilon$, and add dummy users restricted to go to a_0 or a_i, such that for every facility, $all(a_i) = \Delta$.

5   The Total Welfare Perspective

In this section we consider the combined welfare of both the users and the entrepreneur. Recall that the social cost is given by $\sum_{j \in N} C_j + \sum_{i \in M_{active}} c_i$. The social optimum corresponds to a setting in which the profile is determined by an external authority that controls both the users and the entrepreneur. In particular, non-profitable facilities, for which $L_i < c_i$, may be active in the social optimum, but not in a NE, since such facilities will be deactivated by the entrepreneur.

Throughout this section, a profile is given by (p, s), where as described in Sect. 2, p is the assignment of users, and s is a vector giving for each facility its status with regards to the entrepreneur.

5.1   The Total Welfare Problem - Unweighted Users

We start by proving that for any $x < 1$ it is NP-hard to calculate a NE that costs less than $O(n^x)$ times the cheapest NE, even for entrepreneurship games with unweighted users. On the other hand, it is well-known that BRD is guaranteed to converge in polynomial time in every unweighted singleton congestion game [10]. Since every facility is activated and deactivated at most once, and the users play a singleton congestion game in every status vector of the facilities. BRD is guaranteed to converge to a NE in poly-time in our game as well. In Theorem 15 below we prove that $PoA \leq \frac{n}{2}$. In particular, the NE reached by BRD is a $\frac{n}{2}$-approximation to the cheapest NE.

Theorem 12. *For every $\epsilon > 0$, it is NP-hard to find a NE that costs less than $O(n^{1-\epsilon})$ times the cost of the cheapest NE.*

Our proof for Theorem 12 constructs a game with the same activation cost for all facilities. Thus, our hardness of approximation result holds also for the class of games with uniform activation costs.

Next, we show that finding the SO is an NP-complete problem. Since users may be assigned to non-profitable facilities only in the SO, this result is not a direct consequence of Theorem 12.

Theorem 13. *For any entrepreneurship game with unweighted users, finding an SO profile is NP-complete.*

We turn to analyze the equilibrium inefficiency in games with unweighted users. We first give a lower bound example for both the PoA and the PoS.

Theorem 14. *For any $\epsilon > 0$ and $n \geq 4$, there is an entrepreneurship game with unweighted users, G, for which $PoA(G) = \frac{(n-1)^2+2}{2n-2} - O(n\epsilon)$, and $PoS(G) = \frac{(n-2)^2+5}{2n-2} - O(n\epsilon)$.*

Proof. Given $\epsilon > 0$ and $n \geq 4$, let G be an entrepreneurship game with n unweighted users, and $n + 1$ facilities, $a_0, a_1, \ldots, a_n$. Let $c_0 = c_1 = 0$, $c_n = 1$, and $c_i = 1+\epsilon$ for every $2 \leq i \leq n-1$. The users' feasible facilities are defined such that one user can go to any facility, $n-2$ users can go to a single non-civil facility, and one user is restricted to go to the civil facility. Formally, $M_1 = \{a_0, \ldots, a_n\}$, $M_j = \{a_0, a_j\}$ for every $2 \leq j \leq n - 1$, and $M_n = \{a_0\}$.

Due to space constraints, we omit the complete analysis of G. We only state without a proof that $cost(SO) = 2n - 2 + (n - 2)\epsilon$, and the highest cost NE is the profile (p, s) with $M_{active}(p, s) = \{a_0, a_n\}$, such that $cost(p, s) = (n-1)^2+2$. Thus, $PoA(G) = \frac{(n-1)^2+2}{2n-2+(n-2)\epsilon} = \frac{(n-1)^2+2}{2n-2} - O(n\epsilon)$. □

Next, we give an upper bound for the PoA.

Theorem 15. *For any entrepreneurship game G with $n > 12$ unweighted users, $PoA(G) \leq \frac{n}{2}$.*

The upper bound of $\frac{n}{2}$ is not tight with respect to the lower bound of $\frac{(n-1)^2+2}{2n-2} = \frac{n}{2} - \frac{1}{2} + \frac{1}{n} + O(\frac{1}{n^2})$. We note that the upper bound can be reduced to match the PoA and PoS lower bounds for higher values of n.

Symmetric Users. Next, we consider entrepreneurship games with symmetric unweighted users. Throughout this section, we assume the facilities are sorted by their activation cost, that is, $0 = c_0 \leq c_1 \leq \cdots \leq c_m$.

In an entrepreneurship game with symmetric unweighted users, in every NE, for some integer L, m_1 facilities have load L and m_2 facilities have load $L + 1$. Clearly, if the gap between the loads on two facilities is more than 1, a user on the highly loaded facility has a beneficial deviation. It also holds that $m_1 L + m_2 (L + 1) = n$. In addition, given that $m_1 + m_2$ facilities are active, it is preferable for the entrepreneur to activate the cheapest facilities. We therefore look for an L such that $m_1 + m_2$ is maximal, $m_1 L + m_2 (L + 1) = n$, and each of the facilities in a balanced assignment of the users on the cheapest $m_1 + m_2$ facilities is a sound investment for the entrepreneur.

Algorithm 3 is a linear time algorithm for computing a cheapest NE in a game with symmetric unweighted users.

Algorithm 3. Computing a cheapest NE in a game with symmetric unweighted users

---

1: Let $\hat{m}$ be the maximal index such that (i) $\lceil \frac{n}{\hat{m}} \rceil \geq c_{\hat{m}-1}$, and (ii) $n \bmod (\hat{m}) = 0$ or $n \bmod (\hat{m}) \geq |\{i < \hat{m} | c_i > \lfloor \frac{n}{\hat{m}} \rfloor\}|$
2: For each $0 \leq i < \hat{m}$, set $s_i = 1$.
3: Let $h = n \bmod (\hat{m})$, $\ell = \hat{m} - h$.
4: For $0 \leq i \leq \ell - 1$, assign $\lfloor \frac{n}{\hat{m}} \rfloor$ users to facility i.
5: For $\ell \leq i \leq \ell + h - 1$, assign $\lceil \frac{n}{\hat{m}} \rceil$ users to facility i.

Theorem 16. *For any entrepreneurship game G with symmetric unweighted users, Algorithm 3 computes a cheapest NE of G.*

We can bound the PoA and PoS by analyzing the NE profile calculated in Algorithm 3, and calculating the maximum ratio between any two NE profiles.

Theorem 17. *For any entrepreneurship game G with symmetric unweighted users, $PoA(G) \leq O(\sqrt{n})$. Additionally, for every n, there is a game G with n unweighted users for which $PoS(G) = \Theta(\sqrt{n})$.*

Uniform Activation Costs: When all non-civil facilities have the same activation cost, the PoA and PoS upper bounds are slightly lower than in the general unweighted case. The bound of $\frac{n}{2}$ is nearly tight.

Theorem 18. *For every $n \geq 4$, $\epsilon > 0$, there is a game G with n unweighted users and uniform non-civil activation costs for which $PoA(G) = PoS(G) = \frac{(n-2)^2 + 5}{2n - 1} - O(n\epsilon)$.*

We note that the *PoA* upper bound from Theorem 15 is not tight with respect to the lower bound in Theorem 18. The upper bound can be reduced to match the *PoA* and *PoS* lower bounds for uniform activation costs.

5.2   The Total Welfare Problem - Weighted Users

We move on to analyzing games with weighted users. The hardness results we showed for unweighted users clearly hold. On the other hand, for a game with symmetric users, for which we were able to provide optimal algorithms for games with unweighted users (Theorem 16), we show that with weighted users, even the simplest setting of symmetric users and uniform activation cost is intractable.

Theorem 19. *The problem of computing a lowest cost NE profile in an entrepreneurship game with symmetric weighted users and uniform activation cost is strongly NP-complete.*

Recall that with unweighted users the PoA and PoS are $\approx \frac{n}{2}$. We show below that the factor of 2 is lost when the users have variable weights.

Theorem 20. *For any entrepreneurship game G, $PoA(G) < n$. Additionally, for every $n \geq 2$, $\epsilon > 0$, there is a game G with n users, such that $PoA(G) = n - O(n^2\epsilon)$.*

Theorem 21. *For any entrepreneurship game G with $n \geq 12$ users, $PoS(G) < n - 2$. Additionally, for any $\epsilon > 0$ and $n \geq 12$, there is a game G with n users for which $PoS(G) = n - 2 - O(n\epsilon)$.*

For a game with symmetric users, the PoA lower bound example from Theorem 20 holds. However, we show a tighter bound of $\frac{n}{2}$ for the PoS.

Theorem 22. *For any entrepreneurship game G with $n \geq 6$ symmetric users, $PoS(G) < \frac{n}{2}$. Additionally, for any $\epsilon > 0$ and $n \geq 6$, there is an entrepreneurship game G with n symmetric users for which $PoS(G) = \frac{n}{2} - O(\epsilon)$.*

The analysis of the equilibrium inefficiency with uniform activation cost is similar to the variable cost setting. The PoA result from Theorem 20 and the PoS results from Theorems 21, 22, hold for the case of uniform activation costs.

6   Conclusions, Model Considerations, and Future Work

We introduced a new model for analyzing the impacts of entrepreneurship. Entrepreneurship has been extensively studied by economists, but to the best of our knowledge, has not received much attention in the AGT community.

In our model, an entrepreneur decides which facilities to invest in, while users choose a facility in order to minimize their cost, given by the congestion on the facility. This resulting game combines the weighted singleton congestion game, played by the users, with a revenue maximization game, played by the entrepreneur. Our game draws inspiration from both games but it is very different from both.

We studied two different perspectives, starting with the entrepreneurship perspective, who wishes to maximize her profit. We provided asymptotically tight algorithms for this problem, for a setting in which the entrepreneur controls the users as well as for a setting in which the users act selfishly. We also looked at the problem from a total welfare perspective, with the aim of minimizing the total cost of the entrepreneur and all users. For both the weighted and unweighted variant, we provided analysis of the computational complexity of the problem and the equilibrium inefficiency.

The model analyzed in this paper is clearly only one possible model corresponding to an environment that supports entrepreneurship. In our model, the civil facility, a_0, is treated differently. It has an activation cost of 0, it is in the strategy space of every user, it cannot be closed, and users assigned to it do not contribute to the entrepreneur's profit. Moreover, in the baseline profile (p^0, s^0), all users are assigned to the civil facility. The main rational behind this choice, is to guarantee that every user has a fallback in case the entrepreneur does not activate any facilities in its strategy space. Indeed, entrepreneurs in the real world invest in a field in order to become a valid alternative to the existing options. However, the existing options do not disappear. One alternative to a civil facility is giving every user a high cost strategy $\perp$ corresponding to not being a serviced at all. This models a situation where a user always prefers some facility to no facility. Another alternative is disallowing the entrepreneur from deactivating all facilities in the strategy space of a user, corresponding to regulated industries, such as the energy or telecommunications sectors.

Some other natural variations of the model include activity-dependent users' utilization, or using different cost-sharing mechanisms for the facility activation cost, or adding additional entrepreneurs. Due to the many negative results, it is desirable to identify more variants corresponding to a tractable model.

With the breadth of study on entrepreneurship by economists, modelling entrepreneurship can be done in various ways that may lead to different, yet important and interesting results. We hope that our work stimulates further research in this area and contributes to a better understanding of the complexities of entrepreneurship and its impact on economic and social systems.

References

1. Alibeyg, A., Contreras, I., Fernández, E.: Hub network design problems with profits. Transp. Res. Part E Logist. Transp. Rev. **96**, 40–59 (2016)
2. Anshelevich, E., Dasgupta, A., Kleinberg, J., Tardos, E., Wexler, T., Roughgarden, T.: The price of stability for network design with fair cost allocation. SIAM J. Comput. **38**(4), 1602–1623 (2008)
3. Balinski, M.L.: On finding integer solutions to linear programs. Technical report, Prince: Mathematics (1964)
4. Berenbrink, P., Goldberg, L.A., Goldberg, P.W., Martin, R.: Utilitarian resource assignment. J. Discr. Algorithms **4**(4), 567–587 (2006). https://doi.org/10.1016/j.jda.2005.06.009. https://www.sciencedirect.com/science/article/pii/S157086670 5000511

5. Bhawalkar, K., Gairing, M., Roughgarden, T.: Weighted congestion games: the price of anarchy, universal worst-case examples, and tightness. ACM Trans. Econ. Comput. **2**(4), 14:1–14:23 (2014)
6. Carree, M.A., Thurik, A.R.: The impact of entrepreneurship on economic growth. In: Acs, Z.J., Audretsch, D.B. (eds.) Handbook of Entrepreneurship Research International. Handbook Series on Entrepreneurship, vol. 1, pp. 437–471. Springer, Boston (2010). https://doi.org/10.1007/0-387-24519-7_17
7. Chvatal, V.: A greedy heuristic for the set-covering problem. Math. Oper. Res. **4**(3), 233–235 (1979)
8. Desrochers, M., Marcotte, P., Stan, M.: The congested facility location problem. Locat. Sci. **3**(1), 9–23 (1995)
9. Drucker, P.: Innovation and Entrepreneurship. Routledge, New York (2014)
10. Even-Dar, E., Kesselman, A., Mansour, Y.: Convergence time to nash equilibria. In: Proceedings of the 30th International Colloquium on Automata, Languages, and Programming, pp. 502–513 (2003)
11. Gairing, M., Schoppmann, F.: Total latency in singleton congestion games. In: Deng, X., Graham, F.C. (eds.) Internet and Network Economics. LNCS, vol. 4858, pp. 381–387. Springer, Heidelberg (2007). https://doi.org/10.1007/978-3-540-77105-0_42
12. Hajiaghayi, M.T., Mahdian, M., Mirrokni, V.S.: The facility location problem with general cost functions. Netw. Int. J. **42**(1), 42–47 (2003)
13. Harks, T., Klimm, M.: On the existence of pure nash equilibria in weighted congestion games. Math. Oper. Res. **37**(3), 419–436 (2012)
14. Jain, K., Mahdian, M.: Algorithmic Game Theory, Chap. 15: Cost Sharing. Cambridge University Press, Cambridge (2007)
15. Jain, K., Mahdian, M., Saberi, A.: A new greedy approach for facility location problems. In: Proceedings of the Thiry-Fourth Annual ACM Symposium on Theory of Computing, pp. 731–740 (2002)
16. Koutsoupias, E., Papadimitriou, C.: Worst-case equilibria. Comput. Sci. Rev. **3**(2), 65–69 (2009)
17. Krogmann, S., Lenzner, P., Molitor, L., Skopalik, A.: Two-stage facility location games with strategic clients and facilities. arXiv preprint arXiv:2105.01425 (2021)
18. Kuehn, A.A., Hamburger, M.J.: A heuristic program for locating warehouses. Manage. Sci. **9**(4), 643–666 (1963)
19. Mahdian, M., Ye, Y., Zhang, J.: Approximation algorithms for metric facility location problems. SIAM J. Comput. **36**(2), 411–432 (2006)
20. Rosenthal, R.W.: A class of games possessing pure-strategy nash equilibria. Internat. J. Game Theory **2**, 65–67 (1973)
21. Sasaki, M., Campbell, J.F., Krishnamoorthy, M., Ernst, A.T.: A Stackelberg hub arc location model for a competitive environment. Comput. Oper. Res. **47**, 27–41 (2014)
22. Sasaki, M., Fukushima, M.: Stackelberg hub location problem. J. Oper. Res. Soc. Jpn. **44**(4), 390–402 (2001)
23. Shmoys, D.B., Tardos, E., Aardal, K.: Approximation algorithms for facility location problems (extended abstract). In: Proceedings of the Twenty-Ninth Annual ACM Symposium on Theory of Computing, STOC 1997, pp. 265–274 (1997)
24. Taherkhani, G., Alumur, S.A.: Profit maximizing hub location problems. Omega **86**, 1–15 (2019)
25. Vetta, A.R.: Nash equilibria in competitive societies with applications to facility location, traffic routing and auctions. In: Symposium on the Foundations of Computer Science (FOCS), pp. 416–425 (2002)

26. Vöcking, B.: Algorithmic Game Theory, Chap. 20: Selfish Load Balancing. Cambridge University Press, Cambridge (2007)
27. Zuckerman, D.: Linear degree extractors and the inapproximability of max clique and chromatic number. Theory Comput. **3**(6), 103–128 (2007). https://doi.org/10.4086/toc.2007.v003a006. https://theoryofcomputing.org/articles/v003a006

Computational Social Choice

Single-Peaked Jump Schelling Games

Tobias Friedrich, Pascal Lenzner[✉], Louise Molitor, and Lars Seifert

Hasso Plattner Institute, University of Potsdam, Potsdam, Germany
{tobias.friedrich,pascal.lenzner,louise.molitor}@hpi.de,
lars.seifert@student.hpi.de

Abstract. Schelling games model the wide-spread phenomenon of residential segregation in metropolitan areas from a game-theoretic point of view. In these games agents of different types each strategically select a node on a given graph that models the residential area to maximize their individual utility. The latter solely depends on the types of the agents on neighboring nodes and it has been a standard assumption to consider utility functions that are monotone in the number of same-type neighbors, i.e., more same-type neighbors yield higher utility. This simplifying assumption has recently been challenged since sociological poll results suggest that real-world agents actually favor diverse neighborhoods.

We contribute to the recent endeavor of investigating residential segregation models with realistic agent behavior by studying Jump Schelling Games with agents having a single-peaked utility function. In such games, there are empty nodes in the graph and agents can strategically jump to such nodes to improve their utility. We investigate the existence of equilibria and show that they exist under specific conditions. Contrasting this, we prove that even on simple topologies like paths or rings such stable states are not guaranteed to exist. Regarding the game dynamics, we show that improving response cycles exist independently of the position of the peak in the utility function. Moreover, we show high almost tight bounds on the Price of Anarchy and the Price of Stability with respect to the recently proposed degree of integration, which counts the number of agents with a diverse neighborhood. Last but not least, we show that computing a beneficial state with high integration is NP-complete and, as a novel conceptual contribution, we also show that it is NP-hard to decide if an equilibrium state can be found via improving response dynamics starting from a given initial state.

1 Introduction

Residential segregation [32], i.e., the emergence of regions in metropolitan areas that are homogeneous in terms of ethnicity or socio-economic status of its inhabitants, has been widely studied. Segregation has many negative consequences for the inhabitants of a city, for example, it negatively impacts their health [1]. The causes of segregation are complex and range from discriminatory laws to individual action. Schelling's classical agent-based model for residential segregation [28,29] specifies a spatial setting where individual agents with a bias towards

© The Author(s), under exclusive license to Springer Nature Switzerland AG 2023
A. Deligkas and A. Filos-Ratsikas (Eds.): SAGT 2023, LNCS 14238, pp. 111–126, 2023.
https://doi.org/10.1007/978-3-031-43254-5_7

favoring similar agents care only about the composition of their individual local neighborhoods. This model gives a coherent explanation for the widespread phenomenon of residential segregation, since it shows that local choices by the agents yield globally segregated states [15,30]. In Schelling's model two types of agents, placed on a path and a grid, respectively, act according to the following threshold behavior: agents are *content* with their current position if at least a τ-fraction of neighbors, with $\tau \in (0,1)$, is of their own type. Otherwise, they are discontent and want to move, either via swapping with another random discontent agent or via jumping to an empty position. Starting from a random distribution, Schelling showed empirically that the random process drifts towards segregation. This is to be expected if all agents are intolerant, i.e., for $\tau > \frac{1}{2}$. But Schelling's astonishing insight is that this also happens if all agents are tolerant, i.e., for $\tau \leq \frac{1}{2}$.

Many empirical studies have been conducted to investigate the influence of various parameters on the obtained segregation patterns [5,26,27]. In particular, the model has been studied by sociologists [4,11,16] with the help of sophisticated agent-based simulation frameworks such as SimSeg [18]. On the theoretical side, the underlying stochastic process leading to segregation was studied [3,9,21]. Furthermore, Schelling's model recently gained traction within Algorithmic Game Theory, Artificial Intelligence, and Multi-agent Systems [2,6,7,12–14,17,22,23].

Most of these papers are in line with the assumptions made by Schelling and incorporate monotone utility functions, i.e., the agents' utility is monotone in the fraction of same-type neighbors, cf. Fig. 1 (left). Although for $\tau < 1$ it is true that no agent prefers segregation locally, agents are equally content in segregated neighborhoods as they are in neighborhoods that just barely meet their tolerance thresholds. However, recent sociological surveys [31] show that people actually prefer to live in diverse rather than segregated neighborhoods[1]. Based on this, different models in which agents prefer integration have been proposed [26,33,34]. Recently, Bilò et al. [6] introduced the Single-Peaked Swap Schelling Game, where agents have single-peaked utility functions, cf. Fig. 1, and pairs of agents can swap their locations if this is beneficial for both of them.

Based on the model by Bilò et al. [6], we investigate the Jump Schelling Game (JSG), where agents can improve their utility by jumping to empty locations, assuming realistic agents having a single-peaked utility function.

Model. We consider a strategic game played on an undirected, connected graph $G = (V, E)$. For a given node $v \in V$, let $\delta(v)$ be its *degree* and let Δ_G be the *maximum degree* over all nodes $v \in V$. A graph is δ-*regular*, if $\forall v \in V : \delta(v) = \Delta_G$. We denote with $\alpha(G)$ the *independence number* of G, i.e., the cardinality of the maximum independent set in G.

A *Single-Peaked Jump Schelling Game* (G, r, b, p), called the *game*, is defined by a graph G, a pair of integers $r \geq 1$ and $1 \leq b \leq r$, and a single-peaked utility function p. There are two types of agents associated with the colors red and

---

[1] Respondents (on average 78% white) were asked what they think of "Living in a neighborhood where half of your neighbors were blacks?". In 2018 82% responded "strongly favor", "favor" or "neither favor nor oppose".

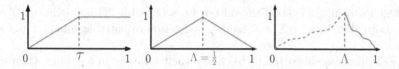

Fig. 1. Left: Schelling's original monotone threshold utility function. Middle+Right: single-peaked utility functions. The dashed line marks the utility of an agent if the fraction of same type neighbors meets the threshold and the peak, respectively

blue. We have r red agents and b blue agents. If $r = b$, we say that the game is *balanced*. Let $c(i)$ the color of agent i.

An agent's *strategy* is her position $v \in V$ on the graph. Each node can only be occupied by at most one agent. The $n = r + b$ strategic agents occupy a strict subset of the nodes in V, i.e., there are $e = |V| - n \geq 1$ *empty nodes*. A *strategy profile* $\sigma \in V^n$ is a vector of n distinct nodes in which the i-th entry $\sigma(i)$ corresponds to the strategy of the i-th agent. We say that an agent i is adjacent to a node v (or an agent j) if G has an edge between $\sigma(i)$ and v (resp. $\sigma(j)$). For convenience, we use σ^{-1} as a mapping from a node $v \in V$ to the agent occupying v or $\ominus$ if v is empty. The set of empty nodes is $\emptyset(\sigma) = \{v \in V \mid \sigma^{-1}(v) = \ominus\}$.

For an agent i, we define $C_i(\sigma) = \{v \in V \setminus \emptyset(V) \mid c(\sigma^{-1}(v)) = c(i)\}$ as the set of nodes occupied by agents of the same color in σ. The *closed neighborhood* of an agent i in a strategy profile σ is $N[i, \sigma] = \{\sigma(i)\} \cup \{v \in V \setminus \emptyset(\sigma) \mid \{v, \sigma(i)\} \in E\}$. The agents care about the fraction $f_i(\sigma)$ of agents of their own color, including themselves, in their closed neighborhood where $f_i(\sigma) = \frac{|N[i,\sigma] \cap C_i(\sigma)|}{|N[i,\sigma]|}$. If $f_i(\sigma) = 1$, we say that agent i is *segregated*. Furthermore, observe that we have $f_i(\sigma) > 0$ for any agent i, since $\sigma(i) \in N[i, \sigma]$. Also, we emphasize that our definition of $f_i(\sigma)$ deviates from similar definitions in related work. In particular, the papers [2,14,17] exclude the respective agent i from her neighborhood, while Kanellopoulos et al. [22] count agent i only in the denominator of $f_i(\sigma)$. The different existing definitions of the homogeneity of a neighborhood all have their individual strengths and weaknesses. We decided to follow the definition of Bilò et al. [6]. The key idea of their definition is that agents contribute to the diversity of their neighborhood. Thus, agents actively strive for integration. We think that this best captures the single-peaked setting.

The *utility* of an agent i is $U_i(\sigma) = p(f_i(\sigma))$, with p being an arbitrary single-peaked function with peak $\Lambda \in (0, 1)$ and the following properties: (1) $p(0) = 0$ and $p(x)$ is strictly monotonically increasing on $[0, \Lambda]$, (2) for all $x \in [\Lambda, 1]$ it holds that $p(x) = p(\frac{\Lambda(1-x)}{1-\Lambda})$, i.e., it is symmetric to the other side of Λ but possibly squeezed. W.l.o.g., we further assume that $p(\Lambda) = 1$. See Fig. 1 (middle and right). We explicitly exclude $\Lambda = 1$ and from our definition follows $p(1) = 0$. Allowing $\Lambda = 1$ would allow monotone utilities, similar to the models in [2,14], where agents actively strive for segregation or passively accept it. In contrast, we assume that agents actively strive for diversity. Thus, a homogeneous neighborhood should not be acceptable. This justifies $p(1) = 0$. Hence, both $\Lambda < 1$ and $p(1) = 0$ model integration-oriented agents and go hand in hand.

The strategic agents attempt to choose their strategy to maximize their utility. The only way in which an agent can change her strategy is to *jump*, i.e., to choose an empty node $v \in \emptyset(\sigma)$ as her new location. We denote the resulting strategy profile after a jump of agent i to a node v as σ_{iv}. A jump is *improving*, if $U_i(\sigma) < U_i(\sigma_{iv})$. A strategy profile σ is a (pure) *Nash Equilibrium* (NE) if and only if there are no improving jumps, i.e., for all agents i and nodes $v \in \emptyset(\sigma)$, we have $U_i(\sigma) \geq U_i(\sigma_{iv})$.

A measure to quantify the amount of segregation in a strategy profile σ is the *degree of integration* (DoI), which counts the number of non-segregated agents, hence $\mathrm{DoI}(\sigma) = |\{i \mid f_i(\sigma) < 1\}|$. For a game (G, r, b, p), let σ^* be a strategy profile that maximizes the DoI and let $\mathrm{NE}(G, r, b, p)$ be its set of Nash Equilibria. We evaluate the impact of the agents' selfishness on the overall social welfare by studying the *Price of Anarchy* (PoA), defined as $\mathrm{PoA}(G, r, b, p) = \frac{\mathrm{DoI}(\sigma^*)}{\min_{\sigma \in NE(G,r,b,p)} \mathrm{DoI}(\sigma)}$ and the *Price of Stability* (PoS), defined as $\mathrm{PoS}(G, r, b, p) = \frac{\mathrm{DoI}(\sigma^*)}{\max_{\sigma \in NE(G,r,b,p)} \mathrm{DoI}(\sigma)}$. If the best (resp. worst) NE has a DoI of 0, the PoS (resp. PoA) is unbounded.

A game has the *finite improvement property* (FIP) if and only if, starting from any strategy profile σ, the game will always reach a NE in a finite number of steps. As proven by Monderer and Shapley [25], this is equivalent to the game being a *generalized ordinal potential game*. In particular, the FIP does not hold if there is a cycle of strategy profiles $\sigma^0, \sigma^1, \ldots, \sigma^k = \sigma^0$, such that for any $k' < k$, there is an agent i and empty node $v \in \emptyset(\sigma^{k'})$ with $\sigma^{k'+1} = \sigma_{iv}^{k'}$ and $U_i(\sigma^{k'}) < U_i(\sigma^{k'+1})$. These cycles are known as *improving response cycles* (IRCs).

Related Work. Game-theoretic models for residential segregation were first studied by Chauhan et al. [14] and later extended by Echzell et al. [17]. There, agents have a monotone utility function as shown in Fig. 1 (left). Additionally, agents may also have location preferences. Agarwal et al. [2] consider a simplified model using the most extreme monotone threshold-based utility function with $\tau = 1$. They prove results on the existence of equilibria, in particular, that equilibria are not guaranteed to exist on trees, and on the complexity of deciding equilibrium existence. Also, they introduce the DoI as social welfare measure and they study the PoA in terms of utilitarian social welfare and in terms of the DoI. The complexity results were extended by Kreisel et al. [24], in particular, they show that deciding the existence of NE in the swap version as well as in the jump version of the simplified model is NP-hard. Bilò et al. [7] strengthen the PoA results for the swap version w.r.t. the utilitarian social welfare function and investigate the model on almost regular graphs, grids and paths. Additionally, they introduce a variant with locality. Chan et al. [13] study a variant of the JSG with $\tau = 1$, where the agents' utility is a function of the neighborhood composition and of the social influence. Kanellopoulos et al. [23] considered a generalized variant, where the agent types are linearly ordered. Another novel variant of the JSG, that includes an agent when counting the neighborhood size, was investigated by Kanellopoulos et al. [22]. This subtle change leads to agents preferring locations with more own-type neighbors. Bullinger et al. [12] measure social welfare via the number of agents with non-zero utility, they prove hardness results for computing the social optimum and discuss other solution concepts.

Most related is the recent work by Bilò et al. [6], which studies the same model as we do, but there only pairs of agents can improve their utility by swapping their locations. They find that equilibria are not guaranteed to exist in general, but they do exist for $\Lambda = \frac{1}{2}$ on bipartite graphs and for $\Lambda \leq \frac{1}{2}$ on almost regular graphs. The latter is shown via an ordinal potential function, i.e., convergence of IRDs is guaranteed. For the PoA they prove an upper bound of $\min\{\Delta(G), \frac{n}{b+1}\}$ and give almost tight lower bounds for bipartite graphs and regular graphs. Also, they lower bound the PoS by $\Omega(\sqrt{n\Lambda})$ and give constant bounds on bipartite and almost regular graphs. Note that due to the existence of empty nodes in our model, our results cannot be directly compared.

Also related are hedonic diversity games [8,10,20] where selfish agents form coalitions and the utility of an agent only depends on the type distribution of her coalition. For such games, single-peaked utility functions yield favorable game-theoretic properties.

Our Contribution. We investigate Jump Schelling Games with agents having a single-peaked utility function. In contrast to monotone utility functions studied in earlier works, this assumption better reflects recent sociological poll results on real-world agent behavior [31]. Moreover, this transition to a different type of utility function is also interesting from a technical point of view since it yields insights into the properties of Schelling-type systems under different preconditions.

Regarding the existence of pure NE, we provide a collection of positive and negative results. On the negative side, we show that NE are not guaranteed to exist on the simplest possible topologies, i.e., on paths and rings with single-peaked utilities with $\Lambda \geq \frac{1}{2}$. This is in contrast to the version with monotone utilities where for the case of rings NE always exist. On the positive side, we give various conditions that enable NE existence, e.g., such states are guaranteed to exist if the underlying graph has a sufficiently large independent set, or if it has sufficiently many degree 1 nodes. The situation is worse for the convergence of game dynamics. We show that even on regular graphs IRCs exist independently of the position of the peak in the utility function. Moreover, this even holds for the special case with $\Lambda = \frac{1}{2}$ and only a single empty node. These negative results for $\Lambda \leq \frac{1}{2}$ also represent a marked contrast to the swap version, where convergence is guaranteed for this case on almost regular graphs.

With regard to the quality of the equilibria, we focus on the DoI as social cost function. This measure has gained popularity since it can be understood as a simple proxy for the obtained segregation strength. For the PoA w.r.t. the DoI, we establish that the technique from Bilò et al. [6] can be carried over to our setting. This yields the same PoA upper bound of $\min\{\Delta(G), n/(b+1)\}$.

Subsequently, we give almost matching PoA lower bounds and we prove that also the lower bounds for the PoS almost match this high upper bound. On the positive side, we show that on graphs with a sufficiently large independent set, the PoS depends on the ratio of the largest and the smallest node degree, which implies a PoS of 1 on regular graphs that also holds for rings with a single empty node.

Last but not least, we consider the complexity aspects of our model. Analogously to previous work on the Jump Schelling Game with monotone utilities and to work on Swap Schelling Games with single-peaked utilities, we focus on the hardness of computing a strategy profile with a high degree of integration. Using a novel technique relying on the MAX SAT problem, we show that this problem is NP-complete, improving on an earlier result by Agarwal et al. [2]. Moreover, as a novel conceptual contribution, we investigate the hardness of finding an equilibrium state via improving response dynamics. As one of our main results, we show that this problem is NP-hard. So far, researchers have studied the complexity of deciding the existence of an equilibrium for a given instance of a Schelling Game. We depart from this, since even if it can be decided efficiently that for some instance an equilibrium exists, guiding the agents towards this equilibrium from a given initial state is complicated, since this would involve a potentially very complex centrally coordinated relocation of many agents in a single step. In contrast, reaching an equilibrium via a sequence of improving moves is much easier to coordinate, since in every step the respective move can be recommended and, since this is an improving move, the agents will follow this advice.

Overall we find that making the model more realistic by employing single-peaked utilities entails a significantly different behavior of the model compared to the variant with monotone utilities but also compared to Single-Peaked Swap Schelling Games.

We refer to the full version [19] for all omitted details.

2   Game Dynamics

We show that even on very simple graph classes improving response dynamics are not guaranteed to converge to stable states. Moreover, we provide IRCs for the entire range of Λ. Note, that given an IRC for a game on a graph G IRCs exist for all games on any graph H that contains G as a node-induced subgraph since we can add empty nodes to G to obtain H without interfering with the IRC. We start with an IRC for $\Lambda \geq \frac{1}{2}$.

Theorem 1. *For $\Lambda \geq \frac{1}{2}$, the FIP does not hold even on rings and paths with $e \geq 2$.*

Proof. Consider a game with five nodes, two red agents and one blue agent on a ring or path. We start with a strategy profile in which the blue agent is adjacent to both red agents. An illustration is given in Fig. 2. As $\Lambda \geq \frac{1}{2}$, the blue agent prefers to be in a neighborhood with only one of the red agents. Hence,

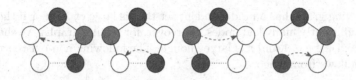

Fig. 2. IRC on a ring (path without the dotted edge) for $\Lambda \geq \frac{1}{2}$.

an improving jump from the blue agent results in one segregated red agent. As a consequence the red agent jumps to the node adjacent to the blue agent. Further, observe that at no point in this cycle does any other agent have an improving jump and none of the jumping agents have an alternative improving jump (except for symmetry).   □

We now show that IRCs also exist if $\Lambda \leq \frac{1}{2}$.

Theorem 2. *For $\Lambda \leq \frac{1}{2}$, the FIP does not hold even on regular graphs.*

Even for $\Lambda = \frac{1}{2}$ and $e = 1$ no convergence is guaranteed.

Theorem 3. *For $\Lambda = \frac{1}{2}$, the FIP does not hold even on regular graphs with $e = 1$.*

On the positive side, convergence is guaranteed on rings.

Theorem 4. *On rings, the game with $e = 1$ and $\Lambda = \frac{1}{2}$ is an ordinal potential game. It converges after at most n steps.*

Proof. We claim that for each improving jump of an agent i to a node v, we have $\mathrm{DoI}(\sigma_{iv}) \geq \mathrm{DoI}(\sigma) + 1$. Hence, $\mathrm{DoI}(\sigma)$ is an ordinal potential function and a NE must be reached after at most n improving jumps.

Assume there is an agent i with an improving jump to v, i.e., $U_i(\sigma) < U_i(\sigma_{iv})$. We claim $U_i(\sigma) = 0$. Assume $U_i(\sigma) > 0$, i.e., either $p\left(\frac{1}{2}\right) = 1$ or $p\left(\frac{1}{3}\right) = p\left(\frac{2}{3}\right)$. In the first case, agent i already has the highest possible utility and thus no incentive to jump. In the second case $\left(U_i(\sigma) = p\left(\frac{1}{3}\right)\right)$, we must have $U_i(\sigma_{iv}) = 1$. But since v is the only empty node this is only possible if $\sigma(i)$ and v are adjacent. However, this requires $|N[i, \sigma]| = 2 \neq 3$.

Therefore, in σ, agent i is not adjacent to any agent of the other color and in σ_{iv} adjacent to at least one agent of the other color. Thus, any agent adjacent to i that has a utility larger than 0 in σ still has a utility larger than 0 in σ_{iv}. Also, no agent adjacent to v can drop to utility 0 because of i jumping to v. Thus, we have $\mathrm{DoI}(\sigma) + 1 \leq \mathrm{DoI}(\sigma_{iv})$.   □

3 Existence of Equilibria

A fundamental question is if NE always exist. We start with a negative result that even on rings existence of equilibria is not guaranteed for $\Lambda \geq \frac{1}{2}$. However, in certain cases, we can provide existential results. In particular, equilibria exist if the underlying graph has an independent set that is large enough or if the graph contains sufficiently many leaf nodes. Moreover, for regular graphs, we show that equilibria exist if $e = 1$ and r is large enough. The following non-existence result for rings follows from Theorem 1.

Corollary 1. *Even on rings, the existence of equilibria for the game is not guaranteed for $\Lambda \geq \frac{1}{2}$.*

If the independence number is at least the number of blue agents plus the number of empty nodes, existence of NE is guaranteed. This result is similar to the swap version [6].

Theorem 5. *Every game on a graph with an independent set of size $\alpha(G) \geq b+e$ has a NE.*

Thus, if r is large enough NE always exist on bipartite graphs.

Corollary 2. *Every game with $r \geq \frac{|V|}{2}$ on a bipartite graph admits an efficiently computable NE.*

Next, we show that for $\Lambda \geq \frac{1}{2}$ games with a low number of empty nodes and a low difference between the number of red and blue agents proportional to the number of empty nodes admit a NE. To this end, we consider a special kind of independent sets.

Definition 1. *A maximum degree independent set (max-deg IS) is an independent set I, such that $\forall u \in I, v \in V \setminus I : \delta(v) \leq \delta(u)$. The size of the largest max-deg IS of a graph G is $\alpha^{\max \delta}(G)$.*

Note that for any graph, it holds that $\alpha^{\max \delta}(G) \geq 1$.

Theorem 6. *Let G be a graph with $e \leq \alpha^{\max \delta}(G)$ and $e \leq \frac{r-b}{\Delta_G}$. For $\Lambda \geq \frac{1}{2}$, the game has a NE.*

Proof. Let I be a max-deg IS of size e. Since $e \leq \alpha^{\max \delta}(G)$, this exists. We place red agents on all nodes adjacent to nodes in I. For this, we need at most $\Delta_G \cdot e$ red agents. We have r' red agents left and $r' \geq r - \Delta_G \cdot e \geq b$.

We claim that we can place the remaining agents on the remaining nodes, such that every blue agent is adjacent to at least one red agent. For this, consider the layer graph rooted at an imaginary node that results from merging all e nodes in I, cf. Fig. 3. Let the root layer be layer 0. Note that therefore, layer 1 is fully occupied by the $r - r'$ red agents we placed in the first step. Let L_2 be the set of nodes in all even layers (except for layer 0) and L_3 be the set of nodes in all odd layers (except for layer 1).

All nodes in L_2 (resp. L_3) have at least one adjacent node not in L_2 (resp. L_3). Also, we have $|L_2| + |L_3| = r' + b$. Hence, $|L_2|$ or $|L_3|$ is at least $\frac{r'+b}{2}$. Since $r' \geq b$, it follows $b \leq \frac{r'+b}{2}$, so there is $L \in \{L_2, L_3\}$ with $|L| \geq b$. We place all blue nodes in L and all red nodes on the remaining empty spots in L_2, L_3. Then, every blue node has at least one red neighbor.

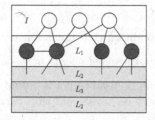

Fig. 3. The layer graph. We first have an independent set I of e nodes, then a layer L_1 of at most $\Delta_G \cdot e$ red agents. The nodes in the following layers are either part of L_2 (for even layers) or L_3 (for odd layers). (Color figure online)

The placement σ is stable. As all empty nodes are adjacent to only red nodes, no red agent wants to jump. Let i be a blue agent and u be an empty node. By construction, $\sigma(i) \notin I$ and $u \in I$. At least one neighbor of $\sigma(i)$ is red, hence i has a non-zero utility. Since $\Lambda \geq \frac{1}{2}$, the worst non-zero utility is $p\left(\frac{1}{\delta(\sigma(i))+1}\right)$. Thus, $U_i(\sigma) \geq p\left(\frac{1}{\delta(\sigma(i))+1}\right)$ and since all neighbors of u are red, $U_i(\sigma_{iu}) = p\left(\frac{1}{\delta(u)+1}\right)$. As I is a max-deg IS, we have $\delta(\sigma(i)) \leq \delta(u)$. Furthermore, it follows from $\Lambda \geq \frac{1}{2}$ that $p\left(\frac{1}{\delta(u)+1}\right) \leq p\left(\frac{1}{\delta(\sigma(i))+1}\right) = U_i(\sigma)$. Hence, i has no improving jump. $\square$

Note that for regular graphs any independent set is a max-deg IS, i.e., $\alpha^{\max \delta}(G) = \alpha(G) \geq \frac{|V|}{\delta+1}$.

Corollary 3. *Any game on a δ-regular graph G with $e \leq \alpha(G)$, $r \geq b + \delta \cdot e$ and $\Lambda \geq \frac{1}{2}$ has NE.*

Next, we show that graphs with a large number of leaves admit NE. In particular, this applies to trees with many leaves, e.g., stars.

Theorem 7. *Every game with $\Lambda \geq \frac{1}{2}$ on a graph with at least b nodes of degree one admits NE.*

While even for regular graphs with $e = 1$ the FIP is violated, we can guarantee the existence of NE with further conditions.

Theorem 8. *For any game on a δ-regular graph with $\Lambda \geq \frac{1}{2}$, $r \geq \delta$ and $e = 1$, equilibria exist and can be computed efficiently.*

4   Price of Anarchy and Stability

We study the PoA and PoS of the game with respect to the DoI. We already showed that the existence of equilibria is not guaranteed for many instances, yet, we still give bounds that apply whenever equilibria do exist.

4.1   Price of Anarchy

We start with a necessary condition that holds for any NE.

Lemma 1. *No NE contains segregated agents of different colors.*

As shown in [6], Lemma 1 can be used to get a bound on the PoA for the swap version. The proofs do not rely on swaps and thus carry over.

Lemma 2. *For any game and σ, we have $DoI(\sigma) \leq \min((\Delta_G + 1)b, n)$.*

With this, we get the same upper bound as in [6].

Theorem 9 ([6]). *For any game, the PoA is at most $\min\left(\Delta_G, \frac{n}{b+1}\right)$.*

It still remains to be shown that this upper bound is tight. We show that this is, asymptotically with respect to Δ_G, the case for general graphs.

Theorem 10. *For any Λ, there exists a game with PoA $\frac{n}{b+1} = \Delta_G - 1$.*

Proof. For some $\delta \geq 4$, consider the game (G, r, b, p) with $b = \delta - 1, r = b^2$ depicted in Fig. 4. The graph G has a node v adjacent to a set B of b nodes. Further, v is adjacent to another node, which lies on a path of altogether b nodes, which at the same time represent the root of a tree. Hence, each node on this path is adjacent to one node in B', each of which is adjacent to b nodes in total. Observe that $\Delta_G = \delta$ and $e = b + 1$.

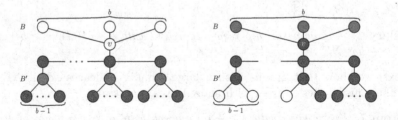

Fig. 4. A game with $b = \Delta_G - 1$ and $r = b^2$. The middle row is a path of b many nodes occupied by red agents. The dots in the lower row are representative for the rest of the $b - 1$ many leaf nodes. Left: Optimum σ^* with $DoI(\sigma^*) = \Delta_G(\Delta_G - 1) = n$. Right: NE σ with $DoI(\sigma) = b + 1 = \Delta_G$. (Color figure online)

There is an optimal strategy profile σ^* in which all nodes in B' are occupied by blue agents and all nodes outside of $B \cup B' \cup \{v\}$ are occupied by red agents. We have that $DoI(\sigma^*) = \Delta_G(\Delta_G - 1) = n$. Also, there is a NE σ in which the blue agents occupy B and $b + 1$ of the leaf nodes adjacent to nodes in B' are empty. Since each blue agent is adjacent to exactly one red agent, we have for any red agent i and empty node u that $U_i(\sigma) = U_i(\sigma_{iu}) = p\left(\frac{1}{2}\right)$. Thus, we have that σ is a NE. Only the blue agents and one red agent are not segregated, hence it holds that $DoI(\sigma) = b + 1 = \Delta_G$. Thus, we have that $PoA(G, r, b, p) \geq \frac{n}{b+1} = \frac{\Delta_G(\Delta_G - 1)}{\Delta_G}$.   □

Single-Peaked Jump Schelling Games   121

We use a similar construction as in [6] to also obtain a lower bound for a regular graph. Yet, in our case the bound holds for all values of Λ.

Theorem 11. *For every $\delta \geq 2$ and Λ, a game (G, r, b, p) on a δ-regular graph with $PoA(G, r, b, p) \geq \frac{\delta(\delta+1)}{2\delta+1} = \frac{\delta+1}{2} - \frac{\delta+1}{4\delta+2}$ exists.*

If $r = b$, Theorem 9 yields that $PoA \leq \frac{2b}{b+1} < 2$. This is tight.

Theorem 12. *For any Λ and b, there is a balanced game (G, b, b, p) with $PoA(G, b, b, p) = \frac{2b}{b+1}$.*

4.2 Price of Stability

We give bounds on the PoS under different conditions. First, we observe from Theorem 9, that for any game the PoS is at most $\min\left(\Delta_G, \frac{n}{b+1}\right)$. We now present a lower bound which is asymptotically tight for $b = 1$.

Theorem 13. *For any $\Lambda \geq \frac{1}{2}$, there is a game on a tree with $PoS = \frac{\Delta_G}{2} = \frac{n-2}{2} = \frac{n-2}{b+1}$.*

Next, we study balanced games. Here, the PoS is upper bounded by a PoA of at most 2. We show that this bound is tight for $\Lambda \geq \frac{1}{2}$.

Theorem 14. *For $\Lambda \geq \frac{1}{2}$, a game (G, b, b, p) with $PoS(G, b, b, p) \geq 2 - \varepsilon$ for any $\varepsilon > 0$ exists.*

Proof. Consider the balanced game (G, b, b, p) as shown in Fig. 5. The graph G has two sets A and B of b nodes each and the i-th node in A is connected to the i-th node in B. Furthermore, the first node $v \in A$ is connected to all nodes in both, A and B. Additionally, the node v is adjacent to $2b$ leaf nodes Z.

In the optimal strategy profile σ^*, all red nodes are located on A and all blue nodes on B. Thus, it holds that $\mathrm{DoI}(\sigma^*) = 2b$. We claim that there is no equilibrium σ in which v is empty or any agent of the opposite color of $\sigma^{-1}(v)$ is adjacent to any agent of $c(\sigma^{-1}(v))$ other than $\sigma^{-1}(v)$.

Suppose that v is empty. There are $2b - 1$ nodes in $B \cup A \setminus \{v\}$. Thus by counting, there must be an agent i on a node in Z. As v is empty, we have

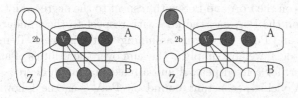

Fig. 5. The PoS of a balanced game with b agents per type. A and B contain b nodes each. Left: Optimum. Right: Best NE, where b nodes in Z are occupied by blue agents. (Color figure online)

that $U_i(\sigma) = 0$. Yet, it holds that $U_i(\sigma_{iv}) = p(\frac{b}{2b}) > 0$, so agent i has an improving jump. W.l.o.g., let there be a red agent on v. Suppose that a blue agent i is adjacent to an additional red agent that is not $\sigma(v)$. Then, we have that $U_i(\sigma) = p(\frac{1}{3})$. As there are $2b$ nodes in Z and neither $\sigma^{-1}(v)$ nor i are on a node in Z, there is an empty node $u \in Z$ and since $U_i(\sigma_{iu}) = p(\frac{1}{2}) > U_i(\sigma)$ agent i has an improving jump. Thus, v is not empty and all red agents except for $\sigma^{-1}(v)$ are segregated. For any equilibrium, it holds that at most the agent on v and the agents of a different color may be non-segregated, i.e., $\text{DoI}(\sigma) \leq b + 1$. Figure 5 shows such a NE: All nodes in A are occupied by red agents, all nodes in B are empty and b nodes in Z are blue. Clearly, no red agent can improve and any blue agent jumping to a node in B will have a utility of either $p(\frac{1}{2})$ or $p(\frac{1}{3})$ which is no improvement. Hence, $\text{PoS}(G, b, b, p) \geq \frac{2b}{b+1}$. Thus, for any $\varepsilon > 0$, we can achieve a $PoS \geq 2 - \varepsilon$ by choosing b large enough. $\qquad \square$

Earlier, in Theorem 5, we proved the existence of equilibria for graphs that have an independent set of size at least $b + e$. Now, we show that on such graphs, we can also bound the PoS.

Theorem 15. *For any game (G, r, b, p) with $b + e \leq \alpha(G)$, we have $PoS(G, r, b, p) \leq \frac{\Delta_G + 1}{\delta_G + 1}$.*

Theorem 15 applies to δ-regular graphs. Note that for any δ-regular graph, we have $\alpha(G) \geq \frac{|V|}{\delta + 1}$.

Corollary 4. *For any game on a δ-regular graph with $b + e \leq \alpha(G)$, we have $PoS(G, r, b, \Lambda) = 1$.*

Furthermore, in Theorem 4, we prove that any game on a ring with $\Lambda = \frac{1}{2}$ and $e = 1$ converges to a NE by proving that $\text{DoI}(\sigma)$ is an ordinal potential function. It follows that every strategy profile that maximizes the degree of integration must be a NE.

Corollary 5. *For any game $(G, r, b, \frac{1}{2})$ on a ring with $e = 1$, we have $PoS(G, r, b, \frac{1}{2}) = 1$.*

4.3   Quality of Equilibria w.r.t. the Utilitarian Welfare

While our main focus in this work is on the quality of equilibria with respect to the degree of integration as social welfare, we close this section by pointing out, that our results on the PoA and PoS with respect to the degree of integration also imply bounds on the PoA and the PoS with respect to the standard utilitarian welfare (PoA^U and PoS^U for short), assuming that p is linear. Remember, that the utilitarian social welfare simply is the sum over the utilities of all the agents.

In particular, for a fixed peak Λ and a fixed maximum degree δ, a constant bound on PoA yields a constant bound on PoA^U, as the following theorem demonstrates.

Theorem 16. *Let p be a linear function. For any game $\Gamma = (G, r, b, \Lambda)$, the following holds:*

- $PoA(\Gamma) \le a \Rightarrow PoA^U(\Gamma) \le a \cdot \max(\Lambda, (1 - \Lambda)) \cdot (\Delta_G + 1)$.
- $PoS(\Gamma) \le s \Rightarrow PoS^U(\Gamma) \le s \cdot \max(\Lambda, (1 - \Lambda)) \cdot (\Delta_G + 1)$.

For the PoA, this bound is asymptotically tight, i.e., $PoA^U(G, b, b, \frac{1}{2}) = PoA(G, b, b, \frac{1}{2}) \cdot \frac{1}{2} \cdot \Delta_G$ holds.

5   Computational Complexity

We discuss the computational complexity of finding equilibria via improving response dynamics and the complexity of computing strategy profiles with a high DoI. Especially the former question is particularly interesting, since finding equilibria via improving moves can be easily coordinated within a society of selfish agents. In contrast, centrally switching from some initial state directly to an equilibrium state requires much more coordination and also that the agents trust the central coordinator.

Settling the complexity of the equilibrium decision problem seems to be very challenging and we leave this as an open problem. However, our hardness proof for finding equilibria via improving response dynamics can be seen as a first step towards proving that deciding the existence of equilibria is NP-hard as well. Moreover, we note in passing that if we would allow for stubborn agents, as in [2], then we can prove that deciding if an equilibrium exists is indeed NP-hard. We suspect that this assumption may be removed, similarly to the approach of [24].

5.1   Finding Equilibria via Improving Response Dynamics

We investigate the problem of finding equilibria. We consider the problem of deciding whether an equilibrium for a given game can be reached through *improving response dynamics (IRDs)* from a given initial strategy profile σ_0. We show that this problem is NP-hard for any value of Λ.

Theorem 17. *For any fixed $\Lambda = \frac{x}{y} \in (0, 1)$, it is NP-hard to decide if a given game played on a graph G with r red and b blue agents can reach a NE through IRDs starting from a given initial placement σ_0.*

5.2   Existence of Strategy Profiles with High DoI

We aim for finding a strategy profile with a DoI larger than some threshold d. This problem is indifferent to the utilities of the agents and thus the same for any Jump Schelling Game. For $d = n$, the hardness of this problem has been studied before by [2]. However, their focus lies on swap games and therefore assumes $|V| = n$. As noted by the authors this result can be generalized to $|V| > n$ by adding isolated empty nodes. We improve on their result by showing that the hardness holds in a more realistic setting without isolated nodes.

Theorem 18. *Given a JSG with r red and b blue agents on a connected graph $G = (V, E)$ with $|V| > n$, it is NP-complete to decide if there is a strategy profile σ^* with $DoI(\sigma^*) \ge d$.*

6 Discussion

Our paper sheds light on Jump Schelling Games with non-monotone agent utilities. With this, we strengthen the recent trend of investigating more realistic residential segregation models.

6.1 Comparison with Single-Peaked Swap Schelling Games

Similarly to other variants of Schelling games, we also observe that our jump version behaves very differently compared to the swap version studied by Bilò et al. [6] and novel techniques are required. The main difference in jump games is that structural properties of the underlying graph cannot be exploited. The reason is that empty nodes are not counted when computing an agent's utility and hence it is impossible to distinguish between an empty node or a missing node. We do carry over some ideas from Single-Peaked Swap Schelling Games, e.g., the PoA upper bound proof, or the idea of considering independent sets, but the main part of our paper, e.g., all lower bound proofs and the proofs of our hardness results, follow entirely new approaches.

We obtained predominantly negative results with regard to convergence towards equilibria, in particular the finite improvement property does not hold for any $\Lambda \in (0,1)$, not even on regular graphs or trees. This is in stark contrast to the swap version, which converges to equilibria even on almost regular graphs for $\Lambda \leq \frac{1}{2}$. Furthermore, on regular graphs with $\Lambda = \frac{1}{2}$, instances of our jump version exist that do not admit equilibria. Also, although we get similar PoA bounds, compared to the swap version, we find that the PoS of the jump version tends to be worse, in particular, while the swap version has a PoS of at most 2 on bipartite graphs for $\Lambda = \frac{1}{2}$, there exists a tree that enforces a PoS that is linear in n for our jump version for this setting.

6.2 The Variant with Self-exclusive Neighborhoods

To enable a better comparison with the models by Chauhan et al. [14] and Agarwal et al. [2], that do not count the agent herself in the computation of the fraction of same-type neighbors, we also considered a variant of our model with self-exclusive neighborhoods, i.e., where the agent herself is not contained in her neighborhood. This self-exclusive variant behaves in some aspects very similarly to our model: the FIP does not hold and there is no equilibrium existence guarantee on regular graphs. Regarding the PoA it gets even worse, since equilibria exist where every agent has utility 0, implying an unbounded PoA. This also holds for the PoA with respect to the utilitarian social welfare. Moreover, also the PoA and the PoS with respect to the utilitarian welfare is unbounded.

References

1. Acevedo-Garcia, D., Lochner, K.A.: Residential Segregation and Health. Oxford University Press (2003). https://doi.org/10.1093/acprof:oso/9780195138382.003.0012

2. Agarwal, A., Elkind, E., Gan, J., Igarashi, A., Suksompong, W., Voudouris, A.A.: Schelling games on graphs. Artif. Intell. **301**, 103576 (2021). https://doi.org/10. 1016/j.artint.2021.103576

3. Barmpalias, G., Elwes, R., Lewis-Pye, A.: Digital morphogenesis via schelling segregation. In: 55th IEEE Annual Symposium on Foundations of Computer Science, FOCS, pp. 156–165. IEEE Computer Society (2014). https://doi.org/10. 1109/FOCS.2014.25

4. Benard, S., Willer, R.: A wealth and status-based model of residential segregation. J. Math. Sociol. **31**(2), 149–174 (2007). https://doi.org/10.1080/ 00222500601188486

5. Benenson, I., Hatna, E., Or, E.: From schelling to spatially explicit modeling of urban ethnic and economic residential dynamics. Sociol. Methods Res. **37**(4), 463– 497 (2009). https://doi.org/10.1177/0049124109334792

6. Bilò, D., Bilò, V., Lenzner, P., Molitor, L.: Tolerance is necessary for stability: single-peaked swap schelling games. In: Proceedings of the 31st International Joint Conference on Artificial Intelligence, IJCAI 2022, pp. 81–87. ijcai.org (2022). https://doi.org/10.24963/ijcai.2022/12

7. Bilò, D., Bilò, V., Lenzner, P., Molitor, L.: Topological influence and locality in swap schelling games. Auton. Agents Multi-Agent Syst. **36**(2), 47 (2022). https:// doi.org/10.1007/s10458-022-09573-7

8. Boehmer, N., Elkind, E.: Individual-based stability in hedonic diversity games. In: 34th AAAI Conference on Artificial Intelligence, AAAI, pp. 1822–1829. AAAI Press (2020). https://ojs.aaai.org/index.php/AAAI/article/view/5549

9. Brandt, C., Immorlica, N., Kamath, G., Kleinberg, R.: An analysis of one-dimensional schelling segregation. In: Proceedings of the 44th Symposium on Theory of Computing Conference, STOC, pp. 789–804. ACM (2012). https://doi.org/ 10.1145/2213977.2214048

10. Bredereck, R., Elkind, E., Igarashi, A.: Hedonic diversity games. In: Proceedings of the 18th International Conference on Autonomous Agents and MultiAgent Systems, AAMAS, pp. 565–573. International Foundation for Autonomous Agents and Multiagent Systems (2019)

11. Bruch, E.E.: How population structure shapes neighborhood segregation. Am. J. Sociol. **119**(5), 1221–1278 (2014). https://doi.org/10.1086/675411

12. Bullinger, M., Suksompong, W., Voudouris, A.A.: Welfare guarantees in schelling segregation. J. Artif. Intell. Res. **71**, 143–174 (2021). https://doi.org/10.1613/jair. 1.12771

13. Chan, H., Irfan, M.T., Than, C.V.: Schelling models with localized social influence: a game-theoretic framework. In: Proceedings of the 19th International Conference on Autonomous Agents and Multiagent Systems, AAMAS, pp. 240–248. International Foundation for Autonomous Agents and Multiagent Systems (2020). https://doi.org/10.5555/3398761.3398794

14. Chauhan, A., Lenzner, P., Molitor, L.: Schelling segregation with strategic agents. In: Deng, X. (ed.) SAGT 2018. LNCS, vol. 11059, pp. 137–149. Springer, Cham (2018). https://doi.org/10.1007/978-3-319-99660-8_13

15. Clark, W.A.V.: Residential segregation in American cities: a review and interpretation. Popul. Res. Policy Rev. **5**(2), 95–127 (1986). http://www.jstor.org/stable/ 40229819

16. Clark, W.A.V., Fossett, M.: Understanding the social context of the schelling segregation model. Proc. Natl. Acad. Sci. **105**(11), 4109–4114 (2008). https://doi.org/ 10.1073/pnas.070815510

17. Echzell, H., et al.: Convergence and hardness of strategic schelling segregation. In: Caragiannis, I., Mirrokni, V., Nikolova, E. (eds.) WINE 2019. LNCS, vol. 11920, pp. 156–170. Springer, Cham (2019). https://doi.org/10.1007/978-3-030-35389-6_12

18. Fossett, M.A.: Simseg-a computer program to simulate the dynamics of residential segregation by social and ethnic status. Race and Ethnic Studies Institute Technical Report and Program, Texas A&M University (1998)

19. Friedrich, T., Lenzner, P., Molitor, L., Seifert, L.: Single-peaked jump schelling games (2023). https://doi.org/10.48550/ARXIV.2302.12107. https://arxiv.org/abs/2302.12107

20. Ganian, R., Hamm, T., Knop, D., Schierreich, S., Suchý, O.: Hedonic diversity games: a complexity picture with more than two colors. In: 36th AAAI Conference on Artificial Intelligence, AAAI, pp. 5034–5042 (2022). https://ojs.aaai.org/index.php/AAAI/article/view/20435

21. Immorlica, N., Kleinberg, R., Lucier, B., Zadomighaddam, M.: Exponential segregation in a two-dimensional schelling model with tolerant individuals. In: Proceedings of the 28th Annual ACM-SIAM Symposium on Discrete Algorithms, SODA, pp. 984–993. SIAM (2017). https://doi.org/10.1137/1.9781611974782.62

22. Kanellopoulos, P., Kyropoulou, M., Voudouris, A.A.: Modified schelling games. Theoret. Comput. Sci. **880**, 1–19 (2021). https://doi.org/10.1016/j.tcs.2021.05.032

23. Kanellopoulos, P., Kyropoulou, M., Voudouris, A.A.: Not all strangers are the same: the impact of tolerance in schelling games. In: 47th International Symposium on Mathematical Foundations of Computer Science, MFCS, vol. 241, pp. 60:1–60:14 (2022). https://doi.org/10.4230/LIPIcs.MFCS.2022.60

24. Kreisel, L., Boehmer, N., Froese, V., Niedermeier, R.: Equilibria in schelling games: computational hardness and robustness. In: 21st International Conference on Autonomous Agents and Multiagent Systems, AAMAS, pp. 761–769 (2022). https://doi.org/10.5555/3535850.3535936. https://www.ifaamas.org/Proceedings/aamas2022/pdfs/p761.pdf

25. Monderer, D., Shapley, L.S.: Potential games. Games Econom. Behav. **14**(1), 124–143 (1996). https://doi.org/10.1006/game.1996.0044

26. Pancs, R., Vriend, N.J.: Schelling's spatial proximity model of segregation revisited. J. Public Econ. **91**(1), 1–24 (2007). https://doi.org/10.1016/j.jpubeco.2006.03.008

27. Rogers, T., McKane, A.J.: A unified framework for schelling's model of segregation. J. Stat. Mech. Theory Exp. **2011**(07), P07006 (2011). https://doi.org/10.1088/1742-5468/2011/07/p07006

28. Schelling, T.C.: Models of segregation. Am. Econ. Rev. **59**(2), 488–493 (1969). http://www.jstor.org/stable/1823701

29. Schelling, T.C.: Dynamic models of segregation. J. Math. Sociol. **1**(2), 143–186 (1971). https://doi.org/10.1080/0022250X.1971.9989794

30. Schelling, T.C.: Micromotives and Macrobehavior. W. W. Norton & Company, New York (1978)

31. Smith, T.W., Davern, M., Freese, J., Morgan, S.L.: General Social Surveys, 1972–2018 Cumulative Codebook. NORC ed. Chicago: NORC 2019, U. Chicago (2019)

32. White, M.J.: Segregation and diversity measures in population distribution. Popul. Index **52**(2), 198–221 (1986). http://www.jstor.org/stable/3644339

33. Zhang, J.: A dynamic model of residential segregation. J. Math. Sociol. **28**, 147–170 (2004). https://doi.org/10.1080/00222500490480202

34. Zhang, J.: Residential segregation in an all-integrationist world. J. Econ. Behav. Org. **54**(4), 533–550 (2004). https://doi.org/10.1016/j.jebo.2003.03.005

Parameterized Complexity
of Gerrymandering

Andrew Fraser[ID], Brian Lavallee[(✉)][ID], and Blair D. Sullivan[ID]

University of Utah, Salt Lake City, UT, USA
bplavallee@gmail.com, sullivan@cs.utah.edu

Abstract. In a representative democracy, the electoral process involves partitioning geographical space into districts which each elect a single representative. These representatives craft and vote on legislation, incentivizing political parties to win as many districts as possible (ideally a plurality). Gerrymandering is the process by which district boundaries are manipulated to the advantage of a desired candidate or party. We study the parameterized complexity of GERRYMANDERING, a graph problem (as opposed to Euclidean space) formalized by Cohen-Zemach et al. (AAMAS 2018) and Ito et al. (AAMAS 2019) where districts partition vertices into connected subgraphs. We prove that GERRYMANDERING is W[2]-hard on trees (even when the depth is two) with respect to the number of districts k. Moreover, we show that GERRYMANDERING remains W[2]-hard in trees with ℓ leaves with respect to the combined parameter $k + \ell$. In contrast, Gupta et al. (SAGT 2021) give an FPT algorithm for paths with respect to k. To complement our results and fill this gap, we provide an algorithm to solve GERRYMANDERING that is FPT in k when ℓ is a fixed constant.

Keywords: gerrymandering · parameterized complexity · graph algorithms

1 Introduction

Many electoral systems around the world divide voters into districts. The votes in each district are tallied separately, and each district elects a representative to a seat in a congressional system. The adversarial manipulation of these districts to favor one political party over another is known as *gerrymandering* and has the potential to greatly skew elections. Gerrymandering has been studied in various contexts, including political science [13], geography [12], and social networks [15, 16]. Many studies focus on the prevention of gerrymandering [3] or calculate a fairness metric on real-world districts [2,6,14]. The increasing role of algorithms in the creation and evaluation of district maps [4,8] motivates the study of the computational complexity of gerrymandering problems.

This work was supported in part by the Gordon & Betty Moore Foundation under award GBMF4560 to Blair D. Sullivan.

In this paper, we study gerrymandering in the graph setting. Cohen-Zemach et al. proposed a model in which the vertices of a graph represent (groups of) voters and edges model proximity and continuity [5]. Compared to a geographic map, this abstraction is more general and therefore more powerful, since a graph can represent complex socio-political relationships in addition to geographical proximity. Ito et al. followed this notion and formally defined the GERRYMANDERING problem [11]. Given a graph, GERRYMANDERING asks if the vertices can be partitioned into connected subsets so that a preferred candidate (or political party) wins the most districts. A candidate wins a district by receiving the most votes, represented by vertex weights, within a district.

Several hardness results have been shown for this problem. In 2019, Ito et al. proved GERRYMANDERING is NP-complete even when restricted to complete bipartite graphs with only $k = 2$ districts and 2 candidates [11]. They also observed a simple $O(n^k)$ algorithm for trees (proving that GERRYMANDERING is XP with respect to k) and gave a polynomial time algorithm for stars. In 2021, Bentert et al. proved that GERRYMANDERING remains NP-hard even on paths where all vertices have unit weight [1]. They also prove that the problem is weakly NP-hard on trees with 3 candidates, but it becomes solvable in polynomial time when there are only 2 candidates.

In 2021, Gupta et al. showed that GERRYMANDERING is fixed parameter tractable (FPT) on paths with respect to the number of districts k (independent of the number of candidates) [10]. They gave an $O(2.619^k (n + m)^{O(1)})$ algorithm for WEIGHTED GERRYMANDERING, a generalization of GERRYMANDERING which allows vertices to split their votes between multiple candidates.

In this paper, we study the parameterized complexity of GERRYMANDERING in trees. We prove that GERRYMANDERING is W[2]-hard on trees (even when the depth is 2) with respect to the number of districts k, suggesting that no FPT algorithm exists. This contrasts sharply with the polynomial time algorithm for stars (trees of depth 1), and answers an open question of Gupta et al. [10]. To better understand the difference in complexity between trees and paths, we also study the problem in trees with only ℓ leaves. In this setting, we prove that GERRYMANDERING is still W[2]-hard with respect to the combined parameter $k + \ell$, even on subdivided stars (i.e. when only one vertex has degree greater than 2). To complement this result, we also provide an algorithm for trees with ℓ leaves. The algorithm is FPT with respect to k when ℓ is a fixed constant. We note that our algorithm and both hardness results apply to the more general setting of WEIGHTED GERRYMANDERING as well.

2   Preliminaries

GERRYMANDERING from [11] is defined on simple, undirected graphs. We use C to denote the set of all candidates, and we annotate a graph $G = (V, E)$ with each vertex v having a candidate preference $\chi(v)$ and number of votes cast $w(v)$. Given a graph, GERRYMANDERING asks for a *district-partition* of G with k districts.

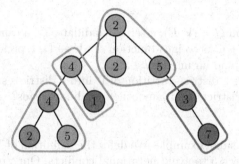

Fig. 1. A district-partition for a GERRYMANDERING instance with $k = 4$ districts and $|C| = 3$ candidates. Each vertex v is labeled with $w(v)$, the number of votes cast by v. Vertices are colored according to which candidate $\chi(v)$ they vote for. Blue indicates the preferred candidate p. Each district is outlined in the color of its winning candidate. Candidate p wins two districts and the other two candidates each win only one, so this is a satisfying district-partition. (Color figure online)

Definition 1. *Given a graph $G = (V, E)$, a **district-partition** of G is a partition of V into sets $D_1, \ldots, D_k$ so that $D_1 \cup \cdots \cup D_k = V$, $D_i \cap D_j = \emptyset$ for all $i \neq j$, and the induced subgraph $G[D_i]$ is connected for all i. We refer to $D_1, \ldots, D_k$ as **districts**.*

Specifically, GERRYMANDERING asks for a district-partition in which a preferred candidate p (equivalently a group of affiliated candidates or a political party) *wins* a plurality of districts. We refer to the following definition from Ito et al. [11].

Definition 2. *Given a graph $G = (V, E)$ and a district-partition $\mathcal{D}$ of G, we define the set of all candidates with the most votes in a district $D \in \mathcal{D}$ as follows:*

$$top(D) := \arg\max_{q \in C} \left\{ \sum_{v \in D : \chi(v) = q} w(v) \right\}$$

We say that a candidate q *leads* a district D if $q \in top(D)$. We note that Definition 2 allows for multiple candidates to lead a single district. If $top(D) = \{q\}$ and therefore q is the only leader of the district, we say that q *wins* the district.

Formally, GERRYMANDERING is defined as follows.

GERRYMANDERING

Input: A graph $G = (V, E)$, a set of candidates C, a candidate function $\chi : V \to C$, a weight function $w : V \to \mathbb{N}$, a preferred candidate $p \in C$, and an integer $k \in \mathbb{N}$.

Problem: Is there a district-partition of V into k districts such that p wins more districts than any other candidate leads?

Figure 1 shows a small example. We defer the definition of WEIGHTED GERRYMANDERING to Sect. 5 to avoid notational conflicts. Our work focuses on the parameterized complexity of GERRYMANDERING on trees. The study of parameterized complexity revolves around two important classes of problems.

Definition 3. *A problem Π is **fixed parameter tractable (FPT)** with respect to a parameter k if it admits an algorithm A which can answer an instance of Π of size n with parameter value k in time $O(f(k) \cdot n^{O(1)})$ for some computable function f. We call A an FPT algorithm. Similarly, Π is **slicewise polynomial (XP)** with respect to k if A runs in time $O(g(k) \cdot n^{h(k)})$ for computable functions g, h. In this case, we call A an XP algorithm.*

Clearly, FPT $\subseteq$ XP, and so the study of parameterized complexity often focuses on determining whether or not a problem is in FPT. Like P $\neq$ NP, FPT $\neq$ W[1] is the basic complexity assumption at the foundation of parameterized algorithms. W[1]-hardness is proven using parameterized reductions which resemble standard NP-hardness reductions but have additional requirements on the translation of the parameter. In this paper, we prove W[2]-hardness (an even stronger notion [7]) via parameterized reductions from SET COVER.

SET COVER

Input: A set of elements $\mathcal{U} = \{e_1, \ldots, e_n\}$, a family of sets $\mathcal{F} = \{S_1, \ldots, S_m\}$, and an integer $t \in \mathbb{N}$.

Problem: Is there a subset $X \subseteq \mathcal{F}$ such that $|X| \leq t$ and $\bigcup_{S \in X} S = \mathcal{U}$?

SET COVER is a well-studied problem in the field of parameterized complexity which is known to be W[2]-hard when parameterized by the natural parameter t [9]. We assume that every element in $\mathcal{U}$ appears in at least one set of $\mathcal{F}$, as otherwise it is trivially a NO-instance. Moreover, we assume that $t \leq |\mathcal{F}|$ since otherwise it is a trivial YES-instance. We refer to the textbook by Cygan et al. [7] for additional reading on parameterized complexity.

3 W[2]-Hardness in Trees of Depth Two

In this section, we prove that the GERRYMANDERING problem is W[2]-hard in trees of depth 2 parameterized by the number of districts k using a reduction from SET COVER. Before describing the reduction, we make the following observation about the frequency of elements in an instance of SET COVER.

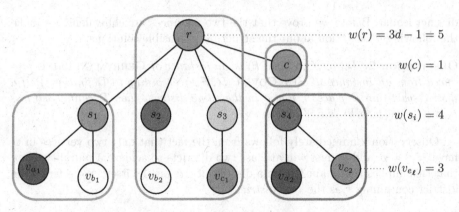

Fig. 2. A YES-instance of GERRYMANDERING constructed from the SET COVER instance $(\mathcal{U} = \{a, b, c\}, \mathcal{F} = \{S_1 = \{a, b\}, S_2 = \{b\}, S_3 = \{c\}, S_4 = \{a, c\}\}, t = 2)$. The vertex labels match those used in Definition 4. Vertex weights are equal for every vertex in each row. Vertices are colored according to which candidate $\chi(v)$ they vote for. The satisfying district-partition corresponding to the set cover $\{S_1, S_4\}$ is shown by the colored borders. (Color figure online)

Observation 1. *Let $(\mathcal{U}, \mathcal{F}, t)$ be an instance of SET COVER, and let f_e denote the frequency of e: the number of sets in $\mathcal{F}$ which contain the element $e \in \mathcal{U}$. There is an equivalent instance $(\mathcal{U}, \mathcal{F}', t)$ in which $f_e = f_{e'}$ for all $e, e' \in \mathcal{U}$.*

The equivalent instance can be constructed by adding additional sets to $\mathcal{F}$ which contain only a single element e. This increases the frequency of e by one and can be repeated until f_e is equal to the maximum frequency of any element. Since the new sets contain only a single element, they can be replaced in a feasible solution by any set in $\mathcal{F}$ which also contains that element.

Now, we describe how to construct an instance of GERRYMANDERING from an instance of SET COVER (see Fig. 2).

Definition 4. *Let $(\mathcal{U}, \mathcal{F}, t)$ be an instance of SET COVER. By Observation 1, we may assume that $f_e = d$ for all $e \in \mathcal{U}$. Note that $d \geq 2$ in non-trivial instances. We construct an instance (G, C, χ, w, p, k) of GERRYMANDERING as follows. Let G be the tree with root vertex r and a child c, and let $|C| = n+m+1$. Set $\chi(r) = \chi(c) = 0$, and set $w(r) = 3d - 1$ and $w(c) = 1$. For each set $S_i \in \mathcal{F}$, add another child s_i to r and set $\chi(s_i) = i$ and $w(s_i) = 4$. We refer to s_i as a set-vertex. For each element e_j, add d element-vertices $v_{j_1}, \dots, v_{j_d}$ and connect one to each s_i such that $e_j \in S_i$. Set $\chi(v_{j_\ell}) = j + m$, and set $w(v_{j_\ell}) = 3$. Finally, set $p = 0$ and $k = t + 2$.*

We note that in instances constructed using Definition 4, there is exactly one candidate corresponding to each set, exactly one candidate corresponding to each element, and finally a single preferred candidate. Also note that we choose $w(s_i) = 4$ and $w(v_{j_\ell}) = 3$ to ensure that all possible districts have a distinct leader. Before we prove that the two instances are equivalent, we make the following observation about the structure of feasible solutions.

Observation 2. *Let (G, C, χ, w, p, k) be an instance of* GERRYMANDERING *produced from an instance of* SET COVER $(\mathcal{U}, \mathcal{F}, t)$ *according to Definition 4. If a district-partition $\mathcal{D}$ places r and c in the same district, then $\mathcal{D}$ cannot witness that (G, C, χ, w, p, k) is a YES-instance.*

Observation 2 immediately follows from the fact that only two vertices in G have $\chi(v) = p$, and p must win at least two districts to achieve a plurality. Note that this implies that c must be in a district of size one by itself. We refer to the district containing r as the *root district*.

Theorem 1. GERRYMANDERING *is W[2]-hard in trees of depth 2 when parameterized by the number of districts k.*

Proof. Let $(\mathcal{U}, \mathcal{F}, t)$ be an instance of SET COVER. We will prove the claim by showing that $(\mathcal{U}, \mathcal{F}, t)$ is equivalent to the instance (G, C, χ, w, p, k) of GERRYMANDERING constructed according to Definition 4. First, we prove that a YES-instance of SET COVER produces a YES-instance of GERRYMANDERING.

Let $X \subseteq \mathcal{F}$ be a set cover of size t witnessing that $(\mathcal{U}, \mathcal{F}, t)$ is a YES-instance. Note that we may assume $|X| = t$ since adding sets to a feasible cover cannot make it infeasible. Let $\mathcal{D}$ be the following district-partition of G. Per Observation 2, create a district containing only the vertex c; candidate p wins this district. For each $S_i \in X$, create a district containing s_i and all of its children; candidate i wins the district created for S_i. Place all remaining vertices (including the root) in the final district.

Note that $\mathcal{D}$ contains exactly $k = t + 2$ districts, each of which is connected. We need only show that candidate p wins the root district. Suppose not. There must exist a candidate which receives at least $3d - 1$ votes since p receives $3d - 1$ votes from r. The candidates corresponding to sets can only receive four votes in the entire instance, and so it must be a candidate corresponding to an element. Without loss of generality, suppose it is candidate $j + m$ corresponding to element e_j. In order to receive $3d - 1$ votes, all d element-vertices $v_{j_1}, \dots, v_{j_d}$ must be in the root district. The construction of $\mathcal{D}$ thus implies that $e_j \notin \bigcup_{S_i \in X} S_i$, contradicting that X is a set cover. Therefore, p wins the root district.

Now, we show that a YES-instance of GERRYMANDERING implies a YES-instance of SET COVER. Let $\mathcal{D}$ be a satisfying district-partition of G. Let $X \subseteq F$ be the set containing each S_i such that a vertex in the subtree rooted at s_i does not appear in the root district of $\mathcal{D}$. Since one district in $\mathcal{D}$ contains only c by Observation 2 and non-root districts can only intersect the subtree of a single s_i, $|X| \leq t$.

Suppose that X is not a set cover of $(\mathcal{U}, \mathcal{F}, t)$. Then there exists some element e_j which is not contained by any set in X. By the construction of X, this implies that all of $v_{j_1}, \dots, v_{j_d}$ appear in the root district of $\mathcal{D}$. However, then candidate $j + m$ would receive $3d$ votes in the root district, and so candidate p could not have won (since it receives only $3d - 1$ votes). This contradicts that $\mathcal{D}$ was a

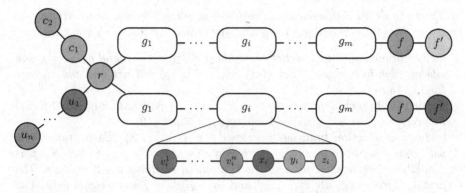

Fig. 3. A GERRYMANDERING instance produced according to Definition 5 from a SET COVER instance with $t = 2$. Each vertex v is colored according to which candidate $\chi(v)$ it votes for. Specifically, blue indicates p, orange indicates q, and yellow and green are branch adversaries. Each set S_j is represented by the group g_j of $n + 3$ vertices, as shown for g_i above. (Color figure online)

satisfying district-partition, since p must win the root district in order to win a plurality of districts.

4 W[2]-Hardness in Trees with Few Leaves

In this section, we prove that GERRYMANDERING is W[2]-hard on subdivided stars parameterized by the combined parameter of $k + \ell$, where ℓ is the number of leaves. We again reduce from the SET COVER problem.

The general idea of our reduction is to create a subdivided star with t branches, each containing groups of vertices representing every set in $\mathcal{F}$. Choosing some group on a branch as an endpoint of the root district corresponds to choosing a set to add to the cover. The hardness of the problem lies in the many choices of endpoints for the root district on each branch. If the root district chooses these boundaries such that the chosen sets are a set cover, p will win the root district and therefore be a YES-instance.

To begin our reduction, we describe how to produce the instance of GERRY-MANDERING from an instance of SET COVER. An example of the construction can be seen in Fig. 3.

Definition 5. *Given an instance* $(\mathcal{U}, \mathcal{F}, t)$ *of* SET COVER, *let* (G, C, χ, w, p, k) *be the following instance of* GERRYMANDERING. *Set* $|C| = 2 + n + t$ *and* $k = t + 3$. *Let* $p = 0$ *be the preferred candidate. Candidates* $1, \ldots, n$ *correspond to the elements* $e_1, \ldots, e_n \in \mathcal{U}$. *The remaining* $t + 1$ *candidates (which we call adversaries) are denoted by symbols for clarity. Let* q *be the* primary adversary *of* p, *and let* $a_1, \ldots, a_t$ *be the* branch adversaries.

Create G as the following subdivided star with $t + 2$ leaves. Start with a root vertex r. Set $\chi(r) = p$ and $w(r) = 3m^2t$. We attach the following branches to r:

- *a child branch with two vertices c_1 and c_2. Set $\chi(c_1) = p$ and $w(c_1) = 1$ and add an edge from r to c_1. Set $\chi(c_2) = q$ and $w(c_2) = 7m^2t$ and add an edge from c_1 to c_2.*
- *an element branch with n vertices $u_1, \ldots, u_n$ in a path with r adjacent to u_1. For vertex u_j, we set $\chi(u_j) = j$ and $w(u_j) = 3m^2t + 2$.*
- *t identical selection branches numbered $b \in \{1, 2, \ldots, t\}$. Each branch is a path consisting of m groups of vertices representing the sets $S_1, \ldots, S_m$ plus 2 additional vertices at the end. Each group g_i contains $n + 3$ vertices. The first n vertices in g_i are $v_i^1, \ldots, v_i^n$ and have $\chi(v_i^j) = j$ and weights defined as follows (assume $S_0 = \emptyset$):*

$$
w(v_i^j) = \begin{cases} 0 & \text{if } e_j \in S_i \wedge e_j \notin S_{i-1} \\ 6 & \text{if } e_j \notin S_i \wedge e_j \in S_{i-1} \\ 3 & \text{otherwise} \end{cases}
$$

The remaining three vertices in g_i are x_i, y_i, and z_i. Set $\chi(x_i) = a_b$, $\chi(y_i) = p$, and $\chi(z_i) = q$. Set $w(x_i) = m + 1$, $w(y_i) = 3$, and $w(z_i) = m + 2$. The last two vertices on the branch are f and f'. Set $\chi(f) = q$ and $\chi(f') = a_b$. Set $w(f) = 5m^2t$ and $w(f') = 5m^2t + m + 1$.

Note that in this construction, we intentionally ensure that no district can be won by both p and another candidate. Thus, any district p leads, it also wins. Before we can prove that the instances produced by this construction are equivalent, we need to show that certain district choices can never result in a satisfying district-partition. In Lemmas 1 through 5, we assume that (G, C, χ, w, p, k) is an instance of GERRYMANDERING constructed from an instance $(\mathcal{U}, \mathcal{F}, t)$ of SET COVER by Definition 5. We call the district containing r the *root district*.

Lemma 1. *In any valid district-partition of G, for every non-root district D won by p which is contained in a branch b, there exists a unique district D' also within b which is won by q.*

Proof. In order for D to be won by p, it must contain some vertex that votes for p. Therefore, we will consider all possible districts that contain some non-root vertex voting for p and show that they must result in another district won by q.

Suppose D contains any of the vertices y_i (which all vote for p). In order for p to win D without containing r, it must only contain y_i. Any other choice of D would contain x_i or z_i which have at least $m + 1$ votes for other candidates, outvoting y_i. This cannot be resolved by extending D to contain all of $y_i, \ldots, y_{i+d}$ for some d, since then D must also include $x_{i+1}, \ldots, x_{i+d}$ and $z_i, \ldots, z_{i+d-1}$. This results in $d(m + 1)$ votes for a_b and $d(m + 2)$ votes for q which will overwhelm the $3(d + 1)$ votes for p for any non-trivial m.

Thus, we may assume D contains only y_i. This necessarily separates z_i from x_i. Let D' be the district which contains z_i. If D' does not include z_{i+1}, then q

will win as all other vertices in each group vote for different candidates and have fewer than $m + 2$ votes. By including z_{i+1}, q gains an additional $m + 2$ votes and the problem persists, as q gains one more vote than candidate a_b per group that is included in D' and will always outvote the other candidates with constant weight. Finally, if D' includes the entire tail of the branch, a_b will have a total of $5m^2t + (m-i)(m+1) + m + 1$ votes. However, q will have $5m^2t + (m-i+1)(m+2)$ total votes, gaining votes relative to a_b from the inclusion of z_i and the exclusion of x_i. Subtracting the two, we get that q will have exactly $m - i + 1$ more votes than a_b, and therefore will also win such a district.

Now consider c_1, the only remaining vertex voting for p outside the root. We need not consider a district containing r, and p will lose D if it contains both c_1 and c_2. Therefore, D must contain only c_1 in order for p to win. However, this forces a second district D' containing only c_2 which is won by q.

This lemma shows that district-partitions where wins for p are greedily chosen cannot help p achieve a plurality. Winning the root district is the only way to ensure a plurality for p.

Lemma 2. *In order to win a plurality, p must win the root district.*

Proof. By Lemma 1, any non-root district won by p results in another district won by q. Therefore, in order to ever win a plurality, the district containing r must be won by p. Otherwise, p will win at most as many districts as q.

Using this information, we rule out district-partitions that prevent p from winning the root district. Note that we index f and f' as f_b and f'_b on branch b when necessary to distinguish between these vertices on separate branches.

Lemma 3. *The preferred candidate p can only win the root district if it does not contain c_2 and f_b on any branch.*

Proof. Consider the total sum of votes for p in the graph. Each branch has m vertices which contribute 3 votes. There are t of these branches, so this adds up to $3mt$ votes. Adding r and c_1, p can get a maximum of $3m^2t + 3mt + 1$ votes. This cannot overcome the $5m^2t$ votes that f_b will contribute to q. It also cannot overcome the $7m^2t$ votes for q in c_2. Therefore, p cannot possibly win any district that contains f_b or c_2.

Lemma 4. *For p to win a plurality, c_1 and c_2 must be in districts by themselves.*

Proof. If the root district contains c_2, then it cannot be won by p by Lemma 3, and therefore p cannot win a plurality by Lemma 2. If instead c_1 and c_2 make up a district or the root district contains c_1, then q wins a district in the child branch but p does not. By Lemma 1, the number of districts won by q in the other branches is at least the number won by p. As a result, p cannot win a strict plurality even if it wins the root district. Thus, c_1 and c_2 must be in separate districts and c_1 cannot be in the root district.

Lemma 5. *For p to win a plurality, the root district must contain the entire element branch $u_1, \ldots, u_n$.*

Proof. By Lemma 4, c_1 and c_2 must each be in districts by themselves. By Lemmas 2 and 3, f_b on each of the t branches cannot be in the same district as the root, so each branch requires another district to disconnect f_b from r. Covering these constraints requires $t + 2$ districts. This leaves us with only the root district. Since we have no districts remaining, the root district must also contain the element branch.

With these lemmas out of the way, we now complete our reduction by proving that the two instances are equivalent.

Theorem 2. GERRYMANDERING *is W[2]-hard in subdivided stars with ℓ leaves when parameterized by the combined parameter $k + \ell$.*

Proof. Let $(\mathcal{U}, \mathcal{F}, t)$ be an instance of SET COVER. We will prove the claim by showing that $(\mathcal{U}, \mathcal{F}, t)$ is equivalent to the instance (G, C, χ, w, p, k) of GERRYMANDERING constructed according to Definition 5. First, we will prove that a YES-instance of SET COVER produces a YES-instance of GERRYMANDERING.

Let $X \subseteq \mathcal{F}$ be a set cover of size t witnessing that $(\mathcal{U}, \mathcal{F}, t)$ is a YES-instance. Note that we may assume $|X| = t$ since adding sets to a feasible cover cannot make it infeasible. Let $\mathcal{D}$ be the following district-partition of G. Per Lemma 4, we put c_1 and c_2 in districts of size one, won by candidates p and q respectively. Now, we will construct t districts based upon the set cover X, each contained in one of the t selection branches. For each $S_i \in X$, we create a district in the ith selection branch starting with the first vertex after g_i and ending with f' at the end of the branch. This district contains $5m^2t + (m - i)(m + 1) + m + 1$ votes for candidate a_b and $5m^2t + (m - i)(m + 2)$ votes for q. Therefore, a_b will win the district by a margin of $1 + i$ votes.

Having chosen $t+2$ districts, we put all remaining vertices in the root district. Note that the element branch is contained within the root district, as required by Lemma 5. Consider the number of votes that candidate j receives in the root district. By construction, candidate j receives either $3i$ or $3(i-1)$ votes along each selection branch depending on its relationship with the set S_i used to create the district on that branch. If $e_j \in S_i$, then candidate j only receives $3(i - 1)$ votes. Since X is a set cover, this must happen to every element candidate at least once. Candidate p and the other element candidates will receive $3i$ votes, q will receive $i(m+2)$ votes, and a_b will receive $i(m+1)$ votes. Let $d = \sum_{S_i \in X} i$. Candidate p receives $3m^2t + 3d$ votes, each candidate j receives at most $3m^2t + 3(d - 1) + 2$ votes, q receives $d(m+2)$ votes, and a_b receives $d(m+1)$ votes. Therefore, p wins the root district and thus two districts overall. Candidate q also wins one district and each a_b wins one district. Therefore, p wins a plurality and (G, C, χ, w, p, k) is a YES-instance.

Now, we must prove that a YES-instance of GERRYMANDERING was produced by a YES-instance of SET COVER. Let $\mathcal{D}$ be a satisfying district-partition of G. By Lemma 4, c_1 and c_2 must each be in districts by themselves. By Lemma 5 and Lemma 2, the root district must contain the element branch and must still be won by p. The root district cannot contain f_b or f_b' from any of the branches b, as per Lemma 3. Each branch must then contain exactly one district besides the root district using pigeonhole. Let Y be the set of groups such that $g_i \in Y$ is an endpoint of the root district in some branch. We consider g_i to be the endpoint if y_i is in the district and y_{i+1} is not. Set X to be the set of all S_i such that $g_i \in Y$. By construction, $|X| \leq t$.

Suppose X is not a set cover of $(\mathcal{U}, \mathcal{F}, t)$. Then there exists some $e_j \in \mathcal{U}$ that is not in any $S_i \in X$. By the construction of X, this means that candidate j will receive $3i$ votes on each branch b, where that branch's endpoint is g_i. Let $d = \sum_{S_i \in X} i$. Consider the sum of votes for p and candidate j in the root district. Candidate p will receive at most $3m^2t + 3d$ votes, while candidate j receives $3m^2t + 3d + 2$ votes and therefore wins the root district. This contradicts that $\mathcal{D}$ was a satisfying district-partition, as p must win the root district to win a plurality by Lemma 2.

5   FPT Algorithm w.r.t k in Trees with Few Leaves

In this section, we provide an algorithm to solve WEIGHTED GERRYMANDERING that is FPT with respect to the number of districts k and XP with respect to the number of leaves ℓ. WEIGHTED GERRYMANDERING is a generalization of GERRYMANDERING which allows a vertex to vote for multiple candidates. In this setting, C denotes the set of candidates, and $w(v)$ is a $|C|$-dimensional vector whose i-th component is the number of votes for candidate i. The definitions of *wins* and *leads* are analogous to GERRYMANDERING.

WEIGHTED GERRYMANDERING

Input: A graph $G = (V, E)$, a set of candidates C, a weight function
$w : V \to C \times \mathbb{N}$, a preferred candidate p, and an integer $k \in \mathbb{N}$.

Problem: Is there a district-partition of V into k districts such that p wins
more districts than any other candidate leads?

We use a modified version of the FPT algorithm for paths from Gupta et al. [10]. Their algorithm creates an instance (H, s, t, k, k^*) of k-LABELED PATH which, given a partially edge-labeled directed graph H with vertices s and t, asks if there exists an st-path with exactly k internal vertices such that no edge label is used more than k^* times. They construct this instance by creating one vertex for each of the $\binom{n}{2}$ possible districts in G, connecting vertices in H corresponding to adjacent districts in G, and labeling those edges by the winner of the preceding district (unless p wins). In this way, a satisfying district-partition of G corresponds to a satisfying st-path in H and vice versa. We slightly modify their construction to solve on a collection of disjoint paths.

Note that the algorithm given by Gupta et al. [10] requires a tie-breaking rule η as a parameter to the problem. For any district $D \in V(G)$, the rule η

must declare a distinct winner from the set arg $\max_{q \in C}\{\sum_{v \in D} w(v)[q]\}$. Their algorithm applies this rule to ensure that no district has more than one winner. The details in our algorithm don't directly apply this rule, as all district decisions are made using Corollary 1.

Corollary 1. *Let (G, C, χ, w, p, k) be an instance of* WEIGHTED GERRYMAN-DERING *with a tie-breaking rule η. If G is a path forest (one or more disconnected paths), then there exists an algorithm which can decide (G, C, χ, w, p, k) in time $O(2.619^k(n + m)^{O(1)})$.*

Proof. We construct a similar instance of k-LABELED PATH as in [10]. First, number the vertices of G such that vertices $[1, a]$ are in the first path, then $[a + 1, b]$ are in the next path, and so forth. For any of the $\binom{n}{2}$ "district" vertices that would usually be created, we only create the vertex if the endpoints i and j are both contained in the same path in G. We add labeled edges between these vertices in the same manner as [10]. By only creating the vertices corresponding to the legal districts of G, feasible solutions to the k-LABELED PATH instance must respect the disconnected structure of G. The remainder of the argument follows as in [10].

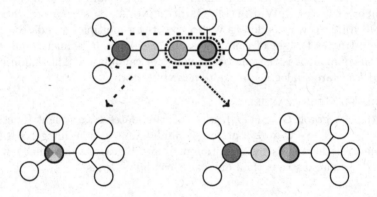

Fig. 4. Two possible ways (shown by dashed borders) for the district containing the current branch vertex (in bold) to overlap the segment shown by the colored vertices. Vertices are colored according to which candidate they vote for. The WEIGHTED GER-RYMANDERING instances produced by our branching strategy are shown below, where vertices with multiple colors split votes between those candidates.

We now relate the parameter ℓ to the *summed branch degree* which we define to be d, the sum of the degree of every vertex with degree $\delta(v) \geq 3$ (which we call *branch vertices*).

Lemma 6. *In a tree T with ℓ leaves, the summed branch degree d is at most 3ℓ.*

Proof. We induct on n, the number of vertices in T. For the base case, a tree with $n = 1$ vertex also has $\ell = 1$ and $d = 0$, so $d \leq 3\ell$ holds. Assume the claim holds for trees with less than n vertices. Let T be a tree with n vertices, and let u be a leaf in T with neighbor v. Let T' be the tree obtained by removing u from T. By the inductive hypothesis, $d' \leq 3\ell'$ in T'. Consider the degree δ' of v in T'. If $\delta'(v) = 1$; then v is not a leaf in T, but $d = d'$ and $\ell = \ell'$. When $\delta'(v) = 2$, $d = d' + 3$ and $\ell = \ell' + 1$, so $d \leq 3\ell$ still holds. In the case that $\delta'(v) \geq 3$, $d = d' + 1$ and $\ell = \ell' + 1$, and so $d \leq 3\ell$ holds.

Before describing the algorithm, we define a *segment* of a tree T to be any subpath of T such that both endpoints are either a leaf or a branch vertex and all internal vertices have degree 2 in T. The algorithm proceeds by selecting a branch vertex b and a segment S containing it. It then branches on how the district D containing b could intersect S (either ending at some vertex along S or containing the entire segment). The vertices in the same district as b are contracted into b and an edge is removed if D does not contain all of S. See Fig. 4 for an example.

Theorem 3. *Let (G, C, χ, w, p, k) be an instance of* WEIGHTED GERRYMAN-DERING *with a tie-breaking rule η. If G is a forest with summed branch degree at most d, then there exists an algorithm which can decide (G, C, χ, w, p, k) in time $O(n^d 2.619^k (n + m)^{O(1)})$.*

Proof. We proceed by induction on d. If $d = 0$, then G is a path forest, and so the instance can be solved in $O(2.619^k (n + m)^{O(1)})$ time by Corollary 1. Assume the claim holds for graphs with summed branch degree less than d.

Consider some branch vertex b in G, and let $S = v_1, \ldots, v_s$ be a segment of G such that $b = v_1$. If (G, C, χ, w, p, k) is a YES-instance, then in any valid district-partition, there exists a district D which contains b. Thus, either D contains all of S or there is a last vertex v_i along S which is still in D. We branch on the choice of v_i and construct a new instance (G', C, χ, w', p, k) in the following manner. First if $i < s$, remove the edge $v_i v_{i+1}$. Then, contract $v_1, \ldots, v_i$ into b so that it is a single vertex with weight vector $w(b) = \sum_{j=1}^{i} w(v_j)$. Any district partition for G' is easily converted to a district partition for G by extending the district containing b along S to v_i.

Finally, we argue the runtime is correct. The new instance (G', C, χ, w', p, k) has summed branch degree at most $d - 1$. Either the degree of b is reduced by removing an edge and contracting part of S, or all of S is contracted into a single vertex with degree $\delta(b) + \delta(v_s) - 2$. Thus, by the inductive hypothesis, the reduced instance can be solved in time $O(n^{d-1} 2.619^k (n + m)^{O(1)})$. Since $|S| \leq n$, we can check every branch in $O(n^d 2.619^k (n + m)^{O(1)})$ time. We note that contracting the edges to create G' can be handled in constant time by checking the branches defined by $v_1, \ldots, v_s$ in that order.

Corollary 2. *Let (G, C, χ, w, p, k) be an instance of* WEIGHTED GERRYMAN-DERING *with a tie-breaking rule η. If G is a tree with at most ℓ leaves, then there exists an algorithm which can answer (G, C, χ, w, p, k) using η in time $O(n^{3\ell} 2.619^k (n + m)^{O(1)})$.*

Proof. This result follows from Theorem 3 and Lemma 6.

6 Conclusion

Identifying and preventing the gerrymandering of political districts is an important social problem that has recently seen significant attention from the algorithmic community. To incorporate socio-political relationships beyond geographic proximity, Ito et al. formalized GERRYMANDERING on graphs [11]. GERRYMANDERING is a natural candidate for FPT algorithms, since the number of districts k is often manageably small in real-world instances (e.g. 10–15). In contrast, XP algorithms are unlikely to be feasible at these parameter values, and so the precise parameterized complexity of GERRYMANDERING has important practical consequences.

Ito et al. spurred interest in GERRYMANDERING on trees specifically by proving NP-completeness for the problem on $K_{2,n}$ (i.e. a graph one vertex deletion away from a tree) [11]. In response, GERRYMANDERING results have been discovered for many restricted settings including a polynomial time algorithm for stars [11], weak NP-hardness for trees with at least 3 candidates [1], and an FPT algorithm for paths parameterized by k [10]. We further characterize the properties of trees that make GERRYMANDERING hard. First, we show that GERRYMANDERING is W[2]-hard with respect to k in trees of depth 2, answering an open question of [10]. Furthermore, we prove that GERRYMANDERING remains W[2]-hard with respect to $k + \ell$ in trees with only ℓ leaves, even if G is a subdivided star (i.e. only has one vertex with degree greater than 2). Complementing these results, we give an algorithm to solve WEIGHTED GERRYMANDERING that is FPT with respect to k when ℓ is a fixed constant. Except for the restricted setting where all vertices have only a single vote, this completely resolves the parameterized complexity of GERRYMANDERING with respect to the number of districts.

Acknowledgements. Thanks to Christopher Beatty for his contributions to a course project that led to this research. We also thank the anonymous reviewers whose comments on a previous version of this manuscript led to significant improvements in notational clarity.

References

1. Bentert, M., Koana, T., Niedermeier, R.: The complexity of gerrymandering over graphs: paths and trees. Discret. Appl. Math. **324**, 103–112 (2023). https://doi.org/10.1016/j.dam.2022.09.009
2. Chen, J., Cottrell, D.: Evaluating partisan gains from congressional gerrymandering: using computer simulations to estimate the effect of gerrymandering in the U.S. house. Elect. Stud. **44**, 329–340 (2016). https://doi.org/10.1016/j.electstud.2016.06.014
3. Chen, J., Rodden, J.: Unintentional gerrymandering: political geography and electoral bias in legislatures. Q. J. Polit. Sci. **8**, 239–269 (2013). https://doi.org/10.1561/100.00012033

4. Cho, W.K.T.: Technology-enabled coin flips for judging partisan gerrymandering. South. Calif. Law Rev. **93**, 11 (2019). https://southerncalifornialawreview.com/wp-content/uploads/2019/06/93_Cho_Final.pdf

5. Cohen-Zemach, A., Lewenberg, Y., Rosenschein, J.S.: Gerrymandering over graphs. In: Proceedings of the 17th Conference on Autonomous Agents and MultiAgent Systems, pp. 274–282. International Foundation for Autonomous Agents and Multiagent Systems (2018). https://doi.org/10.5555/3237383.3237429. https://dl.acm.org/doi/10.5555/3237383.3237429

6. Cottrell, D.: Using computer simulations to measure the effect of gerrymandering on electoral competition in the U.S. congress. Legis. Stud. Q. **44**, 487–514 (2019). https://doi.org/10.1111/lsq.12234

7. Cygan, M., et al.: Parameterized Algorithms. Springer, Cham (2015). https://doi.org/10.1007/978-3-319-21275-3

8. Earle, G.: Political machines: the role of software in enabling and detecting partisan gerrymandering under the whitford standard. N. C. J. Law Technol. **19**, 67 (2018). https://scholarship.law.unc.edu/ncjolt/vol19/iss4/3/

9. Flum, J., Grohe, M.: Parameterized Complexity Theory. Texts in Theoretical Computer Science. Springer, Heidelberg (2006). https://doi.org/10.1007/3-540-29953-x

10. Gupta, S., Jain, P., Panolan, F., Roy, S., Saurabh, S.: Gerrymandering on graphs: computational complexity and parameterized algorithms. In: Caragiannis, I., Hansen, K.A. (eds.) SAGT 2021. LNCS, vol. 12885, pp. 140–155. Springer, Cham (2021). https://doi.org/10.1007/978-3-030-85947-3_10

11. Ito, T., Kamiyama, N., Kobayashi, Y., Okamoto, Y.: Algorithms for gerrymandering over graphs. Theor. Comput. Sci. **868**, 30–45 (2021). https://doi.org/10.1016/j.tcs.2021.03.037

12. Lewenberg, Y., Lev, O., Rosenschein, J.S.: Divide and conquer: using geographic manipulation to win district-based elections. In: Proceedings of the 16th Conference on Autonomous Agents and MultiAgent Systems, pp. 624–632. International Foundation for Autonomous Agents and Multiagent Systems (2017). https://doi.org/10.5555/3091125.3091215. https://dl.acm.org/doi/10.5555/3091125.3091215

13. McGhee, E.: Partisan gerrymandering and political science. Annu. Rev. Political Sci. **23**, 171–185 (2020). https://doi.org/10.1146/annurev-polisci-060118-045351. https://doi.org/10.1146/annurev-polisci-060118-045351

14. Simon, J., Lehman, J.: Antimander: open source detection of gerrymandering though multi-objective evolutionary algorithms. In: Proceedings of the 2020 Genetic and Evolutionary Computation Conference Companion, pp. 51–52. Association for Computing Machinery (2020). https://doi.org/10.1145/3377929.3398156

15. Talmon, N.: Structured proportional representation. Theor. Comput. Sci. **708**, 58–74 (2018). https://doi.org/10.1016/j.tcs.2017.10.028

16. Tsang, A., Larson, K.: The echo chamber: strategic voting and homophily in social networks. In: Proceedings of the 15th Conference on Autonomous Agents and MultiAgent Systems, pp. 368–375. International Foundation for Autonomous Agents and Multiagent Systems (2016). https://doi.org/10.5555/2936924.2936979. https://dl.acm.org/doi/10.5555/2936924.2936979

Coordinating Monetary Contributions in Participatory Budgeting

Haris Aziz[1], Sujit Gujar[2], Manisha Padala[2], Mashbat Suzuki[1(✉)], and Jeremy Vollen[1]

[1] UNSW Sydney, Kensington, Australia
{haris.aziz,mashbat.suzuki,j.vollen}@unsw.edu.au
[2] IIIT Hyderabad, Hyderabad, India
sujit.gujar@iiit.ac.in, manisha.padala@research.iiit.ac.in

Abstract. We formalize a framework for coordinating funding and selecting projects, the costs of which are shared among agents with quasi-linear utility functions and individual budgets. Our model contains the discrete participatory budgeting model as a special case, while capturing other useful scenarios. We propose several important axioms and objectives and study how well they can be simultaneously satisfied. We show that whereas welfare maximization admits an FPTAS, welfare maximization subject to a natural and very weak participation requirement leads to a strong inapproximability. This result is bypassed if we consider some natural restricted valuations, namely laminar single-minded valuations and symmetric valuations. Our analysis for the former restriction leads to the discovery of a new class of tractable instances for the *set-union knapsack* problem, a classical problem in combinatorial optimization.

Keywords: participatory budgeting · social choice · social choice with money

1 Introduction

Participatory budgeting (PB) is an exciting grassroots democratic paradigm in which members of a community collectively decide on which relevant public projects should be funded (see, e.g., [6,27,29]). The funding decisions take into account the preferences and valuations of the members.

The positive influence of PB is apparent in the many implementations across the globe at the country, city and community level. For example, a PB scheme in the Govanhill area of Glasgow, Scotland empowered local residents to direct funds towards projects like addiction family support groups, a community justice partnership, and refurbishment of locally significant public baths.[1] In the 2014-15 New York City PB process, 51,000 people voted to fund $32 million of neighbourhood improvements.[2] As both examples demonstrate, efficient use of

---

[1] local.gov.uk/case-studies/govanhill-glasgow.
[2] hudexchange.info/programs/participatory-budgeting.

A. Deligkas and A. Filos-Ratsikas (Eds.): SAGT 2023, LNCS 14238, pp. 142–160, 2023.
https://doi.org/10.1007/978-3-031-43254-5_9

public funds and a significant improvement in community member involvement are two of the foremost advantages of PB processes around the world.

In all implementations of PB that we are aware of, the process relies upon a central authority to determine and provide a budget to fund projects. In practice, this requirement excludes groups who lack the institutional structure required to pool resources from initiating a PB process. For example, several neighbouring municipalities may wish to collaborate on funding projects which can benefit residents from multiple communities simultaneously. On a smaller scale, a group of flatmates may need to decide which furnishings and appliances to buy. Or, a number of organisations co-hosting an event may need to select a list of speakers, each of which charges their own fee. In each of these cases, while PB seems a natural process of arriving at a mutually beneficial outcome, the classical discrete PB model is insufficient because PB's focus is on project selection and not efficient resource pooling. In this paper, we present a framework which captures both of these components simultaneously.

Furthermore, in the classical PB model, it is typical to assume that agents' utilities depend only on their valuations for selected projects and that agents are indifferent toward the amount of the budget used. While this is appropriate in that setting because the agents do not necessarily believe leftover budget will benefit them, this is not the case in our setting since agents can use their leftover funds directly. For this reason, we model agents with utilities dependent upon their contributions (i.e. *quasi-linear utilities*).

In summary, we consider a flexible and general framework which we term *PB with Resource Pooling* in which (i) agents can have their own budgets, which can be directed to fund desirable projects, and (ii) agents care both about which projects are funded, and how much monetary contribution they make due to quasi-linear utilities. Our framework captures the classical discrete PB model in the following way: an artificial agent can be introduced with budget equal to the central budget and valuations for project bundles equal to their total costs.

Taking cues from what we see as the key successes of PB implementations, we primarily focus on the *efficiency* of the outcome while ensuring each involved agent benefits from the outcome and is thus incentivized to participate in the process. Towards this, we study the possibility of achieving optimal *utilitarian welfare* alongside a very basic participation notion, namely *weak participation*, that guarantees positive utility to all of the agents involved.

Contributions. Our first contribution is a meaningful model of collective decision making that connects various problems including participatory budgeting, cost sharing problems, and crowd-sourcing. The model can also be viewed as a bridge between voting problems and mechanism design with money.

In Sect. 3, we lay the groundwork for axiomatic research for the problem by formalizing meaningful axioms that capture efficiency and participation incentives. To capture a PB program which is both useful and sustainable, we focus on mechanisms that satisfy *weak participation*, which requires that every agent benefits from participation.

In Sect. 4, we show that whereas welfare maximization admits a *fully polynomial time approximation scheme* (FPTAS)[3], welfare maximization subject to weak participation leads to a strong inapproximability for as few as two agents. We then show that the same objective is inapproximable even for the case with identical project costs despite there being an exact, polynomial time algorithm for welfare maximization.

In Sect. 5, we give an FPTAS for welfare maximization subject to participation in the single-minded setting with laminar demand sets, utilizing a result from the *knapsack with conflict graphs* problem. We use the insight from this argument to reveal a tractable case for the *set-union knapsack* problem, making a novel contribution to a well-studied generalization of the knapsack problem. We also present a polynomial time algorithm for *symmetric valuations* (Sect. 6). All missing proofs can be found in the full version of our paper [5], along with experimental results and our treatment of the set-union knapsack problem. Our results are summarized in Table 1.

Table 1. Summary of our computational results

	Welfare Maximization	Welfare Maximization subject to Weak Participation
General case	NP-hard; FPTAS	Inapproximable* for any $n \geq 2$
Identical costs	Polynomial-time exact	Inapproximable*
Laminar Single-minded valuations	NP-hard	FPTAS
Symmetric valuations	Polynomial-time exact	Polynomial-time exact

* Inapproximability results hold assuming $P \neq NP$.

2   Related Work

Funding Public Goods/Projects. Many classical papers from public economics focus on mechanisms for public good provision [19,26]. However, they are primarily concerned with incentives and mostly focus on divisible public goods [18], a setting which differs from ours significantly. Buterin et al. [10] presented a mechanism with quasi-linear utilities, but they consider divisible goods and do not include individual budgets. Other works have considered models with personal contributions [4,8], but they do not allow for quasi-linear utilities and are better suited for charitable coordination.

Discrete Participatory Budgeting. The model we formalize has some connections with discrete PB models [6] in which agents do not make contributions. These models generalize multi-winner voting [16]. Some research has considered PB settings in which agents express budget constraints in addition to preferences [11,20]. Unlike in these works, the agents in our model care how much of their budget is used, better capturing the budgeting trade-offs considered by agents with limited resources.

---
[3] An algorithm which approximates the optimal solution by a factor of at least $1 - \epsilon$ in time polynomial in the instance size and $1/\epsilon$ for any $\epsilon > 0$.

Cost-sharing/Crowdfunding. PB without budget constrained agents overlaps significantly with the study of cost-sharing mechanisms [15,23], an area focused on designing truthful and efficient mechanisms for sharing the cost of availing a certain service or project among the members. Birmpas et al. [7] focused on symmetric submodular valuations and provided a mechanism which approximates social cost. The social cost considered is equivalent to the quasi-linear utility that we consider in our setting, but these works focus on agents without budget restrictions. Additionally, utility-based PB bears resemblance to certain civic crowdfunding models [13,30]. However, these papers consider neither budget constraints nor the multiple project case. In this line of work, the goal is to analyze what happens at equilibrium when the agents are strategic, as opposed to our own goal of determining a welfare maximizing subset of projects to fund provided budget constraints.

3 Preliminaries

In this work, we provide a framework for collective funding decisions in which agents derive quasi-linear utility and lack an exogenously defined shared budget. The setting has the following components.

3.1 Model

An instance of *PB with Resource Pooling* contains a set of participating agents $N = [n]$ and a set of projects, $M = [m]$. $\mathbf{C} = (C_j)_{j \in M}$ denote the project costs. Abusing notation slightly, we let $C(S) = \sum_{j \in S} C_j$ for any $S \subseteq M$. Each agent i has valuation $v_i : 2^M \to \mathbb{R}_{\geq 0}$ and a budget b_i, which is the maximum amount they are willing to contribute. We denote $\mathbf{v} = (v_i)_{i \in N}$ and $\mathbf{b} = (b_i)_{i \in N}$. We assume v_i to be monotonic, that is $v_i(S) \leq v_i(T), S \subseteq T$. Agent i's valuation of a single project j is denoted by v_{ij} for ease. We assume that the overall valuation of each project is higher than its cost, i.e. $\sum_{i \in N} v_{ij} \geq C_j, \ \forall j \in M$, since it will be trivially excluded otherwise.

In summary, a PB with Resource Pooling instance is a tuple $I = \langle N, M, \mathbf{v}, \mathbf{b}, \mathbf{C} \rangle$. A mechanism takes an instance I and computes an outcome $(W, \mathbf{x})$, comprising a set of funded projects $W \subseteq M$ and a vector of agent payments $\mathbf{x} = (x_i)_{i \in N}$. Each agent then derives *quasi-linear utility*, i.e. $u_i(W, x) = v_i(W) - x_i$. We close with an illustrative motivating example, which assumes additive valuations.

Example 1. Three towns perform cost-benefit analyses for three proposed projects: a concert hall, a shelter, and a pool. The particulars are given in Table 2.

While Towns A and B have the funds to pay for the pool on their own, they receive zero utility from doing so. Furthermore, no town can fund either of the other two projects on its own. Together, the three towns have enough funds to build the shelter and the pool, the result of which will be a strictly positive utility for all towns. Lastly, we point out that, while the towns could instead fund the concert hall and generate positive social welfare, Town B will be required to pay at least 2, which exceeds its valuation and it will thus receive negative utility.

Table 2. An example of *PB with Resource Pooling* with three agents and three projects. The table records the costs, budgets, and valuations.

	Budget	Hall	Shelter	Pool
		Cost		
		5	4	2
Town A	2	2	1	2
Town B	3	1	2	2
Town C	1	4	3	1

3.2 Desirable Axioms

We now formalize basic feasibility criteria and desirable properties related to participation incentives and efficiency.

Feasibility. We say that an outcome is *feasible* if (1) no agent's payment exceeds their individual budget, i.e. $x_i \leq b_i$ for all $i \in N$, and (2) it is weakly budget balanced, a property which requires an outcome does not run a deficit and which we will now define.

Definition 1 (Weakly Budget Balanced (WBB)). *An outcome $(W, \mathbf{x})$ is WBB if $C(W) \leq \sum_{i \in N} x_i$. When $C(W) = \sum_{i \in N} x_i$, we say the outcome is Budget Balanced (BB).*

Henceforth, we focus our attention on outcomes which satisfy these basic requirements and will thus refer to feasible outcomes merely as outcomes.

Participation. We now turn our attention to properties that incentivize agents to participate in the mechanism. Weak Participation (WP) ensures that each agent obtains non-negative utility from the mechanism.

Definition 2 (Weak Participation (WP)). *An outcome $(W, \mathbf{x})$ is WP if for each agent $i \in N$, $u_i(W, \mathbf{x}) \geq 0$, i.e., $v_i(W) \geq x_i$.*

We note that WP is a minimal requirement and considerably weaker than Individual Rationality (IR), which ensures that the utility each agent obtains from the mechanism is at least the maximum utility they can obtain with only their budget. In other words, whereas IR captures individual utility maximization, WP ensures that no agent is making a loss. However, the gap between the social welfare of the best WP outcome and that of the best IR outcome can be arbitrarily large (refer to Example 2). This highlights the trade-off between social welfare and participation incentivization. Selecting a weaker participation criterion allows us to pursue a greater social welfare objective. Furthermore, the two notions coincide under the natural circumstance that the cost of every project exceeds the budget of any individual agent.

Hence, we will focus on welfare maximization within the space of WP outcomes. In Sect. 7, we will point out and give intuition for why many of the results in this paper also hold for the problem of welfare maximization subject to IR. The following lemma illustrates that WP and feasibility can be captured simultaneously by a single inequality.

Lemma 1. *A set of projects $W \subseteq M$ can be funded in a feasible and WP manner if and only if $C(W) \leq \sum_{i \in N} \min(b_i, v_i(W))$.*

Proof. Let $W \subseteq M$ be a set of projects which can be funded in a feasible and WP manner. That is, there exists payments $\mathbf{x}$ such that $x_i \leq b_i$ and $x_i \leq v_i(W)$ for each $i \in N$. Combining the two inequalities, $x_i \leq \min(b_i, v_i(W))$ for all $i \in N$. Since $(W, \mathbf{x})$ is WBB, we have that $C(W) \leq \sum_{i \in N} x_i$, and thus $C(W) \leq \sum_{i \in N} \min(b_i, v_i(W))$, as desired.

As for the other direction, we need only show that there exist payments $\mathbf{x}$ such that $(W, \mathbf{x})$ satisfies feasibility and WP. Consider payments $x_i = \min(b_i, v_i(W))$ for each $i \in N$. The payments are clearly feasible and WBB holds since $C(W) \leq \sum_{i \in N} \min(b_i, v_i(W)) = \sum_{i \in N} x_i$. WP is satisfied since $x_i = \min(b_i, v_i(W)) \leq v_i(W)$ for all $i \in N$. $\square$

Efficiency. We measure the efficiency of the outcome with respect to the utilitarian welfare, i.e. the sum of utilities. Since we model quasi-linear utility for each agent, the utilitarian social welfare (which we refer to simply as social welfare) is given by

$$\text{SW}(W, x) = \sum_{i \in N} u_i(W, x) = \sum_{i \in N} v_i(W) - \sum_{i \in N} x_i \tag{1}$$

The utilitarian welfare optimal (UWO) outcome is the social welfare maximizing feasible outcome.

Definition 3 (Utilitarian Welfare Optimal (UWO)). *An outcome $(W, \mathbf{x})$ is UWO if it maximizes social welfare as given by Eq. (1).*

We define UWO-WP to represent the welfare-optimal outcome among outcomes that ensure WP.

Definition 4 (Welfare Optimal among Weak Participation (UWO-WP)). *An outcome $(W, \mathbf{x})$ is UWO-WP if it is welfare optimal among WP outcomes.*

Remark 1. For any outcome (W, x) which is WBB, there is an outcome which is BB, maintains WP, and achieves weakly greater social welfare.

To see why Remark 1 is true, consider for any WBB outcome an alternative outcome with the same project selection, but with some set of agents' payments decreased such that the outcome is BB. By Remark 1 and our objectives stated in Definitions 3 and 4, we can restrict our attention to outcomes which are BB ($\sum_{i \in N} x_i = C(W)$) and refer to social welfare from now on as the following:

$$\text{SW}(W) = \sum_{i \in N} v_i(W) - C(W) \tag{2}$$

In the next section, we prove that the problem of computing a UWO-WP outcome is inapproximable, assuming $P \neq NP$.

4   Inapproximability of UWO-WP

In this section, we first show the hardness of finding a welfare-optimal project bundle, i.e. UWO. We then show that the same objective with the additional constraint of WP, i.e. UWO-WP, is inapproximable. Our inapproximability result is striking: the problem of finding UWO admits an FPTAS but after imposing the very weak requirement of WP, the same problem does not admit any polynomial approximation guarantees, even in the setting with only two agents.

The results in this section focus entirely on the setting with *additive valuations*, under which $v_i(S) = \sum_{j \in S} v_{ij}$ for any $S \subseteq M$. We point out that the negative results that follow also hold in settings with any class of valuations broader than additive (e.g. superadditive, subadditive, general setting). We first make some remarks on computation of UWO (Definition 3). Due to Eq. (2), the UWO problem is given by

$$\max_{W \subseteq M} \quad \sum_{i \in N} v_i(W) - C(W) \qquad s.t. \quad C(W) \leq \sum_{i \in N} b_i.$$

Remark 2. The UWO problem is NP-hard even for a single agent. However, in the setting with additive valuations, UWO admits an FPTAS [22].

Despite the positive approximation results, approximation guarantees to UWO may be possible only with huge costs to certain agents who incur large disutility, thus motivating the search for outcomes which satisfy WP. However, it is impossible to guarantee an outcome that satisfies both UWO and WP[4]. Thus, we are interested in finding solutions which are welfare optimal among those which satisfy WP, i.e., that are UWO-WP (Definition 4). However, the proof of Remark 2 (see full version) can also be used to show that finding a UWO-WP allocation is NP-hard, even for one agent.

4.1   Gap Introducing Reduction for UWO-WP

As finding UWO-WP is NP-hard, we look for an approximation algorithm. To see why finding such an approximation algorithm will be difficult, consider the following example.

---

[4] Consider an instance with two agents and one project with $C_1 = 1$, valuations $v_{11} = 2$ and $v_{21} = 0$, and budgets $b_1 = 0$ and $b_2 = 1$. The UWO outcome is to fund the project, but this violates WP.

Table 3. An instance with $n = 2$ and $m = 4$ where the UWO-WP outcome must contain a unique set of projects (P4) to allow the WP funding of a high-welfare project (P1).

		P1	P2	P3	P4
	Budget	Cost			
		1	2	1	1
Agent 1	2	0	20	2-ϵ	2
Agent 2	0	H	0	20	0

Example 2. Observe that in the example given in Table 3, agent 1 holds the entire collective budget and maximizes her utility by funding project 2, which can be funded in a WP manner. But, no budget remains to fund other projects if project 2 is selected. Project 3, on the other hand, gives positive utility to both agents and leaves enough budget to fund project 4 in a WP manner.

However, note that $W = \{1, 4\}$ can be funded in a WP manner and achieves $SW(W) = H$. Although project 4 seems inferior to projects 2 or 3 on its own, it must be selected in order to fund project 1 in a WP manner. Since H can be arbitrarily high, any algorithm which hopes to give a good approximation of UWO-WP should be able to find the set of projects that makes project 1 affordable if such a project set exists.

Inspired by Example 2, where excess money must be extracted optimally to fund valuable projects, we introduce a related problem.
MAXIMUM EXCESS PAYMENT EXTRACTION (MaxPE):

$$\max_{W \subseteq M} \mathrm{PE}(W) = \sum_{i \in N} \min(b_i, v_i(W)) - C(W)$$

The above quantity measures the amount of excess money we can extract after paying for the costs of the projects in a WP manner. The decision version of the MaxPE problem asks if MaxPE $\geq t$, that is whether t dollars can be extracted while maintaining WP. Note that the decision version of the problem can be used to compute MaxPE simply by using binary search. The following theorem states that any polynomial approximation for UWO-WP can be used to solve the MaxPE decision problem in polynomial time.

Theorem 1. *Let $f(n, m)$ be a polynomial time computable function. Any polynomial time algorithm with $f(n, m)$-approximation guarantee for UWO-WP can be used to decide MaxPE in polynomial time.*

Proof. Consider an arbitrary instance $I = \langle N, M, \mathbf{v}, \mathbf{b}, \mathbf{C} \rangle$ of the MaxPE $\geq t$ problem where there are n agents and m projects. Let $\mathrm{Opt}(I)$ be the social welfare obtained from the UWO-WP solution to instance I. We know that $\mathrm{Opt}(I) \leq \sum_{i \in N} v_i(M)$. We now create a new instance by adding an agent 0 and a project 0 to I such that:

- $v_{00} = (2f(n+1, m+1)) \sum_{i \in N} v_i(M);$ $v_{i0} = 0$ for all $i \in N$
- $v_{0j} = 0$ for all $j \in M;$ $b_0 = 0;$ $C_0 = t$

We denote the transformed instance as I^t. It has $n+1$ agents and $m+1$ projects. Note that the transformation is polynomial time as $f(n, m)$ is polynomial-time computable. The modified instance creates a large gap in the optimal social welfare depending on the cost of project 0, as seen in Fig. 1. As the figure illustrates, any f-approximation algorithm Alg will maintain such a gap and can thus be used to retrieve information about MaxPE. As we will see, this observation can be used to show approximation hardness.

Consider now a polynomial time algorithm Alg for UWO-WP with approximation guarantee $f(n, m)$. Since I^t has one additional agent and project, we have

$$f(n+1, m+1)\, \mathrm{SW}(\mathrm{Alg}(I^t)) \geq \mathrm{Opt}(I^t). \tag{3}$$

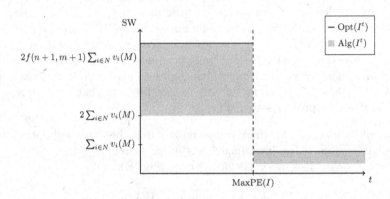

Fig. 1. The modified instance I^t creates a large gap in optimal social welfare, depending on t, as shown by the solid lines. This welfare gap will remain for any f-approximation algorithm Alg, as shown by the shaded regions, and illustrates how such an approximation can be used to solve the MaxPE problem.

We now claim that $\mathrm{MaxPE}(I) \geq t$ accepts (i.e., t dollars can be extracted from agents in I while satisfying WP) if and only if $\mathrm{SW}(\mathrm{Alg}(I^t)) \geq 2 \sum_{i \in N} v_i(M)$. The forward direction follows since if t dollars can be extracted from agents in I then project 0 can be afforded. Hence, $\mathrm{Opt}(I^t) \geq (2f(n+1, m+1)) \sum_{i \in N} v_i(M)$ since there is a WP solution which funds project zero. Thus, combining with Eq. (3), we see that $\mathrm{SW}(\mathrm{Alg}(I^t)) \geq 2 \sum_{i \in N} v_i(M)$.

As for the backward direction, first note that if $\mathrm{SW}(\mathrm{Alg}(I^t)) \geq 2 \sum_{i \in N} v_i(M)$ then $0 \in \mathrm{Alg}(I^t)$. To see this, suppose on the contrary $0 \notin \mathrm{Alg}(I^t)$. Then, $\mathrm{SW}(\mathrm{Alg}(I^t)) \leq \mathrm{Opt}(I) \leq \sum_{i \in N} v_i(M)$, leading to a contradiction. Thus, we have $0 \in \mathrm{Alg}(I^t)$, which implies that the agents in I must be able to pay for project 0 in a WP manner. This is due to the fact that agent 0 cannot contribute towards funding project 0 since she has zero budget, and agents in I do not value project 0. Hence, t dollars can be extracted from agents in I in a WP manner. Thus, we may use Alg to decide MaxPE $\geq t$ in polynomial time.   □

In the subsections that follow, we use Theorem 1 to show that unlike UWO, which admits an FPTAS, UWO-WP does not admit *any* bounded polynomial approximation guarantees in the additive setting, even if we limit the number of agents to two or restrict the costs to be identical.

4.2   Two Agents with Additive Valuations

As Lemma 2 will show, MaxPE is NP-hard even for a single agent with additive valuation. The following theorem uses Lemma 2 to demonstrate a strong inapproximability of UWO-WP in the additive setting, even in the very restricted case with two agents.

Theorem 2. *Let $f(m)$ be a polynomial time computable function. Even for two agents, there is no polynomial time $f(m)$-approximation algorithm for the UWO-WP problem, assuming $P \neq NP$.*

Proof. Suppose, on the contrary, that a polynomial time algorithm exists with approximation guarantee $f(m)$ for UWO-WP with $n = 2$. By the argument used to prove Theorem 1, we see that such an algorithm can be used to solve MaxPE for one agent in polynomial time. However, as we will show in Lemma 2, MaxPE is NP-hard even for one agent, contradicting $P \neq NP$.   □

Lemma 2. *It is NP-hard to decide MaxPE $\geq t$, even for a single agent with additive valuation.*

One might fairly argue that the inapproximability given by Theorem 2 depends on unnatural instances with a zero-budget agent. However, we point out that the result holds even if we constrain agents' budgets to be strictly positive.

Remark 3. Theorem 2 holds even when restricted to instances where every agent has strictly positive budget.

To see this, observe that in the reduction given to prove Theorem 1 we can set $b_0 = b$ (for arbitrary b polynomially bounded in the size of the instance), and if we set $C_0 = t + b$, then the reduction follows as before. The following remark shows that this strong inapproximability is not purely an artifact of our particular choice of social welfare function.

Remark 4. Theorem 2 holds for a broader class of social welfare functions that includes (but is not limited to) Nash social welfare and egalitarian social welfare, in addition to utilitarian.

Though UWO admits an FPTAS, with the inclusion of the simple and intuitive constraint of WP, we obtain the above strong inapproximability results. We next show that the inapproximability holds even if all projects costs are identical.

4.3 Identical Costs Setting

We consider the special case in which all projects have identical costs. In this setting we have $C_j = C$, $\forall j \in M$, for some constant C. We assume $C = 1$ for simplicity. We first note that the UWO allocation in the identical costs setting is computable in polynomial time.[5]

Given UWO is polynomial time computable in the identical costs setting, and the same problem is NP-hard in the general setting, we may take this as an encouraging sign that a tractable algorithm for UWO-WP may exist in our restricted setting. However, as we will show, UWO-WP does not admit any polynomial approximation guarantees, even in this restricted setting. Our argument follows similarly to that used in the general setting. Intuitively, to be able to afford any single project in our setting, we must be able to identify a subset of projects that extracts a single dollar of excess payment when such a subset exists. We define the decision version of the MaxPE problem with $t = 1$ (MaxPE ≥ 1) as $\max_{W \subseteq M} \sum_{i \in N} \min(b_i, v_i(W)) - |W| \geq 1$.

Lemma 3. *It is NP-hard to decide* MaxPE ≥ 1, *even with identical budgets.*

With the preceding lemma, the following inapproximability result follows from an analogous argument to that used in the proof of Theorem 2.

Theorem 3. *Let $f(n, m)$ be a polynomial time computable function. Unless $P \neq NP$, there is no polynomial time $f(n, m)$-approximation algorithm for UWO-WP problem in the identical costs setting.*

Having found a strong inapproximability in various settings with additive valuations, we turn to another well-motivated setting and give an approximation algorithm for UWO-WP.

5 An Algorithm for Laminar Single-Minded Valuations

In this section, we study a setting in which each agent derives non-zero value from a project bundle if and only if the bundle contains the set of projects desired by that agent, which we refer to as the agent's *demand set*. We refer to this as the setting with *single-minded* valuations, following the precedent of single-minded bidders in the combinatorial auctions literature [1,12]. Single-minded agents are also well-studied in the mechanism design literature [3,14] and fair division literature [9]. In contrast to the additive setting, the single-minded setting captures project complementarities in agent valuations. We now define the single-minded setting formally.

---

[5] Specifically, we can sort the projects according to their social welfare and greedily select them until there is no remaining project with non-negative social welfare or until no budget remains.

Definition 5 (Single-minded Valuations). *Valuations* $\mathbf{v} = (v_i)_{i \in N}$ *are single-minded if, for all* $i \in N$, *there exists* $D_i \subseteq M$ *and* $z_i \in \mathbb{R}_{\geq 0}$ *such that* $v_i(W) = z_i$ *if* $D_i \subseteq W$ *and zero otherwise. We refer to* D_i *as agent* i's *demand set.*

First note that for any set of agents with the same demand set, i.e. $D_i = T$ for all $i \in N' \subseteq N$ and some $T \subseteq M$, the problem is equivalent to the problem where N' is replaced by a single agent i' with $b_{i'} = \sum_{i \in N'} b_i$ and $v_{i'}(W) = \sum_{i \in N'} v_i(W)$ for all $W \subseteq M$. After executing this step for all such sets of agents, we have an equivalent instance with distinct demand sets, $\mathbf{D}$. Henceforth, we assume without loss of generality that all demand sets are distinct. We will denote by N_S the set of agents whose demand sets are contained in the set $S \subseteq M$, i.e. $N_S = \{i \in N | D_i \subseteq S\}$. We refer to any set which maximizes the PE quantity, as defined in Sect. 4.1, as a MaxPE *set*.

In this section, we give an FPTAS for a restriction of the single-minded setting, that with *laminar single-minded valuations*, which we will define now.

Definition 6 (Laminar Single-minded Valuations). *Valuations* $\mathbf{v} = (v_i)_{i \in N}$ *are laminar single-minded if they are single-minded and the demand set family* $\mathbf{D} = (D_i)_{i \in N}$ *is a laminar set family, i.e. for every* $D_i, D_j \in \mathbf{D}$, $D_i \cap D_j$ *is either empty or equal to* D_i *or* D_j.

The laminar single-minded case describes instances in which the project set is naturally partitioned into categories and sub-categories. Relating back to Example 1 where neighboring towns fund shared public projects, we might consider a scenario in which each town's budget is constrained to be used toward certain project types, such as infrastructure, housing, or green space. Further, the towns constrained to spend on green space might be divided by whether they want a park with athletic fields or walking trails. In this case, the towns' valuations would comprise a laminar set family.

UWO remains NP-hard in our restricted setting with laminar demand sets. This hardness result follows from a straightforward reduction from KNAPSACK to an instance of our problem with disjoint (and thus, laminar) demand sets which maps knapsack items to agent demand sets. If we set $b_i = z_i$ for all $i \in N$, the UWO-WP outcome will also be UWO and thus the same reduction shows NP-hardness of UWO-WP in the single-minded laminar setting.

Given the hardness results, we search for an approximation of UWO-WP in the laminar single-minded setting. The following is the main result of the section, which provides an FPTAS for UWO-WP in the single-minded setting with laminar demand sets.

Theorem 4. *In the laminar single-minded setting, the UWO-WP problem admits an FPTAS.*

Before we prove this result, we state three key lemmas used in the proof. We first point out that MaxPE, despite being NP-hard for a single agent in the additive setting, is polynomial-time solvable in the single-minded setting.

Lemma 4. *The* MaxPE *problem can be solved in polynomial time in the single-minded setting.*

The following lemma, which states that every MaxPE set is contained in at least one UWO-WP outcome, also holds for the single-minded setting in general.

Lemma 5. *In the single-minded setting, for any MaxPE set* Q, *there exists a UWO-WP outcome* $W^\star$ *such that* $W^\star \supseteq Q$.

Proof. Let Q be any MaxPE set and let W be any UWO-WP outcome. If $Q \subseteq W$, we are done. Assume $Q \not\subseteq W$. Then, there is a non-empty set $Q' = Q \setminus W$. We will now show that $W' = W \cup Q'$ is UWO-WP, which implies that Q is a subset of a UWO-WP outcome and concludes our proof.

First note that because Q is a MaxPE set, we have that $PE(Q) \geq PE(Q \setminus Q')$, which implies that

$$\sum_{i \in N_Q} \min(b_i, z_i) - C(Q) \geq \sum_{i \in N_{Q \setminus Q'}} \min(b_i, z_i) - \sum_{j \in Q \setminus Q'} C_j$$

$$\implies \sum_{i \in N_Q} \min(b_i, z_i) - \sum_{\{i \in N_Q \mid D_i \cap Q' = \emptyset\}} \min(b_i, z_i) - C(Q') \geq 0$$

$$\implies \sum_{\{i \in N_Q \mid D_i \cap Q' \neq \emptyset\}} \min(b_i, z_i) - C(Q') \geq 0 \tag{4}$$

We now show that W' is feasible and WP. Because W and Q' are disjoint and $W \supseteq Q \setminus Q'$, observe that

$$\sum_{i \in N_{W'}} \min(b_i, z_i) - C(W')$$

$$= \sum_{\{i \in N_{W'} \mid D_i \cap Q' = \emptyset\}} \min(b_i, z_i) - C(W) \quad + \sum_{\{i \in N_{W'} \mid D_i \cap Q' \neq \emptyset\}} \min(b_i, z_i) - C(Q')$$

$$\geq \sum_{i \in N_W} \min(b_i, z_i) - C(W) + \sum_{\{i \in N_Q \mid D_i \cap Q' \neq \emptyset\}} \min(b_i, z_i) - C(Q') \geq 0$$

The final inequality follows from Eq. (4) in conjunction with W being WP. All that remains is to show that the addition of Q' to W weakly improves social welfare. By a similar argument as above, it follows that $SW(W')$ equals

$$\left[\sum_{i \in N_W} z_i - C(W) \right] + \left[\sum_{\{i \in N_Q \mid D_i \cap Q' \neq \emptyset\}} z_i - C(Q') \right] \geq$$

$$SW(W) + \sum_{\{i \in N_Q \mid D_i \cap Q' \neq \emptyset\}} \min(b_i, z_i) - C(Q') \geq SW(W).$$

$\square$

We construct an FPTAS in the laminar single-minded setting, by providing an approximation-preserving reduction [28] to another generalization of the classical knapsack problem called *knapsack on conflict graphs* (KCG) [25], which we now describe.

An instance of KCG is defined by a knapsack capacity B and an undirected graph $G = (V, E)$ referred to as a *conflict graph*, where each node $i \in V$ has an associated profit p_i and weight w_i. The KCG problem is then expressed by the following optimization problem: $\max_{S \subseteq V} \sum_{i \in S} p_i$ subject to $\sum_{i \in S} w_i \leq B$ and $|\{(i, j) \in E | i, j \in S\}| = 0$.

The following lemma states the conflict graph defined by a laminar set family is *chordal*, i.e. all cycles of four or more vertices have a chord, which is an edge that is not part of the cycle but connects two vertices of the cycle.

Lemma 6. *Given a laminar set family* $\mathbf{D} = \{D_1, \cdots, D_n\}$, *the graph* $G = (V, E)$ *where* $V = [n]$ *and* $E = \{(i, j) | D_i \subseteq D_j\}$ *is chordal.*

Proof. Consider such a graph $G = (V, E)$. Let $E^c \subseteq E$ be a cycle of length four or more. Pick any edge $(i, j) \in E^c$ and assume without loss of generality that $D_i \subseteq D_j$. Now pick any edge $(i, k) \in E^c$, which must exist because E^c is a cycle. We have that $D_i \cap D_k \neq \emptyset$ by the construction of the graph and thus $D_k \cap D_j \neq \emptyset$. Since $\mathbf{D}$ is a laminar set family, this means that D_j and D_k form a subset relation, which implies $(j, k) \in E$. (j, k) is a chord since it connects two vertices in E^c and cannot be in E^c since it would form a triangle, contradicting E^c being a cycle of length four or more. □

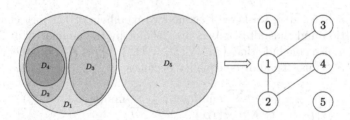

Fig. 2. The mapping from an instance of the laminar single-minded UWO-WP problem to an instance of KCG as described in the proof of Theorem 4.

Proof (Proof of Theorem 4). Let $I = \langle N, M, \mathbf{v}, \mathbf{b}, \mathbf{C} \rangle$ be an instance of UWO-WP problem with laminar single-minded demand sets. Let Q be a MaxPE set computed by the polynomial time algorithm given in the proof of Lemma 4 and let N' be the set of agents whose demand sets are not in Q, i.e. $N' = \{i \in N | D_i \not\subseteq Q\}$. We know that a UWO-WP solution which contains Q is guaranteed to exist by Lemma 5. We proceed by reducing the problem of computing such a UWO-WP solution $W^* \supseteq Q$ to an instance of KCG as follows:

$$- V = \{0\} \cup N; \qquad E = \{(i,j) | D_i \subseteq D_j, \forall i, j \in N\}; \qquad B = PE(Q)$$

$$- \; p_i = \begin{cases} \displaystyle\sum_{j \in N \setminus N'} z_j - C(Q) & \text{if } i = 0 \\ \displaystyle\sum_{j \in N' | D_j \subseteq D_i \cup Q} z_j - C(D_i \setminus Q) & \text{otherwise} \end{cases}$$

$$- \; w_i = \begin{cases} 0 & \text{if } i = 0 \\ C(D_i \setminus Q) - \displaystyle\sum_{\{j \in N' | D_j \subseteq D_i\}} \min(b_j, z_j) & \text{otherwise} \end{cases}$$

See Fig. 2 for an example of the mapping from an instance of UWO-WP to an instance of KCG. In words, each node in the conflict graph besides $\{0\}$ corresponds to an agent in the UWO-WP instance I. The knapsack capacity corresponds to the slack in our feasibility constraint produced by the selection of the MaxPE set. Lastly, node $\{0\}$ corresponds to the agents whose demand sets are in the MaxPE outcome, i.e. $N \setminus N'$. Thus, since we seek a UWO-WP solution containing Q, this node provides profit equal to $SW(Q)$ for zero cost and is not connected by an edge to any other node.

Let S be a feasible solution to the instance of KCG reduced from I and denote $S^0 = S \setminus \{0\}$. We posit that $W = Q \cup \bigcup_{i \in S^0} D_i$ satisfies feasibility and WP. Since S is a feasible KCG solution, we know $\sum_{i \in S} w_i = \sum_{i \in S^0} w_i \leq B$, which we can write as

$$\sum_{i \in S^0} \left[C(D_i \setminus Q) - \sum_{\{j \in N' | D_j \subseteq D_i\}} \min(b_j, z_j) \right] \leq \sum_{i \in N_Q} \min(b_i, z_i) - C(Q).$$

Since S is feasible, we know that no two members of $\{D_i\}_{i \in S}$ can form a subset relation and thus all members are disjoint by the laminarity of $\mathbf{D}$. From this, we can also conclude that $\{j \in N' | D_j \subseteq D_{i_1}\} \cap \{j \in N' | D_j \subseteq D_{i_2}\} = \emptyset$ for all $i_1, i_2 \in S$. Thus, the above inequality becomes

$$\sum_{\substack{j \in \bigcup_{i \in S^0} D_i \setminus Q}} C_j - \sum_{\substack{\{j \in N' | D_j \subseteq \bigcup_{i \in S^0} D_i\}}} \min(b_j, z_j) \leq \sum_{i \in N_Q} \min(b_i, z_i) - C(Q)$$

$$\implies \sum_{i \in N_Q} \min(b_i, z_i) + \sum_{\substack{\{i \in N \setminus N_Q | D_i \subseteq \bigcup_{j \in S^0} D_j\}}} \min(b_i, z_i) - \sum_{\substack{j \in Q \cup \bigcup_{i \in S^0} D_i}} C_j \geq 0$$

$$\implies \sum_{\substack{\{i \in N | D_i \subseteq Q \cup \bigcup_{i \in S^0} D_i\}}} \min(b_i, z_i) - \sum_{\substack{j \in Q \cup \bigcup_{i \in S^0} D_i}} C_j \geq 0$$

which means W is feasible and WP.

All that remains to complete our approximation-preserving reduction is to equate the objective values of corresponding solutions of our original and reduced instances. Since node $\{0\}$ has weight 0 and non-negative profit, we can restrict our attention to KCG solutions containing $\{0\}$ without loss of generality. We now show that the objective value of any feasible KCG solution, S, is equal to that of the resulting project bundle, W:

$$\sum_{i \in S} p_i = \sum_{i \in S^0} \left[\sum_{\{j \in N' | D_j \subseteq D_i \cup Q\}} z_j - C(D_i \setminus Q) \right] + \sum_{j \in N \setminus N'} z_j - C(Q)$$

$$= \sum_{\{i \in N' | D_i \subseteq Q \cup \bigcup_{j \in S^0} D_j\}} z_i + \sum_{i \in N_Q} z_i - \sum_{j \in \bigcup_{i \in S^0} D_i \setminus Q} C_j - C(Q)$$

$$= \sum_{i \in N_W} z_i - C(W) = SW(W)$$

It is apparent that the reduction runs in polynomial time. Pferschy and Schauer [25] provide an FPTAS for KCG on chordal graphs. By Lemma 6, G is a chordal graph. Thus, laminar single-minded UWO-WP admits an FPTAS. □

In the single-minded setting, the problem of welfare maximization resembles the well-studied set-union knapsack problem (SUKP), which is hard to approximate in the general case [2,17,24]. Despite SUKP's resemblance to our problems of interest, approximation results from SUKP or its restricted cases, such as those described by Goldschmidt et al. [17], do not imply any of our results. However, an argument similar to that given to prove Theorem 4 reveals a new restriction under which SUKP admits an FPTAS, namely the restriction to laminar item sets (see full version [5]).

6   An Algorithm for Symmetric Valuations

We now focus our attention on the domain of symmetric valuations. We say that a valuation function v_i is *symmetric* if it depends only on the size of the input, i.e. $v_i(S) = v_i(T)$ whenever $|S| = |T|$. Such valuations describe a setting where multiple units of the same project or item are available and agents' valuations are solely dependent on the quantity of items selected. Note that symmetric valuations are not necessarily additive. For instance, the valuations can be $v_i(S) = \sqrt{|S|}$ or $v_i(S) = e^{|S|} - 1$, which are submodular and supermodular valuations, respectively, and neither of which are additive.

Symmetric valuations are standard restrictions in the mechanism design literature. For example, Hoefer and Kesselheim [21] use symmetric valuations to capture "a spectrum auction of equally sized channels which all offer very similar conditions". Other research has investigated cost sharing mechanisms for symmetric valuations [7].

Theorem 5 *For symmetric valuations, Algorithm 1 finds UWO-WP in polynomial time.*

Algorithm 1 Symmetric Valuation

Input: $\langle N, M, \mathbf{v}, \boldsymbol{b}, \mathbf{C} \rangle$ where valuations are symmetric
Order projects by increasing cost, i.e $C_1 \leq C_2 \leq \cdots \leq C_m$
$\Omega = \emptyset$
for $k = 1$ to m **do**
   if $\sum_{i \in N} \min\{v_i([k]), b_i\} \geq C([k])$ **then**
      $\Omega \leftarrow \Omega \cup k$
$k^* \leftarrow \arg\max_{k \in \Omega} \mathrm{SW}([k])$
for $i = 1$ to n **do**
   if $\sum_{j=1}^{i} \min\{v_j([k^*]), b_j\} < C([k^*])$ **then**
      $x_i \leftarrow \min\{v_i([k^*]), b_i\}$
   else
      $x_i \leftarrow C([k^*]) - \sum_{j=1}^{i-1} \min\{v_j([k^*]), b_j\}$
return $W = [k^*]$ and $\mathbf{x} = (x_1, \cdots, x_n)$

---

7 Discussion

In this paper, we laid the groundwork for an important and general PB framework which captures resource pooling. We focused on welfare maximization subject to minimal participation axioms that agents would expect the mechanism to satisfy and proved several hardness and inapproximability results. We also identified and gave explicit algorithms for two natural classes of instances.

As mentioned in Sect. 3, we chose to study WP outcomes rather than imposing the IR constraint primarily because of the large social welfare gap IR induces. It is worth noting that our inapproximability for the identical costs restricted setting (Theorem 3) still holds even if we instead opt for the IR requirement. This is because the reduction used to show NP-hardness of MaxPE ≥ 1 constructs instances in which the cost of each project exceeds the budget of each individual. For a more detailed argument, refer to the full version. Thus, it is not the case that we would have found more general, positive results if we had instead studied IR outcomes.

Our work leaves interesting open problems, and provides a framework for further exploration of PB with resource pooling. Specifically, while we showed an FPTAS for UWO-WP in the laminar single-minded setting, it remains open whether there exists a bounded approximation algorithm for UWO-WP in the general single-minded case. Furthermore, future work can focus on other restrictions which bypass our inapproximability. Lastly, while our participation axiom captures some notion of fairness, it would be interesting to explore other fairness concepts within our framework.

Acknowledgements. Haris Aziz is supported by the NSF-CSIRO project on "Fair Sequential Collective Decision-Making". Mashbat Suzuki was partially supported by the ARC Laureate Project FL200100204 on "Trustworthy AI".

References

1. Archer, A., Papadimitriou, C., Talwar, K., Tardos, É.: An approximate truthful mechanism for combinatorial auctions with single parameter agents. Internet Math. 129–150 (2004)
2. Arulselvan, A.: A note on the set union knapsack problem. Discret. Appl. Math. **169**, 214–218 (2014)
3. Aziz, H.: Strategyproof multi-item exchange under single-minded dichotomous preferences. In: AAMAS 2020 (2020)
4. Aziz, H., Ganguly, A.: Participatory funding coordination: model, axioms and rules. In: Fotakis, D., Ríos Insua, D. (eds.) ADT 2021. LNCS (LNAI), vol. 13023, pp. 409–423. Springer, Cham (2021). https://doi.org/10.1007/978-3-030-87756-9_26
5. Aziz, H., Gujar, S., Padala, M., Suzuki, M., Vollen, J.: Coordinating Monetary Contributions in Participatory Budgeting. arXiv preprint arXiv:2206.05966 (2022)
6. Aziz, H., Shah, N.: Participatory budgeting: models and approaches. In: Pathways Between Social Science and Computational Social Science (2020)
7. Birmpas, G., Markakis, E., Schäfer, G.: Cost sharing over combinatorial domains: complement-free cost functions and beyond. In: ESA 2019 (2019)
8. Brandl, F., Brandt, F., Greger, M., Peter, D., Stricker, C., Suksompong, W.: Funding public projects: a case for the Nash product rule. J. Math. Econ. **99**, 102585 (2022)
9. Brânzei, S., Lv, Y., Mehta, R.: To give or not to give: fair division for single minded valuations. In: IJCAI 2016, pp. 123–129 (2016)
10. Buterin, V., Hitzig, Z., Weyl, E.G.: A flexible design for funding public goods. Manage. Sci. **65**(11), 5171–5187 (2019)
11. Chen, J., Lackner, M., Maly, J.: Participatory budgeting with donations and diversity constraints. In: AAAI 2022, pp. 9323–9330 (2022)
12. Chen, N., Deng, X., Sun, X.: On complexity of single-minded auction. J. Comput. Syst. Sci. **69**(4), 675–687 (2004)
13. Damle, S., Moti, M.H., Chandra, P., Gujar, S.: Civic crowdfunding for agents with negative valuations and agents with asymmetric beliefs. In: IJCAI 2019, pp. 208–214 (2019)
14. Devanur, N., Goldner, K., Saxena, R., Schvartzman, A., Weinberg, M.: Optimal mechanism design for single-minded agents. In: EC 2020, pp. 193–256 (2020)
15. Dobzinski, S., Mehta, A., Roughgarden, T., Sundararajan, M.: Is shapley cost sharing optimal? Games Econom. Behav. **108**, 130–138 (2018)
16. Elkind, E., Faliszewski, P., Skowron, P., Slinko, A.: Properties of multiwinner voting rules. Social Choice Welfare **48**, 599–632 (2017)
17. Goldschmidt, O., Nehme, D., Yu, G.: Note: on the set-union knapsack problem. Nav. Res. Logist. (NRL) **41**(6), 833–842 (1994)
18. Green, J.R., Laffont, J.J.: Incentives in Public Decision-Making, vol. 1. North-Holland, Amsterdam (1979)
19. Groves, T.: Incentives in teams. Econometrica **41**, 617–631 (1973)
20. Hershkowitz, D.E., Kahng, A., Peters, D., Procaccia, A.D.: District-fair participatory budgeting. In: AAAI 2021, pp. 5464–5471 (2021)
21. Hoefer, M., Kesselheim, T.: Secondary spectrum auctions for symmetric and submodular bidders. In: EC 2012, pp. 657–671 (2012)
22. Lawler, E.L.: Fast approximation algorithms for knapsack problems. Math. Oper. Res. **4**(4), 339–356 (1979)

23. Moulin, H.: Serial cost-sharing of excludable public goods. Rev. Econ. Stud. **61**(2), 305–325 (1994)
24. Nehme-Haily, D.A.: The set-union knapsack problem. Ph.D. thesis, The University of Texas at Austin (1995)
25. Pferschy, U., Schauer, J.: The knapsack problem with conflict graphs. J. Graph Algorithms Appl. **13**(2), 233–249 (2009)
26. Samuelson, P.A.: The pure theory of public expenditure. Rev. Econ. Stat. **36**, 387–389 (1954)
27. Shah, A.: Participatory Budgeting. World Bank Publications, Washington, DC (2007)
28. Vazirani, V.V.: Approximation Algorithms. Springer, Heidelberg (2001). https://doi.org/10.1007/978-3-662-04565-7
29. Vries, M.S.D., Nemec, J., Špaček, D. (eds.): International Trends in Participatory Budgeting. Springer, Cham (2020). https://doi.org/10.1007/978-3-030-79930-4
30. Yan, X., Chen, Y.: Optimal crowdfunding design. In: AAMAS 2021, pp. 1704–1706 (2021)

Robustness of Participatory Budgeting Outcomes: Complexity and Experiments

Niclas Boehmer[1], Piotr Faliszewski[2(✉)], Łukasz Janeczko[2],
and Andrzej Kaczmarczyk[2]

[1] Technische Universität Berlin, Berlin, Germany
niclas.boehmer@tu-berlin.de
[2] AGH University, Krakow, Poland
{faliszew,ljaneczk,andrzej.kaczmarczyk}@agh.edu.pl

Abstract. We study the robustness of approval-based participatory budgeting (PB) rules to random noise in the votes. First, we analyze the computational complexity of the #FLIP-BRIBERY problem, where given a PB instance we ask for the number of ways in which we can flip a given number of approvals in the votes, so that a specific project is selected. This problem captures computing the funding probabilities of projects in case random noise is added. Unfortunately, it is intractable even for the simplest PB rules. Second, we analyze the robustness of several prominent PB rules (including the basic greedy rule and the Method of Equal Shares) on real-world instances from Pabulib. Using sampling, we quantify the extent to which simple, greedy PB rules are more robust than proportional ones, and we identify three types of (very) non-robust projects in real-world PB instances.

1 Introduction

We study the robustness of approval-based participatory budgeting (PB) rules to random noise in the votes. To this end, we first analyze the complexity of the computational problems that capture our approach, and then we perform robustness experiments on real-world PB instances.

In a PB scenario, we are given a set of projects, each with its cost, a collection of voters, and a budget. Each voter indicates which projects he or she approves, and the task is to choose a set of projects that receive sufficient support and whose total cost is within the budget. In particular, participatory budgeting is a common way for cities to let the residents influence their spending: First, the most active citizens submit projects they would like to see implemented, next, the whole electorate votes on these projects, and finally the selected projects are carried out. However, while PB exercises are very appealing in general, they do face several issues, of which we mention two: First, the number of submitted projects is often quite high (in Pabulib [24], a collection of real-world PB instances, over 30% of the instances involve at least 25 projects, and over 10% involve at least 50). Second, usually only a small fraction of the electorate actually votes (as seen in Pabulib [24], typically this is between 4% and 10% of the

A. Deligkas and A. Filos-Ratsikas (Eds.): SAGT 2023, LNCS 14238, pp. 161–178, 2023.
https://doi.org/10.1007/978-3-031-43254-5_10

cities' residents). Hence, PB results may be seen as somewhat shaky. Indeed, it is possible that some citizens did not inform themselves about the full set of submitted projects and would have changed their votes had they done so, while some other citizens might have chosen to vote (or refrain from voting) based on somewhat random criteria (e.g., they saw a PB advertisement at a more or less convenient moment). We study the potential instability of PB results by analyzing their robustness to random noise in the votes.

More specifically, we take the following approach: Given a PB instance, we modify each vote by randomly flipping some of the approvals (i.e., by randomly adding approvals for some of the unsupported projects and randomly removing approvals from some of the supported ones) and, then, we evaluate the probability that the outcome changes. As part of our analysis, we also examine the probability that specific projects are funded if we add noise to the votes like this. On a computational level, we capture this approach through the #FLIP-BRIBERY problem, where we ask for the number of ways in which a given number of approval flips can be performed, so that a specific project is selected. Unfortunately, our complexity results show that #FLIP-BRIBERY is intractable even for the simplest PB rules (often already in the problem's decision variant, where we ask if the problem's solution is non-zero). Consequently, in our numerical experiments, we use sampling to estimate the relevant probabilities: Given a PB instance, we randomly flip approvals in the votes, following the resampling noise model of Szufa et al. [25], parameterized by a noise level parameter $\phi \in [0, 1]$. In our experimental analysis of real-world PB instances, our main robustness measure is the 50%-winner threshold: the smallest value of the noise level for which the outcome changes with probability at least 50% [2,3].

We focus on five prominent PB rules. The first two, GREEDYAV and GREEDYCOST, consider the projects one-by-one, in the non-increasing order of either the number of approvals they receive, or their approval-to-cost ratios (a project's approval-to-cost ratio is the number of approvals this project received divided by its cost); a project is selected if there still are enough unallocated funds at the time when it is considered. We study these two rules because they are among the simplest ones and, more importantly, because GREEDYAV is one of the most commonly used rules in practice. Yet, these two rules are often criticized as providing results that do not represent the voters proportionally. Hence, we also consider a PB variant of the PHRAGMÉN rule [6,16], and two rules from the *Method of Equal Shares* (MES) family, proposed by Peters, Pierczyński, and Skowron [18,19]. The MES rules are particularly attractive both due to their good theoretical properties and the fact that one of them was recently used in a real-world PB exercise [20]. All our rules are computable in polynomial time (at least for appropriate tie-breaking; see the work of Janeczko and Faliszewski for a deeper discussion of this issue [14]).

Contributions. Below we summarize our main contributions:

1. For all our rules, we show that both #FLIP-BRIBERY and its decision variant are, in general, intractable. Somewhat surprisingly, for GREEDYAV, this

Table 1. Computational complexity of FLIP-BRIBERY for our rules when project costs are encoded in binary. Unless stated otherwise, the results are for order-based tie-breaking (see Sect. 2 for definitions). For the counting variant, all intractability results hold already for a single voter and all tractability results hold for arbitrary numbers of voters. The parentheses after FPT, W[1], and XP results indicate for which parameters they hold (m for the number of projects, n for the number of voters, and r for the number of approval flips).

rule	decision variant		counting variant	reference
	1 voter	n voters		
GREEDYAV	NP-com. W[1]-hard(r) FPT(m)	NP-com. W[1]-hard(r) FPT(m)	#P-com. #W[1]-hard(r) FPT(m)	Theorems 1, 2, 4
GREEDYAV(cheaper-first)	P	NP-com. W[1]-hard(n) FPT(m) XP(n)	#P-com. #W[1]-hard(r) FPT(m)	Theorems 2, 3, 4
GREEDYCOST	NP-com. W[1]-hard(r)	NP-com. W[1]-hard(r)	#P-com. #W[1]-hard(r)	Theorem 7, Corollary 2
PHRAGMÉN, MES-APR	P	NP-com (unit costs)	#P-com. #W[1]-hard(r)	Theorem 6, Corollaries 1, 2
MES-COST	NP-com. W[1]-hard(r)	NP-com (unit costs)	#P-com. #W[1]-hard(r)	Theorem 6, Corollaries 1, 2

holds already for a single voter. Nonetheless, we do show some ways to circumvent these intractability results (e.g., an FPT algorithm parameterized by the number of projects, or an XP algorithm parameterized by the number of voters, for a particular tie-breaking scheme). However, generally, these approaches are insufficient for large PB instances, including many of those from Pabulib [24]. We summarize our complexity results in Table 1.

2. We perform a robustness analysis of all our PB rules (except for one of the variants of MES) on PB instances from Pabulib [24]. We find that the greedy rules (i.e., GREEDYAV and GREEDYCOST) are the most robust ones, whereas the proportional rules (i.e., PHRAGMÉN and a variant of MES) are less robust. The extent of the difference between the two kinds of rules is interesting, but the effect itself is expected: By design, proportionality means faster response to changes in the votes.

3. We find many real-world PB instances where random noise quickly changes project's funding probabilities. For example, in a PB instance from Wrzeciono Mlociny from 2019 flipping 0.24% of approvals randomly changes the outcome in a majority of cases. We identify three main types of non-robust projects: Originally selected projects of the first type have low funding probability even for a fairly small noise level, and, as we increase it, their funding probability decreases even further. Such projects can be seen as selected "by luck." (Analogously, projects that originally are not selected, but whose funding probability quickly increases even for small noise levels, can be seen as rejected "by misfortune."). Non-robust projects of the second type quickly reach a funding probability of 50% and stay at this level irrespective of whether further noise is added to the votes. Such projects can be seen as tied with each other. Finally, for projects of the third type the funding probability behaves non-monotonically as the level of noise increases (such projects deserve individual analysis).

We believe that a robustness analysis should always be performed after participatory budgeting exercises. Its results can either be used by the city to fund some additional projects (e.g., the "effectively tied" ones or those "unselected by misfortune"), or by the voters, to understand the performance of a project. All proofs and additional experiments are deferred to our full version [4]. The code for our experiments is available at github.com/Project-PRAGMA/PB-Robustness-SAGT-2023.

Related Work. Approval-based participatory budgeting is an extension of the approval-based (multiwinner) voting framework, where each project (referred to as a candidate) has a unit cost and the goal is to select a fixed-size committee. We point to the works of Rey and Maly [22] and Lackner and Skowron [15] for overviews of the PB and multiwinner voting frameworks, respectively.

Analyses of the probability that election outcomes change under noise were recently pursued by Boehmer et al. [2] and Baumaister and Hogrebe [1]. Both teams analyzed counting variants of various bribery problems, i.e., problems where we ask for the number of ways to modify the votes so that a particular candidate wins, and they both focused on the single-winner, ordinal case, where the voters rank the candidates and the voting rule outputs a single winner. Relevant to our work, Boehmer et al. [2] introduced the notion of the 50%-winner threshold, which they later applied to analyze real-world elections [3].

Another view of election robustness was considered by Shiryaev et al. [23], who instead of asking for the probability that the result changes under a given noise model, asked for the smallest number of modifications in the votes needed for the change (this is also related to computing the margin of victory of particular candidates [7,17,26]). This idea was later pursued by Faliszewski et al. [5] in the ordinal, multiwinner setting, and by Gawron and Faliszewski [13] and Faliszewski et al. [8] in the approval-based one. For multiwinner approval elections, similar types of bribery problem were studied by Faliszewski et al. [11] and while their motivation was different, their technical contributions are similar.

More broadly, the family of bribery problems was first studied by Faliszewski et al. [9]. For an overview, we point to the survey of Faliszewski and Rothe [10].

2   Preliminaries

A *participatory budgeting* instance (a PB instance) is a 5-tuple $E = (C, V, A, B, \text{cost})$, where $C = \{c_1, c_2, \ldots, c_m\}$ is a set of *projects* (also called *candidates* in the literature), $V = (v_1, v_2, \ldots, v_n)$ is a collection of *voters*, $A \colon V \to 2^C$ is a function that associates each voter v_i with the set of projects that v_i *approves*, $B \in \mathbb{N}$ is the available *budget*, and cost$\colon C \to \mathbb{N}$ is a function that associates each project with its cost. For convenience, we overload the function A so that for each project c_i, $A(c_i)$ is the set of voters that approve c_i (i.e., the set of voters $v_j \in V$ with $c_i \in A(v_j)$). We refer to $|A(c_i)|$ as the *approval score* of c_i. Given a set of projects $S \subseteq C$, by cost(S) we mean $\sum_{c_i \in S} \text{cost}(c_i)$, i.e., the total cost of the members of S. Given a PB instance $E = (C, V, A, B, \text{cost})$, a set $S \subseteq C$ is a *feasible outcome* if cost$(S) \leq B$.

A *budgeting rule* is a function f that given a PB instance outputs the winning feasible outcome (we assume that our rules are resolute; we will discuss the used tie-breaking mechanisms later). We focus on sequential budgeting rules, which compute a feasible outcome W starting from an empty set and including projects one-by-one, until a certain condition is met. We consider the following rules:

1. The GREEDYAV rule considers the projects in the order of their non-increasing approval scores (breaking ties between projects according to a given, prespecified rule) and it includes a project into the outcome W if doing so would not exceed the available budget.
2. The GREEDYCOST rule works like GREEDYAV, but it considers the projects in the order of non-increasing ratios of their approval score to their cost.
3. The PHRAGMÉN rule constructs the outcome in a continuous process, in which voters virtually buy the projects to be funded. The voters start with an empty (virtual) bank account and are given (virtual) money at a constant rate as the process runs (the exact value of the constant is irrelevant); slightly abusing the notation, we refer to the balance of voter $v_i \in V$ as $b(v_i)$ (the balance fluctuates over time but we use this notation only at well-defined points of the procedure). As soon as there is a project c who is not yet included in W, such that:

$$\sum_{v_i \in A(c)} b(v_i) = \text{cost}(c), \quad \text{and} \quad \text{cost}(W) + \text{cost}(c) \leq B,$$

(i.e., the voters who approve c have enough money to pay for it and doing so would not exceed the overall budget B), the voters who approve c buy this project (i.e., c is included in W and the bank accounts of the voters who approve c are reset to be empty). The process runs until no more projects can be added to W (i.e., there is no project that is approved by at least one voter, such that adding this project to W would not exceed the overall budget B).
4. The MES-APR and MES-COST rules are two incarnations of the *Method of Equal Shares (MES)*. Just like PHRAGMÉN, these rules are also based on the concept of voters buying the projects, but this time each voter receives $B/|V|$ units of virtual money upfront. Then, the voters sequentially buy the projects with the best price-per-utility value (the difference between the two variants is in how they define this utility). Formally, let $b_i(v)$ be the (virtual) account balance of voter $v \in V$ *just before* stage i of the procedure, and let $u_j(c) \in \mathbb{N}$ be the utility that voter $v_j \in V$ assigns to some project $c \in C$. At each stage i, a project $c \notin W$ is called q-*affordable* if it holds that:

$$\sum_{v_j \in A(c)} \min\{b_i(v_j), u_j(c) \cdot q\} = \text{cost}(c).$$

In other words, project c is q-affordable if the voters who approve it can collect $\text{cost}(c)$ amount of money by spending q units of budget for each unit of utility that they derive from the project, where the voters approving the project who do not have enough money in their accounts give all the money they have left. If there are any q-affordable projects, then the rule includes in W the one which is q-affordable for the smallest q (breaking ties according to a prespecified rule). Otherwise, the rule terminates. Both MES-APR and MES-COST follow the above-described scheme, but under the first one the utility $u_j(c)$ that voter v_j gives to a project c is 1 if the voter approves c and is 0 otherwise; under the second rule, this utility is $\text{cost}(c)$ if the voter approves c and it is 0 otherwise.

Regarding tie-breaking, we assume that each PB instance also comes with a fixed order of projects and whenever we need to resolve a tie between projects, we choose the one that is ranked highest in this order. We refer to this approach as *order-based* tie-breaking. For the case of GREEDYAV we also consider the *cheaper-first* tie-breaking: Whenever there is a tie among a set of projects, we choose the one with the lowest cost (and if there are several projects with the same lowest cost, we choose one of them using order-based tie-breaking). We observe that cheaper-first tie-breaking is a special case of the order-based one, so all algorithms that work for the latter also work for the former, and all hardness results for the former also hold for the latter.

Unlike the other rules we study, MES-APR and MES-COST output only projects which they consider "sufficiently supported". This implies in some instances that the set of funded projects (returned by these rules) can be extended by some additional projects and still fit in the budget. Formally speaking, the MES rules (as defined above) fail exhaustiveness. In our theoretical part, we stick to these variants to focus on the fundamental properties of the MES rules. In the experimental part of the paper we discuss exhaustive variants of MES.

2.1   Computational Complexity

We assume familiarity with both classic and parameterized computational complexity theory, including the P, NP, FPT, W[1], and XP classes, as well as the notions of reductions, hardness, and completeness. The $O^*(\cdot)$ notation is analogous to the classic $O(\cdot)$ one, except that it also omits polynomial terms. Given a decision problem X, where we ask if a mathematical object with some properties exists, we write $\#X$ to denote its counting variant, i.e., the problem where we ask for the number of such objects. If a decision problem belongs to the class NP, its counting analog belongs to $\#P$. Similarly, $\#W[1]$ is the counting analog of W[1] [12].

2.2   Flip-Bribery Problem

We are interested in computing the probability that a given project wins in a given PB instance provided we can flip a given number of approvals. Formally, we capture this problem in the following definition.

Definition 1. *Let f be a budgeting rule. In the f-FLIP-BRIBERY decision problem, given a PB instance $E = (C, V, A, B, \text{cost})$, a preferred project $p \in C$, and a radius $r \in \mathbb{N}$, we ask if there is a PB instance E' such that p belongs to $f(E')$,* *where E' can be obtained from E by performing at most r approval flips. In the counting variant of the problem, denoted $\#f$-FLIP-BRIBERY, we ask for the number of such PB instances E' (obtained by making exactly r approval flips[1]).*

The interpretation of the counting version of the problem is as follows: If our original PB instance has m projects and n voters, and we make exactly r approval flips, then there are $y = \binom{mn}{r}$ different PB instances that we can obtain. If the solution to the counting problem is x (i.e., in x of these y instances p is selected) then the probability of selecting p after making r random approval flips is x/y. This is why we are interested in the complexity of the counting variant of the problem. However, as we will see, even this problem—modeling a rather basic form of noise—is intractable. Thus in our experiments we will use a sampling approach and, taking advantage of that, we will use a more involved noise model that better captures reality (as our intractability proofs work already for a single voter, they imply hardness for any natural model of noise).

We also consider the decision variant of the problem because, on the one hand, if already the decision problem is intractable then so is the counting one, and, on the other hand, because the solution to the decision problem already gives us a first idea regarding how well a particular project performed: The fewer approval flips we need to ensure a project's victory, the stronger it is.

3 Complexity Results for GREEDYAV

We start our complexity analysis of the $(\#)$FLIP-BRIBERY problems by focusing on the GREEDYAV rule. Intuitively, it seems that GREEDYAV-FLIP-BRIBERY is rather simple: If we want some project p to be selected, then we should give it as many approvals as possible and, if we still have some approval flips left (i.e., if p ends up being approved by all the voters before we run out of the available flips), then we should remove approvals from the most expensive, approved-by-all projects that precede p in the tie-breaking order (if such projects exist). However, it turns out that the situation is more involved, and, instead of giving p as many approvals as possible, it may be more beneficial to promote some other project. For example, p may not be selected because some expensive project c is considered and selected earlier, not leaving enough budget for p. However, if we promote some project d to be considered (and selected) before c, then GREEDYAV may first select d and then reject c due to insufficient funds left, and may later select p. Consequently, GREEDYAV-FLIP-BRIBERY can be quite tricky. Indeed, we find that GREEDYAV-FLIP-BRIBERY is NP-complete (and, in fact, para-NP-complete for the parameterization by the number of voters).

Theorem 1. GREEDYAV-FLIP-BRIBERY *is* NP-*complete, even for a single voter, and is* W[1]-*hard for the parameterization by the number of approval flips.*

---

[1] Note that the difference between *at most* r and *exactly* r is immaterial here from the point of view of computational complexity: Both variants are Turing-reducible to each other.

One way to get around the above hardness result is to seek FPT algorithms. However, we have already established in Theorem 1 that such algorithms are (most likely) out of reach for the parameterizations by the number of voters and the number of available approval flips. This leaves us with the number of projects as the remaining most natural parameter and, indeed, we will present a fixed-parameter tractable algorithm for this parameter that even works for the counting variant of the problem. Such algorithms are still useful: At the time of writing this paper, the Pabulib library of real-world PB instances [24] contained 730 instances, of which 224 included at most 10 projects.

Theorem 2. *There are* FPT *algorithms for* #GREEDYAV-FLIP-BRIBERY *parameterized by the number of projects, with running times* $O^*(3^m)$ *and* $O^*(m!)$, *where the latter uses polynomial space.*

Interestingly, switching to the cheaper-first tie-breaking changes the complexity of our problem: For the parameterization by the number of voters, GREEDYAV-FLIP-BRIBERY now lies in XP, yet still is W[1]-hard. In particular, the XP algorithm considers all possible bribery flips if their number is bounded by the number of voters, and follows the simple greedy strategy outlined just before Theorem 1 otherwise (in this case it turns out to be correct). While the parameterization by the number of voters is not practical, it is interesting how the internal tie-breaking scheme affects the complexity of the problem.

Theorem 3. *For cheaper-first tie-breaking and the parameterization by the number of voters,* GREEDYAV-FLIP-BRIBERY *is* W[1]-*hard and belongs to* XP.

Theorem 4. #GREEDYAV-FLIP-BRIBERY *with cheaper-first tie-breaking is* #P-*complete and* #W[1]-*hard for the parameterization by the number of approval flips, even for 1 voter.*

Finally, a very natural way to circumvent the hardness from Theorem 1 would be to consider a variant of the problem where project costs are encoded in unary. Unfortunately, in this case the complexity has, so far, been elusive. Nonetheless, we do have a polynomial-time algorithm for the case of unit prices (while this is a very restricted setting, in the next section we will see that for some other rules even this is too much to hope for).

Theorem 5. *There is a polynomial-time algorithm for* #GREEDYAV-FLIP-BRIBERY *where each project has the same unit cost.*

4   Complexity Results for Rules Beyond GREEDYAV

Next let us move to the analysis of the complexity of FLIP-BRIBERY for our remaining rules. Unfortunately, we mostly obtain fairly strong hardness results. Indeed, for the latter three rules, the problem is NP-complete even for the case where all projects have the same unit cost. These results follow by careful analysis (and, for the case of MES, some adaptation) of proofs already available in the literature [8,14]. GREEDYCOST is polynomial-time computable in this case, as it is then equivalent to GREEDYAV (and so Theorem 5 applies).

Theorem 6. FLIP-BRIBERY *is* NP-*complete for each of* PHRAGMÉN, MES-COST *and* MES-APR, *even if all projects have the same unit cost.* GREEDYCOST *is in* P *in this case.*

For GREEDYCOST, our hardness result requires binary encoding, but works already for a single voter.

Theorem 7. GREEDYCOST-FLIP-BRIBERY *is* NP-*complete, as well as* W[1]-*hard for the parameterization by the number of approval flips, already for a single voter. The counting variant is* #P-*hard and* #W[1]-*hard (for the same parameterization).*

Results in the single-voter case for PHRAGMÉNand MES-APR follow by observing that in this specific case these rules become equivalent to GREEDYAV with cheaper-first tie-breaking (with the exception that GREEDYAV can select projects that do not receive any approvals, whereas PHRAGMÉNand MES-APR disregard such projects). Moreover, for any fixed tie-breaking order MES-COST becomes equivalent to GREEDYAV with the same tie-breaking order (under the same caveat regarding projects without approvals). Consequently, Theorem 1 and Theorem 3 yield the following corollary about the complexity of the discussed rules in the single-voter setting. Theorem 4 gives a similar corollary for the counting variants of the problem.

Corollary 1. MES-APR-FLIP-BRIBERY *and* PHRAGMÉN-FLIP-BRIBERY *are polynomial-time solvable for a single voter, but* MES-COST *is* NP-*complete and* W[1]-*hard for the parameterization by the number of approval flips in this case.*

Corollary 2. *For* PHRAGMÉN, MES-APR, *and* MES-COST, #FLIP-BRIBERY *is* #P-*complete and* #W[1]-*hard for the parameterization by the number of approval flips even for a single voter.*

Notably, as PHRAGMÉN-FLIP-BRIBERY and MES-APR-FLIP-BRIBERY are polynomial-time solvable for a single voter, our results are not sufficient to rule out the existence of FPT (or XP) algorithms for the number of voters for these problems in the decision and counting variants. We have not considered the parameter number of projects in this section, leaving this for future work.

5 Experiments

As discussed in Sect. 1 and Sect. 2.2, counting and decision variants of FLIP-BRIBERY can be used to estimate the robustness of outcomes of budgeting rules. As in most cases these problems are intractable, in this section we resort to a sampling-based approach to assess the robustness of funding decisions in participatory budgeting. In particular, we use real-world participatory budgeting instances from Pabulib [24] (i) to analyze examples of non-robust outcomes and (ii) to evaluate how robust outcomes typically are in practice and how this depends on the used budgeting rule.

Rules. We focus on (i) GREEDYAV, (ii) GREEDYCOST, (iii) PHRAGMÉN, and (iv) MES-COST.[2] As MES-COST regularly does not output exhaustive outcomes, i.e., the leftover funds would be sufficient to include additional projects [20], a completion method is needed in practical applications. In our experiments, we use a variant of MES-COST similar to the rule used in real-world applications [20]:[3] In case the produced outcome is not exhaustive, the initial endowments of the voters are increased (by increasing the total budget by 1%). We continue to do so until the cost of the projects selected by the rule exceeds the original budget. Unfortunately, the produced outcome is still not guaranteed to be exhaustive. In this case, we apply GREEDYAV to spend the remaining budget. We use the implementation provided by the Pabutools library [21] for PHRAGMÉN and MES-COST (and our own implementations for the other rules). In the execution of the rules, we break ties according to the order in which the projects appear in the file on Pabulib.

Noise Model and 50%-Winner Threshold. We use the resampling method introduced by Szufa et al. [25] as our noise model, which is parameterized by a *resampling probability* $\phi \in [0, 1]$ (we will also sometimes refer to ϕ as the noise level). To define the model, for each voter $v_i \in V$, let $p_i := 1/|A(v_i)|$ be the inverse of the number of projects approved by voter v_i. For each voter $v_i \in V$, we execute the following procedure: For every project $c_j \in C$, with probability $1 - \phi$, we do not change whether v_i approves c_j; however, with probability ϕ we "resample" the approval. This means that—independent of whether v_i initially approved c_j—with probability p_i we let v_i approve c_j, and with probability $1 - p_i$ we let v_i disapprove c_j. One advantage of this model is that it does not change the expected number of projects approved by a voter.

In our experiments, to assess the robustness of an outcome produced by rule $\mathcal{R}$ on some participatory budgeting instance $E = (C, V, A, B, \text{cost})$, we execute the following procedure. For each $\phi \in \{0, 1\%, 2\%, \ldots, 24\%, 25\%\}$, we modify E as described above using the resampling model with resampling parameter ϕ and record which projects are funded when rule $\mathcal{R}$ is applied to the modified instance. For each considered value of the resampling probability ϕ, we repeat this process 100 times, and, then, compute for each project its *funding probability*, i.e., the fraction of sampled instances in which the project is included in the computed outcome.[4] Informally speaking, we say that the funding decision on a project is robust if its funding probability does not quickly change when the resampling probability is increased; in contrast, we speak of non-robust funding decisions if

---

[2] To maintain focus, we do not consider MES-APR here. The reason why we examine MES-COST is that this is the variant that has been used in practice [20].

[3] We describe, analyze, and compare other existing completion variants in our full version [4].

[4] Our choice of focusing on resampling probabilities up to 25% is in some sense arbitrary. However, we believe that this range captures practically relevant cases. Indeed, if we need to introduce more than 25% of noise to affect the results, then it is natural to consider the original results to be robust.

already in the case where we perturb votes using a small resampling probability, the project's funding probability changes substantially.

Given a PB instance and a budgeting rule, we quantify this instance's robustness using the notion of 50%-*winner threshold*: Its value is the smallest (considered) value of ϕ for which a majority of sampled instances have a different outcome than the initial one. The idea of the 50%-winner threshold was introduced by Boehmer et al. [2], and was later used by the same team for practical analysis of the robustness in single-winner elections [3].

Data. In our experiments, we analyze instances from the Pabulib platform [24]. Specifically, we consider all instances available on Pabulib as of April 2023 in which approval ballots are used (these can be downloaded at http://pabulib. org/?hash=643d7a7937f76). However, in order to ensure a feasible computation time of our experiments, we discarded all instances for which MES-COST took more than 2 minutes to compute on the initial instance (on a single thread of an Intel(R) Xeon(R) Gold 6338 CPU @ 2.00GHz core). The resulting dataset contains 460 instances and we refer to it as the *full dataset*. In some cases, it will be interesting to focus on instances where some funding decisions are close. For this, we put together a second *selected dataset*, which contains all instances where the 50%-winner threshold for at least one of our rules is smaller or equal to 25%. This selected dataset consists of 257 out of our 460 instances.

Visualization of Results. Examining the robustness of the outcome of a single instance in more detail, we will visualize the funding probabilities of projects as line plots for varying values of the resampling probability (see, e.g., Fig. 2; we always indicate the place where the PB exercise took place in the caption). In these plots, each line corresponds to one project and shows the funding probability of this project (y-axis), depending on the used value of the resampling probability (x-axis).[5] Thus, when moving from left to right on these plots, we move further and further away from the initial instance and increase the level of noise. To ensure the readability of these plots, we only include projects which meet the following criterion: For the initially funded projects, we include those whose funding probability drops below 90% for some resampling probability, and for the initially non-funded ones, we include those whose funding probability reaches at least 10% for some resampling probability. In some cases, these line plots will have legends. In such legends, the entries are of the form x/y, where x is the number of approvals the project got in the initial instance and y is the project's cost. For all instances visualized as line plots, we increased the resolution and sample size of our robustness experiment. Specifically, on these instances, we examine all values $\phi \in \{0, 0.01\%, 0.02\%, \ldots, 24.99\%, 25\%\}$ of the resampling probability and for each of them generate 1000 samples.

---

[5] We sometimes refer to projects by the color of their lines. Doing so for the first time, we often specify the number of approvers of the project and its cost in brackets.

Table 2. Statistical quantities regarding the 50%-winner threshold for different budgeting rules for the full dataset, consisting of 460 instances. The first three columns contain the number of instances with a 50%-winner threshold smaller or equal to 25%/10%/5%. The last two columns give the mean/median 50%-winner threshold among all the instances for which it is smaller or equal to 25%.

budgeting rule	# inst. $\leq$ 25%	# inst. $\leq$ 10%	# inst. $\leq$ 5%	mean (for $\leq$ 25%)	median (for $\leq$ 25%)
GREEDYAV	77	34	17	12%	12%
GREEDYCOST	128	67	41	11%	10%
PHRAGMÉN	151	86	47	10%	9%
MES-COST	187	121	75	9%	7%

5.1   An Aggregate View on Outcome's Robustness

In this section, we take an aggregate look at the robustness of outcomes of real-world participatory budgeting instances, to check how fragile the outcomes are to random noise, and how this depends on the budgeting rule used. Generally speaking, in our analysis we distinguish two types of instances: Those with a 50%-winner threshold above 25%, i.e., in which even for a resampling probability of 25% the probability of a change in the outcome is below 50%, and those whose 50%-winner threshold is smaller than 25%. The former type of instances can be viewed as very robust, whereas the latter ones may exhibit a more complex behavior in terms of robustness and are, thus, of higher interest to our analysis. To get a first overview of the robustness of PB outcomes, in Table 2, we provide some statistical quantities regarding the 50%-winner threshold. We can see here that for all the rules a clear majority of instances has a very robust outcome (their 50%-winner threshold is above 25%). However, there are also numerous instances where funding decisions were closer; in particular, there is a non-negligible number of instances for which already a resampling probability of 5% or even smaller is sufficient to change the outcome in a majority of cases (we will explore those instances in more detail in Sect. 5.2). This contrast between many very robust outcomes and some less robust ones underlines that it might be worthwhile to check for the robustness of outcomes in practice.

Notably, we see in Table 2 that the robustness of outcomes substantially depends on the used budgeting rule. In terms of the 50%-winner threshold, in aggregate, GREEDYAV produces the most robust results, then GREEDYCOST, followed by PHRAGMÉN and MES-COST, which has the lowest robustness. This observation holds irrespective of whether we focus on instances with 50%-winner thresholds up to 25%, 10%, or 5%. Moreover, it also applies to the distribution of the 50%-winner thresholds among the less robust instances (i.e., those with a threshold of at most 25%): For GREEDYAV, the distribution is roughly uniform, and all possible threshold values (below 25%) appear roughly the same number of times, which results both in the mean and the median being around 12%. In contrast, for MES-COST the distribution is significantly skewed towards lower thresholds, which results in a mean of 9% and a median of 7% (in particular, there are 24 instances with a 50%-winner threshold of 1%). Overall, the general

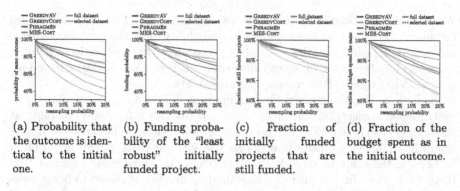

(a) Probability that the outcome is identical to the initial one.

(b) Funding probability of the "least robust" initially funded project.

(c) Fraction of initially funded projects that are still funded.

(d) Fraction of the budget spent as in the initial outcome.

Fig. 1. Some average statistics reflecting the robustness of outcomes for different rules.

gap between GREEDYAV and MES-COST is quite significant: For MES-COST, more than twice as many instances have a 50%-winner threshold smaller or equal to 25% than for GREEDYAV, and among these instances, the fraction of very non-robust ones is substantially higher.

As a rationale for the different behavior of the rules, recall that the 50%-winner threshold is only concerned with whether the outcome changes, and not by how much. For the greedy rules, if the ordering of the projects (according to the number of approvals or the approval-to-cost ratio) does not change, then the outcome also stays fixed. On real-world instances, there is typically only a small number of swaps in this ordering that are both likely to happen and are significant enough to change the outcome of the greedy rules. Thus, practically speaking, whether an outcome is robust often comes down to whether the difference in the approval scores (or the approval-to-cost ratios) of several selected projects is small. In contrast, for PHRAGMÉN and MES-COST, changes in the votes can have a much more subtle influence on the execution of the rules and, thus, on the produced outcome: Here, an additional approval can not only cause a different project to be funded, but also a different distribution of costs to voters, potentially leading to additional follow-up changes. Thus, on a high level, for PHRAGMÉN and MES-COST there are typically more "fragile" moments in the execution of the rules that can have a decisive influence on the outcome.

So far, we have only examined the 50%-winner threshold, which indicates under what level of noise it is likely that the outcome changes. However, it remains unclear how drastic the change is (or, what changes are possible under smaller noise levels). Note that, intuitively, as our rules work in a sequential fashion and thus one change in their execution could potentially lead to selecting completely different outcomes, it is unclear what to expect. To shed some light on this issue, in Fig. 1 we take a more nuanced look at the robustness of outcomes.[6]

---

[6] Note that in these plots we only consider averaged values. We did not include other statistical quantities for the sake of readability and their lack of relevance to the goal of our study.

We examine here both the *full* dataset, as well as the smaller dataset of *selected* instances. First, in Fig. 1a we show the probability that the outcome remains unchanged, depending on the resampling probability. Our observation regarding the relation between the different rules still holds here for both datasets and for all considered values of the resampling probability.

Second, in Fig. 1b we show the funding probability of the "least robust" initially funded project, i.e., the project that has the lowest funding probability at resampling probability 25%. The results here look relatively similar to the results from Fig. 1a, which indicates that in case the outcome changes, this might often be because the same funding decision gets changed. These results suggest that there often is one funded project whose funding decision is closest to being overturned. In fact, we will now show that for a majority of projects the decision of whether or not they are selected is quite robust.

In Fig. 1c, we depict how the fraction of initially funded projects which remain funded depends on the resampling probability. We see here that this fraction is quite high and in particular above 95% for all considered rules and resampling probabilities on the full dataset. It is thus in particular much higher than the probability of the same outcome (see Fig. 1a). Even on the selected dataset, more than 90% of funding decisions do not get reverted. This indicates that even in the case that the outcome changes, most of the originally funded projects remain funded. Together with Fig. 1b, it also highlights that there is a clear gap in the robustness of funding decisions of the "least robust" projects and the other ones. This observation is reassuring for practitioners, as it means that even in case random changes can affect the outcome, these often only regard a limited number of projects; however, it also motivates one to identify which funding decisions are the non-robust ones in practice.

Lastly, in Fig. 1d we show the average fraction of the budget which under a given noise level is spent on the same projects as in the initial instance. Comparing Fig. 1d to Fig. 1c, we see that (except for GREEDYAV) the fraction of still funded projects is generally higher than the fraction of budget spent in the same way: Funding decisions of expensive projects are more fragile to noise

5.2   (Types of) Non-robust Instances

We want to get a sense for how funding probabilities behave in non-robust instances. We find that for all rules there exist examples where the funding probabilities of projects quickly change, which is often due to complex interactions between projects in the selection process that our approach identifies. To this end, in Fig. 2 for each rule we depict an instance where the funding decisions have been particularly non-robust, and where drastic changes in funding probabilities appeared already for a small noise level. Due to limited space, in the following, we only discuss the GREEDYAV rule, but the described effects also apply to the other rules (see our full version [4] for discussions of the other rules).

Figure 2a shows an example of a non-robust instance for GREEDYAV: The outcome quickly changes with non-negligible probability. The pink project

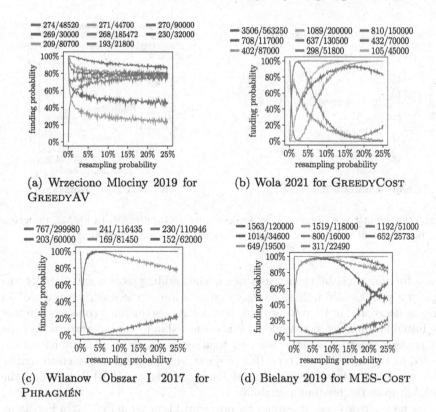

Fig. 2. Examples for non-robust funding decisions for each budgeting rule. For each plot, the caption includes the name of the presented instance from Pabulib and the rule used. Note that some of the lines in these plots largely overlap.

(209/80700) is the least robust initially funded one: Its funding probability is, respectively, 77.4% and 47.5% for resampling probabilities of 0.1% and 1%. In contrast, the purple project (268/185472), initially not funded, has a funding probability of, respectively, 22.4% and 52.5% for resampling probabilities of 0.1% and 1%. Note that in this instance a resampling probability of 0.1% (respectively, 1%) means that in expectation 10.2 (respectively, 102) approvals are flipped (this amounts to a 0.024% or 0.24% fraction of all approvals in the instance). It is quite remarkable that such non-robust instances appear in practice.

In Fig. 2a, we have seen an instance where the funding probability of an initially funded project quickly dropped and continued to drop further when further increasing the resampling probability. Interestingly, there are also initially funded projects with a quickly dropping funding probability that show a different behavior. Three different types of such projects seem to regularly occur: (i) projects whose funding probability further decreases when adding more and more noise to the instance, (ii) projects whose funding probability stays around 50% also when adding more and more noise to the instance, and (iii) projects

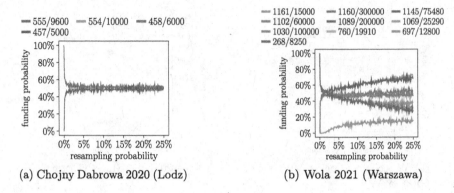

Fig. 3. Different types of non-robust projects under GREEDYAV. In Fig. 3a, the green and blue line and the red and orange line overlap. (Color figure online)

whose funding probability increases again when adding more noise. Notably, the type of a project also influences the interpretation of the non-robustness of its funding decision. For type (i) projects one might raise justified concerns whether the initial funding decision made on this project should not be overturned. Type (ii) projects question whether certain funding decisions should not have been viewed as ties instead. For type (iii) projects, the situation is less clear, and in some cases one might view the initial funding decision as justified despite the initial drop in the funding probability.

We have already seen examples for projects of type (i) in Fig. 2a. In Fig. 3a we present a good example for projects of type (ii): The winning probabilities of the green (458/6000) and blue projects (555/9600) quickly drop from 100% to 50%, and when increasing the resampling probability further, their funding probability stays around 50%. For the red (457/5000) and orange projects (554/10000), we see the reverse of this behavior, as their funding probability quickly goes up from 0% to around 50%, but then stays close to this value. This indicates that the initial decision to select the green and blue projects over the red and orange ones is somewhat arbitrary and one might rather see these four projects as tied (and, perhaps, the city should choose which ones to fund based on external arguments, such as the compatibility between them, or simply fund them all). Turning to Fig. 3b, we see that non-robust projects of different types can even occur in the same instance and may behave identically for very low levels of noise. In particular, the funding probability of the red (1145/75480), blue (268/8250) and purple (1102/60000) initially funded projects all drop to around 50% at a resampling probability of 1%. However, when increasing the noise level, for the blue project (type (i)), the funding probability drops further, for the purple project (type (ii)) it stays roughly constant, and for the red project (type (iii)) it increases again.

6 Conclusions

Our experimental findings illustrate several possible use cases of our approach. First, the 50%-winner threshold allows for a simple quantification of the robustness of an outcome, which sheds some light on how "close" the announced funding decisions are. Our examples of extremely non-robust real-world PB instances provide motivation to carry out such an analysis in practice, to increase the transparency of the process for voters, policymakers, and project proposers. In extreme cases, non-robustness could lead either to audits or reelections. Second, by analyzing how quickly the funding probabilities of different projects change, we can also quantify a project's distance to receiving a different funding outcome on an individual level. In particular, we identified three types of non-robust projects (those that are selected/not-selected "by luck," those that are effectively tied, and those that act non-monotonically). Third, our approach also allowed us to identify situations in which rules made "close" decisions between different (sets) of projects, whose funding probabilities changed simultaneously.

Acknowledgments. NB was supported by the DFG project ComSoc-MPMS (NI 369/22). This project has received funding from the European Research Council (ERC) under the European Union's Horizon 2020 research and innovation programme (grant agreement No 101002854).

References

1. Baumeister, D., Hogrebe, T.: On the complexity of predicting election outcomes and estimating their robustness. In: Proceedings of EUMAS-2021, pp. 228–244 (2021)
2. Boehmer, N., Bredereck, R., Faliszewski, P., Niedermeier, R.: Winner robustness via swap- and shift-bribery: parameterized counting complexity and experiments. In: Proceedings of IJCAI-2021, pp. 52–58 (2021)
3. Boehmer, N., Bredereck, R., Faliszewski, P., Niedermeier, R.: A quantitative and qualitative analysis of the robustness of (real-world) election winners. In: Proceedings of EAAMO-2022, pp. 7:1–7:10 (2022)
4. Boehmer, N., Faliszewski, P., Janeczko, L,, Kaczmarczyk, A.: Robustness of participatory budgeting outcomes: complexity and experiments. Technical report arXiv:2305.08125, arXiv (2023)
5. Bredereck, R., Faliszewski, P., Kaczmarczyk, A., Niedermeier, R., Skowron, P., Talmon, N.: Robustness among multiwinner voting rules. Artif. Intell. **290**, 103403 (2021)
6. Brill, M., Freeman, R., Janson, S., Lackner, M.: Phragmén's voting methods and justified representation. In: Proceedings of AAAI-2017, pp. 406–413 (2017)
7. Cary, D.: Estimating the margin of victory for instant-runoff voting. Presented at 2011 Electronic Voting Technology Workshop/Workshop on Trushworthy Elections (2011)

8. Faliszewski, P., Gawron, G., Kusek, B.: Robustness of greedy approval rules. In: Proceedings of EUMAS-2022, pp. 116–133 (2022)
9. Faliszewski, P., Hemaspaandra, E., Hemaspaandra, L.: How hard is bribery in elections? J. Artif. Intell. Res. **35**, 485–532 (2009)
10. Faliszewski, P., Rothe, J.: Control and bribery in voting. In: Brandt, F., Conitzer, V., Endriss, U., Lang, J., Procaccia, A.D. (eds.) Handbook of Computational Social Choice, chap. 7. Cambridge University Press, Cambridge (2015)
11. Faliszewski, P., Skowron, P., Talmon, N.: Bribery as a measure of candidate success: complexity results for approval-based multiwinner rules. In: Proceedings of AAMAS-2017, pp. 6–14 (2017)
12. Flum, J., Grohe, M.: The parameterized complexity of counting problems. SIAM J. Comput. **33**(4), 892–922 (2004)
13. Gawron, G., Faliszewski, P.: Robustness of approval-based multiwinner voting rules. In: Proceedings of ADT-2019, pp. 17–31 (2019)
14. Janeczko, L., Faliszewski, P.: Ties in multiwinner approval voting. In: Proceedings of IJCAI-2023 (2023, to appear). arxiv.org/abs/2305.01769
15. Lackner, M., Skowron, P.: Multi-Winner Voting with Approval Preferences. SpringerBriefs in Intelligent Systems, Springer, Cham (2023). https://doi.org/10.1007/978-3-031-09016-5
16. Los, M., Christoff, Z., Grossi, D.: Proportional budget allocations: towards a systematization. In: Proceedings of IJCAI-2022, pp. 398–404 (2022)
17. Magrino, T., Rivest, R., Shen, E., Wagner, D.: Computing the margin of victory in IRV elections. Presented at 2011 Electronic Voting Technology Workshop/Workshop on Trushworthy Elections (2011)
18. Peters, D., Pierczynski, G., Skowron, P.: Proportional participatory budgeting with additive utilities. In: Proceedings of NeurIPS-2021, pp. 12726–12737 (2021)
19. Peters, D., Skowron, P.: Proportionality and the limits of welfarism. In: Proceedings of EC-2020, pp. 793–794 (2020)
20. Peters, D., Skowron, P.: Method of equal shares (2023). https://equalshares.net
21. Pierczynski, G.: Pabutools (2023). https://pypi.org/project/pabutools/
22. Rey, S., Maly, J.: The (computational) social choice take on indivisible participatory budgeting. Technical report arXiv:2303.00621, arXiv (2023)
23. Shiryaev, D., Yu, L., Elkind, E.: On elections with robust winners. In: Proceedings of AAMAS-2013, pp. 415–422 (2013)
24. Stolicki, D., Szufa, S., Talmon, N.: Pabulib: a participatory budgeting library. Technical report arXiv:2012.06539, arXiv (2020)
25. Szufa, S., Faliszewski, P., Janeczko, L., Lackner, M., Slinko, A., Sornat, K., Talmon, N.: How to sample approval elections? In: Proceedings of IJCAI-2022, pp. 496–502 (2022)
26. Xia, L.: Computing the margin of victory for various voting rules. In: Proceedings of EC-2012, pp. 982–999 (2012)

Into the Unknown: Assigning Reviewers to Papers with Uncertain Affinities

Cyrus Cousins[ID], Justin Payan[✉][ID], and Yair Zick[ID]

University of Massachusetts Amherst, Amherst, MA 01002, USA
{cbcousins,jpayan,yzick}@umass.edu

Abstract. A successful peer review process requires that qualified and interested reviewers are assigned to each paper. Most automated reviewer assignment approaches estimate a real-valued *affinity score* for each paper-reviewer pair that acts as a proxy for the quality of the match, and then assign reviewers to maximize the sum of affinity scores. Most affinity score estimation methods are inherently noisy: reviewers can only bid on a small number of papers, and textual similarity models and subject-area matching are inherently noisy estimators. Current paper assignment systems are not designed to rigorously handle noise in the peer-review matching market. In this work, we assume paper-reviewer affinity scores are located in or near a high-probability region called an *uncertainty set*. We maximize the worst-case sum of scores for a reviewer assignment over the uncertainty set. We demonstrate how to robustly maximize the sum of scores across various classes of uncertainty sets, avoiding potentially serious mistakes in assignment. Our general approach can be used to integrate a large variety of paper-reviewer affinity models into reviewer assignment, opening the door to a much more robust peer review process.

Keywords: Resource Allocation · Peer Review · Maximin Optimization

1 Introduction

Peer review is a fundamental institution for evaluating scientific knowledge. Over the 20th century, the scientific profession has grown significantly, and the institution of peer review has struggled with the increased scale. Modern computer science conferences receive thousands of submissions, matched to committees of similar size. Due to sheer scale, program chairs rely on automated reviewer assignment platforms, such as Microsoft CMT, OpenReview, and EasyChair, that utilize complex matching algorithms. Reviewing platforms generally implement a two-stage process to largely automate reviewer assignments [5,15,20]. First, the system estimates the "fit" between each paper-reviewer pair, called the *paper-reviewer affinity score*. Next, the system assigns reviewers via constrained optimization, maximizing a function of the computed affinity scores (usually the

---

All authors contributed equally to this work.

© The Author(s), under exclusive license to Springer Nature Switzerland AG 2023
A. Deligkas and A. Filos-Ratsikas (Eds.): SAGT 2023, LNCS 14238, pp. 179–197, 2023.
https://doi.org/10.1007/978-3-031-43254-5_11

sum of scores, or *utilitarian welfare* [5]). Prior work identifies the reviewer assignment process as an important target for improving the overall quality of peer review in computer science [22,27]. Efforts are underway to address shortcomings in reviewer assignment [11–13,15,17,19,21,23,26,29], but none systematically addresses the fundamental issue of *uncertainty* in reviewer assignment.

Uncertainty in affinity score computation is a major source of error in assignment [15]. When we assign a reviewer to a paper, we are interested in ensuring the *quality of the future review*, which is fundamentally noisy. Because of this unpredictability, conferences typically construct affinity scores that reflect reviewer expertise and interest via four main sources of information. These sources include (a) *subject-area matching* (SAM) scores or keyword-based matching, where reviewer-provided areas of expertise are compared against keywords submitted by paper authors, (b) *textual similarity scores*, often implemented by the well-known Toronto Paper Matching System (TPMS) [5] or ACL scores [19], (c) *bidding*, where reviewers express their explicit ability and desire to review papers, and finally (d) *recommendations*, through which program committee members may suggest reviewers for papers. The overall affinity scores are typically computed as a linear combination of these four scores.[1] Recent conferences such as AAAI 2021 took a similar approach, linearly combining TPMS scores, ACL scores, and SAM scores, and raising the sum to some power based on the reviewer bids [15].

Each of these common affinity score components can be missing or inaccurate. State-of-the-art document similarity measures disagree with expert judgments up to 43% of the time [30], and nearly 40% of TPMS scores were completely missing in AAAI 2021 [15].[2] Between 5% and 15% of papers in major AI conferences receive fewer than three positive bids, but there is evidence that many missing bids would be positive if collected [8,17,23]. Although no systematic study has been performed on keyword-based similarity scores, keyword matching accuracy depends on authors and reviewers using consistent terminology, and subtleties are invariably lost in the process. Even reviewers directly suggested by knowledgeable editors or the paper authors have been shown to perform surprisingly poorly on average, as measured by third-party annotators via the Review Quality Index [25,32], showing that recommendations can be noisy as well.

To our knowledge, every reviewer assignment system still relies on affinity score estimates, but does not directly account for the fact that these scores are noisy estimates of assignment quality. Our work takes the first step towards addressing this fundamental gap. We investigate a generalized notion of affinity score, where organizers can implement affinity using any measure of fit between reviewers and papers. These measures may or may not be fully observable; for example, organizers may decide to estimate unknown bids as part of affinity

---

[1] CMT implements their affinity scores this way, which can be seen from https://cmt3.research.microsoft.com/docs/help/chair/auto-assign-reviewers.html, as does OpenReview (source: personal correspondence).

[2] Although the AAAI 2021 organizers do not explain why so many TPMS scores are missing, missing scores occur for several reasons, including reviewers opting out of the system or providing insufficient or empty publication records.

computation. Our approach also enables even more advanced affinity measures, such as predictors of reviewer performance based on historical data.

1.1 Our Contributions

To properly account for uncertainty, we first construct a region called an *uncertainty set* which is close to the true affinities with high probability, then maximize the worst-case welfare over the uncertainty set. Uncertainty sets are a very general construct that allows conference organizers to introduce their own uncertainty models using available data and reasonable assumptions. Uncertainty sets generalize probability distributions—while it is possible to construct an uncertainty set from a probability distribution, non-Bayesian models will frequently *not* specify full probability distributions. In these cases, worst-case guarantees over an uncertainty set are quite natural. We call the problem of maximizing the worst-case welfare over an uncertainty set Reviewer Assignment under Uncertainty, or RAU.

We provide numerous examples of uncertainty sets throughout the paper, starting with axis-aligned, hyperrectangular uncertainty sets in Sect. 3.1 and spherical and ellipsoidal uncertainty sets in Sect. 3.2. Theorems 5 and 6 offer detailed end-to-end examples of how conference organizers can construct ellipsoidal uncertainty sets using bounds on the *square error* of an *affinity score estimator* from historic data or sampled bids (a frequentist approach that precludes optimizing for expected welfare). We also present a *calculus of uncertainty sets*, enabling construction of complex and highly informative uncertainty sets from simple components (Sect. 3.3). Our results are agnostic to the affinity model; organizers can define affinity scores arbitrarily, so long as they can be estimated for all paper-reviewer pairs, and sampled for some pairs.

We show that RAU is NP-hard over convex uncertainty sets (Theorem 9), and present an approximation algorithm called Robust Reviewer Assignment (RRA), which applies to any convex uncertainty set where worst-case welfare can be efficiently computed (Sect. 4). RRA applies *randomized rounding* methods to a *convex relaxation* of the discrete RAU problem, and we analyze both the *optimization error* due to convex programming methods and randomized rounding, and the *minimax error* due to operating with an uncertainty set, rather than known affinity scores (Sect. 4.2). We first give bounds on the true welfare relative to the maximin welfare solution of RAU (Proposition 2), and explore the integrality gap of RAU (Proposition 12). We relegate all proofs to the supplementary material.[3]

We empirically demonstrate the robustness of our approach relative to commonly-used baselines on publicly available data from five recent iterations of ICLR (Sect. 5.1). In addition, we explore synthetic settings where RRA avoids negative consequences faced by the most commonly used baseline (Sect. 5.2). We hope this work draws attention to the ad-hoc nature of affinity scores, spurring improvements to their computation and further study of their robustness.

---

[3] The full version of the paper, including supplementary material, can be found at https://arxiv.org/abs/2301.10816.

1.2   Related Work

Current automated peer review systems compute pointwise, ad-hoc affinity scores and maximize the total sum [5,15,21], the minimum value for papers [13,29], or the minimum value for groups of papers [1].

Two recent studies start from our premise that commonly-used affinity scores may not be as accurate as they seem. Data is now available that directly compares elements of affinity scores to expert judgments of reviewer fit, and the authors of this dataset show that.existing similarity score computation methods make many errors [30]. A recent study leverages randomness in assignment algorithms to directly judge assignment decisions, showing that higher weight should be placed on text similarity metrics over bids [24]. These results encourage further improvements to affinity score computation (especially text similarity), but also justify smarter utilization of the noisy sources of information that are available.

Other works use modern NLP techniques to improve document-based similarity scores [19], encourage reviewers to bid on underbid papers [8,17,23], or disincentivize strategic bidding behavior [10–12]. Although these approaches reduce uncertainty, they do not directly treat uncertainty in affinity scores.

Our robust optimization algorithm is based on an iterative supergradient-ascent approach; similar techniques have been applied to supervised learning with unknown labels [16] and fair learning with unknown group identities [6].

2   Reviewer Assignment Under Uncertainty

Assume we have a set P of n papers submitted to a peer-review venue,[4] and a set R of m reviewers. The key input to the reviewer assignment problem is a paper-reviewer *affinity score matrix* $S^* \in [0,1]^{n \times m}$ (we will also refer to $[0,1]^{n \times m}$ as the *unit hypercube*), where $S^*_{p,r} \in [0,1]$ is the affinity of paper $p \in P$ to reviewer $r \in R$. This matrix S^* encodes the *true* affinities, or the value provided to the venue by assigning each reviewer to each paper. At this point, it is natural to ask, "How can one know the value a paper-reviewer assignment will provide ahead of time?" and "What do we mean by value provided?" These questions directly motivate our work; reviewer assignment is challenging because affinity depends on poorly-defined preferences over uncertain future outcomes.

Despite this fundamental challenge, all prior work assumes direct access to the true affinities [1,5,13,15,21,29]. We relax this assumption, instead assuming only *partial knowledge* of S^*, as represented by an *uncertainty set* $\mathcal{S} \subseteq [0,1]^{n \times m}$ that contains a point near S^* with high probability.

Definition 1 ((δ, γ) Uncertainty Set). *Suppose $S^* \in [0,1]^{n \times m}$ is the true affinity score matrix. A (δ, γ) uncertainty set obeys $\mathbb{P}\big(\inf_{S \in \mathcal{S}} \|S - S^*\|_1 > \gamma\big) < \delta$, i.e., it probably contains some S that is γ-close to S^*.*

---

[4] A peer review venue is any entity which assigns reviewers to papers for the purposes of peer review. The prototypical venue is a peer-reviewed conference, but our approach applies to similar venues such as ACL Rolling Review [18].

Once we compute a (δ, γ) uncertainty set $\mathcal{S}$, our goal is to find an *assignment matrix* A that assigns reviewers to papers with good worst-case guarantees on a score function defined by A and S^*, while satisfying some hard constraints. Assignments are deterministic, i.e. lie on vertices of the unit hypercube, or $\mathcal{A}_0 \doteq \{0,1\}^{n \times m}$. We compute an assignment of reviewers to papers $A \in \mathcal{A}_0$, where $A_{p,r} = 1$ if and only if r is assigned to review the paper p. Hard constraints usually include the number of reviewers required per paper, upper bounds on reviewer loads, and conflicts of interest. Conflicts of interest consist of a set $\mathcal{C} \subseteq (P \times R)$, where $(p,r) \in \mathcal{C}$ implies that r cannot be assigned to p. $\mathcal{A}_{\mathrm{CoI}} \subseteq \mathcal{A}_0$ denotes the set of all assignments respecting conflicts in $\mathcal{C}$. If $A \in \mathcal{A}_{\mathrm{CoI}}$ and $(p,r) \in \mathcal{C}$, then $A_{p,r} = 0$.

Suppose that each paper p requires exactly k_p reviewers and each reviewer r must be assigned no more than u_r papers. Then

$$\mathcal{A}_P \doteq \left\{ A \in \mathcal{A}_0 \,\middle|\, \forall p \in P \colon \sum_{r \in R} A_{p,r} = k_p \right\} \;\&\; \mathcal{A}_R \doteq \left\{ A \in \mathcal{A}_0 \,\middle|\, \forall r \in R \colon \sum_{p \in P} A_{p,r} \leq u_r \right\}$$

define the *paper coverage requirements* and *reviewer load bounds*, respectively. We occasionally refer to the *total review load* $K \doteq \sum_{p \in P} k_p$. Taken together, the hard constraints give us a set of permissible assignments $\mathcal{A} \doteq \mathcal{A}_{\mathrm{CoI}} \cap \mathcal{A}_P \cap \mathcal{A}_R$.

We aim to compute assignments A that maximize a score-based objective function $W(A, S)$, while meeting all hard constraints. Throughout the paper we assume W is utilitarian social welfare $W(A, S) \doteq \frac{1}{n} \sum_{p \in P} \sum_{r \in R} A_{p,r} S_{p,r}$.

In summary, the problem of Reviewer Assignment under Uncertainty (RAU) takes as input a set of papers P, reviewers R, assignment constraints $\mathcal{A}$, and an uncertainty set $\mathcal{S}$. Although ideally we would compute $A^* \doteq \arg\max_{A \in \mathcal{A}} W(A, S^*)$, we cannot since we do not know S^*. Therefore, our goal is to find or approximate

$$A^{\mathrm{MM}} \doteq \arg\max_{A \in \mathcal{A}} \inf_{S \in \mathcal{S}} W(A, S) \;. \tag{1}$$

Here A^{MM} maximizes welfare for adversarial (worst-case) affinity scores over the uncertainty set, which ensures robustness with high probability. Robust guarantees prevent catastrophic failures in exchange for some average case penalty.

We conclude this section with a simple observation relating the worst-case welfare over $\mathcal{S}$ for any assignment A to the true welfare of A with S^*.

Proposition 2 (Relating True and Worst-Case Welfare over $\mathcal{S}$). *Suppose $\mathcal{S}$ is a (δ, γ) uncertainty set with $\|S - S'\|_1 \leq L$ for all $S, S' \in \mathcal{S}$, and the true affinity score matrix is labeled S^*. Consider any assignment $A \in \mathcal{A}$. Then with probability at least $1 - \delta$,*

$$W(A, S^*) - \tfrac{L + \gamma}{n} \leq \inf_{S \in \mathcal{S}} W(A, S) \leq W(A, S^*) + \tfrac{\gamma}{n} \;.$$

Proposition 2 implies that if we aim for low $\mathcal{L}_1$ diameter uncertainty sets $\mathcal{S}$, we can approximately optimize true welfare using the robust objective (1). A similar bound holds when we compare $W(A^{\mathrm{MM}}, S^*)$ to $W(A^*, S^*)$, i.e., to the welfare of the unknown, true optimal assignment A^* (Theorem 13). However,

Proposition 2 states that the maximin objective itself is close to the true welfare under any assignment A, whereas Theorem 13 shows that the specific assignment A^{MM} has low regret against A^*.

3   Uncertainty Models for Affinity Scores

We start by analyzing simple uncertainty sets, namely the case where S is known, as well as hyperrectangular, spherical, and ellipsoidal uncertainty sets. We conclude the section by showing a compositionality rule that allows venue organizers to combine multiple uncertainty sets into a single RAU problem.

The case where S is known, $\mathcal{S} = \{S\}$, is quite straightforward. This corresponds to most current conference management system implementations [5, 15]. When $\mathcal{A} = \mathcal{A}_{\mathrm{CoI}} \cap \mathcal{A}_P \cap \mathcal{A}_R$, the binary integer program $\arg\max_{A \in \mathcal{A}} \mathrm{W}(A, S)$ is known to be polynomial-time solvable, as it is a linear program with totally unimodular constraints. Intuitively, these constraints introduce cuts to the assignment hypercube that never produce new vertices, thus all vertices of the resulting polytope occur on the binary integer lattice. Efficient implementations of this linear program can be found in multiple publicly available sources [13, 21, 29, 31]. Let us now consider hyperrectangular, spherical, and ellipsoidal uncertainty sets.

3.1   Hyperrectangular Uncertainty Sets from Confidence Intervals

Many simple and intuitive models for an uncertainty set take the form of axis-aligned hyperrectangles. A naïve uncertainty set might estimate confidence intervals for each $S_{p,r}$ independently and use a union bound to give a high-probability region for the affinity scores. Venue organizers might also make assumptions about intervals bounding affinity scores with certainty, taking the intersection of multiple such interval bounds. For example, they might start with the global constraints of the unit hypercube. Lower and upper bounds can then be given for pairs based on whether they receive certain bids, whether the program committee recommends the assignment, or whether a threshold on document similarity score is met. This model is ad-hoc and simple, but may be suitable in practice. Furthermore, if we assume that with probability at least $1 - \delta$, only a small constant fraction γ of these bounds can be violated, we can establish a (δ, γ) confidence interval under more realistic assumptions.

If we take all the lower bounds on paper-reviewer scores, we obtain a lower bound affinity score matrix $\underline{S}$. Similarly, taking all the maximal possible values for paper-reviewer scores yields an upper bound affinity score matrix $\bar{S}$. Our uncertainty set is thus $\mathcal{S}_\square \doteq \{X \in \mathbb{R}^{n \times m} \mid \underline{S}_{p,r} \leq X_{p,r} \leq \bar{S}_{p,r} \; \forall p, r\}$. Our first result is that RAU can be solved in polynomial time for axis-aligned, hyperrectangular uncertainty sets.

Theorem 3 (RAU under Hyperrectangular Uncertainty). *When the uncertainty set is an axis-aligned hyperrectangular region $\mathcal{S}_\square$, then*

$$\arg\max_{A \in \mathcal{A}} \inf_{S \in \mathcal{S}_\square} \mathrm{W}(A, S) = \arg\max_{A \in \mathcal{A}} \mathrm{W}(A, \underline{S}) \; .$$

Thus RAU maximizes W for $\underline{S}$, which requires polynomial time via LP reduction.

Axis-aligned, hyperrectangular uncertainty sets correspond to the case where uncertainty is bounded independently across paper-reviewer scores, hence their relative simplicity. Although hyperrectangular uncertainty sets are easy to work with, they are unnecessarily pessimistic, since it is very unlikely that all affinities take extreme values at once (i.e., $\underline{S}$ is actually a very unlikely outcome). We can improve our estimates using uncertainty set models that account for the low probability of many simultaneous extreme values.

3.2 Ellipsoidal Uncertainty Sets with $\mathcal{L}_2$ Error Guarantees

Many standard models directly bound the $\mathcal{L}_1$ or $\mathcal{L}_2$ error of their predictions, which implies uncertainty sets that are more optimistic than hyperrectangular $\mathcal{S}$ (and hence have tighter guarantees for Proposition 2).

We first analyze the case of symmetric uncertainty sets with $\mathcal{L}_2$ error guarantees. For example, we might solicit bids uniformly at random and then predict unsampled bids using collaborative filtering with $\mathcal{L}_2$ error guarantees [4,7,14]. $\mathcal{S}$ could then be constructed as a linear combination of values known with certainty (document-based similarity scores and keyword-based matching scores) and the real and estimated bids, yielding a spherical uncertainty set $\mathcal{S}$.

We can consider a spherical $(\delta, 0)$ uncertainty set to consist of a point estimate S^0 and a radius ε limiting the $\mathcal{L}_2$ error from the point estimate S^0. Formally, we aim to solve the problem $\arg\max_{A \in \mathcal{A}} \inf_{S \in B_\varepsilon(S^0)} W(A, S)$, where $B_\varepsilon(S^0) \doteq \{X \in \mathbb{R}^{n \times m} \mid \|X - S^0\|_F \leq \varepsilon\}$ denotes the ε Frobenius-norm ball around S^0.

Theorem 4 (RAU under Spherical Uncertainty). *When $\mathcal{S}$ is a sphere,*

$$\arg\max_{A \in \mathcal{A}} \inf_{S \in B_\varepsilon(S^0)} W(A, S) = \arg\max_{A \in \mathcal{A}} W(A, S^0),$$

which can be computed in polynomial time. Furthermore, for all $A \in \mathcal{A}$,

$$|W(A, S^0) - W(A, S^*)| \leq \tfrac{\varepsilon \sqrt{K}}{n}.$$

One way of looking at Theorem 4 is that A^{MM} over spherical uncertainty sets provides no additional robustness guarantees over $\arg\max_{A \in \mathcal{A}} W(A, S^0)$. Thus, it seems that in order to obtain meaningful robustness guarantees, we require both a limit to the total amount of variation in affinity scores (Theorem 3) as well as asymmetry between the noise on affinity scores (Theorem 4). We can explain these results intuitively; to decide how best to assign reviewers, we need to be able to make tradeoffs between assigning pairs with potentially high (but also potentially low) affinity or assigning pairs that have an average amount of affinity with higher certainty. Those tradeoffs are only meaningful if uncertainty varies across paper-reviewer pairs, and if there is a limited total amount of uncertainty.

With that intuition in mind, we generalize to the case of ellipsoidal uncertainty sets. In a simple model, we might model affinity scores as multivariate Gaussians, which we explore in greater detail in the experiments of Sect. 5. In this case, we obtain a mean vector[5] $\vec{\mu} \in [0,1]^{nm}$ and a positive semi-definite covariance matrix $\Sigma \in \mathbb{R}^{nm \times nm}$. Given a confidence level $1 - \delta$, we create an uncertainty set

$$\mathcal{S} \doteq \{ S \in \mathbb{R}^{nm} \mid (S - \vec{\mu})^T \Sigma^{-1} (S - \vec{\mu}) \leq \chi_{nm}^2 (1 - \delta) \} \ , \tag{2}$$

where χ_k^2 is the inverse CDF of the χ^2 distribution with k degrees of freedom. If we assume no model error (which is not a safe assumption generally), then the true affinity scores are contained within $\mathcal{S}$ with probability at least $1 - \delta$. We know also that $\chi_{nm}^2(1 - \delta) \leq nm + 2\sqrt{nm \ln \frac{1}{\delta}} + 2 \ln \frac{1}{\delta}$ We can see that the size of the uncertainty set depends only logarithmically on $\frac{1}{\delta}$, and thus we can tradeoff between δ and the $\mathcal{L}_1$ diameter of the uncertainty set.

While the Gaussian model employed in (2) makes a strong modeling assumption, we can use a validation set and a predictive model with provable tail bounds to obtain uncertainty sets that do not require any such assumptions. To accomplish this, we require a predictive model of affinity scores. Venue organizers can then obtain $\mathcal{L}_2$ error bounds using validation data, and this will yield an ellipsoid due to sampling bias (only certain paper-reviewer pairs will be observed for any given venue). In this setting, the uncertainty set is not derived as a confidence interval of a probability distribution, but rather directly comes from a tail bound on total generalization error. Optimizing in this setting *requires* using a robust approach like RAU, and cannot be done with average case analysis.

We now develop this predictive model in more technical detail. Suppose the true affinity score of some paper-reviewer pair is $f^*(p, r)$, and we have access to a predictive model $\hat{f}(p, r)$, perhaps learned on historical venues. In practice, $\hat{f}$ predicts the affinity of reviewer r for paper p based on any information available prior to reviewer assignment, and the specific definition of affinity is left to the venue organizers. For example, a venue may decide that affinity is best measured via reviewer bids, and they may use historical data to train a predictor $\hat{f}$ to predict missing bids from document-based similarity scores and keywords. Alternatively, venue organizers may decide that the ground truth affinity $f^*(p, r)$ should correspond to a meta-reviewer's judgment of review quality, and $\hat{f}$ can then be trained on historical data to predict these judgments.

We will take $\hat{S}_{p,r} \doteq \hat{f}(p, r)$ and $S_{p,r}^* \doteq f^*(p, r)$. We assume that we can evaluate $\hat{f}$ on all paper-reviewer pairs in the current venue, and potentially on pairs from historical venues as well. We may be able to sample $f^*(p, r)$ for some, but not all, pairs in the current venue and historical venues (the validation data). We then probabilistically bound a weighted average of the square error between $\hat{f}$ and f^* in terms of an estimate of expected square error computed on the validation set. The details of the validation set vary by application, but the overall strategy will be to estimate the square error $\mathbb{E}[(s^* - \hat{s})^2]$, where s^* and $\hat{s}$ are given by f^* and $\hat{f}$ on a random paper-reviewer pair. We show two such approaches, the first inductive, using historic or auxilliary data to form the validation set, and the second transductive, assuming a small random sample of true affinity scores (e.g., bids) can be queried within the current peer-review venue.

---

[5] Technically, a sample from this multivariate Gaussian is a vector in $\mathbb{R}^{nm}$, and must be reshaped into a matrix $S \in \mathbb{R}^{n \times m}$. We will convert matrices into vectors in row-major order and ignore the distinction between matrices and vectors when convenient.

Theorem 5 (Ellipsoidal Uncertainty Sets from Inductive Predictors).
*Let $\mathcal{D}'$ be a probability distribution over paper-reviewer pairs, and let $\mathcal{D}^P$ and $\mathcal{D}^R$
be distributions over papers and reviewers, respectively. Suppose we sample T
paper-reviewer pairs i.i.d. (without replacement) from $\mathcal{D}'$ with true and estimated
affinity scores $s^*_{1:T}$ and $\hat{s}_{1:T}$, respectively, and assume that P and R were drawn
i.i.d. (without replacement) from $\mathcal{D}^P$ and $\mathcal{D}^R$, respectively.*[6] *Let*

$$\alpha(p,r) \doteq \frac{\mathbb{P}_{p\sim\mathcal{D}^P}(\boldsymbol{p}=p)\mathbb{P}_{r\sim\mathcal{D}^R}(\boldsymbol{r}=r)}{\mathbb{P}_{(p,r)\sim\mathcal{D}'}((\boldsymbol{p},\boldsymbol{r})=(p,r))} \quad \& \quad \alpha_{\max} \doteq \sup_{p\in P, r\in R} \alpha(p,r)$$

*denote (1) the probability ratio of sampling p from $\mathcal{D}^P$ and r from $\mathcal{D}^R$ to sampling (p,r) from $\mathcal{D}'$, and (2) the supremum probability ratio, respectively. Now
construct the ellipsoid matrix $\Sigma \in \mathbb{R}^{nm\times nm}$ as the diagonal matrix such that
$\Sigma_{pm+r,pm+r} = \alpha(p,r)$ for all $p\in P, r\in R$. Then for any $\delta \in (0,1)$, the ellipsoid*

$$\mathcal{S} \doteq \left\{ S\in\mathbb{R}^{nm} \ \middle| \ (S-\hat{S})\Sigma^{-1}(S-\hat{S}) \le \underbrace{\frac{1}{T}\sum_{i=1}^{T}(s^*_i-\hat{s}_i)^2}_{=\hat{\xi}} + \underbrace{\sqrt{\left(\frac{1}{T}+\frac{(n+m)\alpha^2_{\max}}{nm}\right)\frac{\ln\frac{1}{\delta}}{2}}}_{=\eta} \right\}$$

is a $(\delta,0)$ uncertainty set, where $\hat{\xi}$ denotes the empirical square error *of our
estimated scores, and η denotes the* excess error bound *due to sampling.*

Departing from the standard reviewer assignment setup, Theorem 5 assumes
that both the historic data and the current venue are random. In particular,
historic paper-reviewer pairs are sampled from $\mathcal{D}'$ (modeling the historic data
generation process), and papers and reviewers for the current venue are sampled
from $\mathcal{D}^P$ and $\mathcal{D}^R$ (modeling the processes by which papers are submitted and
reviewers volunteer). We then construct $\alpha(p,r)$ to reweight square error on the
current venue to match expected square error on $\mathcal{D}'$ (i.e., we use importance
sampling to calibrate expectations over $\mathcal{D}'$ versus those over $\mathcal{D}^P$ and $\mathcal{D}^R$). For
example, $\mathcal{D}'$ reflects all elements of historic data generation, most importantly
the availability of historic data from multiple venues with different focuses. We
might then use the (relatively stable) topic areas of papers and reviewers to
model $\mathcal{D}^P$ and $\mathcal{D}^R$, and thus $\alpha(p,r)$ reflects the ratio of the popularity of p and
r's topic areas in the current venue to historic venues.

We show a similar result in the transductive setting. Instead of constructing
a predictive function from historical data, we generalize a small set of known
affinities for the current venue to the unknown affinities for the same venue.
Note that $\mathcal{D}'$ now reflects the process by which we obtain samples for (p,r) pairs
from the current venue, rather than from historical venues.

Theorem 6 (Ellipsoidal Uncertainty Sets from Transductive Predictors). *Suppose a probability distribution $\mathcal{D}'$ over $P \times R$, and a sample of T*

---

[6] Abusing notation slightly, we index the papers $p \in P$ and reviewers $r \in R$ so that p
can represent either a paper in $\mathcal{P}$ or an integer between 1 and n.

paper-reviewer pairs drawn i.i.d. (without replacement) from $\mathcal{D}'$, with true and estimated affinity scores $s_{1:T}^*$ and $\hat{s}_{1:T}$, respectively. Let

$$\alpha(p,r) \doteq \frac{(nm)^{-1}}{\mathbb{P}_{(\boldsymbol{p},\boldsymbol{r})\sim\mathcal{D}'}((\boldsymbol{p},\boldsymbol{r})=(p,r))}$$

denote the probability ratio between sampling (p,r) uniformly at random and sampling (p,r) from $\mathcal{D}'$, and construct the ellipsoid matrix $\Sigma \in \mathbb{R}^{nm \times nm}$ as the diagonal matrix such that $\Sigma_{pm+r,pm+r} = \alpha(p,r)$ for all $p \in P, r \in R$. Then for any $\delta \in (0,1)$, the ellipsoid

$$\mathcal{S} \doteq \left\{ S \,\middle|\, (S-\hat{S})\Sigma^{-1}(S-\hat{S}) \leq \underbrace{\frac{1}{T}\sum_{i=1}^{T}(s_i^* - \hat{s}_i)^2}_{=\hat{\xi}} + \underbrace{\sqrt{\frac{\ln\frac{1}{\delta}}{2T}}}_{=\eta}, \right\}$$

is a $(\delta,0)$ uncertainty set, where $\hat{\xi}$ denotes the empirical square error of our estimated scores, and η denotes the excess error bound due to sampling.

The transductive result can be straightforwardly applied to many different contexts in which venue organizers can solicit samples of f^* on (p,r) pairs from the current venue, rather than historical data. This information must be obtained prior to assigning the majority of reviewers. For example, organizers could define f^* as a reviewer's hypothetical bid and Theorem 6 then requires soliciting a small number of bids to estimate the error of $\hat{f}$. Similarly, f^* could correspond to meta-reviewer judgments of review quality, accomplished by opting for a two-stage reviewing process, in which the reviews and feedback generated in the first stage are used to estimate the error of $\hat{f}$. These definitions of f^* are costly to sample, but organizers can still efficiently target sophisticated affinity models by solving RAU over the uncertainty sets of Theorem 6.

We naturally ask the question, "How many samples are sufficient to obtain a sharp confidence bound?" Observe that, by Proposition 2, the gap between adversarial and true welfare is $\frac{L}{n}$, where L denotes the $\mathcal{L}_1$ diameter of $\mathcal{S}$. For the ellipsoidal uncertainty set of Theorem 6, $\frac{L}{n} \leq 2\alpha_{max}(\hat{\xi}+\eta)\sqrt{\frac{m}{n}}$. Furthermore, the empirical square error $\hat{\xi}$ converges to some ξ as T increases, thus we need only select $T \in \Omega\left(\frac{\log\frac{1}{\delta}}{\xi^2}\right)$ samples to ensure that the uncertainty set is constant-factor optimal, and thus the welfare gap is $\mathbf{O}(\alpha_{max}\xi\sqrt{\frac{m}{n}})$, which is also optimal to within constant factors. Notably, the sufficient sample size T is *independent of the venue size* (i.e., n and m), thus the added burden of soliciting these extra bids is negligible. We also see that the fundamental limitation of this method is the average square error ξ, which depends on the predictor, the venue, and the sampling distribution $\mathcal{D}'$. It is thus paramount to use predictors for which this quantity will be small. Fortunately, this is often the case, as many predictive models are explicitly trained to minimize $\mathcal{L}_2$ error on some task, which motivates the choice of our ellipsoidal uncertainty sets. Note that while this argument pertains to Theorem 6, one can argue similarly for the necessary size of the validation set to ensure $\eta = \mathbf{O}(\xi)$ in Theorem 5.

Finally, we note that it is possible to extend either result under less favorable (more realistic) assumptions about the sampling process using the γ parameter ($\mathcal{L}_1$ error) of our uncertainty set construction. In particular, either result produces a $(\delta, T\gamma)$ uncertainty set if $\hat{s}$, s^*, and the associated (p, r) pairs are subject to *adversarial corruption* of $T\gamma$ of the validation set samples drawn from $\mathcal{D}'$, which has immediate applications in privacy, adversarial robustness, and various notions of strategy-proofness. Furthermore, to model more complicated and potentially not fully understood distribution shift, we obtain via Bennett's inequality [2] a $\left(\delta + \delta', T\gamma + \frac{1}{3} \ln \frac{1}{\delta'} + \sqrt{2T\gamma(1-\gamma) \ln \frac{1}{\delta'}} \right)$ uncertainty set if the validation set is instead drawn from some $\mathcal{D}''$ such that $\text{TVD}(\mathcal{D}', \mathcal{D}'') \leq \gamma$.

3.3 Compositional Rules

We may often have more complicated uncertainty sets than the simple geometries described in the previous sections. For example, we can intersect the constraints of the unit hypercube with an ellipsoidal uncertainty set as described in Sect. 3.2. This produces a *truncated ellipsoid*, a common construction that we will see again in Sect. 5.

Lemma 7 (Uncertainty Set Intersection). *Suppose each $\mathcal{S}_i$ for $i \in [k]$ is a $(\vec{\delta}_i, 0)$ uncertainty set. Then $\mathcal{S}_\cap \doteq \bigcap_{i=1}^{k} \mathcal{S}_i$ is a $(\|\vec{\delta}\|_1, 0)$ uncertainty set.*

We can also use Lemma 8 to convert (δ, γ) uncertainty sets to larger $(\delta, 0)$ uncertainty sets.

Lemma 8 ($\mathcal{L}_1$ Error Terms). *If $\mathcal{S}$ is a (δ, γ) uncertainty set, then for any $\eta \in [0, \gamma]$, it holds that the* Minkowski sum

$$\mathcal{S}' \doteq \mathcal{S} + \{\vec{s} \in \mathbb{R}^{nm} \mid \|\vec{s}\|_1 \leq \eta\} = \{\vec{x} + \vec{s} \mid \vec{x} \in \mathcal{S}, \|\vec{s}\|_1 \leq \eta\}$$

is a $(\delta, \gamma - \eta)$ uncertainty set.

We can apply Lemmas 7 and 8 sequentially to intersect arbitrary (δ, γ) uncertainty sets. We first expand them via Lemma 8 to obtain larger $(\vec{\delta}_i, 0)$ uncertainty sets, and we then apply Lemma 7 to obtain their intersection.

We can also apply these results to the uncertainty sets previously described in Sect. 3. For example, the intersection of multiple axis-aligned, hyperrectangular constraints produces an axis-aligned hyperrectangle. This may occur when structural constraints defined by the venue (e.g., hard upper and lower bounds defined based on topic overlap) intersect with per-pair error bounds. Similarly, we might consider cases with two intersecting ellipsoidal error bounds derived from two different estimators using Theorems 5 and 6. This intersection is uninteresting if the two ellipsoids have the same centroid and one is strictly smaller than the other, but if these ellipsoids have different centroids (as when the estimators have different biases) their intersection can be quite beneficial.

4   Robust Reviewer Assignment (RRA)

We now present a general purpose algorithm for approximately solving the RAU problem over convex uncertainty sets, as long as the adversarial (worst-case) welfare can be computed in polynomial time. We first show in Theorem 9 that RAU is NP-hard in general for convex uncertainty regions of this type.

Theorem 9 (Hardness of RAU). RAU *is NP-hard over a convex uncertainty set* S, *even for* S *with a polynomial-time adversary. In particular, RAU remains NP-hard even when* S *is restricted to bounded polytopes formed by intersections of polynomially many halfspaces.*

Algorithm 1. Robust Reviewer Assignment (RRA)

Require: Error tolerance ε, supergradient norm bound λ, uncertainty set S, constrained allocation space $\tilde{A}$, total review load $K = \sum_{p \in P} k_p$ (i.e., the total number of assignments required)

1: Initialize $S^{(0)} \in S$ arbitrarily
2: $A^{(0)} \leftarrow \arg\max_{A \in \mathcal{A}} \mathrm{W}(A, S^{(0)})$ // Initialize $A^{(0)}$ to optimize $S^{(0)}$ (via LP reduction)
3: $\hat{A} \leftarrow A^{(0)}; \hat{w} \leftarrow -\infty$ // Maintain best allocation $\hat{A}$ and adversarial welfare $\hat{w}$
4: $T \leftarrow \left\lceil \left(\frac{\lambda\sqrt{2K}}{\varepsilon}\right)^2 \right\rceil; \alpha \leftarrow \frac{\varepsilon}{\lambda^2}$ // Compute sufficient *step count* T and *step size* α
5: **for** $t \in \{1, 2, \ldots T\}$ **do**
6:     $S^{(t)} \leftarrow \arg\inf_{S \in S} \mathrm{W}(A^{(t-1)}, S)$ // Adversary selects $S^{(t)}$ from S
7:     **if** $\mathrm{W}(A^{(t-1)}, S^{(t)}) > \hat{w}$ // Update $\hat{A}$ if adversarial welfare beats previous best
8:         $\hat{A} \leftarrow A^{(t-1)}; \hat{w} \leftarrow \mathrm{W}(A^{(t-1)}, S^{(t)})$
9:     $A^{(t)} \leftarrow A^{(t-1)} + \alpha \nabla_{A^{(t-1)}} \mathrm{W}(A^{(t-1)}, S^{(t)})$ // Update allocation with a supergradient step
10:    $A^{(t)} \leftarrow \arg\min_{A \in \tilde{A}} \|A - A^{(t)}\|_2$ // $\mathcal{L}_2$ project onto feasible allocation set $\tilde{A}$
11: **return** ROUND($\hat{A}$)   // Sample integral assignment

---

4.1   Robust Reviewer Assignment

Due to this hardness result, we outline an approach to approximately solve RAU efficiently for convex uncertainty sets with polynomial-time adversaries. We start by allowing *fractional* (rather than binary) assignments. We then apply *supergradient ascent* (analogous to subgradient descent) to approximate $\arg\max_{A \in \tilde{A}} \inf_{S \in S} \mathrm{W}(A, S)$, where $\tilde{A}$ is the convex closure of the feasible set of discrete allocations $\mathcal{A}$ from Sect. 2. When the supergradient ascent algorithm terminates, we randomly round the assignment to a binary assignment.

In particular, we present Algorithm 1, termed RRA. RRA applies an iterative adversarial optimization strategy to the objective. In each iteration t, we take an *adversary step*, which identifies the pessimal $S^{(t)}$ given assignment $A^{(t-1)}$. We then take a *gradient ascent step* from $A^{(t-1)}$ to $A^{(t)}$ assuming the score matrix remains fixed at $S^{(t)}$, followed by a *projection step*, which ensures $A^{(t)}$ remains feasible (i.e., does not violate any constraints on assignments). The gradient ascent step is valid since the gradient $\nabla_A \mathrm{W}(A, \arg\inf_{S \in S} \mathrm{W}(A, S))$ is an element of the supergradient $\nabla_A \inf_{S \in S} \mathrm{W}(A, S)$.

The number of iterations required to prove convergence depends on the *gradient norm bound* λ, which is the smallest term such that $\|\nabla_A W(A, S)\|_2 \leq \lambda$ for all A and S. We approximate the maximin optimal continuous matrix $\tilde{A}^{\mathrm{MM}}$ within an error of ε in number of iterations polynomial in λ, $\frac{1}{\varepsilon}$, and the total review load K. The time complexity of RRA also depends on the *adversarial minimization* and *projection* steps, but so long as these take polynomial time, then so too does RRA. We state the convergence results in Proposition 10. The proof applies standard convergence results for subgradient descent [28].

Proposition 10 (Supergradient Ascent Efficiency). *Let λ denote an upper bound on the $\mathcal{L}_2$ norm of the supergradient elements $\nabla_A W(A, S)$ used in RRA. The supergradient ascent component of RRA converges to within ε of the maximin optimal continuous assignment $\tilde{A}^{\mathrm{MM}}$ in $\left(\frac{\lambda\sqrt{2K}}{\varepsilon}\right)^2$ iterations. RRA runs in time $\mathbf{O}\left(C\left(\frac{\lambda\sqrt{2K}}{\varepsilon}\right)^2\right)$, where C is the time cost of one adversary and projection step.*

Although the bound on the number of iterations can be quite large, it proves the convex relaxation of RAU is solvable in polynomial time, as long as the adversary and projection steps can be solved in polynomial time and λ is bounded. In addition, the required number of iterations until convergence will typically be much smaller in practice.

The complexity result improves in the case of (truncated) ellipsoidal uncertainty sets. The *adversarial minimization* step requires polynomial time under truncated ellipsoidal uncertainty sets, as it is a *linear objective* under *convex quadratic constraints* (and box constraints), which is a *second-order conic program*, and the *projection step* always requires polynomial time, as it is a *convex quadratic* objective under *linear* constraints (i.e., the assignment constraints $\tilde{\mathcal{A}}$). The bound λ can be difficult to compute in the general case, but we show λ is typically well-bounded in the case of truncated ellipsoidal uncertainty sets.

Corollary 11 (Supergradient Ascent Efficiency under Ellipsoidal Uncertainty). *For a truncated ellipsoidal uncertainty set, the supergradient ascent component of RRA converges to within ε of the maximin optimal continuous assignment $\tilde{A}^{\mathrm{MM}}$ in $\mathbf{O}\left(\frac{2Km}{n\varepsilon^2}\right)$ iterations.*

Finally, we can round using the extended Birkhoff von Neumann decomposition sampling algorithm [3,9,12]. This sampling algorithm generates an integral sample $\hat{A}'$ from the distribution defined by the continuous assignment matrix $\hat{A}$. The sample $\hat{A}'$ still satisfies the constraints of $\tilde{\mathcal{A}}$, and $\mathbb{E}_{A'}[\hat{A}] = \hat{A}$. The time complexity of this sampling algorithm is $\mathbf{O}(mn(m+n))$, which is typically negligible compared to the complexity of supergradient ascent.

4.2   Maximin and Integrality Gaps

Aside from the optimization error of RRA (Algorithm 1), there are two more error sources: *maximin error* for working under uncertainty, and *rounding error*.

The integrality gap of RAU can be quite large; similarly, the $\mathcal{L}_1$ difference between a rounded assignment A' and a continuous assignment $\tilde{A}$ may be quite large as well. Surprisingly, we show in this section that although the integrality gap is large, with high probability this does not translate to a large amount of suboptimality in the *true* W of the rounded solution A'. Intuitively, whenever the maximin optimal continuous solution $\tilde{A}^{\mathrm{MM}}$ has a high $\mathcal{L}_1$ distance from any valid binary integer assignment, the decisions made during rounding cancel out on average, and have relatively little impact on the true welfare of the assignment.

Proposition 12 ($\mathcal{L}_1$ Distance to Integral Solution). *Suppose an unrounded assignment $\tilde{A}$ and a randomized rounding A' of $\tilde{A}$ such that $\mathbb{E}[A'] = A$. Then the expected $\mathcal{L}_1$ deviation of the assignment due to rounding obeys*

$$\mathbb{E}_{A'}\left[\|A' - \tilde{A}\|_1\right] = 2\left(\|\tilde{A}\|_1 - \|\tilde{A}\|_2^2\right) \leq nm - 2\left\|\tfrac{1}{2} - \tilde{A}\right\|_1 .$$

Although the assignments may need to be rounded quite significantly, Theorem 13 shows that the rounded assignment produced by RRA has near-optimal true welfare (in expectation). Theorem 13 also allows for ε error in the discrete/continuous maximin assignments. For this, we define $A^\varepsilon \in \mathcal{A}$, representing any ε-optimal discrete solution to RAU and $\tilde{A}^\varepsilon \in \tilde{A}$, any ε-optimal continuous solution to RAU. A^ε and $\tilde{A}^\varepsilon$ are formally defined by the properties

$$\max_{A \in \mathcal{A}} \inf_{S \in \mathcal{S}} W(A, S) - \inf_{S \in \mathcal{S}} W(A^\varepsilon, S) \leq \varepsilon \ \& \ \max_{A \in \tilde{A}} \inf_{S \in \mathcal{S}} W(A, S) - \inf_{S \in \mathcal{S}} W(\tilde{A}^\varepsilon, S) \leq \varepsilon .$$

Theorem 13 (Maximin and Integrality Gaps in Welfare). *Suppose $\mathcal{S}$ is a (δ, γ) uncertainty set with $\mathcal{L}_1$ diameter L. Let A^ε denote an ε-optimal discrete RAU solution, and $\tilde{A}^\varepsilon$ denote an ε-optimal continuous RAU solution. Let A' denote the random variable that arises from applying the randomized rounding procedure* ROUND *to $\tilde{A}^\varepsilon$, and assume that* ROUND *preserves expectation, i.e., $\mathbb{E}_{A'}[A'] = \tilde{A}^\varepsilon$. Suppose also that the true affinity scores are S^*, and denote the optimal solution $A^* \doteq \arg\max_{A \in \mathcal{A}} W(A, S^*)$. The following then hold.*

1. *Maximin Gap:* $\mathbb{P}\big(W(A^*, S^*) - W(A^\varepsilon, S^*) > \varepsilon + \frac{2\gamma + L}{n}\big) < \delta$.
2. *Expected Regret of RRA:* $\mathbb{P}\big(W(A^*, S^*) - \mathbb{E}_{A'}[W(A', S^*)] > \varepsilon + \frac{2\gamma + L}{n}\big) < \delta$.
3. *Probabilistic Regret of RRA:* $\mathbb{P}\big(W(A^*, S^*) - W(A', S^*) > \frac{\varepsilon + (2\gamma + L)/n}{\delta'}\big) < \delta' + \delta$.

Since A' is the result of RRA, Theorem 13 directly bounds the expected and probabilistic regret of RRA. Note that the distribution for the probabilistic regret is over the randomness of the rounding procedure, while all bounds in Theorem 13 are probabilistic with respect to δ of the uncertainty set $\mathcal{S}$.

5   Experiments

We create uncertainty sets using five years of ICLR data, by constructing an asymmetric multivariate Gaussian and taking a confidence interval (as outlined by the example in (2)). We compare the adversarial and average-case performance of our approach to the adversarial and average-case performance of four commonly used baselines. We then demonstrate the importance of optimizing for the adversarial case. Code and data are publicly available on Github.[7]

5.1 Baseline Comparison

We examine the ability of our approach to robustly maximize utilitarian welfare in the case of *truncated* ellipsoidal uncertainty sets $\mathcal{S}$. This experiment is meant to mimic real-world conference scenarios, and thus we do not assume access to a ground truth affinity matrix. Consequently, we can only compare adversarial and average-case welfare for RRA vs. our baselines, but not true welfare.

We use the OpenReview API to collect all papers submitted (both accepted and rejected) to five recent iterations of ICLR (2018–2022). Following recent work, we use the pool of authors for each year as the reviewer pool, since we do not have access to the true reviewer identities for these conferences. The number of reviewers and papers for each conference year is shown in Table 1.

For each author in each year, we collect the multiset of keywords from papers the author submitted to ICLR in the current or previous years. We then follow a procedure similar to that of AAAI 2021 [15] to convert keywords into a mean vector $\vec{\mu} \in \mathbb{R}^{nm}$, and we also construct a covariance matrix $\Sigma \in \mathbb{R}^{nm \times nm}_{\geq 0}$ for paper-reviewer affinity scores. Vector $\vec{p}$ is set so $\vec{p}_i$ is an indicator for keyword i on paper p. Vector $\vec{r}$ is initially set so $\vec{r}_i$ is the number of times the keyword i appears on a paper written by that reviewer in this or previous years' conferences. We then modify the values (but not the ordering) of $\vec{r}$ such that the minimum non-zero value is 0.2, the maximum value is 1, and the remaining non-zero values are evenly-spaced between 0.2 and 1. Let $\vec{\lambda} \in \mathbb{R}^V$ be such that $\vec{\lambda}_i = \left(\frac{1}{2}\right)^{i-1}$. *Sorted* represents the function that sorts values of a vector in decreasing order, $M_{\vec{p}}$ and $M_{\vec{r}}$ denote the number of non-zero entries in $\vec{p}$ and $\vec{r}$ respectively, and $Z = \sum_{i=1}^{M_{\vec{p}}} \left(\frac{1}{2}\right)^{i-1}$. We set $\vec{\mu}_{pr} = \frac{\vec{\lambda} \cdot Sorted(\vec{p} \circ \vec{r})}{Z}$, $\Sigma_{pm+r,pm+r} = (M_{\vec{p}} M_{\vec{r}})^{-2}$, and all off-diagonal entries of Σ are 0. This procedure was chosen to roughly mirror the

Table 1. Adversarial and average welfare (mean ± standard deviation) for the naïve LP, FairFlow, PeerReview4All, FairSequence, and RRA methods on five ICLR conferences. Welfare is scaled by 100 for ease of comparison. Adversarial welfare is consistently highest (**bold**) using RRA, except for 2018, which is within one standard deviation.

Year	m	n	Adversarial USW · 100					Average USW · 100				
			LP	FF	PR4A	FS	RRA	LP	FF	PR4A	FS	RRA
2018	1657	546	**17**±3	7±3	**17**±3	16±3	16±3	**179**±2	134±12	177±2	177±2	160±4
2019	2620	851	22±2	12±2	22±2	22±2	**27**±3	**184**±1	139±9	**184**±1	183±1	161±3
2020	4123	1327	17±2	11±2	18±2	17±2	**23**±2	**187**±1	158±8	**187**±1	186±1	166±5
2021	4662	1557	23±2	18±2	23±2	23±2	**33**±3	**192**±1	177±2	**192**±1	191±1	174±6
2022	5023	1576	28±2	23±2	28±2	27±2	**38**±2	**191**±1	177±1	190±1	190±1	172±3

---

[7] https://github.com/justinpayan/RAU.

procedure used by AAAI 2021. For each year of ICLR, we set the uncertainty set $\mathcal{S}$ for robust optimization to be the 95% confidence interval for the distribution $\mathcal{N}(\vec{\mu}, \Sigma)$ (as in (2)), intersected with the unit hypercube (Lemma 7).

For each year of ICLR, we sample without replacement 60% of the reviewers and 60% of the papers 100 times, to produce more data for statistical robustness of our experiments. We assume that all papers require 3 reviews and all reviewers can review up to 6 papers. There are no conflicts of interest. We then run RRA using our calculated confidence region $\mathcal{S}$, and compare against the assignment given by $\arg\max_{A \in \mathcal{A}} W(A, \vec{\mu})$ (the "LP" solution); that is, the naïve solution that optimizes for the mean score. We also compare against three baselines commonly used for real conferences, FairFlow [13], PeerReview4All [29], and FairSequence [21]. The results of these experiments are shown in Table 1. All baselines lag far behind RRA in adversarial performance.

5.2   The Importance of Adversarial Analysis

To demonstrate the importance of optimizing for the adversarial case, we perform an experiment where we simulate the effect of adding many low-quality, high-variance reviewers to the dataset, and a similar experiment where we systematically overestimate some of the affinities for a subset of papers.

We use the dataset of MIDL 2018, which is publicly available and has been used to validate many reviewer assignment algorithms in the past [13, 21, 29]. This dataset contains an 118×177 affinity score matrix that were used to assign reviewers to papers during the conference. We assume the true affinity of the 177 original reviewers for each paper is equal to the affinity score present in the public dataset, but is *noisily estimated*. Thus we assume that the conference organizers have access to estimated affinity scores which are equal to the original

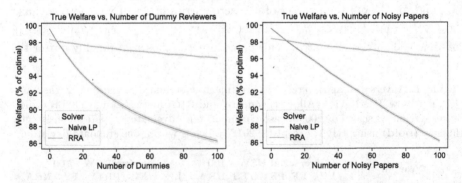

Fig. 1. True welfare (as % of optimal with known S^*) of naïve LP and RRA on MIDL 2018 vs. number of "dummy" reviewers or noisily estimated papers. Dummies have low true affinity for all papers, but high noise in estimated affinity scores. True welfare (which is in practice unknown) decreases sharply for the naïve LP formulation as we add dummies, while RRA welfare only drops slightly. Plot includes min, max, and mean welfare over 100 runs for each number of dummies.

affinity scores plus normally distributed noise, $\mathcal{N}(0, .02)$. We also assume the conference organizers know that the estimation error is distributed according to $\mathcal{N}(0, .02)$ for each paper-reviewer pair. We then add a number of "dummy" reviewers to the dataset. For each dummy reviewer, we set the true affinity of that reviewer to be 0.1 for all papers, and sample the estimated affinity from $\mathcal{N}(0.1, 0.15)$. As with the original reviewers, we assume the conference organizers know the estimation error is distributed according to $\mathcal{N}(0, 0.15)$ for each paper-reviewer pair. This simple setup implies a multivariate Gaussian distribution over the true affinity scores (which are unknown to the conference organizers). We take a 95% confidence interval of this distribution and intersect it with the unit hypercube to define a truncated-ellipsoidal uncertainty set. We then assign reviewers using the naïve LP and RRA, and compare the *true*, but unknown, welfare for each approach. Figure 1 shows that RRA maintains high true welfare, while the welfare of LP decreases with the addition of noisy reviewers. We show a similar result for poorly-estimated papers, with more details on experimental setup in the full version of the paper.

6   Conclusion

Uncertainty is endemic to reviewer assignment. Bias in bids due to partial information, prediction error in text similarity scores, and keyword terminology misalignment all result in inaccurate estimates of reviewers' abilities. Furthermore, fundamental uncertainty about the quality of future reviews can be quantified, but never fully resolved. We treat uncertainty as a first-class citizen, formulating the problem of assigning reviewers under uncertainty as RAU and addressing it under broad conditions with RRA.

We define and explore the concept of uncertainty sets for reviewer assignment; our theory and examples demonstrate the flexibility of uncertainty sets to model real-world uncertainty-aware reviewer assignment workflows. Some special cases of uncertainty sets (singleton, hyperrectangular, or spherical) reduce to problems without uncertainty, which can all be solved via linear programming. The general RAU problem is NP-hard, and our RRA algorithm provides approximate solutions with error guarantees dependent on the uncertainty set.

Because RRA optimizes against an uncertainty-aware adversary, we avoid assigning paper-reviewer pairs with high uncertainty. This method of accounting for uncertainty yields solutions that are more robust than optimizing with pointwise affinity score estimates. We hope this paper serves as a call to further investigate affinity score computation, ensuring affinities correlate with downstream review quality and incorporate the inherent uncertainty present in peer review.

Acknowledgments. Thanks to OpenReview, Vignesh Viswanathan, Elita Lobo, Chang Zeng, Nihar Shah, and the reviewers at GAIW, IJCAI, and SAGT for feedback. Cyrus Cousins acknowledges postdoctoral fellowship support from the Center for Data Science at UMass Amherst. This work was performed using high performance computing equipment obtained under a grant from the Collaborative R&D Fund managed by the Massachusetts Technology Collaborative.

References

1. Aziz, H., Micha, E., Shah, N.: Group fairness in peer review. In: Proceedings of the 22nd AAMAS (2023)
2. Bennett, G.: Probability inequalities for the sum of independent random variables. J. Am. Stat. Assoc. **57**(297), 33–45 (1962)
3. Budish, E., Che, Y.K., Kojima, F., Milgrom, P.: Implementing random assignments: a generalization of the Birkhoff-von Neumann theorem. In: Cowles Summer Conference (2009)
4. Cai, T.T., Zhou, W.X.: Matrix completion via max-norm constrained optimization. Electron. J. Stat. **10**(1), 1493–1525 (2016)
5. Charlin, L., Zemel, R.: The Toronto paper matching system: an automated paper-reviewer assignment system. In: Proceedings of the 2013 ICML Workshop on Peer Reviewing and Publishing Models (2013)
6. Dong, E., Cousins, C.: Decentering imputation: fair learning at the margins of demographics. In: Queer in AI Workshop @ ICML (2022)
7. Fang, E.X., Liu, H., Toh, K.C., Zhou, W.X.: Max-norm optimization for robust matrix recovery. Math. Program. **167**(1), 5–35 (2018)
8. Fiez, T., Shah, N., Ratliff, L.: A SUPER* algorithm to optimize paper bidding in peer review. In: Proceedings of the 36th UAI (2020)
9. Gandhi, R., Khuller, S., Parthasarathy, S., Srinivasan, A.: Dependent rounding and its applications to approximation algorithms. J. ACM (JACM) **53**(3), 324–360 (2006)
10. Jecmen, S., Shah, N.B., Fang, F., Conitzer, V.: Tradeoffs in preventing manipulation in paper bidding for reviewer assignment. In: Proceedings of the 2022 ICLR Workshop on ML Evaluation Standards (2022)
11. Jecmen, S., Yoon, M., Conitzer, V., Shah, N.B., Fang, F.: A dataset on malicious paper bidding in peer review. In: Proceedings of the 2023 WWW (2023)
12. Jecmen, S., Zhang, H., Liu, R., Shah, N., Conitzer, V., Fang, F.: Mitigating manipulation in peer review via randomized reviewer assignments. In: Proceedings of the 34th NeurIPS (2020)
13. Kobren, A., Saha, B., McCallum, A.: Paper matching with local fairness constraints. In: Proceedings of the 25th KDD (2019)
14. Lee, J.D., Recht, B., Srebro, N., Tropp, J., Salakhutdinov, R.R.: Practical large-scale optimization for max-norm regularization. In: Proceedings of the 23rd NeurIPS (2010)
15. Leyton-Brown, K., et al.: Matching papers and reviewers at large conferences. arXiv preprint arXiv:2202.12273 (2022)
16. Mazzetto, A., Cousins, C., Sam, D., Bach, S.H., Upfal, E.: Adversarial multi class learning under weak supervision with performance guarantees. In: International Conference on Machine Learning. PMLR (2021)
17. Meir, R., Lang, J., Lesca, J., Mattei, N., Kaminsky, N.: A market-inspired bidding scheme for peer review paper assignment. In: Proceedings of the 35th AAAI (2021)
18. Neubig, G., the ACL Reviewing Committee: ACL rolling review proposal (2020). http://aclweb.org/adminwiki/index.php?title=ACL_Rolling_Review_Proposal

19. Neubig, G., Wieting, J., McCarthy, A., Stent, A., Schluter, N., Cohn, T.: ACL reviewer matching code (2020). http://github.com/acl-org/reviewer-paper-matching

20. OpenReview: How to do automatic assignments (2023). http://docs.openreview.net/how-to-guides/paper-matching-and-assignment/how-to-do-automatic-assignments

21. Payan, J., Zick, Y.: I will have order! Optimizing orders for fair reviewer assignment. In: Proceedings of the 31st IJCAI (2022)

22. Rogers, A., Augenstein, I.: What can we do to improve peer review in NLP? In: Proceedings of the 2020 EMNLP (2020)

23. Rozenzweig, I., Meir, R., Mattei, N., Amir, O.: Mitigating skewed bidding for conference paper assignment. In: Proceedings of the 2023 International Conference on Autonomous Agents and Multiagent Systems (2023)

24. Saveski, M., Jecmen, S., Shah, N.B., Ugander, J.: Counterfactual evaluation of peer-review assignment policies. arXiv preprint arXiv:2305.17339 (2023)

25. Schroter, S., Tite, L., Hutchings, A., Black, N.: Differences in review quality and recommendations for publication between peer reviewers suggested by authors or by editors. JAMA **295**(3), 314–317 (2006)

26. Shah, N.B.: Principled methods to improve peer review. Technical report, Carnegie Mellon University (2019)

27. Shah, N.B.: Challenges, experiments, and computational solutions in peer review. Commun. ACM **65**(6), 76–87 (2022)

28. Shor, N., Kiwiel, K.C., Ruszcayński, A.: Minimization Methods for Non-differentiable Functions. Springer, Heidelberg (1985). https://doi.org/10.1007/978-3-642-82118-9

29. Stelmakh, I., Shah, N.B., Singh, A.: PeerReview4All: fair and accurate reviewer assignment in peer review. In: Proceedings of the 30th ALT (2019)

30. Stelmakh, I., Wieting, J., Neubig, G., Shah, N.B.: A gold standard dataset for the reviewer assignment problem. arXiv preprint arXiv:2303.16750 (2023)

31. Taylor, C.J.: On the optimal assignment of conference papers to reviewers. Technical report, University of Pennsylvania (2008)

32. Van Rooyen, S., Black, N., Godlee, F.: Development of the review quality instrument (RQI) for assessing peer reviews of manuscripts. J. Clin. Epidemiol. **52**(7), 625–629 (1999)

Diversity-Seeking Jump Games
in Networks

Lata Narayanan and Yasaman Sabbagh[✉]

Department of Computer Science and Software Engineering, Concordia University,
Montreal, Canada
{lata.narayanan,yasaman.sabbaghziarani}@concordia.ca

Abstract. Recently, many researchers have studied strategic games inspired by Schelling's influential model of residential segregation. In this model, agents belonging to k different types are placed at the nodes of a network. Agents can be either stubborn, in which case they will always choose their preferred location, or strategic, in which case they aim to maximize the fraction of agents of their own type in their neighborhood. In the so-called Schelling games inspired by this model, *strategic* agents are assumed to be similarity-seeking: their utility is defined as the fraction of their neighbors of the same type as itself. In this paper, we introduce a new type of strategic jump game in which agents are instead *diversity-seeking*: the utility of an agent is defined as the fraction of its neighbors that is of a *different* type than itself. We show that it is NP-hard to determine the existence of an equilibrium in such games, if some agents are stubborn. However, in trees, our diversity-seeking jump game always admits a pure Nash equilibrium, if all agents are strategic. In regular graphs and spider graphs with a single empty node, as well as in all paths, we prove a stronger result: the game is a potential game, that is, improving response dynamics will always converge to a Nash equilibrium from any initial placement of agents.

1 Introduction

In his seminal work, the economist Schelling proposed an elegant model to explain the phenomenon of residential segregation in American cities [34,35]. In his model, agents of two types are placed uniformly at random on the nodes of a network. An agent is happy if at least some fraction τ of its neighbors are the same type as itself, and unhappy otherwise. An unhappy agent will *jump* to an unoccupied node in the network, or exchange positions with another unhappy agent of a different type. Schelling showed experimentally that this random process would lead to *segregated neighborhoods*, even for values of $\tau < \frac{1}{2}$. His work showed that even small and local individual preferences for one's own type can lead to large-scale and global phenomena such as residential segregation. Schelling's landmark model inspired a significant number of follow-up work in sociology and economics [4,32,33]. Many empirical studies have been conducted to study the influence of different parameters on segregation models [3,9,12,21,37]. Inspired by Schelling's model, there have been a few lines of inquiry pursued by computer scientists. Some researchers attempted to find analytically the conditions under which segregation takes place [7,24]. A more recent line of inquiry uses *game-theoretic* tools to study the problem [10,11,14,16,18,25]. In this setting, strategic agents are placed at arbitrary positions in the network and move to new positions to improve their *utility*. The *utility* of an agent is defined as the fraction of its neighbors which are of the same type as itself. In a *jump* game, an agent moves to a previously unoccupied location which would improve its utility, and in a *swap* game, unhappy agents of different types swap locations. Researchers have studied the computational complexity of finding equilibria, topologies in which a Nash equilibrium always exist, among other results.

In this paper, we introduce a new strategic game called a k-typed Diversity-seeking Jump Game in which the utility of an agent is the fraction of its neighbors of a *different* type to itself. To the best of our knowledge, this is the first time such a utility function has been studied in the context of jump games on a network. Data from the General Social Survey [36] show that people prefer diverse neighborhoods rather than segregated ones. This survey, which is regularly conducted in the US since 1950, shows that the percentage of people preferring diverse neighborhoods has been steadily increasing. There are also other settings that could be modeled using this new utility function; e.g., teams composed of people with diverse backgrounds and skill sets to bring a broader range of perspectives to their business, or research groups composed of people bringing expertise from different disciplines. Indeed, many studies show that ethnically and gender-wise diverse teams lead to better outcomes for business [2,15,17,20,27].

It may seem at first glance that Schelling jump games are intimately related to our diversity-seeking jump games, but the relationship is not obvious. Observe that the utility of a node in the Schelling jump game is not always equal to the complement of its utility in the diversity-seeking setting. To see this, consider an agent placed at a node of degree one, where its neighbor node is empty[1]. Its utility under both games is the same, and not complements of each other. Table 1 shows that the existence (or non-existence) of an equilibrium for the similarity-seeking Jump game in a class of graphs does not guarantee the same (or opposite) result for a diversity-seeking jump game.

1.1   Our Results

For the k-typed Diversity-seeking Jump Game described above, we show that given a network topology and a number of agents drawn from a set of types, it is NP-hard to determine whether there exists a Nash equilibrium if some of the agents are stubborn. In terms of positive results, we show that trees with any number of empty nodes always admit a pure Nash equilibrium, if all agents are strategic. For some classes of graphs, we show a stronger result - the k-typed Diversity-seeking Jump Game is a *potential game* in regular graphs and spider

---

[1] An isolated agent has zero utility in both similarity-seeking and diversity-seeking settings.

graphs with a single empty node, and paths with any number of empty nodes. This means that from any initial placement, improving response dynamics (IRD) by agents converges to a Nash equilibrium. Note that in contrast, for Schelling jump games (whose utility function is similarity-seeking), there are instances on trees that do not admit a Nash equilibrium [18], and there are instances on spider graphs which are not potential games. Table 1 summarizes our results.

Table 1. Summary of results on equilibrium existence and convergence of IRD. Arrows indicate that the result is implied by the indicated result. For results on similarity-seeking games, we use the model of [18]

Graph topology	Empty nodes	Diversity-seeking		Similarity-seeking	
		Potential?	Equilibrium?	Potential?	Equilibrium?
Tree	≥ 1	No (Theorem 2)	Yes (Theorem 3 & Theorem 4)	No $\Leftarrow$	No [18]
Spider graph	1	Yes (Theorem 5)	$\Downarrow$ Yes	No [30]	Yes [31]
	> 1	?	$\Downarrow$ Yes	No [30]	Yes [31]
Graph of degree 2	≥ 1	Yes (Theorem 8)	$\Rightarrow$ Yes	Yes [18]	$\Rightarrow$ Yes
Graph of degree 3	≥ 1	?	?	No $\Leftarrow$	No [31]
Graph of degree ≥ 4	≥ 1	No (Fig. 2)	?	No $\Leftarrow$	No [18]
Regular graph	1	Yes (Theorem 6)	$\Rightarrow$ Yes	Yes [31]	$\Rightarrow$ Yes
	2, 3	?	?	?	?
	4	No (Theorem 7)	?	?	?
	≥ 5	No (Theorem 7)	?	No [16]	?

1.2 Related Work

In the last decade, there have been attempts in the computer science literature [7,24] to theoretically analyze the random process described by Schelling. It was shown that the expected size of the resulting segregated neighborhoods is polynomial in the size of the neighborhood on the line [7] and exponential in its size on the grid [24] but that in both cases it is independent of the overall number of participants.

The study of the above process as a strategic game played by two types of agents rather than as random process appears to have been initiated by Zhang [38], who introduced a game-theoretic model where agents have a noisy single peaked utility function that depends on the ratio of the numbers of agents of two agent types in any local neighborhood. Chauhan et al. [14] introduced a game-theoretic model that incorporates Schelling's notion of a tolerance threshold. In their model, each agent has a threshold parameter $\tau \in (0,1)$ and may have a preferred location. The primary goal of an agent is to find a location where the happiness ratio exceeds τ; if such a location does not exist, the agent aims to maximize its happiness ratio. Its secondary goal is to minimize the distance to its preferred location. Chauhan et al. [14] studied the convergence of best-response dynamics to an equilibrium assignment in both jump and swap games with two types of agents and for various values of the threshold parameter. Among other results, they proved that improving response dynamics (IRD) in a swap Schelling game always converges if $\tau \leq \frac{1}{2}$ for any underlying connected graph, and for arbitrary τ in regular graphs. For jump games, they showed convergence in 2-regular graphs, and that location preferences can lead to improving response cycles. Echzell et al. [16] generalized the model of [14] by considering agents of k different types, Both jump and swap games were studied where agents move only if their utility is under a specified threshold. They provided tight threshold results for the IRD convergence for several versions of the game. Echzell et al. also studied both jump and swap games in a model in which the utility of an agent is the ratio of agents of its own type to the number of agents in the *largest* group of agents of a different type, and also showed results on the computational hardness of finding placements that maximize the number of happy agents.

Elkind et al. [18] studied jump games for the case of $\tau = 1$ for k types of agents. They modeled location preferences by considering two types of agents: those that are strategic and aim to maximize their utility, while others are stubborn and stay at their initial location regardless of the composition of the neighborhood. Elkind et al. [18] showed that while equilibria always exist in stars and graphs of degree 2, an equilibrium assignment does not always exist in this setting, even for trees of degree four. They also showed that computing equilibrium assignments and assignments with optimal social welfare is NP-hard, and bounded the price of anarchy and stability for both general and restricted games. Agarwal et al. [1] used a similar utility function as Elkind et al. [18], but focused on swap games. They showed that while equilibria are known to exist in instances where the topology is highly structured, their existence is not guaranteed in general, and deciding whether a given swap game admits an equilibrium assignment is NP-complete. They prove bounds on the price of anarchy and stability and show that computing assignments that maximize social welfare is NP-hard. They also introduce a new measure called the *degree of integration*, which is the number of agents that are exposed to agents of other types, and show results on the price of anarchy and stability with respect to this measure. Improving the hardness results presented in [18] and [1], Kreisel et al. [26] showed that the determining the existence of equilibria is still hard in jump and swap games even if all the agents are strategic. Bilo et al. [5] investigated the influence of the underlying topology and locality in swap games.

Variations of these models have been studied in [11,13,19,25,28]. The authors of [8] study diversity hedonic games in which some agents have homophilic preferences, while others have heterophilic preferences in coalition formation. However, hedonic games are different to our model as in hedonic games, agents form pairwise disjoint coalitions while in our model, the neighborhoods of different nodes may overlap.

The models most closely related to ours are [6] and [22], which are also motivated by the observation that real-world agents favor diverse neighborhoods. In [6] the authors introduce swap games with a single-peaked utility function with two types of agents which increases monotonically with the fraction of same-type neighbors in the interval $[0, \Lambda]$ for some Λ that lies strictly between 0 and 1, and decreases monotonically afterward. Specifically, Bilo et al. [6] show that for $\Lambda \leq 1/2$, swap equilibria exist on almost-regular graphs, and IRD are guaranteed to converge, while for $\Lambda > 1/2$, there exists games played on 2-regular graphs admitting no equilibria, and for $\Lambda = 1/2$, such games are not potential games on arbitrary graphs. For $\Lambda = 1/2$, equilibria exists and can be efficiently computed on bipartite graphs. They also derive tight bounds on the price of anarchy and stability with respect to the degree of integration defined in [1]. Using the same utility function, but this time for jump games, the authors of [22] investigate the existence of equilibria. They show that improving response cycles exist independently of the position of the peak in the utility function, even for graphs with very simple structures. Furthermore, they show that while equilibria are not guaranteed to exist even on rings for $\Lambda \geq 1/2$, there are conditions under which they are guaranteed to exist, specifically depending on the size of the independent set, the number of empty nodes, and numbers of agents of each color set. They also show bounds on the price of stability and anarchy with respect to the degree of integration and show some hardness results.

While our work is also motivated by the observation that seeking diversity is well-justified in many settings, our model is different from the one considered in [6] and [22]. Indeed they stress that their utility function is *not* monotone; in contrast, in our model, the utility function is monotone, and decreases monotonically with the fraction of same-type agents in the neighborhood. Additionally we consider k types of agents, while they consider only two types of agents. Finally, we also consider location preferences, by considering stubborn agents, while they only consider strategic agents. The model we use is similar to the one used in [1,18] in the sense that the utility function is monotone, $k \geq 2$ agents are considered, and stubborn agents are also considered, but our utility function is diversity-seeking, while theirs is similarity-seeking.

2   The Model and Notation

We have a set of $n \geq 2$ agents, partitioned into $k \geq 2$ different types $T = (T_1, ..., T_k)$. The set of agents is also partitioned into a set of strategic agents R and a set of stubborn agents S. An instance of the *k-typed Diversity-seeking Jump Game* is a tuple $I = (R, S, T, G, \lambda)$, where R is the set of strategic agents, S is the set of stubborn agents, T is the list of k types, G is an undirected graph that satisfies $|V| > |R \cup S|$, and λ is an injective mapping from S to V, that maps the stubborn agents to locations on the nodes of the network.

A strategy for an agent is a location/node in the graph; for a stubborn agent, its only strategy is its location given by λ. In a valid strategy profile, called a *configuration*, no two agents have the same strategy/location. That is, a configuration C is an injective mapping of agents to nodes that respects λ, the placement of the stubborn agents.

Furthermore, we define $n_{T_x}(u, C)$ to be the number of neighbors of node u that are occupied by agents of type T_x in configuration C. Define $n(u, C) = \sum_{T_x \in T} n_{T_x}(u, C)$, that is $n(u, C)$ is the total number of agents in u's neighborhood in configuration C. The *utility function* measures the satisfaction of agents in a given configuration C. Let $v(\mathcal{A}, C)$ denote the node occupied by agent $\mathcal{A}$ in configuration C. The utility of an agent $\mathcal{A}$ of type T_x in a diversity-seeking jump game for a configuration C is defined as the fraction of agents of a type different to $\mathcal{A}$ in $\mathcal{A}$'s neighborhood. That is,

$$u_{\mathcal{A}}(C) = \frac{\sum_{T_y \neq T_x} n_{T_y}(v(\mathcal{A}, C), C)}{n(v(\mathcal{A}, C), C)}$$

By convention, the utility of an agent that has no neighbors is 0.

We are interested in the convergence of improving response dynamics (IRD) in these games: in each step, a single agent tries to change its strategy, that is, it moves to an unoccupied location where it gets a higher utility. We say such a move of an agent $\mathcal{A}$ from configuration C to configuration C' is an *improving move* if $u_{\mathcal{A}}(C) < u_{\mathcal{A}}(C')$. Note that in configuration C, a single agent may have many improving moves available, and multiple agents may have improving moves available. We do not make any assumptions about which improving move will take place if multiple improving moves are available. IRD are said to converge to a pure Nash equilibrium (NE) configuration, if no agent has an improving move. Following [29], a k-typed Diversity-seeking Jump Game is a *potential game* if and only if there exists *a generalized ordinal potential function*, that is, a non-negative real-valued function Φ on the set of configurations such that for any two configurations C and C' where there is an improving move from C to C', we have $\Phi(C') < \Phi(C)$. As observed in [29], such games always admit a Nash equilibrium, and furthermore, regardless of the starting configuration, any sequence of improving moves is finite and will terminate in a Nash equilibrium.

An improving response cycle (IRC) is a sequence of improving moves in which a configuration repeats. Clearly, the presence of an IRC implies that the game cannot be a potential game. Note that the presence of an IRC does not imply the non-existence of a Nash equilibrium.

In this paper, we show that the following function is a generalized ordinal potential function for some specific topologies, for some values of m that depend on the topology and will be specified later. Similar potential functions were used in [14, 16, 18].

Definition 1. *We define the* potential Φ *of a configuration* C *as* $\Phi(C) = \sum_e w_C(e)$, *where weight* $w_C(e)$ *for any edge* $e = \{u, v\} \in E$ *in the configuration* C *is defined as:*

$$w_C(e) = \begin{cases} 1 & \text{if } u \text{ and } v \text{ are occupied by agents of the same type} \\ 0 < m < 1 & \text{if either } u \text{ or } v \text{ is unoccupied} \\ 0 & \text{otherwise.} \end{cases}$$

The following lemma shows that if the k-typed Diversity-seeking Jump Game with no stubborn agents is a potential game in a particular class of networks, then it is also a potential game if some of the agents are stubborn.

Lemma 1. *Given $k \geq 2$, and topology G, if the k-typed Diversity-seeking Jump Game $I = (R, \emptyset, T, G, \lambda)$ is a potential game, then every k-typed Diversity-seeking Jump Game $I' = (R', S', T, G, \lambda)$ where S' and R' form a partition of R, is also a potential game.*

Lemma 1 allows us to consider only the case when all agents are strategic when showing that a k-typed Diversity-seeking Jump Game is a potential game in a class of networks.

All the omitted proofs can be found in the full version of this paper [30].

3   Hardness of Finding Equilibria

In this section, we study the computational complexity of determining if a given k-typed Diversity-seeking Jump Game admits a pure Nash equilibrium.

Theorem 1. *For $k \geq 2$, given a k-typed Diversity-seeking Jump Game $I = (R, S, T, G, \lambda)$, it is NP-complete to decide whether I admits an equilibrium assignment.*

Proof. We give a proof for $k = 2$; it is straightforward to extend it to $k \geq 2$. We will use a reduction from the Independent Set (IS) decision problem [23]. Recall that an independent set in a graph is a subset of vertices of the graph such that no two vertices in the subset are connected by an edge. An instance of the IS problem is an undirected graph $H = (X, Y)$, where X and Y are the set of vertices and edges respectively, and an integer s; it is a yes-instance if and only if H has an independent set of size $\geq s$. We construct an instance I of a k-typed Diversity-seeking Jump Game as follows (see Fig. 1):

1. There are two agent types: red and blue.
2. There are a total of $8s + 16$ agents, of which are there are $s + 1$ strategic red agents, $2s + 4$ stubborn red agents and $5s + 11$ stubborn blue agents.
3. The topology $G = (V, E)$ consists of two components G_1 and G_2.
   (a) $G_1 = (V_1, E_1)$, where $V_1 = X \cup W$, $|W| = 7s + 1$, and $E_1 = Y \cup \{\{v, w\} : v \in X, w \in W\}$. $5s + 1$ stubborn blue agents and $2s$ stubborn red agents are placed on nodes of W.
   (b) G_2 has exactly three empty nodes, denoted x, y, and z, all the other nodes are occupied by stubborn agents. x is connected to y and one blue agent. The node y is connected to six nodes, containing one red agent and five blue agents. Finally z is connected to 7 nodes containing 4 blue agents and 3 red agents. Observe that when the other two nodes in G_2 are unoccupied, x, y, and z offer utilities $1, \frac{5}{6}$, and $\frac{4}{7}$ respectively.
   (c) There is an edge between two (arbitrarily chosen) nodes containing stubborn agents in G_1 and G_2, thereby connecting the graph.

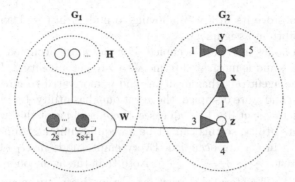

Fig. 1. G_1 and G_2 are the two components of G, connected by a single edge. Every node in H is connected to every node in W. The blue (red) triangle connected to x denotes a set of neighbors of x with blue (red) agents, and the number next to a triangle denotes the number of nodes in the corresponding set. (Color figure online)

The main idea of the reduction is as follows. We will show that if an IS of size $\geq s$ exists in the graph H, then placing s strategic agents on the nodes of the IS and the last strategic agent on node x is an equilibrium assignment in I. Conversely, if no IS of size $\geq s$ exists in H, then we will show with a case analysis that there cannot be an equilibrium assignment in I.

We proceed with the proof that I admits a Nash equilibrium if and only if H has an IS of size $\geq s$. First, suppose that H contains an IS of size $\geq s$. Consider the following assignment in I where s red agents occupy the nodes of that IS and one red agent occupies node x in G_2. We show that this is an equilibrium assignment. The utility of each agent on IS is $\frac{5s+1}{7s+1}$. Note that any remaining empty node on G_1 offers a utility that is at most $\frac{5s+1}{7s+1} < 1$, while the utility of the agent on x is 1. Therefore, the agent on x does not benefit by moving to an empty node in G_1. Also, note that when node x is occupied, the highest utility a red agent can achieve in G_2 is $\frac{5}{7}$ by moving to y. We have $\frac{5s+1}{7s+1} > \frac{5}{7}$, therefore no agent in G_1 has an improving move to an empty node in G_2. Therefore, we have an equilibrium assignment.

On the other hand, suppose H does not contain an IS of size $\geq s$. Suppose for the purpose of contradiction that I admits an equilibrium assignment. There are four possible cases:

1. All empty nodes in G_2 are unoccupied. Then since there is no IS of size s in H, and therefore in G_1, at least one strategic red agent is adjacent to another strategic red agent and has utility at most $\frac{5s+1}{7s+2}$. Note that $\frac{5s+1}{7s+2} < 1$, so that agent will increase its utility by moving to node x in G_2. Therefore, this is not an equilibrium assignment.

2. Exactly one node in G_2 is occupied. Then the strategic agent on G_2 occupies x as it offers the highest utility. Then as in the previous case, since there is no IS of size s, at least one strategic red agent is adjacent to another strategic red agent in G_1 and has utility at most $\frac{5s+1}{7s+2}$. Note that $\frac{5s+1}{7s+2} < \frac{5}{7}$, so that

agent will improve its utility by moving to node y in G_2. Therefore, this is not an equilibrium assignment.

3. Exactly two nodes in G_2 are occupied. If x and y are occupied, the agent on x has utility $\frac{1}{2}$ and is motivated to move to z to get a utility $\frac{4}{7}$. If x and z are occupied, the agent on z has utility $\frac{4}{7}$ and is motivated to move to y to get utility $\frac{5}{7}$. If y and z are occupied, the agent on y has utility $\frac{5}{6}$ and is motivated to move to x to get utility 1. In all cases, there is an agent that wants to move to increase its utility, so this cannot be an equilibrium assignment.

4. All the nodes in G_2 are occupied. Every empty node in G_1 offers a utility that is at least $\frac{5s+1}{(7s+1)+(s-2)} = \frac{5s+1}{8s-1}$. Note that the agent on x has utility $\frac{1}{2}$ and $\frac{5s+1}{8s-1} > \frac{1}{2}$. Therefore, the agent on x is motivated to move to an empty node in G_1. Therefore this cannot be an equilibrium assignment.

We have shown a contradiction in all the possible cases. Therefore, if G does not contain an IS of size s, there is no equilibrium assignment. This completes the proof of the NP-hardness. □

The proof above relies heavily on the existence of stubborn agents, like proofs of similar results for similarity-seeking jump Schelling game in [18]. In a recent paper, Kriesel et al. [26] show that deciding the existence of an equilibria in a jump Schelling game is NP-complete, even if all agents are strategic. Their techniques are not immediately applicable to our setting, and in fact we have not been able to construct a diversity-seeking jump game with only strategic agents that does not have an equilibrium.

4   Seeking Diversity in Tree Topologies

In this section, we consider diversity-seeking jump games restricted to networks with tree topologies. First we show that IRD do not always converge in a tree, even with a single empty node. However, there is always an equilibrium assignment; we give a polytime algorithm to find an NE. In contrast, recall that similarity-seeking games do not always admit an NE in a tree [18]. Finally, in Sect. 4.1, we will show that the diversity-seeking jump game is a potential game in spider graphs (trees in which there is a single node of degree ≥ 3).

Theorem 2. *For every $k \geq 2$, there exists a k-typed Diversity-seeking Jump Game $I = (R, S, T, G, \lambda)$, such that G is a tree and I is not a potential game.*

Proof. Figure 2 shows an IRC in a diversity-seeking jump game on a tree with a single empty node and 2 types of agents. It is easy to verify that each move shown is an improving move. □

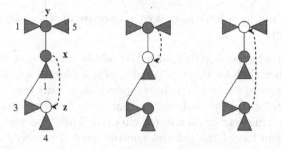

Fig. 2. An IRC in a tree. The blue (red) triangle connected to x denotes a set of neighbors of x with blue (red) agents, and the number next to a triangle denotes the number of nodes in the corresponding set. (Color figure online)

In fact, if the agents in the triangles are all stubborn and only the agents in x, y or z are strategic, the diversity-seeking jump game shown in Fig. 2 does not admit an equilibrium. Thus, equilibria are not guaranteed for diversity-seeking jump games in trees with stubborn agents. Nevertheless, we show that there is always an equilibrium assignment in a tree if all agents are strategic; we give an algorithm to find such a configuration. As a warm-up, we first consider the case when the tree has a single empty node.

Theorem 3. *Given $k \geq 2$, every k-typed Diversity-seeking Jump Game (R, S, T, G, λ) where G is a tree, $|V| = |R| + 1$ and $S = \emptyset$ admits a pure Nash equilibrium.*

Proof. Pick a node r of degree one to be the root of the tree, call its unique neighbor as v. Assume the agents are pre-ordered by type. The algorithm proceeds in two phases. In the first phase, starting with the deepest *odd* level in the tree, place agents in the current level l, moving from left to right. When the current level is completely filled, skip a level, go to level $l - 2$ and repeat, until the unique node v in level 1 is filled, say by an agent of a type T_x: For convenience, we call it a *red agent*. This ends the first phase. In the second phase, move downwards from level 2, filling even levels from left to right.

At the end of this procedure, only the root node is unoccupied. Furthermore, all non-red agents are guaranteed to have utility one, and have no improving move. There may be red agents that have utility less than one, but they cannot improve their utility by moving to the root. This proves that the assignment is an equilibrium.   □

For the case when the number of empty nodes is more than one, we first find a connected sub-tree with one more node than the number of agents, and find an equilibrium assignment for the sub-tree using the method of Theorem 3. Next we adjust this assignment to get an assignment for the original tree, by moving some agents to empty nodes in the original tree that were not present in the sub-tree, in order to ensure that no agent will have an improving move.

We start by noting a few easily seen properties of the assignment for trees described above:

(P1) Every non-red agent is either placed on odd levels or on even levels but not both. This implies that for every non-red agent $\mathcal{A}$ placed in a particular level, there are no agents of its own type in the previous or next levels.

(P2) Except possibly for two red agents, that we call *mixed* agents, a red agent has either all red children[2] or all non-red children. This is because there are only two levels that can have both red and non-red agents, namely the levels where we start and stop placing red agents.

(P3) Every red agent with a non-red parent can only have non-red children, and therefore has utility one.

Theorem 4. *Given $k \geq 2$, every k-typed Diversity-seeking Jump Game (R, S, T, G, λ) where G is a tree, $|V| > |R| + 1$ and $S = \emptyset$ admits an equilibrium.*

Proof. Given the tree $G = (E, V)$, fix a root node of degree one, and repeatedly remove leaf nodes until we have a tree with exactly $|R| + 1$ nodes, call it $G' = (E', V')$. Let $C_{G'}$, denote the equilibrium configuration in G' as described in the proof of Theorem 3. As before, let us call the type of the agent assigned to the unique neighbor of the root a red agent.

Now consider the original tree G, and consider the same placement of agents as in $C_{G'}$, call this configuration C_G. Clearly the utility of agents in C_G is exactly the same as their utility in $C_{G'}$, as acquiring new empty neighbors does not change an agent's utility. From Property (P1), all non-red agents have utility one. As in $C_{G'}$, there may be some red agents that have utility lower than one in C_G, but in G, they may have improving moves available, *i.e.* C_G may not be an equilibrium.

For the preprocessing, we make a local adjustment to the placement of children of $\mathcal{A}$. Let S_1 be the set of red children of $\mathcal{A}$ that are adjacent to at least one more agent, and let S_2 be its non-red children with *no* other agents as neighbors. If $S_2 = \emptyset$, and the second mixed agent $\mathcal{B}$ exists and is a child of $\mathcal{A}$, we swap[3] the position of $\mathcal{B}$ with any non-red child of $\mathcal{A}$. Note that the non-red child in its new position still has utility one, as do all non-red children of $\mathcal{A}$ in this case. Another consequence of this swap is that $\mathcal{B}$ is no longer a mixed agent, so there is only one mixed agent in the tree.

If $S_2 \neq \emptyset$, we swap the positions of $min(|S_1|, |S_2|)$ of the agents in S_2 with the agents in the other set. If $\mathcal{B}$ is child of $\mathcal{A}$ we make sure $\mathcal{B}$ participates in the swap.

Claim. After the preprocessing operation, *at least one* of the following two conditions holds:

---

[2] For brevity, we say an agent is a child (neighbor/parent) of another agent to mean an agent is placed at a node that is the child (neighbor/parent) of the node where the other agent is placed.

[3] Note that this is a jump game, so the swap referred to here is not to be confused with improving response dynamics.

1. All red children of $\mathcal{A}$ have utility 0.
2. All of $\mathcal{A}$'s non-red children have children of their own.

Proof. If $|S_1| \leq |S_2|$, by (P2), the agents in S_2 that swapped positions now have children of a different color than themselves, and still have utility one. The remaining agents in S_2 have no neighbors other than $\mathcal{A}$ and retain utility one. Also, all the red children of $\mathcal{A}$, have no neighbors other than $\mathcal{A}$ and have utility zero. See Fig. 3(a).

If instead $|S_1| > |S_2|$, all non-red children of $\mathcal{A}$ have children of a different type than themselves, by property (P1), and have utility one. And so if $\mathcal{A}$ moves from its position, these non-red agents would still have utility one. Some of the red children of $\mathcal{A}$ may have red children, and others may have non-red children. See Fig. 3(b). □

If there remains another mixed agent in the tree, then this agent $\mathcal{B}$ is not a child of $\mathcal{A}$, and we perform the same pre-processing operation for $\mathcal{B}$'s children as well.

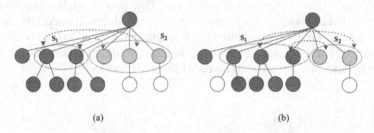

(a)   (b)

Fig. 3. Swapping the red children adjacent to at least one more agent (S_1) with non-red children with no other agents as neighbors (S_2). (a): $|S_1| \leq |S_2|$. (b): $|S_1| > |S_2|$. Red dotted arrows show the swaps. (Color figure online)

We now create an ordered list of *candidate* red agents to move: starting with level one, moving down level by level, we put in red agents that have utility zero in this list. It remains to consider agents of utility strictly between 0 and 1: these are either agents that are mixed agents, or their child red agents who have children of a non-red type.

First consider the agent $\mathcal{A}$. If Condition (1) holds, then all of $\mathcal{A}$'s red children are already in the list of candidates. If they all move, then $\mathcal{A}$'s utility will change to one, so we do not put $\mathcal{A}$ into the candidate list. Otherwise, Condition (2) of Claim 4 holds; we put $\mathcal{A}$ in the list of candidates. Next suppose there was a second mixed agent $\mathcal{B}$. As observed earlier, then $\mathcal{B}$ cannot be a child of $\mathcal{A}$. Because our placement algorithm for the tree G' placed agents from left to right, it can be verified that all of $\mathcal{A}$'s red children can only have red children (see Fig. 4). Condition (1) of Claim 4 is satisfied, and $\mathcal{A}$ was not placed in the candidate list. We follow the same procedure as for $\mathcal{A}$ to decide if $\mathcal{B}$ should be placed in the candidate list. We see that there is at most one mixed agent in the candidate list, and it is the last agent in the list.

Next we describe *where* to move the candidate agents. Before we move any agents, note that all empty nodes have the property that they are adjacent to at most a single node containing an agent. This follows from the manner in which G' was extracted from G by repeatedly removing leaves. Therefore all empty nodes either offer utility 0 or 1 to a red agent. When moving agents, we will maintain this property of the set of empty nodes.

Call a node *available* if it is empty and adjacent only to a non-red agent, and perhaps other empty nodes. Observe that if a candidate red agent moves to an available node, (a) the utility of the candidate increases to one (b) the utility of all other agents stays the same or increases and (c) the number of available nodes decreases by one and (d) the newly vacated node is adjacent only to red agents and possibly empty nodes[4] and therefore offers utility 0 to any red agent and (e) any empty neighbor of the newly occupied node offers utility 0 to any red agent. Thus we maintain the desired property of empty nodes.

We are now ready to describe our procedure to convert C_G to an equilibrium configuration. We repeatedly take the first candidate from the ordered list of candidates and move it to an available node. This process ends when there are no more available nodes or there are no more candidates. If there are no more available nodes, we have an equilibrium configuration, as all other empty nodes offer utility 0 to a red agent. If there are no more candidates, then all red agents have utility one, and we have an equilibrium configuration.   □

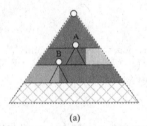 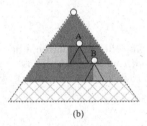

(a)   (b)

Fig. 4. All the red children of $\mathcal{A}$ can only have red children (if any): (a) $\mathcal{B}$ is on the even level at which we finish placing the red agents, then all the red agents that are to the right of $\mathcal{B}$ on the same level (thus children of $\mathcal{A}$) can only have red children (if any) (b) $\mathcal{B}$ is on the odd level at which we start placing the red agents, then all the red agents that are to the left of $\mathcal{B}$ on the same level (thus children of $\mathcal{A}$) can only have red children (if any). The cross hashed levels may or may not exist, but if they do, they are occupied by non-red agents. (Color figure online)

---

[4] Property (d) is not true if a mixed agent vacates its spot, but this happens only in the last step, when there are no more candidates.

4.1 Spider Graphs

A *spider graph*, also called a starlike graph, is a tree in which all the nodes except one, called the *center node* c, have degree of at most 2. We will show that the k-typed Diversity-seeking Jump Game on a spider graph with a single empty node is a potential game. Unfortunately the function Φ from Definition 1 is not a generalized ordinal potential function for the diversity-seeking jump game for any value of m, as there are some improving moves for agents that increase the value of the function. However, we will show that any *long enough sequence of improving moves* is guaranteed to result in a lower value of the function. This will suffice to show convergence of IRD.

We start with a lemma providing upper bounds on the change in potential caused by different types of moves.

Lemma 2. *In every k-typed Diversity-seeking Jump Game (R, S, T, G, λ) where G is a spider graph, for an improving move of an agent $\mathcal{A}$ of type T_x in C_0 that results in C_1, we have:*

1. *$\Phi(C_1) - \Phi(C_0) \leq -m$ if the improving move does not involve the center node*
2. *$\Phi(C_1) - \Phi(C_0) \leq 2m - 1 + n_{T_x}(c, C_1) - m\delta(c)$ if the improving move is from a degree-2 node to center node*
3. *$\Phi(C_1) - \Phi(C_0) \leq m - m\delta(c) + n_{T_x}(c, C_0)$ if the improving move is from a leaf to center node*
4. *$\Phi(C_1) - \Phi(C_0) \leq 1 - 2m + m\delta(c) - n_{T_x}(c, C_0)$ if the improving move is from center node to any other node*

For the remainder of the section, we will assume that $m < \frac{1}{2}$. Lemma 2 then implies that any improving move of an agent that does not involve the center node always *decreases* the value of the potential function Φ. However, an improving move of an agent that moves to or out of the center can increase the potential by a non-constant amount. The change in potential is related to the degree of the center node and the number of neighbors of the same type as the agent that moved to or from the center node. We claim however, that such a move that increases the potential must be followed by moves that collectively decrease the potential *below* its value before the move in question, and that the game is a potential game.

To prove that the diversity-seeking jump game is a potential game in spider graphs, suppose for the purpose of contradiction that there is an IRC. Consider a smallest IRC of length p, and denote the configurations in it by $C_0, C_1, \ldots C_{p-1}$. Since any improving move of an agent that does not involve the center node always decreases the potential, our IRC must involve moves to or out of the center node. Since every move of an agent $\mathcal{A}$ to the center node must be followed by a move of agent $\mathcal{A}$ out of the center node, we calculate the change in potential resulting from the set of moves that includes the move to the center, move out of the center, and any moves in between. Let $C_{j_0}, C_{j_1}, \ldots C_{j_w}$, be the configurations in the cycle in which the center node c is unoccupied, listed in increasing order. Furthermore, define $C_{j_i}^+, C_{j_i}^-$, where $0 \leq i \leq w$ to be the immediate successor and predecessor of C_{j_i}. We will show that for every i, the difference in potential between C_{j_i} and $C_{j_{i+1}}$ is always at most 0[5]. Furthermore, we will show that it impossible for the difference to be zero for *every such pair*, which yields a contradiction to the existence of an IRC.

The following lemma gives an upper bound on the change in potential caused by moves *in between* a move of an agent $\mathcal{A}$ to the center node and the subsequent move out of the center node, that is between the configurations $C_{j_i}^+$ and $C_{j_{i+1}}^-$, for any $0 \leq i \leq w$. Let the center node c be occupied by an agent $\mathcal{A}$ of type T_x in both these configurations and all configurations in between. Assume that $\mathcal{A}$ moved from a source node s in C_{j_i} to the center node and subsequently moved to target node t to reach $C_{j_{i+1}}$ and let $\Delta_{T_x} = n_{T_x}(c, C_{j_{i+1}}^-) - n_{T_x}(c, C_{j_i}^+)$. Then,

Lemma 3.

$$\Phi(C_{j_{i+1}}^-) - \Phi(C_{j_i}^+) \leq \begin{cases} -|\Delta_{T_x}| & \textit{if } s, t \textit{ are not adjacent to } c & (1) \\ -|\Delta_{T_x}| + m & \textit{if only } t \textit{ is adjacent to } c & (2) \\ -|\Delta_{T_x}| + m - 1 & \textit{if only } s \textit{ is adjacent to } c. & (3) \\ -|\Delta_{T_x}| + 2m - 1 & \textit{if } s, t \textit{ are adjacent to } c. & (4) \end{cases}$$

Now we consider the difference in potential between $C_{j_{i+1}}$ and C_{j_i} We analyze separately the cases when s was at a degree-2 node or a leaf node.

Lemma 4. *If s is a degree-2 node, then $\Phi(C_{j_{i+1}}) - \Phi(C_{j_i}) < 0$.*

Lemma 5. *If s is a leaf node, then $\Phi(C_{j_{i+1}}) - \Phi(C_{j_i}) \leq 0$. Furthermore, $\Phi(C_{j_{i+1}}) - \Phi(C_{j_i}) = 0$, only if s is adjacent to the center and $u_{\mathcal{A}}(C_{j_{i+1}}) = \frac{1}{2}$.*

We are now ready to prove the main result of this section:

Theorem 5. *Given $k \geq 2$, every k-typed Diversity-seeking Jump Game (R, S, T, G, λ) where G is a spider graph and $|V| = |R \cup S| + 1$ is a potential game.*

Proof. Suppose instead that k-typed Diversity-seeking Jump Game is not a potential game. Then there exists and IRC, and the net potential change of the moves in this cycle must be zero. By Lemma 2, every improving move that does not involve the center node decreases the potential. It follows that the cycle must involve moves to and out of the center node. Let $C_{j_0}, C_{j_1}, \ldots C_{j_w}$, be the configurations in the cycle in which the center node c is unoccupied, listed in increasing order. Lemmas 4 and 5 show that for every i, the difference in potential between C_{j_i} and $C_{j_{i+1}}$ is at most 0. Since the potential change never increases, and the net potential change must be zero, it must be that in fact, *for every i*, we have $\Phi(C_{j_{i+1}}) - \Phi(C_{j_i})$ is exactly zero. It follows from Lemma 5 that for every i, an agent moved to the center node from a leaf node adjacent to the center, and subsequently moved out to a degree-2 node to get a utility of $\frac{1}{2}$.

---

[5] For readability, we use $i+1$ to mean $(i+1) \bmod (w+1)$ when referring to the indices of the configurations.

Assume without loss of generality that an agent $\mathcal{A}$ of type T_x made such a move from such a leaf node neighbor of the center s, to occupy the center in $C_{j_0}^+$. Before $\mathcal{A}$ moves out of the center node, clearly no agent of type T_x would move to s, as it would get a utility of 0. It follows that if *every* agent that moved to the center in the cycle is of the same type T_x, then the number of neighbors of the center of type T_x must decrease during the moves comprising the cycle, which is a contradiction.

Therefore it must be that for some j_i, an agent $\mathcal{A}$ of type T_x occupies the center node in $C_{j_i}^+$, and an agent $\mathcal{B}$ of type $T_y \neq T_x$ occupies the center in $C_{j_{i+1}}^+$. By Lemma 5, we have $u_{\mathcal{A}}(C_{j_{i+1}}) = \frac{1}{2}$, therefore $u_{\mathcal{A}}(C_{j_{i+1}}^-) < \frac{1}{2}$. Since $\mathcal{B}$ is of a different type to $\mathcal{A}$, it must be that $u_{\mathcal{B}}(C_{j_{i+1}}^+) > \frac{1}{2}$.

Since the change in potential between $C_{j_{i+1}}$ and $C_{j_{i+2}}$ is also zero, by Lemma 5, it must be that $\mathcal{B}$ moved to a node t to get a utility of $\frac{1}{2}$ and so $u_{\mathcal{B}}(C_{j_{i+2}}^-) < \frac{1}{2}$. This means that the number of agents of type T_y that occupy the nodes adjacent to center must have increased, that is, $n_{T_y}(c, C_{j_{i+1}}^+) - n_{T_y}(c, C_{j_{i+2}}^-) < 0$. Now, we have:

$$\Phi(C_{j_{i+2}}) - \Phi(C_{j_{i+1}}) \leq n_{T_y}(c, C_{j_{i+1}}^+) - n_{T_y}(c, C_{j_{i+2}}^-) - |(n_{T_y}(c, C_{j_{i+1}}^+) - n_{T_y}(c, C_{j_{i+2}}^-))|$$

which can be shown to be negative, yielding a contradiction. As such, there can be no cycle in the configuration graph, and we conclude that k-typed Diversity-seeking Jump Game on a spider graph with a single empty node is a potential game.   □

We note that our proof assumes that there is a single empty node; it is unclear if having more empty nodes in the graph could make an IRC possible.

5   Networks of Bounded Degree

In this section, we consider diversity-seeking jump games on networks of fixed degree. We first show that diversity-seeking jump games are potential games in any regular graphs where there is a single empty node.

Theorem 6. *Given $k, \delta \geq 2$, every k-typed Diversity-seeking Jump Game (R, S, T, G, λ) where G is a δ-regular graph and $|V| = |R \cup S| + 1$ is a potential game.*

In contrast to Theorem 6, even in a regular graph, if there are 4 or more empty nodes, then there can be IRCs.

Theorem 7. *For every $\delta > 3$ and $k \geq 2$, there exists a k-typed Diversity-seeking Jump Game $I = (R, S, T, G, \lambda)$ where G is a δ-regular graph and $|V| = |R \cup S| + \delta$ such that I is not a potential game.*

Proof. We start with $\delta = 4$; we show an IRC in a regular graph of degree 4 as shown in Fig. 5. It is easy to verify that the moves shown are improving moves.

We now give an inductive argument for the case of higher δ. Suppose inductively that there is an IRC in a game I on a δ-regular graph G for some $\delta \geq 4$. We now construct a $(\delta + 1)$-regular graph H by duplicating G, call the duplicate graph G' and connecting every node in G' to its counterpart in G. Consider now the $\delta + 1$-regular graph $G \cup G'$, and the following placement of agents. We keep the same assignment of agents in G. The counterpart in G' of the node containing the moving red agent has no agents assigned it, while all other nodes in G' are assigned yellow agents. It can be verified that the same IRC exists in this graph for the same red agent and blue agent visiting the same nodes as in G.   □

Note that there is a gap between the results of Theorems 6 and 7. The question of whether diversity-seeking jump games are potential games in regular graphs of degree 3, or regular graphs of degree 4 with 2 or 3 empty nodes remains open. Finally, we remark that an IRC on a regular graph with $k = 2$ can be constructed from the tree shown in Fig. 2 but the number of empty nodes would be greater than 4.

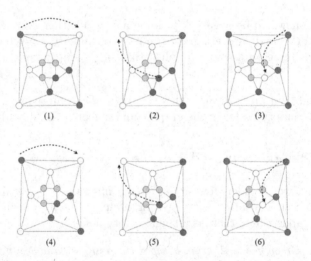

Fig. 5. An IRC in a regular graph of degree 4 with 4 empty nodes

Next we consider networks of maximum degree 2 (that may not be regular), and show that regardless of the number of empty nodes, any k-typed Diversity-seeking Jump Game is a potential game.

Theorem 8. *Given $k \geq 2$, every k-typed Diversity-seeking Jump Game (R, S, T, G, λ) where G is a graph of maximum degree 2 is a potential game.*

6   Discussion

We proposed a new diversity-seeking jump game in networks. We showed that
the complexity of determining if there exists a pure-Nash equilibrium in a given
instance is NP-hard. Our proof relies on the existence of stubborn agents in
the game. Does every game with only strategic agents always admit an equilibrium? If not, what is the complexity of deciding if an equilibrium exists in a
given diversity-seeking jump game with only strategic agents? We showed that
the diversity-seeking jump game is not a potential game in trees; however if
all agents are strategic, there is always a pure Nash equilibrium, regardless of
the number of empty nodes in the tree. It would be interesting to know if the
game is weakly acyclic in trees. In spider graphs with a single empty node,
we showed that the diversity-seeking jump game is a potential game. We conjecture that every diversity-seeking jump game is a potential game on spider
graphs regardless of the number of empty nodes. While diversity-seeking jump
games on 2-regular graphs are always potential games, there are instances of
the game on 4-regular graphs that are not potential games. It would be very
interesting to know whether diversity-seeking jump games on 3-regular graphs
are potential games, and to understand the effect of the number of empty nodes
on the convergence of IRD.

Acknowledgments. The authors gratefully acknowledge many useful discussions
with J. Opatrny, as well as several useful and constructive comments of anonymous
referees.

References

1. Agarwal, A., Elkind, E., Gan, J., Voudouris, A.: Swap stability in Schelling games
   on graphs. In: Proceedings of the AAAI Conference on Artificial Intelligence, vol.
   34, pp. 1758–1765 (2020)
2. Antonio, A.L., Chang, M.J., Hakuta, K., Kenny, D.A., Levin, S., Milem, J.F.:
   Effects of racial diversity on complex thinking in college students. Psychol. Sci.
   15(8), 507–510 (2004)
3. Benard, S., Willer, R.: A wealth and status-based model of residential segregation.
   Math. Sociol. **31**(2), 149–174 (2007)
4. Benenson, I., Hatna, E., Or, E.: From Schelling to spatially explicit modeling of
   urban ethnic and economic residential dynamics. Sociol. Methods Res. **37**(4), 463–
   497 (2009)
5. Bilò, D., Bilò, V., Lenzner, P., Molitor, L.: Topological influence and locality in
   swap Schelling games. Auton. Agent. Multi-Agent Syst. **36**(2), 1–60 (2022)
6. Bilò, D., Bilò, V., Lenzner, P., Molitor, L.: Tolerance is necessary for stability:
   single-peaked swap Schelling games. In: Raedt, L.D. (ed.) Proceedings of the
   Thirty-First International Joint Conference on Artificial Intelligence, IJCAI 2022,
   pp. 81–87. International Joint Conferences on Artificial Intelligence Organization
   (2022)
7. Brandt, C., Immorlica, N., Kamath, G., Kleinberg, R.: An analysis of one-
   dimensional Schelling segregation. In: Proceedings of the Forty-Fourth Annual
   ACM Symposium on Theory of Computing, pp. 789–804 (2012)

8. Bredereck, R., Elkind, E., Igarashi, A.: Hedonic diversity games. In: Proceedings of the 18th International Conference on Autonomous Agents and MultiAgent Systems, pp. 565–573 (2019)
9. Bruch, E.E.: How population structure shapes neighborhood segregation. Am. J. Sociol. **119**(5), 1221–1278 (2014)
10. Bullinger, M., Lenzner, P., Melnichenko, A.: Network creation with homophilic agents. In: Raedt, L.D. (ed.) Proceedings of the Thirty-First International Joint Conference on Artificial Intelligence, IJCAI 2022, pp. 151–157. International Joint Conferences on Artificial Intelligence Organization (2022)
11. Bullinger, M., Suksompong, W., Voudouris, A.A.: Welfare guarantees in Schelling segregation. J. Artif. Intell. Res. **71**, 143–174 (2021)
12. Bursell, M., Jansson, F.: Diversity preferences among employees and ethnoracial workplace segregation. Soc. Sci. Res. **74**, 62–76 (2018)
13. Chan, H., Irfan, M.T., Than, C.V.: Schelling models with localized social influence: a game-theoretic framework. In: AAMAS Conference Proceedings (2020)
14. Chauhan, A., Lenzner, P., Molitor, L.: Schelling segregation with strategic agents. In: Deng, X. (ed.) SAGT 2018. LNCS, vol. 11059, pp. 137–149. Springer, Cham (2018). https://doi.org/10.1007/978-3-319-99660-8_13
15. Dezsö, C.L., Ross, D.G.: Does female representation in top management improve firm performance? A panel data investigation. Strateg. Manag. J. **33**(9), 1072–1089 (2012)
16. Echzell, H., et al.: Convergence and hardness of strategic Schelling segregation. In: Caragiannis, I., Mirrokni, V., Nikolova, E. (eds.) WINE 2019. LNCS, vol. 11920, pp. 156–170. Springer, Cham (2019). https://doi.org/10.1007/978-3-030-35389-6_12
17. Elia, S., Petruzzelli, A.M., Piscitello, L.: The impact of cultural diversity on innovation performance of MNC subsidiaries in strategic alliances. J. Bus. Res. **98**, 204–213 (2019)
18. Elkind, E., Gan, J., Igarashi, A., Suksompong, W., Voudouris, A.A.: Schelling games on graphs. In: Proceedings of the Twenty-Eighth International Joint Conference on Artificial Intelligence, IJCAI 2019, pp. 266–272. International Joint Conferences on Artificial Intelligence Organization (2019)
19. Elkind, E., Patel, N., Tsang, A., Zick, Y.: Keeping your friends close: land allocation with friends. arXiv preprint arXiv:2003.03558 (2020)
20. Filbeck, G., Foster, B., Preece, D., Zhao, X.: Does diversity improve profits and shareholder returns? Evidence from top rated companies for diversity by diversityinc. Adv. Accqunt. **37**, 94–102 (2017)
21. Fossett, M.A.: Simseg-a computer program to simulate the dynamics of residential segregation by social and ethnic status. Race and Ethnic Studies Institute Technical Report and Program, Texas A&M University (1998)
22. Friedrich, T., Lenzner, P., Molitor, L., Seifert, L.: Single-peaked jump Schelling games. arXiv preprint arXiv:2302.12107 (2023)
23. Garey Michael, R., Johnson, D.S.: Computers and intractability. A guide to the theory of NP-completeness. A Series of Books in the Mathematical Sciences (1979)
24. Immorlica, N., Kleinbergt, R., Lucier, B., Zadomighaddam, M.: Exponential segregation in a two-dimensional Schelling model with tolerant individuals. In: Proceedings of the Twenty-Eighth Annual ACM-SIAM Symposium on Discrete Algorithms, pp. 984–993. SIAM (2017)
25. Kanellopoulos, P., Kyropoulou, M., Voudouris, A.A.: Modified Schelling games. In: Harks, T., Klimm, M. (eds.) SAGT 2020. LNCS, vol. 12283, pp. 241–256. Springer, Cham (2020). https://doi.org/10.1007/978-3-030-57980-7_16

26. Kreisel, L., Boehmer, N., Froese, V., Niedermeier, R.: Equilibria in Schelling games: computational hardness and robustness. arXiv preprint arXiv:2105.06561 (2021)

27. Loyd, D.L., Wang, C.S., Phillips, K.W., Lount, R.B., Jr.: Social category diversity promotes premeeting elaboration: the role of relationship focus. Organ. Sci. **24**(3), 757–772 (2013)

28. Massand, S., Simon, S.: Graphical one-sided markets. arXiv preprint arXiv:1911.06757 (2019)

29. Monderer, D., Shapley, L.S.: Potential games. Games Econ. Behav. **14**(1), 124–143 (1996)

30. Narayanan, L., Sabbagh, Y.: Diversity-seeking jump games in networks. arXiv preprint arXiv:2305.17757 (2023)

31. Narayanan, L., Sabbagh, Y.: Equilibria in jump Schelling games (2023, unpublished manuscript)

32. Pancs, R., Vriend, N.J.: Schelling's spatial proximity model of segregation revisited. J. Public Econ. **91**(1–2), 1–24 (2007)

33. Rogers, T., McKane, A.J.: A unified framework for Schelling's model of segregation. J. Stat. Mech. Theory Exp. **2011**(07), P07006 (2011)

34. Schelling, T.C.: Models of segregation. Am. Econ. Rev. **59**(2), 488–493 (1969)

35. Schelling, T.C.: Dynamic models of segregation. J. Math. Sociol. **1**(2), 143–186 (1971)

36. Smith, T.W., Davern, M., Freese, J., Morgan, S.L.: General social surveys, 1972–2018: cumulative codebook. NORC, Chicago (2019)

37. Stivala, A., Robins, G., Kashima, Y., Kirley, M.: Diversity and community can coexist. Am. J. Community Psychol. **57**(1–2), 243–254 (2016)

38. Zhang, J.: A dynamic model of residential segregation. J. Math. Sociol. **28**(3), 147–170 (2004)

Fair Division

Maximin Fair Allocation of Indivisible Items Under Cost Utilities

Sirin Botan, Angus Ritossa, Mashbat Suzuki[✉], and Toby Walsh

UNSW Sydney, Kensington, Australia
{s.botan,mashbat.suzuki,t.walsh}@unsw.edu.au,
a.ritossa@student.unsw.edu.au

Abstract. We study the problem of fairly allocating indivisible goods among a set of agents. Our focus is on the existence of allocations that give each agent their *maximin fair share*—the value they are guaranteed if they divide the goods into as many bundles as there are agents, and receive their lowest valued bundle. An *MMS allocation* is one where every agent receives at least their maximin fair share. We examine the existence of such allocations when agents have *cost utilities*. In this setting, each item has an associated *cost*, and an agent's valuation for an item is the cost of the item if it is useful to them, and zero otherwise.

Our main results indicate that cost utilities are a promising restriction for achieving MMS. We show that for the case of three agents with cost utilities, an MMS allocation always exists. We also show that when preferences are restricted slightly further—to what we call *laminar set approvals*—we can guarantee MMS allocations for any number of agents. Finally, we explore if it is possible to guarantee each agent their maximin fair share while using a strategyproof mechanism.

Keywords: Fair Division · Maximin Fair Share · Resource Allocation

1 Introduction

How to fairly divide a set of indivisible resources is a problem that has been studied by computer scientists, economists, and mathematicians [10,11,25]. Because of the fundamental nature of the problem, there is a large number of applications ranging from course allocations [26], to division of assets [19], and air traffic management [27].

Among the fairness notions studied, two of the most commonly studied are those of envy-freeness—how to ensure no agent envies another, and maximin fair share—our focus in this paper. The notion of the maximin fair share was introduced by Budish [12], and generalises the well known cut-and-choose protocol. Conceptually, an agent's *maximin fair share* is the value they can achieve by partitioning the items into as many bundles as there are agents, and receiving their least preferred bundle. The ideal outcome is of course an *MMS allocation*, where every agent receives at least their maximin fair share.

© The Author(s), under exclusive license to Springer Nature Switzerland AG 2023
A. Deligkas and A. Filos-Ratsikas (Eds.): SAGT 2023, LNCS 14238, pp. 221–238, 2023.
https://doi.org/10.1007/978-3-031-43254-5_13

There has been a significant amount of work on MMS in the general additive valuations setting. Unfortunately, results are often quite negative. In general, MMS allocations cannot be guaranteed to exist, even in the case of three agents [16,24]. Furthermore, for instances where MMS allocations do exist (for example, when agents have identical valuations), computing an MMS allocation is NP-hard. As a result, a large body of work has been focused on establishing the existence of MMS allocations in more restricted settings [4,8,9,15]. In this paper, we study the problem under a natural class of valuation functions–what we call *cost utilities*—that allow us to provide fairness guarantees that are not achievable for general additive valuations. Cost utilities describe the setting where each item has an associated cost. An agent's value for any item is the cost of the item if it is useful to them, and zero otherwise. Our focus in this work is on the existence of MMS allocations under cost utilities.

We are not the first to study this restriction in the context of fair division. Bansal and Sviridenko [7] provided an approximation of egalitarian welfare maximisation under cost utilities, that was then improved upon by Asadpour et al. [5] and Cheng and Mao [14]. Camacho et al. [13] and Akrami et al. [1] focus on envy-freeness, and show that an EFX allocation always exists under cost utilities[1]. There are clear practical advantages to studying this particular class of valuations. In many real-life settings, the price of items are known, and elicitation of preferences boils down to asking an agent whether they want the item or not—a task that can be accomplished easily.

Related Work. Given that MMS allocations cannot be guaranteed for general additive valuations, the work done on MMS in fair division has focused on two main approaches to circumvent this impossibility. The first—which is the route we employ in this paper—is to consider a restriction on the valuations of the agents. Examples of such restrictions under which MMS allocations always exist include binary valuations [9], and ternary valuations [4]—where item values belong to $\{0, 1, 2\}$, and Borda utilities [21]. Existence of MMS allocations also holds for personalised bivalued valuations—where for each agent i, the value of an item belongs to $\{1, p_i\}$ for $p_i \in \mathbb{N}$, and weakly lexicographical valuations—where each agent values each good more than the combined value of all items that are strictly less preferred [15].

The second approach is to examine *how close* we can get to MMS, meaning how far each agent is from receiving their maximin fair share. An allocation is said to be ρ-MMS, if each agent receives a ρ fraction of their MMS value. Garg and Taki [17] show that for instances with more than five agents a $\left(\frac{3}{4} + \frac{1}{12n}\right)$-MMS allocation always exists. On the more negative side, [16] show that there exist instances such that no allocation is 39/40-MMS. For valuations that are beyond additive, the picture is arguably gloomier. [18] show an existence of $\frac{1}{3}$-MMS allocations and a PTAS for computing such allocations. They also show

---

[1] Bansal and Sviridenko [7] call them *restricted assignment valuations*, while Camacho et al. [13] call them *generalised binary valuations*. Akrami et al. [1] study them under the name *restricted additive valuations*. We use the term "cost utilities" as we find it conceptually the most appealing and descriptive.

that for submodular valuations, there exist instances that do not admit any $\frac{3}{4}$-MMS allocation.

There have been several works focused on achieving both fairness along with strategyproofness. Amanatidis et al. [2] show that when there are two agents and m items there is no truthful mechanism that outputs an $\frac{1}{\lceil m/2 \rceil}$-MMS allocation. On the positive side Halpern et al. [20] and Babaioff et al. [6] show that when agents have binary valuations there is a polynomial time computable mechanism that is strategyproof and outputs an MMS allocation along with several other desirable properties.

Our Contribution. We know that for some restricted settings—bivalued and ternary valuations—MMS allocations can always be found. Amanatidis et al. [3] highlight an open problem regarding the existence of other classes of structured valuations for which an MMS allocation is guaranteed to exist. Our paper answers this in the affirmative for a new class of valuation functions. We first show that MMS allocations exist for three agents under cost utilities, in contrast to the case of general additive utilities. We also show that when valuations are restricted slightly further to laminar set approvals, MMS allocations are guaranteed to exist for any number of agents. Additionally, for the case of n agents and $n + 2$ items, we show there is a strategyproof polynomial time algorithm for computing Pareto optimal MMS allocations.

Interestingly, to the best of our knowledge, our results on cost utilities are first of its kind for which (other than identical valuations) the computation of the maximin fair share value is NP-hard, while existence of MMS allocation is still guaranteed. For previously known classes where an MMS allocation is guaranteed, the computation of the maximin fair share value can be done in polynomial time.

Paper Outline. In Sect. 2 we introduce the framework of fair division of indivisible items, and present the central preference and fairness notions of the paper. Section 3 is focused on when we can achieve MMS allocations for cost utilities. Section 4 looks at a strategyproof mechanism for finding MMS allocations. Section 5 concludes.

2   Preliminaries

Let N be a set of n *agents*, and M a set of m indivisible *goods* (or *items*). Our goal is to divide M among the agents in N according to their preferences over the items.

Preferences. Each agent $i \in N$ has a *valuation function* $v_i : 2^M \to \mathbb{R}_{\geq 0}$ that determines how much they value any bundle of items. For all agents i, we assume that v_i is additive, so $v_i(S) = \sum_{g \in S} v_i(g)$. For singleton bundles, we write $v_i(g)$ in place of $v_i(\{g\})$ for simplicity. We write $v = (v_1, \ldots, v_n)$ to denote the vector of all valuation functions for agents in N.

Our focus in this paper is on a restricted domain of preferences—cost utilities. For these preferences, it is easy to think of each agent as submitting an approval set. Let A_i be the *approval set* of agent i. More formally, we say $A_i = \{g \in M \mid v_i(g) > 0\}$. We say agents have *cost utilities* if there exists a *cost function* c such that $v_i(S) = c(S \cap A_i)$ for all $S \subseteq M$ and all agents $i \in N$. We require that the cost function is additive, as well as non-negative.

Allocations and Mechanism. An *allocation* $\boldsymbol{B} = (B_1, \ldots, B_n)$ is an n-partition of the set of items M, where $B_i \subseteq M$ is the *bundle* assigned to agent i under the allocation $\boldsymbol{B}$. We write $\boldsymbol{B}|_{N'}$ to denote the restriction of the allocation $\boldsymbol{B}$ to only the bundles assigned to agents in $N' \subseteq N$. For a set of goods M, we write $\mathcal{B}_n(M)$ to mean all possible allocations of the goods in M to n agents. An *instance* $\mathcal{I} = (N, M, \boldsymbol{v})$ of a fair division problem is defined by a set of agents, a set of goods, and the agents' valuations over those goods.

Given an instance $\mathcal{I}$, our goal is to find an allocation $\boldsymbol{B}$ that satisfies certain normative properties. An *allocation mechanism* for n agents and m items is a function $f : \boldsymbol{V}_n \to \mathcal{B}_n(M)$, where $\boldsymbol{V}_n$ is the set of possible valuation profiles—i.e. vectors of n valuation functions.

Fairness and Efficiency. For an agent $i \in N$, their *maximin fair share* in an instance $\mathcal{I} = (N, M, \boldsymbol{v})$ is defined as

$$\mathsf{MMS}_i^n(\mathcal{I}) = \max_{\boldsymbol{B} \in \mathcal{B}_n(M)} \min_{j \in N} v_i(B_j).$$

We sometimes write $\mathsf{MMS}_i^n(M)$ when the instance is clear from context. When the set of goods and the value of n is fixed, we will also sometimes write MMS_i.

An *MMS allocation* $\boldsymbol{B} \in \mathcal{B}_n(M)$ is an allocation such that $v_i(B_i) \geq \mathsf{MMS}_i$ for all agents $i \in N$.

We say an allocation $\boldsymbol{B} \in \mathcal{B}_n(M)$ is *Pareto efficient* if there is no allocation $\boldsymbol{B}' \in \mathcal{B}_n(M)$ such that $v_i(B_i') \geq v_i(B_i)$ for all $i \in N$ and $v_{i^*}(B_{i^*}') > v_{i^*}(B_{i^*})$ for some $i^* \in N$.

3 Maximin Fair Share Guarantees

In this section, we will look at two settings where cost utilities can aid in finding cases where MMS allocations can be guaranteed to exist. Section 3.1 focuses on cases with only three agents. Section 3.2 considers any number of agents but is limited to laminar approval sets. This is a restriction that captures the idea of items belonging to different categories.

3.1 MMS Allocations for Three Agents

For the case of three agents, restricting our scope to considering only cost utilities yields positive results. As we have seen in the introduction, this is not the case for the more general case of additive preferences. Theorem 1 is therefore a very welcome result.

In this section, we will sometimes speak about items approved exclusively by two agents. We denote by $A_{ij} = (A_i \cap A_j) \setminus A_{i^*}$—where $i^* \in N$ and $i^* \neq i, j$—the set of items approved by agents i and j, and no third agent.

Before we state our main result in this section, we present the following two lemmas that we need in order to prove Theorem 1. Our first lemma simply tells us that adding items approved only by a single agent does not affect the existence of an MMS allocation.

Lemma 1. *If an MMS allocation exists for instance $\mathcal{I} = (N, M, \boldsymbol{v})$, then an MMS allocation also exists for the instance $\mathcal{I}' = (N, M \cup S, \boldsymbol{v})$, where S is a set of items approved by a single agent $i \in N$, and $S \cap M = \emptyset$.*

Proof. Suppose we have an instance $\mathcal{I} = (N, M, \boldsymbol{v})$ where $\boldsymbol{B}$ is an MMS allocation. Suppose further that $\mathcal{I}' = (N, M \cup S, \boldsymbol{v})$ is an instance where S is a set of items approved by a single agent $i \in N$, and $S \cap M = \emptyset$. We show that $\boldsymbol{B}'$ where $B'_j = B_j$ for all $j \neq i$ and $B'_i = B_i \cup S$ is an MMS allocation. Since for any $j \neq i$ we have $v_j(B_j) \geq \mathsf{MMS}^n_j$, we only need to show that agent i gets her MMS fair share.

Suppose for contradiction that we have $v_i(S) + \mathsf{MMS}^n_i(M) < \mathsf{MMS}^n_i(M \cup S)$. Let $\boldsymbol{W} = (W_1, \ldots, W_n)$ be an n-partition of $(M \cup S)$ such that $v_i(W_k) \geq \mathsf{MMS}^n_i(M \cup S)$ for $1 \leq k \leq n$. Note that for any W_k in the partition we have that $W_k = (W_k \cap M) \cup (W_k \cap S)$. Thus we have the following:

$$
\begin{aligned}
\mathsf{MMS}^n_i(M \cup S) &\leq v_i(W_k) \\
&= v_i(W_k \cap M) + v_i(W_k \cap S) \\
&\leq v_i(W_k \cap M) + v_i(S) \\
&< v_i(W_k \cap M) + \mathsf{MMS}^n_i(M \cup S) - \mathsf{MMS}^n_i(M)
\end{aligned}
$$

where the last inequality follows from our assumption that $v_i(S) < \mathsf{MMS}^n_i(M \cup S) - \mathsf{MMS}^n_i(M)$. It follows that $v_i(W_k \cap M) > \mathsf{MMS}^n_i(M)$. As k was chosen arbitrarily, this implies existence of a partition of M into n sets $(W_k \cap M)_{k \in [n]}$ such that each set has value strictly larger than $\mathsf{MMS}^n_i(M)$, a contradiction. $\square$

Our second lemma is a more technical one. In yet another simplification of notation, we write $\mu_{ij} = \mathsf{MMS}^2_i(A_{ij}) = \mathsf{MMS}^2_j(A_{ij})$ to mean the maximin fair share of agents i and j when dividing exactly the goods only the two of them approve among themselves.

Lemma 2. *Let $N = \{1, 2, 3\}$, and let $\boldsymbol{S} = (S_1, S_2, S_3)$ be a 3-partition of A_1 such that $v_1(S_r) \geq \mathsf{MMS}_1$ for all $r \in \{1, 2, 3\}$. Then there exist distinct $k, \ell \in \{1, 2, 3\}$ such that*

$$
\begin{aligned}
c(S_k \cap A_{12}) &\leq \mu_{12}, \text{ and} \\
c(S_\ell \cap A_{13}) &\leq \mu_{13}.
\end{aligned}
$$

Proof. Note that, by the definition of maximin fair share, there cannot be two elements $k_1, k_2 \in \{1,2,3\}$ such that $c(S_{k_1} \cap A_{12}) > \mu_{12}$ and $c(S_{k_2} \cap A_{12}) > \mu_{12}$—this would imply that we could divide A_{12} into two bundles such that both agents 1 and 2 are guaranteed strictly more than their maximin fair share.

Therefore, there must exist at least two distinct $k, k' \in \{1,2,3\}$ such that both $c(S_k \cap A_{12}) \leq \mu_{12}$ and $c(S_{k'} \cap A_{12}) \leq \mu_{12}$. The same argument tells us there are distinct $\ell, \ell' \in \{1,2,3\}$ such that $c(S_\ell \cap A_{13}) \leq \mu_{13}$ and $c(S_{\ell'} \cap A_{13}) \leq \mu_{13}$. Applying a pigeonhole argument, we conclude there must be distinct $k, \ell \in \{1,2,3\}$ such that $c(S_k \cap A_{12}) \leq \mu_{12}$ and $c(S_\ell \cap A_{13}) \leq \mu_{13}$, as desired.   □

We are now ready to state the main result of this section.

Theorem 1. *For three agents with cost utilities, there always exists a Pareto efficient MMS allocation.*

Proof. Given a set of agents $N = \{1,2,3\}$, let $\mathsf{MMS}_i = \mathsf{MMS}_i^3(M)$—the maximin fair share of agent i when dividing the items in M among the three agents. We assume that for any item $g \in M$, we have that g is approved by at least two agents. By Lemma 1, we know the claim will also hold for the remaining cases where there are additional goods approved by a single agent.

Finally, we define the following three values:

$$q_1 = \mathsf{MMS}_1 + \mu_{23}$$
$$q_2 = \mathsf{MMS}_2 + \mu_{13}$$
$$q_3 = \mathsf{MMS}_3 + \mu_{12}$$

Without loss of generality, we assume that $q_1 \geq q_2$ and $q_1 \geq q_3$. We can rewrite this, and express it as follows:

$$\mathsf{MMS}_1 + \mu_{23} - \mu_{13} \geq \mathsf{MMS}_2 \tag{1}$$

$$\mathsf{MMS}_1 + \mu_{23} - \mu_{12} \geq \mathsf{MMS}_3 \tag{2}$$

Our method for finding an allocation that satisfies the maximin property and is Pareto efficient, takes as basis a partition of the goods where each bundle reaches the maximin fair share of agent 1. Let $S = (S_1, S_2, S_3)$ be a 3-partition of A_1 such that $v_1(S_r) \geq \mathsf{MMS}_1$ for all $r \in \{1,2,3\}$. Note that such a partition always exists by definition of MMS_1. By Lemma 2 we know there exist distinct $k, \ell \in \{1,2,3\}$ such that

$$c(S_k \cap A_{12}) \leq \mu_{12}, \tag{3}$$

$$c(S_\ell \cap A_{13}) \leq \mu_{13}. \tag{4}$$

We can now describe the allocation B, which we claim is a Pareto efficient MMS allocation.

We divide A_{23} into two disjoint sets T_1 and T_2 such that $c(T_1) \geq \mu_{23}$ and $c(T_2) \geq \mu_{23}$. Note that such a partition exists by the definition of μ_{23}. Let S_x be the third bundle in S—i.e. $x \in \{1,2,3\} \setminus \{k, \ell\}$. We then allocate the goods in M as follows:

$$B_1 = (S_\ell \setminus A_2) \cup (S_k \setminus A_3) \cup S_x$$
$$B_2 = (S_\ell \cap A_2) \cup T_1$$
$$B_3 = (S_k \cap A_3) \cup T_2$$

In words, agent 2 receives T_1 and everything in S_ℓ that she wants, agent 3 receives T_2 and everything in S_k that she wants, and agent 1 receives the remaining items in S_k and S_ℓ as well as the entire bundle S_x. Note that all items have been allocated as $A_1 \cup A_{23} = M$, and no item is allocated to more than one agent as S_x and A_{23} are disjoint. By definition, we have that $v_1(B_1) \geq$ MMS$_1$—agent 1 clearly receives their maximin fair share as she receives one of the original bundles, S_x, and then some. We now show that the same must hold for the other two agents.

For agent 2, we need to show that $v_2(B_2) \geq$ MMS$_2$. Note that we can express the value of agent 2's bundle using the cost function c as follows (where $S_\ell \cap A_{13}$ is the portion of S_ℓ that agent 2 values at 0).[2]

$$v_2(B_2) = v_2(S_\ell \cap A_2) + v_2(T_1)$$
$$= c(S_\ell \cap A_2) + c(T_1)$$
$$= c(S_\ell) - c(S_\ell \cap A_{13}) + c(T_1)$$

Because of the way we've defined the partition S and A_{13}, we know that $c(S_\ell) \geq$ MMS$_1$ and $c(T_1) \geq \mu_{23}$. Additionally, by Eq. 4, we know that $c(S_\ell \cap A_{13}) \leq \mu_{13}$. From this, we can conclude the following, where the last inequality follows from Eq. 1.

$$v_2(B_2) = c(S_\ell) - c(S_\ell \cap A_{13}) + c(T_1)$$
$$\geq \text{MMS}_1 - \mu_{13} + \mu_{23}$$
$$\geq \text{MMS}_2$$

Putting this all together, we have shown that $v_2(B_2) \geq$ MMS$_2$, as desired. The proof for agent 3 proceeds analogously, using Eqs. 2 and 3. Thus, we have shown that B is an MMS allocation.

Finally, we see that no item has been allocated to an agent who values it at 0, meaning the allocation is indeed Pareto efficient.   □

Theorem 1 establishes a clear improvement when dealing with cost utilities over general additive valuations.

3.2 MMS Allocations for Laminar Set Approvals

In this section we present our results for agents with laminar set approvals. This restriction on the agents' preferences has a very natural interpretation, in that it

---

[2] This is possible because we know that any good in the set is either approved by all three agents, or a subset of two. Agent 2 is a member of any subset of size two except A_{13}.

describes the notion of items falling into categories and subcategories quite well. We can think of agents as approving categories as a whole. For example, one agent might want all vegetarian dishes, while another wants only the seafood. A third agent might want the pasta-based vegetarian dishes, which would constitute a subcategory of vegetarian.

We say agents with cost utilities have *laminar set approvals* if for a vector $\boldsymbol{A} = (A_1, \ldots, A_n)$ of approval sets, we have that for any $i, j \in N$, either $A_i \cap A_j = A_j$, $A_i \cap A_j = \emptyset$, or $A_i \cap A_j = A_i$. In words, for any two agents, one approval set is either a subset of the other, or the sets are disjoint. Note that in this paper, we only examine laminar set approvals within the context of cost utilities.

We first present a technical lemma that we will apply inductively in the proof of Theorem 2. Lemma 3 allows us to carry the existence of an MMS allocation from cases where all agents submit the whole set M of goods as their approval, to cases where fewer and fewer agents do so, until we reach a single agent approving all goods.

Lemma 3. *For n agents with cost utilities and laminar set approvals, and $k \geq 1$, if an MMS allocation exists for all instances where $k+1$ agents approve all items in M, then an MMS allocation exists for any instance where k agents approve all items.*

Proof. Consider an instance $\mathcal{I} = (N, M, \boldsymbol{v})$ where there are $k \geq 1$ agents whose approval set equals M. We call this set of agents N'. Let $i \in N \setminus N'$ be an agent such that $A_i \not\subset A_j$ for all $j \in N \setminus N'$ in the instance $\mathcal{I}$. Note that such an agent must exist, as agents have laminar set approvals. See Fig. 1 for a visual representation. We will continue to use this figure throughout this proof.

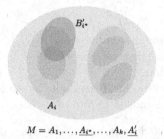

$$M = A_1, \ldots, \underline{A_{i*}}, \ldots, A_k, \underline{A_i'}$$

Fig. 1. An illustration of the sets involved in the proof of Lemma 3. The largest set is M—the set of goods. Note how the approval sets $A_1, \ldots, A_k$ are equivalent to the whole set of goods, and the same holds for A_{i*} and A_i'. The approval set A_i is "one level below" the sets approving all items. The bundle B_{i*}'—represented in blue—is the bundle in the allocation $\boldsymbol{B}|_{N' \cup \{i\}}$ that is highest valued according to v_i.

Our aim is to show that there exists an MMS allocation for the instance $\mathcal{I}$. To this end, we define a second instance $\mathcal{I}' = (N, M, \boldsymbol{v}')$ such that $A_i' = M$, and

$A'_j = A_j$ for all agents $j \neq i$—i.e. the instance $\mathcal{I}'$ only differs from $\mathcal{I}$ in that agent i now approves all items. Thus, we have $k + 1$ agents whose approval set is M in the instance $\mathcal{I}'$.

Suppose $\boldsymbol{B}'$ is an MMS allocation for $\mathcal{I}'$, such an allocation is guaranteed to exist by the assumption of the lemma. We construct an MMS allocation $\boldsymbol{B}$ for our initial instance by building on $\boldsymbol{B}'$. We first define $i^* \in \mathrm{argmax}_{j \in N' \cup \{i\}}\, v_i(B'_j)$. This is an agent who gets the highest value bundle in $\boldsymbol{B}|_{N' \cup \{i\}}$ according to v_i—agent i's valuation in the initial instance. Because the value n is fixed, we will write $\mathsf{MMS}_i(\mathcal{I})$ to mean $\mathsf{MMS}_i^n(\mathcal{I})$. We consider two cases.

Case 1: Suppose $v_i(B'_{i^*}) \geq \mathsf{MMS}_i(\mathcal{I})$. Then agent i values agent i^*'s bundle at least as much as their maximin fair share in the initial instance. We define an allocation $\boldsymbol{B}$ and claim that it is an MMS allocation for the instance $\mathcal{I}$.

$$B_j = \begin{cases} B'_{i^*} & \text{if } j = i \\ B'_i & \text{if } j = i^* \\ B'_j & \text{otherwise} \end{cases}$$

First note that for any agent $j \notin \{i, i^*\}$, their maximin fair share is the same across both instances, and they receive the same bundle under $\boldsymbol{B}$ and $\boldsymbol{B}'$. Thus, they receive at least their maximin fair share in the allocation $\boldsymbol{B}$.

We now show the same holds for i and i^*. For agent i, this follows by assumption since $v_i(B_i) = v_i(B'_{i^*}) \geq \mathsf{MMS}_i(\mathcal{I})$. For agent i^* then, we only need to consider when $i^* \neq i$. In that case, as $i^* \in N'$, we have that $A_{i^*} = A'_i = M$. Then agent i^* must also receive their maximin fair share in the allocation $\boldsymbol{B}$, because $v_{i^*}(B_{i^*}) = v'_i(B'_i) \geq \mathsf{MMS}_i(\mathcal{I}') = \mathsf{MMS}_{i^*}(\mathcal{I})$. Note that this holds because the agents have cost utilities, and both v_{i^*} and v'_i are equivalent to the cost function c since $A_{i^*} = A'_i = M$. As $\boldsymbol{B}$ guarantees everyone at least their maximin fair share, it is an MMS allocation for $\mathcal{I}$.

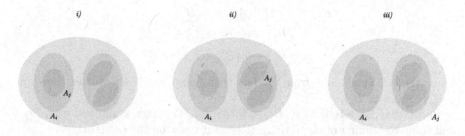

Fig. 2. An illustration of the sets involved in Case 2 of the proof of Lemma 3. The possible approval set of agent j in each case is represented in green.

Case 2: Suppose instead that $v_i(B'_{i^*}) < \mathsf{MMS}_i(\mathcal{I})$. In this case, agent i values agent i^*'s bundle strictly less than their maximin fair share in the initial instance. Recall that $v_i(B'_j) \leq v_i(B'_{i^*})$ for all $j \in N' \cup \{i\}$—agent i^*'s bundle is still the "best" one among those in $\boldsymbol{B}|_{N' \cup \{i\}}$. Given our initial assumption, we then have that

$$v_i(B'_j) < \mathsf{MMS}_i(\mathcal{I}) \text{ for all } j \in N' \cup \{i\}. \tag{5}$$

Before we proceed, we will need to define a third instance over only the goods in A_i. Let $\mathcal{I}^* = (N, A_i, \boldsymbol{v})$ be a restriction of the instance $\mathcal{I}$ to only the items in A_i—meaning $A_j^* = A_j \cap A_i$ for all $j \in N$. Note that in $\mathcal{I}^*$, there are at least $k+1$ agents whose approval set is A_i—the initial k agents who approved all items in $\mathcal{I}$, and agent i. Let $\boldsymbol{B}''$ be an MMS allocation for $\mathcal{I}^*$. We now proceed with defining an allocation $\boldsymbol{B}$ by using both allocations $\boldsymbol{B}'$ and $\boldsymbol{B}''$. In particular, we define

$$B_j = (B'_j \setminus A_i) \cup B''_j \text{ for all } j \in N.$$

Note that no item is allocated more than once because $B''_j \subseteq A_i$ for all $j \in N$. We claim that $\boldsymbol{B}$ is an MMS allocation for the instance $\mathcal{I}$. Because agents have laminar set approvals, there are three possible cases for any agent j: either i) $A_j \subseteq A_i$, or ii) $A_j \cap A_i = \emptyset$, or iii) $A_i \subset A_j$. See Fig. 2 for a visual representation.

i) Suppose $A_j \subseteq A_i$. Then agent j was only approving items in A_i and their approval set remains the same in the restriction $\mathcal{I}^*$, implying that their maximin fair share also remains the same in both instances. Additionally, we have that $v_j(B'_j \setminus A_i) = 0$ given that $A_j \subseteq A_i$, and so $v_j(B_j) = v_j(B''_j)$. Since j receives their maximin fair share in $\boldsymbol{B}''$, they also do so in $\boldsymbol{B}$.

ii) Suppose instead $A_j \cap A_i = \emptyset$. Because agent j does not approve any items in A_i, we have that $v_j(B'_j) = v_j(B'_j \setminus A_i)$ and $v_j(B''_j) = 0$. Then $v_j(B_j) = v_j(B'_j)$, and because $A'_j = A_j$ their maximin fair share is the same in $\mathcal{I}$ and $\mathcal{I}'$. Thus j receives their maximin fair share in $\boldsymbol{B}$.

iii) Finally, suppose $A_i \subset A_j$. This is only possible if $j \in N'$, meaning j is one of the agents approving all items. We know that

$$\begin{aligned} v_j(B_j) &= v_j(B'_j \setminus A_i) + v_j(B''_j) \\ &= (B'_j) - v_j(B'_j \cap A_i) + v_j(B''_j) \\ &= (B'_j) - v_i(B'_j) + v_j(B''_j) \end{aligned} \tag{6}$$

Where the last line follows from the fact that agents have cost utilities, meaning $v_j(B'_j \cap A_i) = v_i(B'_j)$.

Recall that Eq. 5 tells us $v_i(B'_j) < \mathsf{MMS}_i(\mathcal{I})$. This fact, combined with Eq. 6 (and some reshuffling of the terms), tells us it must be the case that

$$v_j(B_j) > v_j(B'_j) - \mathsf{MMS}_i(\mathcal{I}) + v_j(B''_j). \tag{7}$$

Since $\boldsymbol{B}''$ is an MMS allocation for $\mathcal{I}^*$, it follows that $v_j(B''_j) \geq \mathsf{MMS}_j(\mathcal{I}^*)$. Further, since $A_i \subset A_j$, and $\mathcal{I}^*$ is an instance over only A_i, we have that $\mathsf{MMS}_j(\mathcal{I}^*) = \mathsf{MMS}_i(\mathcal{I})$. Thus, $v_j(B''_j) \geq \mathsf{MMS}_i(\mathcal{I})$.

We can then transform Eq. 7 as follows:

$$v_j(B_j) > v_j(B'_j) - \mathsf{MMS}_i(\mathcal{I}) + \mathsf{MMS}_i(\mathcal{I}),$$

meaning it must be the case that $v_j(B_j) > v_j(B'_j)$. Because we know agent j has identical valuations in $\mathcal{I}$ and $\mathcal{I}'$, and B' is an MMS allocation, we can conclude that agent j receives at least their maximin fair share in B.

Thus we have shown for any agent $j \in N$ that they receive their maximin fair share in the allocation B, meaning it must be an MMS allocation. Since $\mathcal{I}$ was an arbitrary instance where exactly k agents submit the approval set M, this concludes the proof. □

We can now (finally) present the main result of this section.

Theorem 2. *For n agents with cost utilities and laminar set approvals, there always exists an MMS allocation.*

Proof. First, note that given agents with laminar set approvals, if no agent has M as their approval set, then we can find a k-partition $(N_1, \ldots, N_k)$ of agents and pairwise disjoint subsets $M_1, \ldots, M_k$ of items such that agents in N_ℓ do not approve any items in $M \setminus M_\ell$, and there is an agent $i \in N_\ell$ such that $A_i = M_\ell$. It is clear—because the agents are partitioned such that each partition considers a distinct set of items from M—that if we find an MMS allocation for each of the k sub-cases, this gives us an MMS allocation in the global case. Therefore, without loss of generality, we assume for any instance that at least one agent submits M as their approval set.

Now suppose there are n agents with cost utilities who all submit M as their approval set. Then an MMS allocation trivially exists. Applying Lemma 3 inductively, we see that for agents with cost utilities and laminar set approvals, an MMS allocation always exists given that at least one agent submits M as their approval set. □

Remark 1. If an MMS allocation exists, then an MMS and PO allocation always exists since after each Pareto improvement agent's utility is weakly increasing. Thus, Theorem 2 implies that under cost utilities and laminar set approvals, MMS and PO allocation always exist.

4   Strategyproof MMS Allocations

In this section, we study the strategic guarantees possible under cost utilities. We first show that for cost utilities, the *Sequential Allocation* mechanism is strategyproof. Let us first define what we mean by strategyproofness.

An allocation mechanism f is *manipulable* if there is some agent $i \in N$ such that $v_i(f(\boldsymbol{v}_{-i}, v'_i)_i) > v_i(f(\boldsymbol{v})_i)$, where $(\boldsymbol{v}_{-i}, v'_i)$ is the valuation that results when v_i is replaced by v'_i. In other words, agent i can misrepresent their preferences by submitting an untruthful valuation v'_i, thereby getting a more preferred outcome. We say f is *strategyproof* if it is not manipulable by any agent.

We now define the *Sequential Allocation mechanism* from previous studies [22,23]. We first define a *picking sequence* as a sequence of agents in N. Note that the sequence of agents can be of any length, and any agent might appear multiple times in the sequence. We can think of Sequential Allocation as proceeding sequentially (as the name indicates), through the ordering of agents. At each step, the agent whose turn it is chooses the item with the highest cost that a) is still available and b) is in their approval set. Note that we "force" agents to pick their most wanted item, as reported in their approvals. If there are no remaining items that an agent finds useful then we skip this agent and continue with the next. The mechanism allows some items to remain unallocated only if they are not approved by any agent.

In fact, Sequential Allocation is a family of mechanisms, each defined by the picking sequence. As we will see, the properties of the mechanism also heavily depend on the picking sequence in question. For example, it is well known that Sequential Allocation is not strategyproof in general unless an agent's picks are all consecutive [23].

In the rest of this section, we will assume that the goods in $M = \{g_1, \ldots, g_m\}$ are ordered from lowest cost to highest cost—i.e. $c(g_k) \leq c(g_\ell)$ for all $k < \ell$.

Proposition 1. *For agents with cost utilities, there exists a picking sequence such that Sequential Allocation is strategyproof and results in a Pareto efficient allocation.*[3]

Proof. We define a sequence S of agents of length $n + 2$, and a sequence T of agents where every agent appears exactly once. Let $S = 1, 2, \ldots, n - 1, n, n, n$, and $T = n, n - 1, \ldots, 2, 1$. Our picking sequence is S, followed by m copies of each element in the sequence T. We can think of this as running through S, then letting each agent in T choose all the items they want when it is their turn in T. We now show that this gives us a strategyproof mechanism.

It is immediately clear that agent n has no incentive to manipulate. They cannot move themselves up in the picking sequence, and once it is their turn, they can essentially grab all the items they want.

For any other agent $i \in N$, let X_i be the items remaining immediately before agent i received their first item, and let x be the item with highest cost in $X_i \cap A_i$. Then, agent i receives x. After this, all items in the approval sets of agents $i+1, i+2, \ldots, n$ are allocated before agent i receives all remaining items in A_i. Thus, agent i receives the bundle $x \cup (A_i \cap (X_i \setminus (A_{i+1} \cup A_{i+2} \cup \ldots \cup A_n)))$. Note that the preferences of agent i do not decide the set X_i. Hence, by misreporting, agent i is unable to gain any additional items that they approve.

Note that the final allocation is Pareto optimal because items are only allocated to agents that want them. As agents have cost utilities, all agents who want an item will value it the same. This concludes the proof.   □

We now consider whether there are picking sequences that can give us an MMS allocation along with truthfulness for a restricted number of items. Such

---

[3] We prove Proposition 1 for a picking sequence used in the proof of Proposition 2, but note that there are simpler picking sequences for which it holds.

a restriction is needed because computation of an agent's MMS value is NP-hard for an arbitrary number of items, which implies that no picking sequence is guaranteed to output an MMS allocation.[4] We start with a lemma that will be used to prove Proposition 2.

Lemma 4. *For n agents and $n+2$ goods, let $|A_i| \geq n+k$ where $k \in \{0, 1, 2\}$. The $(n-k)$-th most valuable item in A_i is guaranteed to give agent i their maximin fair share.*

Proof. Note that for any n-partition of the items in A_i, there is at most k bundles that are not singletons, meaning at least $(n-k)$ of the bundles have just a single item. Any of these bundles will give agent i their maximin fair share. Of these $(n-k)$ singleton bundles, the highest possible value for the lowest valued bundle is the cost of the $(n-k)$-th most valuable item in the agent's approval set.

Proposition 2. *For n agents with cost utilities, and $n+2$ goods, there exists a picking sequence such that Sequential Allocation is strategyproof, and returns a Pareto efficient MMS allocation.*

Proof. We first show that there is a picking sequence such that Sequential Allocation returns an MMS allocation. If an agent approves fewer than n items, they still receive their maximin fair share even when no items are allocated to them. We therefore focus on agents who approve at least n items. We define the picking sequence based on the cost of the items in M.

▶ If $c(g_4) > c(g_2) + c(g_3)$, our picking sequence is $1, 2, \ldots, n-1, n, n, n$.
▶ Otherwise, our picking sequence is $1, 2, \ldots, n-1, n, n, n-1$.

Note that these differ only in who gets to pick the last item. The fact that agents 1 through $n-2$ are guaranteed their maximin fair share for both picking sequences follows from Lemma 4. It remains to show that the same holds for agent $n-1$ and agent n. If agent $n-1$ or agent n approve at most n items, then we already know they are guaranteed their maximin fair share. If agent $n-1$ approves $n+1$ items, their $(n-1)$-th most valuable item is still up for grabs, and by Lemma 4 this will guarantee them their maximin fair share.

We now consider what happens when agent n approves $n+k$ items—for $k \in \{1, 2\}$), and when agent $(n-1)$ approves $n+2$ items. We look at each potential picking sequence separately.

Case 1: Suppose $c(g_4) > c(g_2) + c(g_3)$. If agent n approves $n+k$ items, they will receive at least $k+1$ items, as they pick last and can pick up to three items if they want, given the picking sequence $1, 2, \ldots, n-1, n, n, n$. Clearly a bundle of size $k+1$ guarantees them their maximin fair share.

What remains is to check what happens when agent $(n-1)$ approves all items in M, so suppose this to be the case. We first show that the maximin fair share of agent $n-1$ is $\min(c(\{g_1, g_2, g_3\}), c(g_4))$. Consider a partition B of M into n bundles, where $c(B_i) \geq \mathsf{MMS}_{n-1}^n(M)$ for each $i \in N$. At least

---

[4] This is under the assumption P$\neq$NP.

$n - 2$ of these bundles must contain a single item, and so we know that either *i)* $n - 2$ bundles contain one item and two bundles contain two items, or *ii)* $n - 1$ bundles contain one item and one bundle contains three items. We know that $c(g_4) > c(g_2) + c(g_3)$ by assumption, and the non-singleton bundles will be made up of the four lowest value items—$g_1, \ldots, g_4$. Then the best we can do is one 3-item bundle $B = \{g_1, g_2, g_3\}$ and all the remaining items in singleton bundles. It follows that the maximin fair share of agent $n - 1$ is $\min(c(B), c(g_4))$. When it is agent $n - 1$'s turn to pick, in the worst case, the only remaining goods will be $g_1, \ldots, g_4$, in which case agent $n - 1$ can pick item g_4 to guarantee their maximin fair share.

Case 2: Suppose instead that $c(g_4) \leq c(g_2) + c(g_3)$. If agent n approves $n + 1$ items, they will receive two items, guaranteeing them their maximin fair share. If agent n approves all items in M, their maximin fair share in this case is determined by the lowest value bundle between the two bundles of size two, and the cheapest singleton. In particular, agent n's maximin fair share is $\min(c(\{c_1, c_4\}), c(\{c_2, c_3\}), c(\{g_5\}))$. With this picking sequence, agent n receives two items and in the worst case, this will be the bundle $B = \{g_2, g_3\}$. Clearly this guarantees agent n their maximin fair share.

Finally, we look at when agent $(n - 1)$ approves $n + 2$ items. In this case, we know that their maximin fair share is determined by $\min(c(\{g_1, g_4\}), c(\{g_2, g_3\}), c(\{g_5\}))$, as was the case for agent n. As we did for agent n we know that agent $(n - 1)$ will receive two items, and in the worst case this will be the bundle $B = \{g_4, g_1\}$, which gives the agent their maximin fair share.

Strategyproofness and Pareto efficiency for the first case follows directly from Proposition 1. We now prove strategyproofness and Pareto efficiency for the second case, where $c(g_4) \leq c(g_2) + c(g_3)$. In this case, our picking sequence is $1, 2, \ldots, n - 1, n, n, n - 1$.

For any agent $i \in N$, if $i < n - 1$, it is clear that there is no way for the agent to manipulate as they only get one pick. For agent n, because their picks are right after each other, they also have no incentive to manipulate. Thus, we need only consider agent $n - 1$. Let X be the items remaining immediately before agent $n - 1$ received their first item, and let x be the item with highest cost in $X \cap A_{n-1}$. Agent $n - 1$ will pick x by definition of the mechanism. Agent n then receives their two highest valued remaining items if they exist (call these items y and y'), and then finally agent $n - 1$ potentially receives the last item they approve (call this item z).

First, consider the case where agent $n - 1$ misreports that they approve some item x', and they receive x' instead of x. Then, the bundle of agent $n - 1$ will consist of x' (which they value at 0), and potentially some other item z' with $v_{n-1}(z') \leq v_{n-1}(x)$. Thus, agent $n - 1$ is not better off in this case. Otherwise, if agent $n - 1$ instead misreports that they do not approve item x, then they will pick some other item x'' instead, where $c(x'') \leq c(x)$. If $x'' \neq y$ and $x'' \neq y'$, then we must have $v_{n-1}(x'') \leq v_{n-1}(z)$, and so agent $n - 1$ is not better off. Otherwise, if $x'' = y$ or $x'' = y'$, then agent $n - 1$ will have strictly fewer options for their final pick (compared to the case where they do not misreport), and so they are still not any better off.

Therefore, the mechanism is strategyproof. It is clear that no agent is assigned an item they do not want, and all items that are wanted by at least one agent are assigned to someone. Thus the allocation is Pareto efficient.   □

We remark that Proposition 2 is tight in the sense that it no longer holds when there are n agents and $n + 3$ items.

Proposition 3. *For agents with cost utilities, there exists an instance with $n = 2$ agents and $m = 5$ goods such that no strategyproof mechanism can guarantee a Pareto efficient MMS allocation.*

Proof. Let $n = 2$, and $M = \{g_2, g_3, g_4, g_5, g_6\}$ such that $c(g_i) = i$. We will show that no allocation mechanism can satisfy strategyproofness while also guaranteeing a Pareto Efficient MMS allocation. Our aim is to start from an instance $\mathcal{I}_1$ and—by repeatedly applying the three axioms—reach a contradiction.

First, consider the instance $\mathcal{I}_1$, where both agents approve all items—this corresponds to the top row of Table 1. Then, their maximin fair share is 10, and the only way to reach an MMS allocation is to give g_4 and g_6 to one agent, and g_2, g_3 and g_5 to another. Suppose without loss of generality that $\{g_2, g_3, g_5\}$ is allocated to agent 1, and $\{g_4, g_6\}$ is allocated to agent 2. We will consider 5 further instances.

$\mathcal{I}_2$ differs only on agent 2's approval set—they now only approve items g_4, g_5, and g_6. By strategyproofness, agent 2 must still receive a bundle she values at 10. If this were a higher value the agent could manipulate from $\mathcal{I}_1$, and if it were lower, they could manipulate from $\mathcal{I}_2$ to $\mathcal{I}_1$.

Instance $\mathcal{I}_3$ differs from instance $\mathcal{I}_2$ only on agent 1's approval set—they now only approve items g_3, g_4, g_5, and g_6. As agent 1 is the only one approving item g_3, they must be allocated this item by Pareto efficiency. The maximin value of agent 1 in this instance is 9, so they must receive one of the following bundles: $\{(g_3, g_6\}, \{g_3, g_4, g_5\}, \{g_3, g_4, g_6\}, \{g_3, g_5, g_6\}$, or $\{g_3, g_4, g_5, g_6\}$. All but $\{g_3, g_6\}$ break strategyproofness, as agent 1 would have an incentive to manipulate from $\mathcal{I}_2$ to $\mathcal{I}_3$.

Instance $\mathcal{I}_4$ differs from instance $\mathcal{I}_3$ only on agent 1's approval set—they now only approve item g_6. Agent 1 must be allocated g_6. If this were not the case, they would have an incentive to manipulate from $\mathcal{I}_4$ to $\mathcal{I}_3$ as they do receive item 6 in that instance.

Instance $\mathcal{I}_5$ differs from instance $\mathcal{I}_4$ only on agent 1's approval set—they now approve items g_2, g_3 and g_6. As agent 1 is the only one approving items g_2 and g_3, they must be allocated these items by Pareto efficiency. If agent 1 is not also given g_6, they would have an incentive to manipulate from $\mathcal{I}_4$ to $\mathcal{I}_3$ as their bundle in that instance is valued at 6 (which is greater than $2 + 3$, the value of the bundle $\{g_2, g_3\}$). Note that this gives them a bundle valued at 11.

Finally, instance $\mathcal{I}_6$ differs from instance $\mathcal{I}_5$ only on agent 1's approval set—they now approve all items. If agent 1 is given a bundle valued lower than 11, they would have an incentive to manipulate from $\mathcal{I}_6$ to $\mathcal{I}_5$. Note however that

$\mathcal{I}_6 = \mathcal{I}_2$, and our axioms dictated in that instance that agent 1 must receive utility of 10. This gives us our contradiction.

$\square$

Table 1. Table showing the approval sets corresponding to each instance in the proof of Proposition 3. For example, (23456)(456) denotes the instance where agent 1 approves all items, and agent 2 approves items g_4, g_5, and g_6. The second column describes outcomes consistent with MMS, Pareto efficiency, and strategyproofness. Note that we omit items not approved by either agents, as they can be allocated to anyone without affecting any of the three axioms.

Instance	Approval Sets	Allocation
$\mathcal{I}_1$	(23456)(23456)	(235)(46)
$\mathcal{I}_2$	(23456)(456)	(235)(46)
$\mathcal{I}_3$	(3456)(456)	(36)(45)
$\mathcal{I}_4$	(6)(456)	(6)(45)
$\mathcal{I}_5$	(236)(456)	(236)(45)
$\mathcal{I}_6$	(23456)(456)	(at least 11) (at most 9)

5 Conclusion

Fair division of indivisible resources is a challenging yet important problem with wide-ranging applications. In this paper, we have established that cost utilities are a useful restriction to study, especially in the context of MMS allocations. We have shown that there are several classes of instances where MMS allocations always exist under cost utilities. We also show that cost utilities are helpful in circumventing problems of strategic manipulation.

The topic of MMS allocations in general, and for cost utilities in particular, poses many challenging questions. One might consider various fair division problems with constraints under cost utilities. A prime example is cardinality constraints—or more generally, budget constraints—which are quite natural in this setting.

Our work serves as a further indication that fair division under cost utilities is a fruitful research direction.

Acknowledgements. This project was partially supported by the ARC Laureate Project FL200100204 on "Trustworthy AI".

References

1. Akrami, H., Rezvan, R., Seddighin, M.: An EF2X allocation protocol for restricted additive valuations. In: Proceedings of the 31st International Joint Conference on Artificial Intelligence (IJCAI) (2022)

2. Amanatidis, G., Birmpas, G., Christodoulou, G., Markakis, E.: Truthful allocation mechanisms without payments: characterization and implications on fairness. In: Proceedings of the 18th ACM Conference on Economics and Computation (EC) (2017)
3. Amanatidis, G., Birmpas, G., Filos-Ratsikas, A., Voudouris, A.A.: Fair division of indivisible goods: a survey. In: Proceedings of the 31st International Joint Conference on Artificial Intelligence (IJCAI) (2022)
4. Amanatidis, G., Markakis, E., Nikzad, A., Saberi, A.: Approximation algorithms for computing maximin share allocations. ACM Trans. Algorithms 13(4), 1–28 (2017b)
5. Asadpour, A., Feige, U., Saberi, A.: Santa Claus meets hypergraph matchings. ACM Trans. Algorithms 8(3), 1–9 (2012)
6. Babaioff, M., Ezra, T., Feige, U.: Fair and truthful mechanisms for dichotomous valuations. In: Proceedings of the 35th AAAI Conference on Artificial Intelligence (AAAI) (2021)
7. Bansal, N., Sviridenko, M.: The Santa Claus problem. In: Proceedings of the 38th Annual ACM Symposium on Theory of Computing, p. 31–40 (2006)
8. Bouveret, S., Cechlárová, K., Elkind, E., Igarashi, A., Peters, D.: Fair division of a graph. In: Proceedings of the 26th International Joint Conference on Artificial Intelligence (IJCAI) (2017)
9. Bouveret, S., Lemaître, M.: Characterizing conflicts in fair division of indivisible goods using a scale of criteria. Auton. Agents Multi-Agent Syst. 30(2), 259–290 (2016)
10. Brams, S.J., Taylor, A.D.: Fair Division: From cake-cutting to dispute resolution. Cambridge University Press (1996)
11. Brandt, F., Conitzer, V., Endriss, U., Lang, J., Procaccia, A.D.: Handbook of Computational Social Choice. Cambridge University Press (2016)
12. Budish, E.: The combinatorial assignment problem: approximate competitive equilibrium from equal incomes. J. Polit. Econ. 119(6), 1061–1103 (2011)
13. Camacho, F., Fonseca-Delgado, R., Pino Pérez, R., Tapia, G.: Generalized binary utility functions and fair allocations. Math. Soc. Sci. 121, 50–60 (2022)
14. Cheng, S., Mao, Y.: Integrality gap of the configuration LP for the restricted maxmin fair allocation (2018), http://arxiv.org/abs/1807.04152
15. Ebadian, S., Peters, D., Shah, N.: How to fairly allocate easy and difficult chores. In: Proceedings of the 21st International Conference on Autonomous Agents and Multiagent Systems (AAMAS) (2022)
16. Feige, U., Sapir, A., Tauber, L.: A tight negative example for MMS fair allocations. In: Proceedings of the 17th International Conference on Web and Internet Economics (WINE) (2021)
17. Garg, J., Taki, S.: An improved approximation algorithm for maximin shares. In: Proceedings of the 21st ACM Conference on Economics and Computation (EC) (2020)
18. Ghodsi, M., Hajiaghayi, M., Seddighin, M., Seddighin, S., Yami, H.: Fair allocation of indivisible goods: Improvements and generalizations. In: Proceedings of the 19th ACM Conference on Economics and Computation (EC) (2018)
19. Goldman, J., Procaccia, A.D.: Spliddit: unleashing fair division algorithms. SIGecom Exchanges 13(2), 41–46 (2015)
20. Halpern, D., Procaccia, A.D., Psomas, A., Shah, N.: Fair division with binary valuations: one rule to rule them all. In: Proceedings of the 16th International Conference on Web and Internet Economics (WINE), Springer (2020)

21. Heinen, T., Nguyen, N.-T., Nguyen, T.T., Rothe, J.: Approximation and complexity of the optimization and existence problems for maximin share, proportional share, and minimax share allocation of indivisible goods. Auton. Agents Multi-Agent Syst. **32**(6), 741–778 (2018). https://doi.org/10.1007/s10458-018-9393-0
22. Kalinowski, T., Narodytska, N., Walsh, T.: A social welfare optimal sequential allocation procedure. In: Proceedings of the 23rd International Joint Conference on Artificial Intelligence (IJCAI) (2013)
23. Kalinowski, T., Narodytska, N., Walsh, T., Xia, L.: Strategic behavior when allocating indivisible goods sequentially. In: Proceedings of the 27th AAAI Conference on Artificial Intelligence (AAAI) (2013)
24. Kurokawa, D., Procaccia, A.D., Wang, J.: Fair enough: guaranteeing approximate maximin shares. J. ACM **65**(2), 1–27 (2018)
25. Moulin, H.: Fair division and collective welfare. MIT press (2004)
26. Othman, A., Sandholm, T., Budish, E.: Finding approximate competitive equilibria: efficient and fair course allocation. In: Proceedings of the 9th International Conference on Autonomous Agents and Multiagent Systems (AAMAS) (2010)
27. Vossen, T.: Fair allocation concepts in air traffic management. PhD thesis (2002)

Fair Algorithm Design: Fair and Efficacious Machine Scheduling

April Niu[✉][iD], Agnes Totschnig[iD], and Adrian Vetta[iD]

McGill University, Montreal, Canada
{yuexing.niu,agnes.totschnig}@mail.mcgill.ca, adrian.vetta@mcgill.ca

Abstract. Motivated by a plethora of practical examples where bias is induced by automated decision-making algorithms, there has been strong recent interest in the design of fair algorithms. However, there is often a dichotomy between *fairness* and *efficacy*: fair algorithms may proffer low social welfare solutions whereas welfare optimizing algorithms may be very unfair. This issue is exemplified in the machine scheduling problem where, for n jobs, the social welfare of any fair solution may be a factor $\Omega(n)$ worse than the optimal welfare. In this paper, we prove that this dichotomy between fairness and efficacy can be overcome if we allow for a negligible amount of bias: there exist algorithms that are both "almost perfectly fair" and have a constant factor *efficacy ratio*, that is, are guaranteed to output solutions that have social welfare within a constant factor of optimal welfare. Specifically, for any $\epsilon > 0$, there exist mechanisms with efficacy ratio $\Theta(\frac{1}{\epsilon})$ and where no agent is more than an ϵ fraction worse off than they are in the fairest possible solution (given by an algorithm that does not use personal or type data). Moreover, these bicriteria guarantees are tight and apply to both the single machine case and the multiple machine case. The key to our results is the use of *Pareto scheduling mechanisms*. These mechanisms, by the judicious use of personal or type data, are able to exploit Pareto improvements that benefit every individual; such Pareto improvements would typically be forbidden by fair scheduling algorithms designed to satisfy standard statistical measures of group fairness. We anticipate this paradigm, the judicious use of personal data by a fair algorithm to greatly improve performance at the cost of negligible bias, has wider application.

1 Introduction

The boom in automated decision-making is producing transformative effects on society. In principle, automation should produce lower cost and higher performance outcomes. Moreover, a common presumption was that the use of algorithms based upon big data sets would eliminate the inherent bias in human decision-making. Unfortunately, that has not been the case. Indeed, it appears that in many instances automated decision-making has allowed bias to emerge on a huge scale and also to institutionalize partiality. A particularly nefarious example concerns judicial sentences based upon algorithms that predict

A. Deligkas and A. Filos-Ratsikas (Eds.): SAGT 2023, LNCS 14238, pp. 239–256, 2023.
https://doi.org/10.1007/978-3-031-43254-5_14

the risk of reoffending [23,32]; these risk scores have been claimed to exhibit strong racial bias. Two more classical examples concern bias in the assignment of credit scores [26,38] and in automated hiring systems [44]. Indeed, as technology advances further, such as in facial recognition, the scope and potential dangers of automated decision-making are expanding dramatically [11,45]. Consequently, the issue of fair algorithms is now receiving a considerable amount of attention in the law, politics, philosophy, statistics and, especially, machine learning communities.

But what is a fair algorithm? There is a subtlety here. There are two predominant, but quite distinct, ways to view fairness. First, an algorithm may be considered fair if it produces outcomes that are unbiased across groups. This is the underlying framework when fairness measures based on statistical criteria are applied. Second, an algorithm may be considered fair if its internal workings are unbiased. In particular, such an algorithm cannot use any personal or type information (such as race, sex, sexual orientation, wealth, class, etc.) nor use any correlated attributes. Our approach is to combine these two viewpoints: we present a measure to assess fairness across groups (including individual fairness); furthermore, this measure is calibrated against the fairest outcome achievable by a mechanism that is not allowed to use personal information.

But our purpose is not to proffer a new measure of fairness; there is already an abundance of such definitions in the literature [5]. Nor is our aim simply to design an algorithm that computes fair solutions with respect to the measure. Our objective is more ambitious. We desire fair algorithms that also guarantee high performance. The grail is an algorithm that produces outcomes that are both unbiased **and** efficacious (that is, of high social welfare). Specifically, we are searching for an algorithm $\mathcal{A}$ that outputs solutions that are (i) comparable in performance to those produced by the social welfare maximizing algorithm $\mathcal{A}^*$, and (ii) comparable in fairness to those produced by the fairest algorithm $\mathcal{A}^f$. The reason that our proposed measure is useful is because it will naturally allow us to make such bicriteria comparisons.

The reader may question whether this objective is achievable since there is often a dichotomy between fairness and social welfare. For proof of concept, in this paper we examine the machine scheduling problem. In machine scheduling, personal type data concerns properties of the job to be scheduled, specifically, size. (We remark that whilst size may appear a somewhat trifling characteristic in comparison to race or sex it does have important real-world consequences. For example, net-neutrality is based upon the idea that bandwidth allocation algorithms should not discriminate against agents based upon their size.) Unfortunately, we will see that machine scheduling does indeed suffer from the aforementioned dichotomy: a fair scheduling algorithm that does not use the type data of an agent can produce arbitrarily poor outcomes from a social welfare perspective. Conversely, an optimal scheduling algorithm for social welfare can be arbitrarily unfair. This result appears fatal for our project. But, amazingly, this dichotomy can be circumvented by allowing for a *negligible* amount of bias. Specifically, we prove that very good social outcomes (within a constant factor of optimal) can be obtained by algorithms that are near-perfectly fair (within a $1 + \epsilon$ factor of perfect fairness, for any constant $\epsilon > 0$).

1.1 Overview and Results

In Sect. 2 we provide a brief history concerning the need for fair algorithms and discuss related works in the field. In Sect. 3 we present the classical machine scheduling problem with n jobs (agents). We first explain how the optimal algorithm for social welfare $\mathcal{A}^*$ and the fairest algorithm $\mathcal{A}^f$ perform in the special case of a single machine. We then prove a strong dichotomy between fairness and efficacy by showing the fairest solution can have social cost a factor $\Omega(n)$ worse than that of the optimal solution (see Example I). This motivates the study of ϵ-fair mechanisms. These mechanisms have the property that no individual is allowed to be more than an ϵ fraction worse off than they would be if the fairest algorithm was used. Since the guarantee applies at the individual level it also applies to any group as a whole.

In Sect. 4 we present a class of scheduling algorithms called *priority scheduling mechanisms*. We prove that it suffices to consider only a sub-class of these mechanisms, namely *Pareto scheduling mechanisms*, when searching for an algorithm that is both fair and efficacious. Specifically, these mechanisms can be used to output Pareto optimal solutions.[1] Indeed, the focus on Pareto solutions is also necessary: algorithms based upon statistical group fairness measures may output poor social solutions precisely because they are, typically, forced to output solutions that are Pareto dominated.

Then in Sect. 5, given a target fairness $\epsilon > 0$, we prove that there is always a Pareto optimal scheduling mechanism that is both ϵ-fair and provides social cost within a factor of $\frac{1}{4\epsilon}$ of optimal. Furthermore, we show that these bicriteria guarantees are the best possible. Thus, by allowing a negligible amount of bias, high quality social outcomes can be guaranteed. This is somewhat analogous to differential privacy where, essentially, an individual's data can be included in a database if it does not comprise her individual privacy by more than an ϵ fraction, but with the bonus here that (in using personal data judiciously) we also obtain strong social welfare guarantees. Finally, in Sect. 6 we show how to extend these results to the setting of multiple machines with exactly the same bicriteria guarantees.

All proofs have been omitted from this version of the paper due to page constraints, and interested readers are invited to refer to the full paper.[2]

2   Background and Related Work

The potential for bias in automated decision-making systems has become a critical issue recently in a range of disparate applications. Prominent examples include credit score evaluations [9,26,38], automated recruitment [36,44],

---

[1] An outcome is Pareto optimal if no other outcome exists where at least one agent is better off and no agents are worse off.

[2] https://arxiv.org/abs/2204.06438.

judicial sentencing [2,23,32,37], community policing [24,39], advertising [36], medical treatments [30,43], social services [14], etc. Moreover, these issues have arisen in even the largest and most influential technology companies. For example, Amazon's recruitment engine was found to prefer men over women [17] and its same-day delivery algorithms produced outcomes that disadvantaged communities with large ethnic minority groups [31]. Gender stereotypes abound in Google News [10]. Topically, Twitter recently announced that its amplification algorithms are severely biased in favour of right-wing politicians [29]. Bias in facial recognition software could in the future have calamitous ramifications, so it is worrying that the commercial gender classifiers of IBM, Microsoft, and Megvii (Face++) perform the worst with darker skin females and better with males than females [11,45]. Another example is given by the advertisement algorithms of Facebook; these are specialized for target audiences, leading to lawsuits for violations of multiple civil rights laws [50].

Given the breadth and importance of these applications, the issue of algorithmic fairness has consequently received a considerable amount of attention in the law, politics, philosophy, statistics and, especially, machine learning communities. In this section we will provide only a sample overview of the literature and also highlight the prior research most pertinent to our work; we refer the curious reader to the book *Fairness and Machine Learning* [5] for a much more extensive and technical guide to the existing literature.

The first problem facing the academic community is to decide whether or not an algorithm is fair. Therefore, a major focus has been to devise tests based upon measures of fairness. These have been predominantly group-based statistical measures including the influential measures of *independence*, *separation* and *sufficiency*. The origins of these criteria date back to the works of Darlington [16] and Cleary [15]. These measures are commonly termed *group fairness/statistical parity* [19], *equalized odds* [25], and *calibration within groups* [13], respectively. Furthermore, there are now dozens of fairness criteria in the computer science literature closely related to just independence, separation and sufficiency alone; see Barocas et al. [5]. Follow-up works based on group and individual fairness definitions abound. Dwork et al. [20] studied the composition of cohort pipelines under various individual fairness conditions. The notion of multi-group fairness is defined in Rothblum and Yona [47] where a multi-group agnostic PAC learning algorithm is proposed such that the loss on every sub-population is not much worse than the minimal loss for that population. A reduction from multi-group agnostic PAC learning to outcome indistinguishable learning [22] is used to obtain such an algorithm. In addition, in Hebert-Johnson et al. [27], it is argued that calibration is not enough for achieving fairness; multicalibration is proposed to compute identifiable subpopulations within a collection, on which learning algorithms output predictions that are highly accurate. This model is further used in predicting COVID-19 mortality risk where multicalibration is combined with other baseline models [4]. Other measures based on causal reasoning and the use of counterfactuals have also been proposed [33,35,42]. A stronger theoretical result [21] gives an extraction procedure capable of learning from a fairness oracle with an arbitrary fairness condition.

A consequence of the abundance of tests is that these measures may be mutually incompatible [16]; see also Kleinberg et al. [34] and Chouldechova [13]. This can make assessments of bias somewhat subjective. Consider, for example, *risk assessment scores*. These are widely used in the criminal justice system in the US in assigning bail or remand (pre-trial detention) [32]. ProPublica [2,37] found that COMPAS risk scores, generated using software by Northpointe, were strongly biased against African-Americans. Specifically, African-Americans were twice as likely to be falsely flagged as high risk, while Caucasian defendants were more often mislabeled as low risk. Northpointe [18] counterargued these findings by claiming that the COMPAS risk scores were fair because they satisfy the sufficiency criteria. More detailed discussion on this case and on the incompatibilities and trade-offs between popular statistical fairness criteria can be found in Berk et al [6].

The shift from human to automated decision-making has also added a degree of opacity, as most predictors lack interpretability, tracability and auditability. We tend to view technology as an impartial prediction tool that is less prone to making mistakes than the human judgments it replaces and, consequently, assign it unwarranted legitimacy. Another major issue with black-box predictors is the diffusion of responsibility and the loss of accountability that ensues from a lack of clarity in the automated decision process [39]. The trade-offs between different predictors with respect to interpretability, accuracy and fairness are discussed in Chouldechova et al. [14] for the case of child maltreatment hotline screening processes. A more general discussion about screening decisions and fairness can be found in Rambachan et al. [46].

In addition to modelling and assessing fairness, a major research agenda concerns the practical issues that arise with real-world data. These include the collection, appropriate usage, and dynamic maintenance of data. Consider the findings of Holstein et al. [28] based upon interviews with ML industrial practitioners. In practice, datasets are often both incomplete and inappropriate for assessing fairness. Thus guidance is needed in the data collection stage. Moreover, even if important sensitive data (such as type data) has been collected, it may be withheld from the industrial teams actually developing and running the algorithms, making accurate auditing impossible. Furthermore, humans are involved throughout the development pipeline (including in data collection and data labelling for training) leading to the possible incorporation of human bias. Also, unlike in hiring or judicial sentencing, in many industrial applications the outcomes and objectives are more fuzzy and opaque (e.g. chatbots, tutoring, etc) so are less conducive for evaluation by standard statistical fairness measures. For such practical reasons, thorough auditing and documentation is proposed as essential in remedying bias in computer programs [40,44].

As alluded to, great care has to be taken with real-world data because there may be many components that are highly correlated with a critical or protected attribute. In particular, the naive approach of "*fairness through unawareness*", where the protected attribute is removed, is insufficient to guarantee fair treatment [48]. The dynamic nature of data collection can itself be problematic, for example, in causing negative feedback loops, which can amplify the bias contained in the data sets. Consider a case study on predictive policing in Oakland conducted by Lum and Isaac [39]: a software recommendation of increased policing in a region will lead to an increase in recorded crimes in the dataset; this, in turn, can lead to a recommendation of further increases in policing for that area, etc.; see Ensign et al. [24] for a mathematical model of this phenomenon. Negative feedback loops may also arise in automated hiring systems, where positive information may be added to the database for successful candidates whereas no or negative information may be added for candidates the software rejected [52]. Similar feedback-loop effects have also been observed in credit score calculations [9] and in the polarization of social networks [49].

Let us conclude this overview by discussing the fairness literature most pertinent to our work. Mullainathan [41] discusses the relationships between social welfare and fairness. Dwork et al. [19] highlight two aspects of particular relevance here. One, they emphasize the importance of fairness measures that extend beyond group fairness and apply at the level of an individual. They do this using a Lipschitz condition on the classifier. Two, they propose a bicriteria approach, namely utility optimization subject to a fairness constraint. Our approach follows this framework. In essence, we wish to optimize welfare (minimize social cost) subject to individual fairness constraints, namely ϵ-fairness.

Moreover, we further desire quantitative bicriteria performance guarantees. This is analogous to the concept of the *price of fairness* introduced independently by Caragiannis et al. [12] and Bertsimas et al. [7]. The price of fairness quantifies the loss in social welfare (economic efficiency) incurred under the fairness scheme. Specifically, for a minimization problem, it is the worst case ratio between the cost of the "best" fair solution and the cost of the most efficient solution.[3] We remark that this approach has wide application depending upon the definition of fairness used. For example, in Caragiannis et al. [12] the problem studied is the classical economic problem concerning the fair allocation of a collection of goods, where an outcome is deemed fair if it satisfies the properties of proportionality, envy-freeness, or equitability. For proof of concept, we have chosen to study the machine scheduling problem with n agents and m machines. The price of fairness in machine scheduling has been studied for the special case of two-agents on a single machine [1,53].

Our main result can be viewed through the price of fairness lens. Specifically, for machine scheduling, the price of fairness for the class of perfectly fair (0-fair) schedules is $\Omega(n)$ but the price of fairness for the class of near-perfectly fair (ϵ-fair) schedules is only $\Theta(1/\epsilon)$ for any $\epsilon > 0$.

---

[3] Bertsimas et al. [7] actually use a measure set equal to one minus this ratio, but that is of no significance here.

3   The Machine Scheduling Problem

In the *machine scheduling problem* there are n agents who wish to schedule a single job each on one of m machines. Agent i has a job of *size* (duration) $d_i \geq 0$ and its objective is to minimize the *completion time* $c_i(\mathcal{A})$ of its job, which is a function of the (possibly, randomized) assignment mechanism $\mathcal{A}$ used to assign the jobs to the machines. The *social cost* of an assignment is the sum of the (expected) completion times. Our objective is to design a *fair* allocation mechanism that performs well in comparison to the optimal mechanism for social cost. To begin, in Sects. 3 to 5, we will focus on the case of a single machine, namely $m = 1$. Using the lessons derived from the single machine case, we will study the general case of multiple machines, that is $m \geq 2$, in Sect. 6.

3.1   Fair Schedules and Optimal Schedules

Consider the case of a single machine. Here the completion time for agent i is simply the sum of its size plus the sizes of the jobs that are scheduled on the machine before it is. It is now easy to compute both the fairest schedule and the optimal schedule. The optimal mechanism $\mathcal{A}^*$ for social cost is given by Smith's Rule [51]: *schedule the jobs in increasing order of size.* On the other hand, recall that a fair mechanism may not use any private characteristic of the agent. In this case, the only such characteristic is size. Thus, for machine scheduling a fair mechanism must treat the agents identically. In particular, for any pair of jobs, job i should be equally likely to appear before or after job ℓ. Ergo, the fair solution is given by the Random Assignment Rule: *schedule the jobs in random order.* We remark that for machine scheduling on a single machine there is a unique fair solution. Hence for this application it makes sense to refer to the random assignment rule as the *fairest mechanism* $\mathcal{A}^f$. (For the multiple machine setting we will see that there is more than one fair mechanism. So, for the purpose of comparison, there we define the fairest mechanism $\mathcal{A}^f$ to be the mechanism with the best social welfare among the set of all fair mechanisms.)

We may now calculate the social cost of the optimal assignment mechanism $\mathcal{A}^*$. Without loss of generality, label the agents such that $d_1 \leq d_2 \leq \cdots \leq d_n$. Then, under Smith's Rule, agent i has completion time $c_i(\mathcal{A}^*) = \sum_{\ell=1}^{i} d_\ell$. It follows immediately that the social cost of the optimal assignment is

$$c(\mathcal{A}^*) = \sum_{i=1}^{n} c_i(\mathcal{A}^*) = \sum_{i=1}^{n} \sum_{\ell=1}^{i} d_\ell = \sum_{i=1}^{n} (n - i + 1) \cdot d_i. \tag{1}$$

Next, let's compute the expected social cost of the fairest mechanism $\mathcal{A}^f$. Define $D = \sum_{i=1}^{n} d_i$ to be the sum of the job sizes. Under the randomized assignment mechanism, job ℓ will appear before job i with probability exactly $\frac{1}{2}$. Thus the expected completion time of job i is exactly $c_i(\mathcal{A}^f) = d_i + \sum_{\ell \neq i} \frac{1}{2} \cdot d_\ell = \frac{1}{2} \cdot (D + d_i)$. Consequently, the expected social cost of the fairest mechanism is

$$c(\mathcal{A}^f) = \sum_{i=1}^{n} c_i(\mathcal{A}^f) = \sum_{i=1}^{n} \frac{1}{2} \cdot (D + d_i) = \frac{1}{2} D \cdot (n + 1). \tag{2}$$

We can now formalize how to measure the trade-off between fairness and efficacy. A standard approach to do this is via the *price of fairness*, due to Caragiannis et al. [12]; see also Bertsimas et al. [7]. This is the maximum ratio between the social cost of the best fair solution ($\min_{S \in \mathcal{F}(I)} c(S)$) and that of the optimal solution $c(S^*)$ over all possible instances $\mathcal{I}$. Formally, let $\mathcal{I}$ be the set of instances and let $\mathcal{F}(I)$ be the set of solutions that satisfy the proscribed fairness criteria for an instance $I \in \mathcal{I}$. Then the price of fairness is $\Phi = \max_{I \in \mathcal{I}} \min_{S \in \mathcal{F}(I)} \frac{c(S)}{c(S^*)}$ (3).
We may also define the *price of fairness* $\Phi(\mathcal{A}) = \max_{I \in \mathcal{I}} \frac{c(\mathcal{A})}{c(\mathcal{A}^*)}$ (4) of a mechanism $\mathcal{A}$ as the worst case ratio, over all possible instances, of the social cost of the solution output by the mechanism compared to that of the optimal mechanism $\mathcal{A}^*$. We also call $\Phi(\mathcal{A})$ the *efficacy ratio* (or *social welfare ratio*) of the mechanism $\mathcal{A}$. For machine scheduling, we will see in Sect. 4 that we can compute (3) from (4). That is, under the fairness measure considered, we can find a mechanism $\mathcal{A}$ that for any instance I outputs the best fair solution in $\mathcal{F}(I)$.

3.2 The Dichotomy Between Fairness and Efficacy

Unfortunately, the following example shows that achieving an assignment mechanism that is **both** fair and efficacious is a chimera.

Example I. Let there be $n - 1$ small jobs of size 1 and one large job of size $d_n \gg 1$. By (1), the optimal social cost is

$$c_i(\mathcal{A}^*) = \sum_{i=1}^{n}(n-i+1)\cdot d_i = d_n + \sum_{i=1}^{n-1} n-i+1 = d_n + \sum_{j=2}^{n} j = d_n + \frac{1}{2}n(n+1)-1.$$
(5)

In contrast, by (2), the social cost of the fairest mechanism is

$$c_i(\mathcal{A}^f) = \frac{1}{2}D\cdot(n+1) = \frac{1}{2}\cdot(n-1+d_n)\cdot(n+1) = \frac{1}{2}(n+1)\cdot d_n + \frac{1}{2}(n^2-1).$$
(6)

But, for large d_n, we see from (5) and (6) that $\frac{c(\mathcal{A}^f)}{c(\mathcal{A}^*)}$ tends to $\frac{1}{2}(n+1)$. Thus the price of fairness for machine scheduling is at least $\frac{1}{2}(n+1)$.

This example is troubling as a price of fairness of $\Omega(n)$ is the worst possible. Seemingly, one may conclude that this rules out any possibility of designing a mechanism for scheduling that is both fair and effective. The remainder of the paper is devoted to proving that this conclusion is emphatically incorrect!

3.3 Near-Fair Mechanisms

To show the existence of a fair and efficacious scheduling mechanism, our task is two-fold. First, we desire a scheduling algorithm $\mathcal{A}$ that outputs a solution whose social cost is comparable to that given by the optimal algorithm $\mathcal{A}^*$. Second, the fairness of the solution output by $\mathcal{A}$ must also be comparable to that given by the fairest algorithm $\mathcal{A}^f$.

For the former desiderata it suffices to prove that the efficacy ratio $\Phi(\mathcal{A})$ is small, in particular, our target is a constant efficacy ratio. For the latter desiderata we require a measure of fairness. Our measure will be at the level of the individual. Specifically, for a given instance $I \in \mathcal{I}$, we say that the fairness $f_i(\mathcal{A})$ of the mechanism to agent i is the ratio between the expected completion time $c_i(\mathcal{A})$ and the completion time $c_i(\mathcal{A}^f)$ it receives in the fairest solution. We then define the fairness ratio $f(\mathcal{A})$ for the mechanism $\mathcal{A}$ to be the worst case fairness over all agents and over all instances.

$$f(\mathcal{A}) \;=\; \max_{I \in \mathcal{I}} \max_i \; f_i(\mathcal{A}) \;=\; \max_{I \in \mathcal{I}} \max_i \; \frac{c_i(\mathcal{A})}{c_i(\mathcal{A}^f)}$$

For $\epsilon \geq 0$, we say the mechanism $\mathcal{A}$ is ϵ-near-fair, or more concisely ϵ-fair, if $f(\mathcal{A}) \leq 1 + \epsilon$. This implies that an ϵ-fair algorithm can never output a solution in which the cost to any agent i is more than an ϵ fraction greater than the cost it pays in the fairest solution. Thus if ϵ is large the use of type-data by the algorithm $\mathcal{A}$ significantly harms at least one individual; if ϵ is small the use of type-data does not significantly harm any individual.

In this paper, our target is for ϵ-fair mechanisms where ϵ is close to zero. We call such an algorithm *almost perfectly fair*. Observe that a 0-fair algorithm $\mathcal{A}$ is *perfectly fair* – every agent does at least as well under $\mathcal{A}$ as under the fairest mechanism $\mathcal{A}^f$. Unfortunately, Example I extends to all perfectly fair algorithms. Ergo, all 0-fair algorithms have extremely poor efficacy ratios, namely $\Omega(n)$. Remarkably, we can circumvent this negative result by proving that if we allow for an arbitrarily small amount of unfairness then the efficacy ratio falls to a constant! Specifically, we will show that an ϵ-fair algorithm exists for which the the worst case efficacy ratio is $\Theta(\frac{1}{\epsilon})$. Our result then implies the existence of an algorithm that is able to use type-data in such as way as to massively improve the social performance of the algorithm whilst harming no individual more than a negligible amount.

We remark that, even without the social welfare guarantee, ϵ-fairness itself is an extremely strong guarantee. Because it applies at the individual level it automatically applies at the group level.[4] Moreover, it simultaneously applies to every group no matter how they are defined; in particular this includes groups that a particular study may not even be investigating! We emphasize that the concept of near-fair mechanisms extends beyond applications where there is a unique fairest algorithm $\mathcal{A}^f$. Specifically, it suffices to demand that, for every agent, the mechanism provides a comparable utility to that given in expectation by a collection of fair algorithms $\{\mathcal{A}^{f_1}, \mathcal{A}^{f_2}, \ldots, \mathcal{A}^{f_k}\}$. Thus the bicriteria measure can essentially be applied to any application setting; only a target set of

---

[4] This important property is an immediate consequence of the definition of our measure. We remark that this property does not hold for statistical measures of fairness: typically individual fairness does not imply group fairness, and group fairness does not imply individual fairness. See Binns [8] for detailed discussions on this issue.

criteria (or target set of algorithms/outcomes) are required for the purpose of comparison.

4   Priority Scheduling Mechanisms

In this section, we show that we can refine our search space when looking for a scheduling mechanism that is both fair and efficacious. To wit, we define the class of priority scheduling mechanisms and prove it has a subclass, namely Pareto scheduling mechanisms, that correspond exactly to algorithms that output Pareto optimal solutions. Ergo, it will suffice in Sect. 5 to study only Pareto scheduling mechanisms to obtain the best possible performance guarantees with respect to fairness and efficacy.

The most general scheduling mechanism assigns a probability p_π to each permutation π of the agents and then schedules the agents in the order π with probability p_π. For our purposes it will suffice to consider only the class of *priority scheduling mechanisms*. A priority scheduling mechanism partitions the jobs into priority groups. Every job of priority (group) k must be scheduled before every job of priority $k + 1$. Jobs of the same (priority) group are scheduled in random order. For example, both Smith's rule and the randomized assignment rule are priority scheduling mechanisms. For the former, there are n priority groups with job i alone in priority group i. For the latter, there is just one priority group, that is, every job has the same priority.

Our task now is to show that the priority scheduling mechanisms include the optimal mechanisms in terms of the trade-off between fairness and efficacy.

4.1   Pareto Optimal Mechanisms

We say that scheduling mechanism $\mathcal{A}_1$ Pareto dominates $\mathcal{A}_2$ if $f(\mathcal{A}_1) \leq f(\mathcal{A}_2)$ and $c(\mathcal{A}_1) \leq c(\mathcal{A}_2)$ (with at least one inequality strict). That is, $\mathcal{A}_1$ is both fairer and more efficacious than $\mathcal{A}_2$. To begin, we wish to characterize the mechanisms that are not Pareto dominated. These are the *Pareto optimal mechanisms* – no mechanism exists which yields better fairness and better efficacy. Thus these mechanisms lie on the *Pareto frontier* of all scheduling mechanisms (we will give an illustration of this later in Fig. 1). Our aim is to show this Pareto frontier consists **only** of the Pareto optimal mechanisms. To do this, we consider a series of properties held by Pareto optimal mechanisms.

Lemma 1. *For any priority scheduling mechanism, the worst fairness applies to a job in the lowest priority group.*

Lemma 1 has an important consequence. Because, the overall fairness of the schedule is determined only by the lowest priority grouping, we obtain a Pareto improvement if every job of higher priority is ordered by size in its own singleton priority group. As this coincides with Smith's rule for those items, this can only decrease the social cost. Further, by Lemma 1, because it has no effect on the lowest priority grouping, the fairness of the schedule remains the same.

Henceforth, we need only consider schedules where the lowest priority group has a random ordering and, before them, all other items are ordered by Smith's rule. For ease of exposition, we will also partition the jobs into two *sections*. The second section consists of jobs in the lowest priority group; the first section consists of all the other jobs. Thus jobs in the first section are ordered by Smith's rule and after them the jobs in the second section are ordered randomly.

Now we have seen that the jobs in the lowest priority group have the worst fairness. Amongst them, the smallest job has the worst fairness.

Lemma 2. *For any priority scheduling mechanism, the worst fairness applies to the smallest job in the lowest priority group.*

Lemma 2 also has an important consequence. It implies that the lowest priority group must contain the largest jobs. More specifically, a smaller job should never have higher priority than a larger job.

Lemma 3. *In any Pareto optimal schedule, a smaller job can never have higher priority than a larger job.*

This implies that there are only n Pareto optimal scheduling mechanisms.

4.2   The Pareto Frontier

Let's see an example illustrating how the n Pareto scheduling mechanisms lie on the Pareto frontier. Figure 1 shows the trade-off between fairness and social cost for an example with $2^{9-\ell}$ jobs of size 2^ℓ, for all $0 \leq \ell \leq 9$. In particular, the total duration of all the jobs of each size is constant (512). The y-axis gives the fairness guarantee, ϵ, and the x-axis gives the efficacy ratio for the instance. Each point represents the performance of a given priority scheduling mechanism. But as there are an exponential number of priority scheduling mechanisms and we have $n = 1023$ agents, we have not plotted them all in Fig. 1. Specifically, shown are only those priority scheduling mechanisms that did not place two jobs of identical size in different sections (that is, in both the first section and the second section). Of the 1023 Pareto optimal mechanisms, ten satisfy this property and they are shown in red; observe that these do lie on the Pareto frontier.

We remark that Lemma 1 explains why many of the mechanisms share the same fairness guarantee and, hence, are plotted on the same horizontal line. In addition, in Fig. 1, Smith's rule corresponds to the leftmost red Pareto schedule $\mathcal{A}^{n-1}$ and the random assignment rule corresponds to the rightmost red Pareto schedule $\mathcal{A}^0$.

5   Fair and Efficacious Scheduling

We must now decide on the appropriate trade-off between fairness and social cost. By the results in Sect. 4, it suffices to analyze only the n Pareto optimal

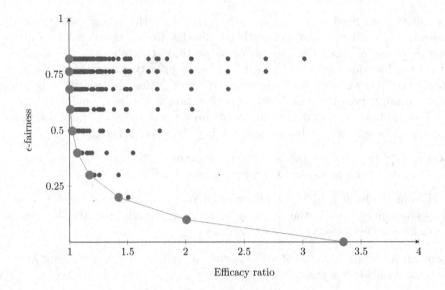

Fig. 1. The Pareto frontier showing the fairness vs social cost trade-off.

mechanisms $\{\mathcal{A}^0, \mathcal{A}^1, \ldots, \mathcal{A}^{n-1}\}$. If we run $\mathcal{A}^{n-1}$ then this is Smith's rule and thus, trivially, we can obtain the optimal solution. But this gives a fairness guarantee where ϵ can be as large as 1, which is extremely unfair. Consequently, our interest lies in smaller values of ϵ. If we run $\mathcal{A}^0$ then this is the random assignment rule. So we have $\epsilon = 0$ giving a perfectly fair assignment. But now we have the opposite problem, the social cost may be extremely high. Specifically, from Example I, the efficacy ratio of this mechanism is $\Omega(n)$. Can we get the best of both worlds? In particular, for a fixed $\epsilon > 0$ what is the best social cost we can guarantee?

5.1 The Fairness of Pareto Scheduling

Let's commence by computing the fairness of each Pareto optimal scheduling mechanism, $\mathcal{A}^k$. Take an instance I with sizes $d_1 \leq d_2 \leq \cdots \leq d_n$ and define

$$\epsilon_k = \frac{\sum_{\ell=1}^{k} d_\ell}{\sum_{\ell=1}^{n} d_\ell} = \frac{\sum_{\ell=1}^{k} d_\ell}{D}.$$

Theorem 1. *The k-th Pareto optimal scheduling mechanism $\mathcal{A}^k$ is ϵ_k-fair.*

5.2 The Efficacy of Pareto Scheduling

So the k-th Pareto optimal schedule $\mathcal{A}^k$ is ϵ-fair, for $\epsilon = \epsilon_k = \frac{\sum_{\ell=1}^{k} d_\ell}{\sum_{\ell=1}^{n} d_\ell}$. But what is its efficacy ratio? Take a worst-case instance I with sizes $d_1 \leq d_2 \leq \cdots \leq d_n$ where $\sum_{\ell=1}^{k} d_\ell = \epsilon \cdot D$. To find its efficacy, we will transform I into an auxiliary instance $\hat{I}$ whose efficacy is at least as bad as I, but which is easier to analyze. To begin, by scaling, we may assume $d_k = 1$. We say that a job i is *small* if $d_i < 1$, is *medium* if $d_i = 1$, and is *large* if $d_i > 1$. Then, given I, define the following parameters:

- Let S be the total size of the small jobs: i.e. $S = \sum_{j:d_j<1} d_j$.
- Let M be the total size of the medium jobs, i.e. $M = \sum_{j:d_j=1} d_j = |\{j : d_j = d_k = 1\}|$.
- Let L be the total size of the large jobs, i.e. $L = \sum_{j:d_j>1} d_j$.
- Let $\lambda \in [0,1]$ be the fraction of the medium jobs in the first section.

These definitions are illustrated in Fig. 2. Observe that, for the k-th Pareto optimal schedule, the jobs corresponding to S are all in the first section and the jobs corresponding to L are all in the second section. Of course, Smith's rule will simply order the jobs by size.

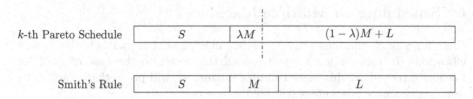

Fig. 2. Two different algorithms on instance I.

We are now ready to transform I into an auxiliary instance $\hat{I}$. Furthermore, $\hat{I}$ will satisfy two properties that will simplify our analyses.

PROPERTY 1. Every small job in $\hat{I}$ has size 0.

PROPERTY 2. There is exactly one large job in $\hat{I}$.

5.3 The Efficacy Ratio

So to calculate the worst case efficacy ratio it suffices to consider an instance $\hat{I}$ where every job is of medium size, that is 1, except for one large job of size $d_n = L$, say. Now let $n_0 = M$ be the number of medium jobs. Thus $n = n_0 + 1$ and $D = n_0 + L$. In addition, let $\hat{\epsilon} = \frac{n_0}{D}$ be the proportion of the total sum of the job sizes due to the medium jobs. Finally, recall that k of the medium jobs are in the first section for the k-th Pareto optimal schedule $\mathcal{A}^k$, and $n_0 - k$ of the medium jobs are in the second section. Let $\epsilon = \epsilon_k = \frac{k}{D}$ signify the dividing point between the first section and the second section; observe $0 \le \epsilon \le \hat{\epsilon}$.

Theorem 2. *The efficacy ratio of $\mathcal{A}^k$ is at most $\frac{1}{4\epsilon} + \left(1 + \frac{\epsilon}{4}\right)$, where $\epsilon = \epsilon_k$.*

So there is always a priority scheduling mechanism that is both ϵ-fair and produces a solution whose social cost is within a factor $\frac{1}{4\epsilon} + \left(1 + \frac{\epsilon}{4}\right)$ of optimal. This upper bound is tight to within an additive term of one half. In particular, the dominant term $\frac{1}{4\epsilon}$ cannot be improved. To see this we present an example (in the full version of the paper) for which any priority scheduling mechanism that is ϵ-fair must output a solution whose social cost is at least a factor $\frac{1}{4\epsilon} + \frac{1}{2}$ greater than optimal.

Theorem 3. *The efficacy ratio of $\mathcal{A}^k$ is at least $\frac{1}{4\epsilon} + \frac{1}{2}$, where $\epsilon = \epsilon_k$.*

Theorem 2 and Theorem 3 apply for the case $\epsilon = \epsilon_k$. But the bound of $\frac{1}{4\epsilon}$ is tight for any $\epsilon > 0$. In particular, we can choose any *target value* $\epsilon > 0$ to be our fairness guarantee. Then we can still apply our worst case analysis. This is because we defined $\epsilon_k = \frac{k}{D}$. Hence for any small ϵ, there is a k such that $\epsilon < \epsilon_k + \frac{1}{D}$. But recall $D \geq n$. Therefore, if we set a target fairness of ϵ then we can obtain an even better fairness guarantee of $\epsilon_k < \epsilon$ for no loss in the dominant term of $\frac{1}{4\epsilon}$ in the efficacy ratio (there is an insignificant loss only in the minor terms).

6   Scheduling on Multiple Machines

Ergo, for a single machine there is a scheduling algorithm that is both fair and efficacious. In this section we will extend this result to the case of multiple machines. Indeed, in this more complex setting, we will prove that exactly the same performance guarantees still hold.

6.1   Optimal Scheduling on Multiple Machines

Our first task is to compute an optimal scheduling mechanism $\mathcal{A}^*$ for minimizing the social cost with multiple machines. We will see that there is a simple algorithm to achieve this: *order the jobs by size and place the next job on the least crowded machine*. For the purposes of designing a fair algorithm, however, it is important to note that there is a class of randomized algorithms that also guarantee an optimal scheduling. Begin by adding dummy jobs of size zero to ensure there are exactly $n = m \cdot \tau$ jobs. Next, order the jobs by size and then group them into blocks of size m. Finally, for each block, independently generate a random perfect matching to assign the m jobs in the block to the m machines.

To analyze this, let M_r be the total size of the jobs in the rth block. The social cost is then $\tau \cdot M_1 + (\tau - 1) \cdot M_2 + \cdots + 2 \cdot M_{\tau-1} + M_\tau$. This is because the jobs in block r are delayed in total by the jobs before them. That this randomized algorithm is optimal follows from the fact its deterministic version is optimal, a fact observed by Baker [3].

Theorem 4. *The optimal schedule has cost*

$$\tau \cdot M_1 + (\tau - 1) \cdot M_2 + \cdots + 2 \cdot M_{\tau-1} + M_\tau.$$

As alluded to, Theorem 4 implies that there is a simple greedy algorithm $\mathcal{A}^*$ to output the optimal schedule. Simply order the jobs by size and, at each step, place the next job on the least crowded machine. Observe this greedy algorithm has the property of assigning the jobs in a block to different machines. This is because when a job is assigned to a machine with the lowest load, that machine now has the highest load because the jobs are ordered by size. This can be shown inductively. Indeed, let Machine 1 be the machine with the lowest load denoted ℓ_1. Let Machine 2 be the machine with the highest load to which we have just added a job of size d_2 and which previously had the lowest load ℓ_2. So in particular, we have that $\ell_2 \le \ell_1$. After adding the next job of size $d_1 \ge d_2$ to Machine 1, it must have higher load than Machine 2, since $\ell_1 + d_1 \ge \ell_2 + d_2$. Consequently, Machine 1 now has the highest load. It follows that every other machine must then receive a job before that machine receives another job. Hence the greedy algorithm can be viewed as scheduling the blocks in order via perfect matchings and thus outputs an optimal schedule.

6.2   Fair Scheduling on Multiple Machines

Of course, as with a single machine, the optimal schedules for multiple machines may be very unfair. But, we can use the ideas developed for the single machine case to design a fair and efficacious algorithm for the multiple machine case. First we must define the fairest scheduling mechanism $\mathcal{A}^f$. Recall a mechanism is fair if it does not use type data. But now, for the multiple machine setting, there is no longer a unique fair mechanism. For example, scheduling all the jobs (in random order) on just one of the m machines is fair! Thus, we define the fairest mechanism $\mathcal{A}^f$ to be the mechanism that minimizes social cost over the set of all fair mechanisms. In particular, $\mathcal{A}^f$ will assign each job to a random machine and then, for each machine, order the jobs assigned to it at random.

Next we must define our scheduling mechanism $\mathcal{A}$. Specifically, we use the randomized perfect matching algorithm to assign τ jobs to each machine but not to order the jobs on those machines. Instead to order the jobs on each individual machine, we use the ϵ-fair scheduling algorithm developed in Sect. 5 for a single machine. We claim $\mathcal{A}$ is ϵ-fair and has efficacy ratio $\Theta(\frac{1}{\epsilon})$ for the multiple machine-scheduling problem.

Theorem 5. *The multiple-machine scheduling mechanism $\mathcal{A}$ is ϵ-fair.*

Theorem 6. *For machine scheduling on multiple machines, the mechanism $\mathcal{A}$ has efficacy ratio at most $\frac{1}{4\epsilon} + \left(1 + \frac{\epsilon}{4}\right)$.*

Again the dominant term $\frac{1}{4\epsilon}$ applies even when the targeted fairness guarantee ϵ does not coincide with any of the ϵ_k. (Note, given a target fairness of ϵ, the mechanism $\mathcal{A}^k$ used may vary on different machines.) Moreover, this efficacy ratio is tight because the single-machine setting is a special case of the multiple-machine setting; so the lower bound of $\frac{1}{4\epsilon} + \frac{1}{2}$ from Theorem 3 applies to the multiple-machine setting.

7 Conclusion

For the machine scheduling problem, we have shown that the dichotomy between fairness and efficacy can be overcome by allowing for a negligible amount of bias in the mechanism. We conjecture that this paradigm extends to a much broader range of applications and also to other classical models in computer science such as matching, the assignment problem, flows and network routing. Accordingly, investigating this hypothesis is the most important line of research arising from this paper.

References

1. Agnetis, A., Chen, B., Nicosia, G., Pacifici, A.: Price of fairness in two-agent single-machine scheduling problems. Eur. J. Oper. Res. **276**(1), 79–87 (2019)
2. Angwin, J., Larson, J., Mattu, S., Kirchner, L.: Machine bias. ProPublica (2016)
3. Baker, K.: Introduction to Sequencing and Scheduling. Wiley (1974)
4. Barda, N. et al.: Developing a COVID-19 mortality risk prediction model when individual-level data are not available. Nature Commun. **11**, 4439 (2020)
5. Barocas, S., Hardt, M., Narayanan, A.: Fairness and Machine Learning. fairmlbook.org (2019)
6. Berk, R., Heidari, H., Jabbari, S., Kearns, M., Roth, A.: Fairness in criminal justice risk assessments: the state of the art. Sociol. Meth. Res. **50**(1), 3–44 (2021)
7. Bertsimas, D., Farias, V., Trichakis, N.: The price of fairness. Oper. Res. **59**(1), 17–31 (2011)
8. Binns, R.: On the apparent conflict between individual and group fairness. In: Proceedings of 3rd Conference on Fairness, Accountability, and Transparency (FAT*). pp. 514–524 (2020)
9. Blattner, L., Nelson, S.: How costly is noise? data and disparities in consumer credit (2021)
10. Bolukbasi, T., Chang, K., Zou, J., Saligrama, V., Kalai, A.: Man is to computer programmer as woman is to homemaker? debiasing word embeddings. In: Proceedings of 30th Conference on Neural Information Processing Systems (NIPS). pp. 4356–4364 (2016)
11. Buolamwini, J., Gebru, T.: Gender shades: intersectional accuracy disparities in commercial gender classification. In: Proceedings of 1st Conference on Fairness, Accountability and Transparency (FAT*). vol. 81, pp. 77–91. PMLR (2018)
12. Caragiannis, I., Kaklamanis, C., Kanellopoulos, P., Kyropoulou, M.: The efficiency of fair division. Theory Comput. Syst. **50**, 589–610 (2012)
13. Chouldechova, A.: Fair prediction with disparate impact: a study of bias in recidivism prediction instruments. Big Data **5**(2), 153–163 (2017)
14. Chouldechova, A., Benavides-Prado, D., Fialko, O., Vaithianathan, R.: A case study of algorithm-assisted decision making in child maltreatment hotline screening decisions. In: Proceedings of 1st Conference on Fairness, Accountability and Transparency (FAT*). vol. 81, pp. 134–148. PMLR (2018)
15. Cleary, A.: Test bias: validity of the scholastic aptitude test for negro and white students in integrated colleges. J. Educ. Measur. **1968**(2), 115–124 (1966)
16. Darlington, R.: Another look at "Cultural Fairness." J. Educ. Measur. **8**(2), 71–82 (1971)

17. Dastin, J.: Amazon scraps secret AI recruiting tool that showed bias against women. Reuters (2018)

18. Dieterich, W., Mendoza, C., Brennan, T.: Compas risk scales: demonstrating accuracy equity and predictive parity. Northpointe Inc 7(4), 1–36 (2016)

19. Dwork, C., Hardt, M., Pitassi, T., Reingold, O., Zemel, R.: Fairness through awareness. In: Proceedings of 3rd Conference on Innovations in Theoretical Computer Science (ITCS). pp. 214–226 (2012)

20. Dwork, C., Ilvento, C., Jagadeesan, M.: Individual fairness in pipelines. In: 1st Symposium on Foundations of Responsible Computing, FORC 2020. vol. 156, pp. 7:1–7:22 (2020)

21. Dwork, C., Ilvento, C., Rothblum, G., Sur, P.: Abstracting fairness: oracles, metrics, and interpretability. In: 1st Symposium on Foundations of Responsible Computing, FORC 2020. vol. 156, pp. 8:1–8:16. Schloss Dagstuhl - Leibniz-Zentrum für Informatik (2020)

22. Dwork, C., Kim, M., O.Reingold, Rothblum, G., Yona, G.: Outcome indistinguishability. In: STOC '21: 53rd Annual ACM SIGACT Symposium on Theory of Computing. pp. 1095–1108. ACM (2021)

23. van Eijk, G.: Socioeconomic marginality in sentencing: the built-in bias in risk assessment tools and the reproduction of social inequality. Punishment Soc. 19(4), 463–481 (2017)

24. Ensign, D., Friedler, S., Neville, S., Scheidegger, C., Venkatasubramanian, S.: Runaway feedback loops in predictive policing. In: Proceedings of 1st Conference on Fairness, Accountability and Transparency (FAT*). vol. 81, pp. 160–171. PMLR (2018)

25. Hardt, M., Price, E., Srebro, N.: Equality of opportunity in supervised learning. In: Proceedings of 30th Conference on Neural Information Processing Systems (NIPS). pp. 3323–3331 (2016)

26. Hassani, B.: Societal bias reinforcement through machine learning: a credit scoring perspective. AI Ethics 1, 239–247 (2021)

27. Hebert-Johnson, U., Kim, M., Reingold, O., Rothblum, G.: Multicalibration: Calibration for the (Computationally-identifiable) masses. In: Proceedings of the 35th International Conference on Machine Learning. pp. 1939–1948. PMLR (Jul 2018)

28. Holstein, K., Wortman Vaughan, J., Daumé, H., Dudik, M., Wallach, H.: Improving fairness in machine learning systems: What do industry practitioners need? In: Proceedings of 37th ACM Conference on Human Factors in Computing Systems (CHI). p. 1–16 (2019)

29. Huszár, F., Ktena, S., O'Brien, C., Belli, L., Schlaikjer, A., Hardt, M.: Algorithmic amplification of politics on Twitter. Proc. Natl. Acad. Sci. 119(1), e2025334119 (2022)

30. Igoe, K.: Algorithmic bias in health care exacerbates social inequities - how to prevent it. Executive and Continuing Professional Education (2021)

31. Ingold, D., Soper, S.: Amazon doesn't consider the race of its customers. should it? Bloomberg (2016)

32. Kehl, D., Kessler, S.: Algorithms in the criminal justice system: Assessing the use of risk assessments in sentencing. Berkman Klein Center for Internet and Society (2017)

33. Kilbertus, N., Rojas-Carulla, M., Parascandolo, G., Hardt, M., Janzing, D., Schölkopf, B.: Avoiding discrimination through causal reasoning. In: Proceedings of 31st Conference on Neural Information Processing Systems (NIPS), pp. 656–666 (2017)

34. Kleinberg, J., Mullainathan, S., Raghavan, M.: Inherent trade-offs in the fair determination of risk scores. In: Proceedings of 8th Conference on Innovations in Theoretical Computer Science (ITCS), pp. 43:1–43:23 (2017)

35. Kusner, M., Loftus, J., Russell, C., Silva, R.: Counterfactual fairness. In: Proceedings of 31st International Conference on Neural Information Processing Systems (NIPS), pp. 4069–4079 (2017)

36. Lambrecht, A., Tucker, C.: Algorithmic bias? an empirical study of apparent gender-based discrimination in the display of stem career ads. Manag. Sci. **65**(7), 2966–2981 (2019)

37. Larson, J., Mattu, S., Kirchner, L., Angwin, J.: How we analyzed the COMPAS recidivism algorithm. ProPublica (2016)

38. Liu, L., Dean, S., Rolf, E., Simchowitz, M., Hardt, M.: Delayed impact of fair machine learning. In: Proceedings of 35th International Conference on Machine Learning (ICML). pp. 3150–3158. PMLR (2018)

39. Lum, K., Isaac, W.: To predict and serve? Significance **13**(5), 14–19 (2016)

40. Mitchell, M., et al.: Model cards for model reporting. In: Proceedings of 2nd Conference on Fairness, Accountability, and Transparency (FAT*), pp. 220–229 (2019)

41. Mullainathan, S.: Algorithmic fairness and the social welfare function. In: Proceedings of the 2018 ACM Conference on Economics and Computation. p. 1. EC '18, Association for Computing Machinery (2018)

42. Nabi, R., Shpitser, I.: Fair inference on outcomes. pp. 1931–1940 (2018)

43. Obermeyer, Z., Powers, B., Vogeli, C., Mullainathan, S.: Dissecting racial bias in an algorithm used to manage the health of populations. Science **366**(6464), 447–453 (2019)

44. Raghavan, M., Barocas, S., Kleinberg, J., Levy, K.: Mitigating bias in algorithmic hiring: evaluating claims and practices. In: Proceedings of 3rd Conference on Fairness, Accountability, and Transparency (FAT*), pp. 469–481 (2020)

45. Raji, I., Buolamwini, J.: Actionable auditing: investigating the impact of publicly naming biased performance results of commercial AI products. In: Proceedings of 2nd Conference on AI, Ethics, and Society (AIES). pp. 429–435 (2019)

46. Rambachan, A., Kleinberg, J., Ludwig, J., Mullainathan, S.: An economic perspective on algorithmic fairness. AEA Papers Proc. **110**, 91–95 (2020)

47. Rothblum, G., Yona, G.: Multi-group agnostic PAC learnability. In: Proceedings of the 38th International Conference on Machine Learning, ICML 2021, 18–24 July 2021, Virtual Event. Proceedings of Machine Learning Research, vol. 139, pp. 9107–9115. PMLR (2021)

48. Ruf, B., Detyniecki, M.: Active fairness instead of unawareness (2020)

49. Santos, F., Lelkes, Y., Levin, S.: Link recommendation algorithms and dynamics of polarization in online social networks. Proc. Natl. Acad. Sci. **118**(50) (2021)

50. Sapiezynski, P., Ghosh, A., Kaplan, L., Mislove, A., Rieke, A.: Algorithms that "don't see color": comparing biases in lookalike and special ad audiences (2019)

51. Smith, W.: Various optimizers for single-stage production. Naval Res. Logistics Q. **3**(1–2), 59–66 (1956)

52. Wachter-Boettcher, S.: Why you can't trust AI to make unbiased hiring decisions. Time (2017)

53. Zhang, Y., Zhang, Z., Liu, Z.: The price of fairness for a two-agent scheduling game minimizing total completion time. J. Comb. Optim. , 1–19 (2020). https://doi.org/10.1007/s10878-020-00581-5

EFX Allocations for Indivisible Chores: Matching-Based Approach

Yusuke Kobayashi[1] , Ryoga Mahara[2(✉)] , and Souta Sakamoto[1]

[1] Kyoto University, Kyoto, Japan
yusuke@kurims.kyoto-u.ac.jp
[2] University of Tokyo, Tokyo, Japan
mahara@mist.i.u-tokyo.ac.jp

Abstract. One of the most important topics in discrete fair division is whether an EFX allocation exists for any instance. Although the existence of EFX allocations is a standing open problem for both goods and chores, the understanding of the existence of EFX allocations for chores is less established compared to goods. We study the existence of EFX allocation for chores under the assumption that all agent's cost functions are additive. Specifically, we show the existence of EFX allocations for the following three cases: (i) the number of chores is at most twice the number of agents, (ii) the cost functions of all agents except for one are identical ordering, and (iii) the number of agents is three and each agent has a personalized bi-valued cost function. Furthermore, we provide a polynomial time algorithm to find an EFX allocation for each case.

Keywords: fair division · chores · EFX

1 Introduction

Fair division theory has significant attention across various fields, including economics, mathematics, and computer science. The classic problem of fairly dividing divisible resources, also known as the cake-cutting problem, dates back to the 1940s [31] and has a long history [9,10,27,30]. In contrast, the fair allocation of indivisible items has been a topic of active research in recent decades (see surveys [2]). Given a set $N = \{1, 2, \ldots, n\}$ of n agents and a set M of m items, the goal is to allocate M to N in a fair manner. We refer to items as *goods* if they are beneficial, such as cars and smartphones, and as *chores* if they are burdens, such as housework and teaching duties. For the case of goods, each agent $i \in N$ has a valuation function $v_i : 2^M \to \mathbb{R}_{\geq 0}$, while for the case of chores, each agent $i \in N$ has a cost function $c_i : 2^M \to \mathbb{R}_{\geq 0}$. In general, v_i and c_i are assumed to be monotone non-decreasing.

One of the most popular and well-studied fairness notions is *envy-freeness* (EF) [20]. Informally speaking, an allocation is called EF if each agent prefers their own bundle at least as much as that of any other agent. In the case of divisible resources, an EF allocation always exists for both goods and chores [5,

258 Y. Kobayashi et al.

17, 18, 32, 33], while in the case of indivisible items, it may not exist (for example, dividing one item among two agents). This has motivated researchers to consider relaxing notions of EF, such as EF1, EFX, and other related notions.

Envy-Freeness up to any Item (EFX) for Goods. One of the most well-studied relaxed notions of EF is EFX, which was proposed by Caragiannis et al. [13,14][1]. An allocation $A = (A_1, A_2, \ldots, A_n)$ of goods is called *EFX* if for all pairs of agents i and j, and for any $g \in A_j$, it holds that $v_i(A_i) \geq v_i(A_j \setminus \{g\})$. In other words, each agent i prefers their own bundle at least as much as the bundle of agent j after the removal of *any* good in j's bundle. EFX is regarded as the best analog of envy-freeness in the discrete fair division: Caragiannis et al. [12] remarked that *"Arguably, EFX is the best fairness analog of envy-freeness for indivisible items."* However, the existence of EFX allocations is not well understood, and it is recognized as a significant open problem in the field of fair division. Procaccia [29] remarked that *"This fundamental and deceptively accessible question (EFX existence) is open. In my view, it is the successor of envy-free cake cutting as fair division's biggest problem."*

There has been a significant amount of research to investigate the existence of EFX allocations in various special cases: For general valuations, i.e., each valuation function v_i is only assumed to be (i) *normalized*: $v_i(\emptyset) = 0$ and (ii) *monotone*: $S \subseteq T$ implies $v_i(S) \leq v_i(T)$ for any $S, T \subseteq M$, Plaut and Roughgarden [28] showed that an EFX allocation always exists when there are two agents, or when all agents have identical valuations. This result was extended to the case where all agents have one of two general valuations [26]. In addition, Mahara showed the existence of EFX allocations when $m \leq n + 3$ in [26]. Chaudhury et al. [15] showed that an EFX allocation always exists when $n = 3$ for additive valuations. This result was extended to the case where all agents have nice-cancelable valuations, which generalize additive valuations [7]. A further generalization was obtained by Akrami et al. [1], who showed the existence of EFX allocations when there are three agents with two general valuations and one MMS-feasible valuation, which generalizes nice-cancelable valuations. In other cases, Amanatidis et al. [3] showed that an EFX allocation always exists when each agent has a bi-valued valuation function. The existence of EFX allocations of goods remains open even when there are four agents with additive valuations.

Envy-Freeness up to any Item (EFX) for Chores. We understand even less about the existence of EFX allocations for chores than for goods. By analogy to goods, EFX for chores can be defined as follows. An allocation $A = (A_1, A_2, \ldots, A_n)$ of chores is called *EFX* if for all pairs of agents i and j, and for any $e \in A_i$, it holds that $c_i(A_i \setminus \{e\}) \leq c_i(A_j)$. In other words, each agent i prefers their own bundle at least as much as the bundle of agent j after the removal of *any* chore in i's bundle. Chen and Liu [16] showed the existence of EFX allocations for n agents with identical valuations and cost functions in the case where goods and

---

[1] A notion similar to EFX has been defined under a different name by Gourvès et al. [22].

chores are mixed. Li et al. [24] showed that an EFX allocation for chores always exists when all agents have an identical ordering cost function by using the top-trading envy graph, which is a tool modified from the envy graph. Gafni et al. [21] showed the existence of EFX allocations when each agent has a leveled cost function where a larger set of chores is always more burdensome than a smaller set. Zhou and Wu [35] showed a positive result when $n = 3$ and the bi-valued instances, in which each agent has at most two cost values on the chores. Yin and Mehta [34] showed that if two of the three agents' functions have an identical ordering of chores, are additive, and evaluate every non-singleton set of chores as more burdensome than any single chore, then an EFX allocation exists. The existence of EFX allocations of chores remains open even when there are three agents with additive valuations.

1.1   Our Results

We study the existence of EFX allocations of chores for some special cases under the assumption that each agent has an additive cost function. We show that an EFX allocation always exists in each of the following three cases:

Result 1 (Theorem 6). *There exists an EFX allocation of chores when $m \leq 2n$ and each agent has an additive cost function. Moreover, we can find an EFX allocation in polynomial time.*

Result 2 (Theorem 7). *There exists an EFX allocation of chores when $n - 1$ agents have identical ordering cost functions. Moreover, we can find an EFX allocation in polynomial time.*

Result 3. *There exists an EFX allocation of chores when $n = 3$ and each agent has a personalized bi-valued cost function. Moreover, we can find an EFX allocation in polynomial time.*

The first result is the case where the number of chores is small compared to the number of agents. If m is at most n, then there is an obvious EFX allocation (each agent should be allocated at most one chore). To the best of our knowledge, Result 1 is the first nontrivial result for a small number of chores. Interestingly, as mentioned before, for the case of goods, positive results are shown only when m is at most $n + 3$ [26].

Result 2 generalizes the result of the case where n agents have identical ordering cost functions in [24]. Informally speaking, an identical ordering means that the agents have the same ordinal preference for the chores. See Sect. 4 for the formal definition of identical ordering. It should be emphasized that, in Result 2, the remaining agent can have a general cost function. Note that our result also extends the result in [34], in which they considered a more restricted case as mentioned above.

In the last result, we consider personalized bi-valued instances, in which each agent has two values for chores that may be different. Thus, personalized bi-valued instances include the bi-valued instances but not vice versa. Result 3 extends the result in [35], where a positive result was shown when $n = 3$ and each agent has a bi-valued cost function.

1.2   Related Work

Envy-Freeness up to one Item (EF1) for Goods. One of the most popular relaxed notions of EF is EF1, which was introduced by Budish [11]. EF1 requires that each agent i prefers their own bundle at least as much as the bundle of agent j after the removal of *some* good in j's bundle. Thus, EF1 is a weaker notion than EFX. While the existence of EFX allocations remains open in general, an EF1 allocation can be computed in polynomial time for any instance [14,25]. There are several studies that find not only EF1, but also efficient (particularly Pareto optimal) allocation. It is known that the maximum Nash social welfare solution satisfies both EF1 and PO (Pareto optimal) [14]. Barman et al. [6] show that an allocation satisfying both EF1 and PO can be computed in pseudo-polynomial time. It remains an open problem whether a polynomial-time algorithm exists to find an allocation that satisfies both EF1 and PO.

Envy-Freeness up to one Item (EF1) for Chores. By analogy to goods, EF1 for chores can be defined as follows. An allocation $A = (A_1, A_2, \ldots, A_n)$ of chores is called *EF1* if for all pairs of agents i and j with $A_i \neq \emptyset$, and for some $e \in A_i$, it holds that $c_i(A_i \setminus \{e\}) \leq c_i(A_j)$. In other words, each agent i prefers their own bundle at least as much as the bundle of agent j after the removal of *some* chore in i's bundle. Bhaskar et al. [8] showed an EF1 allocation of chores always exists and can be computed in polynomial time. It remains open whether there always exists an allocation that satisfies both EF1 and PO for chores.

Approximate EFX Allocations. There are several studies on approximate EFX allocations. In the case of goods, the definition of α-EFX is obtained by replacing $v_i(A_i) \geq v_i(A_j \setminus \{g\})$ with $v_i(A_i) \geq \alpha \cdot v_i(A_j \setminus \{g\})$ in the definition of EFX, where $\alpha \in [0, 1]$. It is known that there are 1/2-EFX allocations for subadditive valuations [28]. For additive valuations, there are polynomial time algorithms to compute 0.618-EFX allocations [4,19]. As for chores, there has been little research done so far. In the case of chores, the definition of α-EFX is obtained by replacing $c_i(A_i \setminus \{e\}) \leq c_i(A_j)$ with $c_i(A_i \setminus \{e\}) \leq \alpha \cdot c_i(A_j)$ in the definition of EFX, where $\alpha \geq 1$. Zhou and Wu [35] showed that there exists a polynomial time algorithm to compute a 5-EFX allocation for 3 agents and a $3n^2$-EFX allocation for $n \geq 4$ agents. It remains open whether there exist constant approximations of EFX allocation for any number of agents.

1.3   Organization

Section 2 provides definitions for terminology and notations, defines the EFX-graph, and discusses its basic properties. In Sect. 3, it is shown that an EFX allocation exists when the number of chores is at most twice the number of agents. In Sect. 4, we consider the case where the cost functions of all agents except for one are identical ordering. We omit to prove Result 3 in this paper. Refer to the full paper [23] for details.

2   Preliminaries

Let $N = \{1, 2, \ldots, n\}$ be a set of n agents and M be a set of m indivisible chores. Each agent $i \in N$ has a cost function $c_i : 2^M \to \mathbb{R}_{\geq 0}$. We assume that (i) any cost function c_i is *normalized*: $c_i(\emptyset) = 0$, (ii) it is *monotone*: $S \subseteq T$ implies $c_i(S) \leq c_i(T)$ for any $S, T \subseteq M$, and (iii) it is *additive*: $c_i(S) = \sum_{e \in S} c_i(e)$ for any $S \subseteq M$.

To simplify notation, we denote $\{1, \ldots, k\}$ by $[k]$. For any $i \in N$, $e \in M$, and $S \subseteq M$, we write $c_i(e)$ to denote $c_i(\{e\})$, and use $S \setminus e, S \cup e$ to denote $S \setminus \{e\}, S \cup \{e\}$, respectively.

For $M' \subseteq M$, an *allocation* $A = (A_1, A_2, \ldots, A_n)$ of M' is an n-partition of M', where $A_i \cap A_j = \emptyset$ for all i and j with $i \neq j$, and $\bigcup_{i \in N} A_i = M'$. In an allocation A, A_i is called a *bundle* given to agent $i \in N$. Given an allocation A, we say that agent i *envies* agent j if $c_i(A_i) > c_i(A_j)$, and agent i *strongly envies* agent j if there exists a chore e in A_i such that $c_i(A_i \setminus e) > c_i(A_j)$. An allocation A is called *EFX* if no agent strongly envies another, i.e., for any pair of agents $i, j \in N$ and $e \in A_i$, $c_i(A_i \setminus e) \leq c_i(A_j)$. It is easy to see that an allocation A is EFX if and only if for any agent $i \in N$, we have $\max_{e \in A_i} c_i(A_i \setminus e) \leq \min_{j \in [n]} c_i(A_j)$.

Let $G = (V, E)$ be a graph. A *matching* in G is a set of pairwise disjoint edges of G. A *perfect matching* in G is a matching covering all the vertices of G. For a matching X in G and a vertex v incident to an edge in X, we write $X(v)$ as the vertex adjacent to v in X. For a subgraph H of G, let $V[H]$ denote all vertices in H and $E[H]$ denote all edges in H. Similarly, $V[H]$ and $E[H]$ are defined also for a digraph H. For finite sets A and B, we denote the symmetric difference of A and B as $A \triangle B = (A \setminus B) \cup (B \setminus A)$.

EFX-Graph. In this paper, we introduce a bipartite graph called an *EFX-graph*, which plays an important role to show Results 1 to 3. Note that as a related concept, Akrami et al. [1] consider *EFX feasibility* for the setting of goods. We now define the EFX-graph and provide its basic properties.

Let U be a set of size n and $M' \subseteq M$. Note that U essentially plays the role of a copy of N. We say that $A = (A_u)_{u \in U}$ is an *allocation to U of M'* if it is an n-partition of M', where each set is indexed by an element in U, i.e., $A_u \cap A_{u'} = \emptyset$ for all u and u' with $u \neq u'$, and $\bigcup_{u \in U} A_u = M'$. For an allocation $A = (A_u)_{u \in U}$ to U, we define a bipartite graph $G_A = (N, U; E_A)$ called *EFX-graph* as follows. The vertex set consists of N and U, and the edge set E_A is defined by

$$(i, u) \in E_A \iff \max_{e \in A_u} c_i(A_u \setminus e) \leq \min_{k \in U} c_i(A_k)$$

for any $i \in N$ and $u \in U$. That is, an edge (i, u) means that agent i can receive A_u without violating the EFX conditions. We define $E_A^{\min}$ by the set of all edges corresponding to the minimum cost chore set in A, i.e., $E_A^{\min} = \{(i, u) \in E_A \mid c_i(A_u) = \min_{k \in U} c_i(A_k), i \in N\}$. See also Example 1.

Example 1. Let $N = \{1, 2, 3\}$ and $M = \{e_1, e_2, e_3, e_4, e_5, e_6\}$, and suppose that each cost function is represented as in Table 1. Consider an allocation

Table 1. The cost of each agent's chores

	e_1	e_2	e_3	e_4	e_5	e_6
agent 1	2	0	5	2	5	2
agent 2	2	4	3	3	0	3
agent 3	1	1	1	1	1	1

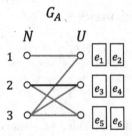

Fig. 1. EFX-graph G_A. The black and gray edges are in E_A, and the gray edges are in $E_A^{\min}$.

$A = (\{e_1, e_2\}, \{e_3, e_4\}, \{e_5, e_6\})$ to U. Then, the corresponding EFX-graph G_A is represented as in Fig. 1.

By simple observation, we see the following properties hold.

Observation 4. *Let $G_A = (N, U; E_A)$ be an EFX-graph for an allocation $A = (A_u)_{u \in U}$. Then, the following properties hold.*

(i) For $u \in U$ with $|A_u| \leq 1$, it holds that $(i, u) \in E_A$ for any $i \in N$.
(ii) For any $i \in N$, there exists $u \in U$ such that $(i, u) \in E_A^{\min}$.
(iii) If G_A has a perfect matching, then G_A has a perfect matching X such that $(i, X(i)) \in E_A^{\min}$ for some $i \in N$.

Proof. (i) If $|A_u| = 0$, the claim is obvious. If $|A_u| = 1$, then $\max_{e \in A_u} c_i(A_u \setminus e) = 0 \leq \min_{k \in U} c_i(A_k)$ for any $i \in N$. Thus, we have $(i, u) \in E_A$.

(ii) For $i \in N$, let $u \in \arg\min_{k \in U} c_i(A_k)$. Then, we have $(i, u) \in E_A^{\min}$.

(iii) Let Y be any perfect matching in G_A. If $(i, Y(i)) \in E_A^{\min}$ for some $i \in N$, then we are done. Suppose that $(i, Y(i)) \notin E_A^{\min}$ for any $i \in N$. We consider a directed bipartite graph $D_A = (N, U; F)$, where the vertex set consists of N and U, and the arc set F is defined by

$$F = \{(i, u) \mid (i, u) \in E_A^{\min}, i \in N\} \cup \{(u, Y(u)) \mid u \in U\}.$$

Since all vertices in D_A have at least one outgoing arc by (ii), D_A has a directed cycle $\vec{C}$ of length more than two by our assumption. Let C be the underlying undirected cycle of $\vec{C}$. We define a new perfect matching $X = Y \triangle E[C]$ in G_A. Then, there exists an edge $(i, X(i)) \in E_A^{\min}$ for some $i \in N$.

It is easy to see that if an EFX-graph has a perfect matching, then an EFX allocation can be obtained as follows.

Observation 5. *Let $M' \subseteq M$ and $A = (A_u)_{u \in U}$ be an allocation to U of M'. Suppose that EFX-graph G_A has a perfect matching. Then, there exists an EFX allocation of M', and it can be found in polynomial time.*

Proof. Let X be a perfect matching in G_A. We construct an allocation $A' = (A'_1, \ldots, A'_n)$ to N as follows. For each agent $i \in N$, A'_i is defined as $A_{X(i)}$, where $A_{X(i)}$ is the chore set corresponding to the vertex matched to i in X. By the definition of E_A, it holds that $\max_{e \in A'_i} c_i(A'_i \setminus e) = \max_{e \in A_{X(i)}} c_i(A_{X(i)} \setminus e) \leq \min_{k \in U} c_i(A_k) \leq \min_{j \in [n]} c_i(A'_j)$ for any $i \in N$. Thus, A' is an EFX allocation of M'.

Let $M' \subsetneq M$ and $A = (A_u)_{u \in U}$ be an allocation to U of M'. Let $e \in M \setminus M'$ be an unallocated chore and A_v be some chore set in A. We say that an allocation $A' = (A'_u)_{u \in U}$ to U of $M' \cup e$ is obtained from A by *adding e to A_v* if

$$A'_u = \begin{cases} A_v \cup e & \text{if } u = v, \\ A_u & \text{otherwise.} \end{cases}$$

The following lemma is a fundamental one that will be used repeatedly later.

Lemma 1. *Let $M' \subsetneq M$ and $A = (A_u)_{u \in U}$ be an allocation to U of M'. Suppose that there exist $i \in N$ and $e \in M \setminus M'$ such that $c_i(e) \leq c_i(e')$ for any $e' \in M'$. Let $(i, u_i) \in E_A^{\min}$ and $A' = (A'_u)_{u \in U}$ be an allocation obtained from A by adding e to A_{u_i}. Then, the following two statements hold.*

(i) $(i, u_i) \in E_{A'}$.
(ii) $(j, u) \in E_A \Rightarrow (j, u) \in E_{A'}$ for any $j \in N$ and $u \in U \setminus u_i$.

Proof. (i) Since $c_i(e) \leq c_i(e')$ for any $e' \in M'$, $\max_{f \in A'_{u_i}} c_i(A'_{u_i} \setminus f) = c_i(A'_{u_i} \setminus e) = c_i(A_{u_i})$. By the fact that $(i, u_i) \in E_A^{\min}$, $c_i(A_{u_i}) = \min_{k \in U} c_i(A_k) \leq \min_{k \in U} c_i(A'_k)$. Therefore, $\max_{f \in A'_{u_i}} c_i(A'_{u_i} \setminus f) \leq \min_{k \in U} c_i(A'_k)$, which implies $(i, u_i) \in E_{A'}$.

(ii) Fix any $j \in N$ and $u \in U \setminus u_i$ with $(j, u) \in E_A$. Since $u \in U \setminus u_i$, we have $A'_u = A_u$. Thus, $\max_{f \in A'_u} c_j(A'_u \setminus f) = \max_{f \in A_u} c_j(A_u \setminus f) \leq \min_{k \in U} c_j(A_k) \leq \min_{k \in U} c_j(A'_k)$, where the first inequality follows from $(j, u) \in E_A$. This implies $(j, u) \in E_{A'}$. $\quad\square$

The following corollary can be obtained by applying Lemma 1 for i, e, and $u_i = X(i)$.

Corollary 1. *Let $M' \subsetneq M$ and $A = (A_u)_{u \in U}$ be an allocation to U of M'. Suppose that G_A has a perfect matching X such that $(i, X(i)) \in E_A^{\min}$, and there exists $e \in M \setminus M'$ such that $c_i(e) \leq c_i(e')$ for any $e' \in M'$. Then, X is a perfect matching also in $G_{A'}$, where $A' = (A'_u)_{u \in U}$ is the allocation obtained from A by adding e to $A_{X(i)}$.*

3   Existence of EFX with at Most $2n$ Chores

In this section, we prove the following theorem by constructing a polynomial-time algorithm to find an EFX allocation when $m \leq 2n$.

Theorem 6. *There exists an EFX allocation of chores when $m \leq 2n$ and each agent has an additive cost function. Moreover, we can find an EFX allocation in polynomial time.*

Our algorithm is described in Algorithm 1. If $m \leq n$, then an EFX allocation can be obtained by allocating at most one chore to each agent. Otherwise, we denote $m = n + l$ with $1 \leq l \leq n$. Our basic idea is as follows. First, we create an allocation $A = (A_u)_{u \in U}$ to U by setting $A_u = \emptyset$ for any $u \in U$. Then, we add chores to one of the chore sets in A one by one while maintaining the condition that G_A has a perfect matching. If this condition is satisfied after all chores have been allocated, we can obtain an EFX allocation of M by Observation 5. However, in general, it is not possible to maintain this condition when adding chores in an arbitrary order. Intuitively, this is because it becomes difficult to keep an edge in G_A if heavy chores are added at the end. To address this issue, we first let l agents (e.g., agents $l, l-1, \dots, 1$) choose the chore with the smallest cost for themselves in turn and hold it. Then, we create an allocation $A = (A_u)_{u \in U}$ for the remaining n chores, such that $|A_u| = 1$ for any $u \in U$. Next, we add the held chores to the smallest chore set for each agent in the reverse order $(1, 2, \dots, l)$. By applying induction, we can show that G_A always has a perfect matching during the entire process of adding chores.

Proof (Proof of Theorem 6). We first show the correctness of Algorithm 1. By Observation 4, it is sufficient to show that G_A has a perfect matching in line 13 of Algorithm 1. If $l = 0$, that is, $m \leq n$, the first and third for-loops are not executed. After the middle for-loop is executed, $|A_u| \leq 1$ for any $u \in U$ and $R = \emptyset$. Hence, $A = (A_u)_{u \in U}$ is an allocation of M to U and G_A becomes a perfect bipartite graph by Observation 4 (i). Thus, G_A has a perfect matching.

Suppose next that $l > 0$. For $t \in \{0\} \cup [l]$, we call the t-th execution of the third for-loop *round t*. Let $A^t = (A_u^t)_{u \in U}$ be the allocation to U immediately after adding a chore in round t. We show the existence of a perfect matching in G_{A^t} by induction on t. More precisely, we show the following claim.

Claim. For any round $t \in \{0\} \cup [l]$, there exists a perfect matching X^t in G_{A^t} such that

$$(i, u) \in X^t \Rightarrow |A_u^t| = 1 \text{ for any } i \in \{t+1, \dots, n\}. \tag{1}$$

Proof (Proof of Claim 3). We show the claim by induction on t. For the base case $t = 0$, after the middle for-loop is executed, $|A_u| = 1$ holds for any $u \in U$. Hence, G_A has a perfect matching and condition (1) obviously holds. For the inductive step, we assume that Claim 3 holds for $t \in \{0\} \cup [l]$. Let X^t be a perfect matching in G_{A^t} satisfying (1). Since the first and third for-loops are executed in the reverse order with respect to i, it holds that

$$c_{t+1}(e_{t+1}) \leq c_{t+1}(e') \text{ for any } e' \in \bigcup_{u \in U} A_u^t.$$

Algorithm 1. Case when $m \leq 2n$

Input: a set of agents N, a set of chores M of size at most $2n$, and a cost function c_i
    for each $i \in N$
Output: an EFX allocation A^* of M.
1: $R \leftarrow M$ ▷ remaining set of chores
2: $A_u \leftarrow \emptyset$ for all $u \in U$, where U is a set of size n.
3: Set $l = \max\{m - n, 0\}$.
4: **for** $i = l, l - 1, \cdots, 1$ **do**
5:     Pick up $e_i \in \arg\min_{e \in R} c_i(e)$
6:     $R \leftarrow R \setminus e_i$
7: **for** $u \in U$ **do**
8:     Pick up $e \in R$ arbitrarily (if it exists).
9:     $A_u \leftarrow \{e\}, R \leftarrow R \setminus e$
10: **for** $i = 1, 2, \cdots, l$ **do**
11:     Pick up $u_i \in \arg\min_{u \in U} c_i(A_u)$
12:     $A_{u_i} \leftarrow A_{u_i} \cup e_i$
13: Find a perfect matching X on G_A.
14: Construct the allocation A^* by allocating each chore set to the matched agent in
    X.
15: **return** A^*

Thus, by applying Lemma 1 for $i = t + 1$ and $e = e_{t+1}$, we obtain the following, where we recall that $u_{t+1} \in \arg\min_{u \in U} c_{t+1}(A_u^t)$.

(i) $(t + 1, u_{t+1}) \in E_{A^{t+1}}$.
(ii) $(j, u) \in E_{A^t} \Rightarrow (j, u) \in E_{A^{t+1}}$ for any $j \in N$ and $u \in U \setminus u_{t+1}$.

We consider two cases separately.

Case 1: $(t + 1, u_{t+1}) \in X^t$
    Let $X^{t+1} = X^t$. By (i) and (ii) above, we obtain $X^{t+1} \subseteq E_{A^{t+1}}$. In addition, for $i \in \{t + 2, \ldots, n\}$, if $(i, u) \in X^{t+1} = X^t$, then $|A_u^{t+1}| = |A_u^t| = 1$ holds by the induction hypothesis. Thus, X^{t+1} is a perfect matching in $E_{A^{t+1}}$ satisfying condition (1).

Case 2: $(t + 1, u_{t+1}) \notin X^t$
    In this case, we create a new perfect matching by swapping two edges in X^t (see Fig. 2). Formally, we define $X^{t+1} = X^t \cup \{(t+1, u_{t+1}), (X^t(u_{t+1}), X^t(t+1))\} \setminus \{(t+1, X^t(t+1)), (X^t(u_{t+1}), u_{t+1})\}$. We see that $(t+1, u_{t+1}) \in E_{A^{t+1}}$ holds by (i) above and $(X^t(u_{t+1}), X^t(t+1)) \in E_{A^{t+1}}$ holds by Observation 4 (i). Hence, $X^{t+1} \subseteq E_{A^{t+1}}$. For any $i \in \{t + 2, \ldots, n\}$, if $i = X^t(u_{t+1})$, then $(i, X^t(t+1)) \in X^{t+1}$, and $|A_{X^t(t+1)}^{t+1}| = |A_{X^t(t+1)}^t| = 1$ by the induction hypothesis and $X^t(t+1) \neq u_{t+1}$. Otherwise, since $A_{X^{t+1}(i)}^{t+1} = A_{X^t(i)}^t$, $|A_{X^{t+1}(i)}^{t+1}| = |A_{X^t(i)}^t| = 1$ by the induction hypothesis. Thus, X^{t+1} is a perfect matching in $E_{A^{t+1}}$ satisfying condition (1).

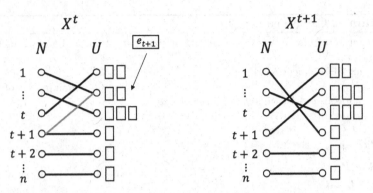

Fig. 2. Situation in Case 2 of Claim 3. The black edge set in the left figure represents X^t, and the black edge set in the right figure represents X^{t+1}. The gray edge in the left figure represents an edge in $E_{A^t}^{\min}$.

By Claim 3, there exists a perfect matching X^l in G_{A^l}. This means that there exists a perfect matching X in G_A in line 13 of Algorithm 1. Therefore, Algorithm 1 returns an EFX allocation.

We next show that Algorithm 1 runs in polynomial time. For the first for-loop, line 5 is executed in $O(m)$ time for each i. Since $l \leq n$, the first for-loop takes $O(mn)$ to execute. The second for-loop takes $O(n)$ to execute since $|U| \leq n$. The last for-loop takes $O(mn)$ to execute. Finally, we can find a perfect matching X on G_A by a maximum matching algorithm on a bipartite graph in $O(mn^2)$ time, because G_A has $O(n)$ vertices and $O(mn)$ edges. Therefore, Algorithm 1 returns an EFX allocation in $O(mn^2)$ time. Note that the running time can be improved by using a sophisticated bipartite matching algorithm, but we do not go into details.

4   When $n-1$ Agents Have Identical Ordering Cost Functions

In this section, we consider the case where $n-1$ agents have identical ordering cost functions. For any pair of agents i and j, we call the cost functions of i and j are *identical ordering* if for any e and e' in M, it holds that $c_i(e) < c_i(e') \iff c_j(e) < c_j(e')$. In other words, we can sort all the chores in non-increasing order of cost for both i and j. For $k \in [n]$, we say that k agents have identical ordering cost functions if the cost functions of any two agents among those k agents are identical ordering. We show the following theorem.

Theorem 7. *There exists an EFX allocation of chores when $n-1$ agents have identical ordering cost functions. Moreover, we can find an EFX allocation in polynomial time.*

From now on, we assume that agents $1, 2, \ldots n-1$ have identical ordering cost functions. Our algorithm is described in Algorithm 2. Our basic idea is quite similar to the approach in Sect. 3. First, we create an allocation $A = (A_u)_{u \in U}$ to U by setting $A_u = \emptyset$ for any $u \in U$. We sort the chores in non-increasing order of cost for agents $1, 2, \ldots, n-1$, which is possible as they have identical ordering cost functions. Then, in this order, we add chores to one of the chore sets in A one by one while maintaining the condition that G_A has a perfect matching. If this condition is satisfied after all chores have been allocated, we can obtain an EFX allocation of M by Observation 5. By applying induction, we can show that G_A always has a perfect matching during the entire process of adding chores.

In order to show that there exists a vertex u^* satisfying the desired condition in lines 4 and 5 of Algorithm 2, we prove the following lemma.

Algorithm 2. Case when $n - 1$ agents have identical ordering cost functions.

Input: a set of agents N, a set of chores M, and a cost function c_i for each $i \in N$, where $c_1, \ldots, c_{n-1}$ are identical ordering.
Output: an EFX allocation A^* of M.
1: $A_u \leftarrow \emptyset$ for all $u \in U$, where U is a set of size n.
2: Sort all the chores in M: $c_i(e_1) \geq c_i(e_2) \geq \cdots \geq c_i(e_m)$ for all $i \in [n-1]$.
3: **for** $t = 1, 2, \cdots, m$ **do**
4:    Find a vertex $u^* \in U$ such that $G_{A'}$ has a perfect matching,
5:    where A' is the allocation to U obtained from A by adding e_t to A_{u^*}.
6:    $A_{u^*} \leftarrow A_{u^*} \cup e_t$
7: Find a perfect matching X on G_A.
8: Construct the allocation A^* by allocating each chore set to the matched agent in X.
9: **return** A^*

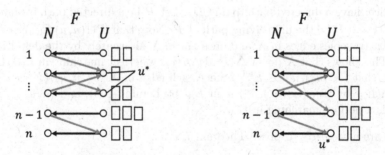

Fig. 3. Two cases in Lemma 2: D_A has a directed cycle (left) and D_A has no directed cycles (right).

Lemma 2. Let $M' \subsetneq M$ and $e \in M \setminus M'$ such that $c_i(e) \leq c_i(e')$ for any $i \in [n-1]$ and $e' \in M'$. Let $A = (A_u)_{u \in U}$ be an allocation to U of M' such that G_A has a perfect matching. Then, there exists a vertex $u^* \in U$ such that $G_{A'}$ has a perfect matching, where A' is the allocation to U of $M' \cup e$ obtained from A by adding e to A_{u^*}.

Proof. Let X be a perfect matching on G_A, and $e \in M \setminus M'$ be an unallocated chore such that $c_i(e) \le c_i(e')$ for any $i \in [n-1]$ and $e' \in M'$. For an allocation $A = (A_u)_{u \in U}$ to U of M', we consider a directed bipartite graph $D_A = (N, U; F)$, where the vertex set consists of N and U, and the arc set F is defined by

$$F = \{(i,u) \mid (i,u) \in E_A^{\min}, i \in [n-1]\} \cup \{(u, X(u)) \mid u \in U\}.$$

We consider two cases separately. See also Fig. 3.

Case 1: D_A has a directed cycle.

Let $\overrightarrow{C}$ be any directed cycle in D_A. Since the vertex $n \in N$ has no outgoing arc in D_A by the construction, we have $n \notin V[\overrightarrow{C}]$. If $|V[\overrightarrow{C}]| = 2$, define a perfect matching $X' = X$ in G_A. Otherwise, define a new perfect matching $X' = X \triangle E[C]$ in G_A, where C is the underlying (undirected) cycle of $\overrightarrow{C}$. In both cases, we pick up $i \in V[\overrightarrow{C}] \cap [n-1]$ and choose $X'(i)$ as u^*. Then, by the definition of F, it holds that $(i, X'(i)) \in E_A^{\min}$. By applying Corollary 1, $G_{A'}$ has a perfect matching X', where A' is the allocation to U of $M' \cup e$ obtained from A by adding e to $A_{X'(i)}$.

Case 2: D_A has no directed cycles.

We choose $X(n)$ as u^*. Let A' be an allocation to U of $M' \cup e$ obtained from A by adding e to $A_{X(n)}$. By the same argument as in Lemma 1 (ii), we can see that

$$(j,u) \in E_A \Rightarrow (j,u) \in E_{A'} \text{ for any } j \in N \text{ and } u \in U \setminus X(n). \tag{2}$$

If $(n, X(n)) \in E_{A'}$, then $X' = X$ is a perfect matching in $G_{A'}$ by (2). Otherwise, there exists $u \ne X(n)$ with $(n,u) \in E_{A'}^{\min}$ by Observation 4 (ii). Since all vertices except n have at least one outgoing arc in the acyclic digraph D_A, all vertices have a directed path to n in D_A. Let $\overrightarrow{P}$ be a directed path from u to n in D_A and P be the underlying path of $\overrightarrow{P}$. Note that $P \cup (n,u)$ forms a cycle, and it traverses edges in X and ones not in X alternately by the definition of F. This shows that $X' := X \triangle (P \cup (n,u))$ is a perfect matching in $E_A \cup (n,u)$ such that $(X'(u^*), u^*) \in E_A^{\min}$. Since each edge in $X' \setminus \{(n,u), (X'(u^*), u^*)\}$ is in $E_{A'}$ by (2), $(X'(u^*), u^*)$ is in $E_{A'}$ by Lemma 1 (i), and $(n,u) \in E_{A'}^{\min}$, X' is a perfect matching in $G_{A'}$.

We are now ready to prove Theorem 7.

Proof (Proof of Theorem 7). We first show the correctness of Algorithm 2. By Lemma 2, we can pick up u^* satisfying the desired condition in lines 4 and 5 of Algorithm 2. During the execution of the for-loop, we maintain the condition that G_A has a perfect matching. Thus, there exists a perfect matching in line 7 of Algorithm 2. Therefore, we can find an EFX allocation by Observation 5.

We next show that Algorithm 2 runs in polynomial time. Line 2 is easily done in polynomial time using a sorting algorithm. Lines 4 and 5 can be executed in polynomial time since we can check the condition by using a maximum matching algorithm for all $u^* \in U$, which can be done in polynomial time. Thus, the for-loop runs in polynomial time. By applying a maximum matching algorithm again, we can find a perfect matching in line 7 in polynomial time. Therefore, Algorithm 2 runs in polynomial time.

We give a remark here that, in our proofs of Lemma 2 and Theorem 7, we do not use the explicit form of the cost function of the remaining agent (agent n). Therefore, we can slightly generalize Theorem 7 so that the remaining agent can have a general (i.e., non-additive) cost function.

Acknowledgments. This work was partially supported by the joint project of Kyoto University and Toyota Motor Corporation, titled "Advanced Mathematical Science for Mobility Society" and by JSPS KAKENHI Grant Number JP20K11692.

References

1. Akrami, H., Alon, N., Chaudhury, B.R., Garg, J., Mehlhorn, K., Mehta, R.: EFX allocations: simplifications and improvements. arXiv preprint arXiv:2205.07638 (2022)
2. Amanatidis, G., et al.: Fair division of indivisible goods: recent progress and open questions. Artif. Intell. 103965 (2023)
3. Amanatidis, G., Birmpas, G., Filos-Ratsikas, A., Hollender, A., Voudouris, A.A.: Maximum nash welfare and other stories about EFX. Theor. Comput. Sci. **863**, 69–85 (2021)
4. Amanatidis, G., Markakis, E., Ntokos, A.: Multiple birds with one stone: beating 1/2 for EFX and GMMS via envy cycle elimination. Theoret. Comput. Sci. **841**, 94–109 (2020)
5. Aziz, H., Mackenzie, S.: A discrete and bounded envy-free cake cutting protocol for any number of agents. In: 2016 IEEE 57th Annual Symposium on Foundations of Computer Science (FOCS), pp. 416–427. IEEE (2016)
6. Barman, S., Krishnamurthy, S.K., Vaish, R.: Finding fair and efficient allocations. In: Proceedings of the 2018 ACM Conference on Economics and Computation, pp. 557–574 (2018)
7. Berger, B., Cohen, A., Feldman, M., Fiat, A.: Almost full EFX exists for four agents. In: Proceedings of the AAAI Conference on Artificial Intelligence, vol. 36, pp. 4826–4833 (2022)
8. Bhaskar, U., Sricharan, A.R., Vaish, R.: On approximate envy-freeness for indivisible chores and mixed resources. In: Approximation, Randomization, and Combinatorial Optimization. Algorithms and Techniques (2021)
9. Brams, S.J., Taylor, A.D.: Fair Division: From Cake-Cutting to Dispute Resolution. Cambridge University Press, Cambridge (1996)
10. Brandt, F., Conitzer, V., Endriss, U., Lang, J., Procaccia, A.D.: Handbook of Computational Social Choice. Cambridge University Press, Cambridge (2016)
11. Budish, E.: The combinatorial assignment problem: approximate competitive equilibrium from equal incomes. J. Polit. Econ. **119**(6), 1061–1103 (2011)
12. Caragiannis, I., Gravin, N., Huang, X.: Envy-freeness up to any item with high Nash welfare: the virtue of donating items. In: Proceedings of the 20th ACM Conference on Economics and Computation, pp. 527–545 (2019)
13. Caragiannis, I., Kurokawa, D., Moulin, H., Procaccia, A.D., Shah, N., Wang, J.: The unreasonable fairness of maximum Nash welfare. In: Proceedings of the 2016 ACM Conference on Economics and Computation, pp. 305–322 (2016)

14. Caragiannis, I., Kurokawa, D., Moulin, H., Procaccia, A.D., Shah, N., Wang, J.: The unreasonable fairness of maximum Nash welfare. ACM Trans. Econ. Comput. (TEAC) **7**(3), 1–32 (2019)

15. Chaudhury, B.R., Garg, J., Mehlhorn, K.: EFX exists for three agents. In: Proceedings of the 21st ACM Conference on Economics and Computation (EC), pp. 1–19 (2020)

16. Chen, X., Liu, Z.: The fairness of leximin in allocation of indivisible chores. arXiv preprint arXiv:2005.04864 (2020)

17. Dehghani, S., Farhadi, A., HajiAghayi, M., Yami, H.: Envy-free chore division for an arbitrary number of agents. In: Proceedings of the Twenty-Ninth Annual ACM-SIAM Symposium on Discrete Algorithms, pp. 2564–2583. SIAM (2018)

18. Edward Su, F.: Rental harmony: Sperner's lemma in fair division. Am. Math. Mon. **106**(10), 930–942 (1999)

19. Farhadi, A., Hajiaghayi, M.T., Latifian, M., Seddighin, M., Yami, H.: Almost envy-freeness, envy-rank, and nash social welfare matchings. In: Proceedings of the AAAI Conference on Artificial Intelligence, vol. 35, pp. 5355–5362 (2021)

20. Foley, D.K.: Resource allocation and the public sector. Yale University (1966)

21. Gafni, Y., Huang, X., Lavi, R., Talgam-Cohen, I.: Unified fair allocation of goods and chores via copies. arXiv preprint arXiv:2109.08671 (2021)

22. Gourvès, L., Monnot, J., Tlilane, L.: Near fairness in matroids. In: ECAI, vol. 14, pp. 393–398 (2014)

23. Kobayashi, Y., Mahara, R., Sakamoto, S.: EFX allocations for indivisible chores: matching-based approach. arXiv preprint arXiv:2305.04168 (2023)

24. Li, B., Li, Y., Xiaowei, W.: Almost (weighted) proportional allocations for indivisible chores. In: Proceedings of the ACM Web Conference 2022, pp. 122–131 (2022)

25. Lipton, R.J., Markakis, E., Mossel, E., Saberi, A.: On approximately fair allocations of indivisible goods. In: Proceedings of the 5th ACM Conference on Electronic Commerce, pp. 125–131 (2004)

26. Mahara, R.: Extension of additive valuations to general valuations on the existence of EFX. In: 29th Annual European Symposium on Algorithms (ESA) (2021)

27. Moulin, H.: Fair Division and Collective Welfare. MIT Press, Cambridge (2004)

28. Plaut, B., Roughgarden, T.: Almost envy-freeness with general valuations. SIAM J. Discret. Math. **34**(2), 1039–1068 (2020)

29. Procaccia, A.D.: Technical perspective: an answer to fair division's most enigmatic question. Commun. ACM **63**(4), 118–118 (2020)

30. Robertson, J., Webb, W.: Cake-cutting algorithms: be fair if you can (1998)

31. Steinhaus, H.: Sur la division pragmatique. Econometrica **17**, 315–319 (1949)

32. Stromquist, W.: How to cut a cake fairly. Am. Math. Mon. **87**(8), 640–644 (1980)

33. Woodall, D.R.: Dividing a cake fairly. J. Math. Anal. Appl. **78**(1), 233–247 (1980)

34. Yin, L., Mehta, R.: On the envy-free allocation of chores. arXiv preprint arXiv:2211.15836 (2022)

35. Zhou, S., Wu, X.: Approximately EFX allocations for indivisible chores. arXiv preprint arXiv:2109.07313 (2021)

The Price of Equity with Binary Valuations and Few Agent Types

Umang Bhaskar[1], Neeldhara Misra[2], Aditi Sethia[2(✉)], and Rohit Vaish[3]

[1] Tata Institute of Fundamental Research, Mumbai, India
umang@tifr.res.in
[2] Indian Institute of Technology Gandhinagar, Gandhinagar, India
{neeldhara.m,aditi.sethia}@iitgn.ac.in
[3] Indian Institute of Technology Delhi, New Delhi, India
rvaish@iitd.ac.in

Abstract. In fair division problems, the notion of price of fairness measures the loss in welfare due to a fairness constraint. Prior work on the price of fairness has focused primarily on envy-freeness up to one good (EF1) as the fairness constraint, and on the utilitarian and egalitarian welfare measures. Our work instead focuses on the price of equitability up to one good (EQ1) (which we term *price of equity*) and considers the broad class of *generalized p-mean* welfare measures (which includes utilitarian, egalitarian, and Nash welfare as special cases). We derive fine-grained bounds on the price of equity in terms of the *number of agent types* (i.e., the maximum number of agents with distinct valuations), which allows us to identify scenarios where the existing bounds in terms of the number of agents are overly pessimistic.

Our work focuses on the setting with binary additive valuations, and obtains upper and lower bounds on the price of equity for p-mean welfare for all $p \leqslant 1$. For any fixed p, our bounds are tight up to constant factors. A useful insight of our work is to identify the *structure* of allocations that underlie the upper (respectively, the lower) bounds *simultaneously* for all p-mean welfare measures, thus providing a unified structural understanding of price of fairness in this setting. This structural understanding, in fact, extends to the more general class of binary submodular (or matroid rank) valuations. We also show that, unlike binary additive valuations, for binary submodular valuations the number of agent types does not provide bounds on the price of equity.

Keywords: Price of Fairness · Equitability · Optimal Welfare

1 Introduction

Tradeoffs are inevitable when we pursue multiple optimization objectives that are typically not simultaneously achievable. Quantifying such tradeoffs is a fundamental problem in computation, game theory, and economics. Our focus in this work is on the "price of fairness" in the context of fair division problems, which is a notion that captures tradeoffs between *fairness* and *welfare*.

A. Deligkas and A. Filos-Ratsikas (Eds.): SAGT 2023, LNCS 14238, pp. 271–289, 2023.
https://doi.org/10.1007/978-3-031-43254-5_16

Recall that a fair division instance in the discrete setting involves a set of n *agents* $N = \{1, 2, \ldots, n\}$, m indivisible *goods* $M = \{g_1, \ldots, g_m\}$, and $\mathcal{V} := \{v_1, v_2, \ldots, v_n\}$, a *valuation profile* consisting of each agent's valuation of the goods. For any agent $i \in N$, its valuation function $v_i : 2^M \to \mathbb{N} \cup \{0\}$ specifies its numerical value (or *utility*) for every subset of goods in M. We will assume that the valuations are normalised, that is, for all $i \in N$, $v_i(M) = W$, where W is the normalisation constant. Our goal is to devise an *allocation* of goods to agents; defined as an ordered partition[1] of the m goods into n "bundles", where the bundles are (possibly empty) subsets of M, and the convention is that the ith bundle in the partition is the set of goods assigned to the agent i.

The *welfare* of an allocation is a measure of the utility that the agents derive from the allocation. For additive valuations, the individual utility that an agent i derives from their bundle A_i is simply the sum of the values that they have for the goods in A_i. The overall welfare of an allocation A is typically defined by aggregating individual utilities in various ways. Not surprisingly, there are several notions of welfare corresponding to different approaches to consolidating the individual utilities. For instance, the *utilitarian social welfare* is the sum of utilities of agents under A; the *egalitarian social welfare* is the lowest utility achieved by any agent with respect to A; and the *Nash social welfare* is the geometric mean of utilities of agents under A. One may view all of these welfare notions as special cases of the *p-mean welfare* (where $p \in (-\infty, 0) \cup (0, 1]$), which is defined as the generalized p-mean of utilities of agents under A, i.e., $W_p(A) := \left(\frac{1}{n}\sum_{i \in N}\left(v_i(A_i)\right)^p\right)^{1/p}$. Note that for $p > 1$, the p-mean optimal allocation tends to concentrate the distribution among fewer agents (consider the simple case of two identical agents with additive valuations who value each of two goods at 1), which is contrary to the spirit of fairness. Hence we focus on $p \leqslant 1$.

A natural goal for a fair division problem is to obtain an allocation that maximizes the overall welfare. However, observe that optimizing exclusively for welfare can lead to undesirable allocations. To see this, consider an instance with additive valuations where all the valuation functions are the same, i.e., the utility of any good g is the same for all agents in N. In this case, *every* allocation has the same utilitarian welfare. So, when we only optimize for—in this example, utilitarian—welfare, we have no way of distinguishing between, say, the allocation that allocates all goods to one agent and one that distributes the goods more evenly among the agents. To remedy this, one is typically interested in allocations that not only maximize welfare, but are also "fair".

There are several notions of fairness studied in the literature. Consider an allocation $A = (A_1, \ldots, A_n)$. We say that A is *envy-free* (EF) if for any pair of agents i and k, we have that i values A_i at least as much as they value A_k, i.e., $v_i(A_i) \geqslant v_i(A_k)$; and *equitable* (EQ) if every pair of agents i and k value their respective bundles equally, i.e., $v_i(A_i) = v_k(A_k)$. While both these fairness goals are natural, they may not be achievable, such as in a trivial instance with one good valued positively by two agents. This has motivated several approximations,

---

[1] Unless otherwise specified, we implicitly assume that allocations are *complete*, i.e., every good is assigned to some agent.

and in particular, the notions of *envy-freeness up to one good* and *equitability up to one good* have been widely studied. The allocation A is *envy-free up to one good* (EF1) if for any pair of agents $i, k \in N$ such that $A_k \neq \emptyset$, there is a good $g \in A_k$ such that $v_i(A_i) \geqslant v_i(A_k \setminus \{g\})$. Analogously, A is *equitable up to one good* (EQ1) if for any pair of agents $i, k \in N$ such that $A_k \neq \emptyset$, there is a good $g \in A_k$ such that $v_i(A_i) \geqslant v_k(A_k \setminus \{g\})$. For instances with additive valuations (and somewhat beyond), EF1 (and, similarly, EQ1) allocations are guaranteed to exist.

The price of fairness is informally the cost of achieving a specific fairness notion, where the cost is viewed through the lens of a particular welfare concept. For a fairness notion $\mathcal{F}$ (such as EQ1 or EF1) and a welfare notion $\mathcal{W}$ (such as egalitarian or utilitarian welfare), the price of fairness is the "worst-case ratio" of the maximum welfare (measured by $\mathcal{W}$) that can be obtained by *any* allocation, to the maximum welfare that can be obtained among allocations that are fair according to $\mathcal{F}$. For example, it is known from the work of Caragiannis et al. [15] that under additive valuations, any allocation that maximizes the Nash social welfare satisfies EF1. Thus, the price of fairness of EF1 with respect to Nash social welfare is 1. Further, Barman et al. [5] show that the price of EF1 with respect to utilitarian welfare is $O(\sqrt{n})$ for normalised subadditive valuations.

In this contribution, we focus on bounds for the price of fairness in the context of EQ1, a notion that we will henceforth refer to as the *price of equity* (PoE) when there is no ambiguity. Much of the existing literature on price of fairness analysis focuses on *specific* welfare measures (e.g., utilitarian, egalitarian, and Nash social welfare). Our work deviates from this trend by analyzing the *entire* family of generalized p-mean welfare measures (i.e., for *all* $p \leqslant 1$); recall that this captures the notions of egalitarian, utilitarian, and Nash welfare as special cases. Our results therefore address the behavior of the PoE for a wide spectrum of welfare notions.

Further, we obtain bounds in terms of the *number of agent types*—which we denote by r—rather than the total number of agents. The number of agent types of a fair division instance is the largest number of agents whose valuations are mutually distinct: in other words, it is the number of distinct valuation functions in the instance. Note that the number of agent types is potentially *much* smaller than the total number of agents. The notion of agent types has been popular in the fair division literature for the reason that it is a natural quantification of the "simplicity" of the structure of the instance as given by the valuations. Note that the well-studied special case of identical valuations is equivalent to the class of instances for which $r = 1$, and therefore one might interpret parameterizing by r as a smooth generalization of the case of identical valuations. For a representative selection of studies that focus on instances with a bounded number of agent types, we refer the reader to [10–12, 22].

We restrict ourselves to the setting of *binary submodular* (also known as matroid rank) valuations. A valuation function v_i is submodular if for any subsets of goods $S, S' \subseteq M$ such that $S \subseteq S'$, and for any good $g \notin S'$, $v_i(S \cup g) - v_i(S) \geqslant v_i(S' \cup g) - v_i(S')$. That is, the marginal value of adding g to S is at least that of

Table 1. Summary of results for the price of equity (PoE). Each cell indicates either the lower or the upper bound (columns) on PoE for a specific welfare measure (rows) as a function of the number of *agent types* r. Our contributions are highlighted by shaded boxes. The lower bounds are from Theorem 2, while the upper bounds are shown in Theorem 3 and Theorem 4. The full version of the paper [9] presents the upper and lower bounds graphically as a function of r, for $p = 1$, $p = 0$, $p = -1$, and $p = -10$.

PoE	Agent types (r)	
	Lower bound	Upper bound
Utilitarian welfare ($p = 1$)	$r - 1$	r
Nash welfare ($p = 0$)	$\frac{(r-1)/e}{\ln(r-1)}$	$\frac{(r-1)}{\ln(r-1)/e}$
Egalitarian welfare ($p \to -\infty$)	1	1 [34]
$p \in (0,1)$	$p(r-1)/e$	$2r - 1$
$p \in (-1,0)$	$2^{1/p}(r-1)^{1/(1-p)}$	$2^{-1/p}(-p)^{1/p(1-p)}(r-1)^{1/(1-p)}$
$p \leqslant -1$	$2^{1/p}(r-1)^{1/(1-p)}$	$2(r-1)^{1/(1-p)}$

adding g to a superset of S. Valuation v_i is binary submodular if for any subset of goods $S \subseteq M$ and any good g, the marginal value $v_i(S \cup g) - v_i(S) \in \{0,1\}$. Binary submodular valuations are frequently studied in fair division and are considered to be a useful special case such as in allocating items under a budget, or with exogenous quotas [7,36]. It also provides algorithmic leverage: many computational questions of interest that are hard in general turn out to be tractable once we restrict our attention to binary submodular valuations. As an example, while it is NP-hard to compute a Nash social welfare maximizing allocation even for identical additive valuations [30], such an allocation can be computed in polynomial time under binary submodular valuations in conjunction with other desirable properties such as strategyproofness, envy-freeness up to any good, and ex-ante envy-freeness [4].

A strict subset of binary submodular valuations is the class of *binary additive* valuations—this is a subclass of additive valuations wherein each value $v_i(g)$ is either 0 or 1. Binary additive valuations provide a simple way for agents to express their preferences as they naturally align with the idea of agents "approving" or "rejecting" goods. These are also widely studied in the literature on fair division, for example, see [1,3,4,25,29]. In the case of voting too, binary additive valuations play a role. Darmann and Schauer [16] consider the complexity of maximizing Nash social welfare when scores inherent in classical voting procedures are used to associate utilities with the agents' preferences, and find that the case of approval ballots—which happen to lead to binary additive valuations—are a tractable subclass.

Our Contributions and Techniques

We now turn to a discussion of our findings (see Table 1 for a summary of our results for binary additive valuations). Given an instance of fair division with binary submodular valuations, let $A^\star$ be an allocation that maximizes the Nash social welfare. It is implicit from the results of Benabbou et al. [7] that $A^\star$ also has maximum p-mean welfare for all $p \leqslant 1$ (for details, refer to Sect. 3.1). We show an analogous result for EQ1 allocations, by demonstrating that there exists an EQ1 allocation (which we call B, or the *truncated allocation*) that maximizes the p-mean welfare for all p. To this end, in allocation $A^\star$, let i be an agent with the minimum value, and let $\ell = v_i(A_i^\star)$. If the allocation is not already EQ1, then we reallocate "excess" goods from the bundles of agents who value their bundles at more than $\ell + 1$ and give them to agent i. Notice that agent i must have marginal value 0 for all these excess goods, otherwise this reallocation would improve the Nash welfare. It turns out that this allocation B is EQ1 and also has—among EQ1 allocations—the highest p-mean welfare.

Theorem 1 ($\star$). *For any $p \in \mathbb{R} \cup \{-\infty\}$ and binary submodular valuations, the p-mean welfare of the truncated allocation B is at least that of any other EQ1 allocation.*

Notice that together with the result of Benabbou et al. [7], Theorem 1 allows us to focus only on the maximum Nash social welfare allocation $A^\star$ and the truncated allocation B to obtain upper bounds on the PoE for all $p \leqslant 1$ simultaneously.

We now describe our bounds on the PoE for binary additive valuations. Our lower bounds are based on varying parameters in a single basic instance. The parameters are r, the number of agent types, and W, the normalisation constant for the agents. Given r and W, the instance has $m = rW$ goods, divided into r groups of W goods each. The groups are $M_1, M_2, \ldots, M_r$. There are $W + 1$ agents who value all the goods in M_1 at 1 each and everything else at 0. Further, for each $2 \leqslant i \leqslant r$, we have exactly one agent who values the goods in M_i and nothing else. To summarize, we have $W + 1$ agents of the first type, who have a common interest in W goods. Any allocation must leave one of these agents with zero value. Beyond these coveted goods, each of the remaining goods is valued by exactly one agent. A welfare maximizing allocation will allocate each good in $M_2 \cup \cdots \cup M_r$ to the unique agent who values it; however, an EQ1 allocation is constrained by the fact that an agent of the first type must get value 0.[2] It turns out that using this family of instances, we can obtain the following bounds.

Theorem 2 (PoE lower bounds). *Let $s := r - 1$. The price of equity for binary additive valuations is at least:*

1. *s, for $p = 1$,*
2. *$\frac{p}{e} s$, for $p \in (0, 1)$,*
3. *$\frac{s}{e \ln s}$, for $p = 0$,*
4. *$2^{1/p} s^{1/(1-p)}$, for $p < 0$.*

---

[2] For $p \leqslant 0$, we use the standard convention that allocation A is a p-mean optimal allocation if (a) it maximizes number of agents with positive value, and (b) among all allocations that satisfy (a), maximizes the p-mean welfare when restricted to agents with positive value.

We now turn to the upper bounds for binary additive valuations. It turns out that the PoE for utilitarian welfare is bounded by the *rank* of the instance, where the rank is simply the rank of the $n \times m$ matrix $\{v_i(g_j)\}_{1 \leqslant i \leqslant n; 1 \leqslant j \leqslant m}$. Observe that the rank is a lower bound for the number of agent types, so this result also implies an upper bound of r on the PoE. In fact, the rank could be logarithmic in the number of agent types, and hence this is a significantly tighter bound than the number of agent types.

To obtain this upper bound, in allocation B (which, as shown in Theorem 1, maximizes the utilitarian welfare among EQ1 allocations) we show that the number of wasted goods is at most $m(1 - \frac{1}{k})$, where k is the rank of the instance. This implies the theorem.

Theorem 3 ($(\star)$ Utilitarian PoE upper bound). *Under binary additive valuations and utilitarian welfare as the objective, the price of equity is at most the rank of the instance.*

Theorem 4 ($(\star)$ PoE upper bounds). *Let $s := r - 1$. The price of equity for binary additive valuations is at most*

1. $1 + s$ *for* $p = 1$
2. $1 + 2s$ *for* $p \in (0, 1)$
3. $\frac{s}{\ln(s/e)}$ *for* $p = 0$ *(i.e., the Nash social welfare)*
4. $s^{1/(1-p)} 2^{-1/p} (-1/p)^{1/p(p-1)}$ *for* $p \in (-1, 0)$
5. $2s^{1/(1-p)}$ *for* $p \leqslant -1$

We note that for any fixed p, the lower bounds (Theorem 2) and upper bounds (Theorem 4) are within a constant factor of each other.

Conceptually, for the proof of the upper bounds, we show that the worst case for the PoE is in fact the family of instances used for showing our lower bounds in Theorem 2. In particular, any instance can be transformed into one belonging to the lower bound family, without improving the PoE. Note that for the PoE, we can focus on the allocations $A^\star$ and B irrespective of the p-mean welfare measure, since these maximize the p-mean welfare for all $p \leqslant 1$ simultaneously. For a given instance, let l be the minimum value of any agent in $A^\star$. We divide the agent types into two groups: types for which every agent has value at most $l + 1$ in $A^\star$, and types for which an agent has value $> l + 1$. Note that for a type in the first group, each agent of this type retains its value in B, while for a type in the second group, the value of each agent of this type is truncated to $l + 1$. Our proof shows that agents in the first group must have total value at least W, as in the lower bound example. We also use W as an upper bound for the total value of each agent type in the second group. Then letting α be the fraction of agents in the first group, and optimizing over α, gives us the required upper bounds.

We then consider the PoE for binary additive valuations with the additional structure that both the rows and the columns are normalised. That is, each agent values exactly W goods, and each good is valued by exactly W_c agents. For such *doubly normalised* instances, we show the PoE is 1.

Theorem 5. *For doubly normalised instances under binary additive valuations, the PoE for the p-mean welfare is 1 for all $p \leqslant 1$.*

Finally, we obtain bounds on the PoE for binary submodular valuations. For identical valuations, it follows from similar results for EF1 that the PoE is 1.

Proposition 1 ($\star$). *When all agents have identical binary submodular valuations, the PoE is 1 for p-mean welfare measure for all $p \leqslant 1$.*

However, this is the best that can be obtained, in the sense that even with just *two* agent types, the PoE for utilitarian welfare is at least $n/6$, where n is the number of agents. Hence we cannot obtain bounds on the PoE that depend on the number of agent types, as we did for binary additive valuations.

Theorem 6 ($\star$). *The PoE for utilitarian welfare when agents have binary submodular valuations is at least $n/6$ (where n is the number of agents), even when there are just two types of agents.*

Nonetheless, we do obtain an upper bound of $2n$ on the PoE for binary submodular valuations.

Theorem 7 ($\star$). *For binary submodular valuations and any $p \leqslant 1$, the PoE for p-mean welfare is at most $2n$.*

Related Work

The notion of *price of fairness* was proposed in the works of Bertsimas et al. [8] and Caragiannis et al. [14]. These formulations were inspired from similar notions in game theory—specifically, *price of stability* and *price of anarchy*—that capture the loss in social welfare due to strategic behavior.[3] Caragiannis et al. [14] studied the price of fairness for divisible and indivisible resources under three fairness notions: *proportionality* [33], *envy-freeness* [19,21], and *equitability* [17]. For indivisible resources, they defined price of fairness only with respect to those instances that admit some allocation satisfying the fairness criterion.

Recently, Bei et al. [6] studied price of fairness for indivisible goods for fairness notions whose existence is guaranteed; in particular, they studied *envy-freeness up to one good* (EF1) and *maximum Nash welfare* allocations.[4] In a similar vein, Sun et al. [35] studied price of fairness for allocating indivisible *chores* for different relaxations of envy-freeness and maximin share. Perhaps closest to

---

[3] Price of anarchy was defined by Koutsoupias and Papadimitriou [24] and subsequently studied in the notable work of Roughgarden and Tardos [31], while price of stability was defined by Anshelevich et al. [2].

[4] The EF1 notion was formulated by Budish [13] although subsequently it was observed that an algorithm of Lipton et al. [26] achieves this guarantee for monotone valuations. The Nash social welfare function was originally proposed in the context of the bargaining problem [28] and subsequently studied for resource allocation problems by Eisenberg and Gale [18].

our work is a recent paper by Sun et al. [34]. This work studies PoE and price of equitability for any item (EQX) for indivisible goods as well as indivisible chores under utilitarian and egalitarian welfare. The valuations are assumed to be additive but not necessarily binary. For indivisible goods, the PoE is shown to be between $n - 1$ and $3n$, where n is the number of agents, while for egalitarian welfare, a tight bound of 1 is provided.

2   Preliminaries

Problem Instance. An instance of the fair division problem is specified by a tuple $\langle N, M, \mathcal{V} \rangle$, where $N = \{1, 2, \ldots, n\}$ is a set of $n \in \mathbb{N}$ *agents*, $M = \{g_1, \ldots, g_m\}$ is a set of m indivisible *goods*, and $\mathcal{V} := \{v_1, v_2, \ldots, v_n\}$ is the *valuation profile* consisting of each agent's valuation function. For any agent $i \in N$, its valuation function $v_i : 2^M \to \mathbb{N} \cup \{0\}$ specifies its numerical value (or *utility*) for every subset of goods in M. For simplicity, for a valuation function v, we will denote $v(\{g\})$ as $v(g)$.

Agents i and j are said to be of the same *type* if their valuation functions are identical, i.e., if for every subset of goods $S \subseteq M$, $v_i(s) = v_j(S)$. We will use r to denote the number of distinct agent types in an instance. Further, an instance is *normalised* if for some constant W, $v_i(M) = W$ for all agents i. Our work focuses on instances with normalised valuations, since there are trivial instances where the PoE for any p-mean welfare for $p \in \mathbb{R}$ is large without this assumption (e.g., the simple instance with 2 agents and k goods, where agent 1 has value 1 for the first good and zero for the others, and agent 2 has value 1 for all goods, has PoE $k/3$ for the utilitarian welfare).

Classes of Valuation Functions. A valuation function v is:

- *monotone* if for any two subsets of goods S and T such that $S \subseteq T$, we have $v(S) \leqslant v(T)$,
- *monotone submodular* (or simply submodular) if it is monotone and for any two subsets of goods S and T such that $S \subseteq T$ and any good $g \in M \setminus T$, we have $v(S \cup \{g\}) - v(S) \geqslant v(T \cup \{g\}) - v(T)$,
- *additive* if for any subset of goods $S \subseteq M$, we have $v(S) = \sum_{g \in S} v(g)$,
- *binary submodular* (or *matroid rank*) if it is submodular and for any subset $S \subseteq M$ and any good $g \in M \setminus S$, we have $v(S \cup \{g\}) - v(S) \in \{0, 1\}$, and
- *binary additive* if it is additive and for any good $g \in M$, $v(\{g\}) \in \{0, 1\}$.

The containment relations between these classes are as follows:

$$\text{Binary additive} \subseteq \text{Additive} \subseteq \text{Submodular} \subseteq \text{Monotone}$$

and

$$\text{Binary additive} \subseteq \text{Binary submodular} \subseteq \text{Submodular} \subseteq \text{Monotone}$$

The domains of additive and binary submodular valuations are incomparable in the sense that an instance belonging to one class may not belong to the other.

We will primarily focus on binary submodular valuations in Sect. 3 and 7, and on binary additive valuations in Sect. 4, 5, and 6.

Allocation. A *bundle* refers to any (possibly empty) subset of goods. An allocation $A := (A_1, \ldots, A_n)$ is a partition of the set of goods M into n bundles; here, A_i denotes the bundle assigned to agent i. Given an allocation A, we say that agent i values good g if $v_i(A_i \cup \{g\}) > v_i(A_i \setminus \{g\})$. Thus if $g \in A_i$, then removing g decreases i's value. Else, assigning g to A_i increases i's value. For additive valuations, specifying an allocation is unnecessary, and we say i values g if $v_i(\{g\}) = 1$. Further, for an allocation A, we say a good $g \in A_i$ is *wasted* if $v_i(A_i \setminus \{g\}) = v_i(A_i)$, i.e., if removing it does not change the value of agent i. For additive valuations, this implies that $v_i(g) = 0$. We say an allocation (possibly partial) is *wasteful* if some good is wasted (and is *non-wasteful* or *clean* otherwise). If A is a clean allocation, then for binary submodular valuations, for each agent i, $v_i(A_i) = |A_i|$.

Fairness Notions. An allocation $A = (A_1, \ldots, A_n)$ is said to be:

- *envy-free* (EF) if for any pair of agents $i, k \in N$, we have $v_i(A_i) \geqslant v_i(A_k)$ [19, 21],
- *envy-free up to one good* (EF1) if for any pair of agents $i, k \in N$ such that $A_k \neq \emptyset$, there is a good $g \in A_k$ such that $v_i(A_i) \geqslant v_i(A_k \setminus \{g\})$ [13,26],
- *equitable* (EQ) if for any pair of agents $i, k \in N$, we have $v_i(A_i) = v_k(A_k)$ [17], and
- *equitable up to one good* (EQ1) if for any pair of agents $i, k \in N$ such that $A_k \neq \emptyset$, there is a good $g \in A_k$ such that $v_i(A_i) \geqslant v_k(A_k \setminus \{g\})$ [20,23].

Pareto Optimality. An allocation $A = (A_1, \ldots, A_n)$ is said to be Pareto dominated by another allocation $B = (B_1, \ldots, B_n)$ if for every agent $i \in N$, $v_i(B_i) \geqslant v_i(A_i)$ and for some agent $k \in N$, $v_k(B_k) > v_k(A_k)$. A *Pareto optimal* allocation is one that is not Pareto dominated by any other allocation.

Welfare Measures. We will now discuss various welfare measures associated with an allocation A.

- *Utilitarian social welfare* is the sum of utilities of agents under A, i.e., $\mathcal{W}^{\text{util}}(A) := \sum_{i \in N} v_i(A_i)$.
- *Egalitarian social welfare* is the utility of the least-happy agent under A, i.e., $\mathcal{W}^{\text{egal}}(A) := \min_{i \in N} v_i(A_i)$.
- *Nash social welfare* is the geometric mean of utilities of agents under A, i.e., $\mathcal{W}^{\text{Nash}}(A) := \left(\Pi_{i \in N} v_i(A_i) \right)^{1/n}$, and
- for any $p \in \mathbb{R}$, the *p-mean welfare* is the generalized p-mean of utilities of agents under A, i.e., $\mathcal{W}_p(A) := \left(\frac{1}{n} \sum_{i \in N} v_i^p(A_i) \right)^{1/p}$.

For any $p \in \mathbb{R}$, the p-mean welfare is a strictly increasing, symmetric function of the agent values. It can be observed that utilitarian, egalitarian, and Nash welfare are all special cases of p-mean welfare for $p = 1$, $p \to -\infty$, and $p \to 0$, respectively [27].

Given an instance, it may be that in every allocation, some agent gets zero value. In this case, we need to redefine the p-mean welfare. We fix a largest subset of agents S that can simultaneously get positive value in an allocation, and then define $\mathcal{W}_p(A) = \left(\frac{1}{|S|} \sum_{i \in S} v_i^p(A_i)\right)^{1/p}$. This follows prior work on the Nash welfare, e.g., [7,15].

A *leximin* allocation is one which maximizes the minimum utility, then subject to that, it maximizes the second minimum, and so on. Thus a leximin allocation also maximizes the egalitarian welfare.

Price of Fairness. Given a fairness notion $\mathcal{F}$ (e.g., EF1, EQ1) and a p-mean welfare measure, the price of fairness of $\mathcal{F}$ with respect to a welfare measure $\mathcal{W}_p$ is the supremum over all fair division instances with n agents and m goods of the ratio of the maximum welfare (according to $\mathcal{W}_p$) of any allocation and the maximum welfare of any allocation that satisfies $\mathcal{F}$.

Formally, let $\mathcal{I}_{n,m}$ denote the set of all fair division instances with n agents and m items. Let $\mathcal{A}(I)$ denote the set of all allocations in the instance I, and further let $\mathcal{A}_{\mathcal{F}}(I)$ denote the set of all allocations in the instance I that satisfy the fairness notion $\mathcal{F}$. Then, the price of fairness (PoF) of the fairness notion $\mathcal{F}$ with respect to the welfare measure $\mathcal{W}_p$ is defined as $\mathrm{PoF}(\mathcal{F}, \mathcal{W}_p) :=$ $\sup_{I \in \mathcal{I}_{n,m}} \frac{\max_{A^* \in \mathcal{A}(I)} \mathcal{W}_p(A^*)}{\max_{B \in \mathcal{A}_{\mathcal{F}}(I)} \mathcal{W}_p(B)}$.

As indicated earlier, throughout this paper we will focus on equitability up to one good (EQ1) as the fairness notion of choice (i.e., $\mathcal{F}$ is EQ1). For notational simplicity, we will just write PoF instead of $\mathrm{PoF}(\mathcal{F}, \mathcal{W})$ whenever the welfare measure $\mathcal{W}$ is clear from context, and we will refer to this ratio as the price of equity (PoE) whenever the fairness notion in question is EQ1.

2.1   Some Properties of p-Mean Welfare

We state here some basic properties of the p-mean welfare that will be useful. For the proof of the results marked $\star$, we refer the reader to the full version of the paper [9].

Claim 1 ($\star$). For all $p < 1$, the p-mean welfare is a concave function of the agent valuations.

Corollary 1. *Given a vector of values for n agents $x \in \mathbb{R}_+^n$ and a subset $S \subseteq N$ of agents, let x' be the vector where $x_i' = x_i$ if $i \notin S$, and $x_i' = \sum_{j \in S} x_j / |S|$ if $i \in S$. Then for all $p \leqslant 1$, $\left(\frac{1}{n} \sum_{i=1}^n (x_i)^p\right)^{1/p} \leqslant \left(\frac{1}{n} \sum_{i=1}^n (x_i')^p\right)^{1/p}$ i.e., averaging out the value for a subset of agents weakly increases the p-mean welfare.*

Claim 2 ($\star$). Given $l \in \mathbb{N}$, and a vector $(x_1, \ldots, x_l) \in \mathbb{R}_+^l$, for $p \in [0,1]$, $\frac{1}{l} \sum_{i=1}^l x_i^{1-p} \leqslant \left(\frac{1}{l} \sum_{i=1}^l x_i\right)^{1-p}$ while for $p < 0$, the opposite inequality holds.

3   Optimal Allocations for Binary Submodular Valuations

We first show that for obtaining bounds on the PoE for the class of binary submodular valuations (and hence, for binary additive valuations), we can focus on two allocations: the first is the Nash welfare optimal allocation A^*, which obtains the optimal p-mean welfare for all $p \leqslant 1$, and the second is the truncated allocation B, which obtains the optimal p-mean welfare among all EQ1 allocations for all $p \in \mathbb{R} \cup \{-\infty\}$.

3.1   An Optimal p-Mean Welfare Allocation

Benabbou et al. [7] show the following results.

Proposition 2 ([7], **Theorem 3.14**). *Let $\Phi : \mathbb{Z}^n \to \mathbb{R}$ be a symmetric strictly convex function, and let $\Psi : \mathbb{Z}^n \to \mathbb{R}$ be a symmetric strictly concave function. Let A be some allocation. For binary submodular valuations, the following statements are equivalent:*

1. *A is a minimizer of Φ over all the utilitarian optimal allocations,*
2. *A is a maximizer of Ψ over all the utilitarian optimal allocations,*
3. *A is a leximin allocation, and*
4. *A maximizes Nash social welfare.*

Proposition 3 ([7], **Theorem 3.11**). *For binary submodular valuations, any Pareto optimal allocation is utilitarian optimal.*

For $p \leqslant 1$, if the p-mean welfare function was strictly concave, then it would follow immediately that the Nash welfare optimal allocation A^* in fact simultaneously maximizes the p-mean welfare for all $p \leqslant 1$. However, in general the p-mean welfare is concave (Claim 1), but not strictly concave. E.g., for any $p \leqslant 1$ and any vector of values $v = (v_1, \ldots, v_n)$ with $v_i > 0$ for all agents i, let us overload notation slightly and define $\mathcal{W}_p(v) = \left(\frac{1}{n} \sum_{i=1}^n v_i^p\right)^{1/p}$. Then $\mathcal{W}_p(2v) = (\mathcal{W}_p(v) + \mathcal{W}_p(3v))/2$, violating strict concavity. However, we can slightly modify the proof of Theorem 3.14 from [7], to obtain the following result. The modified proof is in the full version [9].

Proposition 4 (⋆). *For binary submodular valuations, any Nash welfare maximizing allocation (and hence, leximin allocation) simultaneously maximizes the p-mean welfare for all $p \leqslant 1$.*

The following property of leximin allocations is useful in the proof of Proposition 4.

Proposition 5 (⋆). *For agents with binary submodular valuations, let A be a utilitarian optimal allocation so that $\max_i v_i(A_i) \leqslant \min_i v_i(A_i) + 1$. Then A is a leximin allocation.*

3.2 An Optimal p-Mean Welfare EQ1 allocation

We now show that similarly, there exists an EQ1 allocation B that maximizes the p-mean welfare for all p. Given $A^\star$, allocation B is obtained as follows, which we call the *truncated allocation*. Let $l = \min_i v_i(A_i^\star)$ be the smallest value that any agent obtains in $A^\star$, and let i_l be an agent that has this minimum value. Note that for any agent i, if $v_i(A_i^\star) \geqslant l+2$, then all goods allocated to i must have marginal value 0 for the agent i_l, i.e., for all $g \in A_i^\star$, $v_{i_l}(A_{i_l}^\star \cup \{g\}) = v_{i_l}(A_{i_l}^\star)$ (else we can increase the Nash social welfare by re-allocating any good that violates this to agent i_l).

For the EQ1 allocation that we would like to construct, for any agent i with $v_i(A_i^\star) \geqslant l+2$, we remove goods from $A_i^\star$ until i's value for the remaining bundle is $l+1$. We allocate the removed goods to agent i_l (that has marginal value 0 for these goods). Let B be the resulting allocation. Then clearly, if $v_i(A_i^\star) \in \{l, l+1\}$, then $v_i(B_i) = v_i(A_i^\star)$, else $v_i(B_i) = l+1$. Thus, allocation B, our truncated NSW allocation, is EQ1.

Theorem 1 ($\star$). *For any $p \in \mathbb{R} \cup \{-\infty\}$ and binary submodular valuations, the p-mean welfare of the truncated allocation B is at least that of any other EQ1 allocation.*

4 Lower Bounds on the PoE for Binary Additive Valuations

Theorem 2 (PoE lower bounds). *Let $s := r - 1$. The price of equity for binary additive valuations is at least:*

1. s, *for $p = 1$,*
2. $\frac{p}{e}s$, *for $p \in (0, 1)$,*
3. $\frac{s}{e \ln s}$, *for $p = 0$,*
4. $2^{1/p}s^{1/(1-p)}$, *for $p < 0$.*

Note that as $p \to -\infty$, $2^{1/p}s^{1/(1-p)} \to 1$.

Proof. All our lower bounds are based on varying parameters in a single instance. The parameters are r, the number of agent types, and W, the normalisation constant for the agents. Given r, W, the instance has $m = rW$ goods, divided into r groups of W goods each. The groups are M_1, M_2, ..., M_r. There are $W + 1$ agents of the first agent type, and 1 agent each of the remaining $r - 1$ types (thus, $n = W + r$). Agents of type t have value 1 for the goods in group M_t, and value 0 for all other goods. The instance is thus *disjoint*; no good has positive value for agents of two different types.

We use Λ_p to denote the PoE for this instance. Then Λ_p is exactly

$$\Lambda_p = \left(\frac{\frac{1}{W+r-1}(W \times 1^p + (r-1) \times W^p)}{\frac{1}{W+r-1}(W \times 1^p + (r-1) \times 1^p)} \right)^{1/p} = \left(\frac{W + s \times W^p}{W + s} \right)^{1/p}.$$

For each of the cases in the theorem, we will now show how to choose W to obtain the bound claimed. For $p = 1$, choose $W = s^2$. For $p \in (0,1)$, choose $W = ps$. For $p = 0$, choose $W = s/\ln s$. For $p < 0$, choose W so that $W = sW^p$, or $W = s^{1/(1-p)}$.

Due to lack of space, we defer the details of the calculations to the full version [9]. □

5   Upper Bounds on the PoE for Binary Additive Valuations

5.1   Upper Bounds on the PoE for $p = 1$

Theorem 3 ((⋆) Utilitarian PoE upper bound). *Under binary additive valuations and utilitarian welfare as the objective, the price of equity is at most the rank of the instance.*

It follows immediately from the theorem that the PoE is also bounded by the number of agent types.

Corollary 2. *Under binary additive valuations and utilitarian welfare as the objective, the price of equity is at most r, the number of agent types.*

5.2   Upper Bounds on the PoE for $p < 1$

From Proposition 2 and Theorem 1, to bound the PoE for any $p < 1$, it suffices to obtain an upper bound on the ratio of the p-mean welfare for the two allocations $A^\star$ (which maximizes the Nash welfare) and B (the truncated allocation). We will use various properties of the allocations $A^\star$ and B in the following proofs. To state these, define T_k as the set of agents of type k, and let S_k be the set of goods allocated to agents in T_k by $A^\star$. That is, $S_k := \cup_{i \in T_k} A_i^\star$. Let $m_k := |S_k|$, and $n_k := |T_k|$. Then note that for each agent $i \in T_k$, $v_i(A_i^\star) = |A_i^\star| \in \left\{ \left\lfloor \frac{m_k}{n_k} \right\rfloor, \left\lceil \frac{m_k}{n_k} \right\rceil \right\}$.

We reindex the types in increasing order of the averaged number of goods assigned by $A^\star$, so that $m_i/n_i \leqslant m_{i+1}/n_{i+1}$. Now define

$$\lambda := \begin{cases} \left\lceil \frac{m_1}{n_1} \right\rceil & \text{if } m_1/n_1 \text{ is fractional} \\ 1 + \frac{m_1}{n_1} & \text{if } m_1/n_1 \text{ is integral.} \end{cases}$$

Thus λ is integral, $\lambda > m_1/n_1$, and $\lambda \geqslant 2$ (since the p-mean welfare is only taken over agents with positive valuation, $m_1 \geqslant n_1$). Note that in $A^\star$, the smallest value of any agent is $\lfloor m_1/n_1 \rfloor$, and $\lambda \leqslant 1 + \lfloor m_1/n_1 \rfloor$. Hence agents with value at most λ in $A^\star$ will retain their value in allocation B, while other agents will have their values truncated to λ. Now let ρ be the highest index so that $\lambda \geqslant m_\rho/n_\rho$. Thus,

$$\lambda \geqslant \frac{\sum_{i=1}^{\rho} m_i}{\sum_{i=1}^{\rho} n_i}. \tag{1}$$

As stated above, any agent of type $k \leqslant \rho$ will retain their value, i.e., $v_i(B_i) = v_i(A_i^\star)$ for an agent i of type $k \leqslant \rho$. We claim that agents of the first ρ types must have got at least W goods under $A^\star$.

Claim 3 ($\star$). $\sum_{i=1}^{\rho} m_i \geqslant W$.

Then from (1) and Claim 3, we obtain

$$\lambda \geqslant W / \sum_{i=1}^{\rho} n_i. \tag{2}$$

We now obtain a general expression for bounding the PoE for all $p \leqslant 1$. We will then optimize this expression for different ranges of p, to obtain upper bounds on the PoE.

Lemma 1 ($\star$). *The price of equity for p-mean welfare for instances with r types is at most*

1. $\sup_{\alpha \in [0,1]} \left(\alpha + \alpha^p s^p (1-\alpha)^{1-p} \right)^{1/p}$ *for $p < 0$*
2. $\sup_{\alpha \in [0,1]} \left(\frac{s\alpha}{1-\alpha} \right)^{(1-\alpha)}$ *for $p = 0$,*
3. $\sup_{\alpha \in [0,1]} \left(\alpha + 2^p \alpha^p s^p (1-\alpha)^{1-p} \right)^{1/p}$ *for $p \in (0,1)$.*

where as before, $s = r - 1$.

Theorem 4 (($\star$) PoE upper bounds). *Let $s := r - 1$. The price of equity for binary additive valuations is at most*

1. $1 + s$ *for $p = 1$*
2. $1 + 2s$ *for $p \in (0,1)$*
3. $\frac{s}{\ln(s/e)}$ *for $p = 0$ (i.e., the Nash social welfare)*
4. $s^{1/(1-p)} 2^{-1/p} (-1/p)^{1/p(p-1)}$ *for $p \in (-1,0)$*
5. $2s^{1/(1-p)}$ *for $p \leqslant -1$*

6   PoE Bounds for Doubly Normalised Instances

So far, we have considered instances with binary additive normalised valuations, where each agent values the same number W of goods. In this case, for the utilitarian welfare, we have seen that the PoE can be as bad as r, the number of types of agents. In this section, we consider instances with further structure. In *doubly normalised* instances, each good g is valued by the same number W_c of agents. Thus, $v_i(M) = W$ for all $i \in N$, and $\sum_{i \in N} v_i(g) = W_c$ for every good $g \in M$. The valuation matrix V is thus both row and column normalised. Such instances are intuitively "balanced," and we ask if this balance is reflected in the PoE for such instances. This indeed turns out to be the case.

Theorem 5. *For doubly normalised instances under binary additive valuations, the PoE for the p-mean welfare is 1 for all $p \leqslant 1$.*

For an undirected graph, the edge-incident matrix X has entry $X_{i,e} = 1$ if edge e is incident on vertex i, and $X_{i,e} = 0$ otherwise. We will use the following well-known property of edge-incidence matrices for bipartite graphs.

Proposition 6 (e.g., [32]). *If G is a bipartite graph, then the edge-incidence matrix of G is totally unimodular.*

Proof of Theorem 5. Let V be the valuation matrix for a doubly normalised instance, where each row sums to W and each column sums to W_c. Divide each entry by W_c. Let V^f be the resulting matrix. Then V^f satisfies: (i) each entry is either 0 or $1/W_c$, (ii) each column sums to 1, and (iii) each row sums to W/W_c. We will show that the matrix V^f can be represented as the convex combination of nonnegative integer matrices $X^1, \ldots, X^t$ so that for any matrix X^k in this decomposition, each column sums to 1 and each row sums to either $\lceil W/W_c \rceil$ or $\lfloor W/W_c \rfloor$. Assuming such a decomposition, fix any such matrix X^k in this decomposition. Clearly, due to (ii) and nonnegativity, each entry of X^k is either 1 or 0. Further if the entry $X^k_{i,g} = 1$, then $V^f_{i,g} = 1/W_c$ since V^f is a convex combination of the M-matrices, and hence $V_{i,g} = 1$. Consider then the allocation A that assigns good g to agent i if $X^k_{i,g} = 1$. In this allocation, following the properties of X^k, each good is assigned to an agent that has value 1 for it, and each agent is assigned either $\lceil W/W_c \rceil$ or $\lfloor W/W_c \rfloor$ goods. The allocation is thus EQ1 and maximizes the utilitarian welfare. Further by Proposition 5 this is also a leximin allocation, and hence by Proposition 4 and Proposition 2 this maximizes the p-mean welfare for all $p \leqslant 1$, proving the theorem. It remains to show that V can be decomposed as stated. We defer that to the full version [9]. □

In the full version [9], we offer an alternate proof of Theorem 5, based on a so-called "eating argument" and an extension of Hall's theorem.

7 PoE Bounds for Binary Submodular Valuations

We now consider the more general case of binary submodular valuations. Here we focus on the utilitarian welfare, and show that our results for binary additive valuations that bound the PoE by the number of types of agents do not extend to binary submodular valuations. We first show that from prior work (see Proposition 7 below), it follows that if the agents have identical valuations, then PoE is 1 for the p-mean welfare objective for all $p \leqslant 1$.

Proposition 1 ($\star$). *When all agents have identical binary submodular valuations, the PoE is 1 for p-mean welfare measure for all $p \leqslant 1$.*

As earlier, an allocation $A = (A_1, \ldots, A_n)$ is *clean* if for all agents i, $v_i(A_i) = |A_i|$, that is, no good is wastefully allocated. We note that, given any allocation A, we can obtain a clean (possibly partial) allocation $\hat{A}$ so that $v_i(A_i) = v_i(\hat{A}_i)$ for all agents i by repeatedly removing wasted items from the allocation A. We will use the following result due to Benabbou at al. [7].

Proposition 7 ([7], Corollary 3.8). *For binary submodular valuations, any clean, utilitarian optimal (partial) allocation that minimizes $\Phi(A) := \sum_i v_i(A_i)^2$ among all utilitarian optimal allocations is EF1.*

The bound in Proposition 1 is, in a certain sense, the best that can be obtained. We will now show that with more than one type of agent under binary submodular valuations, the PoE is at least $n/6$ for utilitarian welfare. Hence we cannot obtain bounds on the PoE that depend on the number of agent types for all $p \leqslant 1$, as we did for binary additive valuations.

Theorem 6 ($\star$). *The PoE for utilitarian welfare when agents have binary submodular valuations is at least $n/6$ (where n is the number of agents), even when there are just two types of agents.*

Theorem 7 ($\star$). *For binary submodular valuations and any $p \leqslant 1$, the PoE for p-mean welfare is at most $2n$.*

8 Some Concluding Remarks on Chores

Our focus in the paper has been on goods, where agents have non-negative marginal utility for all items. We briefly remark on the case of bads or chores, where all marginal utilities are non-positive. Consider any instance with binary additive valuations, i.e., the value of each item is either 0 or -1. It is not hard to see that in these instances, there is always a utilitarian optimal EQ1 allocation: if chore c has value 0 for an agent i, assign c to i. The remaining chores have value -1 for all agents, and can be assigned using the round robin procedure. This allocation is clearly EQ1 and also achieves the best possible utilitarian welfare.

For more general additive instances with chores, we now show that the PoE is unbounded, even in very simple cases.[5] To this end, consider the following example with $2n$ items and $n + 1$ agents. The first n agents mildly dislike the first n chores, at $-\epsilon$ and severely dislike the last n at -1, while it is the opposite for the $(n + 1)$th agent, who strongly dislikes the first n items at -1 and mildly dislikes the last n at $-\epsilon$. In this example, the maximum utility is $-2n\epsilon$: assign the first n chores to the first agent and the last n chores to the last agent. On the other hand, in any EQ1 allocation, the last agent can get at most 2 chores, and hence some agent gets a chore that they value at -1. The PoE is thus at least $1/(2n\epsilon)$, which can be made arbitrarily large by choosing ϵ appropriately. Note that this instance has two item types, two agent types, and only two distinct entries in the valuation matrix. Relaxing any of these conditions implies identical valuations, where the PoE is 1; so, in some sense, this is a "minimally complex" example that already exhibits unbounded PoE. There is thus a sharp change in the PoE between instances where the values are in $\{0, -1\}$ and those where the values are in $\{-\epsilon, -1\}$. While the PoE is unbounded as ϵ approaches 0, it "snaps back" to 1 at $\epsilon = 0$.

To conclude, we obtain nearly tight bounds on the PoE in terms of agent types for the p-mean welfare spectrum. This captures, as special cases, the notions of

---

[5] For chores, we adopt the natural definition of PoE: the ratio of the utilitarian welfare of the best EQ1 allocation, to the maximum utilitarian welfare obtainable in any allocation. Note that if the denominator is 0, then so is the numerator (and this can be identified in polynomial time).

utilitarian, egalitarian, and Nash welfare. Our bounds are in terms of agent types (r) rather than the number of agents. Overall, our results provide a fine-grained perspective on the behavior of the PoE parameterized by p and r. In future work, it would be interesting to extend the insights that we obtain in this work beyond the domain of binary valuations. We also propose obtaining bounds on the PoE parameterized by other structural parameters, such as the number of item types. We note that for additive valuations, the rank of the valuation matrix is a lower bound on the number of item types, and hence Theorem 3 bounds the PoE in this case by the number of item types as well.

Acknowledgments. We thank the anonymous reviewers from SAGT 2023 and COMSOC 2023 for helpful comments. We are especially grateful to an anonymous reviewer from COMSOC 2023 who pointed out an error in the proof of Lemma 1 in an earlier version of the draft and provided several other helpful comments. RV acknowledges support from DST INSPIRE grant no. DST/INSPIRE/04/2020/000107 and SERB grant no. CRG/2022/002621.

References

1. Amanatidis, G., Birmpas, G., Filos-Ratsikas, A., Hollender, A., Voudouris, A.A.: Maximum nash welfare and other stories about EFX. Theoret. Comput. Sci. **863**, 69–85 (2021)
2. Anshelevich, E., Dasgupta, A., Kleinberg, J., Tardos, É., Wexler, T., Roughgarden, T.: The price of stability for network design with fair cost allocation. SIAM J. Comput. **38**(4), 1602–1623 (2008)
3. Aziz, H., Rey, S.: Almost group envy-free allocation of indivisible goods and chores. In: Proceedings of the 29th International Conference on International Joint Conferences on Artificial Intelligence, pp. 39–45 (2021)
4. Babaioff, M., Ezra, T., Feige, U.: Fair and truthful mechanisms for dichotomous valuations. In: Proceedings of the 35th AAAI Conference on Artificial Intelligence, vol. 35, pp. 5119–5126 (2021)
5. Barman, S., Bhaskar, U., Shah, N.: Optimal bounds on the price of fairness for indivisible goods. In: Proceedings of the 16th International Conference on Web and Internet Economics, pp. 356–369 (2020)
6. Bei, X., Lu, X., Manurangsi, P., Suksompong, W.: The price of fairness for indivisible goods. Theory Comput. Syst. **65**(7), 1069–1093 (2021). https://doi.org/10.1007/s00224-021-10039-8
7. Benabbou, N., Chakraborty, M., Igarashi, A., Zick, Y.: Finding fair and efficient allocations for matroid rank valuations. ACM Trans. Econ. Comput. **9**(4), 1–41 (2021)
8. Bertsimas, D., Farias, V.F., Trichakis, N.: The price of fairness. Oper. Res. **59**(1), 17–31 (2011)
9. Bhaskar, U., Misra, N., Sethia, A., Vaish, R.: The Price of Equity with Binary Valuations and Few Agent Types. arXiv preprint arXiv:2307.06726 (2023)
10. Bliem, B., Bredereck, R., Niedermeier, R.: Complexity of efficient and envy-free resource allocation: few agents, resources, or utility levels. In: Proceedings of the 25th International Joint Conference on Artificial Intelligence, pp. 102–108 (2016)

11. Bouveret, S., Cechlárová, K., Elkind, E., Igarashi, A., Peters, D.: Fair division of a graph. In: Proceedings of the 26th International Joint Conference on Artificial Intelligence, pp. 135–141 (2017)
12. Brânzei, S., Lv, Y., Mehta, R.: To give or not to give: fair division for single minded valuations. In: Proceedings of the Twenty-Fifth International Joint Conference on Artificial Intelligence, pp. 123–129 (2016)
13. Budish, E.: The combinatorial assignment problem: approximate competitive equilibrium from equal incomes. J. Polit. Econ. **119**(6), 1061–1103 (2011)
14. Caragiannis, I., Kaklamanis, C., Kanellopoulos, P., Kyropoulou, M.: The efficiency of fair division. Theory Comput. Syst. **50**(4), 589–610 (2012)
15. Caragiannis, I., Kurokawa, D., Moulin, H., Procaccia, A.D., Shah, N., Wang, J.: The unreasonable fairness of maximum nash welfare. ACM Trans. Econ. Comput. **7**(3), 1–32 (2019)
16. Darmann, A., Schauer, J.: Maximizing nash product social welfare in allocating indivisible goods. Eur. J. Oper. Res. **247**(2), 548–559 (2015)
17. Dubins, L.E., Spanier, E.H.: How to cut a cake fairly. Am. Math. Mon. **68**(1P1), 1–17 (1961)
18. Eisenberg, E., Gale, D.: Consensus of subjective probabilities: the Pari-Mutuel method. Ann. Math. Stat. **30**(1), 165–168 (1959)
19. Foley, D.: Resource Allocation and the Public Sector. Yale Economic Essays, pp. 45–98 (1967)
20. Freeman, R., Sikdar, S., Vaish, R., Xia, L.: Equitable allocations of indivisible goods. In: Proceedings of the 28th International Joint Conference on Artificial Intelligence, pp. 280–286 (2019)
21. Gamow, G., Stern, M.: Puzzle-Math (1958)
22. Garg, J., Kulkarni, P., Murhekar, A.: On fair and efficient allocations of indivisible public goods. In: Proceedings of the 41st IARCS Annual Conference on Foundations of Software Technology and Theoretical Computer Science. LIPIcs, vol. 213, pp. 22:1–22:19 (2021)
23. Gourvès, L., Monnot, J., Tlilane, L.: Near fairness in matroids. In: Proceedings of the 21st European Conference on Artificial Intelligence, pp. 393–398 (2014)
24. Koutsoupias, E., Papadimitriou, C.: Worst-case equilibria. Comput. Sci. Rev. **3**(2), 65–69 (2009)
25. Kyropoulou, M., Suksompong, W., Voudouris, A.A.: Almost envy-freeness in group resource allocation. Theoret. Comput. Sci. **841**, 110–123 (2020)
26. Lipton, R.J., Markakis, E., Mossel, E., Saberi, A.: On approximately fair allocations of indivisible goods. In: Proceedings of the 5th ACM Conference on Electronic Commerce, pp. 125–131 (2004)
27. Moulin, H.: Fair Division and Collective Welfare. MIT Press, Cambridge (2004)
28. Nash Jr., J.F.: The bargaining problem. Econometrica 155–162 (1950)
29. Ortega, J.: Multi-unit assignment under dichotomous preferences. Math. Soc. Sci. **103**, 15–24 (2020)
30. Roos, M., Rothe, J.: Complexity of social welfare optimization in multiagent resource allocation. In: Proceedings of the 9th International Conference on Autonomous Agents and Multiagent Systems, pp. 641–648 (2010)
31. Roughgarden, T., Tardos, É.: How bad is selfish routing? J. ACM **49**(2), 236–259 (2002)
32. Schrijver, A.: Theory of Linear and Integer Programming. Wiley, Hoboken (1998)
33. Steinhaus, H.: The problem of fair division. Econometrica **16**(1), 101–104 (1948)
34. Sun, A., Chen, B., Doan, X.V.: Equitability and welfare maximization for allocating indivisible items. Auton. Agents Multi-Agent Syst. **37**(8) (2023)

35. Sun, A., Chen, B., Vinh Doan, X.: Connections between fairness criteria and efficiency for allocating indivisible chores. In: Proceedings of the 20th International
Conference on Autonomous Agents and MultiAgent Systems, pp. 1281–1289 (2021)
36. Viswanathan, V., Zick, Y.: A general framework for fair allocation with matroid
rank valuations. In: Proceedings of the 24th ACM Conference on Economics and
Computation, pp. 1129–1152 (2023)

The Frontier of Intractability for EFX with Two Agents

Paul W. Goldberg[1], Kasper Høgh[2], and Alexandros Hollender[3](✉)

[1] University of Oxford, Oxford, UK
paul.goldberg@cs.ox.ac.uk
[2] Aarhus University, Aarhus, Denmark
kh@cs.au.dk
[3] EPFL, Lausanne, Switzerland
alexandros.hollender@epfl.ch

Abstract. We consider the problem of sharing a set of indivisible goods among agents in a fair manner, namely such that the allocation is envy-free up to any good (EFX). We focus on the problem of computing an EFX allocation in the two-agent case and characterize the computational complexity of the problem for most well-known valuation classes. We present a simple greedy algorithm that solves the problem when the agent valuations are weakly well-layered, a class which contains gross substitutes and budget-additive valuations. For the next largest valuation class we prove a negative result: the problem is **PLS**-complete for submodular valuations. All of our results also hold for the setting where there are many agents with identical valuations.

1 Introduction

The field of fair division studies the following fundamental question: given a set of resources, how should we divide them among a set of agents (who have subjective preferences over those resources) in a fair way? This question arises naturally in many settings, such as divorce settlement, division of inheritance, or dissolution of a business partnership, to name just a few. Although the motivation for studying this question is perhaps almost as old as humanity itself, the first mathematical investigation of the question dates back to the work of Banach, Knaster and Steinhaus [29, 30].

Of course, in order to study fair division problems, one has to define what exactly is meant by a *fair* division. Different fairness notions have been proposed to formalize this. Banach, Knaster and Steinhaus considered a notion which is known today as *proportionality*: every agent believes that it obtained at least a fraction $1/n$ of the total value available, where n is the number of agents. A generally[1] stronger notion, and one which seems more adapted to the motivating examples we mentioned above, is that of *envy-freeness* [16, 18, 33]. A division of

---

[1] As long as agents' valuations are subadditive, every envy-free division also satisfies proportionality.

A. Deligkas and A. Filos-Ratsikas (Eds.): SAGT 2023, LNCS 14238, pp. 290–307, 2023.
https://doi.org/10.1007/978-3-031-43254-5_17

the resources is said to be envy-free, if no agent is envious, i.e., no agent values the bundle of resources obtained by some other agent strictly more than what it obtained itself.

As our motivating examples already suggest, the case with few agents – in fact, even just with two agents – is very relevant in practice. When the resources are divisible, such as for example money, water, oil, or time, the fair division problem with two agents admits a very simple and elegant solution: the cut-and-choose algorithm, which already appears in the Book of Genesis. As its name suggests, in the cut-and-choose algorithm one agent cuts the resources in half (according to its own valuation), and the other agent chooses its preferred piece, leaving the other piece to the first agent. It is easy to check that this guarantees envy-freeness, among other things. The case of divisible resources, which is usually called *cake cutting*, has been extensively studied for more than two agents. One of the main objectives in that line of research can be summarized as follows: come up with approaches that achieve similar guarantees to cut-and-choose, but for more than two agents. This has been partially successful, and notable results include the proof of the existence of an envy-free allocation for any number of agents [31,32,34], as well as a finite, albeit very inefficient, protocol for computing one [5].

In many cases, however, assuming that the resources are divisible might be too strong an assumption. Indeed, some resources are inherently *indivisible*, such as a house, a car, or a company. Sometimes these resources can be made divisible by sharing them over time, for example, one agent can use the car over the weekend and the other agent on weekdays. But, in general, and in particular when agents are not on friendly terms with each other, as one would expect to often be the case for divorce settlements, this is not really an option.

Indivisible resources make the problem of finding a fair division more challenging. First of all, in contrast to the divisible setting, envy-free allocations are no longer guaranteed to exist. Indeed, this is easy to see even with just two agents and a single (indivisible) good that both agents would like to have. No matter who is given the good, the other agent will envy them. In order to address this issue of non-existence of a solution, various relaxations of envy-freeness have been proposed and studied in the literature. The strongest such relaxation, namely the one which seems closest to perfect envy-freeness, is called *envy-freeness up to any good* and is denoted by EFX [11,19]. An allocation is EFX if for all agents i and j, agent i does not envy agent j, after removal of *any* single good from agent j's bundle. In other words, an allocation is *not* EFX, if and only if there exist agents i and j, and a good in j's bundle, so that i envies j's bundle even after removal of that good.

For this relaxed notion of envy-freeness, it is possible to recover existence, at least in some cases. An EFX allocation is guaranteed to exist for two agents with any monotone valuations [27], and for three agents if we restrict the valuations to be additive [12]. It is currently unknown whether it always exists for four or more agents, even just for additive valuations.

Surprisingly, proving the existence of EFX allocations for two agents is non-trivial. In order to use the cut-and-choose approach, we need to be able to "cut in half". In the divisible setting, this is straightforward. But, in the indivisible setting, we need to "cut in half in the EFX sense," i.e., divide the goods into two bundles such that the first agent is EFX with either bundle. In other words, we first need to show the existence of EFX allocations for two identical agents, namely two agents who share the same valuation function, which is not a trivial task.

Plaut and Roughgarden [27] provided a solution to this problem by introducing the *leximin++ solution*. Given a monotone valuation function, they defined a total ordering over all allocations called the leximin++ ordering. They proved that for two identical agents, the leximin++ solution, namely the global maximum with respect to the leximin++ ordering, must be an EFX allocation. As mentioned above, using the cut-and-choose algorithm, this shows the existence of EFX allocations for two, possibly different, agents. Unfortunately, computing the leximin++ solution is computationally intractable[2] and so, while this argument proves the existence of EFX allocations, it does not yield an efficient algorithm.

Nevertheless, for two agents with *additive* valuations, Plaut and Roughgarden [27] provided a polynomial-time algorithm based on a modification of the Envy-Cycle elimination algorithm of Lipton et al. [23]. They also provided a lower bound for the problem in the more general class of submodular valuations, but not in terms of computational complexity (i.e., not in the standard Turing machine model). Namely, they proved that for two identical agents with submodular valuations computing an EFX allocation requires an exponential number of queries in the query complexity model.

Their work naturally raises the following two questions about the problem of computing an EFX allocation for two agents:

1. What is the *computational* complexity of the problem for submodular valuations?
2. What is the computational complexity of the problem for well-known valuation classes lying between additive and submodular,[3] such as gross substitutes, OXS, and budget-additive?

Note that it does not make sense to study the query complexity for additive valuations, since a polynomial number of queries is sufficient to reconstruct the whole valuation functions (and the amount of computation then needed to determine a solution is not measured in the query complexity). However, it does make sense to study the computational complexity of the problem for submodular valuations, as well as other classes beyond additive. The query lower bound

---

[2] Computing the leximin++ solution is NP-hard, even for two identical agents with additive valuations. This can be shown by a reduction from the PARTITION problem (see [27, Footnote 7] and note that their argument, which they use for leximin, also applies to leximin++).

[3] In particular, Plaut and Roughgarden [27, Section 7] propose studying the complexity of fair division problems with respect to the hierarchy of complement-free valuations (additive $\subseteq$ OXS $\subseteq$ gross substitutes $\subseteq$ submodular $\subseteq$ XOS $\subseteq$ subadditive) introduced by Lehmann et al. [22].

by Plaut and Roughgarden essentially says that many queries are needed in order to gather enough information about the submodular valuation function to be able to construct an EFX allocation. But it does not say anything about the *computational* hardness of finding an EFX allocation. Their lower bound does not exclude the possibility of a polynomial-time algorithm for submodular valuations in the standard Turing machine model. Studying the problem in the computational complexity model allows us to investigate how hard it is to solve when the valuation functions are given in some succinct representation, e.g., as a few lines of code, or any other form that allows for efficient evaluation.

Our Contribution. We answer both of the aforementioned questions:

1. For submodular valuations, we prove that the problem is PLS-complete in the standard Turing machine model, even with two identical agents.
2. We present a simple greedy algorithm that finds an EFX allocation in polynomial time for two agents with *weakly well-layered* valuations, a class of valuation functions that we define in this paper and which contains all well-known strict subclasses of submodular, such as gross substitutes (and thus also OXS) and budget-additive.[4]

Together, these two results resolve the computational complexity of the problem for all valuation classes in the standard complement-free hierarchy (*additive* ⊆ *OXS* ⊆ *gross substitutes* ⊆ *submodular* ⊆ *XOS* ⊆ *subadditive*) introduced by Lehmann et al. [22]. Furthermore, just like in the work of Plaut and Roughgarden [27], our negative and positive results also hold for any number of *identical* agents.

Regarding the PLS-completeness result, the membership in PLS is easy to show using the leximin++ ordering of Plaut and Roughgarden [27]. The PLS-hardness is more challenging. The first step of our hardness reduction is essentially identical to the first step in the corresponding query lower bound of Plaut and Roughgarden [27]: a reduction from a local optimization problem on the Kneser graph to the problem of finding an EFX allocation. The second step of the reduction is our main technical contribution: we prove that finding a local optimum on a Kneser graph is PLS-hard[5], which might be of independent interest.

Further Related Work. The existence and computation of EFX allocations has been studied in various different settings, such as for restricted versions of valuation classes [3,6], when some items can be discarded [8,10,13,14], or when valuations are drawn randomly from a distribution [24].

---

[4] The class of weakly well-layered valuations also contains the class of *cancelable* valuations which have been recently studied in fair division [1,4,8].

[5] We note that proving a tight computational complexity lower bound is more challenging than proving a query lower bound, because we have to reduce from problems with more structure. Indeed, the exponential query lower bound for the Kneser problem (and thus also for the EFX problem) can easily be obtained as a byproduct of our reduction.

A weaker relaxation of envy-freeness is *envy-freeness up to one good* (EF1) [9,23]. It can be computed efficiently for any number of agents with monotone valuations using the Envy-Cycle elimination algorithm [23]. If one is also interested in economic efficiency, then it is possible to obtain an allocation that is both EF1 and Pareto-optimal in pseudopolynomial time for additive valuations [7]. For more details about fair division of indivisible items, we refer to the recent survey by Amanatidis et al. [2].

Outline. We begin with Sect. 2 where we formally define the problem and solution concept, as well as some standard valuation classes of interest. In Sect. 3 we introduce *weakly well-layered* valuation functions, and present our simple greedy algorithm for computing EFX allocations. Finally, in Sect. 4 we prove our main technical result, the PLS-completeness for submodular valuations.

2   Preliminaries

We consider the problem of discrete fair division where an instance consists of a set of agents N, a set of goods M, and for every agent $i \in N$ a valuation function $v_i \colon 2^M \to \mathbb{R}_{\geq 0}$ assigning values to bundles of goods. All valuation functions will be assumed to be *monotone*, meaning that for any subsets $S \subseteq T \subseteq M$ it holds that $v(S) \leq v(T)$, and *normalized*, i.e., $v(\emptyset) = 0$.

We now introduce the different types of valuation functions that are of interest to us. A valuation $v \colon 2^M \to \mathbb{R}_{\geq 0}$ is *additive* if $v(S) = \sum_{g \in S} v(\{g\})$ for every $S \subseteq M$. The hardness result we present in Sect. 4 holds for *submodular* valuations. These are valuations that satisfy the following diminishing returns condition that whenever $S \subseteq T$ and $x \notin T$ it holds that $v(S \cup \{x\}) - v(S) \geq v(T \cup \{x\}) - v(T)$.

Next, for our results in the positive direction, we introduce the classes of *gross substitutes* and *budget-additive* valuations, both contained in the class of submodular valuations. Before defining gross substitutes valuations, we have to introduce some notation. For a price vector $p \in \mathbb{R}^m$ on the set of goods, where $m = |M|$, the function v_p is defined by $v_p(S) = v(S) - \sum_{g \in S} p_g$ for any subset $S \subseteq M$, and the demand set is $D(v, p) = \arg\max_{S \subseteq M} v_p(S)$. A valuation v is *gross substitutes* if for any price vectors $p, p' \in \mathbb{R}^m$ with $p \leq p'$ (meaning that $p_g \leq p'_g$ for all $g \in M$), it holds that if $S \in D(v, p)$, then there exists a demanded set $S' \in D(v, p')$ such that $\{g \in S \colon p_g = p'_g\} \subseteq S'$. That is to say, if some good g is demanded at prices p and the prices of some *other* goods increase, then g will still be demanded. These valuations have various nice properties, for instance guaranteeing existence of Walrasian equilibria [20]. Lastly, a valuation v is *budget-additive* if it is of the form $v(S) = \min\{B, \sum_{g \in S} w_g\}$ for reals $B, w_1, \ldots, w_m \geq 0$. [22] show that a budget-additive valuation need not satisfy the gross substitutes condition. See Fig. 1 for the relationship between the valuation classes.

Envy-Freeness Up to Any Good (EFX). The goal of fair division is to find an allocation of the goods to the agents (i.e., a partitioning $M = X_1 \sqcup \cdots \sqcup X_n$)

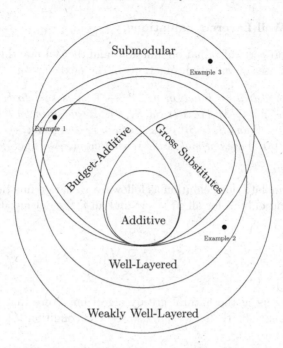

Fig. 1. Inclusions of valuation classes

satisfying some notion of fairness. One might hope for an *envy-free* division in which every agent prefers his own bundle over the bundle of any other agent, that is, $v_i(X_i) \geq v_i(X_j)$ for all $i, j \in N$. Such a division need not exist, however, as can be seen in the case where one has to divide one good among two agents, as already mentioned in the introduction. Therefore various weaker notions of fairness have been studied. In this paper we consider the notion of *envy-freeness up to any good* (EFX) introduced by Caragiannis et al. [11], and before that by Gourvès et al. [19] under a different name. An allocation $(X_1, \ldots, X_n)$ is said to be EFX if for any $i, j \in N$ and any $g \in X_j$ it holds that $v_i(X_i) \geq v_i(X_j \setminus \{g\})$.

3 Polynomial-Time Algorithm for Weakly Well-Layered Valuations

In this section we present our positive result, namely the polynomial-time algorithm for computing an EFX allocation for two agents with weakly well-layered valuations. To be more precise, our algorithm works for any number of agents that all share the same weakly well-layered valuation function. As a result, using cut-and-choose it can then be used to solve the problem with two possibly *different* agents. We begin with the definition of this new class of valuations, and then present the algorithm and prove its correctness.

3.1   Weakly Well-Layered Valuations

We introduce a property of valuation functions and then situate this with respect to well-known classes of valuation functions in the next section.

Definition 1. *A valuation function* $v\colon 2^M \to \mathbb{R}_{\geq 0}$ *is said to be* weakly well-layered *if for any* $M' \subseteq M$ *the sets* $S_0, S_1, S_2, \ldots$ *obtained by the greedy algorithm (that is, $S_0 = \emptyset$ and $S_i = S_{i-1} \cup \{x_i\}$ where $x_i \in \arg\max_{x \in M' \setminus S_{i-1}} v(S_{i-1} \cup \{x\})$ for $1 \leq i \leq |M'|$) are optimal in the sense that $v(S_i) = \max_{S \subseteq M'\colon |S| = i} v(S)$ for all i.*

We can reformulate this definition as follows: a valuation function v is weakly well-layered if and only if, for all $M' \subseteq M$ and all i, the optimization problem

$$\begin{aligned} \max \quad & v(S) \\ \text{s.t.} \quad & S \subseteq M' \\ & |S| \leq i \end{aligned} \tag{1}$$

can be solved by using the natural greedy algorithm. Note that since we only consider monotone valuations, we can also use the condition $|S| = i$ instead of $|S| \leq i$.

The reformulation of the definition in terms of the optimization problem (1) is reminiscent of one of the alternative definitions of a matroid. Consider the optimization problem

$$\begin{aligned} \max \quad & v(S) \\ \text{s.t.} \quad & S \in \mathcal{F} \end{aligned} \tag{2}$$

where $v\colon 2^M \to \mathbb{R}_{\geq 0}$ is a valuation function and $\mathcal{F}$ is an independence system on M. Then, it is well-known that $\mathcal{F}$ is a matroid, if and only if, for all additive valuations v, the optimization problem (2) can be solved by the natural greedy algorithm [15,17,28]. In other words, the class of set systems (namely, matroids) is defined by fixing a class of valuations (namely, additive). The alternative definition of weakly well-layered valuations given in (1) can be viewed as doing the opposite: the class of valuations (namely, weakly well-layered) is defined by fixing a class of set systems (namely, all uniform matroids on subsets $M' \subseteq M$, or, more formally, $\mathcal{F} = \{S \subseteq M' : |S| \leq i\}$ for all $M' \subseteq M$ and all i).

3.2   Relationship to Other Valuation Classes

Gross Substitutes. We begin by showing that any gross substitutes valuation is weakly well-layered. In particular, this also implies that OXS valuations, which are a special case of gross substitutes, are also weakly well-layered. Paes Leme [26] proved that gross substitutes valuation functions satisfy the stronger condition of being *well-layered*, that is, for any $p \in \mathbb{R}^m$ it holds that if $S_0, S_1, S_2, \ldots$ is constructed greedily with respect to the valuation v_p, where $v_p(S) := v(S) - \sum_{g \in S} p_g$, then S_i satisfies that $S_i \in \arg\max_{S \subseteq M\colon |S|=i} v_p(S)$.

Lemma 1. *If* $v\colon 2^M \to \mathbb{R}_{\geq 0}$ *is well-layered, then it is also weakly well-layered. In particular, gross substitutes valuations are weakly well-layered.*

Proof. Assume that $v\colon 2^M \to \mathbb{R}_{\geq 0}$ is well-layered and let $M' \subseteq M$. Assume that the sequence $S_0, S_1, S_2, \ldots$ is constructed via the greedy algorithm: that is $S_0 = \emptyset$ and $S_i = S_{i-1} \cup \{x_i\}$ where $x_i \in \arg\max_{x \in M' \setminus S_{i-1}} v(S_{i-1} \cup \{x\})$ for $1 \leq i \leq |M'|$. We have to show that $v(S_i) = \max_{S \subseteq M'\,:\,|S|=i} v(S)$.

In order to exploit the assumption that v is well-layered, we introduce a price vector $p \in \mathbb{R}^m$ given by

$$p_g = \begin{cases} 0 & g \in M' \\ v(M) + 1 & g \notin M' \end{cases}$$

One sees that the sequence $S_0, S_1, S_2, \ldots$ can occur via the greedy algorithm for the valuation v_p, because goods not in M' cannot be chosen as their prices are too high. As v is well-layered, we have that $v_p(S_i) = \max_{S \subseteq M\,:\,|S|=i} v_p(S)$. As $p_g = 0$ for all $g \in M'$, this implies that $v(S_i) = \max_{S \subseteq M'\,:\,|S|=i} v(S)$. We conclude that v is weakly well-layered. $\qed$

Closure Properties and Budget-Additive Valuations. We note that the class of weakly well-layered valuations is closed under two natural operations.

Lemma 2. *Let* $v\colon 2^M \to \mathbb{R}_{\geq 0}$ *be weakly well-layered and let* $f\colon \mathbb{R}_{\geq 0} \to \mathbb{R}_{\geq 0}$ *strictly increasing. Then the composition* $f \circ v\colon 2^M \to \mathbb{R}_{\geq 0}$ *is weakly well-layered.*

Proof. Let $M' \subseteq M$ and assume that $S_0, S_1, S_2, \ldots$ are constructed greedily, that is $S_0 = \emptyset$ and $S_i = S_{i-1} \cup \{x_i\}$ where $x_i \in \arg\max_{x \in M' \setminus S_{i-1}} f(v(S_{i-1} \cup \{x\}))$ for $1 \leq i \leq |M'|$. As f is strictly increasing, we see that $x_i \in \arg\max_{x \in M'} f(v(S_{i-1} \cup \{x\}))$ if and only if $x_i \in \arg\max_{x \in M'} v(S_{i-1} \cup \{x\})$. Therefore $S_0, S_1, S_2, \ldots$ could also arise via the greedy construction based on the valuation v. As v is weakly well-layered, this implies that $v(S_i) = \max_{S \subseteq M'\,:\,|S|=i} v(S)$ for all i. As f is increasing, this shows that $f(v(S_i)) = \max_{S \subseteq M'\,:\,|S|=i} f(v(S))$ for all i. We conclude that $f \circ v$ is weakly well-layered. $\qed$

Lemma 3. *Let* $v\colon 2^M \to \mathbb{R}_{\geq 0}$ *be weakly well-layered and* $B \geq 0$. *Then the valuation* $u\colon 2^M \to \mathbb{R}_{\geq 0}$ *given by* $u(S) = \min(v(S), B)$ *is weakly well-layered.*

Proof. Let $S_0, S_1, S_2, \ldots$ be constructed greedily from the valuation u. Suppose that $S_0, S_1, \ldots, S_k$ have utility $< B$ and that $S_{k+1}, S_{k+2}, \ldots$ have utility B. As $x \mapsto \min(x, B)$ is strictly increasing on $[0, B)$, the sets $S_0, S_1, \ldots, S_k$ could have been constructed greedily from v. As v is weakly well-layered, they are therefore optimal of their given size for v and therefore also for u. The sets $S_{k+1}, \ldots$ all have maximal utility B and are therefore optimal of their given sizes. $\qed$

As a corollary, since additive valuations are weakly well-layered, it follows that the class of budget-additive valuations satisfies the weakly well-layered property.

Corollary 1. *Any budget-additive valuation is weakly well-layered.*

In contrast, it is known that budget-additive valuations are not necessarily gross substitutes, and, as the following example shows, not even well-layered.

Example 1. Consider the budget-additive valuation on three goods a, b, c with values $v_a = v_b = 2$, $v_c = 4$ and a budget of $B = 4$. Let $p = (1, 1, 2)$ be a price vector. Under these prices, the greedy algorithm would pick good c as its first item. However, $\{a, b\}$ is the unique optimal bundle of size 2, and so the greedy algorithm would fail in this case. As a result, the valuation is not well-layered.

Cancelable Valuations. The class of weakly well-layered valuations also contains the class of cancelable valuations recently defined by Berger et al. [8], which contains budget-additive, unit-demand, and multiplicative valuations as special cases. A valuation function $v : 2^M \to \mathbb{R}_{\geq 0}$ is said to be *cancelable* if $v(S \cup \{x\}) > v(T \cup \{x\}) \implies v(S) > v(T)$ for any $S, T \subseteq M$ and $x \in M \setminus (S \cup T)$.

Lemma 4. *Any cancelable valuation is weakly well-layered.*

Proof. Let v be cancelable, $M' \subseteq M$, and let $S_0, S_1, S_2, \ldots$ be obtained by the greedy algorithm on v and M' (see Definition 1). We prove by induction that $v(S_i) = \max_{S \subseteq M' : |S| = i} v(S)$ for all i. Clearly, this holds for $i = 1$.

Now assume that the induction hypothesis holds for some $i \geq 1$ and consider $S_{i+1} = S_i \cup \{x_{i+1}\}$. If there existed $T \subseteq M'$ with $|T| = i + 1$ such that $v(T) > v(S_{i+1})$, then, letting y be any element in $T \setminus S_i$, we would obtain

$$v((T \setminus \{y\}) \cup \{y\}) = v(T) > v(S_{i+1}) = v(S_i \cup \{x_{i+1}\}) \geq v(S_i \cup \{y\})$$

where we used the fact that x_{i+1} was added greedily to S_i. Since v is cancelable, it follows that $v(T \setminus \{y\}) > v(S_i)$, which contradicts the induction hypothesis for i. As a result, the set S_{i+1} must also be optimal.

The results of this subsection are summarised in Fig. 1. Note also that the classes of submodular valuations and weakly well-layered valuations are incomparable. For an example of a valuation function that is submodular but not weakly well-layered, see Example 3 in the next section. For the other direction, see the following example of a valuation that is well-layered (and thus weakly well-layered), but not submodular.

Example 2. Consider the valuation function v on two goods a, b given by $v(\{a, b\}) = 1$ and $v(\emptyset) = v(\{a\}) = v(\{b\}) = 0$. This valuation function is seen to be well-layered (and thus weakly well-layered), because subsets of equal size have the same valuation. However, it is not submodular, because $v(\{a\} \cup \{b\}) - v(\{a\}) = 1 > 0 = v(\emptyset \cup \{b\}) - v(\emptyset)$.

Algorithm 1. Greedy EFX

Input: N, M, v
Output: EFX allocation
  Let $A_i = \emptyset$ for $i \in N$.
  Let $R = M$.
  while $R \neq \emptyset$ **do**
    $i = \arg\min_{j \in N} v(A_j)$
    $g = \arg\max_{x \in R} v(A_i \cup \{x\})$
    $A_i = A_i \cup \{g\}$
    $R = R \setminus \{g\}$
  end while
  return $(A_1, \ldots, A_n)$

3.3 The Greedy EFX Algorithm

We now present a simple algorithm that computes an EFX allocation for many agents that all share the same weakly well-layered valuation function v.

Theorem 1. *If the valuation function v is weakly well-layered, then the output of Algorithm 1 is EFX. In particular, by using the cut-and-choose protocol one may compute an EFX allocation for two agents with different valuations as long as one of these valuations is weakly well-layered.*

Proof. We show that the algorithm maintains a partial EFX allocation throughout. Initially the partial allocation is empty and so clearly EFX. Suppose that at the beginning of some round the current partial allocation $(X_1, \ldots, X_n)$ is EFX and that some agent $i \in N$ receives a good g in this round. We have to show that the new (partial) allocation $(X'_1, \ldots, X'_n)$ is EFX, where $X'_i = X_i \cup \{g\}$ and $X'_j = X_j$ for $j \neq i$. Clearly, the only thing we have to argue is that $v(X'_i \setminus \{g'\}) \leq v(X'_j)$ for all $j \in N$ and all $g' \in X'_i$. As i received a good in the current round we have that $v(X_i) \leq v(X_j) = v(X'_j)$. Therefore, it suffices to argue that $v(X'_i \setminus \{g'\}) \leq v(X_i)$ for all $g' \in X'_i$. This last inequality follows from v being weakly well-layered by taking $M' = X'_i$. With this M', the set X_i could namely be produced by running the greedy algorithm. Therefore, X_i is an optimal subset of $M' = X'_i$ of size $|X_i| = |X'_i| - 1$, meaning that $v(X'_i \setminus \{g'\}) \leq v(X_i)$ for all $g \in X'_i$.

The algorithm can fail to provide an EFX allocation for submodular valuations that are not weakly well-layered, as the following example shows.

Example 3. Consider an instance with two agents and four goods denoted a, b, c, d, where the valuation function v is given by: $v(\{a\}) = 11, v(\{b\}) = v(\{c\}) = 10, v(\{d\}) = 16, v(\{a,b\}) = 15, v(\{a,c\}) = 15, v(\{b,c\}) = 17, v(\{a,b,c\}) = 18$, and $v(S) = 18$ for all sets S that satisfy $d \in S$ and $|S| \geq 2$. It can be checked by direct computation that v is indeed submodular. The greedy EFX algorithm yields: agent 1 gets good d, and then agent 2 gets goods a, b, c. This allocation is not EFX, because $v(\{d\}) < v(\{b,c\})$.

4   PLS-completeness for Submodular Valuations

Total NP search problems (TFNP). A total search problem is given by a relation $R \subseteq \{0,1\}^* \times \{0,1\}^*$ that satisfies: for all $x \in \{0,1\}^*$, there exists $y \in \{0,1\}^*$ such that $(x,y) \in R$. The relation R is interpreted as the following computational problem: given $x \in \{0,1\}^*$, find some $y \in \{0,1\}^*$ such that $(x,y) \in R$. The class TFNP [25] is defined as the set of all total search problems R such that the relation R is polynomial-time decidable (i.e., given some x, y we can check in polynomial time whether $(x,y) \in R$) and polynomially balanced (i.e., there exists some polynomial p such that $|y| \leq p(|x|)$ whenever $(x,y) \in R$).

Let R and S be two problems in TFNP. We say that R reduces to S if there exist polynomial-time functions $f : \{0,1\}^* \to \{0,1\}^*$ and $g : \{0,1\}^* \times \{0,1\}^* \to \{0,1\}^*$ such that for all $x, y \in \{0,1\}^*$: if $(f(x), y) \in S$, then $(x, g(y,x)) \in R$. In other words, f maps an instance of R to an instance of S, and g maps back any solution of the S-instance to a solution of the R-instance.

Polynomial Local Search (PLS). Johnson et al. [21] introduced the class PLS, a subclass of TFNP, to capture the complexity of computing locally optimal solutions in settings where local improvements can be computed in polynomial time. In order to define the class PLS, we proceed as follows: first, we define a set of basic PLS problems, and then define the class PLS as the set of all TFNP problems that reduce to a basic PLS problem.

A *local search problem* Π is defined as follows. For every instance[6] $I \in \{0,1\}^*$, there is a finite set $F_I \subseteq \{0,1\}^*$ of *feasible solutions*, an objective function $c_I \colon F_I \to \mathbb{N}$, and for every feasible solution $s \in F_I$ there is a neighborhood $N_I(s) \subseteq F_I$. Given an instance I, one seeks a *local optimum* $s^* \in F_I$ with respect to c_I and N_I, meaning, in case of a maximization problem, that $c_I(s^*) \geq c_I(s)$ for all neighbors $s \in N_I(s^*)$.

Definition 2. *A local search problem Π is a basic PLS problem if there exists some polynomial p such that $F_I \subseteq \{0,1\}^{p(|I|)}$ for all instances I, and if there exist polynomial-time algorithms A, B and C such that:*

1. *Given an instance I, algorithm A produces an initial feasible solution $s_0 \in F_I$.*
2. *Given an instance I and a string $s \in \{0,1\}^{p(|I|)}$, algorithm B determines whether s is a feasible solution and, if so, computes the objective value $c_I(s)$.*
3. *Given an instance I and any feasible solution $s \in F_I$, the algorithm C checks if s is locally optimal and, if not, produces a feasible solution $s' \in N_I(s)$ that improves the objective value.*

Note that any basic PLS problem lies in TFNP.

Definition 3. *The class PLS is defined as the set of all TFNP problems that reduce to a basic PLS problem.*

---

[6] A more general definition would also include a polynomial-time recognizable set $D_\Pi \subseteq \{0,1\}^*$ of valid instances. The assumption that $D_\Pi = \{0,1\}^*$ is essentially without loss of generality. Indeed, for $I \notin D_\Pi$ we can define $F_I = \{0\}$, $c_I(0) = 1$ and $N_I(0) = \{0\}$. Note that this does not change the complexity of the problem.

A problem is PLS-complete if it lies in PLS and if every problem in PLS reduces to it. Johnson et al. [21] showed that the so-called FLIP problem is PLS-complete. We will define this problem later when we make use of it to prove our PLS-hardness result.

4.1 PLS-membership

Plaut and Roughgarden [27] prove the existence of an EFX allocation when all agents share the same monotone valuation, by introducing the leximin++ solution. In this section, we show how their existence proof can be translated into a proof of PLS-membership for the following problem.

Definition 4 (Identical-EFX). *An instance* $I = (N, M, C)$ *of the* IDENTICAL-EFX *search problem consists of a set of agents* $N = [n]$, *a set of goods* $M = [m]$, *and a boolean circuit* C *with* m *input gates. The circuit* C *defines a valuation function* $v: 2^M \to \mathbb{N}$ *which is the common valuation of all the agents. A solution is one of the following:*

1. *An allocation* $(X_1, \ldots, X_n)$ *that is EFX.*
2. *A pair of bundles* $S \subseteq T$ *that violate monotonicity, that is,* $v(S) > v(T)$.

The reason for allowing the violation-of-monotonicity solutions is that the circuit C is not guaranteed to define a monotone valuation, and in this case an EFX allocation is not guaranteed to exist. Importantly, we note that our PLS-hardness result (presented in the next section) does not rely on violation solutions. In other words, even the version of the problem where we are promised that the valuation function is monotone remains PLS-hard.

Theorem 2. *The* IDENTICAL-EFX *problem lies in* PLS.

The problem of computing an EFX allocation for two non-identical agents with valuations v_1 and v_2 is reducible to the problem of computing an EFX allocation for two identical agents via the cut-and-choose protocol. As a result, we immediately also obtain the following:

Corollary 2. *Computing an EFX allocation for two not necessarily identical agents is in* PLS.

Proof. To show that the IDENTICAL-EFX problem is in PLS, we reduce it to a basic PLS problem. An instance of this basic PLS problem is just an instance of the IDENTICAL-EFX problem, i.e., a tuple $I = (N, M, C)$. The set of feasible solutions F_I is the set of all possible allocations of the goods in M to the agents in N. As an initial feasible solution, we simply take the allocation where one agent receives all goods. It remains to specify the objective function c_I and the neighborhood structure N_I, and then to argue that a local optimum corresponds to an EFX allocation.

Plaut and Roughgarden [27, Section 4] introduce the *leximin++* ordering on the set of allocations, and show that the maximum element with respect to that ordering must be an EFX allocation. In fact, a closer inspection of their proof reveals that even a *local* maximum with respect to the leximin++ ordering must be an EFX allocation. As a result, we construct an objective function that implements the leximin++ ordering and then use the same arguments as Plaut and Roughgarden [27, Theorem 4.2]. The details can be found in the full version of our paper.

4.2 PLS-Hardness

In this section we prove the following theorem.

Theorem 3. *The problem of computing an EFX allocation for two identical agents with a submodular valuation function is* PLS-*hard.*

The reduction consists of two steps. First, following Plaut and Roughgarden [27], we reduce the problem of local optimization on an odd Kneser graph to the problem of computing an EFX allocation for two agents sharing the same submodular valuation function. Then, in the second step, which is also our main technical contribution, we show that the PLS-complete problem FLIP reduces to local optimization on an odd Kneser graph.

Kneser $\leq$ Identical-EFX For $k \in \mathbb{N}$, the odd Kneser graph $K(2k+1, k)$ is defined as follows: the vertex set consists of all subsets of $[2k+1]$ of size k, and there is an edge between two vertices if the corresponding sets are disjoint. We identify the vertex set of $K(2k+1, k)$ with the set $\{x \in \{0,1\}^{2k+1} : ||x||_1 = k\}$, where $||x||_1 = \sum_{i=1}^{2k+1} x_i$ denotes the 1-norm. Note that there is an edge between x and x' if and only if $\langle x, x' \rangle = 0$, where $\langle \cdot, \cdot \rangle$ denotes the inner product.

Definition 5 (Kneser). *The* KNESER *problem of local optimization on an odd Kneser graph is defined as the following basic* PLS *problem. An instance of the* KNESER *problem consists of a boolean circuit C with $2k+1$ input nodes for some $k \in \mathbb{N}$. The set of feasible solutions is $F_C = \{x \in \{0,1\}^{2k+1} : ||x||_1 = k\}$, and the neighborhood of some $x \in F_C$ is given by $N_C(x) = \{x' \in F_C : \langle x, x' \rangle = 0\}$. The goal is to find a solution that is a local maximum with respect to the objective function $C(x) = \sum_{i=0}^{m-1} y_i \cdot 2^i$, where $y_0, \ldots, y_{m-1}$ denote the output nodes of the circuit C.*

Lemma 5. KNESER *reduces to* IDENTICAL-EFX *with two identical submodular agents.*

Proof. Our proof of this lemma closely follows the corresponding proof of Plaut and Roughgarden [27, Theorem 3.1], with some minor modifications due to the different computational model. The proof is omitted due to space constraints, but can be found in the full version of our paper.

Flip $\leq$ Kneser Johnson et al. [21] introduced the computational problem FLIP and proved that it is PLS-complete. We will now reduce from FLIP to KNESER to show that KNESER, and thus IDENTICAL-EFX, are PLS-hard. In particular, this also establishes the PLS-completeness of KNESER, which might be of independent interest.

Definition 6 (Flip). *The* FLIP *problem is the following basic* PLS *problem. The instances of* FLIP *are boolean circuits. For an instance* C *with* n *input nodes* $x_0, \ldots, x_{n-1}$ *and* m *output nodes* $y_0, \ldots, y_{m-1}$, *the set of feasible solutions is all the possible inputs to the circuit:* $F_C = \{0,1\}^n$. *For any* $x \in \{0,1\}^n$, *the neighborhood is all the inputs that can be obtained from* x *by flipping one bit:* $N_C(x) = \{x' \in \{0,1\}^n : \Delta(x, x') = 1\}$ *where* $\Delta(\cdot, \cdot)$ *denotes the Hamming distance. The goal is to find a solution that is locally minimal with respect to the objective function defined by* $C(x) = \sum_{i=0}^{m-1} y_i \cdot 2^i$.

Lemma 6. FLIP *reduces to* KNESER.

Proof. We construct a reduction from FLIP to the minimization version of KNESER. The minimization version of KNESER is seen to be equivalent to its maximization version by negating the output nodes of the original circuit. Let C_F be an instance of FLIP. Denote by $p = \mathrm{poly}(|C_F|)$ the length of the feasible solutions of C_F. The map of instances f now takes C_F to an instance C_K of the KNESER-problem whose feasible solutions are $F_K = \{x \in \{0,1\}^{2p+1} : ||x||_1 = p\}$. A typical feasible solution will be written as $s = uvb$ where $u, v \in \{0,1\}^p$ and $b \in \{0,1\}$. We will use the notation $\overline{u}$ to denote the bitwise negation of $u \in \{0,1\}^p$. The circuit C_K is defined as follows:

1. $C_K(u\overline{u}0) = 2 \cdot C_F(u)$,
2. $C_K(uv1) = 2 \cdot \min(C_F(\overline{u}), C_F(v)) + 1$ if $\Delta(\overline{u}, v) = 1$,
3. $C_K(uvb) = M + \Delta(\overline{u}, v)$ otherwise.

Here M denotes a number chosen to be sufficiently large so that it dominates any cost $2 \cdot C_F(w)$. Note that the circuit C_K is well-defined and that it can be constructed in polynomial time given the circuit C_F. At a high level, the definition of the cost of a vertex of the third type is meant to ensure that for any such vertex uvb, there is a sequence of neighbors with decreasing costs that ends in a vertex of the form $u\overline{u}0$. The costs of the first and second vertex types are then meant to ensure that for a vertex $u\overline{u}0$, there is a sequence of neighbors with decreasing costs that ends in a vertex $w\overline{w}0$ where w is an improving neighbor of u in the original FLIP-instance.

Below we show that the only local minima of C_K are of the form $u\overline{u}0$ where u is a local minimum for C_F. Therefore, upon defining the solution-mapping by $g(uvb) = u$ we have that (f, g) is a reduction from FLIP to KNESER.

No Optimal Solutions of Type (3). If a feasible solution $s = uvb$ is of type (3), then we claim that it must have a neighbor of lower cost. First of all, note that since s is not of type (1) or (2), and since $||s||_1 = p$, it follows that $\Delta(\overline{u}, v) \geq 2$. Now, because $\Delta(\overline{u}, v) \geq 2 > 0$ and $||uv||_1 \leq p$, there must exist an i such that $u_i = v_i = 0$. Otherwise one would find that $||uv||_1 > p$, which contradicts s being a feasible solution. Now, let $s' = u'v'b'$, where $u' = \overline{u}$, $b' = \overline{b}$, and $v'_j = \overline{v}_j$ for all $j \neq i$, but $v_i' = v_i = 0$. We note that $||s'||_1 = ||\bar{s}||_1 - 1 = (p+1) - 1 = p$, so s' is a valid vertex in the Kneser graph. Further, we see that s' is a neighbor of s, because $s_j's_j = 0$ for all j. If s' is not of type (3), then it has lower cost than s by construction of C_K and choice of M. Finally, if s' is of type (3), then the observation that $\Delta(\overline{u'}, v') < \Delta(\overline{u}, v)$ again yields that s' has lower cost than s.

No Optimal Solutions of Type (2). Suppose $s = uv1$ is of type (2). As $||s||_1 = p$ and $\Delta(\overline{u}, v) = 1$, there is some i with $v_i = 0$ and $\overline{u}_i = 1$, and $v_j = \overline{u}_j$ for $j \neq i$. This implies that $\sum_i u_i v_i = 0$, and so both $s' = \overline{u}u0$ and $s'' = v\overline{v}0$ are neighbors of s. Furthermore, by construction of C_K, the cost of s' or of s'' is strictly less than the cost of s.

Optimal Solutions. Consider a feasible solution of the form $u\overline{u}0$. If u is not a local minimum for C_F, then let w be an improving neighbor of u. As $\Delta(u, w) = 1$, there are now two cases to consider. If $u_i = 0$ and $w_i = 1$ for some i, then $s' = \overline{w}u1$ is a type (2) neighbor of lower cost. If $u_i = 1$ and $w_i = 0$ for some i, then $s' = \overline{u}w1$ is a type (2) neighbor of lower cost. Therefore, if $u\overline{u}0$ is a local minimum for C_K, then u is a local minimum for C_F.

Corollary 3. *Let $n \geq 2$ be an integer. Computing an EFX allocation for n identical agents with a submodular valuation function is PLS-hard.*

Proof. By Theorem 3 it suffices to produce a reduction from the problem of computing an EFX allocation for two identical agents to the problem of computing an EFX allocation for n identical agents. We sketch this reduction. Let $u: 2^M \to \mathbb{R}$ denote the common submodular valuation function of the two agents. Construct an EFX-instance with n agents by adding $n-2$ agents and $n-2$ goods, $M' = M \cup \{g_1, \ldots, g_{n-2}\}$. Define the valuation function of the n agents to be $u' = \overline{u} + v$ where $\overline{u}: 2^{M'} \to \mathbb{R}$ is the extension of u given by $\overline{u}(S) = u(S \cap M)$ and where $v: 2^{M'} \to \mathbb{R}$ is additive given by $v(\{g_i\}) = u(M) + 1$ for $i = 1, \ldots, n-2$ and $v(\{g\}) = 0$ for $g \in M$. One may verify that $\overline{u}$ is submodular, and so that u' is the sum of two submodular valuations and therefore itself submodular.

Let $(X_1, \ldots, X_n)$ denote an EFX allocation of this instance. We claim that after permuting the bundles, we may assume that $X_{i+2} = \{g_i\}$ for $i = 1, \ldots, n-2$ and $X_1 \cup X_2 = M$. At least one bundle, say X_1, receives no good from $\{g_1, \ldots, g_{n-2}\}$, and so $u'(X_1) = u(X_1) \leq u(M)$. Now suppose some other bundle X_i contains some good g_j. If X_i contained another good g, then

$$u'(X_i \setminus \{g\}) \geq u'(\{g_j\}) = u(M) + 1 > u'(X_1),$$

contradicting $(X_1, \ldots, X_n)$ being EFX. Hence, $X_i = \{g_j\}$, and the claim follows. Now, one sees that (X_1, X_2) is an EFX allocation of the original two-agent instance.

Acknowledgements. We thank all the reviewers of SAGT 2023 for their comments and suggestions that improved the presentation of the paper. In particular, we thank one reviewer for pointing out that weakly well-layered valuations also generalize cancelable valuations.

P. W. Goldberg was supported by a JP Morgan faculty award. K. Høgh was supported by the Independent Research Fund Denmark under grant no. 9040-00433B. Most of this work was done while he was visiting Oxford thanks to a STIBO IT Travel Grant. A. Hollender was supported by the Swiss State Secretariat for Education, Research and Innovation (SERI) under contract number MB22.00026.

References

1. Akrami, H., Alon, N., Chaudhury, B.R., Garg, J., Mehlhorn, K., Mehta, R.: EFX: a simpler approach and an (almost) optimal guarantee via rainbow cycle number. In: Proceedings of the 24th ACM Conference on Economics and Computation (EC), p. 61 (2023). https://doi.org/10.1145/3580507.3597799
2. Amanatidis, G., et al.: Fair division of indivisible goods: recent progress and open questions. Artif. Intell. **322** (2023). https://doi.org/10.1016/j.artint.2023.103965
3. Amanatidis, G., Birmpas, G., Filos-Ratsikas, A., Hollender, A., Voudouris, A.A.: Maximum Nash welfare and other stories about EFX. Theoret. Comput. Sci. **863**, 69–85 (2021). https://doi.org/10.1016/j.tcs.2021.02.020
4. Amanatidis, G., Birmpas, G., Lazos, P., Leonardi, S., Reiffenhäuser, R.: Round-robin beyond additive agents: Existence and fairness of approximate equilibria. In: Proceedings of the 24th ACM Conference on Economics and Computation (EC), pp. 67–87 (2023). https://doi.org/10.1145/3580507.3597796
5. Aziz, H., Mackenzie, S.: A discrete and bounded envy-free cake cutting protocol for any number of agents. In: Proceedings of the 57th IEEE Symposium on Foundations of Computer Science (FOCS), pp. 416–427 (2016). https://doi.org/10.1109/focs.2016.52
6. Babaioff, M., Ezra, T., Feige, U.: Fair and truthful mechanisms for dichotomous valuations. In: Proceedings of the 35th AAAI Conference on Artificial Intelligence (AAAI), pp. 5119–5126 (2021). https://ojs.aaai.org/index.php/AAAI/article/view/16647
7. Barman, S., Krishnamurthy, S.K., Vaish, R.: Finding fair and efficient allocations. In: Proceedings of the 19th ACM Conference on Economics and Computation (EC), pp. 557–574 (2018). https://doi.org/10.1145/3219166.3219176
8. Berger, B., Cohen, A., Feldman, M., Fiat, A.: Almost full EFX exists for four agents. In: Proceedings of the 36th AAAI Conference on Artificial Intelligence (AAAI), pp. 4826–4833 (2022). https://doi.org/10.1609/aaai.v36i5.20410
9. Budish, E.: The combinatorial assignment problem: approximate competitive equilibrium from equal incomes. J. Polit. Econ. **119**(6), 1061–1103 (2011). https://doi.org/10.1086/664613
10. Caragiannis, I., Gravin, N., Huang, X.: Envy-freeness up to any item with high Nash welfare: the virtue of donating items. In: Proceedings of the 20th ACM Conference on Economics and Computation (EC), pp. 527–545 (2019). https://doi.org/10.1145/3328526.3329574
11. Caragiannis, I., Kurokawa, D., Moulin, H., Procaccia, A.D., Shah, N., Wang, J.: The unreasonable fairness of maximum Nash welfare. ACM Trans. Econ. Comput. **7**(3), 12:1–12:32 (2019). https://doi.org/10.1145/3355902

12. Chaudhury, B.R., Garg, J., Mehlhorn, K.: EFX exists for three agents. In: Proceedings of the 21st ACM Conference on Economics and Computation (EC), pp. 1–19 (2020). https://doi.org/10.1145/3391403.3399511

13. Chaudhury, B.R., Garg, J., Mehlhorn, K., Mehta, R., Misra, P.: Improving EFX guarantees through rainbow cycle number. In: Proceedings of the 22nd ACM Conference on Economics and Computation (EC), pp. 310–311 (2021). https://doi.org/10.1145/3465456.3467605

14. Chaudhury, B.R., Kavitha, T., Mehlhorn, K., Sgouritsa, A.: A little charity guarantees almost envy-freeness. SIAM J. Comput. **50**(4), 1336–1358 (2021). https://doi.org/10.1137/20m1359134

15. Edmonds, J.: Matroids and the greedy algorithm. Math. Program. **1**(1), 127–136 (1971). https://doi.org/10.1007/bf01584082

16. Foley, D.K.: Resource Allocation and the Public Sector. Ph.D. thesis, Yale University (1966)

17. Gale, D.: Optimal assignments in an ordered set: an application of matroid theory. J. Comb. Theory **4**(2), 176–180 (1968). https://doi.org/10.1016/s0021-9800(68)80039-0

18. Gamow, G., Stern, M.: Puzzle-Math. Viking Press (1958)

19. Gourvès, L., Monnot, J., Tlilane, L.: Near fairness in matroids. In: Proceedings of the 21st European Conference on Artificial Intelligence (ECAI), pp. 393–398 (2014). https://doi.org/10.3233/978-1-61499-419-0-393

20. Gul, F., Stacchetti, E.: Walrasian equilibrium with gross substitutes. J. Econ. Theory **87**(1), 95–124 (1999). https://EconPapers.repec.org/RePEc:eee:jetheo:v:87:y:1999:i:1:p:95-124

21. Johnson, D.S., Papadimitriou, C.H., Yannakakis, M.: How easy is local search? J. Comput. Syst. Sci. **37**(1), 79–100 (1988). https://doi.org/10.1016/0022-0000(88)90046-3

22. Lehmann, B., Lehmann, D., Nisan, N.: Combinatorial auctions with decreasing marginal utilities. Games Econom. Behav. **55**(2), 270–296 (2006). https://doi.org/10.1016/j.geb.2005.02.006

23. Lipton, R.J., Markakis, E., Mossel, E., Saberi, A.: On approximately fair allocations of indivisible goods. In: Proceedings of the 5th ACM Conference on Electronic Commerce (EC), pp. 125–131 (2004). https://doi.org/10.1145/988772.988792

24. Manurangsi, P., Suksompong, W.: Closing gaps in asymptotic fair division. SIAM J. Discret. Math. **35**(2), 668–706 (2021). https://doi.org/10.1137/20m1353381

25. Megiddo, N., Papadimitriou, C.H.: On total functions, existence theorems and computational complexity. Theoret. Comput. Sci. **81**(2), 317–324 (1991). https://doi.org/10.1016/0304-3975(91)90200-L

26. Paes Leme, R.: Gross substitutability: an algorithmic survey. Games Econom. Behav. **106**, 294–316 (2017). https://doi.org/10.1016/j.geb.2017.10.016

27. Plaut, B., Roughgarden, T.: Almost envy-freeness with general valuations. SIAM J. Discret. Math. **34**(2), 1039–1068 (2020). https://doi.org/10.1137/19m124397x

28. Rado, R.: Note on independence functions. Proc. Lond. Math. Soc. **s3-7**(1), 300–320 (1957). https://doi.org/10.1112/plms/s3-7.1.300

29. Steinhaus, H.: The problem of fair division. Econometrica **16**(1), 101–104 (1948). https://www.jstor.org/stable/1914289

30. Steinhaus, H.: Sur la division pragmatique. Econometrica **17**(Suppl.), 315–319 (1949). https://doi.org/10.2307/1907319

31. Stromquist, W.: How to cut a cake fairly. Am. Math. Mon. **87**(8), 640–644 (1980). https://doi.org/10.1080/00029890.1980.11995109

32. Su, F.E.: Rental harmony: Sperner's lemma in fair division. Am. Math. Mon. **106**(10), 930–942 (1999). https://doi.org/10.1080/00029890.1999.12005142
33. Varian, H.R.: Equity, envy, and efficiency. J. Econ. Theory **9**(1), 63–91 (1974). https://doi.org/10.1016/0022-0531(74)90075-1
34. Woodall, D.R.: Dividing a cake fairly. J. Math. Anal. Appl. **78**(1), 233–247 (1980). https://doi.org/10.1016/0022-247x(80)90225-5

Matching and Mechanism Design

Computational Complexity of k-Stable Matchings

Haris Aziz[1] , Gergely Csáji[2,3] , and Ágnes Cseh[3,4(✉)]

[1] UNSW Sydney, Sydney, Australia
[2] Eötvös Loránd University, Budapest, Hungary
[3] Institute of Economics, Centre for Economic and Regional Studies, Budapest, Hungary
cseh.agnes@krtk.hu
[4] University of Bayreuth, Bayreuth, Germany

Abstract. We study deviations by a group of agents in the three main types of matching markets: the house allocation, the marriage, and the roommates models. For a given instance, we call a matching k-*stable* if no other matching exists that is more beneficial to at least k out of the n agents. The concept generalizes the recently studied majority stability (Thakur, 2021). We prove that whereas the verification of k-stability for a given matching is polynomial-time solvable in all three models, the complexity of deciding whether a k-stable matching exists depends on $\frac{k}{n}$ and is characteristic to each model.

Keywords: Majority stability · stable matching · popular matching · complexity

1 Introduction

In matchings under preferences, agents seek to be matched among themselves or to objects. Each agent has a preference list on their possible partners. When an agent is asked to vote between two offered matchings, they vote for the one that allocates the more desirable partner to them. The goal of the mechanism designer is to compute a matching that guarantees some type of optimality. A rich literature has emerged from various combinations of input type and optimality condition. In our paper, we study three classic input types together with a new, flexible optimality condition that incorporates already defined notions as well.

Input Types. Our three input types differ in the structure of the underlying graph and the existence of objects as follows.

- *House allocation model.* One side of a two-sided matching instance consists of agents who have strictly ordered, but possibly incomplete preferences and cast votes, while the other side is formed by objects with no preferences or votes.

- *Marriage model.* Vertices on both sides of a two-sided matching instance are agents, who all have strictly ordered, but possibly incomplete preferences and cast votes.
- *Roommates model.* The matching instance is not necessarily two-sided, all vertices are agents, who have strictly ordered, but possibly incomplete preferences and cast votes.

Optimality Condition. For a given k, we say that a matching M is k-*stable* if there is no other matching M' that at least k agents prefer to M. Notice that this notion is highly restrictive, as the number of agents who prefer M to M' is not taken into account. Some special cases of k express very intuitive notions. The well-known notion of weak Pareto optimality is equivalent to n-stability; majority stability (Thakur, 2021) is equivalent to $\frac{n+1}{2}$-stability, and finally, 1-stability asks whether there is a matching that assigns each agent their most preferred partner.

Structure of the Paper and Techniques. We summarize relevant known results in Sect. 2 and lay the formal foundations of our investigation in Sect. 3. We then turn to our complexity results for the house allocation model in Sect. 4 and provide analogous proofs for the marriage and roommates models in Sect. 5. We conclude in Sect. 6. Our proofs rely on tools from matching theory such as the famous Gallai-Edmonds decomposition, stable partitions, or scaling an instance with carefully designed gadgets. Due to space restrictions, we had to omit some of these proofs in this version—for them, please consult the full version (Aziz et al., 2023) of the paper.

2   Related Work

Matchings under preferences have been actively researched by both Computer Scientists and Economists (Roth, 1982, Manlove, 2013). In this section, we highlight known results on the most closely related optimality concepts from the field.

2.1   Pareto Optimal Matchings

Pareto optimality is a desirable condition, most typically studied in the house allocation model. It is often combined with other criteria, such as lower and upper quotas. A matching M is *Pareto optimal* if there is no matching M', in which no agent is matched to a object they consider worse, while at least one agent is matched to a object they consider better than their object in M. A much less restrictive requirement implies *weak Pareto optimality*: M is weakly Pareto optimal if no matching M' exists that is preferred by all agents. This notion is equivalent to n-stability.

Weak Pareto optimality is mainly used in continuous and multi-objective optimization (Ehrgott and Nickel, 2002) and in economic theory (Warburton,

1983, Florenzano et al., 2006). Pareto optimality is one of the most studied concepts in coalition formation and hedonic games (Aziz et al., 2013, Bullinger, 2020, Elkind et al., 2020, Balliu et al., 2022), and has also been defined in the context of various matching markets (Cechlárová et al., 2014, 2016, Aziz et al., 2018, Biró and Gudmundsson, 2020). As shown by Abraham et al. (2004), in the house allocation model, a maximum size Pareto optimal matching can be found in polynomial time.

2.2 Stable Matchings

Possibly the most studied optimality notion for the marriage and roommates models is stability. A matching is *stable* if it is not *blocked* by any edge, that is, no pair of agents exists who are mutually inclined to abandon their partners for each other. There is a striking difference between the definitions of stability and k-stability: while the existence of a blocking edge is an inherently local property, k-stability is defined in relation with other matchings.

The existence of stable matchings was shown in the seminal paper of Gale and Shapley (1962) for the marriage model. Later, Irving (1985) gave a polynomial-time algorithm to decide whether a given roommates instance admits a stable matching. Tan (1991) improved Irving's algorithm by providing an algorithm that always finds a so-called stable partition, which coincides with a stable matching if any exists. Stability was later extended to various other input settings in order to suit the growing number of applications such as employer matching markets (Roth and Sotomayor, 1990), university admission decisions (Balinski and Sönmez, 1999, Braun et al., 2010), campus housing matchings (Chen and Sönmez, 2002, Perach et al., 2008), and bandwidth matching (Gai et al., 2007).

2.3 Popular Matchings

Popular matchings translate the simple majority voting rule into the world of matchings under preferences. Given two matchings M and M', matching M is more popular than M' if the number of vertices preferring M to M' is larger than the number of vertices preferring M' to M. A matching M is *popular* in an instance if there is no matching M' that is more popular than M. The main difference between k-stability and popularity is that in the earlier, only agents are counted who benefit from switching to an alternative matching, while in popularity, agents can vote both for and against the alternative matching.

The concept of popularity was first introduced by Gärdenfors (1975) for the marriage model, and then studied by Abraham et al. (2007) in the house allocation model. Polynomial-time algorithms to find a popular matching were given in both models. In the marriage model, it was already noticed by Gärdenfors that all stable matchings are popular, which implies that in this model, popular matchings always exist. In fact stable matchings are the smallest size popular matchings, as shown by Biró et al. (2010), while maximum size popular matchings can be found in polynomial time as well (Huang and Kavitha, 2013a, Kavitha, 2014).

Only recently Faenza et al. (2019) and Gupta et al. (2021) resolved the long-standing (Biró et al., 2010, Huang and Kavitha, 2013b, Manlove, 2013, Cseh, 2017, Huang and Kavitha, 2021) open problem on the complexity of deciding whether a popular matching exists in a popular roommates instance and showed that the problem is NP-complete. This hardness extends to graphs with complete preference lists (Cseh and Kavitha, 2021).

Besides the three matching models, popularity has also been defined for spanning trees (Darmann, 2013), permutations (van Zuylen et al., 2014, Kraiczy et al., 2021), the ordinal group activity selection problem (Darmann, 2018), and very recently, for branchings (Kavitha et al., 2022a). Matchings nevertheless constitute the most actively researched area of the majority voting rule outside of the usual voting scenarios.

2.4   Relaxing Popularity

The two most commonly used notions for near-popularity are called *minimum unpopularity factor* (McCutchen, 2008, Kavitha et al., 2011, Huang and Kavitha, 2013a, Kavitha, 2014, Bhattacharya et al., 2015, Kavitha et al., 2022a, Ruangwises and Itoh, 2021) and *minimum unpopularity margin* (McCutchen, 2008, Huang et al., 2011, Kavitha et al., 2022a, 2022b). Both notions express that a near-popular matching is never beaten by too many votes in a pairwise comparison with another matching. We say that matching M' *dominates* matching M by a margin of $u - v$, where u is the number of agents who prefer M' to M, while v is the number of agents who prefer M to M'. The *unpopularity margin* of M is the maximum margin by which it is dominated by any other matching. As opposed to k-stability, the unpopularity margin takes the number of both the satisfied and dissatisfied agents into account when comparing two matchings.

Checking whether a matching M' exists that dominates a given matching M by a margin of k can be done in polynomial time by the standard popularity verification algorithms in all models (Abraham et al., 2007, Biró et al., 2010, Ruangwises and Itoh, 2021). Finding a least-unpopularity-margin matching in the house allocation model is NP-hard (McCutchen, 2008), which implies that for a given (general) k, deciding whether a matching with unpopularity margin k exists is also NP-complete. A matching of unpopularity factor 0, which is a popular matching, always exists in the marriage model, whereas deciding whether such a matching exists in the roommates model is NP-complete (Faenza et al., 2019, Gupta et al., 2021).

The unpopularity margin of a matching expresses the degree of undefeatability of a matching admittedly better than our k-stability. We see a different potential in k-stability and majority stability. The fact that, compared to M, there is no alternative matching in which at least k agents improve simultaneously, is a strong reason for choosing M—especially if $k = \frac{n+1}{2}$. The decision maker might care about minimizing the number of agents who would mutually improve by switching to an alternative matching. If there is a matching, where a significant number of agents can improve simultaneously, then they may protest together against the central agency to change the outcome—even though it would make some other agents worse off—out of ignorance or lack of information about the preferences of others. The unpopularity margin and factor give no information on this aspect, as they only measure the relative number of improving and disimproving agents.

2.5 Majority Stability

The study of majority stable matchings was initiated very recently by Thakur (2021). The three well-known voting rules plurality, majority, and unanimity translate into popularity, majority stability, and Pareto optimality in the matching world. A matching M is called *majority stable* if no matching M' exists that is preferred by more than half of all voters to M. The concept is equivalent to $\frac{n+1}{2}$-stability in our terminology.

Thakur observed that majority stability, in sharp contrast to popularity, is strikingly robust to correlated preferences. Based on this, he argued that in application areas where preferences are interdependent, majority stability is a more desirable solution concept than popularity. He provided examples and simulations to illustrate that, unlike majority stable matchings, the existence of a popular matching is sensitive to even small levels of correlations across individual's preferences. Via a linear programming approach he also showed that the verification of majority stability is polynomial-time solvable in the house allocation model.

3 Preliminaries

In this section, we describe our input settings, formally define our optimality concepts, and give a structured overview of all investigated problems.

3.1 Input

In the simplest of our three models, the house allocation model, we consider a set of agents $N = \{1, \ldots, n\}$ and a set of objects O. Each agent $i \in N$ has strict preferences $\succ_i$ over a subset of O, called the set of *acceptable* objects to i, while objects do not have preferences. The notation $o_1 \succ_i o_2$ means that agent i prefers object o_1 to object o_2. Being unmatched is considered worse by agents than being matched to any acceptable object or agent. To get a more complete picture, we also explore cases, where ties are allowed in the preference lists. A *matching* assigns each object to at most one agent and gives at most one acceptable object to each agent.

In the marriage model, no objects are present. Instead, the agent set $N = U \cup W$ is partitioned into two disjoint sets, and each agent seeks to be matched to an acceptable agent from the other set. In the roommates model, an agent from the agent set N can be matched to any acceptable agent in the same set.

For clearer phrasing, we often work in a purely graph theoretical context. The *acceptability graph* of an instance consists of the agents and objects as vertices and the acceptability relations as edges between them. This graph is bipartite in the house allocation and marriage models.

For a matching M, we denote by $M(i)$ the object or agent assigned to agent $i \in N$. Each agent's preferences over objects or agents can be extended naturally to corresponding preferences over matchings. According to these extended preferences, an agent is indifferent among all matchings in which they are assigned to the same object or agent. Furthermore, agent i prefers matching M' to matching M if $M'(i) \succ_i M(i)$.

3.2 Optimality

Next, we define some standard optimality concepts from the literature. A matching M is

- *weakly Pareto optimal* if there exists no other matching M' such that $M'(i) \succ_i M(i)$ for all $i \in N$;
- *majority stable* if there exists no other matching M' such that $|i \in N : M'(i) \succ_i M(i)| \geq \frac{n+1}{2}$;
- *popular* if there exists no other matching M' such that $|i \in N : M'(i) \succ_i M(i)| > |i \in N : M(i) \succ_i M'(i)|$.

In words, weak Pareto optimality means that, compared to M, no matching is better for all agents, majority stability means that no matching is better for a majority of all agents, while popularity means that no matching is better for a majority of the agents who are not indifferent between the two matchings. It is easy to see that popularity implies majority stability, which in turn implies weak Pareto optimality.

We refine this scale of optimality notions by adding k-stability to it. A matching M is

- *k-stable* if there exists no other matching M' such that $|i \in N : M'(i) \succ_i M(i)| \geq k$.

In words, k-stability means that no matching M' is better for at least k agents than M—regardless of how many agents prefer M to M'. Weak Pareto optimality is equivalent to n-stability, while majority stability is equivalent to $\frac{n+1}{2}$-stability. It follows from the definition that k-stability implies $(k+1)$-stability.

We demonstrate k-stability on an example instance, which we will also use in our proofs later.

Example 1 (An $(n-1)$-stable matching may not exist). Consider an instance in which $N = \{1, 2, \ldots, n\}$ and $O = \{o_1, o_2, \ldots, o_n\}$. Each agent has identical preferences of the form $o_1 \succ o_2 \succ \ldots \succ o_n$, analogously to the preferences in the famous example of Condorcet (1785). For an arbitrary matching M, each agent i of the at least $n-1$ agents, for whom $M(i) \neq o_1$ holds, could improve by switching to the matching that gives them the object directly above $M(i)$ in the preference list (or any object if i was unmatched in M). Therefore, no matching is majority stable or $(n-1)$-stable.

3.3 Our Problems and Contribution

Now we define our central decision problems formally. We are particularly interested in the computational complexity and existence of k-stable matchings depending on the value $c = \frac{k}{n}$, so in our problems we investigate cn-stability for all constants $c \in (0, 1)$. One problem setting is below.

---

c-HAI

Input: Agent set N, object set O, a strict ranking $\succ_i$ over the acceptable objects for each $i \in N$ and a constant $c \in (0, 1)$.

Question: Does a cn-stable matching exist?

In most hardness results, we will choose the constant c not to be part of the input, but to be a universal constant instead. Our further problem names also follow the conventions (Manlove, 2013). For majority stability instead of cn-stability, we add the prefix MAJ. We substitute HA by SM for the marriage model, and by SR for the roommates model. If the preference lists are complete, that is, if all agents find all objects acceptable, then we replace the I standing for incomplete by a C standing for complete. If ties are allowed in the preference lists, we add a T. Table 1 depicts a concise overview of the problem names.

Table 1. Each problem name consists of four components, as shown in the columns of the table.

Optimality criterion	Model	Presence of ties	Completeness of preferences
c or MAJ	HA or SM or SR	T or $\emptyset$	C or I

For each of the two optimality criteria, there are $3 \cdot 2 \cdot 2 = 12$ problem variants. Our goal was to solve all 12 variants for all $0 \le c \le 1$ values, and also majority stability (which corresponds to cn-stability for $c = \frac{1}{2} + \varepsilon$, if $\varepsilon < \frac{1}{n}$). Our results are summarized in Table 2. We remark that our positive results are also existencial results, that is we show that a majority stable matching always exists in the SM model and a $\left(\frac{5}{6}n + \varepsilon\right)$-stable matching always exists in the SR model for any $\varepsilon > 0$. We only leave open the complexity of the four variants of c-SR for $\frac{2}{3} < c \le \frac{5}{6}$.

Table 2. Our results on the complexity of deciding whether a k-stable matching exists.

Problem	HA	SM		SR	
variant	NP-complete	NP-complete for $c \le \frac{1}{2}$	P for $c > \frac{1}{2}$	NP-complete for $c \le \frac{2}{3}$	P for $c > \frac{5}{6}$
C, I, TC, TI	Theorems 6, 7	Theorem 15		Theorem 14	Theorem 15	Theorem 13

In order to draw a more accurate picture in the presence of ties, we also investigate two standard input restrictions (Bogomolnaia and Moulin, 2004, Peters, 2016, Cseh et al., 2017), see Table 3.

- DC: dichotomous and complete preferences, which means that agents classify all objects or other agents as either "good" or "bad", and can be matched to either one of these.
- STI: Possibly incomplete preferences consisting of a single tie, which again means that agents classify all objects or other agents as either "good" or "bad", and consider a bad match to be unacceptable.

Note that these two cases can be different, because if the preferences are DC, then each agent can be in one of three situations: matched to a good partner, matched to a bad partner or remain unmatched. In STI, each agent is either matched or unmatched.

Table 3. Results for the two restricted settings in the presence of ties. NP-c abbreviates NP-complete.

Problem	HA			SM and SR		
variant	$c \leq \frac{1}{2}$	$\frac{1}{2} < c \leq \frac{2}{3}$	$c > \frac{2}{3}$	$c \leq \frac{1}{3}$	$\frac{1}{3} < c \leq \frac{1}{2}$	$c > \frac{1}{2}$
DC	NP-c: Theorem 11	NP-c: Theorem 11	P: Theorem 9	NP-c: Theorem 19	NP-c: Theorem 19	P: Theorem 17
STI	NP-c: Theorem 8	P: Theorem 9		NP-c: Theorem 18	P: Theorem 16	P: Theorem 16

4 The House Allocation Model

In this section, we examine the computational aspects of k-stability and majority stability in the house allocation model. We first present positive results on verification in Sect. 4.1 and then turn to hardness proofs on existence and some solvable restricted cases in Sect. 4.2.

4.1 Verification

Thakur (2021) constructed an integer linear program to check whether a given matching is majority stable. He showed that the underlying matrix of the integer linear constraints is unimodular and hence the problem can be solved in polynomial time. Here we provide a simple characterization of majority stable matchings, which also delivers a fast and simple algorithm for testing majority stability.

In this subsection, we investigate k-stability for an arbitrary, but fixed $k \in \mathbb{N}$, which does not depend on n. Our first observation characterizes 1-stable matchings.

Observation 1. *A matching is 1-stable if and only if each agent gets their most preferred object.*

To generalize this straightforward observation to k-stability and majority stability, we introduce the natural concept of an improvement graph. For a given matching M, let $G_M = (N \cup O, E)$ be the corresponding *improvement graph*, where $(i, o) \in E$ if and only if $o \succ_i M(i)$. In words, the improvement graph consists of edges that agents prefer to their current matching edge. We also say that agent i *envies* object o if $(i, o) \in E$.

Observation 2. *Matching M is k-stable if and only if G_M does not admit a matching of size at least k. In particular, M is majority stable if and only if G_M does not admit a matching of size at least $\frac{n+1}{2}$.*

Proof. It follows from the definition of G_M that G_M admits a matching M' of size at least k if and only if in M', at least k agents get a better object than in M. The non-existence of such a matching M' defines k-stability for M. $\square$

Observation 2 delivers a polynomial verification method for checking k-stability and majority stability. Constructing G_M to a given matching M takes at most $O(m)$ time, where m is the number of acceptable agent-object pairs in total. Finding a maximum size matching in G_M takes $O(\sqrt{n}m)$ time (Hopcroft and Karp, 1973).

Corollary 3. *For any $k \in \mathbb{N}$, it can be checked in $O(\sqrt{n}m)$ time whether a given matching is k-stable. In particular, verifying majority stability can be done in $O(\sqrt{n}m)$ time.*

4.2   Existence

By Corollary 3, all decision problems on the existence of a k-stable matching in the house allocation model are in NP. Our hardness proofs rely on reductions from the problem named exact cover by 3-sets (X3C), which was shown to be NP-complete by Garey and Johnson (1979). First we present our results for the problem variants with possibly incomplete preference lists, then extend these to complete lists, and finally we discuss the case of ties in the preferences.

X3C

Input: A set $\mathcal{X} = \{1, \dots, 3\hat{n}\}$ and a family of 3-sets $\mathcal{S} \subset \mathcal{P}(\mathcal{X})$ of cardinality $3\hat{n}$ such that each element in $\mathcal{X}$ is contained in exactly three sets.

Question: Are there $\hat{n}$ 3-sets that form an exact 3-cover of $\mathcal{X}$, that is, each element in $\mathcal{X}$ appears in exactly one of the $\hat{n}$ 3-sets?

4.2.1   Incomplete Preferences

Theorem 4. *c-HAI is NP-complete even if each agent finds at most two objects acceptable.*

Proof. Let I be an instance of X3C, where $\mathcal{S} = \{S_1, \ldots, S_{3\hat{n}}\}$ is the family of 3-sets and $S_j = \{j_1, j_2, j_3\}$. We build an instance I' of c-HAI as follows. For each set $S_j \in \mathcal{S}$ we create four agents s_j^1, s_j^2, s_j^3, t_j and an object p_j. For each element $i \in \mathcal{X}$ we create an object o_i and two dummy agents d_i^1, d_i^2. Altogether we have $12\hat{n} + 6\hat{n} = 18\hat{n}$ agents and $3\hat{n} + 3\hat{n} = 6\hat{n}$ objects. The preferences are described and illustrated in Fig. 1.

$$s_j^\ell : o_{j_\ell} \succ p_j \quad \text{for } j \in [3\hat{n}], \ell \in [3]$$
$$t_j : p_j \qquad\qquad \text{for } j \in [3\hat{n}]$$
$$d_i^1, d_i^2 : o_i \qquad\quad \text{for } i \in [3\hat{n}]$$

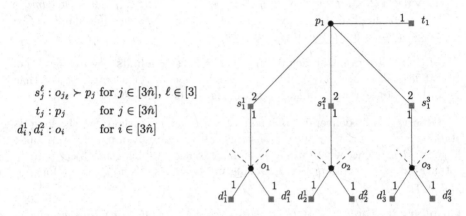

Fig. 1. The preferences and a graph illustration of a gadget of a set $S_1 = \{1,2,3\}$ in the proof of Theorem 4. Red squares are agents, black disks are objects, and the numbers on the edges indicate the preferences to the left of the graph. Dashed edges run to other gadgets. Each agent finds at most two objects acceptable.

We prove that there is a $(5\hat{n}+1)$-stable matching M in I' if and only if there is an exact 3-cover in I.

Claim. If I admits an exact 3-cover, then I' admits a $(5\hat{n}+1)$-stable matching.

Proof: Suppose that $S_{l^1}, \ldots, S_{l^{\hat{n}}}$ form an exact 3-cover. Construct a matching M as follows: for each $j \in [3\hat{n}]$ match t_j with p_j. For each $j \in \{l^1, \ldots, l^{\hat{n}}\}$ match s_j^ℓ with o_{j_ℓ} for $\ell \in [3]$. As each object is covered exactly once, M is a matching.

We claim that M is $(5\hat{n}+1)$-stable. Due to Observation 2 it is enough to show that at most $5\hat{n}$ objects are envied by any agent, so the improvement graph has at most $5\hat{n}$ objects with non-zero degree. For each $j \in \{l^1, \ldots, l^{\hat{n}}\}$, the object p_j is not envied by anyone, as all of s_j^1, s_j^2, s_j^3 got their best object and t_j got p_j. Hence, at most $2\hat{n}$ objects of type p_j and at most $3\hat{n}$ objects of type o_i are envied, proving our claim. ∎

Claim. If I' admits a $(5\hat{n}+1)$-stable matching, then I admits an exact 3-cover.

Proof: Let M be a $(5\hat{n}+1)$-stable matching. First we prove that in M at most $5\hat{n}$ objects are envied by any agent, because we can construct a matching M' that gives all envied objects to an agent who envies them. Each object o_i is envied in any matching by at least one of d_i^1 and d_i^2 and can be given to the envious agent in M'. Regarding envied objects of type p_j, one agent only finds at most one p_j object acceptable, which implies that each envied p_j can be assigned to an envious agent in M'. Therefore, M' is indeed a matching.

As at most $5\hat{n}$ objects can be envied and all o_i objects are envied in M, at most $2\hat{n}$ envied objects are of type p_j. This implies that at least $\hat{n}$ objects of type p_j are not envied by any agent. As these objects are the first choices of their s_j^ℓ, $\ell \in [3]$ agents, those agents must all get their first-choice object of type o_i. As M is a matching, these sets constitute an exact 3-cover. ∎

□

Theorem 5. MAJ-HAI *is NP-complete even if each agent finds at most two objects acceptable.*

We now apply a more general scaling argument than in the proof of Theorem 5 to show that finding a cn-stable matching is NP-complete for any non-trivial choice of c.

Theorem 6. c-HAI *is NP-complete for any fixed constant $0 < c < 1$.*

4.2.2 Complete Preferences
We now extend our hardness proof in Theorem 6 to cover the case of complete preference lists as well.

Theorem 7. c-HAC *is NP-complete for any fixed constant $0 < c < 1$. In particular,* MAJ-HAC *is NP-complete.*

4.2.3 Ties in the Preference Lists
From Theorems 6 and 7 follows that c-HATI and c-HATC are both NP-complete for any constant $0 < c < 1$. Therefore, we investigate the preference restrictions DC and STI.

Theorem 8. c-HATI *is NP-complete even if each agent puts their two acceptable objects into a single tie. This holds for any fixed constant $0 < c \leq \frac{1}{2}$.*

We complement Theorem 8 with positive results in some restricted cases. For example, while c-HATI is hard if each agent is indifferent between their acceptable objects (restriction STI), MAJ-HATI becomes solvable in this case.

Theorem 9. *The following statements hold:*

1. *If each agent's preference list is a single tie in* MAJ-HATI*, a majority stable matching exists and can be found in $O(\sqrt{n}m)$ time.*
2. *If each agent's preference list is dichotomous and complete in* MAJ-HATC *with $|O| \geq |N|$, then a majority stable matching exists and can be found in $O(\sqrt{n}m)$ time.*

3. *If each agent's preference list is dichotomous and complete in* MAJ-HATC *with* $|O| < |N|$, *a* $\left(\frac{2n}{3} + 1\right)$-*stable matching exists and can be found in* $O(\sqrt{n}m)$ *time.*

The first two statements and the fact that k-stable matchings are also $k+1$-stable imply the following.

Corollary 10. c-HATI *is solvable in* $O(\sqrt{n}m)$ *time for any* $c > \frac{1}{2}$ *when each preference list is a single tie. The same holds for* c-HATC *with dichotomous preferences.*

Our last result for the house allocation model is valid for the preference restriction DC.

Theorem 11. c-HATC *with dichotomous preferences is NP-complete*

1. *for any fixed* $c \leq \frac{1}{2}$ *even if* $|N| = |O|$;
2. *if* $|O| < |N|$, *then even for any fixed constant* $c \leq \frac{2}{3}$.

5   The Marriage and Roommates Models

In this section, we settle most complexity questions in the marriage and roommates models. Just as in Sect. 4, we first prove that verification can be done in polynomial time in Sect. 5.1 and then turn to the existence problems in Sect. 5.2.

5.1   Verification

Theorem 12. *Verifying whether a matching is* k-stable *can be done in* $O(n^3)$ *time for any* $k \in \mathbb{N}$, *both in the marriage and roommates models, even the preference lists contain ties.*

Proof. Let M be a matching in a c-SRI instance. We create an edge weight function ω, where $\omega(e)$ is the number of end vertices of e who prefer e to M. From the definition of k-stability follows that M is k-stable if and only if maximum weight matchings in this graph have weight less than k. Such a matching can be computed in $O(n^3)$ time (Gabow, 1976). $\square$

5.2   Existence

To show that a $\left(\frac{5}{6}n + 1\right)$-stable matching exists even in the roommates model with ties, we first introduce the concept of stable partitions, which generalizes the notion of a stable matching. Let $(N, \succ)$ be a stable roommates instance. A *stable partition* of $(N, \succ)$ is a permutation $\pi : N \to N$ such that for each $i \in N$:

1. if $\pi(i) \neq \pi^{-1}(i)$, then $(i, \pi(i)), (i, \pi^{-1}(i)) \in E$ and $\pi(i) \succ_i \pi^{-1}(i)$;
2. for each $(i, j) \in E$, if $\pi(i) = i$ or $j \succ_i \pi^{-1}(i)$, then $\pi^{-1}(j) \succ_j i$.

A stable partition defines a set of edges and cycles. Tan (1991) showed that a stable partition always exists and that one can be found in polynomial time. He also showed that a stable matching exists if and only if a stable partition does not contain any odd cycle.

Theorem 13. *For any $c > \frac{5}{6}$, a cn-stable matching exists in c-SRI and can be found efficiently.*

Proof. We present an algorithm to construct such a matching. We apply Tan's algorithm to obtain a stable partition. Then, for each odd cycle of length at least three, we remove an arbitrary vertex from the cycle. This leaves us with components that are either even cycles, or paths on an even number of vertices, or single vertices, as the odd cycles become paths on an even number of vertices after the removal of a vertex. In all these components except the single vertices, we choose a perfect matching.

Denote the matching obtained in this way by M. Clearly, M has at most $\frac{n}{2}$ edges. We claim that M is $\left(\frac{5}{6}n + 1\right)$-stable. Let M' be any matching. Observe that if an edge $e \in M'$ has the property that both of its end vertices prefer it to M, then e must be adjacent to one of the deleted vertices. This is because otherwise both end vertices of e would prefer e to their worst partner (if there is any) in the stable partition, but this is a contradiction to it being a stable partition in the first place. Also, observe that the number of deleted vertices x just the number of odd cycles, which is at most $\frac{n}{3}$. Combining these, we get that the number of agents who prefer M' to M is at most $2x + \left(\frac{n}{2} - x\right) = \frac{n}{2} + x \le \frac{5}{6}n$.

Hence, M is $\left(\frac{5}{6}n + 1\right)$-stable, which proves our statement. □

As c-SRC, c-SMI, and c-SMC are subcases of c-SRI the existence of a cn-stable matching follows from Theorem 13. In the marriage model, even majority stable matchings are guaranteed to exist.

Theorem 14. *In the marriage model, a majority stable matching exists and can be found in $O(m)$ time. Thus, for any $c > \frac{1}{2}$, a cn-stable matching exists and can be found in $O(m)$ time.*

Proof. Even in the presence of ties, a stable matching can be found in $O(m)$ time with the Gale-Shapley algorithm (by breaking the ties arbitrarily). Such a matching is cn-stable for any $c > \frac{1}{2}$. To see this, let M be stable and suppose that there is a matching M' where more than half of the agents improve. Then, there must be two agents, who both improve and are matched to each other to M', as all improving agents must get a partner. But they would be a blocking pair to M, contradicting the stability of M. □

As majority stable matchings always exist in the marriage model, it is natural to ask whether we can find a majority stable matching that is a maximum size matching as well. We denote the problem of deciding if such a matching exists by MAX-MAJ-SMI. In the case of complete preferences, a maximum size and majority stable matching exists and can be found efficiently, as popular matchings are both majority stable and maximum size. Otherwise, the situation is less preferable, as the following theorem shows.

Theorem 15. *The following problems are NP-complete:*

1. MAX-MAJ-SMI *even if* $|U| = |W|$;
2. *c*-SMC *and c*-SMI *for any fixed constant* $c \leq \frac{1}{2}$ *even if* $|U| = |W|$;
3. *c*-SRC *and c*-SRI *for any fixed constant* $c \leq \frac{2}{3}$.

We now turn to the preference-restricted cases DC and STI.

Theorem 16. *If each preference list consists of a single tie, then a cn-stable matching can be found* $O(\sqrt{n}m)$ *time for any* $c > \frac{1}{3}$.

Proof. Let M be a maximum size matching in the acceptability graph $G = (N, E)$, which can be found in $O(\sqrt{n}m)$ time (Micali and Vazirani, 1980). We claim that M is $\left(\frac{n}{3} + 1\right)$-stable. Suppose there is a matching M', where at least $\frac{n}{3}+1$ agents improve. As the preferences consist of a single tie, this is only possible if all of them were unmatched in M and they can be matched simultaneously. By the famous Gallai-Edmonds decomposition, we know that there is a set $X \subset N$ such that:

- each maximum size matching matches every vertex of X;
- every vertex in X is matched to a vertex in distinct odd components in $G \backslash X$;
- G has exactly $q(X) - |X|$ unmatched vertices, each of which are in distinct odd components in $G \backslash X$, where $q(X)$ denotes the number of odd components in $G \backslash X$.

As $\frac{n}{3} + 1$ agents can improve, we get that $q(X) - |X| > \frac{n}{3}$. Let s denote the number of singleton components in $G \backslash X$. If such a vertex was unmatched in M, then it can only improve by getting matched to someone in X. Let $x \leq s$ be the number of agents in singleton components who improve in M'. Then, $|X| \geq x$ by our observation. Also, at least $\frac{n}{3} - x + 1$ agents must improve from the other odd components, which all have size at least 3. Furthermore, there must be at least x odd components, whose vertices are all matched by M according to the Gallai-Edmonds characterization. Hence, we get that the number of vertices of G is at least $x + 3 \cdot \left(\frac{n}{3} - x + 1\right) + 2 \cdot x \geq n + 3$, which is a contradiction. $\square$

Theorem 17. *If the preferences are complete and dichotomous, then a cn-stable matching exists and can be found in* $O(n^3)$ *time for any* $c > \frac{1}{2}$.

Theorem 18. *c*-SMI *is NP-complete for any fixed constant* $c \leq \frac{1}{3}$ *even if each preference list is a single tie.*

Theorem 19. *c*-SMC *is NP-complete for any fixed constant* $c \leq \frac{1}{2}$, *even if the preferences are dichotomous.*

6   Conclusion and Open Questions

We have settled the main complexity questions on the verification and existence of k-stable and majority stable matchings in all three major matching models.

We derived that the existence of a k-stable solution is the easiest to guarantee in the marriage model, while it cannot be guaranteed for any non-trivial k at all in the house allocation model. Only one case remains partially open: in the roommates model, the existence of a cn-stable solution is guaranteed for $c \geq \frac{5}{6}$ (Theorem 13), whereas NP-completeness was only proved for $c < \frac{2}{3}$ (Theorem 15, point 3). We conjecture polynomial solvability for $\frac{2}{3} \leq c < \frac{5}{6}$.

A straightforward direction of further research would be to study the strategic behavior of the agents. It is easy to prove that k-stability, as stability and popularity, is fundamentally incompatible with strategy proofness. However, mechanisms that guarantee strategyproofness for a subset of agents might be developed. Another rather game-theoretic direction would be to investigate the price of k-stability.

A much more applied line of research involves computing the smallest k for which implemented solutions of real-life matching problems are k-stable. For example: given a college admission pool and its stable outcome, how many of the students could have gotten into a better college in another matching? We conjecture that the implemented solution can only be improved for a little fraction of the applicants simultaneously. Simulations supporting this could potentially strengthen the trust in the system.

Acknowledgments. We thank Barton E. Lee for drawing our attention to the concept of majority stability and for producing thought-provoking example instances. We also thank the reviewers of the paper for their suggestions that helped improving the presentation of the paper. Haris Aziz acknowledges the support from NSF-CSIRO grant on 'Fair Sequential Collective Decision-Making'. Gergely Csáji acknowledges the financial support by the Hungarian Academy of Sciences, Momentum Grant No. LP2021-1/2021, and by the Hungarian Scientific Research Fund, OTKA, Grant No. K143858. Ágnes Cseh's work was supported by OTKA grant K128611 and the János Bolyai Research Fellowship.

References

Abraham, D.J., Cechlárová, K., Manlove, D.F., Mehlhorn, K.: Pareto optimality in house allocation problems. In: Fleischer, R., Trippen, G. (eds.) ISAAC 2004. LNCS, vol. 3341, pp. 3–15. Springer, Heidelberg (2004). https://doi.org/10.1007/978-3-540-30551-4_3

Abraham, D.J., Irving, R.W., Kavitha, T., Mehlhorn, K.: Popular matchings. SIAM J. Comput. **37**, 1030–1045 (2007)

Aziz, H., Brandt, F., Harrenstein, P.: Pareto optimality in coalition formation. Games Econ. Behav. **82**, 562–581 (2013)

Aziz, H., Chen, J., Gaspers, S., Sun, Z.: Stability and Pareto optimality in refugee allocation matchings. In: AAMAS'18, pp. 964–972 (2018)

Aziz, H., Csáji, G., Cseh, A.: Computational complexity of k-stable matchings. arXiv preprint arXiv:2307.03794 (2023)

Balinski, M., Sönmez, T.: A tale of two mechanisms: student placement. J. Econ. Theory **84**(1), 73–94 (1999)

Balliu, A., Flammini, M., Melideo, G., Olivetti, D.: On Pareto optimality in social distance games. Artif. Intell. **312**, 103768 (2022)

Bhattacharya, S., Hoefer, M., Huang, C.-C., Kavitha, T., Wagner, L.: Maintaining near-popular matchings. In: Halldórsson, M.M., Iwama, K., Kobayashi, N., Speckmann, B. (eds.) ICALP 2015. LNCS, vol. 9135, pp. 504–515. Springer, Heidelberg (2015). https://doi.org/10.1007/978-3-662-47666-6_40

Biró, P., Gudmundsson, J.: Complexity of finding Pareto-efficient allocations of highest welfare. Eur. J. Oper. Res. (2020)

Biró, P., Irving, R.W., Manlove, D.F.: Popular matchings in the marriage and room-mates problems. In: Calamoneri, T., Diaz, J. (eds.) CIAC 2010. LNCS, vol. 6078, pp. 97–108. Springer, Heidelberg (2010). https://doi.org/10.1007/978-3-642-13073-1_10

Bogomolnaia, A., Moulin, H.: Random matching under dichotomous preferences. Econometrica **72**(1), 257–279 (2004)

Braun, S., Dwenger, N., Kübler, D.: Telling the truth may not pay off: an empirical study of centralized university admissions in Germany. B.E. J. Econ. Anal. Policy **10**, article 22 (2010)

Bullinger, M.: Pareto-optimality in cardinal hedonic games. In: AAMAS'20, pp. 213–221 (2020)

Cechlárová, K., Eirinakis, P., Fleiner, T., Magos, D., Mourtos, I., Potpinková, E.: Pareto optimality in many-to-many matching problems. Discret. Optim. **14**, 160–169 (2014)

Cechlárová, K., et al.: Pareto optimal matchings in many-to-many markets with ties. Theory Comput. Syst. **59**(4), 700–721 (2016)

Chen, Y., Sönmez, T.: Improving efficiency of on-campus housing: an experimental study. Am. Econ. Rev. **92**, 1669–1686 (2002)

Condorcet, M.: Essai sur l'application de l'analyse à la probabilité des décisions rendues à la pluralité des voix. L'Imprimerie Royale (1785)

Cseh, Á.: Popular matchings. Trends Comput. Soc. Choice **105**(3) (2017)

Cseh, Á., Kavitha, T.: Popular matchings in complete graphs. Algorithmica **83**(5), 1493–1523 (2021)

Cseh, Á., Huang, C.-C., Kavitha, T.: Popular matchings with two-sided preferences and one-sided ties. SIAM J. Discret. Math. **31**(4), 2348–2377 (2017)

Darmann, A.: Popular spanning trees. Int. J. Found. Comput. Sci. **24**(05), 655–677 (2013)

Darmann, A.: A social choice approach to ordinal group activity selection. Math. Soc. Sci. **93**, 57–66 (2018)

Ehrgott, M., Nickel, S.: On the number of criteria needed to decide Pareto optimality. Math. Methods Oper. Res. **55**(3), 329–345 (2002). https://doi.org/10.1007/s001860200207

Elkind, E., Fanelli, A., Flammini, M.: Price of Pareto optimality in hedonic games. Artif. Intell. **288**, 103357 (2020)

Faenza, Y., Kavitha, T., Powers, V., Zhang, X.: Popular matchings and limits to tractability. In: Proceedings of SODA '19: the Thirtieth Annual ACM-SIAM Symposium on Discrete Algorithms, pp. 2790–2809. ACM-SIAM (2019)

Florenzano, M., Gourdel, P., Jofré, A.: Supporting weakly Pareto optimal allocations in infinite dimensional nonconvex economies. Econ. Theor. **29**, 549–564 (2006)

Gabow, H.: An efficient implementations of Edmonds' algorithm for maximum matching on graphs. J. ACM **23**(2), 221–234 (1976)

Gai, A.-T., Lebedev, D., Mathieu, F., de Montgolfier, F., Reynier, J., Viennot, L.: Acyclic preference systems in P2P networks. In: Kermarrec, A.-M., Bougé, L., Priol, T. (eds.) Euro-Par 2007. LNCS, vol. 4641, pp. 825–834. Springer, Heidelberg (2007). https://doi.org/10.1007/978-3-540-74466-5_88

Gale, D., Shapley, L.S.: College admissions and the stability of marriage. Am. Math. Monthly **69**, 9–15 (1962)

Gärdenfors, P.: Match making: assignments based on bilateral preferences. Behav. Sci. **20**, 166–173 (1975)

Garey, M.R., Johnson, D.S.: Computers and Intractability. Freeman, San Francisco (1979)

Gupta, S., Misra, P., Saurabh, S., Zehavi, M.: Popular matching in roommates setting is NP-hard. ACM Trans. Comput. Theory **13**(2) (2021). ISSN 1942-3454

Hopcroft, J., Karp, R.: A $n^{5/2}$ algorithm for maximum matchings in bipartite graphs. SIAM J. Comput. **2**, 225–231 (1973)

Huang, C.-C., Kavitha, T.: Popular matchings in the stable marriage problem. Inf. Comput. **222**, 180–194 (2013)

Huang, C.-C., Kavitha, T.: Near-popular matchings in the roommates problem. SIAM J. Discret. Math. **27**(1), 43–62 (2013)

Huang, C.-C., Kavitha, T.: Popularity, mixed matchings, and self-duality. Math. Oper. Res. **46**(2), 405–427 (2021)

Huang, C.-C., Kavitha, T., Michail, D., Nasre, M.: Bounded unpopularity matchings. Algorithmica **61**(3), 738–757 (2011)

Irving, R.W.: An efficient algorithm for the "stable roommates" problem. J. Algorithms **6**, 577–595 (1985)

Kavitha, T.: A size-popularity tradeoff in the stable marriage problem. SIAM J. Comput. **43**, 52–71 (2014)

Kavitha, T., Mestre, J., Nasre, M.: Popular mixed matchings. Theoret. Comput. Sci. **412**, 2679–2690 (2011)

Kavitha, T., Király, T., Matuschke, J., Schlotter, I., Schmidt-Kraepelin, U.: Popular branchings and their dual certificates. Math. Program. **192**(1), 567–595 (2022)

Kavitha, T., Király, T., Matuschke, J., Schlotter, I., Schmidt-Kraepelin, U.: The popular assignment problem: when cardinality is more important than popularity. In: SODA '22: Proceedings of the 2022 Annual ACM-SIAM Symposium on Discrete Algorithms, pp. 103–123. SIAM (2022b

Kraiczy, S., Cseh, Á., Manlove, D.: On weakly and strongly popular rankings. In: Proceedings of the 20th International Conference on Autonomous Agents and MultiAgent Systems, AAMAS '21, Richland, SC, pp. 1563–1565. International Foundation for Autonomous Agents and Multiagent Systems (2021). ISBN 9781450383073

Manlove, D.F., Algorithmics of Matching Under Preferences. World Scientific (2013)

McCutchen, R.M.: The least-unpopularity-factor and least-unpopularity-margin criteria for matching problems with one-sided preferences. In: Laber, E.S., Bornstein, C., Nogueira, L.T., Faria, L. (eds.) LATIN 2008. LNCS, vol. 4957, pp. 593–604. Springer, Heidelberg (2008). https://doi.org/10.1007/978-3-540-78773-0_51

Micali, S., Vazirani, V.: An $O(\sqrt{|V|} \cdot |E|)$ algorithm for finding maximum matching in general graphs. In: Proceedings of FOCS '80: The 21st Annual IEEE Symposium on Foundations of Computer Science, pp. 17–27. IEEE Computer Society (1980)

Perach, N., Polak, J., Rothblum, U.G.: A stable matching model with an entrance criterion applied to the assignment of students to dormitories at the Technion. Internat. J. Game Theory **36**, 519–535 (2008)

Peters, D.: Complexity of hedonic games with dichotomous preferences. Proceedings AAAI Conf. Artif. Intell. **30**, 1 (2016)

Roth, A.E.: Incentive compatibility in a market with indivisible goods. Econ. Lett. **9**, 127–132 (1982)

Roth, A.E., Sotomayor, M.A.O.: Two-Sided Matching: A Study in Game-Theoretic Modeling and Analysis. Econometric Society Monographs, vol. 18. Cambridge University Press, Cambridge (1990)

Ruangwises, S., Itoh, T.: Unpopularity factor in the marriage and roommates problems. Theory Comput. Syst. **65**(3), 579–592 (2021)

Tan, J.J.: A necessary and sufficient condition for the existence of a complete stable matching. J. Algorithms **12**(1), 154–178 (1991)

Thakur, A.: Combining social choice and matching theory to understand institutional stability. In: The 25th Annual ISNIE / SIOE Conference. Society for Institutional and Organizational Economics (2021)

van Zuylen, A., Schalekamp, F., Williamson, D.: Popular ranking. Discret. Appl. Math. **165**, 312–316 (2014)

Warburton, A.R.: Quasiconcave vector maximization: connectedness of the sets of Pareto-optimal and weak Pareto-optimal alternatives. J. Optim. Theory Appl. **40**, 537–557 (1983)

Optimizing over Serial Dictatorships

Ioannis Caragiannis$^{(\boxtimes)}$ and Nidhi Rathi

Department of Computer Science, Aarhus University, Åbogade 34, 8200 Aarhus N, Denmark
{iannis,nidhi}@cs.au.dk

Abstract. Motivated by the success of the *serial dictatorship* mechanism in social choice settings, we explore its usefulness in tackling various combinatorial optimization problems. We do so by considering an abstract model, in which a set of agents are asked to *act* in a particular ordering, called the *action sequence*. Each agent acts in a way that gives her the maximum possible value, given the actions of the agents who preceded her in the action sequence. Our goal is to compute action sequences that yield approximately optimal total value to the agents (a.k.a., *social welfare*). We assume *query access* to the value $v_i(S)$ that the agent i gets when she acts after the agents in the ordered set S.

We establish tight bounds on the social welfare that can be achieved using polynomially many queries. Even though these bounds show a marginally sublinear approximation of optimal social welfare in general, excellent approximations can be obtained when the valuations stem from an underlying combinatorial domain. Indicatively, when the valuations are defined using bipartite matching and satisfiability of Boolean expressions, simple query-efficient algorithms yield 2-approximations. Furthermore, we introduce and study the *price of serial dictatorship*, a notion that provides an optimistic measure of the quality of combinatorial optimization solutions generated by action sequences.

1 Introduction

Serial dictatorship (SD) is arguably the most straightforward algorithm with numerous applications in many different settings [1,6,10,16,21,25,26]. In the economics literature (e.g., see [1]), it was first considered as a solution to the *house allocation* problem, where a set of houses have to be matched to agents who have strict preferences for them. The algorithm considers the agents in a fixed order and assigns the most-preferred available house to each agent considered.

Crucially, SD can be used in a much more general context. Consider a scenario with a set of agents, each having a menu of available actions and preferences for them. The objective is to compute a set of collective actions, with one action per agent. SD can perform the task by asking the agents to act in a predefined order. Whenever it is an agent's turn to act, she does so by selecting the action that is best possible, given the actions of agents who acted before. Previous actions may render some action of an agent unavailable and they can furthermore change her initial preferences.

© The Author(s), under exclusive license to Springer Nature Switzerland AG 2023
A. Deligkas and A. Filos-Ratsikas (Eds.): SAGT 2023, LNCS 14238, pp. 329–346, 2023.
https://doi.org/10.1007/978-3-031-43254-5_19

This is a paradigm with several advantages. From the computational point of view, SD is as simple as possible. Furthermore, it is easily explainable to the agents, who are expected to have a minimal interaction with it. As SD never uses any input from the agents besides their actions, they have no other option but to select their best available action. On the negative side, the predefined order in which the agents are considered may lead to inefficiencies [10]. An agent who acts early may block actions which might be highly beneficial to agents acting later. *Random serial dictatorship* [1,6,16,21] is an attempt to address this inefficiency without deviating from the main principles of SD. The main idea is to consider the agents in a uniformly random order in the hope that problematic orderings will be used only rarely. However, inefficiencies may still happen [16].

We attempt a radical improvement of SD and instead ask: what is the ordering of the agents which SD must use in order to obtain the *best* possible results? In other words, we are interested in *optimizing* over serial dictatorships for a given problem. Of course, this task cannot be performed without using the agent preferences. Starting with no information about the problem at hand, our algorithms learn (part of) the preferences by *posing queries* to the agents. A typical query to an agent asks for the value of her best possible action in an agent ordering. Our objective is to study the *query complexity* of optimizing over serial dictatorships and to seek algorithms that use as few queries as possible.

Our Contribution. At the highest level of abstraction, we define the problem OPTIMALSEQUENCE that captures the essence of optimizing over serial dictatorships (see Sect. 3). Instances of OPTIMALSEQUENCE consist of a set of n agents. Each agent i has a valuation function which returns the value $v_i(S)$ she gets by her best available action after the agents in the sequence S have acted before i. Our aim is to design algorithms that compute an agent ordering that gives high value to the agents. Our benchmark is the *social welfare*, i.e., the total value of all agents. An important restriction is low query complexity; we seek algorithms that use only polynomially many value queries. Our main result (under a mild monotonicity assumption) is an asymptotically tight bound of $\Theta\left(\frac{n \ln \ln n}{\ln n}\right)$ on the best approximation ratio that can be achieved by such algorithms that use randomization.

Next, in Sect. 4 we consider refined OPTIMALSEQUENCE instances that may be relevant for practical applications. We do so by assuming an underlying combinatorial structure which defines the valuations. Indicatively, we present two specific valuation structures, motivated by matching markets and constraint satisfaction. These define two special cases of OPTIMALSEQUENCE, which we call OSM and OSS (see Sects. 5 and 6). In OSM, the agents have a set of items as their available actions. Whenever it is an agent's turn to act, she picks the available item that is of highest value to her. In OSS, each agent controls a Boolean variable and has two actions: setting her variable to either True or False. These variables appear in a collection of weighted clauses. Whenever it is an agent's turn, she acts so that the weight of new satisfied clauses is maximized.

It turns out that OSM and OSS admit much better algorithms. We present simple 2-approximation algorithms for them and leave open the question of better approximation results or lower bounds on the approximation ratio that can be achieved by algorithms with polynomial query complexity. We furthermore study computational questions related to the existence of serial dictatorships that produce a given solution to the underlying combinatorial problem. We prove that whether a given perfect matching for OSM can be produced by serial dictatorships can be decided in polynomial time. In contrast, for OSS, we show that deciding whether a given Boolean assignment can be produced by a serial dictatorship is an NP-hard problem.

We also consider serial dictatorship as a *solution concept* and quantify the restrictions it poses on the solutions of optimization problems by introducing the notion of the *price of serial dictatorship* (PoSD). The PoSD of a combinatorial optimization problem is the worst-case ratio over all instances of the benefit of the optimal solution over the best social welfare obtained by a serial dictatorship. We prove that the PoSD of maximum-weight bipartite matching is 1 while, in contrast, for maximum satisfiability, it is between 3/2 and 2.

Our work reveals many open problems; we give a list with the most important ones later. We remark that the approach can be naturally extended to many other combinatorial problems than the ones considered here.

Further Related Work. Serial dictatorship and its variations have been well-studied in the matching literature [23]. It seems however that the approach we consider here has not received attention therein. As an attempt to optimize serial dictatorships, one can view the notion of greedy weighted matchings in [15]. A greedy weighted matching is one that can be produced by an algorithm which starts from an empty matching and iteratively puts an edge of maximum weight that is consistent with it. This is a restricted way to optimize over serial dictatorships. Furthermore, the authors in [15] study the computational complexity of the problem assuming that the graph information (i.e., the edge weights) is given to the algorithm upfront. The notion of picking sequence in fair division [5,9,18,20] is close to the action sequences that we consider here; the crucial difference is that each agent can appear several times in a picking sequence.

Optimizing over serial dictatorships can be thought of as a particular way of exploiting greediness in computation. There have been several attempts to formally define greedy algorithms, including their relations to matroids, which are covered in classical textbooks on algorithm design [13]. In relation to combinatorial optimization, the work on incremental priority algorithms [7,8,14] has conceptual similarities. Furthermore, for maximum satisfiability, there is an ongoing research line (e.g., see [24]) that aims to design simple greedy-like algorithms that achieve good approximation ratios. However, all these studies neglect query complexity questions.

Finally, we remark that value queries, similar in spirit to those we consider here, have been used to solve the maximum welfare problem in combinatorial auctions [22]. The PoSD notion is inspired by the price of stability in strategic games [3] and the price of fairness in allocation problems [4,11].

2 Preliminaries

We consider scenarios where a set of agents are asked to *act* in a particular order. Whenever it is the turn of an agent to act, she selects an action that gives her the maximum possible value, given the actions of agents who acted before her. In this section, we present basic definitions and notation for an abstract model that captures such scenarios. Later, in Sect. 4, we refine this model further to bring it closer to well-known combinatorial optimization problems.

We denote by n the number of agents, which we assume to be identified by the integers in set $[n] = \{1, 2, ..., n\}$. An *action sequence* (respectively, *action subsequence*) S is an ordering $S = (S(1), S(2), ...)$ of the agents in $[n]$ (respectively, some of the agents in $[n]$). For a subset of agents $C \subseteq [n]$, we denote by $\mathcal{S}_C$ the set of all action (sub)sequences of the agents in C. For an agent $i \in [n]$, we write $\mathcal{S}_{-i}$ to denote all possible action subsequences consisting of agents from the set $[n] \setminus \{i\}$. We reserve the letters S and π for use as action (sub)sequences.

For two action subsequences S and S', we write $S' \leq S$ if S' is an ordered subset of S, i.e., if all agents in S' are also in S and have the same relative ordering. We use $S\|i$ to denote the action (sub)sequence which is obtained by appending agent i to the action subsequence S. We use $S \setminus j$ to denote the action subsequence obtained by removing agent j from S, and preserving the order of the remaining agents. For an action (sub)sequence S, we write S^i to denote the action subsequence consisting of the ordered set of agents that are ranked ahead of agent i in S. We sometimes use the term *prefix* to refer to agents at the beginning of an action (sub)sequence. Clearly, for any agent i who appears in action subsequence S, it is $S^i \leq S$. For an integer $c \in [n]$, we denote by $S|_c$ the action subsequence consisting of the first c agents of S.

Every agent $i \in [n]$ has a *valuation function* $v_i : \mathcal{S}_{-i} \mapsto \mathbb{R}_{\geq 0}$ which, for every action subsequence $S \in \mathcal{S}_{-i}$, returns the value $v_i(S)$ that agent i gets when acting immediately after the agents in the action subsequence[1] S. We say that the valuations of an agent i are *monotone* if for any two action subsequences $S, S' \in \mathcal{S}_{-i}$, $S' \leq S$ implies $v_i(S') \geq v_i(S)$. The *social welfare* SW(S) of an action sequence S is the total value of the agents in the sequence, i.e., SW$(S) = \sum_{i \in [n]} v_i(S^i)$.

We study the problem of computing an action sequence having maximum social welfare, which we call OPTIMALSEQUENCE. In particular, an instance of OPTIMALSEQUENCE consists of the valuation functions of n agents and the objective is to compute an action sequence of maximum social welfare. An important limitation of our model is that the valuation functions are not given to the algorithm as part of the input. Instead, the algorithms for solving OPTIMALSEQUENCE can access the entry $v_i(S)$ of the valuation function through a query. We are interested in algorithms that solve OPTIMALSEQUENCE using a polynomial number of queries. In other words, we are interested in understanding the *query complexity* of OPTIMALSEQUENCE. Notice that exponentially many queries (for

---

[1] Note that agents are *myopic*, i.e., they choose their best available action in a given round without thinking how their peers will behave in subsequent rounds.

each agent i and each action subsequence in $\mathcal{S}_{-i}$) can always be used to learn the valuation functions. Then, OPTIMALSEQUENCE can be solved exactly. We remark that computational limitations are not our concern in this work and we assume to have unlimited computational resources to process the valuations once these are available.

As we will see, solving OPTIMALSEQUENCE exactly using polynomially many queries is a challenge. So, we are interested in algorithms that compute approximately optimal solutions. On input an OPTIMALSEQUENCE instance, a ρ-*approximate* action sequence (for $\rho \geq 1$) is one which has a social welfare that is at most ρ times smaller than the maximum possible (or *optimal*) social welfare over all action sequences. We refer to ρ as the *approximation ratio* of an algorithm which always returns ρ-approximate action sequences. We are interested in OPTIMALSEQUENCE algorithms that make only polynomially many queries and achieve an approximation ratio that is as low as possible.

3   The Query Complexity of Approximate Serial Dictatorships

We devote this section to studying the query complexity of approximation algorithms for OPTIMALSEQUENCE, presenting both positive and negative results. It is not hard to see that non-monotone valuations are notoriously hard to cope with and any finite approximation may require to examine almost all the $n!$ action sequences.[2] However, as we will see later in Sect. 6, excellent approximations for special cases of non-monotone valuations are possible.

So, in the rest of this section, we focus on instances with monotone valuations. On the positive side, we present two algorithms for OPTIMALSEQUENCE, one deterministic and one randomized, called DET and RAND, respectively. Both algorithms use an integer parameter $c \geq 1$ and apply to n-agent OPTIMALSEQUENCE instances. We denote by N_c the collection consisting of all sets of c distinct agents from $[n]$. Algorithm DET considers all c-sets in N_c. For each set $C \in N_c$, it considers every action subsequence $S \in \mathcal{S}_C$ and selects the one, call it S', that maximizes the quantity $\sum_{i \in C} v_i(S^i)$. Finally, it returns an action sequence that contains S' as a prefix (by filling the last $n - c$ positions in the action sequence with agents in $[n] \setminus C$ in arbitrary order).

Theorem 1. *On input n-agent monotone* OPTIMALSEQUENCE *instances,* DET *makes $\binom{n}{c} \cdot c \cdot c!$ queries and has an approximation ratio of at most $\frac{n}{c}$.*

Proof. Consider an n-agent OPTIMALSEQUENCE instance and notice that the algorithm enumerates all the $\binom{n}{c}$ elements of N_c and for each element $C \in N_c$ and each of the $c!$ action subsequences $S \in \mathcal{S}_C$, it makes c queries to compute the value of the sum $\sum_{i \in C} v_i(S^i)$. The bound on the number of queries follows.

---

[2] Indeed, consider instances in which a special agent i has valuation $v_i(S) = 1$ if S contains all $n-1$ other agents in a specific hidden order and all other agent valuations are zero. To compute the only action sequence with non-zero social welfare, an algorithm needs to "guess" the hidden order.

Given an n-agent OPTIMALSEQUENCE instance, let $\widetilde{\pi}$ be the optimal action sequence, π be the action sequence returned by algorithm DET, and $S = \pi|_c$. Denote by $\widetilde{S} \leq \widetilde{\pi}$ the action subsequence consisting of those c agents that have the c highest values $v_i(\widetilde{\pi}^i)$ (breaking ties arbitrarily). By the definition of DET,

$$\sum_{i \in S} v_i(S^i) \geq \sum_{i \in \widetilde{S}} v_i(\widetilde{S}^i). \tag{1}$$

Furthermore, by monotonicity, the fact that $\widetilde{S}^i \leq \widetilde{\pi}^i$ implies that $v_i(\widetilde{S}^i) \geq v_i(\widetilde{\pi}^i)$ for every agent i and, thus,

$$\sum_{i \in \widetilde{S}} v_i(\widetilde{S}^i) \geq \sum_{i \in \widetilde{S}} v_i(\widetilde{\pi}^i). \tag{2}$$

Finally, by the definition of $\widetilde{S}$, we have $\sum_{i \in \widetilde{S}} v_i(\widetilde{\pi}^i) \geq \frac{c}{n} \cdot \sum_{i \in [n]} v_i(\widetilde{\pi}^i)$. Using the inequalities (1), (2) and the definition of the social welfare, we get

$$\mathrm{SW}(\pi) = \sum_{i \in [n]} v_i(\pi^i) \geq \sum_{i \in S} v_i(S^i) \geq \frac{c}{n} \cdot \sum_{i \in [n]} v_i(\widetilde{\pi}^i) = \frac{c}{n} \cdot \mathrm{SW}(\widetilde{\pi}),$$

as desired.   □

Theorem 1 implies the following using $c = 1/\epsilon$ for constant $\epsilon > 0$.

Corollary 1. *For every constant $\epsilon > 0$, on input n-agent monotone OPTIMALSEQUENCE instances, algorithm DET has an approximation ratio at most $\epsilon \cdot n$ by making $O\left(n^{2/\epsilon}\right)$ queries.*

Algorithm RAND is similar to DET; it uses randomization to avoid the enumeration over all elements of N_c. First, it selects a c-set C from N_c uniformly at random. Then, it considers every action subsequence $S \in \mathcal{S}_C$ and selects the one, call it S', that maximizes the quantity $\sum_{i \in C} v_i(S^i)$. Finally, it returns an action sequence that contains S' as a prefix.

Theorem 2. *On input n-agent monotone OPTIMALSEQUENCE instances, RAND makes $c \cdot c!$ queries and has an approximation ratio of at most $\frac{n}{c}$.*

Proof. The bound on the number of queries is due to the fact that RAND considers all the $c!$ action subsequences with the agents in C and computes the sum $\sum_{i \in C} v_i(S^i)$ by making c queries for each of them.

To bound the approximation ratio, consider an n-agent OPTIMALSEQUENCE instance and let $\widetilde{\pi}$ and π be the optimal action sequence and the (random) action sequence returned by RAND, respectively. Also, let S_C be the action subsequence consisting of agents in C so that $S_C \leq \widetilde{\pi}$. Since RAND prefers the prefix $\pi|_c$ to S_C, we have

$$\sum_{i \in C} v_i(\pi^i) \geq \sum_{i \in C} v_i(S_C^i) \geq \sum_{i \in C} v_i(\widetilde{\pi}^i). \tag{3}$$

The last inequality follows by monotonicity of valuations, which implies that $v_i(S_C^i) \geq v_i(\tilde{\pi}^i)$ since $S_C^i \leq \tilde{\pi}^i$ for every agent $i \in C$. Since C is selected uniformly at random from N_c, an agent from $[n]$ belongs to C with probability $\frac{c}{n}$. Using linearity of expectation, inequality (3), and the last observation,

$$\mathbb{E}\left[\mathrm{SW}(\pi)\right] \geq \mathbb{E}\left[\sum_{i \in C} v_i(\pi^i)\right] \geq \mathbb{E}\left[\sum_{i \in C} v_i(\tilde{\pi}^i)\right]$$

$$= \frac{c}{n} \cdot \mathbb{E}\left[\sum_{i \in [n]} v_i(\tilde{\pi}^i)\right] = \frac{c}{n} \cdot \mathbb{E}\left[\mathrm{SW}(\tilde{\pi})\right],$$

as desired. □

For $c = \Theta\left(\frac{\ln n}{\ln \ln n}\right)$, Theorem 2 yields the following.

Corollary 2. *On input n-agent monotone* OPTIMALSEQUENCE *instances,* RAND *makes* poly(n) *queries and has an approximation ratio of* $O\left(\frac{n \ln \ln n}{\ln n}\right)$.

We show RAND is (asymptotically) optimal through the following lower bound.

Theorem 3. *For every integer $c \geq 1$, any (possibly randomized) algorithm for monotone* OPTIMALSEQUENCE *that makes at most $\frac{c!}{n} - 1$ queries when applied on instances with n agents has an approximation ratio at least $\frac{n}{c+1}$.*

Proof. For an integer $c \geq 1$, we will define a probability distribution Q_c over n-agent instances of OPTIMALSEQUENCE with an optimal social welfare of n, and will prove that the expected social welfare of any deterministic algorithm that makes at most $\frac{c!}{n} - 1$ queries on these instances is at most $c + 1$. Then, by Yao's principle [27], the quantity $\frac{n}{c+1}$ will be a lower bound on the approximation ratio of randomized algorithms for OPTIMALSEQUENCE.

We define the family $\mathcal{F}_c$ consisting of instances I_π for every $\pi \in \mathcal{S}_{[n]}$. Instance I_π is defined by the following valuation functions. For any agent $i \in [n]$ and any action subsequence S from $\mathcal{S}_{-i}$:

$$v_i(S) = \begin{cases} 1 \text{ if } |S| < c \text{ or } S \leq \pi \\ 0 \text{ otherwise} \end{cases}$$

Hence, the valuation functions are binary. An agent gets a value of 1 only in the following two cases: (a) when she has fewer than c agents ahead of her, or (b) when the agents ranked ahead of her have the same relative ordering as in the action sequence π. In all other cases, her value is 0. Notice that the action sequence π has optimal social welfare of n for instance I_π.

Let us prove that the instances in $\mathcal{F}_c$ are indeed valid ones, i.e., the valuations defined are monotone. Fix any agent $i \in [n]$ and any action subsequence $S \in \mathcal{S}_{-i}$. To prove monotonicity, we need to show that $v_i(S') \geq v_i(S)$ for any action subsequence $S' \leq S$. This follows trivially when $|S| < c$ or when $v_i(S) = 0$. Therefore, let us assume that $|S| \geq c$ and $v_i(S) = 1$. This implies that S is an

336 I. Caragiannis and N. Rathi

action subsequence of π, i.e., $S \leq \pi$. By transitivity, we have $S' \leq \pi$ as well, and the definition of v_i yields $v_i(S') = 1$, thereby proving that v_i is monotone.

For integer $c \geq 1$, the probability distribution Q_c simply selects a *magic action sequence* $\hat{\pi}$ uniformly at random and produces the instance $I_{\hat{\pi}}$. Consider a deterministic algorithm $\mathcal{A}$ that makes at most $k = \frac{c!}{n} - 1$ queries; we will show that the expected social welfare of its output on the (random) instances produced by distribution Q_c is at most $c+1$. Assume that, on input the instance $I_{\hat{\pi}}$, algorithm $\mathcal{A}$ makes k queries of the form (i, S) and eventually returns the action sequence $\bar{\pi} \in \mathcal{S}_{[n]}$. We say that an action (sub)sequence S *hits* the magic action sequence $\hat{\pi}$ when $|S| \geq c$ and $S|_c \leq \hat{\pi}$. We define the *enhanced* version of $\mathcal{A}$, denoted by $\mathcal{A}_{\hat{\pi}}$, that works as follows when applied on instance $I_{\hat{\pi}}$. Algorithm $\mathcal{A}_{\hat{\pi}}$ simulates algorithm $\mathcal{A}$, performing the following additional steps. Whenever $\mathcal{A}$ makes a query (i, S) so that S hits the magic action sequence $\hat{\pi}$, $\mathcal{A}_{\hat{\pi}}$ returns $\hat{\pi}$ and terminates. Also, if the action sequence $\bar{\pi}$ returned by $\mathcal{A}$ hits $\hat{\pi}$, algorithm $\mathcal{A}_{\hat{\pi}}$ returns $\hat{\pi}$ instead. Otherwise, it returns $\bar{\pi}$.

Observe that, the social welfare of algorithm $\mathcal{A}$ when applied on the instance $I_{\hat{\pi}}$ is never higher than the social welfare of the enhanced algorithm $\mathcal{A}_{\hat{\pi}}$. This is due to the fact that $\mathcal{A}_{\hat{\pi}}$ returns a suboptimal action sequence (i.e., one that is different than $\hat{\pi}$) only when this sequence is returned by $\mathcal{A}$. Hence, it suffices to bound the social welfare of algorithm $\mathcal{A}_{\hat{\pi}}$ when applied on instance $I_{\hat{\pi}}$.

For an action (sub)sequence S, observe that $\mathcal{S}_{[n]}$ contains $\frac{n!}{c!}$ action sequences π' such that $S|_c \leq \pi'$. Since $\hat{\pi}$ is selected uniformly at random among the $n!$ action sequences of $\mathcal{S}_{[n]}$, the probability that S hits $\hat{\pi}$ is $\frac{1}{c!}$. By applying the union bound, we obtain that the probability that either some of the k action subsequences that algorithm $\mathcal{A}$ uses in its k queries or the action sequence $\bar{\pi}$ it outputs hit the magic action sequence $\hat{\pi}$ is at most $\frac{k+1}{c!}$. We conclude that the enhanced algorithm $\mathcal{A}_{\hat{\pi}}$ returns $\hat{\pi}$ with probability at most $\frac{k+1}{c!}$ and gets social welfare n. Notice that if this is not the case, the social welfare of the action sequence returned is exactly c. Then, the expected welfare of algorithm $\mathcal{A}$ is

$$\mathbb{E}_{I \sim Q_c}[\mathrm{SW}(\mathcal{A}(\mathcal{I}))] \leq \mathbb{E}_{\hat{\pi} \sim Q_c}[\mathrm{SW}(\mathcal{A}_{\hat{\pi}}(I_{\hat{\pi}}))] \leq c + (n-c) \cdot \frac{k+1}{c!} \leq c+1,$$

as desired. The last inequality follows by the definition of k. □

By applying Theorem 3 with $c = \Theta\left(\frac{\ln n}{\ln \ln n}\right)$, we obtain that RAND is essentially best possible.

Corollary 3. *Any (possibly randomized) algorithm for monotone* OPTIMALSE-QUENCE *that makes* $\mathrm{poly}(n)$ *queries has approximation ratio* $\Omega\left(\frac{n \ln \ln n}{\ln n}\right)$.

4 Specific Valuation Structures

We now explore specific instances of OPTIMALSEQUENCE, in which valuations have a combinatorial structure. In particular, the definition of valuations assumes that each agent i has a set X_i from which she can select her *actions*. A *collection of actions* is a set of agent-action pairs (i, a), each consisting of an agent i and an action $a \in X_i$. An agent i may appear in at most one agent-action pair of a collection. A collection of actions that includes all agents is called *full*. A constraint F defines which collections of actions are *feasible*. F is called *downward closed* if every subset of a feasible collection of actions is feasible.

An action (sub)sequence S produces a collection of actions A as follows. Initially, A is empty. When it is the turn of agent i to act, she selects an action $\widehat{a}$ from X_i which is best possible among all actions a in X_i such that $A \cup \{(i,a)\}$ is feasible. The agent-action pair $(i, \widehat{a})$ is then included in the collection of actions A. To decide which action is best possible, agent i uses a strict ranking of the actions in X_i (possibly dependent on other agent-action pairs in A when this decision is made) and corresponding valuations for them that are consistent to it. We call the ranking of an agent and the corresponding valuations for their action *endogenous* when it is independent of actions by other agents. For an agent i who acts after a collection of actions by other agents, we denote her best possible action as $\mathrm{BR}(i, A)$.

We consider two different feasibility constraints, which define two different classes of valuations and corresponding restricted classes of OPTIMALSEQUENCE instances; others can be defined analogously. Essentially, with each class, we restrict our attention to OPTIMALSEQUENCE instances that may appear in practical applications and which are hopefully easier to solve than the very general ones. The two valuation structures we consider are described in the next two subsections.

4.1 Matchings in Bipartite Graphs

The valuations are defined using a complete bipartite graph $G = K_{n,n}$, equipped with a function $w : [n]^2 \to \mathbb{R}_{\geq 0}$, that assigns non-negative weights to its edges. The nodes in the left part of the bipartition correspond to the n agents. The nodes in the right part correspond to items, which are to be given to the agents, under the restriction that each agent can get (at most) one item and each item will be given to (at most) one agent. Such an assignment of items to agents is represented by a *matching* in G. The weight $w(i,j)$ denotes the value agent i has for item j. Agents pick their items according to an action sequence. When it is the turn of an agent to act, she picks the item of highest value among those that have not been picked by agents who acted before her.

Formally, each agent i has a strict ranking r_i that ranks the items in non-increasing order with respect to the value of agent i for them, breaking ties in a predefined (agent-specific) manner. We denote by $r_i(j)$ the rank of item j for agent i. The items of rank 1 and n for agent i are ones for which she has highest and lowest values, respectively. Also, $r_i(j) < r_i(j')$ implies that $w(i,j) \geq w(i,j')$. For an action subsequence $S \in \mathcal{S}_{-i}$, denote by $\mu_i(S)$ the item agent i gets when she acts immediately after the agents in S. By overloading notation, we use $\mu(S)$ to denote the set of items picked by the agents who acted before agent i, i.e., $\mu(S) = \cup_{k \in S} \mu_k(S^k)$. Clearly, $\mu(\emptyset) = \emptyset$. Then, the action of agent i when acting after the action subsequence $S \in \mathcal{S}_{-i}$ is to pick item

$\mu_i(S) = \arg \min_{j \in [n] \setminus \mu(S)} r_i(j)$, which gives her value $v_i(S) = w(i, \mu_i(S))$. Notice that, when all agents have acted, the items picked form a *perfect matching* in G.

We denote by OSM the special cases of OPTIMALSEQUENCE when applied on instances with the specific valuation structure as defined above. To make a connection with the general combinatorial structure described above, each agent i has the set of all items as its set of available actions X_i. The feasibility constraint F requires that the collection of actions form a matching in G. Clearly, F is downward closed. All agents have endogenous rankings/valuations. It is easy to see that OSM valuations are monotone.

4.2   Satisfiability of Clauses

The valuations are defined using n Boolean variables $x_1, x_2, ..., x_n$, a set $\mathcal{C}$ of m clauses[3] $C_1, C_2, ..., C_m$, and a function $w : \mathcal{C} \to \mathbb{R}_{\geq 0}$ that assigns a non-negative weight to each clause. Agent $i \in [n]$ controls the variable x_i. Informally, when acting according to an action sequence, an agent sets the value of her variable to either True or False, so that the additional weight in the newly satisfied clauses is maximized. The value of an agent is then simply this additional weight of clauses that became satisfied due to her action.

Formally, for agent $i \in [n]$ and a set of clauses M, we denote by $P(i, M)$ (respectively, $N(i, M)$) the total weight of the clauses in M which contain the positive literal x_i (respectively, the negative literal $\overline{x_i}$). For an action subsequence S, we denote by C_S the set of clauses that are not satisfied by the actions of the agents in S. Clearly, $C_\emptyset = \mathcal{C}$. The action of agent i when acting after the agents in the action subsequence $S \in \mathcal{S}_{-i}$ is to set her variable x_i to True if $P(i, C_S) > N(i, C_S)$ and to False if $P(i, C_S) < N(i, C_S)$. Ties, i.e., when $P(i, C_S) = N(i, C_S)$, are resolved by setting x_i to a predefined value (True or False). Then, the valuation $v_i(S)$ is simply $P(i, C_S)$ or $N(i, C_S)$, whichever is higher, i.e., $v_i(S) = \max\{P(i, C_S), N(i, C_S)\}$.

According to the terminology above, each agent i has True and False as her two available actions in X_i and there is no feasibility constraint. In contrast to the two classes above, the agent rankings/values of the two actions are non-endogenous. We denote by OSS the special cases of OPTIMALSEQUENCE when applied on satisfiability instances. It is easy to see that OSS valuations are not monotone.

4.3   Three Key Questions

We devote the last part of this section to introduce the three *key questions* that we consider, using the term OSF as a proxy for a valuation structure defined by a feasibility constraint F.

With specific valuation structures, we hope to be able to achieve considerably better approximations with polynomially many queries, compared to the upper bounds for general OPTIMALSEQUENCE instances in Theorem 2. We remark that,

---

[3] A clause is the disjunction of literals of the variables e.g., $C_4 = x_1 \vee \overline{x_2} \vee \overline{x_4}$.

like in our algorithms in Sect. 3, the only tool that is available to algorithms for these problems is query access to the valuations. However, knowledge of the fact that the valuations have a specific underlying structure may prove useful.

> **Question 1:** How well can algorithms that use polynomially many queries approximate OSF?

Note that the computational complexity of the underlying optimization problem does not have any implications for the query complexity of (approximating) the corresponding OPTIMALSEQUENCE instance. We demonstrate this with a tailored class of instances (defining the special case OSI of OPTIMALSEQUENCE) that use independent sets to define the valuations. Does the fact that the maximum independent set problem is NP-hard (even to approximate) imply any lower bound on the query complexity of OSI? The answer is negative.[4]

Next, we would like to understand how rich the space of action sequences is with respect to all feasible solutions to the underlying combinatorial problem.

> **Question 2:** What is the computational complexity of the following problem? Given a collection of actions that satisfies the feasibility constraint F, decide whether it can be produced by an action sequence.

An action sequence can be viewed as a greedy algorithm for computing a solution to the combinatorial optimization problem MAXF, whose objective is to compute a feasible collection of actions of maximum total value for the agents. An important question about the quality of action sequences is then:

> **Question 3:** How well can the best action sequence approximate the optimal solution to the underlying MAXF combinatorial optimization problem?

We introduce the concept of the *price of serial dictatorship* (PoSD) of MAXF to quantify the answer to Question 3. The price of serial dictatorship of an instance of MAXF is the ratio of the maximum total value for the agents among all the feasible collections of actions over the social welfare of the best action sequence. Then, the price of serial dictatorship of MAXF is the worst-case PoSD over all MAXF instances. Note that PoSD is a number higher or equal to 1.

---

[4] An OSI instance is defined with an n-node undirected graph G. Each node corresponds to an agent. For an agent $i \in [n]$, the value $v_i(S)$ for an action subsequence $S \in S_{-i}$ is 1 if the nodes in $S \cup \{i\}$ form an independent set and 0 otherwise. It is not difficult to see that these valuations are monotone. Furthermore, the social welfare $SW(\pi)$ of an action sequence π is equal to the length of the maximal prefix of π consisting of agents whose corresponding nodes form an independent set in G. Hence, the optimal social welfare among all action sequences is equal to the size of the maximum independent set. Now, notice that a simple algorithm that uses only $O(n^2)$ queries can learn the underlying graph G, compute a maximum independent set in it, and, consequently, an action sequence with maximum social welfare. It just suffices to query the value $v_i(j)$ for every pair of agents i and j. Then, the edge (i,j) exists in G if $v_i(j) = 0$ and does not exist if $v_i(j) = 1$.

5   Matchings in Bipartite Graphs

We now present answers to these three key questions for OSM. An answer to Question 1 can be obtained using Algorithm 1, which is presented in the following. It builds the action sequence π gradually in steps. In the k-th step, it selects the agent i^* (among those in the set variable R, which contains the agents not included in π yet) who attains maximum value if she acts immediately after the action subsequence built so far. Notice that π is an empty action subsequence initially and is augmented in each execution of the for loop of Algorithm 1.

ALGORITHM 1: A 2-approximation algorithm for OSM

Input: Query access to an n-agent OSM instance
Output: An action sequence π
1: Initialize $\pi \leftarrow \emptyset$; $R \leftarrow [n]$;
2: **for** $k \leftarrow 1$ to n **do**
3:     Let $i^* \leftarrow \arg\max_{i \in R} v_i(\pi)$;
4:     Update $\pi(k) \leftarrow i^*$; $R \leftarrow R \setminus \{i^*\}$;
5: **end for**
6: **return** π;

Theorem 4. *On input n-agent OSM instances, Algorithm 1 uses $O(n^2)$ queries and computes a 2-approximate solution.*

Proof. The bound on the number of queries is obvious: the algorithm makes n executions of the for loop and, in each of them, it makes a query (i, π) for each of the at most n agents in set R.

Let $\widehat{\pi}$ be an optimal action sequence for a given OSM instance consisting of a complete bipartite graph $G = K_{n,n}$, edge-weight function $w : [n]^2 \to \mathbb{R}_{\geq 0}$, and rank information $\{r_i\}_{i \in [n]}$ and π the action sequence returned by Algorithm 1. Let M and $\widehat{M}$ be the sets of edges defined by the items picked in action sequences π and $\widehat{\pi}$. Let e_i be the edge that is incident to node i in $\widehat{M}$. Let C be the set of agents who pick a different item in π and $\widehat{\pi}$. For each agent $i \in C$, denote by e_i^+ and e_i^- the two edges of M which are incident to edge e_i. Notice that the definition of Algorithm 1 implies that, for any $i \in C$, the agent who picks the first among those incident to edges e_i^+ and e_i^- gets a value that is at least as high as the weight of edge e_i (since e_i was available at that point and agent i had not picked any item yet). Hence, $w(e_i) \leq w(e_i^+) + w(e_i^-)$ and

$$\mathrm{SW}(\widehat{\pi}) = \sum_{i \in [n]} w(e_i) = \sum_{i \in C} w(e_i) + \sum_{i \in [n] \setminus C} w(e_i)$$

$$\leq \sum_{i \in C} (w(e_i^+) + w(e_i^-)) + \sum_{i \in [n] \setminus C} w(e_i)$$

$$= 2 \cdot \sum_{i \in C} w(i, \mu_i(\pi^i)) + \sum_{[n] \setminus C} w(i, \mu_i(\pi^i)) \leq 2 \cdot \mathrm{SW}(\pi),$$

as desired.   □

Despite the simplicity of Algorithm 1, improvements seem to be technically challenging:

> **Open Question 1:** Are there algorithms that solve OSM optimally using polynomially many queries?

We suspect that the answer to Open Question 1 is positive, at least for the special case of OSM where each agent has different valuations for the items. Unfortunately, our attempts to design an algorithm that learns the underlying valuations in polynomial time have not been successful so far. In our answer to Question 2, we will first use our more general terminology as we intend to provide an answer for a large class of valuation structures; our answer to Question 2 for OSM will follow as a corollary.

Theorem 5. *Consider an OSF instance defined by a downward closed feasibility constraint F and endogenous valuations, and let $A = \{(i, a_i)\}_{i \in [n]}$ be a full feasible collection of actions. Deciding whether there exists an action sequence π that produces A can be done in polynomial time.*

We prove Theorem 5 using Algorithm 2, which constructs the action sequence π in a greedy way. It uses the set variable P to keep the agents whose actions have not been checked yet; the set variable M keeps the agent-action pairs with agents in P. The action sequence is stored in variable π, which is returned at the end. In case no action sequence can be computed, the algorithms returns a Fail report.

ALGORITHM 2: Deciding whether a full collection of actions can be produced by an action sequence

---

Input: A feasibility constraint F, a feasible full collection of actions $\{i, a_i\}_{i \in [n]}$, rank information $\{r_i\}_{i \in [n]}$
Output: An action sequence that produces $\{i, a_i\}_{i \in [n]}$ or Fail report
1: Initialize $\pi \leftarrow \emptyset$; $P \leftarrow [n]$; $M \leftarrow \emptyset$; $k \leftarrow 1$;
2: **while** $P \neq \emptyset$ **do**
3:    Top $\leftarrow \{i \in P : a_i = \text{BR}(i, M)\}$;
4:    **if** Top $\neq \emptyset$ **then**
5:       Let $i^* \in$ Top;
6:       $\pi(k) \leftarrow i^*$; $P \leftarrow P \setminus \{i^*\}$; $M \leftarrow M \cup \{(i^*, a_{i^*})\}$; $k \leftarrow k + 1$;
7:    **else**
8:       **return** Fail;
9:    **end if**
10: **end while**
11: **return** π;

Proof. Clearly, the algorithm runs in polynomial time assuming we have polynomial-time access to $BR(i, M)$. To prove its correctness, first notice that it indeed outputs an action sequence that produces the collection of actions A if it never fails. Now, assume that A can be produced by an action sequence $\widehat{\pi}$; we will show that the algorithm never fails. Indeed, at the beginning of any execution of the while loop, let i be the agent in set P that acts earliest in $\widehat{\pi}$. Denote by $\widehat{M}$ the collection of actions decided by the action subsequence $\widehat{\pi}^i$ (while M is the collection of actions that have been checked prior to the current while loop execution. Since $M \cup \{(i, a_i)\} \subseteq A$, downward closedness of F implies that $M \cup \{(i, a_i)\}$ is feasible. Furthermore, since $\widehat{M} \cup \{(i, x)\} \subseteq M \cup \{(i, x)\}$ for any $x \in X_i$, we conclude that any action that is available to agent i in π^i was also available in $\widehat{\pi}^i$. Endogeneity of valuations then implies that $a_i = BR(i, M)$. □

For OSM, Theorem 5 implies the following corollary.

Corollary 4. *Given an instance of OSM and a perfect matching μ in the underlying bipartite graph G, deciding whether there exists an action sequence π that produces μ can be done in polynomial time.*

Corollary 4 implies that with a full access to the agents valuations, we can compute the optimal action sequence in polynomial time. We can use Algorithm 2 together with Corollary 4 to rediscover a characterization of Abdulkadiroğlu and Sönmez [1] (see also [2]) about matchings that can be computed by serial dictatorships. To do so, we need to adapt Pareto-optimality to our case.

Definition 1. *Given a complete bipartite graph $G = K_{n,n}$ and rank $\{r_i\}_{i \in [n]}$ representing strict preferences of agent $i \in [n]$ for n items, a perfect matching μ is Pareto-optimal if there is no other perfect matching μ' such that $r_i(\mu'_i) \leq r_i(\mu_i)$ for all $i \in [n]$ and $r_i(\mu'_{i*}) < r_i(\mu_{i*})$ for some agent $i^* \in [n]$.*

Theorem 6 (Abdulkadiroğlu and Sönmez [1]). *Given an instance of OSM consisting of a complete bipartite graph $G = K_{n,n}$ and rank information $\{r_i\}_{i \in [n]}$, a perfect matching can be produced by an action sequence if and only if it is Pareto-optimal.*

To answer Question 3, it suffices to use Theorem 6 and observe that there is always a maximum-weight perfect matching that is Pareto-optimal. In this way, we obtain the following corollary.

Corollary 5. *The price of serial dictatorship of maximum weight perfect matching in bipartite graphs is 1.*

6   Satisfiability

It turns out that the case of OSS is fundamentally different from OSM.

Theorem 7. *Any action sequence yields a 2-approximate solution to OSS.*

Proof. Consider an action sequence π. Then, the quantity $P(i, C_{\pi^i}) + N(i, C_{\pi^i})$ is the total weight of the clauses in which variable x_i appears and which are unsatisfied when it is the turn of agent i to act. Hence, $\sum_{i \in [n]} (P(i, C_{\pi^i}) + N(i, C_{\pi^i}))$ is an upper bound on the total weight in all clauses. In addition, the value agent i gets is $v_i(\pi^i) \geq \frac{1}{2}(P(i, C_{\pi^i}) + N(i, C_{\pi^i}))$. Denoting $\hat{\pi}$ to be the optimal action sequence for the OSS instance, we obtain

$$\mathrm{SW}(\pi) = \sum_{i \in [n]} v_i(\pi^i) \geq \frac{1}{2} \sum_{i \in [n]} (P(i, C_{\pi^i}) + N(i, C_{\pi^i}))$$

$$\geq \frac{1}{2} \sum_{j \in [m]} w(C_j) \geq \frac{1}{2}\mathrm{SW}(\hat{\pi}),$$

as desired. $\square$

Given Theorem 7, the obvious next step would be to design more sophisticated algorithms for achieving a better-than-2 approximation ratio with polynomially many queries. However, we believe that there are important obstacles in doing so for OSS, summarized in the next question:

> **Open Question 2:** Is there an exponential lower bound on the query complexity of (approximating) OSS?

Next, we denote by SAT-AS the problem of deciding whether a given Boolean assignment for the underlying satisfiability instance of OSS can be produced by an action sequence. In contrast to the easiness of deciding whether a given perfect matching can be produced by an action sequence, SAT-AS turns out to be intractable.

Theorem 8. SAT-AS *is NP-hard.*

Proof. We prove the theorem by presenting a polynomial-time reduction from EXACT-3COVER (X3C). An instance of X3C consists of a universe $\mathcal{U}$ of $3q$ elements and a collection $\mathcal{T}$ of t sets that each contains exactly three elements from $\mathcal{U}$. The problem of deciding whether there exists an *exact 3-cover*, i.e., a subcollection of q sets from $\mathcal{T}$ that includes all elements of $\mathcal{U}$, is a well-known NP-hard problem [17].

For an element $x \in \mathcal{U}$, we write $f(x) = |T \in \mathcal{T} : x \in T|$ to denote the frequency of x in collection $\mathcal{T}$. We construct a satisfiability instance which contains one *element variable* for each element in $\mathcal{U}$, one *set variable* for each set in $\mathcal{T}$, and one auxiliary variable Q. Additionally, there are five types of clauses, each of which contains at most two literals:

- Type A: Clause $(T_i \vee T_j)$ of weight 1 for each pair of distinct sets $T_i, T_j \in \mathcal{T}$. There are a total of $t(t-1)/2$ such clauses.
- Type B: Clauses $(T \vee \overline{x}), (T \vee \overline{y})$, and $(T \vee \overline{z})$, each of weight 1, for each set $T = \{x, y, z\} \in \mathcal{T}$. There are a total of $3t$ such clauses.
- Type C: Clause $(x \vee \overline{Q})$ of weight $f(x) - 1/3$ for each element $x \in \mathcal{U}$. There are a total of $3q$ such clauses.

- Type D: Clauses $(Q \vee \overline{T_1}), (Q \vee \overline{T_2}), \ldots, (Q \vee \overline{T_t})$, each of weight $t - q + 7/3$. There are a total of t such clauses.
- Type E: Clause (with singleton literal) $\overline{Q}$ of weight $t^2 - qt + 7t/3 - 1/3$.

Hence, the satisfiability instance consists of $n = 3q + t + 1$ variables and $m = t^2/2 + 7t/2 + 3q + 1$ clauses. We now show that there is an action sequence which assigns the value of True to each variable of the satisfiability instance if and only if the X3C instance has an exact 3-cover. The next lemma state important properties an action sequence must have so that all variables are set to True. We use the terms *set agent* and *element agent* to refer to the agents who control the corresponding variables.

Lemma 1. *For the above construction, the following properties hold true.*

1. *Agent Q should act after all element agents.*
2. *Element agent x should act after at least one set agent T such that $x \in T$ has acted.*
3. *At most q many set agents can act before agent Q.*

Proof. We prove the three stated properties in order. For property (1), notice that variable Q appears as positive literal in clauses of total weight $t^2 - qt + 7t/3$. Denoting by w_C the total weight of all type C clauses, we have that Q appears as negative literal in clauses of total weight $t^2 - qt + 7t/3 - 1/3 + w_C$. Since $w_C \geq 2/3$, agent Q can act and set its variable to True only after all type C clauses are satisfied, which implies that all element agents have acted before (and set their variable to True).

Next, for property (2), observe that element variable x appears as positive and negative literal in clauses of total weight $f(x) - 1/3$ and $f(x)$, respectively. As literal $\overline{x}$ appears only in type B clauses, the element agent x can set variable x to True only if at least one set agent T such that $x \in T$ acted before (and set her variable to True).

For property (3), consider when q set agents have acted; denote them by set R. Every set agent T not belonging to R appears as positive and negative literal in clauses of total weight $t - q + 2$ and $t - q + 7/3$, respectively, and would set their variable to False if they acted before agent Q acts (and decreases the total weight of unsatisfied clauses that include T as a negative literal).   □

Lemma 1 proves the structure of the action sequence that assigns each variable to True: it starts with a set R of at most q set agents corresponding to an exact 3-cover of the X3C instance, then come all the $3q$ element agents, followed by agent Q, and finally the remaining set agents. We can verify that such a structure works for any R that forms an exact 3-cover, completing the proof. □

Finally, we show that the PoSD for maximum satisfiability is higher than 1.

Theorem 9. *There is an OSS instance in which no action sequence produces better than 3/2-approximate solution to the underlying satisfiability instance.*

Proof. Let $\varepsilon > 0$ be a negligibly small value. Consider the OSS instance defined by three Boolean variables x_1, x_2, x_3 and the following six clauses: $(x_1 \vee \overline{x_2} \vee \overline{x_3})$, $(\overline{x_1} \vee x_2 \vee \overline{x_3})$, $(\overline{x_1} \vee \overline{x_2} \vee x_3)$, each of weight 1, and (x_1), (x_2), (x_3), each of weight $1 - \varepsilon$. It is easy to verify that any action sequence sets the first two variables to 0 and the third one to 1, producing an assignment that satisfies clauses of total weight at most $4 - \varepsilon$ while the assignment $x_1 = x_2 = x_3 = 1$ has maximum total weight of $6 - 3\varepsilon$. □

Closing the gap between 3/2 and 2 is an important open problem.

> **Open Question 3:** What is the tight bound on the price of serial dictatorship for maximum satisfiability?

Better upper bound on the price of serial dictatorship for maximum satisfiability should exploit simple greedy algorithms. An algorithm we have studied considers the agents in monotone non-increasing order in terms of the total weight in singleton clauses containing their variable. Proving that this algorithm has an approximation ratio, say, 3/2, would be enough to close the PoSD gap. Notice that this would match a known 3/2 bound by Chen *et al.* [12] for a slightly more complicated greedy algorithm proposed by Johnson [19].

References

1. Abdulkadiroğlu, A., Sönmez, T.: Random serial dictatorship and the core from random endowments in house allocation problems. Econometrica **66**(3), 689–701 (1998)
2. Abraham, D.J., Cechlárová, K., Manlove, D.F., Mehlhorn, K.: Pareto optimality in house allocation problems. In: Proceedings of the 16th International Symposium on Algorithms and Computation (ISAAC), pp. 3–15 (2005)
3. Anshelevich, E., Dasgupta, A., Kleinberg, J.M., Tardos, É., Wexler, T., Roughgarden, T.: The price of stability for network design with fair cost allocation. SIAM J. Comput. **38**(4), 1602–1623 (2008)
4. Bertsimas, D., Farias, V.F., Trichakis, N.: The price of fairness. Oper. Res. **59**(1), 17–31 (2011)
5. Beynier, A., Bouveret, S., Lemaître, M., Maudet, N., Rey, S., Shams, P.: Efficiency, sequenceability and deal-optimality in fair division of indivisible goods. In: Proceedings of the 18th International Conference on Autonomous Agents and MultiAgent Systems (AAMAS), pp. 900–908 (2019)
6. Bogomolnaia, A., Moulin, H.: A new solution to the random assignment problem. J. Econ. Theory **100**(2), 295–328 (2001)
7. Borodin, A., Boyar, J., Larsen, K.S., Mirmohammadi, N.: Priority algorithms for graph optimization problems. Theor. Comput. Sci. **411**(1), 239–258 (2010)
8. Borodin, A., Nielsen, M.N., Rackoff, C.: Incremental priority algorithms. Algorithmica **37**(4), 295–326 (2003)
9. Bouveret, S., Lang, J.: A general elicitation-free protocol for allocating indivisible goods. In: Proceedings of the 22nd International Joint Conference on Artificial Intelligence (IJCAI), pp. 73–78 (2011)

10. Caragiannis, I., Filos-Ratsikas, A., Frederiksen, S.K.S., Hansen, K.A., Tan, Z.: Truthful facility assignment with resource augmentation: an exact analysis of serial dictatorship. In: Proceedings of the 12th Conference on Web and Internet Economics (WINE), pp. 236–250 (2016)

11. Caragiannis, I., Kaklamanis, C., Kanellopoulos, P., Kyropoulou, M.: The efficiency of fair division. Theory Comput. Syst. **50**(4), 589–610 (2012)

12. Chen, J., Friesen, D., Zheng, H.: Tight bound on Johnson's algorithm for max-sat. In: Proceedings of the 12th Annual IEEE Conference on Computational Complexity (CCC), pp. 274–281 (1997)

13. Cormen, T.H., Leiserson, C.E., Rivest, R.L., Stein, C.: Introduction to Algorithms, 3rd edn. The MIT Press, Cambridge (2009)

14. Davis, S., Impagliazzo, R.: Models of greedy algorithms for graph problems. In: Proceedings of the 15th Annual ACM-SIAM Symposium on Discrete Algorithms (SODA), pp. 381–390 (2004)

15. Deligkas, A., Mertzios, G.B., Spirakis, P.G.: The computational complexity of weighted greedy matching. In: Proceedings of the 31st AAAI Conference on Artificial Intelligence (AAAI), pp. 466–472 (2017)

16. Filos-Ratsikas, A., Frederiksen, S.K.S., Zhang, J.: Social welfare in one-sided matchings: random priority and beyond. In: Proceedings of the 7th International Symposium on Algorithmic Game Theory (SAGT), pp. 1–12 (2014)

17. Garey, M.R., Johnson, D.S.: Computers and Intractability: A Guide to the Theory of NP-Completeness (Series of Books in the Mathematical Sciences). W. H. Freeman (1979)

18. Gourvès, L., Lesca, J., Wilczynski, A.: On fairness via picking sequences in allocation of indivisible goods. In: Proceedings of the 7th International Conference on Algorithmic Decision Theory (ADT), pp. 258–272 (2021)

19. Johnson, D.S.: Approximation algorithms for combinatorial problems. J. Comput. Syst. Sci. **9**(3), 256–278 (1974)

20. Kalinowski, T., Narodytska, N., Walsh, T.: A social welfare optimal sequential allocation procedure. In: Proceedings of the 24th International Joint Conference on Artificial Intelligence (IJCAI), pp. 227–233 (2013)

21. Krysta, P., Manlove, D.F., Rastegari, B., Zhang, J.: Size versus truthfulness in the house allocation problem. Algorithmica **81**(9), 3422–3463 (2019)

22. Lehmann, B., Lehmann, D., Nisan, N.: Combinatorial auctions with decreasing marginal utilities. Games Econom. Behav. **55**(2), 270–296 (2006)

23. Manlove, D.F.: Algorithmics of Matching Under Preferences. World Scientific (2013)

24. Poloczek, M., Schnitger, G., Williamson, D., Zuylen, A.: Greedy algorithms for the maximum satisfiability problem: simple algorithms and inapproximability bounds. SIAM J. Comput. **46**, 1029–1061 (2017)

25. Roth, A.E., Sotomayor, M.A.O.: Two-Sided Matching: A Study in Game-Theoretic Modeling and Analysis. Cambridge University Press, Cambridge (1990)

26. Svensson, L.G.: Strategy-proof allocation of indivisible goods. Soc. Choice Welfare **16**(4), 557–567 (1999)

27. Yao, A.C.C.: Probabilistic computations: toward a unified measure of complexity. In: Proceedings and the 18th Annual Symposium on Foundations of Computer Science (FOCS), pp. 222–227 (1977)

Repeatedly Matching Items to Agents
Fairly and Efficiently

Ioannis Caragiannis[1,2] and Shivika Narang[1,2(✉)]

[1] Aarhus University, Aarhus, Denmark
iannis@cs.au.dk
[2] Indian Institute of Science, Bengaluru, India
shivika@iisc.ac.in

Abstract. We consider a novel setting where a set of items are matched to the same set of agents repeatedly over multiple rounds. Each agent gets exactly one item per round, which brings interesting challenges to finding efficient and/or fair *repeated matchings*. A particular feature of our model is that the value of an agent for an item in some round depends on the number of rounds in which the item has been used by the agent in the past. We present a set of positive and negative results about the efficiency and fairness of repeated matchings. For example, when items are goods, a variation of the well-studied fairness notion of envy-freeness up to one good (EF1) can be satisfied under certain conditions. Furthermore, it is intractable to achieve fairness and (approximate) efficiency simultaneously, even though they are achievable separately. For mixed items, which can be goods for some agents and chores for others, we propose and study a new notion of fairness that we call *swap envy-freeness* (swapEF).

1 Introduction

The problem of fairly dividing indivisible items among agents has received enormous attention by the EconCS research community in the recent years. The standard setting involves a set of items and agents who have values for them. The objective is to compute an allocation which gives each item to a single agent so that some notion of fairness is satisfied. A diverse set of fairness objectives has been explored in the past; some of the most well known of these are envy-freeness and its relaxations. Prior work has typically explored various settings where agents' allocations do not change with time. Typically, the number of items allocated to an agent is not explicitly restricted, with the exception of some very recent work [7,10,13].

However, sometimes in practice, the same set of items must be allocated to the same set of agents repeatedly. More crucially, another feature that distinguishes such scenarios from the standard setting is that the value of an agent for

This work was supported by the Independent Research Fund Denmark (DFF) under grant 2032-00185B (IC) and by a Tata Consultancy Services research scholarship (SN).

A. Deligkas and A. Filos-Ratsikas (Eds.): SAGT 2023, LNCS 14238, pp. 347–364, 2023.
https://doi.org/10.1007/978-3-031-43254-5_20

an item changes over time and typically depends on how many times the agent has received the item in the past. This can make solutions that were fair when the agents were allocated the items once, no longer fair.

To give an example, consider different research labs that all need access to several expensive research facilities in a university. How should the access of the labs to the facilities be fairly coordinated/scheduled throughout the year? This is a fair division problem with the labs and the facilities playing the role of the agents and the items, respectively. To be fair among labs and efficient overall, such a scheduling should take into account the values the labs have for facilities, which typically change over time. For instance, during the first few weeks of access to a facility, the researchers in a lab may need time to learn how to operate it. During that time, the value the lab gets by accessing a facility can be very low, even negative. As the researchers gain more experience, their research output increases, and so does the lab's value for the facility. Once the researchers have run their intended experiments, the lab's value for the facility decreases again until the next experiment.

To capture such situations, we introduce a new model of *repeated matchings* with n agents who must be matched with exactly one of n items[1] in each of T rounds, repeatedly. An important novelty of our model is that valuations are *history-dependent*: the value an agent has for an item in a round depends on how many times the agent has used the item in previous rounds. Such valuations reveal many interesting hurdles to achieving efficiency and fairness. We use *social welfare* (the total value of the agents from the items they get in all rounds) to assess the efficiency of repeated matchings. We also use relaxations of *envy-freeness* as fairness concepts. We adapt the well-known *envy-freeness up to one item* (EF1) and use it when all valuations are non-negative (i.e., when items are *goods*). A repeated matching is EF1 if the value of every agent i for her bundle is at least as high as her value for the bundle of any other agent j after removing the last *copy* of an item from j's bundle. We observe that EF1 is not suitable when valuations can be positive or negative (i.e., when items are *mixed*), and introduce the notion of *swap envy-freeness* to assess fairness of repeated matchings for mixed items.

Our Contribution. More specifically, our technical contribution is as follows. We prove that the problem of computing a repeated matching with maximum social welfare is NP-hard, even for only two rounds ($T = 2$). Our hardness reduction defines instances with non-monotone valuations. The problem becomes solvable in polynomial time when the valuations are monotone. This is when the value an agent has for an item can only decrease or increase, but not both, in terms of the number of rounds the agent had the item in the past. For the case of monotone non-increasing valuations, earlier work on b-matchings can be leveraged to find the optimal solution. When the valuations are monotone non-decreasing, we find a neat reduction to the case of time-constant valuations which can be solved efficiently.

---

[1] This assumption is without loss of generality since, whenever there are more agents or items, we can add dummy items or agents with zero values, respectively.

We also consider fair repeated matchings, first using EF1 as fairness concept. We find that under identical valuations, EF1 repeated matchings always exist and can be found in polynomial time. Furthermore, we show that any instance with general valuations and $T \bmod n \in \{0, 1, 2, n-1\}$ (i.e., including all instances with at most four agents/items) has an EF1 repeated matching, which can be computed efficiently. We establish that, unfortunately, EF1 is not compatible with social welfare maximization, and even approximating the maximum social welfare over EF1 repeated matchings is NP-hard. This holds even for settings where EF1 solutions and social welfare maximizing solutions can be found in polynomial time separately.

Moreover, at a conceptual level, we propose and study a new fairness notion called swap envy-freeness (swapEF). Here, we find that under identical valuations, swapEF repeated matchings can be found using the same algorithm as used for EF1. Furthermore, we show that swapEF repeated matchings always exist and can be computed efficiently on instances with $T \bmod n \in \{0, 1, 2, n-2, n-1\}$ (i.e., including all instances with at most five agents/items). Our hardness results are proved on instances with goods. Our positive results besides those for EF1, apply to instances with mixed items.

Related Work. In fair division with indivisible items (see [1] for a recent survey of the area), EF1 has been established as a key fairness concept. It was defined by Budish [8] (and, implicitly, a few years earlier by Lipton et al [15]). In contrast to envy-freeness which is usually impossible to achieve, EF1 is always achievable in the standard setting and is also compatible with notions of economic efficiency [4, 9]. These papers assume that items are goods, i.e., agents have non-negative valuations for them. Non-positive valuations, i.e., indivisible chores, have also received attention. More importantly, a series of recent papers consider mixed items that can be goods for some agents and chores for others [2,5,6].

The main assumption in the standard setting is that each item is given to exactly one agent with no explicit cap on the number of items one agent can get. Biswas and Barman [7] consider an extension where the items are partitioned into categories and there are cardinality constraints on how many items an agent can be allocated from each category. They show how to compute an EF1 allocation by extending the envy-cycle elimination algorithm of Lipton et al [15]. Even though cardinality constraints can restrict allocations to repeated matchings, our history-dependent valuations cannot be expressed by their model.

The concept of repeated matching has been considered before, actually using EF1 as fairness concept. However, history-dependent valuations have not. Hosseini et al [14] look at a dynamic one-sided repeated matching model with ordinal preferences that change over time. They study strategyproofness and give a mechanism that is EF1. As the model of preferences studied is entirely different, their results are not applicable to our model. Gollapudi et al [13] study a two-sided repeated matching setting where the agent values may change in each round, but do not take into account how often the two agents have been matched in the past. In addition, due to the two-sided nature of their setting, their results are not applicable to our case.

Roadmap. The rest of the paper is structured as follows. We begin with setting up the notation and relevant definitions in Sect. 2. Section 3 focuses on maximizing social welfare. Here, we give our hardness result for maximizing social welfare in general and polynomial-time algorithms for monotone valuations. In Sect. 4, we explore settings under which we can satisfy EF1 and algorithms that find EF1 solutions. In Sect. 5, we find that even in settings where EF1 repeated matchings can be found in polynomial time, maximizing social welfare over the space of EF1 repeated matchings is intractable. We devote Sect. 6 to the study of swap envy-freeness. We conclude with a discussion on open problems in Sect. 7. Due to lack of space, many proofs are omitted.

2   Notation and Preliminaries

Our setting involves a set $\mathcal{A}$ of n agents and a set $\mathcal{G}$ of n items. We use the term *matching* to refer to an allocation of the items to the agents, so that each agent gets exactly one item and each item is given to exactly one agent. We particularly focus on *repeated matchings*, where the items are matched to the agents in multiple rounds. More formally, we consider instances of the form $I = \langle \mathcal{A}, \mathcal{G}, \{v_i\}_{i\in\mathcal{A}}, T \rangle$, where T denotes the number of rounds and, for each agent $i \in \mathcal{A}$, v_i is a function from $\mathcal{G} \times [T]$ to $\mathbb{R}$, where $v_i(g,t)$ denotes the *valuation* of agent i for item g when it is matched to the item for the tth time. A repeated matching $A = (A^1, ..., A^T)$ is simply a collection of matchings, with one matching A^t per each round $t \in [T]$. Furthermore, we denote by A_i the multiset (or *bundle*) which contains copies of the items to which agent $i \in \mathcal{A}$ is matched in the T rounds.

Hence, defining the bundles A_i for $i \in \mathcal{A}$ given the repeated matching A is trivial. The opposite task is also straightforward. Let $N(B, g)$ be the multiplicity of item g in bundle B. Given bundles of items A_i for $i \in \mathcal{A}$ with $|A_i| = T$ (i.e., each agent gets T copies of items) and $\sum_{i\in\mathcal{A}} N(A_i, g) = T$ (i.e., T copies of each item g are allocated), a consistent repeated matching[2] for instance I is obtained as follows. We construct the bipartite multigraph $G = (\mathcal{A}, \mathcal{G}, E)$ so that the set of edges E consists of (a copy of) edge (i, g) for every (copy of) item g such that $g \in A_i$. The graph G is T-regular and, thus, by Hall's matching theorem (see [16]), can be decomposed into T matchings of edges $M_1, ..., M_T$. These matchings correspond to a repeated matching by interpreting the edge (i, g) in matching M_t as the assignment of item g to agent i in the tth round.

With a slight abuse of notation, we use $v_i(B)$ to denote the *value* agent $i \in \mathcal{A}$ has when she gets the bundle B, i.e.,

$$v_i(B) = \sum_{g\in\mathcal{G}} \sum_{t=1}^{N(B,g)} v_i(g,t).$$

---

[2] We remark that this repeated matching is not unique. However, this does not affect the values of each agent for her bundle and the bundle of any other agent, which are the same in all different consistent repeated matchings.

Hence, for a repeated matching A, $v_i(A_i)$ is the total value from each item copy agent i receives in all rounds. The *social welfare* of A is simply the sum of the agents' values for their bundle, i.e., $SW(A) = \sum_{i \in \mathcal{A}} v_i(A_i)$.

We shall look at specific types of valuations under which we will try to find efficient and/or fair repeated matchings. A well-motivated setting is that of *identical* valuations where $v_1 = v_2 = \cdots = v_n$. This assumption proves particularly useful in finding fair solutions. Another important class of valuation functions is that of *monotone* valuations.

Definition 1 (monotone valuations). *The valuation function v_i is monotone non-increasing (respectively, monotone non-decreasing) if for every item $g \in \mathcal{G}$, and $t \in [T-1]$, we have that $v_i(g,t) \geq v_i(g,t+1)$ (respectively, $v_i(g,t) \leq v_i(g,t+1)$).*

These two classes of valuation functions intersect in the class of (time) *constant* valuations where the value any agent has for an item does not change with the number of copies received.

Definition 2 (constant valuations). *Valuation function v_i is said to be constant if for every item $g \in \mathcal{G}$, we have that $v_i(g,1) = v_i(g,2) = \cdots = v_i(g,T) = v_i(g)$.*

We extend to repeated matchings the well-known fairness notion of *envy-freeness of up to one item* (EF1) as follows.

Definition 3 (EF1). *A repeated matching A is EF1 if for every pair of agents $i,j \in \mathcal{A}$, there exists an item $g \in \mathcal{G}$ such that $v_i(A_i) \geq v_i(A_j \setminus \{g\})$.*

We remark that the operation $A_j \setminus \{g\}$ removes one copy of item g from the bundle A_j if g belongs to A_j and leaves A_j intact otherwise.

We refer to the items as *goods* on instances where all valuations are non-negative, i.e., when $v_i(g,t) \geq 0$ for every $i \in \mathcal{A}$, $g \in \mathcal{G}$, and $t \in [T]$. When there are no restrictions on the valuations, we refer to the items as *mixed*.

3 Maximizing Social Welfare

We first study the complexity of the problem of computing a repeated matching of maximum social welfare. Clearly, if $T = 1$, this task can be easily done by computing a maximum-weight perfect matching in the complete bipartite graph $G = (\mathcal{A}, \mathcal{G}, \mathcal{A} \times \mathcal{G})$, in which edge (i,g) has weight $v_i(g,1)$. For $T > 1$, an approach that seems natural computes gradually a maximum-weight perfect matching for each round, taking into account the matching decisions in previous rounds. This approach cannot find a social welfare maximizing matching.

Example 1. Consider an instance with three agents and two rounds (i.e., $n = 3$, $\mathcal{A} = \{1,2,3\}$, $\mathcal{G} = \{g_1, g_2, g_3\}$, and $T = 2$). The agent valuations are as follows: $v_1(g_2,1) = v_1(g_3,1) = 1 - \epsilon$ (for small but strictly positive ϵ), $v_2(g_2,1) =$

$v_3(g_3, 1) = 1$, while all other valuations are 0. A maximum-weight perfect matching on the complete bipartite graph $G = (\mathcal{A}, \mathcal{G}, \mathcal{A} \times \mathcal{G})$ with weight $v_i(g, 1)$ on edge (i, g) assigns item g_i to agent i in the first round; this gives value 1 to agents 2 and 3, while agent 1 receives value 0.

Then, the natural way to compute the matching of the second round is to compute a maximum-weight perfect matching in the complete bipartite graph $G = (\mathcal{A}, \mathcal{G}, \mathcal{A} \times \mathcal{G})$ with weight $v_i(g_i, 2)$ to edge (i, g_i) (because agent i already uses item i in the first round) and weight $v_i(g, 1)$ to edge (i, g) for $g \neq g_i$. In this way, the matching of the second round will give value of $1 - \epsilon$ to agent 1 only, by matching her to either item g_2 or item g_3. Thus, the social welfare is $3 - \epsilon$.

In contrast, consider the repeated matching in which the first-round matching assigns item g_2 to agent 1, item g_1 to agent 2, and item g_3 to agent 3, and the second-round matching assigns item g_3 to agent 1, item g_2 to agent 2, and item g_1 to agent 3. Agent 1 gets value $1 - \epsilon$ in both rounds, agent 2 gets value 1 in the second round, and agent 3 gets value 1 in the first round. Hence, the social welfare is now $4 - 2\epsilon$.

This example demonstrates that computing a repeated matching of maximum social welfare can be a challenging task. Actually, as our first result indicates, the problem is computationally hard, even for $T = 2$.

Theorem 1. *Given a repeated matching instance, computing a repeated matching of maximum social welfare is NP-hard.*

Proof. We present a polynomial-time reduction from three dimensional matching (3DM). Given a tripartite hypergraph $G = (X, Y, Z, E)$ s.t. $|X| = |Y| = |Z| = k$ and $|E| = p$, we must decide where there exists a subset of size k of edges in E such that each node is incident on exactly one edge. This is a well-known NP-hard problem [12]. Such a subset is a three-dimensional perfect matching. When such a subset exists, we shall say that a 3DM exists. Given such a graph, we shall construct a repeated matchings instance such that a 3DM exists if and only if there is a repeated matching of social welfare at least $8p + k$.

We construct an instance $I = \langle \mathcal{A}, \mathcal{G}, \{v_i\}_{i \in \mathcal{A}}, T \rangle$ with $T = 2$ and $n = \max(2k + p, k + 2p)$ agents/items. The set of agents $\mathcal{A}$ has a *node agent* x for every $x \in X$ and one *node agent* y for every $y \in Y$. There is also an *edge agent* i_e for every $e = (x, y, z) \in E$. The set of items $\mathcal{G}$ has a *node item* for every node $z \in Z$, and two *edge items* g_e^1 and g_e^2 for every $e \in E$. The remaining items or agents are dummy agents and items, which never give any agent any value or have any value of their own. Let $e = (x, y, z) \in E$. The valuations are as follows:

- Node agent x has value 3 for the second copy of edge item g_e^1.
- Node agent y has value 3 for the second copy of edge item g_e^2.
- Edge agent i_e has value 3 for the second copy of node item z.
- Edge agent i_e has value 4 for the first copy of g_e^1 and g_e^2.
- All other valuations are 0 (including the valuation of any agent for a dummy item or of any dummy agent for any item).

This is illustrated in Fig. 1. Thus, for node agents x or y to get any value, they must be matched to an edge item for both rounds. Analogously for z to generate

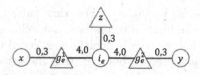

Fig. 1. Edge gadget, values in each round are written on the edges

any value, it must be matched to an edge agent for both rounds. This item/agent must be corresponding to an edge on which they are incident. If an edge item is matched to an edge agent for one round, it cannot generate any social welfare in the other round.

Consequently, in a social welfare maximizing matching, for each edge $e = (x, y, z)$, either the edge items are matched to the edge agent i_e for one round each, giving a combined social welfare of 8, or g_e^1 is matched to x, g_e^2 is matched to y and z is matched to i_e giving a combined social welfare of 9. For an edge $e = (x, y, z)$, if a repeated matching matches both edge items to the corresponding node agents and the edge agent to the node item z, all for two rounds, we say that the edge gadget is matched completely. If a repeated matching matches both edge items to the edge item for one round each, we say that the edge gadget is matched internally. Any other matching, matches the edge gadget partially.

As any node agent can gain value by being matched to an edge item only, and a node item gives value only to a edge agent, it is enough to see how each edge gadget is matched to calculate the social welfare. Each constructed instance can always generate social welfare $8p$ by matching each of the p edge gadgets internally. To get any additional welfare, some edge gadgets must be matched completely. Each completely matched edge gadget gives social welfare 9. Thus, if a repeated matching has social welfare $8p + k$, it must match k edge gadgets completely. The nodes agents and items of these selected edge gadgets must all be distinct. Thus, the corresponding edges form a 3DM.

Now, if a 3DM M exists, we can match the edge gadgets for the edges in M completely and all other edge gadget internally. All other matches are arbitrary. Thus each gadget generates a social welfare of at least 8 and all the edges in M generate an additional social welfare of 1, for total social welfare of 9 each. Thus, the social welfare of the repeated matching is $8p + k$.   □

Fortunately, the problem of computing a repeated matching of maximum social welfare can be solved in polynomial time for monotone valuations, even when the items are mixed. Notice that the instance in Example 1 belongs to the category of monotone non-increasing valuations. Further, in the instance constructed in the proof of Theorem 1, all agents have monotone valuations, only some are monotone non-decreasing and monotone non-increasing. Thus, it is intractable to find a social welfare maximizing repeated matching even when all agents have monotone valuations but not all are monotone non-increasing.

Monotone Non-increasing Valuations. For this particular case, well-known results on b-matchings can be used to find a social welfare maximizing repeated matching. In the following, we briefly explain how; recall that a b-matching in a bipartite graph is just a subset of the edges that includes at most b edges that are incident to any given node. [11] shows how to compute a maximum-weight b-matching on input an edge-weighted bipartite multigraph in polynomial time.

Given a repeated matching instance $I = \langle \mathcal{A}, \mathcal{G}, \{v_i\}_{i \in \mathcal{A}}, T \rangle$ where each $\{v_i\}_{i \in \mathcal{A}}$ is monotone non-increasing, construct the bipartite multigraph graph $G = (\mathcal{A}, \mathcal{G}, E)$ where E consists of T copies of edge (i, g) for each $i \in \mathcal{A}$ and each $g \in \mathcal{G}$. For each $t \in [T]$, $i \in \mathcal{A}$ and $g \in \mathcal{G}$, we set the edge weight of the tth copy of edge (i, g) to $v_i(g, t)$. Now, since the v_is are monotone non-increasing, we can assume that a maximum-weight T-matching in G has the following *consecutive edge copies* property: if it contains k copies of an edge (i, g), these are the first k copies of weights $v_i(g, 1)$, ..., $v_i(g, k)$. Notice that, if this is not the case, we can redistribute the edge copies of (i, g) between agents appropriately without violating weight maximality. Now, a maximum-weight T-matching M in G naturally defines a repeated matching A_M in I, where each i is matched to each g as many times as the number of copies of edge $(i, g)M$ contains. Furthermore, the social welfare of A_M is equal to the weight of M and can be seen to be optimal. The reason is that any repeated matching corresponds to a T-matching with the consecutive edge copies property.

Monotone Non-decreasing Valuations. The above approach cannot be used when all the valuation functions are monotone non-decreasing. Somewhat surprisingly, it suffices to resort to an even simpler ordinary matching computation in this case.

We remark that, on repeated matching instances with constant valuations, there is always a repeated matching of maximum social welfare in which every agent gets the same item in all rounds. To see why, consider any repeated matching A and let t be that round in which the total value the agents get from the items they get in matching A^t is maximum. Then, the repeated matching which uses matching A^t in all rounds has at least as high social welfare as A. Hence, a straightforward maximum-weight matching computation can be used to compute a social welfare maximizing repeated matching for instances with constant valuations. The proof of the next theorem exploits a connection of instances with monotone non-decreasing valuations and instances with constant valuations.

Theorem 2. *Given a repeated instance with monotone non-decreasing valuations, a repeated matching of maximum social welfare can be computed in polynomial time.*

Proof. Consider a repeated matching instance $I = \langle \mathcal{A}, \mathcal{G}, \{v_i\}_{i \in \mathcal{A}}, T \rangle$ with monotone non-decreasing valuations. For each agent $i \in \mathcal{A}$, we construct the constant valuation function v_i^c with $v_i^c(g) = \frac{1}{T} \sum_{t=1}^{T} v_i(g, t)$ for each item $g \in \mathcal{G}$. That is, the value that agent i gets from a copy of item g under valuation v_i^c is i's average value from g under v_i in T rounds. Observe that, by the definition of the valuation v_i, $v_i(A_i) \leq v_i^c(A_i)$ for any repeated matching A and any agent $i \in \mathcal{A}$. This implies that the social welfare of A under the valuations v_i is not higher than the social welfare under the valuations v_i^c. Hence, the maximum social welfare among all repeated matchings with respect to valuations v_i is not higher than the maximum social welfare among all repeated matchings with respect to valuations v_i^c. Furthermore, the maximum social welfare under v_i^c is achieved by a repeated matching $\widehat{A}$ that uses the same matching in all rounds. Finally, note that $v_i(\widehat{A}_i) = \sum_{t=1}^{T} v_i(g_i, t) = v_i^c(\widehat{A}_i)$, where g_i is the item agent i gets in all rounds under $\widehat{A}$. I.e., the social welfare of $\widehat{A}$ is the same with respect to the original valuations v_i and the modified valuations v_i^c. Thus, to maximize the social welfare, it suffices to compute a single-round matching of maximum social welfare according the valuations v_i^c and repeat it for T rounds.   □

4   Computing Fair Repeated Matchings

In this section, we focus on repeated matching instances with goods (i.e., non-negative valuations) and present algorithms that compute EF1 repeated matchings under different conditions. We first consider identical valuations.

Our algorithm for repeated matching instances with identical valuations works as follows. It starts by assigning $\lfloor T/n \rfloor$ copies of each item to each agent. If $T \bmod n > 0$ (i.e., additional copies have to be assigned to the agents so that the repeated matching is correct), the algorithm works in a round robin fashion for $T \bmod n$ phases. In these phases, it uses a fixed ranking of the items according to the value $v(g, \lceil T/n \rceil)$ of their $\lceil T/n \rceil$-th copy. The ranking assigns to each item a distinct integer rank(g) in $[n]$ such that rank$(g_1) <$ rank(g_2) implies that $v(g_1, \lceil T/n \rceil) \geq v(g_2, \lceil T/n \rceil)$. In each round-robin phase, the agents act according to the ordering $1, 2, ..., n$. When it is agent i's turn, she picks a copy of the lowest-rank item that is available.

The algorithm (Algorithm 1) has access to function rank() defined as above and uses the matrix f to store the number of copies of each item an agent gets. The final step is to call routine GenerateFromFreq() to transform f to the repeated matching A; this routine essentially implements the transformation described in Sect. 2 and is called at the final step of every algorithm we present in the paper.

Theorem 3. *Given a repeated matching instance with identical valuations, an EF1 repeated matching exists and can be computed in polynomial time.*

Proof. Algorithm 1 clearly runs in polynomial time. It remains to prove that it always returns an EF1 repeated matching. Consider its application to a repeated matching instance $I = \langle \mathcal{A}, \mathcal{G}, v, T \rangle$, where v is non-negative. The repeated matching returned is clearly EF1 if T is an integer multiple of n; in this case, all agents get the same number of copies of all items and nobody is envious.

Otherwise, since $T \bmod n \leq n - 1$ copies of each item are available in the round-robin phases and all the remaining $T \bmod n$ copies of each item are picked

---

Algorithm 1: EF1 repeated matching under identical valuations

---

Input: Identical Valuations Instance $I = \langle \mathcal{A}, \mathcal{G}, v, T \rangle$ with $|\mathcal{A}| = n$

Output: A repeated matching A

1 $f(i,g) \leftarrow \lfloor T/n \rfloor, \forall i \in \mathcal{A}, \forall g \in \mathcal{G}$;

2 **if** $T \bmod n > 0$ **then**

3     $x_g \leftarrow T \bmod n, \forall g \in G$;

4   **for** $t = 1$ *to* $T \bmod n$ **do**

5   **for** $i = 1$ *to* n **do**

6           $g' \leftarrow \arg\min_{g: x_g > 0} \operatorname{rank}(g)$;

7           $x_{g'} \leftarrow x_{g'} - 1$;

8           $f(i,g') \leftarrow \lceil T/n \rceil$;

9 $A \leftarrow \operatorname{GenerateFromFreq}(f)$;

---

in consecutive round-robin steps, no agent gets more than one copy of the same item in the round robin phases. Let $g_{i,t}$ be the item agent i gets in the round robin phase $t \in \{1, 2, ..., T \bmod n\}$. Consider two agents i and j and observe that the repeated matching A returned by Algorithm 1 satisfies

$$v(A_i) - v(A_j \setminus \{g_{j,1}\})$$

$$= \sum_{t=1}^{(T \bmod n)-1} (v(g_{i,t}, \lceil T/n \rceil) - v(g_{j,t+1}, \lceil T/n \rceil)) + v(g_{i,T \bmod n})$$

$$\geq \sum_{t=1}^{(T \bmod n)-1} (v(g_{i,t}, \lceil T/n \rceil) - v(g_{j,t+1}, \lceil T/n \rceil)) \geq 0,$$

as EF1 requires. The equality follows since both agents i and j get $\lfloor T/n \rfloor$ copies of each item at the beginning of the algorithm and, then, the valuation difference is due to the $\lceil T/n \rceil$-th copies of items allocated in the round-robin phases. The first inequality is due to the non-negativity of valuations. The second one follows since the item that agent i picks at the round-robin phase t has not higher rank than the item agent j picks in the next phase $t + 1$. $\qquad\square$

We now prove that EF1 repeated matchings can be computed in polynomial time for general non-negative valuations when the number T of rounds and the number n of agents/items satisfy a particular condition.

Theorem 4. *Given a repeated matching instance I with n agents/goods and T rounds such that $T \bmod n \in \{0, 1, 2, n-1\}$, an EF1 repeated matching exists and can be computed in polynomial time.*

We prove Theorem 4 constructively, by defining two algorithms for the cases $T \bmod n \in \{0, 1, 2\}$ (Algorithm 2) and $T \bmod n = n - 1$ (Algorithm 3).

Algorithm 2 computes the number of copies of each item that each agent gets as follows. First, it gives to each agent $\lfloor T/n \rfloor$ copies of each item (line 1). If

---

Algorithm 2: Computing an EF1 repeated matching

Input: Instance $I = \langle \mathcal{A}, \mathcal{G}, \{v_i\}_{i \in \mathcal{A}}, T \rangle$ with $|\mathcal{A}| = n$ and $T \bmod n \in \{0, 1, 2\}$
Output: A repeated matching A

1 $f(i, g) \leftarrow \lfloor T/n \rfloor, \forall i \in \mathcal{A}, \forall g \in G$;
2 **if** $T \bmod n > 0$ **then**
3     $P \leftarrow \mathcal{G}$;
4   **for** $i = 1$ *to* n **do**
5        $\widehat{g} \leftarrow \arg\max_{g \in P} v_i(g, \lceil T/n \rceil)$;
6        $f(i, \widehat{g}) \leftarrow \lceil T/n \rceil$;
7        $P \leftarrow P \setminus \{\widehat{g}\}$;

8 **if** $T \bmod n = 2$ **then**
9     $P \leftarrow \mathcal{G}$;
10   **for** $i = n$ *to* 1 **do**
11       $\widehat{g} \leftarrow \arg\max_{g \in P} v_i(g, f(i, g) + 1)$;
12       $f(i, \widehat{g}) \leftarrow f(i, \widehat{g}) + 1$;
13       $P \leftarrow P \setminus \{\widehat{g}\}$;

14 $A \leftarrow \text{GenerateFromFreq}(f)$;

$T \bmod n \neq 0$, it then runs a round-robin phase (lines 2–7) and then, if $T \bmod n = 2$, it runs an additional reverse round-robin phase (lines 8–13). In the round-robin phase, the agents act according to the ordering $1, 2, ..., n$ (see the for-loop in lines 4–7). When it is agent i's turn to act, she gets the item $\widehat{g}$ (identified in line 5) for which her value for the $\lceil T/n \rceil$-th copy is maximum among the items that have not been given to agents who acted before i in the round-robin phase (the set variable P is used to identify these items). In the reverse round-robin phase, the agents act according to the ordering $n, n - 1, ..., 1$ (see the for-loop in lines 10–13). When it is agent i's turn to act, she gets the item $\widehat{g}$ (identified in line 11) for which her value for the next copy is maximum among the items that have not been given to agents who acted before i in the reverse round-robin phase. Finally, the algorithm transforms the matrix f indicating the number of copies of each item each agent gets to a repeated matching by calling routine GenerateFromFreq(). Algorithm 2 clearly runs in polynomial time.

Lemma 1. *The repeated matching $A = (A_1, ..., A_n)$ produced by Algorithm 2 is EF1.*

Proof. Let S denote the multiset that contains each item with multiplicity $\lfloor T/n \rfloor$. If $T \bmod n = 0$, then $A_i = S$ for every agent i and, hence, agents are not envious of each other. If $T \bmod n = 1$, the final repeated matching is obtained after the execution of the round-robin phase. Consider two agents i and j. Denoting by g_j the item agent j gets in this phase, agent i has value $v_i(A_i) \geq v_i(S) = v_i(A_j \setminus \{g_j\})$, i.e., she satisfies the EF1 condition.

If $T \bmod n = 2$, the final repeated matching is obtained after the execution of the reverse round-robin phase. Consider two agents i and j with $i < j$. Let g_i^1

Algorithm 3: Computing an EF1 repeated matching

Input: Instance $I = \langle \mathcal{A}, \mathcal{G}, \{v_i\}_{i \in \mathcal{A}}, T \rangle$ with $|\mathcal{A}| = n$ and $T \bmod n = n - 1$
Output: A repeated matching A

1 $f(i, g) \leftarrow \lceil T/n \rceil, \forall i \in \mathcal{A}, \forall g \in \mathcal{G}$;
2 $P \leftarrow \mathcal{G}$;
3 **for** $i = 1$ *to* n **do**
4 $\quad \hat{g} \leftarrow \arg\min_{g \in P} v_i(g, \lceil T/n \rceil)$;
5 $\quad f(i, \hat{g}) \leftarrow f(i, \hat{g}) - 1$;
6 $\quad P \leftarrow P \setminus \{\hat{g}\}$;
7 $A \leftarrow$ GenerateFromFreq(f);

---

and g_j^1 be the items the agents i and j get in the round-robin phase and g_i^2 and g_j^2 be the items they get in the reverse round-robin phase, respectively. Here,

$$v_i(A_i) \geq v_i(S) + v_i(g_i^1, \lceil T/n \rceil) \geq v_i(S) + v_i(g_j^1, \lceil T/n \rceil) = v_i(A_j \setminus \{g_j^2\}).$$

The second inequality follows since agent i prefers item g_i^1 to item g_j^1 in the round-robin phase. For agent j, we distinguish between two cases. Let μ denote the multiplicity of item g_j^2 in A_j. If $g_j^1 \neq g_i^2$, we have that, in the reverse round-robin phase, agent j prefers the μ-th copy of g_j^2 to the $\lceil T/n \rceil$-th copy of g_i^2, i.e., $v_j(g_j^2, \mu) \geq v_j(g_i^2, \lceil T/n \rceil)$. Then, we have

$$v_j(A_j) \geq v_j(S) + v_j(g_j^2, \mu) \geq v_j(S) + v_j(g_i^2, \lceil T/n \rceil) = v_j(A_i \setminus \{g_i^1\}).$$

If $g_j^1 = g_i^2$, we have

$$v_j(A_j) \geq v_j(S) + v_j(g_j^1, \lceil T/n \rceil) = v_j(S) + v_j(g_i^2, \lceil T/n \rceil) = v_j(A_i \setminus \{g_i^1\}).$$

Thus, the EF1 conditions for agents i and j are satisfied. $\square$

Algorithm 3 uses a similar structure. It starts by giving $\lceil T/n \rceil$ copies of each item to each agent (in line 1) and then removes the copy of a distinct item from each agent by running a round-robin phase (lines 2–6). When it is agent i's turn to act, she gets rid of a copy of the item $\hat{g}$ (identified in line 4) for which her value for the $\lceil T/n \rceil$-th copy is minimum among the items that have not been gotten rid by agents who acted before i in the round-robin phase.

Lemma 2. *The repeated matching $A = (A_1, ..., A_n)$ produced by Algorithm 3 is EF1.*

Proof. Let i and j be two agents and denote by g_i and g_j the items that are removed from their bundles in the round-robin phase. We have

$$v_i(A_i) = v_i(A_j) + v_i(g_j, \lceil T/n \rceil) - v_i(g_i, \lceil T/n \rceil)$$
$$\geq v_i(A_j) - v_i(g_i, \lceil T/n \rceil) = v_i(A_j \setminus \{g_i\})$$

as desired. The last equality follows as A_j has exactly $\lceil T/n \rceil$ copies of g_i. $\square$

Corollary 1. *In repeated matching instances with up to four agents/goods, an EF1 repeated matching always exists.*

5 Are Fairness and Efficiency Compatible?

In this section, we show that achieving the concepts of efficiency and fairness simultaneously is computationally intractable. In particular, we show in Theorem 5 below that even approximating the maximum social welfare of EF1 repeated matching is hard. Our proof is inspired by a reduction by Barman et al. [3] but is more involved. Interestingly, it uses instances with constant valuations and comes in sharp contrast to achieving the two concepts separately. For such instances, an EF1 repeated matching can be computed in polynomial time [7], while a polynomial time algorithm for computing social welfare maximizing repeated matchings follows by Theorem 2.

Theorem 5. *For every constant $\epsilon > 0$, approximating the maximum social welfare of EF1 repeated matchings on instances with n agents/goods and T rounds within a factor of $O\left(\min\{n^{1/3-\epsilon}, T^{1-\epsilon}\}\right)$ is NP-hard.*

Proof. We present a polynomial-time reduction, which, given a graph $G = (V, E)$, constructs a repeated matching instance $I(G)$ in which the maximum social welfare over EF1 repeated matchings is in $[K, K+1)$ if and only if the maximum independent set in graph G has size K. Our construction leads to instances with $n \leq |V|^3$ agents/items and $T = |V|$ rounds. Then, the theorem follows by the next well-known result by [17].

Theorem 6 (Zuckerman [17]). *For every constant $\epsilon > 0$, approximating the maximum independent set of a graph $G = (V, E)$ within a factor of $|V|^{1-\epsilon}$ is NP-hard.*

Let δ be such that $0 < \delta < |V|^{-2}$. Let $G = (V, E)$ be a graph. Without loss of generality, we can assume that G has no isolated nodes, as the existence of such nodes just makes the independent set problem easier. Given graph $G = (V, E)$, the instance $I(G)$ has $T = |V|$ rounds and $n = (2|V| + 1)|E| + 1$ agents/items. For every edge $e \in E$, $I(G)$ has $2|V| + 1$ *edge agents* identified as (e, i) for $i = 1, 2, ..., 2|V| + 1$. There is also a *special agent* s. For every node $u \in V$, there is a *node item* g_u. The instance also has $n - |V|$ *dummy items*. For edge $e = (x, y) \in E$, $i \in [2|V| + 1]$, and $t \in [T]$, the valuation of the edge agent (e, i) for the tth copy of the node item g_u is $v_{e,i}(g_u, t) = \delta$ if $u = x$ or $u = y$, and $v_{e,i}(g_u, t) = 0$ otherwise. For node $u \in V$ and $t \in [T]$, the valuation of the special agent for the tth copy of the node item g_u is $v_s(g_u, t) = 1$. All agents have zero valuations for the dummy items.

Let K be the size of the maximum independent set in G. We claim that any EF1 repeated matching of $I(G)$ has social welfare less than $K + 1$. This will follow by two observations for any EF1 repeated matching A. First, for every edge e, there is some $i \in [2|V| + 1]$ such that the edge agent (e, i) has value 0. Assume that this is not true for edge $e = (x, y)$. Hence, $2|V| + 1$ copies of the node items g_x and g_y have been given to the edge agents corresponding to edge e. However, we only have $|V|$ copies of each item. Second, consider the node items the special agent gets. As for each edge $e = (x, y)$, there is some agent

(e, i) who has zero value, the special agent can get at most one copy of node items g_x or g_y. As this holds for every $e \in E$, the node items that the special agent gets-correspond to the nodes in an independent set in G. Hence, her value is at most K. The total value the edge agents get from the $|V|$ node items they get is at most $|V|^2 \cdot \delta < 1$. Hence, the social welfare of repeated matching A is less than $K + 1$.

We now show that an EF1 repeated matching of social welfare in $[K, K + 1)$ does exist, when the graph G has an independent set S of size K. First, the special agent gets a single copy of node item g_x for each $x \in S$. The remaining copies of the node items are given to the edge agents in such a way that each edge agent corresponding to edge $e = (x, y)$ gets at most one copy of either g_x or g_y. This is always possible, since for every edge $e = (x, y)$, there are $2|V| + 1$ edge agents to get at most one copy of either node item g_x or node item g_y. Then, the copies of the dummy items are distributed so that each agent has exactly $|V|$ item copies. As every edge agent has at most one copy of a node item, the EF1 conditions between any two of them are satisfied. Finally, the EF1 is satisfied between any edge agent and the special agent since the special agent gets at most one item copy for which the edge agent has positive value.   □

6   Swap Envy-Freeness

We now specifically turn our attention to repeated matching instances with mixed items. Consider the following instance with $n = 2$ and $T = 1$. One of the items is a good and the other is a chore. There are exactly two possible matchings. In either, the classical extension of EF1 for mixed items from the fair division literature (e.g., see [2]), which requires that the value of an agent is higher than that of another either by removing a single item from either one of the two bundles, is not satisfied. Motivated by this simple example, we propose and investigate an alternate notion of fairness to EF1 for repeated matchings, which we call *swap envy-freeness* (swapEF).

Definition 4 (swapEF). *Let $I = \langle \mathcal{A}, \mathcal{G}, \{v_i\}_{i \in \mathcal{A}}, T \rangle$ be a repeated matching instance with mixed items. A repeated matching $A = (A_1, ..., A_n)$ in I is swapEF if for every pair of agents $i, j \in \mathcal{A}$, either (i) or (ii) is true:*

(i) $v_i(A_i) \geq v_i(A_j)$;
(ii) There exist items $g_i \in A_i$ and $g_j \in A_j$ such that $v_i(A_i \cup \{g_j\} \setminus \{g_i\}) \geq v_i(A_j \cup \{g_i\} \setminus \{g_j\})$.

Condition (ii) requires that the value agent i has for her bundle A_i after replacing a copy of item g_i with an extra copy of item g_j is at least as high as her value for the bundle A_j of agent j after exchanging a copy of item g_j with a copy of item g_i. For instance, in the example of one good and one chore with $T = 1$, we find that while EF1 cannot be satisfied, each of the two repeated matchings are actually swapEF. This is because the agent who is matched to the chore will envy the other agent, but should the two be swapped, this envy would be mitigated. Now if $T = 2k + 1$ in this example with valuations staying constant with time, any repeated matching that matched one agent to the chore for $k + 1$ rounds will be swapEF. The agent matched to the chore for $k + 1$ rounds, will envy the other agent, but exchanging just one copy of the chore for one of the good would mitigate this envy. We first find that Algorithm 1 successfully finds a swapEF repeated matching, even without the non-negativity constraint on valuations (the rank definition can be trivially adapted).

Lemma 3. *Given a repeated matching instance $I = \langle \mathcal{A}, \mathcal{G}, v, T \rangle$ with identical valuations, the repeated matching returned by Algorithm 1 is swapEF.*

We now turn our attention to general valuations.

Theorem 7. *Given a repeated matching instance I with mixed items, n agents, and T rounds such that $T \bmod n \in \{0, 1, 2, n - 2, n - 1\}$, a swapEF repeated matching exists and can be computed in polynomial time.*

The proof of Theorem 7 uses Algorithm 2 from Sect. 4 for instances with $T \bmod n \in \{0, 1, 2\}$. For instances with $T \bmod n \in \{n - 2, n - 1\}$, we use an extension of Algorithm 3 from Sect. 4, which runs an additional reverse round robin phase to remove one more distinct item from each agent when $T \bmod n = n - 2$. We refer to this as Algorithm 4; the lines 7–12 implement the reverse round-robin phase, while the lines 1–6 are identical to Algorithm 3. The properties of Algorithms 2 and 4 regarding swapEF are given by the next two lemmas, which, together with the fact that both algorithms run in polynomial time, complete the proof of Theorem 7.

Algorithm 4: Computing a swapEF repeated matching

Input: Instance $I = \langle \mathcal{A}, \mathcal{G}, \{v_i\}_{i \in \mathcal{A}}, T \rangle$ with $|\mathcal{A}| = n$, $T \bmod n \in \{n - 1, n - 2\}$

Output: A repeated matching A

1   $f(i, g) \leftarrow \lceil T/n \rceil, \forall i \in \mathcal{A}, \forall g \in G$;

2   $P \leftarrow \mathcal{G}$;

3   **for** $i = 1$ *to* n **do**

4      $\widehat{g} \leftarrow \arg\min_{g \in P} v_i(g, \lceil T/n \rceil)$;

5      $f(i, \widehat{g}) \leftarrow f(i, \widehat{g}) - 1$;

6      $P \leftarrow P \setminus \{\widehat{g}\}$;

7   **if** $T \bmod n = n - 2$ **then**

8      $P \leftarrow \mathcal{G}$;

9   **for** $i = n$ *to* 1 **do**

10        $\widehat{g} \leftarrow \arg\min_{g \in P} v_i(g, f(i, g))$;

11        $f(i, \widehat{g}) \leftarrow f(i, \widehat{g}) - 1$;

12        $P \leftarrow P \setminus \{\widehat{g}\}$;

13   $A \leftarrow \text{GenerateFromFreq}(f)$;

Lemma 4. *The repeated matching $A = (A_1, ..., A_n)$ produced by Algorithm 2 is swapEF.*

Lemma 5. *The repeated matching $A = (A_1, ..., A_n)$ produced by Algorithm 4 is swapEF.*

Proof. Let S denote the multiset that contains each item with multiplicity $\lceil T/n \rceil$. We first consider the case where $T \bmod n = n - 1$. Let i and j be two agents and denote by g_i and g_j the items that are removed from their bundles in the round-robin phase. If $v_i(g_i, \lceil T/n \rceil) \geq v_i(g_j, \lceil T/n \rceil)$, then

$$v_i(A_i \cup \{g_i\} \setminus \{g_j\}) = v_i(S) - v_i(g_j, \lceil T/n \rceil) \geq v_i(S) - v_i(g_i, \lceil T/n \rceil)$$
$$= v_i(A_j \cup \{g_j\} \setminus \{g_i\}).$$

Otherwise, if $v_i(g_i, \lceil T/n \rceil) < v_i(g_j, \lceil T/n \rceil)$, then

$$v_i(A_i) = v_i(S) - v_i(g_i, \lceil T/n \rceil) > v_i(S) - v_i(g_j, \lceil T/n \rceil) = v_i(A_j).$$

Thus, swapEF is satisfied by Algorithm 4 whenever $t \bmod n = n - 1$. If $T \bmod n = n - 2$, the final repeated matching is obtained after the execution of the reverse round-robin phase. Consider two agents i and j. Let g_i^1 and g_j^1 be the items agents i and j remove in the round-robin phase and g_i^2 and g_j^2 be the items they remove in the reverse round-robin phase, respectively. We distinguish between three cases. If $|\{g_i^1, g_i^2\} \cap \{g_j^1, g_j^2\}| = 2$, then A_i and A_j are identical and agent i does not envy agent j. If $|\{g_i^1, g_i^2\} \cap \{g_j^1, g_j^2\}| = 1$, assume, without loss of generality, that $g_i^1 = g_j^2 = g$ and observe that A_i has $\lfloor T/n \rfloor$ copies of g_i^2 and $\lceil T/n \rceil$ copies of g_j^1 and A_j has $\lfloor T/n \rfloor$ copies of g_j^1 and $\lceil T/n \rceil$ copies of g_i^2. If $v_i(g_i^2, \lceil T/n \rceil) \leq v_i(g_j^1, \lceil T/n \rceil)$, then

$$v_i(A_i) = v_i(S \setminus \{g\}) - v_i(g_i^2, \lceil T/n \rceil) \geq v_i(S \setminus \{g\}) - v_i(g_j^1, \lceil T/n \rceil) = v_i(A_j).$$

Otherwise, if $v_i(g_i^2, \lceil T/n \rceil) > v_i(g_j^1, \lceil T/n \rceil)$, then

$$v_i(A_i \cup \{g_i^2\} \setminus \{g_j^1\}) = v_i(S) - v_i(g, \lceil T/n \rceil) - v_i(g_j^1, \lceil T/n \rceil)$$
$$> v_i(S) - v_i(g, \lceil T/n \rceil) - v_i(g_i^2, \lceil T/n \rceil)$$
$$= v_i(A_j \cup \{g_j^1\} \setminus \{g_i^2\}).$$

So, the swapEF conditions are satisfied in this case. The remaining case is where g_i^1, g_i^2, g_j^1, and g_j^2 are distinct. Then, A_i contains $\lfloor T/n \rfloor$ copies of g_i^1 and g_i^2 and $\lceil T/n \rceil$ copies of g_j^1 and g_j^2 and A_j contains $\lfloor T/n \rfloor$ copies of g_j^1 and g_j^2 and $\lceil T/n \rceil$ copies of g_i^1 and g_i^2. If $i < j$, agent i acts before agent j in the round-robin phase and, hence, $v_i(g_i^1, \lceil T/n \rceil) \leq v_i(g_j^1, \lceil T/n \rceil)$. If $v_i(g_i^2, \lceil T/n \rceil) \leq v_i(g_j^2, \lceil T/n \rceil)$, then

$$v_i(A_i) = v_i(S) - v_i(g_i^1, \lceil T/n \rceil) - v_i(g_i^2, \lceil T/n \rceil)$$
$$\geq v_i(S) - v_i(g_j^1, \lceil T/n \rceil) - v_i(g_j^2, \lceil T/n \rceil) = v_i(A_j),$$

and agent i does not envy agent j. Else, if $v_i(g_i^2, \lceil T/n \rceil) > v_i(g_j^2, \lceil T/n \rceil)$, then

$$
\begin{aligned}
v_i(A_i \cup \{g_i^2\} \setminus \{g_j^2\}) &= v_i(S) - v_i(g_i^1, \lceil T/n \rceil) - v_i(g_j^2, \lceil T/n \rceil) \\
&> v_i(S) - v_i(g_j^1, \lceil T/n \rceil) - v_i(g_i^2, \lceil T/n \rceil) \\
&= v_i(A_i \cup \{g_j^2\} \setminus \{g_i^2\}),
\end{aligned}
$$

and the swapEF condition is satisfied. If $i > j$, agent i acts before j in the reverse round-robin phase and, hence, $v_i(g_i^2, \lceil T/n \rceil) \le v_i(g_j^2, \lceil T/n \rceil)$. If $v_i(g_i^1, \lceil T/n \rceil) \le v_i(g_j^1, \lceil T/n \rceil)$, then

$$
\begin{aligned}
v_i(A_i) &= v_i(S) - v_i(g_i^1, \lceil T/n \rceil) - v_i(g_i^2, \lceil T/n \rceil) \\
&\ge v_i(S) - v_i(g_j^1, \lceil T/n \rceil) - v_i(g_j^2, \lceil T/n \rceil) = v_i(A_j),
\end{aligned}
$$

and agent i does not envy agent j. Else, if $v_i(g_i^1, \lceil T/n \rceil) > v_i(g_j^1, \lceil T/n \rceil)$, then

$$
\begin{aligned}
v_i(A_i \cup \{g_i^1\} \setminus \{g_j^1\}) &= v_i(S) - v_i(g_i^2, \lceil T/n \rceil) - v_i(g_j^1, \lceil T/n \rceil) \\
&> v_i(S) - v_i(g_j^2, \lceil T/n \rceil) - v_i(g_i^1, \lceil T/n \rceil) \\
&= v_i(A_i \cup \{g_j^1\} \setminus \{g_i^1\}),
\end{aligned}
$$

and the swapEF condition is again satisfied.   □

Corollary 2. *In repeated matching instances with mixed items and up to five agents/items, a* swapEF *repeated matching always exists.*

We conclude this section with a comparison of EF1 and swapEF. While the two fairness notions have similar definitions, they are actually incomparable. Clearly, swapEF does not imply EF1 as it is trivially satisfied in the simple motivating example with one good and one chore presented at the beginning of this section. However, given that we use largely the same algorithms for swapEF as we did for EF1, one may believe intuitively that for goods alone, EF1 implies swapEF. This is not the case though. Consider an instance with three rounds and two agents with identical constant valuations $v(1, t) = 3$ and $v(2, t) = 2$ for two items. Giving item 1 to one agent and item 2 to the other for all three rounds is EF1 but not swapEF.

7 Open Problems

Our work leaves several interesting open questions that deserve investigation. What about approximation algorithms when the items are goods and valuations are not necessarily monotone? Is a constant approximation ratio possible? Regarding fairness, the most important open question is whether EF1 repeated matchings exist for any instance with goods. Furthermore, is EF1 compatible with different notions of efficiency than the utilitarian social welfare we have used here? For example, what about the egalitarian or Nash social welfare? Is EF1 compatible with Pareto-efficiency? For instances with mixed items, do swapEF repeated matchings always exist? Again, how do they interplay with Pareto-efficiency? In general, swapEF deserves investigation in other fair division settings that involve mixed items.

References

1. Amanatidis, G., et al.: Fair division of indivisible goods: a survey. CoRR abs/2208.08782 (2022)
2. Aziz, H., Caragiannis, I., Igarashi, A., Walsh, T.: Fair allocation of indivisible goods and chores. Auton. Agents Multi Agent Syst. **36**(1), art. 3 (2022)
3. Barman, S., Ghalme, G., Jain, S., Kulkarni, P., Narang, S.: Fair division of indivisible goods among strategic agents. In: Proceedings of the 18th International Conference on Autonomous Agents and MultiAgent Systems (AAMAS), pp. 1811–1813 (2019)
4. Barman, S., Krishnamurthy, S.K., Vaish, R.: Finding fair and efficient allocations. In: Proceedings of the 19th ACM Conference on Economics and Computation (EC), pp. 557–574 (2018)
5. Bérczi, K., et al.: Envy-free relaxations for goods, chores, and mixed items. CoRR abs/2006.04428 (2020)
6. Bhaskar, U., Sricharan, A.R., Vaish, R.: On approximate envy-freeness for indivisible chores and mixed resources. In: Proceedings of the 25th International Conference on Randomization and Computation and the 24th International Conference on Approximation Algorithms for Combinatorial Optimization Problems (APPROX/RANDOM), pp. 1:1–1:23 (2021)
7. Biswas, A., Barman, S.: Fair division under cardinality constraints. In: Proceedings of the 27th International Joint Conference on Artificial Intelligence (IJCAI), pp. 91–97 (2018)
8. Budish, E.: The combinatorial assignment problem: approximate competitive equilibrium from equal incomes. J. Polit. Econ. **119**(6), 1061–1103 (2011)
9. Caragiannis, I., Kurokawa, D., Moulin, H., Procaccia, A.D., Shah, N., Wang, J.: The unreasonable fairness of maximum nash welfare. ACM Trans. Econ. Comput. **7**(3), 1–32 (2019)
10. Freeman, R., Micha, E., Shah, N.: Two-sided matching meets fair division. In: Proceedings of the 30th International Joint Conference on Artificial Intelligence (IJCAI), pp. 203–209 (2021)
11. Gabow, H.N., Tarjan, R.E.: Faster scaling algorithms for network problems. SIAM J. Comput. **18**(5), 1013–1036 (1989)
12. Garey, M.R., Johnson, D.S.: Computers and Intractability: A Guide to the Theory of NP-Completeness. W. H. Freeman (1979)
13. Gollapudi, S., Kollias, K., Plaut, B.: Almost envy-free repeated matching in two-sided markets. In: Proceedings of the 16th International Conference on Web and Internet Economics (WINE), pp. 3–16 (2020)
14. Hosseini, H., Larson, K., Cohen, R.: Matching with dynamic ordinal preferences. In: Proceedings of the 29th AAAI Conference on Artificial Intelligence (AAAI), pp. 936–943 (2015)
15. Lipton, R.J., Markakis, E., Mossel, E., Saberi, A.: On approximately fair allocations of indivisible goods. In: Proceedings of the 5th ACM Conference on Electronic Commerce (EC), pp. 125–131 (2004)
16. Plummer, M.D., Lovász, L.: Matching Theory. Elsevier Science (1986)
17. Zuckerman, D.: Linear degree extractors and the inapproximability of max clique and chromatic number. Theory Comput. **3**(6), 103–128 (2007)

Truthful Two-Facility Location with Candidate Locations

Panagiotis Kanellopoulos, Alexandros A. Voudouris^(⊠), and Rongsen Zhang

School of Computer Science and Electronic Engineering, University of Essex,
Colchester, UK
{panagiotis.kanellopoulos,alexandros.voudouris,rz19109}@essex.ac.uk

Abstract. We study a truthful two-facility location problem in which a set of agents have private positions on the line of real numbers and known approval preferences over two facilities. Given the locations of the two facilities, the cost of an agent is the total distance from the facilities she approves. The goal is to decide where to place the facilities from a given finite set of candidate locations so as to (a) approximately optimize desired social objectives, and (b) incentivize the agents to truthfully report their private positions. We focus on the class of deterministic strategyproof mechanisms and pinpoint the ones with the best possible approximation ratio in terms of the social cost (i.e., the total cost of the agents) and the max cost. In particular, for the social cost, we show a tight bound of $1 + \sqrt{2}$ when the preferences of the agents are homogeneous (i.e., all agents approve both facilities), and a tight bound of 3 when the preferences might be heterogeneous. For the max cost, we show tight bounds of 2 and 3 for homogeneous and heterogeneous preferences, respectively.

Keywords: Facility location · Mechanism design · Approximation

1 Introduction

In the well-studied *truthful single-facility location problem*, there is a set of agents with private positions on the line of real numbers, and a facility (such as a park or a school) that is to be located somewhere on the line. Given such a location, its distance from the position of an agent is interpreted as the individual cost that the agent would suffer by having to travel to the facility in order to be serviced by it. The goal is to determine the facility location so that the agents are given the right incentives to *truthfully* report their positions (that is, not being able to affect the outcome to decrease their cost), and, at the same time, a social function of the individual agent costs (such as the total or the maximum cost) is (approximately) optimized. Since the work of Procaccia and Tennenholtz [19], who were the first to consider facility location problems through the prism of *approximate mechanism design without money*, research on this topic has flourished and a large number of more complex variants of the problem have been introduced and analyzed; see the survey of [4] for an overview.

© The Author(s), under exclusive license to Springer Nature Switzerland AG 2023
A. Deligkas and A. Filos-Ratsikas (Eds.): SAGT 2023, LNCS 14238, pp. 365–382, 2023.
https://doi.org/10.1007/978-3-031-43254-5_21

The original work of Procaccia and Tennenholtz [19] focused on a *continuous* model, where the facility is allowed to be placed at any point of the line, and showed tight bounds on the approximation ratio of deterministic and randomized *strategyproof* mechanisms in terms of the *social cost* (total individual cost of the agents) and the *max cost* (maximum individual cost among all agents). The *discrete* model, where the facility can be placed only at a given set of candidate points of the line, has also been studied, most notably by Feldman et al. [9]. They observed that this setting is equivalent to voting on a line, and the strategyproofness constraint leads to deterministic mechanisms that make decisions using only the ordinal preferences of agents over the candidate points; an assumption typically made in the distortion literature [3]. Many other truthful single-facility location models have been studied under different assumptions, such as that the location space is more general than a line [1,14,18], that the facility location must be decided in a distributed way [10,11], or that the facility is obnoxious and the agents aim to be as far from it as possible [5].

Aiming to locate multiple facilities is a natural generalization. Most of the work in this direction has focused on the fundamental case of two facilities, under several different assumptions about the types of the facilities, the preferences of the agents for them, the agent-related information that is public or private, and whether the setting is continuous or discrete, aiming to capture different applications. In the *homogeneous* case, where the facilities are assumed to be of the same type and serve the same purpose (for example, they might correspond to two parks), with only a few exceptions, the typical assumption is that each agent cares about one of them, such as the facility placed closest to her position (i.e., the agent would like to have a shortest path to a facility) [12,17,19], or the facility farthest from her position (i.e., the agent would like to be in a short radius from both facilities) [25]. More generally, the facilities might be of different types and serve a different purpose (for example, they might correspond to a park and a school), in which case the agents might have different, *heterogeneous* preferences over them. For example, some agents might be interested in both facilities, some agents might be interested in only one of them, or some agents might consider one facility to be useful and the other to be obnoxious [2,6,8,13,15,16,20,26].

In this paper, we consider the case of two facilities that can be placed only at candidate locations. For each agent, we assume that her position on the line is private, she has approval preferences over the facilities which are publicly known, and her individual cost is given by the total distance from the facilities she approves (rather than the distance from the closest or farthest such facility). To the best of our knowledge, these assumptions have not been considered in combination before in the literature. We provide more details below.

1.1   Our Contribution

We study a truthful two-facility location problem, in which there is a set of agents with *known approval preferences* (0 or 1) over two facilities $\{F_1, F_2\}$, so that each agent approves at least one facility; we can safely ignore agents that approve neither facility. The agents have *private positions* on the line of real

Table 1. An overview of the tight bounds that we show in this paper on the approximation ratio of deterministic strategyproof mechanisms for the different combinations of social objectives functions (social cost and max cost) and agent preferences (homogeneous or heterogeneous).

	Social cost	Max cost
Homogeneous	$1 + \sqrt{2}$	2
Heterogeneous	3	3

numbers, and the facilities can only be placed at *different* locations chosen from a given set of *candidate* locations. Once the facilities have both been placed, the individual cost of each agent is the *total* distance from the facilities she approves.

Our goal is to design mechanisms that take as input the positions reported by the agents, and, using also the available information about the preferences of the agents, decide where to place the two facilities, so that (a) a social objective function is (approximately) optimized, and (b) the agents are incentivized to truthfully report their positions. As in previous work, we consider the well-known *social cost* (the total individual cost of the agents) and the *max cost* (the maximum individual cost over all agents) as our social objective functions. We also treat separately the class of instances in which the preferences of the agents are *homogeneous* (that is, when all agents approve both facilities) and the general class of instances in which the preferences might be *heterogeneous*. For all possible combinations of objectives and types of preferences, we design *deterministic* strategyproof mechanisms that achieve the best possible approximation ratio. An overview of our results is given in Table 1. Due to space constraints, the proofs of some of our statements have been omitted.

We start by focusing on the social cost in Sect. 3. For homogeneous instances, we show a tight bound of $1 + \sqrt{2}$ by considering a natural mechanism, which, for a parameter $\alpha \in (0, 1/2)$, places the first facility at the candidate location closest to the αn-leftmost agent, and then places the second facility at the available candidate location that is closest to the $(1 - \alpha)n$-leftmost agent, where n is the number of agents. We show that the desired bound is achieved for $\alpha = \sqrt{2} - 1$. For general instances, we first observe that no strategyproof mechanism can achieve an approximation ratio better than 3; this follows from the fact that instances in which all agents approve just one of the facilities lead to a version of the problem that is essentially equivalent to single-facility location (for which 3 is the best possible bound [9]). We then show a matching upper bound of 3 by considering a mechanism that places each facility at the available candidate location closest to the median agent among those that approve it. To decide the order in which the facilities are placed, we first perform a voting step that allows the agents that approve each facility to decide if they prefer the closest or second-closest candidate location to the respective median agent; this is necessary since just blindly choosing the order of placing the facilities leads to a mechanism with a rather large approximation ratio.

In Sect. 4, we turn our attention to the max cost objective. For homogeneous instances, we show a best possible bound of 2 by considering a simple mechanism that places the facilities at the available candidate locations closest to the leftmost and rightmost agents. For general instances, we show a best possible bound of 3 by considering two mechanisms that work under different approval profiles. The first mechanism is a direct extension of the mechanism used for homogeneous instances and works when there is at least one agent that approves both facilities. The second mechanism works when each agent approves just one facility (that is, some agents approve only the first facility, while the others approve only the second facility). This case is harder to tackle since the straightforward variant of the mechanism for homogeneous instances does not work well. The bottleneck lies in that, after placing the first facility at the candidate location closest to one of the agents that approve it (such as the leftmost), we then need to dynamically decide whether the second facility can be placed closer to the leftmost or rightmost among the agents that approve it, or neither of them. This again is done by a voting-like procedure that is used to decide the order of the agents that approve the second facility relative to the two candidate locations that are closest to where the first facility has been placed.

1.2   Related Work

For an overview of the many different truthful facility location problems that have been considered in the literature, we refer the reader to the survey of [4]. Here, we briefly discuss papers that are mostly related to our work.

The truthful two-facility location problem was first considered in the original work of Procaccia and Tennenholtz [19], where the agents were assumed to have homogeneous preferences over the two facilities, their individual costs were equal to the distance from the closest facility to their positions, and the facilities were allowed to be placed anywhere on the line, even at the same point. For deterministic mechanisms, Procaccia and Tennenholtz showed a constant lower bound and a linear upper bound on the approximation ratio in terms of the social cost, and a tight bound of 3 in terms of the maximum cost. They also showed how randomization can lead to further improvements. Lu et al. [17] improved the lower bound for the social cost and deterministic mechanisms to an asymptotically linear one, before Fotakis and Tzamos [12] finally showed that the exact bound for this case is $n - 2$.

Sui and Boutilier [21] were among the first to consider truthful facility location problems with candidate locations (referred to as constrained facility location), with a focus on achieving approximate strategyproofness by bounding the incentives of the agents to manipulate; for multiple facilities, they considered only the homogeneous case where each agent's individual cost is the distance to the closest facility. As already mentioned, Feldman et al. [9] considered a candidate selection problem with a fixed set of candidates, a model which translates into a single-facility location problem where the facility can only be placed at a location from a given set of discrete candidate locations. They focused on the social cost objective and, among other results, proved that the MEDIAN mechanism that places the facility at the location closest to the position reported by the median agent, achieves an upper bound of 3; they also showed that this is the best possible bound among deterministic mechanisms.

Serafino and Ventre [20] considered a slightly different discrete facility location problem, where agents occupy nodes on a line graph and have approval preferences over two facilities that can only be placed at different nodes of the line. In contrast to our work here, where we assume that the agents have private positions and public preferences, Serafino and Ventre assumed that the positions are known and the preferences unknown. They showed several bounds on the approximation ratio for deterministic and randomized strategyproof mechanisms for the social cost and the max cost. Some of their results for deterministic mechanisms were improved by Kanellopoulos et al. [15].

Tang et al. [22] considered a setting with agents that have homogeneous preferences over two facilities, which can be placed at locations chosen from a set of candidate ones, allowing the facilities to be placed even at the same location. The positions of the agents are assumed to be private information and an agent's individual cost is defined as her distance from the closest facility. They proved an upper bound of $2n - 3$ for the social cost objective and a tight bound of 3 for the maximum cost. They also considered the case of a single facility and the max cost objective, for which they showed a bound of 3 (extending the work of Feldman et al. [9] who only focused on the social cost). Walsh [23] considered a similar setting, where one or more facilities can only be placed at different subintervals of the line, and showed bounds on the approximation ratio of strategyproof mechanisms for many social objective functions, beyond the classic ones. Zhao et al. [25] studied a slightly different setting, in which the agents have known approval preferences over the two facilities and their individual costs are defined as their distance from the farthest facility among the ones they approve. For homogeneous agent preferences, they showed a tight bound of 3 for both the social cost and the max cost objectives, while for general, heterogeneous preferences, they showed an upper bound of $2n + 1$ for the social cost, and an upper bound of 9 for the maximum cost.

Xu et al. [24] considered a setting where two facilities must be located so that there is a minimum distance between them. They showed results for two types of individual costs. The first one is, as in our case, the total distance (assuming that the facilities play a different role, and thus the agents are interested in both of them) and showed that, for any minimum distance requirement, the optimal solution for the social cost or the maximum cost can be attained by a strategyproof mechanism. The second one is the minimum distance (assuming that the facilities are of the same type, and thus the agents are interested only in their closest one), and showed that the approximation ratio of strategyproof mechanisms is unbounded. They also considered the case where the facility is obnoxious and showed a bound that depends on the minimum distance parameter. Duan et al. [7] later generalized the minimum distance setting by allowing for private fractional preferences over the two facilities.

2   Preliminaries

We consider the two-facility location problem with candidate locations. An instance I of this problem consists of a set N of $n \geq 2$ agents and two facilities $\{F_1, F_2\}$. Each agent $i \in N$ has a *private position* $x_i \in \mathbb{R}$ on the line of real numbers, and a *known approval preference* $p_{ij} \in \{0, 1\}$ for each $j \in [2]$, indicating whether she approves facility F_j ($p_{ij} = 1$) or not ($p_{ij} = 0$), such that $p_{i1} + p_{i2} \geq 1$. There is also a set of $m \geq 2$ candidate locations C where the facilities can be located. To be concise, we denote an instance using the tuple $I = (\mathbf{x}, \mathbf{p}, C)$, where $\mathbf{x} = (x_i)_{i \in N}$ is the *position profile* of all agent positions, and $\mathbf{p} = (p_{ij})_{i \in N, j \in [2]}$ is the *preference profile* of all agent approval preferences.

A *feasible solution* (or, simply, *solution*) is a pair $\mathbf{c} = (c_1, c_2) \in C^2$ of candidate locations with $c_1 \neq c_2$, where the two facilities can be placed; that is, for each $j \in [2]$, F_j is placed at c_j. A *mechanism* M takes as input an instance I of the problem and outputs a feasible solution $M(I)$. Our goal is to design mechanisms so that (a) some objective social function is (approximately) optimized, and (b) the agents truthfully report their private positions.

The *individual cost* of an agent $i \in N$ for a solution $\mathbf{c}$ is her total distance from the locations of the facilities she approves:

$$\text{cost}_i(\mathbf{c}|I) = \sum_{j \in [2]} p_{ij} \cdot d(x_i, c_j),$$

where $d(x, y) = |x - y|$ denotes the distance between any two points x and y on the line. Since the line is a special metric space, the distances satisfy the *triangle inequality*, which states that $d(x, y) \leq d(x, z) + d(z, y)$ for any three points x, y and z on the line, with the equality being true when $z \in [x, y]$. We consider the following two natural objective social functions that have been considered extensively within the truthful facility location literature:

– The *social cost* of a solution $\mathbf{c}$ is the total individual cost of the agents:

$$\text{SC}(c|I) = \sum_{i \in N} \text{cost}_i(\mathbf{c}).$$

– The *max cost* of a solution $\mathbf{c}$ is the maximum individual cost over all agents:

$$\text{MC}(c|I) = \max_{i \in N} \text{cost}_i(\mathbf{c}).$$

The *approximation ratio* of a mechanism M in terms of an objective social function $f \in \{\text{SC}, \text{MC}\}$ is the worst-case ratio (over all possible instances) of the f-value of the solution computed by the mechanism over the minimum possible f-value over all possible solutions:

$$\sup_I \frac{f(M(I)|I)}{\min_{\mathbf{c} \in C^2} f(c|I)}.$$

A mechanism is said to be *strategyproof* if the solution $M(I)$ it returns when given as input any instance $I = (\mathbf{x}, \mathbf{p}, C)$ is such that there is no agent i with incentive to misreport a position $x_i' \neq x_i$ to decrease her individual cost, that is,

$$\text{cost}_i(M(I)|I) \leq \text{cost}_i(M((x_i', \mathbf{x}_{-i}), \mathbf{p}, C)|I),$$

where $(x_i', \mathbf{x}_{-i})$ is the position profile obtained by $\mathbf{x}$ when only agent i reports a different position x_i'.

Finally, let us introduce some further notation and terminology that will be useful. For each $j \in [2]$, we denote by N_j the set of agents that approve facility F_j, i.e., $i \in N_j$ if $p_{ij} = 1$. Any agent that approves both facilities belongs to the intersection $N_1 \cap N_2$. We pay particular attention to the subclass of instances in which all agents approve both facilities, i.e., instances with $N = N_1 \cap N_2$. Since all agents have the same preference for both facilities, we will refer to such instances as *homogeneous*; the remaining instances are part of the general class of all instances. We will also denote by m_j, ℓ_j, and r_j the (leftmost) median, leftmost, and rightmost, respectively, agent in N_j. In addition, for any agent i we denote by $t(i)$ and $s(i)$ the closest and the second closest, respectively, candidate location to i.

3   Social Cost

3.1   Homogeneous Instances

We start by considering homogeneous instances, in which all agents approve both facilities, and show a tight bound of $1 + \sqrt{2}$ on the approximation ratio of strategyproof mechanisms in terms of the social cost.

Before we show the best possible approximation ratio, let us first discuss for a bit a straightforward idea. Recall that for the single-facility location problem, Feldman et al. [9] previously showed that the best possible approximation ratio of 3 is achieved by the MEDIAN mechanism, which places the facility at the candidate location closest to the position reported by the median agent m. We can generalize this mechanism by simply placing the two facilities at the two candidate locations that are closest to the position reported by m; that is, F_1 is placed at $w_1 = t(m)$ and F_2 is placed at $w_2 = s(m)$. It is not hard to show that this mechanism still achieves an approximation ratio of at most 3, even when there are two facilities, but cannot do better.

Theorem 1. *For homogeneous instances,* MEDIAN *achieves an approximation ratio of at most* 3, *and this is tight.*

Proof. Let $\mathbf{o} = (o_1, o_2)$ be an optimal solution. Since the position of the median agent minimizes the total distance of all agents, we have that

$$\sum_{i \in N} d(i, m) \leq \sum_{i \in N} d(i, x)$$

for any point x of the line (including o_1 and o_2), and thus

$$2\sum_{i\in N} d(i,m) \le \sum_{i\in N} d(i,o_1) + \sum_{i\in N} d(i,o_2) = \mathrm{SC}(\mathbf{o}).$$

Also, since $t(m)$ and $s(m)$ are the two closest candidate locations to m, we have that $d(m,t(m)) \le d(m,x)$ for any candidate location x, and there exists $o \in \{o_1,o_2\}$ such that $d(m,s(m)) \le d(m,o)$; let $\tilde{o} \in \{o_1,o_2\} \setminus \{o\}$. Therefore, using these facts and the triangle inequality, we obtain

$$\mathrm{SC}(\mathbf{w}) = \sum_{i\in N} \Big(d(i,t(m)) + d(i,s(m)) \Big)$$

$$\le 2\sum_{i\in N} d(i,m) + \sum_{i\in N} d(m,t(m)) + \sum_{i\in N} d(m,s(m))$$

$$\le \mathrm{SC}(\mathbf{o}) + \sum_{i\in N} d(m,\tilde{o}) + \sum_{i\in N} d(m,o)$$

$$\le \mathrm{SC}(\mathbf{o}) + 2\sum_{i\in N} d(i,m) + \sum_{i\in N} d(i,\tilde{o}) + \sum_{i\in N} d(i,o)$$

$$\le 3 \cdot \mathrm{SC}(\mathbf{o}).$$

The analysis of the mechanism is essentially tight due to the following instance: There are four candidate locations at 0, ε, $1 - \varepsilon$, and 1, for some infinitesimal $\varepsilon > 0$. There are also two agents positioned at $1/2 - \varepsilon$ and 1, respectively. Let the first agent be the median one (in case the second agent is the median, there is a symmetric instance). Then, the two facilities are placed at 0 and ε for a social cost of approximately $3/2$, whereas the optimal solution is to place the facilities at $1 - \varepsilon$ and 1 for a social cost of approximately $1/2$, leading to a lower bound of nearly 3.   □

To improve upon the bound of the MEDIAN mechanism, we focus on a family of parameterized mechanisms, which, for a parameter $\alpha \in (0,1/2)$, place one facility at the candidate location closest to the position reported by the αn-leftmost agent, and the other facility at the available candidate location closest to the position reported by the $(1-\alpha)n$-leftmost agent[1]. We refer to such mechanisms as α-STATISTIC; see Mechanism 1 for a description using pseudocode.

Theorem 2. *For any $\alpha \in (0,1/2)$, α-STATISTIC is strategyproof.*

Proof. It is not hard to see that no agent has an incentive to misreport as either the outcome remains the same, or at least one of the facilities is moved farther away from the agent. For example, let x_i and x_j be the positions of agents i

---

[1] Formally, it would be the $\lceil \alpha n \rceil$-leftmost and the $\lceil (1-\alpha)n \rceil$-leftmost agent, respectively, and we require that $\lceil \alpha n \rceil < \lceil (1-\alpha)n \rceil$. This can be guaranteed by creating an identical number of copies for each agent and running the mechanism on the modified instance; the approximation ratio for the modified instance is exactly the same as for the original instance. We omit the ceilings to make the exposition clearer.

Mechanism 1: α-STATISTIC

Input: Reported positions of agents;
Output: Facility locations $\mathbf{w} = (w_1, w_2)$;
$i \leftarrow \alpha n$-leftmost agent;
$j \leftarrow (1 - \alpha)n$-leftmost agent;
$w_1 \leftarrow t(i)$;
if $t(j)$ is available **then**
  $\quad | \quad w_2 \leftarrow t(j)$;
else
  $\quad \lfloor \quad w_2 \leftarrow s(j)$;

---

and j, respectively, and consider an agent z whose true position x_z is such that $x_z \leq x_i$. Then, reporting another position $x_z' < x_i$ does not change the outcome at all, while reporting a position $x_z' > x_i$ may move either both facilities (in case $x_z' > x_j$) or facility F_1 (when $x_z' < x_j$) farther away from x_z; in any case, agent z has no incentive to misreport. $\qquad \square$

Theorem 3. *For homogeneous instances, $(\sqrt{2} - 1)$-STATISTIC achieves an approximation ratio of at most $1 + \sqrt{2}$.*

We next show that the bound of $1 + \sqrt{2}$ is the best possible that any strategyproof mechanism can achieve for homogeneous instances.

Theorem 4. *For homogeneous instances, the approximation ratio of any strategyproof mechanism is at least $1 + \sqrt{2} - \delta$, for any $\delta > 0$.*

Proof. Let $\varepsilon > 0$ be an infinitesimal. To show the theorem, we will consider instances with four candidate locations, two in the ε-neighborhood of 0 (for example, $-\varepsilon$ and ε) and two in the ε-neighborhood of 2 (for example, $2 - \varepsilon$ and $2 + \varepsilon$). To simplify the calculations in the remainder of the proof, we will assume that there can be candidate locations at the same point of the line, so that we have two candidate locations at 0 and two at 2.

First, consider the following generic instance I with the aforementioned candidate locations: There is at least one agent at 0, at least one agent at 2, while each remaining agent is arbitrarily located at a location from $\{0, 1 - \varepsilon, 1 + \varepsilon, 2\}$. We make the following observation: Any solution returned by a strategyproof mechanism when given as input I must also be returned when given as input any of the following two instances:

- J_1: Same as I with the difference that an agent j_1 has been moved from 0 to $1 - \varepsilon$.
- J_2: Same as I with the difference that an agent j_2 has been moved from 2 to $1 + \varepsilon$.

Suppose towards a contradiction that this is not true for J_1; similar arguments can be used for J_2. We consider the following cases:

- Both facilities are placed at 2 in I. If this is not done in J_1, then j_1 can misreport her position as $1 - \varepsilon$ in I so that the instance becomes J_1 and at least one facility moves at her true position 0.
- Both facilities are placed at 0 in I. If this is not done in J_1, then j_1 can misreport her position as 0 in J_1 so that the instance becomes I and both facilities move to 0 which is closer to her true position $1 - \varepsilon$, a contradiction.
- One facility is placed at 0 and the other is placed at 2 in I. Observe that it cannot be the case that both facilities are placed at 0 in J_1 since that would mean that j_1 can misreport her position in I as $1 - \varepsilon$ so that the instance becomes J_1 and both facilities move to her true position 0. So, the only possibility of having a different solution in I and J_1 is that both facilities are placed at 2 in J_1. But then, j_1 can misreport her true position as 0 in J_1 so that the instance becomes I and one of the facilities moves to 0 which is closer to her true position.

Hence, the same solution must be computed by the mechanism when given I or J_1 as input.

Now, consider an arbitrary strategyproof mechanism and let $\alpha = \sqrt{2} - 1$; recall that α is such that $\frac{1+\alpha}{1-\alpha} = \frac{1}{\alpha} = 1+\sqrt{2}$. Let I_1 be the following instance with the aforementioned candidate locations: αn agents are at 0 and $(1 - \alpha)n$ agents are at 2. We consider the following cases depending on the solution returned by the mechanism when given I_1 as input:

Case 1: The mechanism places both facilities at 0. We consider the sequence of instances obtained by moving one by one the αn agents that are positioned at 0 in I_1 to $1 - \varepsilon$. By the observation above, the mechanism must return the same solution for any two consecutive instances of this sequence (essentially, the first one is of type I and the second one is of type J_1), which means that the mechanism must eventually return the same solution for all of them. Therefore, the mechanism must place both facilities at 0 in the last instance of this sequence, where αn agents are at $1 - \varepsilon$ and the remaining $(1 - \alpha)n$ agents are at 2. This solution has social cost $2\alpha n + 4(1 - \alpha)n = 2(2 - \alpha)n$. However, the solution that places both facilities at 2 has social cost $2\alpha n$, leading to an approximation ratio of $\frac{2}{\alpha} - 1 > 1 + \sqrt{2}$.

Case 2: The mechanism places both facilities at 2. Similarly to Case 1 above, we now consider the sequence of instances obtained by moving one by one the $(1 - \alpha)n$ agents that are positioned at 2 in I_1 to $1 + \varepsilon$. Again, by the observation above, the mechanism must return the same solution for any two consecutive instances of this sequence (the first one is of type I and the second one is of type J_2), which means that the mechanism must eventually return the same solution for all of them. Therefore, the mechanism must place both facilities at 2 in the last instance of this sequence, where αn agents are at 0 and the remaining $(1-\alpha)n$ agents are at $1 + \varepsilon$. This solution has social cost $4\alpha n + 2(1 - \alpha)n = 2(1 + \alpha)n$. However, the solution that places both facilities at 0 has social cost $2(1 - \alpha)n$, leading to an approximation ratio of $\frac{1+\alpha}{1-\alpha} = 1 + \sqrt{2}$.

Case 3: The mechanism places one facility at 0 and the other at 2. We consider the same sequence of instances as in Case 1. This results in that the mechanism must place one facility at 0 and the other at 2 when given as input the instance where αn agents are at $1 - \varepsilon$ while the remaining $(1 - \alpha)n$ agents are at 2. This solution has social cost $2\alpha n + 2(1 - \alpha)n = 2n$. However, the solution that places both facilities at 2 has social cost $2\alpha n$, leading to an approximation ratio of $\frac{1}{\alpha} = 1 + \sqrt{2}$. □

3.2 General Instances

Having completely resolved the homogeneous case, we now turn our attention to general, possibly heterogeneous instances. It is not hard to observe that the problem is more general than the single-facility location problem studied by Feldman et al. [9]; indeed, there are instances in which all agents approve just one facility and the other facility does not affect their social cost nor the approximation ratio. Consequently, we cannot hope to achieve an approximation ratio better than 3.

Theorem 5. *For general instances, the approximation ratio of any strategyproof mechanism is at least $3 - \delta$, for any $\delta > 0$.*

Since there is an adaptation of the MEDIAN mechanism that achieves an approximation ratio of 3 for homogeneous instances (see Theorem 1), one might wonder if there is a variant that can do so for heterogeneous instances as well. In particular, the natural extension of MEDIAN is to place F_1 at the candidate location closest to the (leftmost) median agent m_1 of N_1, and F_2 at the available candidate location closest to the (leftmost) median agent m_2 of N_2. While this seems like a good idea at first glance, the following example shows that it fails to achieve the desired approximation ratio bound.

Example 1. Consider an instance with two candidate locations at 0 and 2. For some $x \geq 1$, there are $2x + 1$ agents that approve only F_1 such that $x + 1$ of them are located at $1 - \varepsilon$ and the other x are located at 2. There are also $2x + 1$ agents that approve only F_2 and are all located at 0. According to the definition of the mechanism, F_1 is placed at 0 (which is the candidate location closest to the median agent in N_1), and then F_2 is placed at 2 as 0 is now occupied and 2 is available. This solution has social cost approximately $(x+2x)+4x = 7x$, whereas the solution that places F_1 at 2 and F_2 at 0 has social cost approximately x, leading to an approximation ratio of nearly 7.

The issue with the aforementioned variant of the MEDIAN mechanism is the order in which it decides to place the facilities. If it were to place F_2 first and F_1 second then it would have made the optimal choice in the example. However, there is a symmetric example that would again lead to a lower bound of approximately 7. So, the mechanism needs to be able to dynamically determine the order in which it places F_1 and F_2. This brings us to the following idea: We will again place each facility one after the other at the closest candidate location

---

Mechanism 2: STRONGER-MAJORITY-MEDIAN

Input: Reported positions of agents;
Output: Facility locations $\mathbf{w} = (w_1, w_2)$;
for $j \in [2]$ **do**
$\quad\lfloor\ S_j \leftarrow$ set of agents in N_j (weakly) closer to $t(m_j)$ than to $s(m_j)$;
if $2|S_1| - |N_1| \geq 2|S_2| - |N_2|$ **then**
$\quad|\ j \leftarrow 1$;
else
$\quad\lfloor\ j \leftarrow 2$;
$w_j \leftarrow t(m_j)$;
if $t(m_{3-j})$ is available **then**
$\quad|\ w_{3-j} \leftarrow t(m_{3-j})$;
else
$\quad\lfloor\ w_{3-j} \leftarrow s(m_{3-j})$;

---

to the median among the agents that approve it. However, the facility that is placed first (and thus has priority in case the median agents of N_1 and N_2 are closer to the same candidate location) is the one with stronger majority in terms of the number of agents that approve it who are closer to the top choice of the median agent rather than her second choice; ties are broken in favor of the facility that is approved by most agents, which is assumed to be F_1 without loss of generality. We refer to this mechanism as STRONGER-MAJORITY-MEDIAN; see Mechanism 2 for a more formal description.

We first show that this mechanism is strategyproof and then bound its approximation ratio. It is not hard to observe that this must be true as the mechanism is a composition of variants of two simple strategyproof mechanisms (median plus majority voting).

Theorem 6. STRONGER-MAJORITY-MEDIAN *is strategyproof.*

Proof. Clearly, if $t(m_1) \neq t(m_2)$ then no agent has incentive to deviate as then the facilities are placed at $t(m_1)$ and $t(m_2)$ independently of whether $2|S_j| - |N_j| \geq 2|S_{3-j}| - |N_{3-j}|$ or not for $j \in [2]$. So, it suffices to consider the case where $t(m_1) = t(m_2)$ and $2|S_j| - |N_j| \geq 2|S_{3-j}| - |N_{3-j}|$ for some $j \in [2]$, leading to $w_j = t(m_j)$ and $w_{3-j} = s(m_{3-j})$, solving ties in favor of F_1.

- m_j and any agent $i \in N_j$ that is closer to $t(m_j)$ than to $s(m_j)$ have no incentive to deviate as $t(m_j)$ is the best choice for them.
- Any agent $i \in N_j$ that is closer to $s(m_j)$ than to $t(m_j)$ has no incentive to deviate, as going closer to $t(m_j)$ can only increase the quantity $2|S_j| - |N_j|$ and cannot change the outcome.
- m_{3-j} and any agent $i \in N_{3-j}$ that is closer to $t(m_{3-j})$ than to $s(m_{3-j})$ have no incentive to deviate as moving closer to $s(m_{3-j})$ would decrease the quantity $2|S_{3-j}| - |N_{3-j}|$ and would not change the outcome.
- Any agent $i \in N_{3-j}$ that is closer to $s(m_{3-j})$ than to $t(m_{3-j})$ has no incentive to deviate as $s(m_j)$ is the best choice for them.

Mechanism 3: LEFTMOST-PRIORITY

Input: Reported positions of agents;
Output: Facility locations $\mathbf{w} = (w_1, w_2)$;
$\ell_{12} \leftarrow$ leftmost agent in $N_1 \cap N_2$;
$r_{12} \leftarrow$ rightmost agent in $N_1 \cap N_2$;
$w_1 \leftarrow t(\ell_{12})$;
if $t(r_{12})$ is available **then**
$\quad \mid \quad w_2 \leftarrow t(r_{12})$;
else
$\quad \lfloor \quad w_2 \leftarrow s(r_{12})$;

So, the mechanism is strategyproof.   □

Theorem 7. STRONGER-MAJORITY-MEDIAN *achieves an approximation ratio of at most* 3.

4 Max Cost

In this section, we turn our attention to the max cost objective for which we again show tight bounds on the approximation ratio of deterministic strategyproof mechanisms. In particular, we show a bound of 2 for homogeneous instances and a bound of 3 for general instances.

4.1 Homogeneous Instances

For homogeneous instances, we consider a simple mechanism that places F_1 at the candidate location closest to the leftmost agent ℓ_{12}, and then F_2 at the available candidate location closest to the rightmost agent r_{12}. We refer to this mechanism as LEFTMOST-PRIORITY; see Mechanism 3. It is not hard to show that this mechanism is strategyproof and that it achieves a best possible approximation ratio of 2 among deterministic strategyproof mechanisms.

Theorem 8. *For homogeneous instances,* LEFTMOST-PRIORITY *is strategyproof.*

Proof. Consider any agent i; recall that i approves both facilities. To affect the outcome, agent i would have to either report a position that lies at the left of ℓ_{12} or at the right of r_{12}. Changing the leftmost or rightmost positions, however, can only lead to placing the facilities at locations farther away from i and, hence, i has no incentive to misreport.   □

Theorem 9. *For homogeneous instances,* LEFTMOST-PRIORITY *achieves an approximation ratio of at most* 2.

Proof. Let i be the agent that determines the maximum cost of the mechanism, i.e., $MC(\mathbf{w}) = d(i, w_1) + d(i, w_2)$. Clearly, $i \in \{\ell_{12}, r_{12}\}$; let $j \in \{\ell_{12}, r_{12}\} \setminus \{i\}$. Let $\mathbf{o} = (o_1, o_2)$ be an optimal solution. We consider the following two cases: If $w_1 = t(\ell_{12})$ and $w_2 = t(r_{12})$, then by the triangle inequality and the definition of $t(\cdot)$, we have

$$
\begin{aligned}
MC(\mathbf{w}) &= d(i, t(i)) + d(i, t(j)) \\
&\leq d(i, t(i)) + d(i, o_2) + d(j, o_2) + d(j, t(j)) \\
&\leq d(i, o_1) + d(i, o_2) + d(j, o_2) + d(j, o_1) \leq 2 \cdot MC(\mathbf{o}).
\end{aligned}
$$

If $w_1 = t(\ell_{12})$ and $w_2 = s(r_{12})$, then there exists $x \in \{o_1, o_2\}$ such that $d(r_{12}, w_2) \leq d(r_{12}, x)$. Let $y \in \{o_1, o_2\} \setminus \{x\}$.

– If $i = \ell_{12}$, then

$$
\begin{aligned}
MC(\mathbf{w}) &= d(\ell_{12}, w_1) + d(\ell_{12}, w_2) \\
&\leq d(\ell_{12}, w_1) + d(\ell_{12}, y) + d(r_{12}, y) + d(r_{12}, w_2) \\
&\leq d(\ell_{12}, x) + d(\ell_{12}, y) + d(r_{12}, y) + d(r_{12}, x) \leq 2 \cdot MC(\mathbf{o}).
\end{aligned}
$$

– If $i = r_{12}$, then

$$
\begin{aligned}
MC(\mathbf{w}) &= d(r_{12}, w_1) + d(r_{12}, w_2) \\
&\leq d(r_{12}, y) + d(\ell_{12}, y) + d(\ell_{12}, w_1) + d(r_{12}, w_2) \\
&\leq d(r_{12}, y) + d(\ell_{12}, y) + d(\ell_{12}, x) + d(r_{12}, x) \leq 2 \cdot MC(\mathbf{o}).
\end{aligned}
$$

Therefore, the approximation ratio is at most 2 in any case.   □

Theorem 10. *For homogeneous instances, the approximation ratio of any deterministic strategyproof mechanism is at least $2 - \delta$, for any $\delta > 0$.*

4.2   General Instances

To tackle the general case, we split the set of instances into those with at least one agent that approves both facilities, and those in which each agent approves just one facility. It is not hard to observe that LEFTMOST-PRIORITY can still be applied when there is at least one agent that approves both facilities, and is strategyproof since its decision is fully determined by the leftmost and rightmost such agents. In addition, LEFTMOST-PRIORITY can be shown to achieve an approximation ratio of at most 3.

Theorem 11. *For instances with at least one agent that approves both facilities, the approximation ratio of LEFTMOST-PRIORITY is at most 3.*

Proof. We consider cases depending on the preference of the agent i that determines the max cost of the mechanism.

(**Case 1**). The max cost is determined by an agent $i \in N_1 \setminus N_2$. Then, by the triangle inequality and since $d(\ell_{12}, w_1) \leq d(\ell_{12}, o_2)$, we have

$$\mathrm{MC}(\mathbf{w}) = d(i, w_1) \leq d(i, o_1) + d(\ell_{12}, o_1) + d(\ell_{12}, w_1)$$
$$\leq d(i, o_1) + d(\ell_{12}, o_1) + d(\ell_{12}, o_2)$$
$$\leq 2 \cdot \mathrm{MC}(\mathbf{o}).$$

(**Case 2**). The max cost is determined by an agent $i \in N_2 \setminus N_1$. Since w_2 is either $t(r_{12})$ or $s(r_{12})$, there exists $x \in \{o_1, o_2\}$ such that $d(r_{12}, w_2) \leq d(r_{12}, x) \leq \mathrm{MC}(\mathbf{o})$. Hence, by the triangle inequality, we have

$$\mathrm{MC}(\tilde{\mathbf{w}}) = d(i, w_2) \leq d(i, o_2) + d(r_{12}, o_2) + d(r_{12}, w_2) \leq 3 \cdot \mathrm{MC}(\mathbf{o}).$$

(**Case 3**). The max cost is determined by an agent $i \in N_1 \cap N_2$. Then, following the proof of Theorem 9 for homogeneous instances, we can show an upper bound of 2. □

Next, we focus on instances with only agents that have singleton preferences, that is, $N_1 \cap N_2 = \varnothing$. There are multiple ways for LEFTMOST-PRIORITY to work in such instances, for example, by placing F_1 at the closest candidate location to the leftmost agent ℓ_1 of N_1, and F_2 at the closest available candidate location to an agent of N_2, such as the leftmost agent ℓ_2 or the rightmost agent r_2. While such mechanisms are clearly strategyproof, it is not hard to observe that they cannot achieve a good enough approximation ratio.

Example 2. If we place F_1 at $t(\ell_1)$ and F_2 at $t(r_2)$ or $s(r_2)$ depending on availability, then consider the following instance: There are three candidate locations at 0, 2, and 6. There is an agent ℓ_1 that approves F_1 at $1 + \varepsilon$, an agent ℓ_2 that approves F_2 at 1, and another agent r_2 that approves F_2 at $3 + \varepsilon$, for some infinitesimal $\varepsilon > 0$. So, we place F_1 at 2 and F_2 at 6 for a max cost of 5 (determined by ℓ_2). On the other hand, we could place F_1 at 0 and F_2 at 2 for a max cost of approximately 1, leading to an approximation ratio of 5. Clearly, if we chose ℓ_2 instead of r_2 to determine the location of F_2, there is a symmetric instance leading again to the same lower bound.

The above example illustrates that it is not always a good idea to choose a priori ℓ_2 or r_2 to determine where to place F_2, especially when the closest candidate location to them might not be available after placing F_1. Instead, we need to carefully decide whether ℓ_2 or r_2 or neither of them is the best one to choose where to place F_2. We make this decision as follows: We "ask" ℓ_2 and r_2 to "vote" over two candidate locations; the candidate location L that is the closest at the left of $t(\ell_1)$ (where F_1 is placed) and the candidate location R that is the closest at the right of $t(\ell_1)$. If ℓ_2 and r_2 "agree", then they are both on the same side of the midpoint of the interval defined by L and R, and thus depending on whether they are on the left side (agree on L) or the right side (agree on R), we allow r_2 or ℓ_2, respectively, to make the choice of where to place

---

Mechanism 4: VOTE-FOR-PRIORITY

Input: Reported positions of agents;
Output: Facility locations $\mathbf{w} = (w_1, w_2)$;
$w_1 \leftarrow t(\ell_1)$;
$L \leftarrow$ closest candidate location at the left of w_1;
$R \leftarrow$ closest candidate location at the right of w_1;
// **(case 1)** ℓ_2 and r_2 agree that L is closer: r_2 gets to choose
if ℓ_2 and r_2 are both closer to L than to R **then**
    if $t(r_2)$ is available **then**
        | $w_2 \leftarrow t(r_2)$;
    else
        | $w_2 \leftarrow s(r_2)$;
// **(case 2)** ℓ_2 and r_2 agree that R is closer: ℓ_2 gets to choose
else if ℓ_2 and r_2 are both closer to R than to L **then**
    if $t(\ell_2)$ is available **then**
        | $w_2 \leftarrow t(\ell_2)$;
    else
        | $w_2 \leftarrow s(\ell_2)$;
// **(case 3)** ℓ_2 and r_2 disagree: choose the closest of L and R to w_1
else
    | $w_2 \leftarrow \arg\min_{x \in \{L,R\}} \{|w_1 - x|\}$;

F_2. If they "disagree", they are on different sides of the interval's midpoint, so neither ℓ_2 nor r_2 should make a choice of where to place F_2; in this case, the closest of L and R to $t(\ell_1)$ is a good candidate location to place F_2. This idea is formalized in Mechanism 4, which we call VOTE-FOR-PRIORITY.

Theorem 12. *For instances with only agents that have singleton preferences,* VOTE-FOR-PRIORITY *is strategyproof and achieves an approximation ratio of at most 3.*

Based on the above discussion, we have the following statement.

Corollary 1. *For general instances, there is a deterministic strategyproof mechanism with approximation ratio at most 3.*

Proof. Since the preferences of the agents are known, we can determine whether there is at least one agent that approves both facilities. If this is indeed the case, we run LEFTMOST-PRIORITY. Otherwise, we run VOTE-FOR-PRIORITY. The desired properties of the mechanism follow by the fact that both mechanisms are strategyproof and achieve approximation ratio at most 3 in their respective cases. □

The bound of 3 is in fact the best possible among all deterministic strategyproof mechanisms. As argued at the beginning of Sect. 3.2, instances in which all agents approve one of the facilities are equivalent to having just this one facility to place. Consequently, by the work of Tang et al. [22], we cannot hope to achieve an approximation ratio better than 3.

Theorem 13. *For general instances, the approximation ratio of any deterministic strategyproof mechanism is at least $3 - \delta$, for any $\delta > 0$.*

5 Conclusion

In this paper we studied a truthful two-facility location problem with candidate locations and showed tight bounds on the best possible approximation ratio of deterministic strategyproof mechanisms in terms of the social cost and the max cost. An obvious question that our work leaves open is the design of randomized strategyproof mechanisms with improved approximation guarantees. There are also multiple ways to extend our model. One such way is to change the assumption about what type of information is public or private, and instead of considering the case where the positions are private and the preferences are known as we did in this paper, focus on the case where the positions are public and the preferences are private (which is a generalization of the models studied in [15,20]). Other ways of extending our model include settings with more than just two facilities to place, and more general metric spaces than just the line.

References

1. Alon, N., Feldman, M., Procaccia, A.D., Tennenholtz, M.: Strategyproof approximation of the minimax on networks. Math. Oper. Res. **35**(3), 513–526 (2010)
2. Anastasiadis, E., Deligkas, A.: Heterogeneous facility location games. In: Proceedings of the 17th International Conference on Autonomous Agents and MultiAgent Systems (AAMAS), pp. 623–631 (2018)
3. Anshelevich, E., Filos-Ratsikas, A., Shah, N., Voudouris, A.A.: Distortion in social choice problems: the first 15 years and beyond. In: Proceedings of the 30th International Joint Conference on Artificial Intelligence (IJCAI), pp. 4294–4301 (2021)
4. Chan, H., Filos-Ratsikas, A., Li, B., Li, M., Wang, C.: Mechanism design for facility location problems: a survey. In: Proceedings of the Thirtieth International Joint Conference on Artificial Intelligence (IJCAI), pp. 4356–4365 (2021)
5. Cheng, Y., Yua, W., Zhang, G.: Strategy-proof approximation mechanisms for an obnoxious facility game on networks. Theoret. Comput. Sci. **497**, 154–163 (2013)
6. Deligkas, A., Filos-Ratsikas, A., Voudouris, A.A.: Heterogeneous facility location with limited resources. Games Econom. Behav. **139**, 200–215 (2023)
7. Duan, L., Gong, Z., Li, M., Wang, C., Wu, X.: Facility location with fractional preferences and minimum distance. In: Proceedings of the 27th International Conference on Computing and Combinatorics (COCOON), pp. 499–511 (2021)
8. Feigenbaum, I., Sethuraman, J.: Strategyproof mechanisms for one-dimensional hybrid and obnoxious facility location models. In: AAAI Workshop on Incentive and Trust in E-Communities, vol. WS-15-08 (2015)
9. Feldman, M., Fiat, A., Golomb, I.: On voting and facility location. In: Proceedings of the 2016 ACM Conference on Economics and Computation (EC), pp. 269–286 (2016)

10. Filos-Ratsikas, A., Kanellopoulos, P., Voudouris, A.A., Zhang, R.: Settling the distortion of distributed facility location. In: Proceedings of the 22nd International Conference on Autonomous Agents and Multiagent Systems (AAMAS), pp. 2152–2160 (2023)
11. Filos-Ratsikas, A., Voudouris, A.A.: Approximate mechanism design for distributed facility location. In: Proceedings of the 14th International Symposium on Algorithmic Game Theory (SAGT), pp. 49–63 (2021)
12. Fotakis, D., Tzamos, C.: Strategyproof facility location for concave cost functions. Algorithmica 76(1), 143–167 (2016)
13. Gai, L., Liand, M., Wang, C.: Obnoxious facility location games with candidate locations. In: Proceedings of the 16th International Conference on Algorithmic Aspects in Information and Management (AAIM), pp. 96–105 (2022)
14. Goel, S., Hann-Caruthers, W.: Coordinate-wise median: not bad, not bad, pretty good. CoRR abs/2007.00903 (2020)
15. Kanellopoulos, P., Voudouris, A.A., Zhang, R.: On discrete truthful heterogeneous two-facility location. SIAM J. Discret. Math. 37, 779–799 (2023)
16. Li, M., Lu, P., Yao, Y., Zhang, J.: Strategyproof mechanism for two heterogeneous facilities with constant approximation ratio. In: Proceedings of the 29th International Joint Conference on Artificial Intelligence (IJCAI), pp. 238–245 (2020)
17. Lu, P., Sun, X., Wang, Y., Zhu, Z.A.: Asymptotically optimal strategy-proof mechanisms for two-facility games. In: Proceedings of the 11th ACM Conference on Electronic Commerce (EC), pp. 315–324 (2010)
18. Meir, R.: Strategyproof facility location for three agents on a circle. In: Fotakis, D., Markakis, E. (eds.) SAGT 2019. LNCS, vol. 11801, pp. 18–33. Springer, Cham (2019). https://doi.org/10.1007/978-3-030-30473-7_2
19. Procaccia, A.D., Tennenholtz, M.: Approximate mechanism design without money. ACM Trans. Econ. Comput. 1(4), 18:1–18:26 (2013)
20. Serafino, P., Ventre, C.: Heterogeneous facility location without money. Theoret. Comput. Sci. 636, 27–46 (2016)
21. Sui, X., Boutilier, C.: Approximately strategy-proof mechanisms for (constrained) facility location. In: Proceedings of the 2015 International Conference on Autonomous Agents and Multiagent Systems (AAMAS), pp. 605–613 (2015)
22. Tang, Z., Wang, C., Zhang, M., Zhao, Y.: Mechanism design for facility location games with candidate locations. In: Proceedings of the 14th International Conference on Combinatorial Optimization and Applications (COCOA), pp. 440–452 (2020)
23. Walsh, T.: Strategy proof mechanisms for facility location at limited locations. In: Proceedings of the 8th Pacific Rim International Conference on Artificial Intelligence (PRICAI), pp. 113–124 (2021)
24. Xu, X., Li, B., Li, M., Duan, L.: Two-facility location games with minimum distance requirement. J. Artif. Intell. Res. 70, 719–756 (2021)
25. Zhao, Q., Liu, W., Nong, Q., Fang, Q.: Constrained heterogeneous facility location games with max-variant cost. J. Comb. Optim. 45(3), 90 (2023)
26. Zou, S., Li, M.: Facility location games with dual preference. In: Proceedings of the 2015 International Conference on Autonomous Agents and Multiagent Systems (AAMAS), pp. 615–623 (2015)

Threshold Mechanisms for Dynamic Procurement with Abandonment

Ali Khodabakhsh[1], Evdokia Nikolova[1], Emmanouil Pountourakis[2]([✉]),
and Jimmy Horn[3]

[1] University of Texas at Austin, Austin, TX 78712, USA
ali.kh@utexas.edu, nikolova@austin.utexas.edu
[2] Drexel University, Philadelphia, PA 19104, USA
manolis@drexel.edu
[3] Horn Wind LLC, Austin, TX 78704, USA

Abstract. We study a dynamic model of procurement auctions in which
the agents (sellers) will abandon the auction if their utility does not
satisfy their private target, in any given round. We call this "abandonment" and analyze its consequences on the overall cost to the mechanism
designer (buyer), as it reduces competition in future rounds of the auction
and drives up the price. We show that in order to maintain competition
and minimize the overall cost, the mechanism designer has to adopt an
inefficient (per-round) allocation, namely to assign the demand to multiple agents in a single round. We focus on threshold mechanisms as a
simple way to achieve ex-post incentive compatibility, akin to reserves
in revenue-maximizing forward auctions. We then consider the optimization problem of finding the optimal thresholds. We show that even though
our objective function does not have the optimal substructure property
in general, if the underlying distributions satisfy some regularity properties, the global optimal solution lies within a region where the optimal
thresholds are monotone and can be calculated with a greedy approach,
or even more simply in a parallel fashion.

Keywords: mechanism design · auctions · procurement · threshold
mechanisms

1 Introduction

The wide applicability of auctions in real life, from the simple traditional sealed-
bid and ascending/descending price auctions, to the modern sponsored search
and eBay auctions, to government-run auctions for spectrum and carbon emissions, has inspired the development of a rich theory of auctions and mechanism
design. The more prevalent auction design focuses on the so called 'regular' auctions, where the bidders are buyers wishing to buy an item from the mechanism

Emmanouil Pountourakis was partially supported by NSF grant CCF-2218813. Part
of the research was conducted when the authors were hosted by the Simon's Institute
for the Theory of Computing.

designer (seller), who tries to maximize her revenue (see, e.g. [15]). Less prevalent are 'reverse' or 'procurement' auctions where the bidders are sellers and the mechanism designer is a buyer wanting to minimize cost.

A principal example of procurement auctions is public procurement—the process by which governments purchase goods, services and construction—which comprises a significant fraction, 10–20%, of a country's GDP [5]. Some of the more complex procurement auctions include the above mentioned spectrum and carbon emissions auctions, as well as the procurement of energy, a key motivation of this work.

Thus, while the large majority of literature on auction and mechanism design focuses on *static* mechanisms that optimize the designer goals with a single round in mind, there has been a recent rise in the study of *dynamic mechanism design* which attempts to model and analyze mechanisms across time [1].

In the context of procurement, different strands of literature investigate different types of interdependencies, such as caused by a capacity constraint [21,22], a switching cost from one service provider to another [9,17], a backlog cost in dynamic inventory control models [18,23], learning through experience [16,20] and piecewise procurement where the subprojects of a large project have to be procured in a predetermined order [2,24]. Yet very simple and basic models for dynamic procurement remain unexplored that provide fertile ground for theory exploration and progress. We propose one such model which takes the most basic reverse auction of multiple sellers needing to provide a unit of divisible good or service over repeated rounds, with the condition that a seller must make at a minimum her overhead cost in order to remain present in future rounds of the auction. This provides a coupling or interdependency of the different rounds of the auction that precludes existing mechanisms from applying and calls for new tools in mechanism design.

Our motivation for this model comes from the process for energy procurement called "economic dispatch": Electricity generation is currently managed by Independent System Operators (ISO) in a myopic way (day by day). Each generator submits a supply curve, namely one or more bids of how much it is able to generate at what unit cost, for the following day. The ISO then allocates generation, based on demand (and subject to any system constraints), so as to minimize the total generation cost. Economic dispatch is thus effectively a generalized version of the standard procurement auction.

In a lot of US markets, wind is typically the least expensive form of generation, thus it is favored by the current selection mechanism over conventional generation (nuclear, coal and gas). Coal, as the least competitive conventional generation, is gradually being driven out of business due to underuse. Wind though has higher variability and uncertainty, and requires increased use of expensive back-up generation, while conventionals are reliable and do not need to be backed up. Ultimately, this is pushing the system to the two extremes of cheap, variable renewables and expensive, back-up generation. As a result, this short-term cost-minimization approach yields a higher long-term cost and compromises system reliability [14].

In reality, a less competitive generator whose economic viability is threatened might be "saved" by the ISO if it is considered critical to system reliability, by entering a side contract with the ISO that guarantees it sufficient allocation and payment to help it remain viable. Such contracts are currently done behind closed doors in an ad hoc way, including the ISO's decision which generators it considers critical.

To improve system efficiency and transparency, our model here makes a first step toward providing a framework for systematic allocation and payments that minimize cost over multiple periods. Specifically, two issues stand out from the brief background on energy procurement above. One issue is the need to capture the agents' overhead costs necessary to stay in business as a model feature to make transparent the process of identifying and saving a needed agent. We call the phenomenon of permanently leaving the auction due to not having met the overhead cost in a given round as "abandonment". The second, related issue, is the tension of cost vs competition, or short- vs long-term outlook, namely that being optimal in the current round might be suboptimal from a long-term perspective. That is because cost minimization in a given round might result in fewer agent allocations and thus reduced competition in future rounds, which would lead to a higher cost in the future. We discuss these two issues in more detail in the context of our model and results below.

Modeling Choices and Assumptions. Our goal is to frame the above real-life situation as a simplified auction theory model that abstracts away many engineering components, which are important but not central to the core mechanism design challenges. What are the minimal features our model can be stripped down to, that make it as simple as possible yet expressive of the two above-mentioned issues of (i) abandonment and (ii) tradeoff of cost and competition?

We focus on a two-round model with n symmetric agents (sellers), each of whom can meet the entire demand of 1 unit of divisible good/service per round, and each of whom submits a bid for her overhead cost, namely the amount she needs to make this round to "be saved" and remain in the next round of the auction. The overhead costs are private values, independent and identically distributed according to some known distribution F, across agents and across rounds.

To keep the model tractable, we assume that a per unit production cost that sellers incur for providing the good/service is known and constant (which turns out mathematically equivalent to it being zero). For example, in the energy application above, the cost of producing energy can easily be estimated by the technology; however, the overhead costs of generators (such as financing, labor costs, maintenance, etc.) are private information.

In a given round, the auctioneer or mechanism designer collects the bids and decides on the allocations and payments which in turn determine which agents are going to be saved for the following round. We will argue later that in the last day, the mechanism designer is going to allocate the entire demand to a single agent (since there is no need to maintain the competition anymore). Further, to more succinctly capture the challenges that abandonment and competition issues present, we assume that even in that final round, the mechanism should satisfy the overhead cost constraint of that single agent: this is also equivalent to removing this assumption and having one extra round, namely a 3-round auction setting.

Abandonment. In both forward and reverse auctions, when the auction is repeated over several iterations, it has been noted that the agents may leave the platform. The typical assumptions used in the literature are of dynamic arrival and departure that are exogenous and are not related to the outcome of the auction [11,12]. In a regular auction the agent may prefer to change her auction platform if she is not receiving enough utility. Similarly, in a reverse or procurement auction, for example in the energy sector, if the generators do not meet their overhead costs they are forced to close down.

Two natural modeling choices for the utility function of an agent stand out to capture the abandonment: the utility for being allocated zero or, more generally, for being paid less than one's overhead cost could be modeled as zero or as negative infinity (or, equivalently, a large negative constant). The first choice may appear more natural on the surface but it fails to align the incentives with the phenomenon of abandonment—specifically, it fails to represent the negative repercussions of a bankruptcy in reality, which is what we are trying to model with agents abandoning the auction. Indeed, if an agent ever goes out of business, the agent should not be incentivized to stay in the auction. Furthermore, zero utility for zero allocation is inaccurate in the energy context where power plants continue having overhead expenses (such as employee salaries and power plant maintenance) even if they are not allocated and not producing in a given time period, so effectively a zero or even insufficient positive allocation implies losses which are what ultimately drives plants to retire. We thus opt for the negative infinity model, which also emphasizes the "finality" of an agent's participation in the auction if she is not allocated or has not met her overhead cost in a given round.

We remark that with this modeling choice, the utility function will not satisfy individual rationality, in that participating in the auction may have lower expected utility than not participating. Again, this is consistent with the energy and likely a number of other applications where starting a business such as building and operating a power plant entails risk and is not guaranteed to break even. We note the relation of our utility function choice to regular auctions where a buyer has a budget and receives a utility of negative infinity for exceeding it (e.g., [6,10]). Indeed, we can view the overhead cost that needs to be met each period as a reverse budget where, once the budget is exceeded, or in our case the reverse budget is not met, the agent is forced to abandon the auction.

Summary of our results. Our goal is to design the optimal bid-sensitive mechanisms, i.e., to find the optimal thresholds for allocating the service to various number of agents at every round. Specifically, for our two-round auction, it suffices to set the corresponding thresholds for round one, as the final round has a trivial optimal mechanism. We denote by t_i the threshold for saving i agents in round one. Our main result is to show that the global optimization for the thresholds $t_2, t_3, \ldots$ can be done in a greedy fashion, even though the objective function does not have the optimal substructure property that usually leads to optimality of greedy approach (see Theorem 3). Our results can be summarized as follows:

(a) We model a two-round dynamic procurement auction with abandonment, where the agents leave the auction if they do not meet their overhead costs in a given round. We focus on threshold mechanisms, as they are widely used in practice, and show that they are ex-post incentive compatible for our dynamic auction model. The thresholds are similar to setting reserves for revenue maximization in regular auctions.

(b) Next, we study the optimization problem for finding the optimal set of thresholds. We show that if the distribution F for overhead costs is regular (as defined later), the optimal thresholds are independent of the number of agents participating in the auction. In other words, we do not need to know the number of agents to determine the optimal set of thresholds.

(c) We prove that if the underlying distribution F satisfies certain properties, the optimal thresholds will be monotone, meaning that the optimal threshold for saving i agents is lower than the optimal threshold for saving j agents for any $i > j$. Moreover, we show that this monotonicity helps divide the optimization problem into n separate problems, which ultimately leads to an efficient algorithm to calculate the optimal thresholds in parallel.

2 Related Work

Single-parameter mechanism design has been extensively studied in theoretical computer science over the last decade and lead to several interesting results in the intersection of approximation and mechanism design (e.g. [13] and references therein). Over the last few years there has been an increased interest in dynamic mechanism design and specifically, revenue maximization in repeated auctions [3,19]. The challenge in this line of work has been that depending on the assumptions about when the agents obtain their information, these models become multi-dimensional, leading to a notoriously hard problem in mechanism design (see [4] for a survey).

For example, Ashlagi *et al.* [3] study incentive compatible mechanisms for revenue maximization. In contrast to prior economic literature they require that the mechanism is strongly individually rational, namely the utility of each agent should be non-negative at any stage of the game. One interpretation of strong individual rationality in the context of a dynamic auction is that agents would abandon the service if they ever receive negative utility. Our model of abandonment in a procurement auction setting can be thought of as a relaxation of individual rationality, where each agent expects to achieve a specific level of utility and if she does not meet her target then she abandons the platform.

Different models of dynamic procurement auctions have been studied in the past. The common aspect between these different models is an intertemporal dependency, either on the procurer/buyer side or the suppliers/bidders, that ties the outcomes of the individual auctions. Examples of such dependencies include:

Capacity constraint: When the bidders are capacity-constrained, their costs increase if they win the current auction (due to higher future capacity utilization). Therefore, capacity-constrained firms face an intertemporal trade-off in sequential auctions: higher profits in the current period lead to lower profits in future periods. This model has been studied over both a finite [21] and an infinite horizon [22].

Switching cost: When a procurer buys goods from competing suppliers repeatedly over time, she may incur an additional switching cost each time she switches from one supplier to another. These costs arise because the buyer must acquire skill at using a new supplier's product, and affect the competition between the incumbent supplier and his rivals [9,17].

Backlog/holding cost: In dynamic inventory control models, the procurer becomes a retailer who has to repeatedly run a procurement auction among a number of potential suppliers before observing the actual demand. At the end of each period, any unsatisfied demand will be backlogged with a backlog cost and any unsold inventory will be carried over to the next period with a holding cost [18,23].

Learning through experience: In many industries learning by doing or learning through production experience enables suppliers to provide better service at lower costs. Lewis and Yildirim [16] consider such model in which the cost of each supplier at each round consists of a (public) intrinsic cost of production, which decreases every time that producer supplies the procurer, and a (private) transitory cost drawn according to a prior distribution. They study how buyer optimally manages dynamic competition among rival suppliers to exploit learning economies.

Piecewise procurement: Sometimes sequential procurement auctions belong to a large-scale project whose subprojects have to be procured in a predetermined order. The project yields its full value once it is completed. The question is then how the procurer optimally designs a procurement auction for each subproject, especially when she cannot write long-term contracts [2,24].

In comparison to these previous models, we introduce the notion of **abandonment** to the procurement auction, meaning that the suppliers may leave the auction if their received payments do not cover their internal costs. Under this model, it is no longer true that repeating a single-round-optimal auction will lead to assigning the demand to the best set of agents at the best price [14]. To the best of our knowledge, this fundamental model has not been studied in the literature.

3   Preliminaries

There are 2 periods and a set of agents N, where $|N| = n$. Each period the mechanism designer wants to allocate a unit of production to a subset of agents. In period $j = 1, 2$, each agent i is characterized by her overhead cost M_i^j and her production cost c_i^j. We assume that the overhead costs are private and independently identically distributed according to a distribution F (independent across both agents and rounds). We will assume that F is a continuous distribution supported on $[0, 1]$.

Let x_i^j be the production percentage allocated to agent i in round j and p^j the anonymous payment rate for round j. The utility of agent i in round j is given by:

$$u_i^j(M_1^j, M_2^j, \cdots, M_n^j) = \begin{cases} x_i^j(p^j - c_i^j) & x_i^j(p^j - c_i^j) \geq M_i^j, \\ -\infty, & x_i^j(p^j - c_i^j) < M_i^j. \end{cases} \quad (1)$$

Agent i seeks to maximize her aggregate utility $u_i^1 + u_i^2$ from both rounds. The utility function is capturing the fact that if an agent does not meet her overhead cost M_i^j in round j, she goes out of business and loses everything she gained today. In addition we assume that if an agent receives $-\infty$ utility she will abandon the auction.

We further focus on the case where the individual production costs c_i^j are known to the designer and homogeneous across the agents. For simplicity all our results will assume $c_i^j = 0$ for all i and j but, as we show in the full version of the paper, this can be generalized if they are the same for all agents in a particular round but not necessarily 0, and can vary across rounds. Hence, without loss of generality, the utility of agent i becomes:

$$u_i^j(M_1^j, M_2^j, \cdots, M_n^j) = \begin{cases} x_i^j \cdot p^j & x_i^j \cdot p^j \geq M_i^j, \\ -\infty, & x_i^j \cdot p^j < M_i^j. \end{cases} \quad (2)$$

The mechanism designer does not know the overhead costs, M_i^j, which are all identically and independently distributed according to a distribution F, i.e., $M_i^j \sim F$ independent across rounds $j = 1, 2$ and across agents $i = 1, \ldots, n$.

Mechanism. Each agent reports her current overhead cost M_i^j to the designer during round j and the designer decides on the allocation $x_i^j(M_1^j, \cdots, M_n^j)$ for all $i \in N$ and the anonymous payment rate $p^j(M_1^j, \cdots, M_n^j)$. We seek to design a mechanism that minimizes the expected total cost of the outcome

$$\mathbb{E}_{M_i^j \sim F}\left[p^1(M_1^1, \ldots, M_n^1) + p^2(\hat{M}_1^2, \ldots, \hat{M}_n^2)\right],$$

where $\hat{M}_i^2 = M_i^2$ if $x_i^1 \cdot p^1 \geq M_i^1$ and $\hat{M}_i^2 = \infty$ otherwise.

Truthfulness. There are several generalizations of truthfulness once we depart from the standard single-shot environment. Ex-post incentive compatibility requires that agents want to report truthfully their overhead costs if this maximizes their aggregate utility even if they have access to the realization of their overhead costs in advance. For example, in our setting with two rounds, agent i should not have an incentive to report a different value than M_i^1 in round 1 despite knowing the value M_i^2. Periodic ex-post incentive compatibility relaxes this condition to agents having access to the history of the game and having only distributional assumptions for their future overhead costs. Nevertheless, the natural class of threshold mechanisms that we analyze in this paper satisfies the stronger notion of ex-post incentive compatibility[1]. Each round j is characterized by a choice of n different thresholds $(t_1^j, t_2^j, \ldots, t_n^j)$, where t_i^j represents the maximum amount that the mechanism is willing to pay to save the i-th agent in round j. This is more precisely described in the following definition.

Definition 1. *A single threshold mechanism using thresholds* $t_1, \ldots, t_n \in [0,1]$ *is defined as follows: Assume* $M_1 < M_2 < \cdots < M_n$ *and let us define the predicate* $T_k(M_1, \ldots, M_n) = 1$ *if and only if* $M_k \leq t_k$, *in other words the* k^{th} *smallest value is less than the* k^{th} *threshold.[2] Let* k *be the highest index such that* $T_k = 1$. *Then the mechanism allocation is:*

$$x_i = \begin{cases} 1/k & \text{if } i \leq k \\ 0 & \text{otherwise} \end{cases} \tag{3}$$

and the payment to agent i *is* $x_i \cdot p$, *where* p *is the total mechanism payment (also the per unit cost of providing the demand) defined as* $p = k \cdot \min\{t_k, M_{k+1}\}$. *In other words, the cheapest* k *agents equally provide the service, while each receiving a payment of* $\min\{t_k, M_{k+1}\}$.

The mechanism uses the thresholds to determine the number of agents it wishes to allocate the service to. Note that allocating the service to more than one agent is inefficient. Allocating to multiple agents and respecting their overhead costs means that for every agent such that $x_i > 0$ it must be that the agent payment is at least her overhead cost, $x_i \cdot p \geq M_i$.

Proposition 1. *Any threshold mechanism is truthful[3] in the corresponding single-shot game and each agent that has non-zero allocation has non-negative utility.*

---

[1] We conjecture that threshold mechanisms are optimal for this setting among mechanisms that satisfy ex-post incentive compatibility.

[2] In the case of ties we need to slightly adjust the description of the mechanism. We refer the reader to the full version of the paper for the general version of the mechanism. Since we assume continuous distributions, we can assume no ties for optimizing our objective, without loss of generality.

[3] Assuming no ties.

Proof. If an agent i is not allocated the service, she receives utility of $-\infty$. Bidding a lower overhead cost may result in her being allocated some part of the demand. There are two scenarios in which this may happen: (1) If there exists some k such that T_k is the highest true predicate both before and after agent i lowered her bid. In this case, it must be that her lower bid is less than or equal to $M_k < M_i$. This results in a payment equal to M_k, which makes her utility $-\infty$ again. (2) If T_k is not the highest true predicate after agent i lowers her bid. Assume that the new highest predicate satisfied is T_w for some $w > k$. Since T_w was not true before, it must be that the threshold t_w is now the critical value, therefore each agent receives a payment equal to t_w. But since T_w was false before, we know that $t_w < M_i$, meaning that agent i will receive $-\infty$ utility.

If agent i is allocated the service, notice that her payment is independent of her actual overhead cost. Reporting a lower overhead cost does not change her allocation nor payment. Similarly, if she reports a higher amount, she will receive the same payment, as long as she is still being allocated the service. If her increase makes her not being allocated, then her utility becomes $-\infty$. In neither case is deviating from reporting the true overhead cost profitable.

We now define a threshold mechanism for a two-round game.

Definition 2. *A threshold mechanism for a two round game is characterized by two sets of thresholds* $\mathbf{t}^1 = (t_1^1, \ldots, t_n^1)$ *and* $\mathbf{t}^2 = (t_1^2, \ldots, t_n^2)$. *For any round j, we allocate the demand to at least i agents, if there are i bids below t_i^j.*

While technically the threshold mechanism defined in the second round could depend on the number of surviving agents, the optimal mechanism in the last round is oblivious to this fact; it will always allocate the service to a single agent and offer her a payment equal to the second lowest bid or the top of the distributional support if only one agent has survived. Since the mechanism is only feasible if it always allocates the entire demand, we need to have that $t_1^j = 1$ (the upper bound of the support of F) and therefore we will be omitting t_1 from now on.

Proposition 2. *A threshold mechanism for a dynamic game is ex-post incentive compatible.*

Proof. It is easy to see that for $j = 2$ (the last round), truthfulness of the threshold mechanism in the single-shot version implies that reporting the truth in the last round is optimal for each agent. For $j = 1$, we have to argue that deviating from the truth does not increase the aggregate utility for the agent. Since the mechanism is independent of the outcome of round 1, the only way that the reported overhead cost in round 1 affects the second round is if the agent is not allocated in the first round, hence has to abandon the auction. Instead, the agent could misreport a smaller overhead cost in order to ensure some allocation in round 1 so as to be considered in round 2. But in this case the aggregate utility of this agent remains $-\infty$, hence she cannot benefit from the deviation.

As mentioned earlier, our objective in designing a threshold mechanism is to minimize the total payment of our allocation. In other words, we seek a mechanism (x, p) with thresholds $(\mathbf{t^1}, \mathbf{t^2})$ such that it minimizes the total payment. The optimal mechanism for the second round is independent of what happens during the first round and there is no reason to allocate the production of the service to more than one agent.

Proposition 3. *The optimal threshold mechanism for the second round of a two-round auction is always equal to $t_2^2 = t_3^2 = \cdots = t_n^2 = 0$.*

Proof. Setting $t_2^2 > 0$ means that with some probability two agents will be allocated the service resulting in a payment more than the second lowest bid. Note that allocating the service to the second lowest agent does not result in any benefit in the future (since this is the last round). On the contrary, setting all thresholds for round two to 0 ensures that we allocate the service to the agent with the lowest bid, and the payment would be equal to the second lowest bid. Similarly, setting any t_i^2 to a non-zero value is a sub-optimal choice. Therefore, the optimal mechanism in round 2 is to set all thresholds t_i^2 to zero for $i \geq 2$. (As always we have $t_1^2 = 1$.)

Note that when the threshold mechanism allocates to an agent, it ensures that the payment she receive is at least her reported overhead cost so she will not abandon the auction. This is not necessarily needed for the second round according to the definition of our objective. If we allow the mechanism to allocate to an agent and not respect her overhead cost, then we could simply add an additional round.

In that case, any feasible mechanism must ensure that one agent survives to the third round; therefore, the payments should satisfy her overhead cost in the second round as well. Thus our analysis exactly captures this case when we only focus on the first two rounds.

The main result of our paper is to characterize the first round optimal threshold mechanism for dynamic procurement. It is important to note the connection of our problem to revenue maximization where effectively we use a similar analysis in terms of virtual costs. An alternative way to interpret our mechanism is that it implements a form of supply increase to reduce the aggregate cost of the mechanism. Our results hold for natural assumptions on the distribution of the overhead cost defined below.

Definition 3 (Regularity [7]). *We say that a probability distribution f (with cumulative distribution function F) supported on $[0, 1]$ is regular if its virtual cost function defined as $x + \frac{F(x)}{f(x)}$ is monotone increasing.*

Definition 4 (Order Statistics [8]). *Let $X_1, ..., X_n$ be a random sample of size n (independent) from a distribution F and $X_{1:n} \leq X_{2:n} \leq ... \leq X_{n:n}$ be the order statistics obtained by arranging X_i's in non-decreasing order. We denote by $\mu_{r:n}$ the expectation of the rth order statistic, i.e.:*

$$\mu_{r:n} = \mathbb{E}[X_{r:n}]$$

Definition 5 (Diminishing Returns of Order Statistics). *We say that the rth order statistic of a distribution F has the diminishing returns property if*

$$\mu_{r:n-1} - \mu_{r:n} \geq \mu_{r:n} - \mu_{r:n+1}, \quad \forall n > r.$$

Our main theorem is stated below. A surprising property we find is that the mechanism does not need to know the initial number of agents that participate in any round of the auction.

Theorem 1. *If distribution F satisfies the regularity condition (Definition 3), and its second order statistic has the diminishing returns property (Definition 5), then the optimal threshold mechanism can be found in polynomial time.*

The remainder of our paper is organized as follows. In Sect. 4 we define the canonical threshold mechanism. In Sect. 5 we present the main theorem of our paper proving the optimality of the canonical threshold mechanism. Finally, in Sect. 6 we discuss significant departures from our setting via breaking various types of homogeneity and symmetry and propose future directions.

4 Mechanism

Our objective in designing a threshold mechanism is to minimize the payment of our allocation. We will use $C_n(t_2, ..., t_n)$ to denote the aggregate cost of two rounds given a specific set of thresholds $(t_2, \ldots, t_n)$ for the first round, where n is the number of agents in round 1.

Definition 6 (Canonical Thresholds). *The canonical threshold for saving i agents, denoted by $\hat{t}_i$, is the optimal value for t_i when all previous thresholds are set to one, and all remaining thresholds are set to zero. More precisely,*

$$\hat{t}_i \equiv \underset{t_i}{argmin} \quad C_n(t_2, ..., t_n)$$
$$s.t. \quad t_2 = \cdots = t_{i-1} = 1, \tag{4}$$
$$t_{i+1} = \cdots = t_n = 0.$$

In Sect. 5 we show that the canonical thresholds defined above are indeed optimal thresholds for minimizing the objective function $C_n(t_2, ..., t_n)$. To prepare the ground for this result, we first establish some properties of our objective function. In particular, in Theorem 2, we calculate the partial derivative of the objective function with respect to any threshold t_i. For this theorem, we have to define the following notation.

Notation. Recall that we defined the predicate $T_k(M_1, ..., M_n) = 1$ if there are at least k bids below t_k. We define the vector $\mathbf{M} = (M_1, ..., M_n)$ to be the vector of all private values and we write $T_k(\mathbf{M}) = 1$, or for short $T_k = 1$, if the kth predicate is satisfied. Otherwise, we write $T_k = 0$.

Given that the first i bids are below t_i (hence predicate i is satisfied), we define $P_{i,n}$ as the probability that the remaining bids are above t_i so as not to satisfy any higher predicate $(T_{i+1}, ..., T_n)$.

More precisely, we define

$$P_{i,n} = \Pr\left[M_{i+1}, ..., M_n > t_i, T_{i+1} = ... = T_n = 0 \mid M_1, ..., M_i \le t_i\right], \quad (5)$$

where we assume $P_{n,n} = 1$ (since higher bids/thresholds do not exist for this case). An important property that we use in our proofs is that by this definition, $P_{i,n}$ is independent of all lower thresholds $(t_2, ..., t_{i-1})$.

Finally, given a vector of all private values $\mathbf{M}$, we define $g(\mathbf{M}, t_2, ..., t_n)$ to be the total cost of the mechanism using thresholds $t_2, ..., t_n$. This total cost consists of a deterministic cost for the current round (since the bids are given by $\mathbf{M}$) and an expected cost for the future round(s). With our earlier notation, $C_n(t_2, ..., t_n) = \mathbb{E}_{\mathbf{M}}[g(\mathbf{M}, t_2, ..., t_n)]$. We are now ready to calculate the partial derivative of the objective function. The proof of the theorem can be found in the full version of the paper.

Theorem 2. *The derivative of the cost with respect to any threshold t_i is given by:*

$$\frac{\partial C_n(t_2, ..., t_n)}{\partial t_i} = i\binom{n}{i} P_{i,n} \times \left[F(t_i)^i + F(t_i)^{i-1} f(t_i) \right. \quad (6)$$

$$\mathbb{E}_{\mathbf{M}}\left[i \times t_i + \mu_{2:i} - g(\mathbf{M}, t_2, ..., t_n) \mid T_i = ... = T_n = 0, t_i < M_{i:n} < t_i + \epsilon \right] \Big],$$

where $\epsilon \to 0$.

Let us provide some intuition on different parts of this expression. Roughly speaking, the cost $C_n(t_2, ..., t_n)$ is determined by the "active" threshold, which corresponds to the highest predicate that is satisfied. As long as we do not change the active threshold, perturbing the remaining thresholds should not change the cost, therefore the derivative should be zero with respect to them. When we think of the derivative with respect to a particular t_i, we want to know how much the cost would increase/decrease if we change t_i to $t_i + \epsilon$. There are two scenarios where this perturbation changes the cost:

1. The first scenario is when there are exactly i agents below t_i. This corresponds to $\binom{n}{i} F(t_i)^i$ in (6). We also want the remaining bids to be above t_i in a way that higher predicates are not satisfied (so that t_i is active), which is captured by $P_{i,n}$. Finally in this case, when we add ϵ to t_i, all those i agents receive ϵ more payment, which corresponds to the multiplicative term i in (6).

2. The second scenario is when t_i becomes active after we add ϵ to it. This requires that the ith bid is between t_i and $t_i + \epsilon$, which is why we get $i\binom{n}{i} F(t_i)^{i-1} f(t_i)$. We again need the remaining bids to be above $t_i + \epsilon$ and to not satisfy any higher predicate $(P_{i,n})$. The change in the cost is more complicated in this scenario. We know that at $t_i + \epsilon$ we are going to save i

agents and therefore the cost would be roughly $i \times t_i$ for this round, and $\mu_{2:i}$ for the next round. However, it is not clear how many agents we were saving at t_i. That is why we have the expectation of the cost with negative sign, while the expectation is conditioned to this particular scenario in which there are exactly $i - 1$ agents with bids below t_i.

5 Optimality of Canonical Thresholds

In this section, we study the optimality of the canonical thresholds. We first begin by showing that canonical thresholds form a monotone decreasing sequence. While this property seems intuitive, it is not necessarily true if the underlying distribution F does not satisfy our two assumptions of regularity and diminishing returns property of the second-order statistic, discussed in Sect. 3.

Lemma 1. *For a regular distribution F that its second order statistic has the diminishing returns property (Definition 5), the canonical thresholds are monotone non-increasing and independent of the number of agents n.*

Proof. By definition, $\hat{t}_i$ is the optimal value for t_i when $t_2 = \cdots = t_{i-1} = 1$ and $t_{i+1} = \cdots = t_n = 0$.

To find the optimal t_i, we start from the general expression (6) for the derivative and show that it simplifies as follows whenever $t_i \leq t_{i-1}$ (which is true here since $t_{i-1} = 1$). When the ith bid is between t_i and $t_i + \epsilon$, $T_i = \ldots = T_n = 0$, and $t_i \leq t_{i-1}$, we would save $i - 1$ agents and therefore $g(\mathbf{M}, t_2, ..., t_n) = (i - 1)t_i + \mu_{2:i-1}$. This simplifies equation (6) to:[4]

$$\frac{\partial C_n(t_2, ..., t_n)}{\partial t_i} = i\binom{n}{i}P_{i,n} \times \left[F(t_i)^i + F(t_i)^{i-1}f(t_i)[t_i + \mu_{2:i} - \mu_{2:i-1}] \right]$$

$$= i\binom{n}{i}P_{i,n}F(t_i)^{i-1}f(t_i)\left[t_i + \frac{F(t_i)}{f(t_i)} + \mu_{2:i} - \mu_{2:i-1} \right], \quad \forall t_i \leq t_{i-1}. \quad (7)$$

Other than the trivial roots $t_i = 0$ and $t_i = 1$ (which are local maximizers), there is a single root for this derivative that determines $\hat{t}_i$ as follows:

$$\hat{t}_i + \frac{F(\hat{t}_i)}{f(\hat{t}_i)} = \mu_{2:i-1} - \mu_{2:i}. \quad (8)$$

Therefore, we have $\hat{t}_i \geq \hat{t}_j$ for all $i \leq j$, since the left-hand side is a monotone increasing function and the right-hand side is a constant, monotone non-increasing in i. Also note that (8) makes $\hat{t}_i$ independent of n (as long as $n \geq i$). This concludes the proof.

Now, we prove that the canonical thresholds provide the global optimal solution for minimizing the expected cost of the auction. In Lemma 2 we show that when the previous thresholds are set to 1, as we increase threshold t_i from zero to its canonical value $\hat{t}_i$, the expected cost $C_n(t_2, ..., t_n)$ decreases; and as we increase t_i beyond $\hat{t}_i$, the cost increases again.

---

[4] For consistency of notation, we define $\mu_{2:1} = 1$. This is because when we save i agents in round one, the expected cost of the second round would be $\mu_{2:i}$ for $i \geq 2$, and 1 if $i = 1$.

Lemma 2. *If $t_k = 1$ for all $k \leq i - 1$, then $\frac{\partial}{\partial t_i}C(t_2, ..., t_n)$ is non-positive for $t_i \in (0, \hat{t}_i)$, zero at $t_i = \hat{t}_i$, and non-negative for $t_i \in (\hat{t}_i, 1)$.*[5]

Proof. Since $t_{i-1} = 1$, we can again use the simplified version of the derivative (7) instead of the general version (6) for all t_i. Since $P_{i,n}$, $F(t_i)$, and $f(t_i)$ are all non-negative, we have to show that $t_i + \frac{F(t_i)}{f(t_i)} + \mu_{2:i} - \mu_{2:i-1}$ is non-positive for $t_i \in (0, \hat{t}_i)$, zero at $t_i = \hat{t}_i$, and non-negative for $t_i \in (\hat{t}_i, 1)$. Assuming that the virtual cost is monotone non-decreasing, it suffices to show that $t_i + \frac{F(t_i)}{f(t_i)} + \mu_{2:i} - \mu_{2:i-1} = 0$ at $t_i = \hat{t}_i$, which is true due to (8). (Note that $t_i + \frac{F(t_i)}{f(t_i)} + \mu_{2:i} - \mu_{2:i-1}$ is strictly negative/positive at $0/1$, therefore $\hat{t}_i$ is a fractional point.)

The previous lemma shows that the canonical threshold $\hat{t}_i$ is the global minimizer of the cost when $t_2 = ... = t_{i-1} = 1$, independent of the values of the remaining thresholds $t_{i+1}, ..., t_n$. However, in the following lemma and its corollary, we show that this holds even if we lower the value of the previous thresholds from 1 to their canonical values.

Lemma 3. *If $t_k = \hat{t}_k$ for all $k \leq i - 1$, then $\frac{\partial}{\partial t_i}C(t_2, ..., t_n)$ is non-positive for $t_i \in (0, \hat{t}_i)$, zero at $t_i = \hat{t}_i$, and non-negative for $t_i \in (\hat{t}_i, 1)$.*

Proof. Note that compared to the previous lemma, we only lowered the value of $t_2, ..., t_{i-1}$ from 1 to their canonical value $t_k = \hat{t}_k$. One can argue from (6) that this lowering of thresholds does not change the derivative for any $t_i \in [0, \hat{t}_{i-1}]$. This is true because we can use Eq. (7) in this region, which shows that the derivative is independent of $t_2, ..., t_{i-1}$, whenever $t_i \leq t_{i-1}$ (remember that $P_{i,n}$ is independent of $t_2, ..., t_{i-1}$). Figure 1 shows an example of how lowering the thresholds $t_2, ..., t_{i-1}$ affects the derivative with respect to t_i.

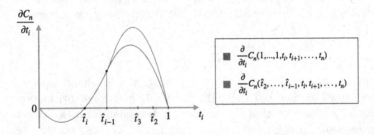

Fig. 1. Derivative of the cost with respect to t_i when: (blue) the previous thresholds are set to one, (red) the previous thresholds are lowered to their canonical values. (Color figure online)

---

[5] Note that whenever $t_{i-1} = 1$, the previous thresholds $t_2, ..., t_{i-2}$ are irrelevant. Therefore, this lemma holds even if we only had $t_{i-1} = 1$. However, we state the lemma as is for the sake of the next lemma.

Note that from Lemma 1 we know that $\hat{t}_i \leq \hat{t}_{i-1}$. This immediately implies that $\frac{\partial}{\partial t_i} C(t_2, ..., t_n)$ is non-positive for $t_i \in (0, \hat{t}_i)$, zero at $t_i = \hat{t}_i$, and non-negative for $t_i \in (\hat{t}_i, \hat{t}_{i-1})$. Therefore, we only need to show that the derivative is non-negative for $t_i \geq \hat{t}_{i-1}$. To do this, we show that the lowering of thresholds $t_2, ..., t_{i-1}$ indeed increases the derivative in this region, i.e.,

$$\frac{\partial}{\partial t_i} C(\hat{t}_2, ..., \hat{t}_{i-1}, t_i, t_{i+1}, ..., t_n) \geq \frac{\partial}{\partial t_i} C(1, ..., 1, t_i, t_{i+1}, ..., t_n), \quad \forall t_i \geq \hat{t}_{i-1} \quad (9)$$

which implies the non-negativity of the derivative, since the right hand side is non-negative due to Lemma 2. To prove (9), note that from (6), comparing the above two derivatives is equivalent to showing that

$$\mathbb{E}_{\mathbf{M}}\left[g(\mathbf{M}, \hat{t}_2, ..., \hat{t}_{i-1}, t_i, t_{i+1}, ..., t_n) \mid A\right] \leq \mathbb{E}_{\mathbf{M}}\left[g(\mathbf{M}, 1, ..., 1, t_i, t_{i+1}, ..., t_n) \mid A\right],$$

where A is the event that there are exactly $i - 1$ bids below t_i and we save at most those $i - 1$ agents. Note that this expected cost is exactly equal to the situation if we had only $i - 1$ agents in the auction, and we knew that their bids are upper bounded by t_i. In other words, it suffices to show that

$$\tilde{C}_{i-1}(\hat{t}_2, ..., \hat{t}_{i-1}) \leq \tilde{C}_{i-1}(1, ..., 1), \quad (10)$$

where $\tilde{C}_{i-1}$ is the expected cost in a game with $i - 1$ agents with distribution $\tilde{F}$ which is obtained from truncating F to have the support $[0, t_i]$ (note that distribution $\tilde{F}$ only applies to the first day, and on day 2 the bids are again drawn according to the original distribution F).

To show 10, we use the following set of inequalities:

$$\tilde{C}_{i-1}(\hat{t}_2, \hat{t}_3, \hat{t}_4, ..., \hat{t}_{i-1}) \leq \tilde{C}_{i-1}(1, \hat{t}_3, \hat{t}_4, ..., \hat{t}_{i-1})$$

$$\tilde{C}_{i-1}(1, \hat{t}_3, \hat{t}_4, ..., \hat{t}_{i-1}) \leq \tilde{C}_{i-1}(1, 1, \hat{t}_4, ..., \hat{t}_{i-1})$$

$$\vdots$$

$$\tilde{C}_{i-1}(1, 1, ..., 1, \hat{t}_{i-1}) \leq \tilde{C}_{i-1}(1, 1, ..., 1, 1)$$

Each of the above inequalities is implied by Lemma 2, since this lemma says that the derivative with respect to any t_k is non-negative for $t_k \geq \hat{t}_k$, as long as the previous thresholds are all equal to one. Therefore, increasing any t_k from $\hat{t}_k$ to 1 cannot decrease the cost. The only concern here is that the thresholds $\hat{t}_k$ were calculated for the auction with n agents and distribution F, while we are using the same thresholds here for the auction with $i - 1$ agents and truncated distribution $\tilde{F}$. The reason why we are allowed to do this is that neither changing the number of agents nor truncating the distribution can affect the optimality of $\hat{t}_k$. This is because $\hat{t}_k$ is the solution of the following equation:

$$t_k + \frac{F(t_k)}{f(t_k)} + \mu_{2:k} - \mu_{2:k-1} = 0$$

In addition to being independent of n, this equation is invariant to conditioning F from above. In other words, for the truncated distribution $\tilde{F}$ we have:

$$\tilde{F}(t) = \frac{F(t)}{F(t_i)}, \qquad \tilde{f}(t) = \frac{f(t)}{F(t_i)}, \quad \forall t \le t_i$$

Hence $\frac{\tilde{F}(t)}{\tilde{f}(t)} = \frac{F(t)}{f(t)}$, which implies having $t_k = \hat{t}_k$ (for $k = 2, ..., i-1$) gives a lower cost compared to $t_k = 1$, regardless of having distribution F or $\tilde{F}$.[6]

Since we showed that the derivative (with respect to t_i) is non-positive up to $\hat{t}_i$ and non-negative afterwards, we arrive at the optimality of $\hat{t}_i$.

Corollary 1. *If $t_k = \hat{t}_k$ for all $k \le i - 1$, then $C_n(t_2, ..., t_n)$ is minimized at $t_i = \hat{t}_i$, independent of the values of the remaining thresholds $t_{i+1}, ..., t_n$.*

So far we showed that as long as the previous thresholds are set to their canonical values, $\hat{t}_i$ is the global optimal value for t_i. To achieve the global optimal values for the entire set of thresholds $(t_k, k = 2, ..., n)$ it suffices to use the previous lemma in an inductive manner.

Theorem 3. *If distribution F satisfies the regularity condition (Definition 3), and its second order statistic has the diminishing returns property (Definition 5), then the global optimal thresholds that minimize $C_n(t_2, ..., t_n)$ are*

$$t_k^* = \hat{t}_k, \quad \forall k.$$

Proof. Let us assume that this is not true and there exists another set of thresholds $(t_2', ..., t_n')$ with cost smaller than $C_n(\hat{t}_2, ..., \hat{t}_n)$. Looking at t_2, Corollary 1 can be used without any condition on the remaining thresholds, which immediately implies that either $t_2' = \hat{t}_2$, or we can change it to $\hat{t}_2$ without increasing the cost. Given $t_2' = \hat{t}_2$, we can now use this argument again for t_3 and conclude that $t_3' = \hat{t}_3$. Repeating this argument, we arrive at $C_n(t_2', ..., t_n') = C_n(\hat{t}_2, ..., \hat{t}_n)$, which contradicts our starting assumption.

6   Conclusion and Future Work

In this paper we studied a dynamic procurement auction for n symmetric agents. We assumed 3 different properties for the agents that were crucial to achieve the optimality of the canonical thresholds: (i) we assumed a common distribution F for the overhead costs, (ii) we assumed that the per-unit cost of providing the service is the same for all agents, and (iii) we assumed that each agent can provide the entire demand. Relaxing any of these assumptions breaks the symmetry of the agents and opens a new research question for future work.

---

[6] This is similar to revenue maximization where if we condition F to be above a certain value v and obtain the conditional distribution $\tilde{F}$, we have that $1 - \tilde{F}(x) = \frac{1-F(x)}{1-F(v)}$ and $\tilde{f}(x) = \frac{f(x)}{1-F(v)}$. This implies that the inverse hazard rate and as a result the virtual value functions of these distributions remain the same.

If we assume a different distribution F_i for each agent's overhead cost, then the savings from allocating the service to k agents and having them participate in the future rounds depend on the identity of those agents. This could potentially lead to having a different threshold for any subset of agents, which would make the problem computationally intractable. On the other hand, if we assume that agents have different per-unit costs, the optimal assignment would not be trivial, even if the set of agents with non-zero assignments are known. In other words, if we want to save a particular set of k agents, the optimal assignment is not necessarily $1/k$, and it depends on the per-unit costs of those particular k agents. The same challenge holds when we consider different capacities for the agents, as equal assignments of $1/k$ may not even be feasible in that setting.

References

1. Agrawal, S., Daskalakis, C., Mirrokni, V., Sivan, B.: Robust repeated auctions under heterogeneous buyer behavior. In: 19th ACM Conference on Economics and Computation (2018)
2. Anton, J.J., Yao, D.A.: Second sourcing and the experience curve: price competition in defense procurement. RAND J. Econ. 57–76 (1987)
3. Ashlagi, I., Daskalakis, C., Haghpanah, N.: Sequential mechanisms with ex-post participation guarantees. In: Proceedings of the 2016 ACM Conference on Economics and Computation, pp. 213–214 (2016)
4. Bergemann, D., Välimäki, J.: Dynamic mechanism design: an introduction. J. Econ. Lit. **57**(2), 235–74 (2019)
5. Bosio, E., Djankov, S.: How large is public procurement? (2020). https://blogs. worldbank.org/developmenttalk/how-large-public-procurement. Accessed 5 Jun 2020
6. Chawla, S., Malec, D.L., Malekian, A.: Bayesian mechanism design for budget-constrained agents. In: Proceedings of the 12th ACM Conference on Electronic Commerce, pp. 253–262 (2011)
7. Chen, F.: Auctioning supply contracts. Manage. Sci. **53**(10), 1562–1576 (2007)
8. David, H.A., Nagaraja, H.N.: Order statistics. John Wiley & Sons (2004)
9. Farrell, J., Klemperer, P.: Coordination and lock-in: competition with switching costs and network effects. Handbook ind. organ. **3**, 1967–2072 (2007)
10. Feldman, J., Muthukrishnan, S., Nikolova, E., Pál, M.: A truthful mechanism for offline ad slot scheduling. In: Monien, B., Schroeder, U.-P. (eds.) SAGT 2008. LNCS, vol. 4997, pp. 182–193. Springer, Heidelberg (2008). https://doi.org/10. 1007/978-3-540-79309-0_17
11. Garrett, D.F.: Intertemporal price discrimination: dynamic arrivals and changing values. Am. Econ. Rev. **106**(11), 3275–99 (2016). https://doi.org/10.1257/aer. 20130564, https://www.aeaweb.org/articles?id=10.1257/aer.20130564
12. Garrett, D.F.: Dynamic mechanism design: dynamic arrivals and changing values. Games Econ. Behav. **104**, 595–612 (2017). https://doi.org/10.1016/j.geb.2017.04. 005, http://www.sciencedirect.com/science/article/pii/S0899825617300696
13. Hartline, J.D.: Mechanism design and approximation (2011)
14. Horn, J., Wu, Y., Khodabakhsh, A., Nikolova, E., Pountourakis, E.: The long-term cost of energy generation. In: Proceedings of the Eleventh ACM International Conference on Future Energy Systems, pp. 74–85 (2020)

15. Krishna, V.: Auction Theory. Academic Press (2009)

16. Lewis, T.R., Yildirim, H.: Managing dynamic competition. Am. Econ. Rev. **92**(4), 779–797 (2002)

17. Lewis, T.R., Yildirim, H.: Managing switching costs in multiperiod procurements with strategic buyers. Int. Econ. Rev. **46**(4), 1233–1269 (2005)

18. Liu, S., Liu, C., Hu, Q.: Optimal procurement strategies by reverse auctions with stochastic demand. Econ. Model. **35**, 430–435 (2013)

19. Papadimitriou, C.H., Pierrakos, G., Psomas, C., Rubinstein, A.: On the complexity of dynamic mechanism design. In: Proceedings of the Twenty-Seventh Annual ACM-SIAM Symposium on Discrete Algorithms, pp. 1458–1475 (2016). https://doi.org/10.1137/1.9781611974331.ch100

20. Pavan, A., Segal, I., Toikka, J.: Dynamic mechanism design: a myersonian approach. Econometrica **82**(2), 601–653 (2014)

21. Saini, V.: Reserve prices in a dynamic auction when bidders are capacity-constrained. Econ. Lett. **108**(3), 303–306 (2010)

22. Saini, V.: Endogenous asymmetry in a dynamic procurement auction. RAND J. Econ. **43**(4), 726–760 (2012)

23. Van Ryzin, G., Vulcano, G.: Optimal auctioning and ordering in an infinite horizon inventory-pricing system. Oper. Res. **52**(3), 346–367 (2004)

24. Yildirim, H.: Piecewise procurement of a large-scale project. Int. J. Ind. Organ. **22**(8–9), 1349–1375 (2004)

Strategy-Proof Budgeting via a VCG-Like Mechanism

Jonathan Wagner$^{(\boxtimes)}$ and Reshef Meir

Technion - Israel Institute of Technology, Haifa, Israel
`sjwagner@campus.technion.ac.il`, `reshefm@technion.ac.il`

Abstract. We present a strategy-proof public goods budgeting mechanism where agents determine both the total volume of expenses and specific allocation. It is constructed as a modification of VCG to a non-typical environment, where we do not assume quasi-linear utilities or direct revelation. We further show that under plausible assumptions it satisfies strategyproofness in strictly dominant strategies, and consequently implements the social optimum as a Coalition-Proof Nash Equilibrium. A primary (albeit not an exclusive) motivation of our model is Participatory Budgeting, where members of a community collectively decide the spending policy of public tax dollars. In that scenario, charging individual payments from voters as the VCG method instructs would be undesirable, thus our second main result provides that, under further specifications relevant in that context, these payments will vanish in large populations, and can further be constructed as non-positive in some cases.

Keywords: VCG · Participatory Budgeting

1 Introduction

We study a model where a population of n agents face the decision of funding several public goods or investments that serve their collective objectives. Formally, we start with an available budget of $B_0 \geq 0$ that should be allocated among $m \geq 1$ different alternatives. The *budget decision* we seek is a pair (x, t) where $t \in [-\frac{B_0}{n}, \infty)$ is a monetary sum ("tax") that each agent adds to (or subtracts from) the budget, and $x \in \Delta^m := \{x \in \mathbb{R}^n | x_j \geq 0 \; \forall j, \; \sum_j x_j = 1\}$ represents the allocation of the resulting budget $B_t = B_0 + nt$ among the m alternatives. Note that we allow $t < 0$, meaning that some of the initial budget B_0 will be distributed equally among agents rather than fund public investments. We are interested in constructing a collective decision mechanism to which every agent submits her preferred budget decision, and one that is incentive compatible (IC) particularly. Table 1 demonstrates how agents might report to such a mechanism their preferences for budget allocations among three municipal services. Note e.g. that agent b suggests an individual payment of $t = 20$ each, and so to allocate a total of $B_0 + 3t = 100 + 3 \cdot 20 = 160$. Also note that agents b and c propose the same normalized allocation $x_b = x_c \in \Delta^3$ but differ in their preferred tax.

A. Deligkas and A. Filos-Ratsikas (Eds.): SAGT 2023, LNCS 14238, pp. 401–418, 2023.
https://doi.org/10.1007/978-3-031-43254-5_23

Table 1. An example voting profile for three alternatives and three agents, with an initial budget $B_0 = 100$.

	Tax (t)	Education (x_1)	Parks (x_2)	Transport (x_3)
agent a	0	60 (0.6)	30 (0.3)	10 (0.1)
agent b	20	32 (0.2)	48 (0.3)	80 (0.5)
agent c	-20	8 (0.2)	12 (0.3)	20 (0.5)

1.1   Motivation

Incentives alignment has long been a major interest in Social Choice and Mechanism Design research. While the Gibbard-Satterthwaite's Theorem [18,28] provides a negative result for preference aggregation without monetary transfers, positive results do exist when the preference space is contracted somehow (mainly to single-peaked [24]). Indeed, several works in the field of computational social choice introduced strategy-proof divisible PB mechanisms [1,9,16,19]. These works typically model individual preferences as an extension to the PB setting of conventional notions from Social Choice Theory, which, generally speaking, measure utility in terms of similarity between the implemented outcome an one's subjective optimum (e.g. spatial models [16] or overlap in approval voting [9]). The approach we take here, however, is that when agents have concrete measurable utility from decisions, as in PB, that may be an over-simplification to the true preference underlying their observed votes. We thus adopt the conventional economic assumption of additive concave utilities [21,32], that was previously applied in a PB framework in [14]. As this model is fairly broad, we can no longer hope for a strategy-proof mechanism without incorporating monetary transfers. In that area, the VCG mechanism [12] is the canonical paradigm and, moreover, Roberts' Theorem [27] shows that for a general preferences domain, any strategy-proof mechanism is in a sense a generalized version of the VCG principle. However, the application of VCG to our setting is not straight-forward, and requires for much of the technical effort in our work.

Challenges in applying VCG to our model. Firstly, VCG is built upon an assumed model of quasi-linear utilities, meaning that the overall satisfaction of agent i when the mechanism outputs the decision Ω and charges her with a payment p_i is expressed as $u_i(\Omega, p_i) = v_i(\Omega) - p_i$ where $v_i(\Omega)$ is the value she attributes to Ω. While plausible in many economic situations, quasi-linearity is in particular violated if agents do not assess their benefits from different outcomes in monetary terms (making the subtraction of p_i from $v_i(\Omega)$ a meaningless expression), whether because these are purely non-financial or just difficult to quantify. When we consider investments in public goods, that is likely to be the case. Furthermore, VCG is a *"Direct Revelation"* mechanism in which agents explicitly report a full description of their preferences [25]. This is reasonable when, for example, we ask agents to specify a value — that is, the maximum price they are willing to pay — for each item offered at an auction. In our case, the space of optional outcomes is a multidimensional continuum and the "value" is quite an abstract concept, non-linear in particular. As should be obvious when we later introduce our model in full details, a direct revelation mechanism becomes unlikely in this context and we thus only collect optimal allocations, as demonstrated in Table 1. Beyond these technical incompatibilities, the strategy-proofness of VCG is achieved via individual payments the mechanism collects from agents, which is unreasonable in a PB context — meaning, paying money "to the mechanism" on top of the tax t that is a part of the chosen outcome and finances shared expenditures.

1.2   Paper Structure and Results

Nevertheless, we show that for the budgeting problem described above we can construct a "VCG-like" mechanism all the same. At the beginning of Sect. 3, we show how full information can in fact be extracted from the preferences that agents report. Section 4 introduces our proposed mechanism. We will show that formulating VCG-like payments that similarly align incentives is in fact quite simple under our assumed model even though it brutally violates quasi-linearity. The key insight here is that what really matters is that we have full information on agents' preferences over monetary transfers, and not that they would be quasi-linear in particular. In our case, the sole fact that makes that information accessible to the mechanism is that the decision space itself involves monetary transfers, thus letting agents express these preference in their vote. In Sect. 4.3 we show that, under certain conditions, our mechanism satisfies IC in strictly dominant strategies and consequently Coalition-proof [6]. In Sect. 5 we show that, for a relevant subclass of utility functions, the payments we charge on top of the collected tax become negligible in large populations, and can further be constructed as non-positive in some cases. Due to space constraints, most of the proofs are omitted from the paper and appear in its full version, as well as a broader discussion on our modelling choices and assumptions.[1]

1.3   Possible Applications

A few examples of environments where our mechanism may be useful are listed below, starting with the one standing at the center of our focus.

Participatory Budgeting. Our model falls naturally within a Participatory Budgeting (PB) framework, where members of a community determine the allocation of their shared budget via some voting mechanism.[2] While most PB implementations worldwide, and accordingly much of the PB literature [26], involve the allocation of a given budget among several public indivisible goods, several previous works were dedicated to divisible PB models [10,14,16,17,19], where "projects" may correspond to city departments, e.g. education, transportation, parks and recreation and so on. Our model moreover involves taxation in the collective decision, in which we find several advantages. Technically,

---

[1] https://arxiv.org/pdf/2303.06923.pdf.
[2] 'The Participatory Budget Project': https://www.participatorybudgeting.org/.

our adjustment of VCG payments to non quasi-linear utilities is enabled solely owing to this feature. Conceptually, it expands the scope of control delegated to society through direct democracy, and also brings a more valuable feedback to the designer on the true value that public expenditures create, rather than just a comparison between them. Being our primary motivation, the terminology we use and our approach to modelling is mainly driven by the PB application, however intended to represent a wider range of real-life economic situations.

Shared financing among nearby businesses. A group of nearby businesses (for example in the same shopping center) might cofinance some facilities and services that are more public or regional by nature, e.g. security, costumers' parking, shared dining areas, public activities that increase exposure, etc.

Environmental or other non-financial investments. That could apply to governments imposing an environmental (or other) tax on firms or different countries deciding on their coordinated actions [7]. Other pursued goals might include border controls of neighbouring countries, for example.

Joint R&D and Human Capital ventures. R & D and Human Capital investments are typically long-term and require considerable resources. Thus, firms in the same or related industries might benefit from joining forces in funding e.g. the training of required professions or the development of new technologies and methods. Such collaborations might scale from a small number of businesses deciding to cooperate, through a unionized industry and up to being run by the government state-wide.

Non-monetary "Currencies". As the concept of "value" of different outcomes is more abstract in our model, it may also apply to situations where the investments themselves, and thereby the collected tax payments, are not necessarily monetary. Examples may include members in a community willing to dedicate an agreed amount of working hours within their community, or firms that allocate resources such as land (e.g. agricultural land dedicated to cooperative experimental planting), or technological resources such as storage space or computation force.

1.4   Our Modelling Approach

As mentioned above, we see divisible budget allocation as similar in nature to problems typically treated within microeconomic framework [5,29,34], especially when assigning budgets to departments etc. rather than to specific projects with variable costs.[3] We thus follow conventional economic assumptions regarding demand and utility, in particular:

- *Additive concave utilities.* We adopt the additive concave utilities model [14, 21,32] that expresses convex preference over goods bundles [22]. Its most

---

[3] See e.g. https://pbstanford.org/boston16internal/knapsack.

closely related version to ours is found in a former work by Fain et al. [14]. There, the utility of agent i in allocation $X = (X_1, X_2 \ldots)$ is expressed as

$$U_i(X) = \sum_j \alpha_{i,j} \theta_j(X_j) \tag{1}$$

where X_j is the amount spent on public good j, the $\{\theta_j\}_j$ functions are monotonically increasing in X_j for all j and strictly concave, (smoothly) expressing the plausible assumption of decreasing marginal gains, and $\alpha_{i,j}$ are scalars that vary between agents. As we assume that part of the budget is collected via a tax-per-agent t, our model adds on the above the disutility $-\alpha_{i,f} f(t)$ of a voter i from the tax payment t.

- *Optimal points characterized by the MRS conditions*, that follows form the concavity and some additional conventions on utilities [22].
- *Utility depends on public investment per capita*. (that we add to the model in Sect. 5). On a large scale, it is reasonable that the quality of public goods depends more on spending per capita rather than on the nominal amount.[4]

In contrast, *elicitation* is an issue that has received much more attention in the literature of mechanism design and computational social choice than in microeconomics. For example there is a live discussion in the context of indivisible PB on the tradeoff between expressiveness of the ballot and effort required for elicitation [4,15]. Similarly, we argue that it does not make sense to assume that we have direct access to voters' preferences, and here we adopt from computational social choice the assumptions that voters simply report their most preferred allocation, as in [16].

In terms of applicability, however, the obvious shortcoming of our model is that it requires us to explicitly specify the functions $\{\theta_j\}_j$ and the disutility f, which are fairly abstract. Importantly, we **do not** assume that agents are aware of their assumed utility function, but, conventionally, only know their preferences regarding the decision space, that presumably can be interpreted as derived from an underlying utility model [22]. Of course, any such model would be an approximation at best. Nevertheless, it is fair to assume that any choice of monotonically increasing concave functions probably better approximates individuals' preferences—and thereby incentives—than previously introduced models such as the spatial model or linear additive utilities [10].

1.5 Further Related Literature

The Economic literature on public goods markets, equilibria and optimal taxation is abundant. ([5,29,32], to name just a few). While our work adopts a similar approach to modelling and also optimizes social welfare, this brunch of the literature rarely discusses mechanisms. One exception that we know of is

---

[4] See for example https://data.oecd.org/gga/general-government-spending.htm, and [29].

found in [23], in which the socially optimal outcome is implemented in strictly dominant strategies using a method very similar to ours, however for quite a different utility model.

The literature on divisible PB, on the other hand, is relatively narrow. To the best of our knowledge, the only existing PB mechanism that included tax in the collective decision previously to ours was studied by Garg et al. [17] in the context of experimenting *"iterative voting"* mechanisms. Interestingly, it may suggest some supporting evidence in favour of the additive concave utility model over spatial models in that context. Other previous works [2,9,10] incorporated private funding into a PB model, albeit in the form of voluntary donations that every agent can choose freely and not as a collectively decided sum that is collected from (or paid to) everyone, as we consider here. In terms of incentive compatibility, [16] presented the soundest results, under a spatial utility model. Alternatively, Fain et al. [14] offer a randomized mechanism that is 'approximately-truthful' for the special case of 1-degree homogeneous additive utilities. The *Knapsack Voting* mechanism introduced in [19] also satisfies some weaker notion of strategyproofness under a similar model. Aziz et al. [1] presented IC mechanisms for additive linear utilities, although their model is primarily motivated by randomized approval mechanisms. A similar utility model is also found in [30]. Overall, in relation to the divisible PB field, this work offers an SDSIC mechanism under concave additive utilities, to the best of our knowledge for the first time.

Our desire for diminishing the (modified) VCG payments resembles the idea of *redistribution* in mechanism design [11,20]. Such methods are especially relevant in a discrete decision space and can eliminate surplus only partially, while in our model the complete (asymptotic) vanishing is much thanks to the continuity of the decision space.

2   Model and Preliminaries

We denote by Δ^m the set of distributions over m elements, and use $[m]$ as a shortcut for $\{1, \ldots, m\}$. A set of n agents (voters) need to collectively reach a *budget decision* (x, t) described as follows. $t \in \mathbb{R}$ is a lump-sum tax collected from every agent. $x \in \Delta^m$ is an allocation of the total available budget $B_t := B_0 + nt$ among some m pre-given public goods, where B_0 is an external, non tax-funded source of public funds. t is restricted only by $t > -\frac{B_0}{n}$, meaning that voters can decide either to finance a budget larger than B_0 through positive taxation, or allocate some of it to themselves directly as cash (negative taxation). The collective decision is taken through some voting mechanism to which every agent submits her most preferred budget decision $(x^{(i)}, t^{(i)})$.

2.1   Preferences

We now introduce the utility function step by step. We start with agents' valuation for public expenditures alone that follows from [14]:

$$\Theta_i(X) := \sum_{j=1}^{m} \alpha_{i,j} \theta_j(X_j)$$

where $X = (X_1, \dots, X_m) \in \mathbb{R}_+^m$ and X_j is the amount spent on project j. For all $j \in [m]$, an agent i gains $\alpha_{i,j} \theta_j(X_j)$ from an X_j spending on public good j. $\{\theta_j\}_{j=1}^{m}$ are identical across agents while agents differ one from another in their coefficients $(\alpha_{i,1} \dots, \alpha_{i,m}) \in \Delta^m$.

assumption 1. *For all $1 \le j \le m$, $\theta_j : \mathcal{D} \to \mathbb{R}, \mathcal{D} \in \{\mathbb{R}_+, \mathbb{R}_{++}\}$ is increasing and strictly concave, and $\lim_{X_j \to 0} \theta(X_j) \le 0$, where $\mathbb{R}_+ := \{x \in \mathbb{R} | x \ge 0\}$, $\mathbb{R}_{++} := \{x \in \mathbb{R} | x > 0\}$.*

As mentioned earlier in the Introduction, our model includes monetary transfers of two types. One is the collectively decided tax that will be collected from every agent, and beyond that, a mechanism may charge payments in order to align incentives, where these payments are not affecting public expenditure. Thus we include in our model the value agents attribute to reduction (or increment) in their overall wealth,

$$\pi_i(\delta_w) := -\alpha_{i,f} \cdot f(\delta_w)$$

where δ_w is the monetary loss (gain when negative) and the coefficient $\alpha_{i,f} > 0$ varies between agents. Our formulation of the disutility function f will follow Kahneman and Tversky's Prospect Theory [31]. Their and others' empirical findings [8,31] demonstrate that people tend to exhibit *loss aversion* in relation to monetary gains or losses, meaning: (a) valuating monetary transfers with reference to their current status presumably located at the origin; and (b) exhibit risk-aversion with respect to monetary losses, and risk-seeking with respect to gains. Meaning, we shall assume that $f(0) = 0$ and that it is strictly convex in $(-\infty, 0]$ and strictly concave in $[0, \infty)$. In principle, our analysis requires differentiable utility functions. However, the most natural examples of elementary increasing concave functions, the logarithmic and power functions, are not differentiable at zero, which still allows for our results. Thus, for the sake of giving more intuitive and simple examples, we will allow a diverging derivative at zero.[5]

assumption 2. *$f : \mathbb{R} \to \mathbb{R}$ is increasing, strictly convex in $(-\infty, 0]$ and strictly concave in $[0, \infty)$. $f(0) = 0$. We assume that f is either continuously differentiable in all $\mathbb{R}$ or anywhere but the origin, in which case $\lim_{z \to 0_-^+} f'(z) = \infty$.*

---

[5] Kahneman and Tversky themselves suggested a functional form built on power functions (See [31], p. 309) that has been adopted widely ever since [8]. Our Assumption 2 thus includes their class of functions and extends beyond it.

Now, by adding Θ_i and π_i together we get the full description of an agent's *utility function*:

$$u_i(X, \delta_w) := \Theta_i(X) + \pi_i(\delta_w) = \sum_{j=1}^{m} \alpha_{i,j}\theta_j(X_j) - \alpha_{i,f}f(\delta_w).$$

In particular, the problem at hand is reaching a collective *budget decision* (x, t) via some voting mechanism that aggregates the collective preferences on the whole decision space $\Delta^m \times [-\frac{B_0}{n}, \infty)$. We therefore specifically define an agent's valuation for a budget decision (i.e. with no regard to payments on top of the collected tax):

$$\forall x \in \Delta^m, \ t \in \mathbb{R}, \quad v_i(x, t) := u_i(x \cdot B_t, t) = \sum_{j=1}^{m} \alpha_{i,j}\theta_j(x_j \cdot B_t) - \alpha_{i,f}f(t)$$

Thus the *type* of i is defined by the coefficients:

$$\alpha_i := (\alpha_{i,1} \ldots, \alpha_{i,m}, \alpha_{i,f}) \in \Delta^m \times \mathbb{R}_{++} \tag{2}$$

In a more general sense, we also write u_α, Θ_α and v_α for functions of a hypothetical "type α" agent.

Optimal budget decisions. Finally, we would reasonably want to assume that every agent would like to fund *some* level of public expenditures, whereas no agent favors an infinite budget funded by infinite tax. For abbreviation, we employ here a slightly stronger demand, that every agent's optimal budget decision, as well as the social optimum, allocates a strictly positive amount to every public good j such that $\alpha_j > 0$. We refer the reader to the full version of the paper [33] where we discuss the justifications for that assumption (or its technical equivalencies), and the extensions of the model when it is relaxed.

assumption 3. *For every type $\alpha \in \Delta^m \times \mathbb{R}$ there exists an optimal budget decision $(x^{(\alpha)}, t^{(\alpha)}) \in \arg\max_{(x,t)} v_\alpha(x, t)$, and for every such point, $\forall j \in [m]$, $x_j^{(\alpha)} \cdot t^{(\alpha)} > 0 \iff \alpha_j > 0$.*

Hence, a *budgeting instance* $\mathcal{I} = \{m, n, B_0, \vec{\alpha}, \{\theta_j\}_{j\in[m]}, f\}$ is defined by the number of public goods m, number of agents n, initial budget B_0, the *type profile* $\vec{\alpha} = (\alpha_i, \ldots, \alpha_n)$ and functions $\{\theta_j\}_{j\in[m]}, f$ that respect Assumptions 1,2,3. For example,

Example 1 (Running example). Consider an instance with $B_0 = 0, m = 2, n = 3$, where for every agent $i \in [3]$, the valuation is:

$$v_i(x, t) := \sum_{j=1}^{2} \alpha_{i,j} \ln(x_j \cdot 3t) - \alpha_{i,f}\sqrt{t} \tag{3}$$

That is, $\theta_j(X_j) := \ln(X_j)$ for both $j \in \{1, 2\}$, and $f(t) := \sqrt{t}$. One can easily varify that for every type α, $\arg\max_{(x,t)} v_\alpha = \left((\alpha_1, \alpha_2), \left(\frac{2}{\alpha_f}\right)^2\right)$ which admits Assumption 3.

3   Mechanisms

Preference Elicitation. The mechanism we introduce in the next section is designed to maximize the social welfare $\sum_i v_i(x, t)$. However, agents do not report their full valuations $v_i(\cdot, \cdot)$ explicitly but rather their optimal budget decisions $(x^{(i)}, t^{(i)})$ $\forall i \in [n]$. Thus, we must first elicit the underlying types. The next lemma and corollary describe how this is done.

Lemma 1. *In every budgeting instance $\mathcal{I}$, for every type α, $(x^{(\alpha)}, t^{(\alpha)})$ satisfies*

$$\frac{n\theta'_j(x_j^{(\alpha)} B_{t^{(\alpha)}})}{f'(t^{(\alpha)})} = \frac{\alpha_f}{\alpha_j} \quad \forall j \ s.t. \ \alpha_j > 0$$

This equality is merely the first order conditions for the optimization of $v_\alpha(x, t)$, that can be solved via a natural reduction where we first optimize $x \in \Delta^m$ for any given t — which is a convex optimization problem— and then differentiate with respect to t (See the paper's full version for a full proof). These m linear equations, along with $\sum_j \alpha_j = 1$, have a unique solution α for any reported optimum $(x^{(\alpha)}, t^{(\alpha)})$ which allows the full and decisive recovery of the underlying types.

Corollary 1 (Preferences Elicitation). *In any budgeting instance (that in particular respects Assumption 3) types can be fully and decisively extracted from votes by solving for α_i, $i \in [n]$:*

1. $x_j^{(i)} B_{t^{(i)}} > 0 \implies \frac{n\theta'_j(x_j^{(i)} B_{t^{(i)}})}{f'(t^{(i)})} = \frac{\alpha_{i,f}}{\alpha_{i,j}}$
2. $x_j^{(i)} B_{t^{(i)}} = 0 \implies \alpha_j = 0$
3. $\sum_j \alpha_{i,j} = 1$

Example 2 (Running example, cont.). Every agent submits the optimal budget decision w.r.t. her valuation function, i.e. some $(x^{(i)}, t^{(i)}) \in \Delta^m \times [-\frac{B_0}{n}, \infty)$ that maximizes $v_i(x, t)$. Using the above Corollary, we infer every agent's underlying type α_i from $\frac{(x_j^{(i)} \cdot 3t^{(i)})^{-1}}{(2\sqrt{t^{(i)}})^{-1}} = \frac{\alpha_{i,f}}{\alpha_{i,j}}$ if $x_j^{(i)} B_{t^{(i)}} > 0$, and $\alpha_{i,j} = 0$ otherwise. For example, the voting profile on the left can only be induced by the preference profile α^{RE} on the right (RE for Running Example):

(votes)	t	$X_1^{(i)}$ $(x_1^{(i)})$	$X_2^{(i)}$ $(x_2^{(i)})$	(types)	$\alpha_{i,1}$	$\alpha_{i,2}$	$\alpha_{i,f}$
voter 1	6.25	13.125 (0.7)	5.625 (0.3)	$i = 1$	0.7	0.3	0.8
voter 2	2.36	0 (0)	7.1 (1)	$i = 2$	0	1	1.3
voter 3	4	6 (0.5)	6 (0.5)	$i = 3$	0.5	0.5	1

Mechanisms. We now want to define a class of mechanisms for our budgeting problem. The first step in every such mechanism must be eliciting the types based on Corollary 1. However, for the sake of a more convenient exposition, we formally define a class of *Direct Revelation* [25] mechanisms that take the explicit type profile as input, which by Corollary 1 will bring to no loss of generality.

Definition 1 (mechanisms). *A* **mechanism** *for budgeting instance* $\mathcal{I}$ *is a pair* $M = (\phi, P)$ *where:*

- $\phi : (\Delta^m \times \mathbb{R})^n \mapsto \Delta^m \times [-\frac{B_0}{n}, \infty)$ *is a social choice function that inputs the type profile* $\vec{\alpha} = (\alpha_1, \ldots, \alpha_n)$ *and outputs a budget decision* $(x, t) \in \Delta^m \times [-\frac{B_0}{n}, \infty)$;
- $P : (\Delta^m \times [-\frac{B_0}{n}, \infty))^n \mapsto \mathbb{R}^n$ *is a function of the type profile that assigns a payment* P_i *for every agent* $i \in [n]$.

Note again that in our model, the outcome itself includes a tax payment t that every agent pays to fund the public budget, and the individual payments $(P_i, \ldots, P_n)$ are charged on top of that. Hereinafter we abuse notation a little when writing $u_i((x, t), P_i)$ or $u_i(M)$, $u_i(\phi, P)$ for the overall utility of agent i from budget decision (x, t) and payment P_i (that are determined by $M = (\phi, P)$).

Incentive Compatibility requires that no agent could benefit from reporting some false preferences $\alpha_i' \neq \alpha_i$ to the mechanism.

Definition 2. *A mechanism M is* **dominant strategy incentive compatible (DSIC)** *in budgeting instance* $\mathcal{I}$ *if for all* $i \in [n]$ *and every* $\alpha' \neq \alpha_i$,

$$u_i(M(\alpha_i, \vec{\alpha}_{-i})) \geq u_i(M(\alpha', \vec{\alpha}_{-i}))$$

If that inequality is strict for all i and α' we say that M is **strictly dominant strategy incentive compatible (SDSIC)** *in* $\mathcal{I}$.

4   Utility-Sensitive VCG

In this section we present our proposed mechanism (Def. 5) and discuss its properties. We start with the payment function P.

4.1   Payments

Essentially, the payments we define are VCG payments adjusted to our non quasi-linear setup. In general, the social choice function in a VCG mechanism ϕ^{VCG} outputs the socially optimal outcome $\Omega^* = argmax_\Omega \sum_i v_i(\Omega)$ and payments are defined as follows [12].

Definition 3 (VCG payments)

$$p_i^{VCG} = -\sum_{k \neq i} v_k(\Omega^*) + h(\vec{\alpha}_{-i}) \quad \forall i \in [n]$$

where $h(\vec{\alpha}_{-i})$ could be any function of $\vec{\alpha}_{-i}$, the partial preferences profile submitted by all agents excluding i. The VCG model assumes *Quasi-linear* utility functions, meaning that

$$(*) \quad u_i(VCG(\vec{\alpha})) = v_i(\Omega^*) - p_i^{VCG} = \sum_k v_k(\Omega^*) - h(\vec{\alpha}_{-i})$$

The above expression is the key property on which the DSIC of a VCG mechanism relies. Since Ω^* maximizes $\sum_k v_k(\cdot)$ and $h(\vec{\alpha}_{-i})$ is independent of i's vote, an agent can never (strictly) increase her utility by manipulating the outcome Ω^*. In our model, however, the quasi-linearity assumption is violated. If we write $\Omega^* := (x^*, t^*)$ then our model assumes

$$u_i(M(\vec{\alpha})) = \sum_j \alpha_{i,j} \theta_j\big(x_j^* B_{t^*}\big) - \alpha_{i,f} f\big(t^* + P_i\big),$$

for any mechanism M. Clearly, naïvely setting $P_i = p_i^{VCG}$ will not result in anything as useful as $(*)$. However, our utility model does entail some significant information we can exploit. While individuals in our model no more exhibit the simple, linear relation between utility gains (or losses) that stem from monetary transfers and those that come from the chosen outcome itself, their true relation *is* in fact described in the utility function, thanks to the introducing of f in it. Relying on that, we can adjust the payments appropriately so that the key property $(*)$ is maintained. We do that in the next definition and lemma.

Definition 4 (Utility-Sensitive VCG Payments). *Let* $\Omega^* = (x^*, t^*) \in$ $\arg\max_{(x,t)} \sum_{i \in [n]} v_i(x,t)$ *be the socially optimal budget decision. For every agent* i, *we define the **utility-sensitive VCG payment** as*

$$P_i = -t^* + f^{-1}\Big(f(t^*) + \frac{1}{\alpha_{i,f}} p_i^{VCG}\Big). \tag{4}$$

Lemma 2. *Let* $\Omega^* = (x^*, t^*)$ *be the social optimum and* P_i *the utility sensitive VCG payment given in 4 above. Then* $u_i(\Omega^*, P_i) = \sum_k v_k(\Omega^*) - h(\vec{\alpha}_{-i})$.

4.2 Definition of the Mechanism

Definition 5 (Utility-Sensitive VCG). *The* Utility-Sensitive VCG *(US-VCG) mechanism* $\mathcal{M}$ *is a tax-involved PB mechanism defined by:*

$$\forall \vec{\alpha} \in (\Delta^m \times \mathbb{R})^n, \quad \mathcal{M}(\vec{\alpha}) := \big(\Omega^*, P\big)$$

where $\Omega^* = (x^*, t^*) \in \arg\max_\Omega \sum_i v_i(\Omega)$ *is the social optimum and* P *is the utility-sensitive VCG payment assignment given in Def. 4.*

4.3 Incentive Compatibility

Mean-dependency. We now point out some very useful characteristic of our model that plays a major role in both of our main results . Namely, that the outcome Ω^* depends solely on the average of types reported by all agents. Let $\bar{\alpha} := \frac{1}{n} \sum_{i \in [n]} \alpha_i$ denote the types mean. Now, simply changing the order of summation in the social welfare

$$\sum_i v_i(x,t) = \sum_i \Big[\sum_j \alpha_{i,j} \theta_j(x_j B_t) - \alpha_{i,f} f(t) \Big] = \sum_j \Big[\sum_i \alpha_{i,j} \theta_j(x_j B_t) - \alpha_{i,f} f(t) \Big]$$

$$= \sum_j n\bar{\alpha}_j \theta_j(x_j B_t) - n\bar{\alpha}_f f(t) = n \cdot v_{\bar{\alpha}}(x,t)$$

shows that:

observation 1 *In any budget decision* (x,t), *the social welfare is given by* $\sum_i v_i(x,t) = n \cdot v_{\bar{\alpha}}(x,t)$. *Consequently,* $\Omega^* = (x^*,t^*)$ *maximizes the social welfare if and only if it maximizes* $v_{\bar{\alpha}}(x,t)$, *the valuation function defined by the average type* $\bar{\alpha}$.

Note that in addition, the above observation means that the social optimum Ω^* is computed in linear time. As for payments, the typical choice for $h(\alpha_{-i})$ is the "Clarke Pivot Rule" that charges every agent with the social welfare of others in her absence. With that choice, computing every agent's payment is as hard as computing the outcome Ω^*.

Example 3 (Running example, cont.). For the utility functions from Eq. (3) we have $\arg\max_{(x,t)} v_\alpha = \left((\alpha_1,\alpha_2),\left(\frac{2}{\alpha_f}\right)^2\right)$. The average type in the type profile α^{RE} from Example 2 is $\bar{\alpha} = (0.4, 0.6, 1.03)$, and thus the budget decision chosen by $\mathcal{M}$ is $\Omega^* = \left((0.4, 0.6), 3.74\right)$.

Following Observation 1, we can use the definition below for a more convenient presentation.

Definition 6. *For all types* $\alpha \in \Delta^m \times \mathbb{R}_{++}$, *define* $g(\alpha) : \Delta^m \times \mathbb{R}_{++} \to \Delta^m \times [-\frac{B_0}{n}, \infty)$ *such that*

$$g(\alpha) = (x^{(\alpha)}, t^{(\alpha)}) \in \arg\max_{(x,t)} v_\alpha(x,t)$$

Meaning, g maps every preferences vector $\alpha = (\alpha_1, \ldots, \alpha_m, \alpha_f)$ to an optimal budget decision w.r.t. the corresponding valuation function v_α. If that optimum is not unique, g chooses one arbitrarily. In some places we use this notation somewhat abusively, ignoring that indecisiveness in the specific choice of $g(\alpha)$. In particular, by Observation 1, $\Omega^* = g(\bar{\alpha})$. We now proceed to our main result of this section.

Theorem 1. *The US-VCG mechanism is SDSIC in any budgeting instance that respects assumption 3.*

Proof. Fix i, α_i and $\bar{\alpha}_{-i}$. Note that by Observation 1 the US-VCG mechanism outputs $g(\bar{\alpha})$, and, by Lemma 2,

$$u_i(\mathcal{M}(\vec{\alpha})) = \sum_k v_k(g(\bar{\alpha})) - h(\vec{\alpha}_{-i}) = n \cdot v_{\bar{\alpha}}(g(\bar{\alpha})) - h(\vec{\alpha}_{-i})$$

Now, assume that i falsely reports $\alpha_i' \neq \alpha_i$. Inevitably, that shifts the mean preferences to some $\bar{\alpha}' \neq \bar{\alpha}$, and the social optimum that $\mathcal{M}$ outputs to $g(\bar{\alpha}')$. By corollary 1, optimal points define the underlying types uniquely, meaning that $g(\bar{\alpha}')$ cannot be an optimum for $v_{\bar{\alpha}}$. Therefore,

$$u_i(\mathcal{M}(\alpha_i', \vec{\alpha}_{-i})) = n \cdot v_{\bar{\alpha}}(g(\bar{\alpha}')) - h(\vec{\alpha}_{-i})$$
$$< n \cdot v_{\bar{\alpha}}(g(\bar{\alpha})) - h(\vec{\alpha}_{-i}) = u_i(\mathcal{M}(\alpha_i, \vec{\alpha}_{-i}))$$

$\square$

Manipulations By Coalitions. In general, VCG mechanisms are known to be highly prone to group manipulations [3,13]. While individuals cannot benefit from reporting false preferences when the reports of all others are fixed, a group of agents can sometimes coordinate their misreports in such way that each of them (or some at least) benefits from the untruthful reports of others. The US-VCG is no different in this regard.[6] However, the SDSIC property ensures that any such coalition would not be sustainable in the sense that colluding agents cannot trust each other to follow the agreed scheme. Thus, it may suggest that such coalitions are unlikely to form in the first place. That softer robustness demand where we allow for manipulating coalitions as long as they are unsustainable in the above sense is captured in the *Coalition Proof Nash Equilibrium* (CPNE) solution concept [6]. Since the original term is quite involved, we omit in this short version the statement of formal result and proof as the application to our context is much intuitive: in an SDSIC mechanism, no sustainable coalition could exist since the individual unique best response, under any circumstances, is for every agent to report her true preference. We refer the reader to the full version of the paper for a complete technical discussion.[7]

5   Vanishing Payments Under Per-Capita Utilities

In this section we show that payments are negligible for large populations. While these payments are essential for aligning incentives, charging additional money from voters would be undesired in a PB context, which primarily motivates our model. For the technical proofs, we will have to further specify the utility model so that it captures some important feature of divisible PB which has been (justifiably) overlooked in past PB literature, as well as in this study up to this point. That is, that the utility achieved from a given spending X_j on some public good j must also depend on the number of people that enjoy it, n.[8] The reason we only have to address that now is that in this section we analyse the asymptotic behavior of payments w.r.t. n, and in our model the overall budget $B_t = B_0 + nt$ depends on it directly. The following example illustrates this problem.

Example 4. Consider a budgeting instance where $m = 1, B_0 = 0, \theta(nt) = (nt)^p$ and $f(t) = t^q$ for some $0 < p < q < 1$. A type α_f agent thus maximizes her utility $u_{\alpha_f} = (nt)^p - \alpha_f t^q$ at

$$t = \Big[\frac{\alpha_f q}{p}\Big]^{\frac{1-q}{1-p}} \cdot n^{1-q} \xrightarrow[n \to \infty]{} \infty$$

This is a very unlikely result, whatever that sole public good may be. There is no reason to expect that larger populations would wish to pay infinitely larger

---

[6] For example, if $h(\vec{\alpha}_{-i}) = \sum_{j \neq i} v_k(g(\bar{\alpha}_{-i}))$ and all agents collude and report $\bar{\alpha}$, the outcome does not change while their payments will be eliminated.

[7] https://data.oecd.org/gga/general-government-spending.htm.

[8] In applications other than PB this may not be plausible. However, in such applications charging payments from agents could be acceptable.

taxes, nor is it the situation found in reality. The model allows that because every tax unit payed by an individual is presumably "matched" $n - 1$ times by others, thus making the substitution rate grow proportionally with n. However, while larger societies probably do have larger available resources, they are also likely to have greater needs. Just as a country's economic state is conventionally measured by its GDP index, on the large scale the quality of public goods should be associated with spending per capita rather than with nominal spending.[9] Hence, we now narrow down the definition of $\Theta_i(X)$ to

Definition 7 (per capita valuations of public expenditures)

$$\Theta_i(X, n) = \sum_{j=1}^{m} \alpha_{i,j} \theta_j(X_j/n) = \sum_{j=1}^{m} \alpha_{i,j} \theta_j(x_j b_t) \ where \ b_t := \frac{B_0 + nt}{n}.$$

Note that all of our previous results follow through since for any fixed n, $\theta_j(X_j/n)$ is a particular case of $\theta_j(X_j)$.

Moreover, in this section we define $h(\vec{\alpha}_{-i})$ in the VCG payments as the conventional Clarke pivot-rule [12] function that charges a voter with the (normalized) social welfare of all others in her absence $h(\vec{\alpha}_{-i}) = \sum_{k \neq i} v_k(g(\bar{\alpha}_{-i}))$, making the VCG payments

$$p_i^{VCG} = -\sum_{k \neq i} v_k(g(\bar{\alpha})) + \sum_{k \neq i} v_k(g(\bar{\alpha}_{-i})) = (n-1)\left(v_{\bar{\alpha}_{-i}}(g(\bar{\alpha}_{-i})) - v_{\bar{\alpha}_{-i}}(g(\bar{\alpha})) \right)$$

where the second equality is by Observation 1. Our main results in this section (Theorems 2 and 3) are basically the convergence of that expression to zero, at different rates. Essentially, convergence requires that as $\bar{\alpha}_{-i} \to \bar{\alpha}$ with n, $v_{\bar{\alpha}_{-i}}(g(\bar{\alpha}_{-i})) \to v_{\bar{\alpha}_{-i}}(g(\bar{\alpha}))$ as well, and faster than $\frac{1}{n}$ in particular. The next lemma takes us one step towards that.

Lemma 3. *Let* $V(x,t) := (\theta_1(x_1 b_t), \ldots, \theta_m(x_m b_t), -f(t))$. *Then for every two types* $\alpha, \beta \in \Delta^m \times \mathbb{R}_{++}$,

$$0 \leq v_\alpha(g(\alpha)) - v_\alpha(g(\beta)) \leq |\alpha - \beta| \cdot |V(g(\alpha)) - V(g(\beta))|$$

where $|\cdot|$ *could be any norm on* $\mathbb{R}^{m+1}$.

Proof. First note that $v_\alpha(x,t) = \alpha \cdot V(x,t) \ \forall(x,t)$. Thus, since $g(\alpha) \in \arg\min v_\alpha$,

$$0 \leq v_\alpha(g(\alpha)) - v_\alpha(g(\beta)) = \alpha \cdot (V(g(\alpha)) - V(g(\beta)))$$

On the other hand,

$$\alpha \cdot (V(g(\alpha)) - V(g(\beta))) = \beta \cdot (V(g(\alpha)) - V(g(\beta))) + (\alpha - \beta) \cdot (V(g(\alpha)) - V(g(\beta)))$$
$$\leq (\alpha - \beta) \cdot (V(g(\alpha)) - V(g(\beta)))$$
$$\leq |\alpha - \beta| \cdot |V(g(\alpha)) - V(g(\beta))|.$$

where the first inequality is due to $g(\beta) \in \arg\min v_\beta$ and in the second we used Cauchy-Shwartz.

---

[9] See for example https://data.oecd.org/gga/general-government-spending.htm, and [29].

By the above, $p_i^{VCG} \le (n-1)|\bar{\alpha}_{-i}-\bar{\alpha}| \cdot |V(g(\bar{\alpha}_{-i}))-V(g(\bar{\alpha}))|$. Since $|\bar{\alpha}_{-i}-\bar{\alpha}| \propto \frac{1}{n}$ and $V(x,t)$ is continuously differentiable, the convergence of p_i^{VCG} relies on the guarantees we can provide for g's smoothness around the solution $g(\bar{\alpha})$. In our running example (1), for instance, $g(\alpha) = ((\alpha_1, \alpha_2), (\frac{2}{\alpha_f})^2)$ is as smooth as you can wish for in all $\Delta^m \times \mathbb{R}_{++}$. The next preliminary lemma establishes the continuity of g at the solution $g(\bar{\alpha})$ when that is uniquely defined, which is sufficient for Theorem 2 that follows.

Lemma 4. *For any given $\alpha \in \Delta^m \times \mathbb{R}$, if v_α has a unique global maximum then*

$$\lim_{\beta \to \alpha} g(\beta) = g(\alpha).$$

Note that (a) this statement is not obvious because we did not assume that g is continuous, and (b) it holds for any function g that follows Definition 6, i.e. the specific arbitrary choice of $g(\beta)$ in case v_β has multiple optima is irrelevant.

5.1   Bounding Individual Payments

We need one more definition before stating our main result in this section.

Definition 8. *A characteristic triplet in a budgeting instance $\mathcal{I}$ is $\sigma = (b_0, \mu, \bar{\alpha})$ where*

- $b_0 := \frac{B_0}{n} \ge 0$ *is the non tax funded budget source per capita.*
- $\bar{\alpha} := \frac{1}{n}\sum_k \alpha_k \in \Delta^m \times \mathbb{R}$ *is the mean preferences vector of all agents.*
- $\mu > 0$ *such that $1/\mu < \alpha_{i,f} < \mu \; \forall i \in [n]$.*

Theorem 2. *Let $\sigma = (b_0, \mu, \bar{\alpha})$ such that $v_{\bar{\alpha}}$ has a unique global maximum at $g(\bar{\alpha})$. Then for every $\epsilon > 0$ there exists $n_\epsilon(\sigma)$ such that in every budgeting instance with characteristic triplet σ and $n > n_\epsilon(\sigma)$,*

$$|P_i| < \epsilon \quad \forall i \in [n].$$

As stated, Theorem 2 means that prices vanish if the population is sufficiently large while not taking into account the likely possibility that in reality, new members that join a community might change it's characteristic parameters b_0, μ and $\bar{\alpha}$. That is, we are saying that in any given community with known parameters $(b_0, \mu, \bar{\alpha})$, prices will be arbitrarily small if the population is large enough. Thus, as there is no reason to assume some correlation between these parameters and the population's size, the theorem essentially implies that prices are likely to be small, even negligible, in larger societies.

A proof sketch. The proof idea is fairly immediate given the preliminary Lemmas. By 3, $p_i^{VCG} \le (n-1)|\bar{\alpha}_{-i}-\bar{\alpha}| \cdot |V(g(\bar{\alpha}_{-i}))-V(g(\bar{\alpha}))|$. Now since $(n-1)$ and $|\bar{\alpha}_{-i} - \bar{\alpha}| = \frac{1}{n}|\bar{\alpha}_{-i} - \alpha_i|$ cancel out and thanks to Lemma 4 $V \circ g(x,t)$ is continuous at $\bar{\alpha}$, $p_i^{VCG} \to 0$ as $\bar{\alpha}_{-i} \to \bar{\alpha}$ with n, which implies the same for P_i (as given in Definition 4).

5.2   Non-Positive Payments

The theorem above shows that individual payments vanish with n. Our next goal is to formulate them as non positive for all agents. Meaning, we want no agent to add any payment on top of the tax t, even negligible. Instead, they might be paid a "negative payment" that we can view as a bonus or a "tax discount" for their participation. We begin with introducing a stronger convergence result than Theorem 2, that further bounds the payments by an $O(\frac{1}{n})$ factor.

Theorem 3. *Let* $\sigma = (b_0, \mu, \bar{\alpha})$ *and assume that g is differentiable at $\bar{\alpha}$.[10] Then there exist some $\mathcal{B} \in \mathbb{R}$ and $n(\sigma)$ such that in every population with characteristic triplet σ and size $n > n(\sigma)$, $|P_i| \le \frac{\mathcal{B}}{n}$ for all $i \in [n]$.*

That stronger result is thanks to the differentiability of g which allows, by linear approximation, bounding $|V(g(\bar{\alpha}_{-i})) - V(g(\bar{\alpha}))|$ by an $O(1/n)$ factor, whereas in the proof of Theorem 2 we could only guarantee its convergence. Relying on that result, we construct non-positive payments the following way. We add to the VCG payments an amount that we pay back to every agent and equals the maximum payment she could have been charged with, given the partial type profile of her peers α_{-i}. Theorem 3 not only provides that bound, but also guarantees that the total amount paid to all agents will not diverge as $n \to \infty$. Corollary 2 states the final result (See [33] for full details).

Corollary 2. *In any budgeting instance with characteristic triplet σ such that g is differentiable at $\bar{\alpha}$ and $n > n(\sigma)$, there exist a payment assignment P that satisfies:*

1. $P_i \le 0 \ \forall i \in [n]$
2. $\sum_{i \in [n]} P_i \ge -\tilde{\mathcal{B}}$ *for some* $\tilde{\mathcal{B}} \in \mathbb{R}_+$.

6   Concluding Remarks

We presented a collective decision budgeting mechanism, the US-VCG mechanism, that concerns both the allocation and total volume of expenses. It is essentially a VCG mechanism adjusted to our setting, in which we had to tackle a few issues. Mainly, we had to reformulate the payments to suit our preference model of non quasi-linear utilities. The US-VCG mechanism is welfare-maximizing and DSIC in the most general setup, and we specified the conditions in which it further satisfies strict DSIC and consequently also resistance against coalition manipulations. In Sect. 5, we showed that the modified VCG payments the mechanism charges become negligible in large populations, and that in some cases we can construct non-positive payments tp all agents.

---

[10] In the full version of the paper we show some preliminary regularity condition that implies differentiability given that $g(\bar{\alpha})$ is unique.

Future Directions. In the introduction, we discussed the theoretic advantages of an additive concave utility model over other examples from the literature. The obvious downside is, when considering a mechanism that aggregates preferences, is the difficulty in assessing the concrete functions we should assume. While we can nevertheless argue that any such functions are probably a better approximation for the true underlying preferences than previous suggestions, future experimental research attempting to evaluate, similarly to those performed in relation to the disutility monetary function f [8], could make a valuable contribution to the field.

References

1. Aziz, H., Bogomolnaia, A., Moulin, H.: Fair mixing: the case of dichotomous preferences. In: ACM-EC 2019, pp. 753–781 (2019)
2. Aziz, H., Ganguly, A.: Participatory funding coordination: model, axioms and rules. In: Fotakis, D., Ríos Insua, D. (eds.) ADT 2021. LNCS (LNAI), vol. 13023, pp. 409–423. Springer, Cham (2021). https://doi.org/10.1007/978-3-030-87756-9_26
3. Bachrach, Y.: Honor among thieves: collusion in multi-unit auctions. In: AAMAS'10, pp. 617–624 (2010)
4. Benade, G., Nath, S., Procaccia, A.D., Shah, N.: Preference elicitation for participatory budgeting. Manage. Sci. 67(5), 2813–2827 (2021)
5. Bernard, A.: Optimal taxation and public production with budget constraints. In: The Economics of Public Services: Proceedings of a Conference held by the International Economic Association at Turin, Italy, pp. 361–389. Palgrave Macmillan, London (1977). https://doi.org/10.1007/978-1-349-02917-4_15
6. Bernheim, B.D., Peleg, B., Whinston, M.D.: Coalition-proof nash equilibria i. concepts. J. Econ. Theory 42(1), 1–12 (1987)
7. Bjorvatn, K., Schjelderup, G.: Tax competition and international public goods. Int. Tax Public Finan. 9, 111–120 (2002)
8. Booij, A.S., Van Praag, B.M., Van De Kuilen, G.: A parametric analysis of prospect theory's functionals for the general population. Theory Decis. 68(1–2), 115–148 (2010)
9. Brandl, F., Brandt, F., Peters, D., Stricker, C.: Distribution rules under dichotomous preferences: two out of three ain't bad. In: Proceedings of the 22nd ACM Conference on Economics and Computation, pp. 158–179 (2021)
10. Brandl, F., Brandt, F., Peters, D., Stricker, C., Suksompong, W.: Funding public projects: a case for the nash product rule. arXiv preprint arXiv:2005.07997 (2020)
11. Cavallo, R.: Optimal decision-making with minimal waste: strategyproof redistribution of VCG payments. In: Proceedings of the Fifth International Joint Conference on Autonomous Agents and Multiagent Systems, pp. 882–889 (2006)
12. Clarke, E.H.: Multipart pricing of public goods. Public choice, pp. 17–33 (1971)
13. Conitzer, V., Sandholm, T.: Failures of the VCG mechanism in combinatorial auctions and exchanges. In: AAMAS'06, pp. 521–528 (2006)
14. Fain, B., Goel, A., Munagala, K.: The core of the participatory budgeting problem. In: Cai, Y., Vetta, A. (eds.) WINE 2016. LNCS, vol. 10123, pp. 384–399. Springer, Heidelberg (2016). https://doi.org/10.1007/978-3-662-54110-4_27
15. Fairstein, R., Lauz, A., Gal, K., Meir, R.: Modeling peoples voting behavior with poll information. arXiv preprint arXiv:1909.10492 (2019)

16. Freeman, R., Pennock, D.M., Peters, D., Wortman Vaughan, J.: Truthful aggrega-
    tion of budget proposals. In: ACM-EC'19, pp. 751–752 (2019)
17. Garg, N., Kamble, V., Goel, A., Marn, D., Munagala, K.: Iterative local voting for
    collective decision-making in continuous spaces. J. Artif. Intell. Res. **64**, 315–355
    (2019)
18. Gibbard, A.: Manipulation of voting schemes: a general result. Econometrica: J.
    Econ. Soc., pp. 587–601 (1973)
19. Goel, A., Krishnaswamy, A.K., Sakshuwong, S., Aitamurto, T.: Knapsack voting
    for participatory budgeting. ACM Trans. Econ. Comput. (TEAC) **7**(2), 1–27 (2019)
20. Guo, M., Conitzer, V.: Worst-case optimal redistribution of VCG payments in
    multi-unit auctions. Games Econ. Behav. **67**(1), 69–98 (2009)
21. Jain, K., Vazirani, V.V.: Eisenberg-gale markets: algorithms and structural prop-
    erties. In: STOC'07, pp. 364–373 (2007)
22. Krugman, P., Wells, R.: Microeconomics. Macmillan (2008)
23. Lahkar, R., Mukherjee, S.: Dominant strategy implementation in a large population
    public goods game. Econ. Lett. **197**, 109616 (2020)
24. Nehring, K., Puppe, C.: The structure of strategy-proof social choice-part i: general
    characterization and possibility results on median spaces. J. Econ. Theory **135**(1),
    269–305 (2007)
25. Nisan, N., Roughgarden, T., Tardos, E., Vazirani, V.V.: Algorithmic game theory,
    2007. Book available for free online (2007)
26. Rey, S., Maly, J.: The (computational) social choice take on indivisible participa-
    tory budgeting. arXiv preprint arXiv:2303.00621 (2023)
27. Roberts, K.: The characterization of implementable choice rules. Aggregation Rev-
    elation Preferences **12**(2), 321–348 (1979)
28. Satterthwaite, M.A.: Strategy-proofness and arrow's conditions: existence and cor-
    respondence theorems for voting procedures and social welfare functions. J. Econ.
    Theory **10**(2), 187–217 (1975)
29. Stiglitz, J.E.: The theory of local public goods. In: The Economics of Public Ser-
    vices: Proceedings of a Conference Held by the International Economic Association
    at Turin, Italy. pp. 274–333. Springer (1977). https://doi.org/10.1007/978-1-349-
    02917-4_12
30. Talmon, N., Faliszewski, P.: A framework for approval-based budgeting methods.
    In: AAAI'19, vol. 33, pp. 2181–2188 (2019)
31. Tversky, A., Kahneman, D.: Advances in prospect theory: cumulative representa-
    tion of uncertainty. J. Risk Uncertainty **5**(4), 297–323 (1992)
32. Vazirani, V.V., Yannakakis, M.: Market equilibrium under separable, piecewise-
    linear, concave utilities. J. ACM (JACM) **58**(3), 1–25 (2011)
33. Wagner, J., Meir, R.: Strategy-proof budgeting via a VCG-like mechanism. arXiv
    preprint arXiv:2303.06923 (2023)
34. Wildasin, D.E.: Nash equilibria in models of fiscal competition. J. Public Econ.
    35(2), 229–240 (1988)

Author Index

A. Deligkas and A. Filos-Ratsikas (Eds.): SAGT 2023, LNCS 14238, pp. 419–420, 2023.
https://doi.org/10.1007/978-3-031-43254-5

Printed in the United States
by Baker & Taylor Publisher Services